Youth Justice and Social Work

**PAUL DUGMORE AND
JANE PICKFORD**

with contributions from Sally Angus

Series Editors: Jonathan Parker and Greta Bradley

LearningMatters

First published in 2006 by Learning Matters Ltd.
Reprinted in 2007.

British Library Cataloguing in Publication Data
A CIP record for this book is available from the British Library.

ISBN: 978 1 84445 066 4

Cover and text design by Code 5 Design Associates
Project management by Deer Park Productions
Typeset by Pantek Arts Ltd, Kent
Printed and bound in Great Britain by Bell & Bain Ltd, Glasgow

Learning Matters Ltd
33 Southernhay East
Exeter EX1 1NX
Tel: 01392 215560
info@learningmatters.co.uk
www.learningmatters.co.uk

Contents

In memory of Alma Pickford

Acknowledgements

We are grateful to all our colleagues, students, friends and families who have contributed in some way to the production of this book. Thank you to the team at Learning Matters, particularly Kate and Jonathan for their help and support. Special thanks from Paul Dugmore to Shelley Greene and Mark Owers for their proof-reading and comments and to Daniel Lane for his continued support.

Introduction

Social work practice within the youth justice setting can be complex, challenging and laden with ethical dilemmas. However, it is also one of the areas in which social workers can really engage in significant work with young people in order to effect positive change. This can involve working with a wide range of service users aged from 10 to 18, as well as working closely with parents and carers all from a variety of social and cultural backgrounds. Young people will also present with many diverse experiences and needs and engage in a whole host of offending behaviour from first-time, trivial nuisance to persistent and serious offences. Social workers in this area have to work closely with a wide group of professionals including those making up multi-agency Youth Offending Teams (YOTs) such as the police, health and education staff to solicitors, judges, magistrates and prison officers. Working within youth justice can be both challenging and incredibly rewarding by being able to build important relationships and make a difference to the lives of young people.

In order to be able to carry out the roles and responsibilities in this area of social work practice, social workers need to employ a range of skills as well as acquire the relevant knowledge and display appropriate values and qualities in order to work effectively with young people who find themselves in trouble as a result of criminal behaviour. This includes:

- The National Occupational Standards for Social Work.

- The General Social Care Council's (GSCC) Code of Practice for Social Care Workers.

- The relevant legislative frameworks in relation to children and criminal justice.

- The ever-changing social and political context.

- Inter-agency and inter-professional working.

- Working with difference.

- Working with young people charged with, but not convicted of, criminal acts.

This book considers all of these areas of knowledge in relation to working within youth justice social work practice.

The subject benchmark statement for social work identifies four key areas in which students need to acquire knowledge, understanding and skills:

- Social work services and service users.

- Values and ethics.

- Social work theory.

- The nature of social work practice.

Working within youth justice requires a wide range of transferable skills. These include communication, gathering information, preparation, engagement, assessment of need and risk, record-keeping, analysis, report writing, time management, team working, decision-making, problem-solving, and intervention. These skills will be considered over the next nine chapters. Instrumental to these skills being employed effectively is the ability to practise in an anti-oppressive way that takes into account difference. This will also be addressed throughout.

Youth justice has been the subject of considerable change over the last eight years and it seems highly likely that this will continue to be the case as the government introduces and implements a raft of new legislation in relation to children and criminal justice such as the Children Act 2004 and the pending youth justice reform proposals.

This book is designed for social work degree students and those studying youth justice qualifications as well as those involved in the education of social work and youth justice and practitioners within the youth justice system.

Book structure

Chapter 1 discusses the values and ethics involved in working in youth justice. It considers some of the issues social workers have to wrestle with in this area of practice and places these within the context of the regulatory bodies involved in social work and youth justice such as the GSCC Codes of Practice. You will be encouraged to explore the value base that you approach your social work practice with and how your beliefs and prejudices might impact upon your practice with young people who offend.

Chapter 2 examines the development of youth justice theory, policy and practice. In order to understand the rationales underpinning any area of social work practice, it is vital to have an insight into the way your area of practice has been shaped by its history. The structure of the youth justice industry has been imbued by dominant philosophies that have seeped into the roots of the foundations of youth justice practice and govern contemporary practice. This chapter reviews the bedrock of youth justice theory and practice and traces the evolution of our unique youth justice system over the last hundred years.

Chapter 3 analyses theories of criminality that may be useful for practitioners within the youth justice system. These theories relate to understanding why young people commit crimes and take part in anti-social or delinquent behaviour. In this chapter we undertake a basic theoretical tour of some of the mainstream criminological theories.

Chapter 4 outlines the policy discussions and legislation that shape contemporary youth justice practice. As a social worker within the youth justice industry, you will need to be familiar with the law underpinning your practice and the rationales that justify the current legal framework. We will examine the contemporary legal framework governing youth justice and set out the current sentencing options for young offenders. We will also analyse non-criminal orders, which have the force of civil law constraints on young people who take part in anti-social and disorderly behaviour.

Chapter 5 considers the professional context that social workers practise within. This includes an examination of the youth justice system and the process a young person who commits an offence goes through, from arrest to sentence. We will look at the role of each of the key agencies in the youth justice system: the police, Crown Prosecution Service (CPS), courts and secure estate. The role and function of the multi-agency YOTs will also be explored, including each of the main professionals: social workers, probation officers, police officers and education and health officers. It will consider some of the issues social workers face when working within the same team as a wealth of other different professionals.

Chapter 6 focuses on the purpose, nature and process of assessment within youth justice. The assessment tool, Asset, used by YOTs is discussed and the interrelation between Asset and pre-sentence reports (PSRs) and risk assessments is considered. The chapter also looks at the relationship between Asset and the Common Assessment Framework introduced by the 2004 Children Act.

Chapter 7 addresses the different types of work that YOT social workers undertake with young people who have offended or are at risk of offending. This will include issues of diversity, equality and working with difference. This chapter considers the importance of planning, reviewing, ending and evaluating interventions with young people and the frameworks in place for achieving this, all of which follow from assessment. Finally, consideration is given to the different approaches to working with young people, such as one-to-one work, group work and restorative justice.

Chapter 8 considers the role of the social worker working with parents and carers of young people who offend. The chapter also focuses on working with volunteers in the youth justice system and the potential challenges this presents to practitioners. Finally the chapter addresses the role of victims of crime within youth justice and considers how social workers balance the needs of young people while acknowledging the issues facing victims in restorative justice interventions.

Chapter 9 examines three key areas relating to effective future practice as a youth justice professional: transferable skills, continuing professional education and the possibilities for future legislation in the youth justice arena. As a youth justice practitioner you will become aware that laws and procedures are regularly subject to change. In order to face the challenges of change within your professional environment, you must keep abreast of contemporary policy debates, reports, reviews and proposals. This chapter informs you of future proposed reforms and of ways of keeping on top of professional and legal changes.

Throughout the book, each chapter refers to the relevant National Occupational Standards and subject benchmark statement for social work and contains activities, case studies and research summaries to assist you in reflecting upon your values, beliefs and practice with young people who offend.

Chapter 1

Values and ethics in youth justice social work

by Paul Dugmore, Jane Pickford and Sally Angus

A C H I E V I N G   A   S O C I A L   W O R K   D E G R E E

This chapter will help you begin to meet the following National Occupational Standards.
Key Role 6: Demonstrate professional competence in social work practice.
- Work within agreed standards of social work practice and ensure own professional development.
- Manage complex ethical issues, dilemmas and conflicts.

It will also introduce you to the following academic standards as set out in the social work subject benchmark statement:

3.1.1 Social work services and service users
- The social processes (associated with, for example, poverty, unemployment, poor health, disablement, lack of education and other sources of disadvantage) that lead to marginalisation, isolation and exclusion and their impact on the demand for social work services.

3.1.3 Values and ethics
- The nature, historical evolution and application of social work values.
- The moral concepts of rights, responsibility, freedom, authority and power inherent in the practice of social workers as moral and statutory agents.
- The complex relationships between justice, care and control in social welfare and the practical and ethical implications of these, including roles as statutory agents and in upholding the law in respect of discrimination.
- Aspects of philosophical ethics relevant to the understanding and resolution of value dilemmas and conflicts in both interpersonal and professional contexts.
- The conceptual links between codes defining ethical practice, the regulation of professional conduct and the management of potential conflicts generated by the codes held by different professional groups.

3.2.2 Problem-solving skills
- Analyse and take account of the impact of inequality and discrimination in work with people in particular contexts and problem situations.

3.2.3 Communication skills
- Communicate effectively across potential barriers resulting from differences (for example, in culture, language and age).

3.2.4 Skills in working with others
- Act with others to increase social justice by identifying and responding to prejudice, institutional discrimination and structural inequality.

Introduction

This chapter explores the concept of social work values and ethics and their application to work with children and young people who offend. The first part of the chapter provides a detailed look at the values and ethics underpinning social work practice and the regulatory bodies that ensure the transmission of values and ethics to social work practice. Later in the chapter there is reference to the legislative and policy framework that promotes the ethical base of social work practice and also the rights of children and young people. The remainder of the chapter considers the application of social work values to practice and potential ethical dilemmas facing social workers in their practice with children and young people who offend.

So exactly what do we mean by values and ethics? The *Collins English Dictionary* defines values as 'the moral principles or accepted standards of a person or group' and defines ethics as 'a code of behaviour considered correct, especially that of a particular group, profession or individual' (1993). As individuals we have our own set of values, which are informed by our own beliefs and those of our family and friends. Different professions may not share the same value base and in the case of youth justice, there are a number of different professions, all sharing the same 'client base' (Yelloly and Henkel, 1995), but all having a different value and ethically based practice. These clashes of values were identified in the evaluation of the pilot YOTs. Researchers found that youth justice staff had difficulty in transferring 'philosophically and practically' to the newly formed Youth Offending Teams (Holdaway et al., 2001, p6).

Values and ethics are fundmental components of social work practice. Reference to values and ethics are integral to social work training and feature prominently within the regulatory framework for social work. Detailed below are a number of documents relating to social work practice, all of which address the application of social work values and ethics as fundamental to social work practice. All those working in social care, including youth justice, are required to work to standards set down by the General Social Care Council (GSCC).

What is the GSCC?

The General Social Care Council is the 'workforce regulator and guardian of standards for the social care workforce in England' (**www.gscc.org.uk**). The GSCC was established in 2001 under the Care Standards Act 2000 and is responsible for regulating social work education and training and maintaining the social care register.

GSCC Code of Practice

In 2003 the GSCC published the Code of Practice for both employers and employees to contribute to the raising of standards in social care services. The codes comprise a list of statements that define the standards of professional conduct required of all practitioners working within social care. The six standards relating to employees are:

- Protect the rights and promote the interests of service users and carers.

- Strive to establish and maintain trust and confidence of service users and carers.

- Promote the independence of service users while protecting as far as possible from danger or harm.

- Respect the rights of service users, while seeking to ensure that their behaviour does not harm themselves or other people.

- Uphold public trust and confidence in social care services.

- Be accountable for the quality of your work and take responsibility for maintaining and improving your knowledge and skills.

As you can see, there is a clear expectation that social work practitioners are required to work with service users in a way that is principled, honest and conscientious – in other words in an 'ethically' legitimate way.

GSCC registration

As from 1st April 2005 all qualified social workers are required to register with the GSCC. All practising social workers have to register and there are no exemptions or exclusions. Under Section 61 of the Care Standards Act 2001 it is a criminal offence for an unregistered person to use the title 'social worker' with the intent to deceive. Doing so is a criminal offence and carries the sanction of a fine of up to £5000. Initially, registration was only mandatory for qualified social workers, but this requirement has now been extended to other groups of social care workers and social work students.

Social work training

The GSCC is also responsible for regulating the education and training of social workers. Training is undertaken at either undergraduate or postgraduate level and has both academic and practice elements. All students will be expected to demonstrate competence across all the National Occupational Standards.

What are the National Occupational Standards?

They are six key roles that 'set out what employers require social workers to be able to do on entering employment' (Department of Health, *Requirements for social work training*, 2002). They were drawn up by the Training Organisation for the Personal Social Services (TOPSS, now called Skills for Care) and effectively provide a 'benchmark of best practice' in social work competence. The standards were developed and informed by the *Statement of Expectations* (TOPSS, 2002) which was compiled in consultation with service users and carers.

These key roles are:

- Prepare for, and work with individuals, families, carers, groups and communities to assess their needs and circumstances.

- Plan, carry out, review and evaluate social work practice, with individuals, families, carers, groups, communities and other professionals.

- Support individuals to represent their needs, views and circumstances.

- Manage risk to individuals, families, carers, groups, communities, self and colleagues.

- Manage and be accountable, with supervision and support, for your own social work practice within your organisation.

- Demonstrate professional competence in social work practice.

When you undertake your 200 days of assessed practice learning, it is against these standards that you will be assessed to demonstrate that you are competent to practise as a social worker.

Values and ethics

Included in the National Occupational Standards are a set of values and ethics that are central to, and underpin, the six key roles that make up the National Occupational Standards. Social work students must be able to critically analyse and evaluate their practice in relation to the six core values and ethics listed below:

- Awareness of your own values, prejudices, ethical dilemmas and conflicts of interest and their implications on your practice.

- Respect for, and the promotion of:

  - each person as an individual;

  - independence and quality of life for individuals, while protecting them from harm;

  - dignity and privacy of individuals, families, carers, groups and communities.

- Recognise and facilitate each person's use of the language and form of communication of their choice.

- Value, recognise and respect the diversity, expertise and experience of individuals, families, carers, groups and communities.

- Maintain the trust and confidence of individuals, families, carers, groups and communities by communicating in an open, accurate and understandable way.

- Understand, and make use of, strategies to challenge discrimination, disadvantage and other forms of inequality and injustice.

So you can see that your ability to practise in a way that is grounded in a strong, ethical value based framework will be crucial to your development as a good social worker.

QAA benchmark statement

Training for social work is monitored by the Quality Assurance Agency for Higher Education (QAA) and sets out academic standards for social work. The social work benchmark refers to social work as a 'moral activity' that requires students to potentially make and implement decisions that may be difficult and which may 'involve the potential for benefit or harm' (QAA, 2001, 2.4). The QAA states that programmes offering the social work degree should include the study of the 'application of and reflection upon ethical principles' (2.4). In terms of subject knowledge in relation to values and ethics, the QAA states that during their degree studies in social work, students should 'critically evaluate, apply and integrate knowledge and understanding' to:

- The nature, historical evolution and application of social work values.

- The moral concepts of rights, responsibility, freedom, authority and power inherent in the practice of social workers as moral and statutory agents.

- The complex relationships between justice, care and control in social welfare and the practical and ethical implications of these, including roles as statutory agents and in upholding the law in respect of discrimination.

- Aspects of philosophical ethics relevant to the understanding and resolution of value dilemmas and conflicts in both interpersonal and professional contexts.

- The conceptual link between codes defining ethical practice, the regulation of professional conduct and the management of potential conflicts generated by the codes held by different professional groups. (3.1.3).

In this chapter we consider a number of issues that may challenge the values that underpin the National Occupational Standards and the ethical principles that are integral to the QAA benchmark statement. Your role as a social worker within a youth justice setting presents you with an array of standards and principles that may appear to conflict with each other. As already mentioned, the GSCC requires all practitioners to work to a code of practice. However, in addition to this there is the BASW code of ethics.

British Association of Social Workers

Many qualified social workers belong to the British Association of Social Workers (BASW). This is one of the largest professional organisations allied to social work practice in the UK. Part of the role of BASW is to ensure that its members 'discharge their ethical obligations and are afforded the professional rights which are necessary for the safeguarding and promotion of the rights of service users' (www.basw.co.uk).

BASW produce a code of ethics, which consists of a set of five basic values and six principles to guidance on ethical practice. The values are:

- Human dignity and worth

- Social justice

- Service to humanity

- Integrity

- Competence

The principles are:

- Respect basic human rights as expressed in the United Nations Universal Declaration of Human Rights and other international conventions derived from that Declaration.

- Show respect for all persons, and respect service users' beliefs, values, culture, goals, needs, preferences, relationships and affiliations.

- Safeguard and promote service users' dignity, individuality, rights, responsibilities and identity.

- Foster individual well-being and autonomy, subject to due respect for the rights of others.

- Respect service users' rights to make informed decisions, and ensure that service users and carers participate in decision-making processes.

- Ensure the protection of service users, which may include setting appropriate limits and exercising authority, with the objective of safeguarding them and others.

Social workers are, therefore, subject to several guiding standards: the GSCC Code of Practice, the values and ethics within the National Occupational Standards, the guiding values and principles of BASW. In addition, social workers working within a YOT are required to work to the *National Standards for youth justice services* (YJB, 2004a).

National Standards for youth justice

The National Standards for youth justice services are set by the Home Secretary and issued by the Youth Justice Board. The standards provide a basis for promoting good practice with children and young people who offend, as well as their families and victims. Like the National Occupational Standards for social work, they provide a benchmark against which the effectiveness of work can be measured. They provide a minimal level of service for those working within the youth justice services. There are ten key National Standards that practitioners should adhere to:

1 Set clear requirements for supervision, which include quality of work, frequency of contact and response to non-compliance.

2 Help to speed up court processes so that sanctions against offending will be experienced more immediately.

3 Improve the effectiveness of information sharing and exchange.

4 Ensure that the victims of crime are central to restorative processes and their needs are respected.

5 Prioritise the protection of the public from re-offending and harm, and increase public confidence in the delivery of youth justice services.

6 Ensure that Youth Offending Teams and secure establishments take a lead in the planning and provision of services designed to prevent offending by children and young people, such as education, training and health, which the Crime and Disorder Act 1998 and other legislation requires to be in place locally.

7 Require that all interventions are delivered fairly, consistently and without improper discrimination, in a way that values and respects the cultural and racial diversity of the whole community.

8 Require Youth Offending Teams and secure establishments to measure the effectiveness of their performance and report on outcomes to the Youth Justice Board.

9 Set out standards for the running of secure establishments.

10 Require that Youth Offending Teams and secure facilities ensure exchange of information relating to young people in custody within prescribed timescales, and that work begun in custody is carried on following release.

ACTIVITY **1.1**

The National Standards make reference to processes; for example, number 2 refers to the importance of speeding up the youth justice process. Is this at odds with the values and ethics that underpin the National Occupational Standards for social work?

Should, for example, the welfare of the child be at the forefront of your practice or should we deal with youth offenders more speedily? Is it possible to do both?

Victims of crime

While the main focus of social work intervention is direct work with children and young people who offend, practitioners may also have some contact with victims of these offences. The National Standards for Youth Justice Services make reference to work with victims, ensuring that their needs are respected in restorative processes. This area of work may be very new to many working in youth justice, and working with victims may present a challenge to practitioners. Historically, services for victims of crime have been provided by the voluntary sector and this is still the case today. Victim Support is the largest charitable organisation providing support to victims of crime, although there are many smaller agencies offering support to victims of specific crimes such as Rape Crisis and Women's Aid. In its policy report of 1995, *The Rights of Victims of Crime*, Victim Support set out five main principles for those working with victims within the criminal justice system:

- To be free of the burden of decisions relating to the offender.

- To receive information and explanation about the progress of their case, and to have the opportunity to provide their own information about the case for use in the criminal justice process.

- To be protected in any way necessary.

- To receive compensation.

- To receive respect, recognition and support.

In 1990 the government published the first Victim's Charter, which set out the service victims of crime should expect from those agencies represented in the criminal justice system. This was superseded in 1996 with a second charter, effectively an updated version of the 1990 charter but with a commitment to 'provide better information' for victims. In December 2005 the government published *The Code of Practice for Victims of Crime* (Home Office, 2005a) which was issued under Section 32 of the Domestic Violence, Crime and Victims Act 2004. After a number of amendments, the Code was finally implemented in April 2006.

The Code of Practice defines public expectations for those services in England and Wales working within the criminal justice system, including Youth Offending Teams. It effectively represents a minimum standard of service to victims involved in the criminal justice system. The GSCC Code of Practice refers to the importance of protecting the rights and promoting the interests of service users. Within youth justice, clearly the service user is the young person. However the Victims' Code of Practice requires all practitioners in the criminal justice system, including those in a YOT, to 'take account of victims' needs' (Home Office, 2005a, p14).

The nature of social work is such that there will always be issues around values and ethics, including your own values. However, there is a clear and explicit message for professionals working within social care reinforced by training, agency policy and regulatory bodies: you must reflect on 'how' you work with service users and consider how your values and beliefs may impact on work with service users. In a youth justice setting we mean children and young people who offend and those who are affected by those actions, including their families as well as the victims.

ACTIVITY *1.2*

Take a look at the GSCC Code of practice for social care workers *and the* National Standards for youth justice services *and consider the differences as well as the similarities between the two.*

The interface between law and ethics

International obligations: human rights and youth justice

In this section we consider our youth justice system in relation to international legislation and conventions, as well as examining how it may stand up to the provisions of our own Human Rights Act 1998. Is the way we treat young people who come into contact with the criminal justice system comparable to juvenile justice systems in other legal cultures? How well do we fare when we scrutinise our brand of youth justice and test its compliance with international legal requirements? We analyse how the implementation of human rights legislation into our domestic law should have impacted upon our practice of youth justice. Do some of the practices introduced by recent youth justice legislation breach fundamental principles of human rights?

But first we must examine international law on the rights of the child and the many protections that have developed over the past two decades. Some countries have taken international provisions on requirements in relation to youth justice systems more seriously than others. How does our system fare when we put it to the test of international conventions? Have we developed a child-oriented system when we deal with young people who are accused of breaching our criminal law?

International human rights law should offer protections for young offenders, if provisions are adhered to at a domestic level. You should be aware of them to check whether procedures your client has been subject to might be in breach of these safeguards. The most significant examples include:

- United Nations Convention on the Rights of the Child (1989).

- United Nations Rules for the Administration of Juvenile Justice (1985) (Beijing Rules).

- United Nations Rules for the Protection of Juveniles Deprived of their Liberty (1990b).

- United Nations Guidelines for the Prevention of Juvenile Delinquency (1990a) (Riyadh Guidelines).

and also:

- Article 5 of the European Convention on Human Rights – the right to liberty and security (now part of our Human Rights Act 1998).

- Article 6 – the right to a fair trial (now part of our Human Rights Act 1998).

- International Covenant on Civil and Political Rights (ICCPR) (1966) – Article 14 (4): ' . . . in the case of juvenile persons, the procedure shall be such as will take account of their age and the desirability of promoting their rehabilitation'.

The most far-reaching is the Convention on the Rights of the Child; this is due to its binding character and the fact that it has been ratified by 191 states/countries (the USA and Somalia have not ratified this Convention).

Article 40 is one of the most significant parts. It states that:

> State Parties recognise the right of every child alleged as, accused of, or recognised as having infringed the penal law to be treated in a manner consistent with the promotion of the child's sense of dignity and worth . . .

This includes minimum due process guarantees, including:

- The presumption of innocence.

- The right to be informed promptly of the charges against him or her.

- The right to have legal assistance in the preparation of his or her defence.

- The right to be tried without delay by a competent legal authority.

- A requirement to set a reasonable minimum age of criminal responsibility.

- The need to provide non-judicial methods of dealing with children in conflict with the law.

- The need to establish alternatives to institutional care.

These provisions are supplemented by Article 37, which prohibits the death penalty and life imprisonment without the possibility of release. Article 37 also requires that imprisonment 'shall be used as a measure of last resort' and where children are imprisoned it must be for the shortest possible period of time.

Article 39 requires the countries to promote physical and psychological recovery and reintegration of child victims.

The Convention also has general principles, which should be considered in addition to specific principles. These include:

- All procedures should be in the best interests of the child (Article 3).
- Judicial bodies/tribunals must take into account the evolving capacities of the child (Article 5).
- Judicial bodies/tribunals must give due weight to the views of the child (Article 12).
- Procedures must be free of discrimination (Article 2).

The Human Rights Act 1998

The Human Rights Act 1998 came into force in October 2000. This Act in effect incorporates the European Convention on Human Rights into domestic law so that all current and planned legislation must be implemented in a manner consistent with the rights and freedoms set out in the Convention. Additionally, the Act includes the adoption into domestic law of the United Nations Convention and linked protocols including (very significantly from a youth justice standpoint) the Beijing Rules (the United Nations Standard Minimum Rules for the Administration of Juvenile Justice 1985).

Has the inclusion of these international provisions affected the practice of youth justice in this country? Could legal challenges be mounted under the Human Rights Act about the way we treat young people who are deemed to be anti-social or who are suspected of or convicted for a criminal offence? You should be aware of these protections in your work with clients and be prepared to challenge any breaches.

In 1999 the European Court of Human Rights, in the case of Thompson and Venables (the killers of toddler James Bulger), even prior to the implementation of the Human Rights Act ruled that:

- The process in the Crown Court was unfair because it was unsuitable for the two defendants (aged 11 at the time) in that it was intimidating and incomprehensible for the boys.
- Sentencing should be left to judges to decide and recommendations should not be overruled by politicians (the boys were originally sentenced to eight years by the trial judge; this was raised to ten years by the Lord Chief Justice and then to 15 years by Michael Howard, the then Home Secretary).
- Decisions about release should not be decided by the Home Secretary but by an independent judicial body such as the Parole Board.

As a result of the ruling in this case, in March 2000 Jack Straw handed over the decision on how long Thompson and Venables would remain in custody to Lord Bingham, the Lord Chief Justice. The sentencing of juveniles convicted of the gravest crimes will now be set by the Lord Chief Justice on a recommendation of the trial judge.

It is noteworthy that the European Court's ruling regarding Crown Courts being unsuitable places for dealing with young people (the Crown Court is essentially an adult court) has been ignored by the Labour Government. Young people who are alleged to have committed serious offences are still tried in this unsuitable and confusing environment. Since October 2000, however, young offenders do not have to go to Strasbourg to obtain such rights. The implication seems clear: children should not be subject to adult court procedures. Changes must be made to the system of trial of children and young suspects in the crown court, especially those at the youngest end of criminal responsibility (i.e. 10 to 13 year olds).

The above decision highlights how the government can be challenged for breaches of human rights and international protections in relation to young offenders. There are other possible breaches that could impact upon your social work practice in advising young people and their parents. Further challenges that could possibly be taken in relation to the provisions in the Crime and Disorder Act 1998 and the Youth Justice and Criminal Evidence Act 1999 include:

- *Anti-social behaviour orders (ASBOs), anti-social behaviour contracts (ABCs) and local child curfews.* A magistrate can order an anti-social behaviour order in respect of any person over the age of 10. The police, in conjunction with the local authority, make the application for an ASBO. The local authority can also impose ABCs on young people (and adults) before an ASBO application is made. Young people may feel pressurised to accept the terms of an ABC, for fear that a formal ASBO application might be made to the court if they decline. (See Chapter 4 for more information about ASBOs and ABCs). Although an ASBO is civil in nature, its breach can involve criminal sanctions. Such an order can now be made for beyond the original two year limit and its potential for constituting an intrusion of individual and family privacy seems clear. Furthermore, the local child curfew, which can be imposed on a group of children under the age of 10 for an extendable period of 90 days, appears similarly intrusive. As with the anti-social behaviour order, no criminal behaviour need be proved before a curfew is imposed.

It is noteworthy that Alvaro Gil-Robles, the Human Rights Commissioner for the Council of Europe, alleged in his report in June 2005 that the UK was suffering from 'asbomania'. Also, Shami Chakrabarti, the current director of Liberty, when asked to comment on the practice of some local authorities to 'name and shame' young people subject to ASBOs said that this practice was: 'More akin to the medieval stocks than a 21st century law and order strategy. We are in danger of transforming Britain into Asboland' (*Observer*, 12 June 2005).

Recently, successful challenges have been mounted by individual 'defendants' to allegedly unreasonable ASBO restrictions. In May 2005, a 16 year old from Collyhurst Village near Manchester became the first person to be banned under an ASBO from wearing a hooded top. However, in August 2005 a youth in Portsmouth, who was banned from wearing a hooded top or a baseball cap under the terms of an ASBO, had this part of the order set aside by a district judge when his solicitor successfully argued that this restriction breached his human rights. Similarly, in July 2005 the High Court backed a 15 year old's claim that ASBO powers that sanctioned the police to remove him from curfew zones breached the Human Rights Act in that it unreasonably interfered with his freedom of movement.

- *Article 8 of the European Convention on Human Rights, which is incorporated into domestic law by the Human Rights Act 1998, states that every person has the right to respect for their individual, private and family life*, unless an intrusion is necessary for (among other things) the prevention of crime. It may be difficult to justify severe restrictions on the liberty of a child who has not yet been convicted of committing any criminal act. Article 8 may also cover situations where a young person has been remanded into local authority accommodation and, due to shortage of specialised places (especially of secure accommodation), they are placed some considerable distance from their family, possibly for a number of months while awaiting trial.

- *Article 6 of the Convention covers the right to a fair trial*: possible issues arising under this provision are threefold.

First, it has been noted earlier that criminal sanctions can be applied for breaches of civil orders under the Crime and Disorder Act 1998 (e.g. anti-social behaviour and local child curfews). For a civil order to be made, the standard of proof is on the balance of probabilities – a much lower standard than the criminal law requirement of proof beyond reasonable doubt. Furthermore, parental bind-overs are deemed to be civil in nature and criminal sanctions can accrue for breach. Additionally, the referral order established by the Youth Justice and Criminal Evidence Act 1999 enables a court to refer a young person to a Youth Offender Panel, a body outside the 'official' criminal justice system, where there is no right to legal representation, yet which is authorised to pass criminal sanctions. Arguably, as such provisions and procedures are either in reality criminal in nature or have criminal consequences, they legitimately fall into the ambit for scrutiny by Articles 6 and 8 of the Convention (particularly as no rights of appeal are set out in either the Crime and Disorder Act 1998 or the Youth Justice and Criminal Evidence Act 1999).

Second, Section 35 of the Crime and Disorder Act 1998 permits an adverse inference to be drawn from a defendant's silence at interview or trial stage: this provision now applies from the age of ten. Article 6, in its assertion of the presumption of innocence and the right to a fair procedure, arguably sits uneasily with Section 35 in relation to young suspects. Also, it can perhaps be implied that Article 6 requires that an appropriate adult be present when the young person is cautioned, so that they can be properly instructed as to the full implications of their silence.

The third possible challenge in relation to Article 6 concerns reprimands and final warnings under Section 65 of the Crime and Disorder Act 1998. Issues about proportionality in relation to such sanctions, coupled with the continued debate about the possibility that young people, in eagerness to rid themselves of any further involvement with the criminal justice process, may confess to things they might not be found guilty of in a court of law, may be open to question in relation to fairness of procedure. Additionally, any failure to co-operate with the requirements of a final warning may result in the breach being cited in court and possibly lead to a harsher sentence being given in any future court appearances.

- *Article 3 of the European convention covers the prohibition of torture*, which includes degrading treatment or punishment. Linked to this, the Beijing Rules state that when a young person is sentenced it should amount to a 'fair reaction' – in other words, it should adhere to the principle of proportionality. It could possibly be argued that the Crime and Disorder Act 1998 implicitly sanctions the use of deterrent sentences in order to dissuade others from certain behaviours and that such sentences may, therefore, fall foul of the Human Rights Act 1998.

- *The consequences of being a young person refused bail*. This may mean that their relationship with their parents is severely affected. In an adversarial process where there may have been only a short time to respond to an application to refuse bail, the parent may not be involved at all in the decision-making process. Certain decisions to refuse bail may possibly breach Article 8 (noted above) and Article 5 of the Convention, which covers the right to security and liberty.

So it appears that there is potential for a number of challenges to our youth justice system that could be mounted under the Human Rights Act. The Youth Justice Board, lawyers representing young offenders and Youth Offending Teams should perhaps have made such challenges a priority but unfortunately we still await the testing of many of these possible Human Rights Act breaches. As a well-informed, proactive practitioner, you must be aware of any potential challenges.

The National Association of Youth Justice: the philosophical base

The National Association of Youth Justice (NAYJ) reflects many of the guiding principles of youth justice set out in international treaties and human rights legislation in their statement of basic philosophy (see www.nayj.org.uk for the full list of guiding principles). Their starting point is reminiscent of the 'welfare principle' that has been enshrined in our law relating to the treatment of young offenders since 1933. Section 44 of the Children and Young Persons Act 1933 states that when dealing with a young person the court shall 'have regard to the welfare of the child or young person and shall in a proper case take steps for removing him from undesirable surroundings or for securing that proper provision is made for his education or training'.

The NAYJ philosophy states from the outset that the welfare of the young person is paramount in proceedings and that a young person being dealt with by the criminal justice system must be regarded 'first and foremost' as a 'child'. The Association's second statement of belief specifically states that 'The establishment, application and protection of children's rights within national and international law and convention is essential'.

To summarise this section, international legal regulations, NAYJ principles and human rights legislation seem to afford extra layers of protection for children and young people who come before our criminal justice system. However, the extent to which our youth justice system conforms to the letter of these requirements should be a matter for continued investigation and legal challenge by professionals within the youth offending system.

ACTIVITY 1.3

Legal case study

Karim (aged 12) and Simon (aged 11) decide not to return to school after lunchtime but instead go to their local shopping mall in Kenchester. They enter Woolworths and Simon suggests that they steal some sweets from the pick 'n' mix counter. While they are stuffing confectionery into their rucksacks, Ken, a security guard, approaches them and asks them to open their bags. Karim complies with this request and reveals the chocolate he has stolen. Simon refuses to open his bag, and when Ken tries to take it from him Simon takes a baseball bat from the side pocket of the bag, hits Ken on the head and runs out of the shop. The police are called and Simon is apprehended while running from the shopping centre and arrested. Karim is also arrested and both boys are taken to the police station for questioning. Ken goes to hospital suffering from a split lip and a broken nose.

Simon is charged with grievous bodily harm (under Section 20 of the Offences Against the Person Act 1861) and theft (under S1 of the Theft Act 1968) and Karim is charged with theft.

As Karim already has a previous final warning for another matter of shoplifting six months earlier, Kenchester Youth Court sentence him to a four-month referral order. At the Youth Offender Panel meeting, the panel state that Karim must sign a contract that requires him to attend community reparation sessions for six hours every other Saturday for the duration of the order. In addition he must attend two one-and-a-half hour meetings with the YOS worker on Mondays and Wednesdays at 2.30 p.m. Karim's mother tells the panel that this will interfere with his school attendance, his extra-curricular sports activities, his homework time and family social time and that she feels that the requirements seem to be quite harsh for the theft of sweets worth £2.50. The panel tell Karim's mother that if he does not sign the contract the matter will be referred back to court for non co-operation and that if this happened Karim could be sentenced to a custodial sentence. Reluctantly, Karim signs the contract. After the court hearing the police and the local authority successfully obtain an ASBO on Karim that bans him from the shopping mall and from anywhere within a two-mile radius of the mall, and prevents him from wearing a hooded top. Karim usually attends a youth club half a mile from the mall on Friday evenings. Also, Karim was scalded as a child and is embarrassed of a large red scar on his neck. He regularly wears hooded tops to cover this mark.

Simon, who has previous convictions for shoplifting and robbery of a mobile phone, has learning difficulties. He initially goes to the Youth Court, but as the injuries to Ken were serious his case is referred to the Crown Court. He is refused bail as it is argued by the prosecution that he is a persistent offender, that this is a serious offence and that he might offend again. As there are no secure remand placements in Kenchester, he is placed in a centre in Durham, 300 miles away from his family. As his parents are on benefits, they can't afford to go to see him. The trial takes place six months later. At the trial, Simon is very worried and confused. He tells his lawyer that he doesn't understand the legal jargon or the procedure.

Advise Karim and Simon regarding legal challenges that might be brought in relation to any possible breaches of their rights.

As a practitioner dealing with these youths the issues that you might raise include:

Regarding Karim

- Karim's referral order seems to breach Article 6 of the European Convention on Human Rights (ECHR) as it is questionable whether he has had a fair hearing and there is no appeal.

- The level of restriction in the referral order on his liberty seems to breach Article 3 of the ECHR as it arguably is not a 'fair reaction' to the crime, as is required.

- The many requirements of the referral order arguably breach Article 8 of the ECHR as they seem to unnecessarily interfere with his private and family life, preventing him from undertaking his educational, sporting and social activities.

- In relation to Karim's ASBO, this is a civil order and if he breaches it he could receive a criminal sanction. This too is possibly a breach of Article 6, above.

- There have been some recent successful court challenges in relation to very restrictive ASBOs that the courts have held have breached the human rights of recipients. The two-mile radius ban and the subsequent impact upon his attendance at the youth club is arguably unreasonable, given the nature of the offence and that he has no other record of anti-social behaviour. The hooded top ban is also possibly a breach of his human rights.

Regarding Simon

- His placement in Durham is possibly in contravention of Article 8 of the ECHR as it interferes with his private and family life.

- The length of detention is also an issue under Article 8 as this is a young man who is on remand and has not yet been convicted of the offence.

- As Simon is only 11 years old and finds the trial in the Crown Court (an adult court) confusing, this seems to contravene one of the decisions of the Euopean Court of Human Rights in *Thompson and Venables* [1999] which stated that a Crown Court was an unsuitable place for the defendants (who were aged 11 at the time of the case) to be tried.

The dual agenda of youth justice and social work: justice vs welfare

Are young people who come before the criminal justice system offenders, who have chosen to break society's rules and so deserve to be punished, or are they (as the Children Act 1989 asserts) children 'in need'? Should we expect them to take full responsibility for the consequences of their actions or should we view them as being less capable than adults of understanding and sticking to the rules of society? Should they be dealt with in the same courts as adults and be eligible to the same punishments, or should they be dealt with by specialist courts and personnel who have been trained to understand and remedy their needs? Should there be a wider range of disposals available to judges and magistrates who deal with young offenders than there is for adult offenders? Should we help and guide young people to move away from law-breaking behaviour or should we provide an optimum deterrent in the form of commensurate punishment? Should we punish the young offender's crime or the young offender himself/herself? These are just some of the questions that highlight the dilemmas facing those who structure and work within the youth justice system and form part of what youth justice theorists and practitioners call the 'justice vs welfare' debate. These two approaches have dominated youth justice philosophy for a hundred years and though other valid perspectives have been developed (we will examine these in Chapter 2) the justice vs welfare debate still rages in academic, media, governmental and professional practice fields.

The introduction of a distinct system for dealing with young offenders in 1908 represented, in essence, a 'modification' of adult justice – a 'compromise' which resulted in the cross-fertilisation of principles of adult responsibility with notions of welfarism and protectionism. A justice approach, based upon classicist ideas of culpability and responsibility, would involve a strict legal due process system, which sentenced using notions of proportionality and seriousness, providing a sanction that befitted the offence, rather than the offender. A welfare-based approach would involve a less formal and adaptable procedure, one that would conceptualise the offending behaviour, allow for mitigation and a recognition of the possibility of limited responsibility (part of neo-classicism), and allow for non-legal experts to enter the decision-making process and produce a disposal that would fit the offender, rather than the offence. The Children Act 1908 effectively opened up the possibility of these two styles being blended (or possibly muddled) in the context of dealing with young offenders.

This early discovery of the potential of conflict between the polemic welfare vs justice dichotomy was to produce various forms of compromise solutions over the course of the century. We examine in detail these philosophies, legislative developments and features of systems based on principles of justice and those based on principles of welfare in Chapter 2.

As a youth justice practitioner, you will become familiar with the dilemmas between justice and welfare approaches. Primarily, your social work training will have taught you to regard the best interests and welfare of the young person you are working with as paramount considerations. You will soon be aware that in youth justice, while the law sometimes protects and supports those interests (such as in relation to international and human rights protections outlined above), often the application of law conflicts with your guiding social work ethics. For example, you might view a young offender as primarily a child in need and feel that community intervention and offence counselling might be the best way to deal with a troubled young person who is 'acting out' through offending behaviour. Judges, magistrates and the police might have a different opinion and decide that the offence is serious and/or that the only way to protect the public is to put your client behind bars.

The conflict between social work ethics and legal principles is arguably more tangible in the practice of youth justice than in any other area of social work.

Using values and ethics in your practice

The vast array of standards, codes and legal frameworks can appear overwhelming for practitioners. How can you ensure your practice takes account of values and ethical issues in accordance with these? When working within youth justice it is important to consider how society views young people generally and young people who offend specifically. We all have personal views about young people and of what expectations are seen as the 'norm'. These may be based on our own experiences of adolescence, drawn from young people with whom we are in contact or from wider society.

ACTIVITY **1.4**

Think about how you view young people. What assumptions do you make about them? What expectations do you have about young people? Are these different from the views, assumptions and expectations you have about young people who offend? Where do your views come from? Look for newspaper headlines about young people. What do they say? How are young people/offenders described? Are these views representative?

Your answers to the questions in this Activity will be determined by a range of factors; they may be partly as a result of your age, your experience of adolescence, how you feel about your own children or those of others in your family or network of friends. Your own experience of adolescence may be very different from young people in contemporary society and you may find it hard to empathise. You may have been positive in thinking about young people, describing them as lively, inquiring, exciting and fun. Your responses may have been neutral, such as innocent, naive and impressionable; or negative, such as rebellious, troublesome, argumentative and difficult.

Your responses will more than likely also be shaped by external factors such as the television, newspapers and social policy. Young people are often presented in negative ways by the media, particularly those involved in offending. Recently in the UK much attention has been paid by the government and the media to the rise of anti-social behaviour, particularly among young people. Various shopping centres and schools have gone so far as to ban young people from wearing 'hoodies' because some young people walk around in groups wearing them and a proportion of these young people allegedly commit crime. This has led to the government announcing a drive to put the 'respect' back into British society, introducing a raft of measures designed to combat 'yobbish' behaviour. It could be argued that another 'moral panic' is being created similar to that in the 1970s when the term 'mugging' was designed to describe street robberies, leading to the use of stop and search powers by the police. These powers effectively discriminated against black and minority ethnic people, who were stopped disproportionately by the police (Hall et al., 1978). The term 'moral panic' was coined by Cohen (1973) as a way of emphasising the media's role in amplifying crime and deviance, particularly in relation to youths. It seems ironic that youth crime is so high on the political agenda when recent Home Office figures and the British Crime Survey both show a decline in youth crime over the last few years (Home Office, 2005b). However, public opinion polls suggest that there is an erroneous belief that youth crime is increasing at an alarming rate (Bateman, 2005).

When working with young people who offend it is important to be aware of the attitudes and feelings you have about and towards them. It may be that you have pre-conceived ideas about how young people behave based on what you have learned from the news. Your views may be stereotypical and unfair representations of young people who offend who are, in reality, as diverse a group of people as any other. Young people are often discriminated against because of their age, with their behaviour often described negatively.

ACTIVITY *1.5*

How might a young offender feel if the overriding picture that is painted of them by society is negative? What impact could this have on the offender and their behaviour?

Young people may internalise what they hear said about them and begin to think that society or adults only see or acknowledge 'bad' behaviour. This might lead them to think that anything else is not recognised. It may also create a divide between young people and adults that could exacerbate the problem. Adults may feel uncomfortable walking past a group of young people on the streets but how does this make law-abiding young people feel? Many young people involved in offending behaviour are likely to have issues of low self-esteem and the effects of labelling (as discussed in Chapter 3), only seek to exacerbate this. It is essential that young people are considered within life-course perspectives on adolescence, which take into account psychological, social and physical factors. As Crawford and Walker (2003, p71) state: 'For some young people, the challenges of adolescence result in choices, which lead to a number of problems, and some problems peak at this time.' Thus, social workers need to be aware of what kind of behaviour might be expected, taking into account the developmental stage they are at.

It is important as a social worker to be aware of the reasons you want to work with a particular service user group and what qualities and values are important in being able to work with that group. It may be useful to identify what you see as the opportunities of working within a youth justice setting as well as what some of the difficulties may be. Social work practice in this area can be extremely varied and could involve working with young people at risk of offending, those in trouble with the police for the very first time, right through to young people with significant criminal records who may have been convicted of extremely serious offences.

ACTIVITY *1.6*

Read the following cases. How would you feel working with each young person? What might some of the moral/ethical issues be for you personally and professionally?

Imran, aged 16, has been charged with indecently assaulting his three-year old brother. He is not allowed to return home while the police investigation is undertaken. You have to liaise with the children and families team and work in partnership with his family to identify an appropriate placement for him.

ACTIVITY 1.6 *continued*

*Sarah, aged 15, is in a local authority children's home as her mother has left
and her father is in prison. She has committed numerous offences of burglary a
writing the pre-sentence report for the court. The judge has indicated that Sara
to receive a custodial sentence. When you discuss this with Sarah she breaks   in
tears saying that if she goes into custody she will kill herself.*

*Andrew, aged 17, is serving a three-year custodial sentence. He is to be released in
three months' time. He has nowhere to live on release and he does not want to engage
in college, training or employment. He is content to sit around with his friends all day
smoking cannabis.*

Each of the cases requires quite different responses. You may find it difficult working with
Imran as the abuse of children is always likely to provoke an emotional action. You have to
remember that at this stage Imran has not been convicted and therefore it is only an allegation. However you may feel about an offence, it is your role to work with the young
person and to see him or her as an individual who *may* have carried out an offence, rather
than as an offender. Imran may be very scared about what is going to happen to him,
about being separated from his family and being placed somewhere else. You will have
to work with his family too, who will undoubtedly be finding the situation very difficult to
deal with. The case may raise unresolved issues for you as an individual. You have to ensure
that your practice is professional at all times despite the feelings this raises for you.

In cases such as Sarah's, you may feel helpless to stop young people like her having their
liberty removed. You can only do what is within your power, and this would probably
involve ensuring that your report for the court addresses all the difficulties that she has
encountered. You will be required to assess her needs in order to make a proposal that will
deal with the issues that caused her to offend, thereby reducing the risk she poses. It may
be that the judge will still sentence Sarah to a period of detention and your role then
would be to work with the secure establishment she is sent to so that she is closely monitored and any risk of harm is minimised.

Andrews' case illustrates the care and control aspect of social work practice in this area.
You may think that at 17 Andrew is almost an adult and therefore capable of making decisions about how he is to live his life. However, as your role is to prevent him from
re-offending and to look after his welfare, you need to work with his motivation levels and
self-esteem as well as provide practical support around accommodation and education or
employment. The reasons why he does not want to do anything may be related to how he
feels let down by his family or because he does not have a stake in society.

Working with young people in the criminal justice system will evoke many different feelings in you and challenge your ethical and moral code of practice. It is important to be
aware of how you feel about a particular case in order to know if it is impacting upon
your practice. This is where reflective practice (Schon, 1983) is essential so that you can
examine the decisions you have made and the actions you have taken in order to analyse
the effect of these upon a case. Being able to relate theory to your practice is also an

portant part of reflective practice. Supervision is one forum where these sorts of issues can be discussed with a manager, or you may choose to talk about cases with your colleagues. Ensuring you are undertaking continual professional development, in line with GSCC registration requirements, will assist you in developing new skills and knowledge, as will being informed by evidenced-based practice and considering new perspectives. These fundamental issues of good social work practice will be revisited throughout this book.

Discrimination

It is clear that young people as a group may be discriminated against based on the stereotypes that are held by individuals and society. Discrimination and oppression are often complex issues, with some young people facing multiple oppressions, for instance based on their culture and sex. Having an awareness of how oppression and discrimination manifest themselves is especially important in the youth justice system.

Anti-discriminatory practice

Thompson (2001) has developed a conceptual framework in order to understand how inequalities and discrimination feature in the social circumstances and interactions of service users. This is called the PCS analysis. The *P* refers to the personal or psychological level, *C* refers to the cultural level and *S* to the structural level. He suggests that all three levels overlap and that it is important to recognise that our views are partly individualised (*P*) but also shaped by our cultural world (*C*) and our experience of socialisation (*S*). That social workers are in a position to play an important role in practising in a way that seeks to redress and challenge discrimination is a point vehemently articulated:

> *Social workers occupy positions of power and influence, and so there is considerable scope for discrimination and oppression, whether this is intentional or by default. Anti-discriminatory practice is an attempt to eradicate discrimination and oppression from our own practice and challenge them in the practice of others and the institutional structures in which we operate. In this respect, it is a form of emancipatory practice.* (Thompson, 2001, p34)

Thompson offers a useful theoretical framework for social work practitioners to develop the required 'skills, values and attitudes' necessary to practise in an anti-discriminatory approach.

According to Home Office statistical data produced in response to Section 95 of the Criminal Justice Act 1991, young people from minority ethnic backgrounds are over-represented within the criminal justice system (Home Office, 2005d). Section 95 of the Criminal Justice Act 1991 requires the Home Secretary to publish statistical data on race and gender with a view to helping the criminal justice system avoid discriminating on the grounds of race, gender or any other improper ground.

RESEARCH SUMMARY

The Youth Justice Board, the organisation that oversees youth justice services in England and Wales, commissioned research to look at whether young people from minority ethnic backgrounds are differentially treated within the criminal justice system. The research examined how young people from minority ethnic backgrounds were dealt with compared to their white counterparts at each stage of the youth justice process. Eight YOTs were selected for the study and information was obtained on 17,054 cases involving males and females aged 12–17 over 15 months in 2001–02. The study, Differences or Discrimination?, *found that there were considerable variations in the extent of over- or under-representation of particular ethnic groups in relation to the proportions served by the YOTs included in the study.*

The research found at various stages of the youth justice process differences in outcome in the treatment of people from different ethnic backgrounds as well as between males and females. Sometimes this was due to relevant variations in the cases; however, there were also differences consistent with 'discriminatory treatment'. These included:

- *A higher rate of prosecution and conviction of mixed-parentage young males.*

- *A higher proportion of prosecutions involving black young males.*

- *A higher probability that a black male would, if convicted in a Crown Court, receive a sentence of 12 months or more.*

- *A greater proportion of black and Asian males remanded in custody prior to sentence.*

- *A much greater proportion of mixed-parentage females who were prosecuted.*

The researchers concluded by stating that 'young black people were substantially overrepresented in the caseloads of the police, prosecutors, YOTs and the courts in relation to their numbers in the local population'. *They voice* 'considerable concern about whether there is always fair treatment of minority ethnic young people'. *Moreover, they believe the evidence of the research to be consistent with* 'a more complex phenomenon of justice by race and geography'.

(YJB, 2004a)

The *Differences or Discrimination*? study did not look at why such differences had occurred but this is clearly an area that needs to be explored. The researchers felt that there needed to be a concerted effort to understand the phenomenon of differential patterns within the youth justice system which could only be achieved by a detailed analysis of local sentencing practices, based on a careful analysis of case records and local crime rates, and on close observations of practices at all stages of the system.

Other research offers similar findings (Goldson, 2002; Wilson and Moore, 2004); however, the general view is that studies into discrimination levels within the youth justice system are few and far between. Kalunta-Crumpton (2005) suggests that given the increased incarceration of black and some other ethnic minority young people, there is a need for comprehensive ethnic monitoring of the use made by courts of the more punitive sanctions available, custody in particular. Youth Offending Teams are now required to undertake a race audit and develop an action plan to address discrimination as a specific area on which their performance is measured, in accordance with the Race Relations (Amendment) Act 2000.

The other significant area of research into differential treatment within the youth justice system is in relation to sex. While offending rates by girls are swamped by those of their male counterparts, there is evidence to suggest they are rising, particularly in relation to the use of custody where the increase over the period 1992–2002 was as high as 600 per cent (NACRO cited in Bateman and Pitts, 2005). The Home Office has established a working party looking at the discrimination of women by the criminal justice system. Historically girls and young women have been treated differently by a system that has struggled to see them as anything other than mad or bad and in need of welfare services. Hudson (2002) suggests that the difficulties faced by girls in trouble are that they are perceived as emotional and more difficult to work with. She suggests that social workers need to view the girl's behaviour as a response to their oppression and a way of surviving, and that emotionality should be seen as a positive resource. Hudson suggests that the recent drive towards the justice model has meant that girls are being treated less along welfare lines; this could be pushing them up the sentencing framework quicker than boys. A common problem for YOTs is the inability to offer suitable programmes for girls because of the lower number of girls in the criminal justice system. This needs to be addressed if girls are to receive a fair service and one that meets their needs effectively. This issue is exacerbated in the case of black and ethnic minority girls.

There are other groups discriminated by and within the youth justice system, such as asylum-seekers, 'looked after' children and travellers. Social work practitioners need to be aware of the issues facing these groups when assessing for and providing services, as well as signalling their discrimination to other agencies within the youth justice system. Social workers also need to listen to the experiences of individuals from such oppressed groups in order to be able to empower them, work in partnership, seek feedback from them and evaluate their interventions to ensure their practice does not discriminate.

ACTIVITY *1.7*

Read the following case studies and identify the significant issues.

Gemma is 15 years old and from a traveller family. She has been sentenced by the court for shoplifting offences. Her parents have not attended appointments with you and Gemma tells you that they will not be attending even though the court has ordered them to. Gemma does not attend school as her family want her at home looking after her younger siblings with her mother.

Andrei is 17 and from Eastern Europe. He has appeared in court having been arrested for attempted theft from a cashpoint. The court is considering whether to grant him bail and you are assessing his suitability. He tells you that he is homeless, has no family and came to the UK six months ago to seek asylum. When you ask him where he has been staying he is very evasive and will not disclose any information.

ACTIVITY **1.7** *continued*

John is 16 and lives in local authority accomodation. He is placed in a children's home in the local area on a temporary basis while a long-term placement is found. You are working with him while he is in the area. John has had six placements in the 18 months that he has been 'looked after'. While he attends his appointments with you, he is feeling very low and is not really engaging with you.

In Gemma's case you may have approached the issues from a legal perspective: her parents have been ordered to attend court, and in accordance with the Education Act 1988 Gemma has to be in education at the age of 15. Both issues carry consequences. However, you are working with Gemma who cannot be held responsible for her parents' behaviour. Alternatively you may have looked at the case from the perspective of assessing why Gemma is offending, and found that her non-school attendance and family may be seen to be contributing factors. In either approach it is essential that you meet her parents and explain the situation and try to gain an understanding of their situation. It may be that their previous contact with authorities has been negative and they are reluctant to engage as a result of this. Your local area may have specific services for travellers, including education provision, that you can put them in touch with for support.

Andrei's case might be best approached in a similar way, in that you do not know what he has experienced in his home country. His previous contact with authorities may also have been negative and he may well have experienced trauma of some kind. He could be in the UK as an unaccompanied minor with no adult care and supervision, he could be connected to a larger criminal group, or he could be an illegal immigrant. Whatever his situation, he is probably scared and confused about what will happen to him in a strange country. An interpreter will be needed to communicate with him if his English is not fluent, in order that he is made to feel at ease, his situation explained fully and as much information as possible obtained to ensure he is placed appropriately and given support.

John is probably feeling that he is not wanted as he is being moved about so often. You are probably one of many social workers and other professionals that he has had to speak to in that time. You need to acknowledge how he is feeling and let him talk about that. You can offer him support in your sessions and advocate on his behalf to the accommodating local authority so that permanent plans can be made as soon as possible. In any event, you need to have some idea about how long he is likely to be in his current placement as this will affect what provision you can put into place around his education, leisure etc. It may be that John is offending as a result of being in care and this is something you could work with him on.

C H A P T E R   S U M M A R Y

In this chapter we have identified the relevant frameworks setting out the expected conduct of workers within a youth justice setting and observed how values and ethics underpin social work education and practice. We have also considered the implications of the Human Rights Act and international guidelines in relation to working with young people who offend. You have explored your attitudes towards youth and young offenders and you have looked at your own prejudices as well of those of society at large. You have thought about what some of the ethical dilemmas may be in working with young people. The impact of the media and the affect that labelling may have on young people has been considered, as has the importance of being able to place young people according to their stage of life-course development. The issue of discrimination of young people within the youth justice system has been examined and the need for anti-discriminatory practice identified. It is essential that future practice is enhanced by the integration of theories of working with young people, young people in trouble as well as evidence-based best practice. Ensuring that this is done within the context of recognising and valuing difference and the impact that such differences have on young people is vital in becoming a fully reflective practitioner.

FURTHER READING

Youth Justice Board (2004) *Differences or discrimination?* London: Youth Justice Board.
Provides a full account of the research highlighted in this chapter.

Thompson, N (2006) *Anti-discriminatory practice, 4th edn*. Basingstoke: Palgrave Macmillan.
Provides a useful introduction to issues of discrimination, equality and diversity.

Monaghan, G (2005) Children's human rights and youth justice, in Bateman, T and Pitts, J (eds) *The RHP companion to youth justice*. Lyme Regis: Russell House Publishing.

WEBSITES

www.homeoffice.gov.uk/rds/section951.html.
For more information on statistical information in relation to ethnicity, gender and crime.

Chapter 2

The development of youth justice philosophies, laws and polices

Jane Pickford

A C H I E V I N G   A   S O C I A L   W O R K   D E G R E E

This chapter will help you begin to meet the following National Occupational Standards.

Key Role 6: Demonstrate professional competence in social work practice

- Review and update your own knowledge of legal, policy and procedural frameworks.
- Identify and assess issues, dilemmas and conflicts that might affect your practice.
- Assess needs, risks and options, taking into account legal and other requirements.

It will also introduce you to the following academic standards as set out in the social work subject benchmark statement:

3.1.1 Social work services and service users

- The social processes (associated with, for example, poverty, unemployment, poor health, disablement, lack of education and other sources of disadvantage) that lead to marginalisation, isolation and exclusion and their impact on the demand for social work services.
- The relationship between agency policies, legal requirements and professional boundaries in shaping the nature of services provided in inter-disciplinary contexts and the issues associated with working across professional boundaries and within different disciplinary groups.

3.1.2 The service delivery context

- The complex relationships between public, social and political philosophies, policies and priorities and the organisation and practice of social work, including the contested nature of these.
- The issues and trends in modern public and social policy and their relationship to contemporary practice and service delivery in social work.
- The significance of legislative and legal frameworks and service delivery standards (including the nature of legal authority, the application of legislation in practice, statutory accountability and tensions between statute, policy and practice).
- The significance of interrelationships with other social services, especially education, housing, health, income maintenance and criminal justice.

3.1.3 Values and ethics

- The moral concepts of rights, responsibility, freedom, authority and power inherent in the practice of social workers as moral and statutory agents.
- The complex relationships between justice, care and control in social welfare and the practical and ethical implications of these, including roles as statutory agents and in upholding the law in respect of discrimination.

- Aspects of philosophical ethics relevant to the understanding and resolution of value dilemmas and conflicts in both interpersonal and professional contexts.
- The conceptual links between codes defining ethical practice, the regulation of professional conduct and the management of potential conflicts generated by the codes held by different professional groups.

3.1.4 Social work theory

- Research-based concepts and critical explanations from social work theory and other disciplines that contribute to the knowledge base of social work, including their distinctive epistemological status and application to practice.

3.1.5 The nature of social work practice

- The place of theoretical perspectives and evidence from international research in assessment and decision-making processes in social work practice.
- The integration of theoretical perspectives and evidence from international research into the design and implementation of effective social work intervention with a wide range of service users, carers and others.
- The processes of reflection and evaluation, including familiarity with the range of approaches for evaluating welfare outcomes, and their significance for the development of practice and the practitioner.

Introduction

In this chapter we examine the development of youth justice theory, policy and practice. In order to understand the rationales underpinning any area of social work practice, it is always vital to have an insight into the way your area of practice has been shaped by its history. It is arguable that the study of youth justice, more than any other area of social work practice, is a creature of its historical development. Though new perspectives have emerged over the recent history of juvenile justice policy, the whole structure of the youth justice industry has been imbued by dominant philosophies that have seeped into the roots of the foundations of youth justice practice and thus still monopolise and govern contemporary practice. It is necessary, therefore, to review the bedrock of youth justice theory and practice and trace the evolution of our unique youth justice system over the last century. Only when we understand the origins and maturation processes of a system can we understand the logic behind contemporary practice.

In Chapter 1, we referred to the two (arguably polemic) philosophies that appear to have dominated youth justice theory over almost a hundred years, namely the justice and welfare perspectives. We also noted that, as these standpoints seem to be directly oppositional to each other, the historical development of youth justice has been peppered with manifestations of conflicts between these approaches, conflicts that have, perhaps, hindered any cohesive advancement in youth justice practice. I have argued elsewhere that the divergent natures of these two leading philosophies of youth justice render any attempt at fusion at the level of practice futile (Pickford, 2000).

This chapter is split into three parts: in Part 1 we examine the historically dominant approaches of justice and welfare; Part 2 analyses other philosophies that have emerged and arguably superseded the justice and welfare perspectives; and in Part 3 we briefly chronicle the historical development of youth justice legislation.

Part 1: The two historically dominant philosophies – justice and welfare

In this section we examine the two perspectives of youth justice that dominated policy developments over most of the twentieth century, before going on to examine further perspectives (in Part 2) that have developed since the latter part of the last century. In order to understand these approaches, it is useful to analyse how features of each become manifest in practice. As I have posited that they are polemical positions, the features of each in terms of contrasting characteristics are outlined below.

Justice vs welfare

- *Due process vs adaptable procedures*. In the justice approach, adherence to a fixed procedure is paramount in order to ensure that all accused persons are treated in the same manner; whereas using the welfare approach there is no fixed procedure – procedures are adaptable to the case/issues being discussed.

- *Legalisic vs holistic*. The justice perspective emphasises 'formal justice' where legal procedures and legal representation by lawyers are used to ensure that all young people who come before the court are treated equally and fairly; whereas using the welfare perspective, lawyers will generally not be required – other professionals may take part in the hearing (e.g. social worker, teacher, youth worker, health worker) in order to discuss possible solutions to the young person's problematic behaviour.

- *Adversarial vs inquisitorial*. The justice philosophy requires a traditional focus on legal battles between the defence and prosecution lawyers in an effort to find the truth; whereas the welfare philosophy adopts a minimalist approach to fact-finding, avoiding conflictual confrontations.

- *Formalism vs informality*. The justice standpoint requires a sombre procedure in a courtroom, which purportedly reinforces the serious nature of matters being raised – in a Crown Court, lawyers wear gowns, in all courts complex legal language is used; whereas using the welfare standpoint, hearings will take place in an informal atmosphere and there may, for example, be a discussion of the alleged offending event and possible solutions where all parties, including the young person and parent(s) are encouraged to speak.

- *Proportionate vs tailor-made sentence*. To ensure fairness and consistency, using the justice approach the defendant should be sentenced in proportion to the seriousness of the offence; whereas the welfare approach requires that the sentence primarily should fit the needs of the offender rather than reflect the seriousness of the offence – emphasis is placed upon what kind of intervention is needed to help the young person desist from negative behaviour patterns, and disposals should be aimed at the need to reform.

- *Responsibility and blame vs explanation and causation*. Using the justice perspective, any person aged ten or above (in England and Wales) is presumed capable of forming the level of culpability (*mens rea*) required for the crime and so logically should be made to face up to the full consequences of their behaviour; whereas under the welfare perspective, the reasons behind the offending behaviour are investigated in order to provide suitable interventions and the young person's capacity to form the required level of culpability is considered.

- *Act orientation vs actor orientation.* In the justice paradigm, the emphasis is on the crime – on the action performed rather than on the person who performed it, and appropriate disposals will be decided upon with regard to the act rather than the actor; whereas during welfare-based proceedings, the emphasis is upon the actor rather than the act.

ACTIVITY 2.1

Now that you have some idea of the different dominant approaches of justice and welfare, let's examine a case study where dilemmas might arise due to the divergences of the dominant philosophies:

Darren, aged 12, has been arrested for writing graffiti on the walls of his local police station. This is his first offence but the police believe that, given the extent of the damage and the cost of repair, the matter should be referred to Youth Court. Darren is sentenced to a six-month referral order and you, as a youth offending social worker, have been asked by your manager to write the referral report and arrange a youth Offender Panel. While interviewing Darren he discloses to you that he and his sister, aged nine, have been physically and sexually abused by their father over a number of years and that their father regularly 'beats up' their mother. You believe that this offence was effectively a 'cry for help'. This is the first time this abuse has come to the attention of any authority.

- *What ethical dilemmas are you faced with by this case?*
- *How do the justice and welfare approaches relate to this case?*
- *Is the youth justice system the proper place for such a case?*
- *Should Darren be punished for his criminal act?*
- *What recommendations regarding the content of the referral order would you propose? (see Chapter 4).*

Incompatibility of dominant philosophies?

There have been many attempts by successive governments to fuse the justice and welfare approaches, in the belief that these contrasting philosophies could melt together to form a seamless, merged practice. This has arguably never succeeded. When you examine the history of youth justice legislation (below) you will realise that each government has failed dismally at its attempt, and on every occasion both approaches have been unhappily forced together by the growing weight of ill-conceived legislation, the result being a piecemeal mish-mash of justice and welfare measures lying uneasily together at different points of youth justice practice. Should we be surprised that a happy alliance has never been forged? If we put oil into water or squeeze lemon into milk do they mix? The oil floats on top of the water and the milk curdles. It is impossible to fuse two divergent substances that are composed of completely different elements. Similarly, the enforced union of two oppositional philosophies will not result in a joined practice. The problem with this attempted merger is that they are opposing approaches. They cancel each other out. Any attempted merger is, therefore, inevitably doomed to failure. (Even the most cursory critical analysis of the history of youth justice policy and legislation exposes this failure – see Part 3 of this chapter.)

Prior to Labour's election success in 1997 the incompatibility of the two paradigms had been recognised. The then Shadow Home Secretary Jack Straw stated that at the root of the problem with the youth justice system was a fundamental confusion over philosophy:

> *At the heart of the crisis in youth justice is confusion and conflict between welfare and punishment. Too many people involved with the system are unclear whether the purpose is to punish and to signify society's disapproval of offending or whether the welfare of the young offender is paramount.* (Home Office, 1997g, p9)

The solution proposed was a reworking of philosophy: 'This confusion cannot continue. A new balance has to be struck between the sometimes conflicting interests of welfare and punishment', which would involve 'resolving some of the confusion between the relationship of welfare and punishment in dealing with young offenders' (Home Office, 1997g, pp9,18).

However, as noted by Fionda (2005) by 1997, in order to justify their proposals to mix justice and welfare initiatives in the Crime and Disorder Act, the Government appeared to have changed their mind and denied any incompatibility between 'protecting the welfare of the young offender and preventing that individual from offending again' (Home Office, 1997d, para 2.2). In Chapter 4 we look at whether this confusion has been resolved by sweeping reforms that have taken place since 1997.

In addition to Labour's recognition of the contradictory nature of justice and welfare approaches, various prominent academics in the area of youth justice have also clearly noted the antagonism between the dominant paradigms.

> *The history of youth justice is a history of conflict, contradictions, ambiguity and compromise. Conflict is inevitable in a system that has traditionally pursued the twin goals of welfare and justice . . . As a result it continually seeks the compromise between youth as a special deserving case and youth as fully responsible for their own actions.* (Muncie and Hughes, 2002, p1)

Muncie and Hughes further argue that the conflict has given rise to an expansion of the remit of the youth justice industry while in pursuit of a compromise. Perhaps as a result of these irresolvable philosophical tensions, theoreticians (but not yet practitioners) seem to have abandoned the justice vs welfare debate, contending that it is 'moribund' and arguing that attempted legislative solutions to this dilemma have resulted in broadening levels of state control of young people, as witnessed in youth justice legislation in the last 25 years (Muncie, 2004). The creation and expansion of civil orders against children and young people in the form of anti-social behaviour contracts, orders and curfew orders are key examples of the widening of social control measures.

Fionda also refers to 'internal conflicts within policy' producing 'ambiguous legislation' that can 'badly misfire' due to 'an inability to choose one approach over the other' (2005, pp40, 43). Rutherford (1992) and Pratt (1989) have also discussed the incompatibility of these two ideologies.

In an attempt to evidence the contradictory nature of justice and welfare approaches, I have noted elsewhere (Pickford, 2000) examples of the various strategies that have been adopted by successive governments in an attempt to fuse justice and welfare approaches. Each has failed and each arguably represents evidential proof of the impossibility of merger at both levels of theory and practice. The failed strategies include:

- *Bifurcation strategy*. Distinguishing between different types of children and young people who come before the justice system. This involves differentiating those who need help from those who deserve punishment; serious offenders from non-serious offenders; persistent offenders from those whose behaviour, it is believed, can be 'nipped in the bud';

- *Sequencing strategy*. Creating different types of procedures/processes that utilise divergent approaches, e.g. a justice approach in relation to trial and conviction – a welfare approach in relation to mitigation and sentencing; pre-trial/court diversionary schemes.

- *Institutional strategy*. Developing practices whereby different institutions/organisations will deal with different types of young offenders, e.g. Youth Offender Panels or courts; social services or the formal youth justice system.

- *Double-edged strategy*. The introduction of measures that have both a welfare and a justice function, e.g. the criminal care order introduced by the Children and Young Persons Act 1969 (now abolished).

- *Career criminal strategy*. A young offender may experience a more welfare-oriented approach at the start of their offending career, e.g. by the use of reprimands and final warnings or other diversionary measures. If they continue to offend, more justice-oriented procedures and sanctions will be implemented.

All the above forms of compromise amount to techniques or splitting strategies which attempt to distribute incompatible elements across the system in different ways (Pickford, 2000, pxxxiv).

When we examine the history of youth justice legislation (in Part 3, below) you should be able not only to assess the legislations in terms of justice and/or welfare measures, but also to identify any of the 'splitting strategies' that might have occurred in order to facilitate implementation.

Given the tendency of academics to deal with these inevitable and unsolvable tensions by moving away from an incessant focus on justice and welfare paradigm (see below) is it not time for the government too to overhaul youth justice theory and provide some consistency?

ACTIVITY 2.2

In groups, discuss whether, in your opinion, justice and welfare approaches can work together and succeed under the same system. Can you think of any strategies/approaches that might assist a seamless merging of these approaches?

Part 2: Other perspectives of youth justice

In addition to the traditional dominating dual perspectives of justice and welfare, academics over recent history have developed/spotted a veritable smorgasbord of approaches to youth justice. Their analyses cover recognition of a number of youth justice styles.

Preventionism

It could be suggested that a further principle of youth justice was born (in embryonic form) at the end of the 1960s: the prevention principle, which has arguably always been a nascent feature of welfarism, emerged in the Children and Young Persons Act 1969 and, in a distinctly overt form, in preventative measures introduced by the Crime and Disorder Act 1998, such as anti-social behaviour, curfew and child safety orders (ASBOs, COs and CSOs). Its rationale is that pre-emptive early intervention should prevent potential future offending behaviour. This approach was given further momentum by the Anti-Social Behaviour Act 2003, which entrenched and expanded police and local authorities' powers to obtain civil orders against young people, whether or not they had committed a criminal offence, and further extended powers relating to parenting orders (POs) introduced by the Crime and Disorder Act 1998. Broader measures, in the form of acceptable behaviour contracts (ABCs) as an interim measure issued prior to a full ASBO, coupled with the introduction of individual support orders (ISOs) targeted at young people subject to ASBOs (from May 2004), are evidence of a government willing to stretch out the tentacles of state control and draw non-offenders into the youth justice net.

We noted in Chapter 1 the legal implications of these measures, and the issues in terms of human rights legislation of civil orders issued by a government which, if breached, result in criminal sanctions. We also referred to some challenges that had been mounted by lawyers, in particular regarding ASBOs and human rights breaches. As social work practitioners, this is an area where you should be constantly vigilant in order to ensure that state bodies do not issue controls on your clients in breach of their human rights. Although purportedly welfare-based, it is arguable that preventionism produces labelling and net-widening effects (see Chapter 3) pulling young people who may not yet have committed any criminal offences into the ambit of the criminal justice system; it is, therefore, essentially a latent form of social control.

Such measures are part of what Ashworth (1994) has called a 'pincer movement' in youth justice, which has been in evidence since the 1970s; this movement gained momentum following the death of toddler James Bulger in 1993 and the ensuing media moral panic that led to what various criminologists have called the 'demonisation' of youth (Jenks, 1996). Hendrick (2002) asserts that this case was transformative in that it led to the abandonment of the 'romantic' model of childhood innocence that had been dominant for many decades and caused a resurgence of the 'evangelical child' model – the notion that children are born evil and that we should be wary of them. Fionda states that current youth justice law 'ensures that more devils are drawn into a wider net with a thinner mesh' from which it is harder to escape (Fionda, 2005, p58).

The growth of the youth justice industry over recent years, produced by a focus on preventionism, has been vast, with prevention teams performing major roles in most Youth Offending Teams across the country. In addition to this, the introduction of preventative orders (noted above) since 1998 and the expansion of the preventionism rationale have led to the setting up of various new organisations, for example:

- Youth Intervention Programmes (YIPs), aimed at 13–16 year olds in a community who are deemed most at risk of offending.

- Youth Intervention and Support Panels (YISPs), consisting of 13 schemes across the country aimed at 8–13 year olds who are deemed most at risk of offending.

- On Track Scheme.

- Sure Start.

- Locally based prevention projects run by local authorities and/or local police authorities, including summer activity schemes.

- Positive Futures Programmes.

- Safer Schools Partnerships.

- Anti-social behaviour action teams attached to local authorities.

Although we have noted some of the dangers of a focus on prevention in terms of expansionism, for potential youth justice practitioners, there has never been a better time for you to enter this growth industry!

Corporatism/managerialism/partnerships/systems management

This approach to youth justice practice has been differently named by various academics, hence the broad heading. However, in essence, following negative feedback from the Audit Commission's report (1996) into the old Youth Justice Teams (Misspent Youth, 1996) in relation to the disparate and often lax management processes, systematic and corporate-style management techniques that had already begun to emerge in some quarters were pushed to the foreground in an effort to improve and standardise the practice of youth justice. This was formalised in the Crime and Disorder Act 1998 by the setting-up of multi-disciplinary Youth Offending Teams across England and Wales from April 2000 and the creation of the Youth Justice Board to standardise best practice and monitor the youth justice profession. Furthermore, local areas were required to establish multi-agency panels of key managers in police, probation, youth justice, education, youth services and social services, in order to address issues of crime and disorder and construct local crime strategies. Local authorities were given a statutory obligation to prevent youth crime. In addition, the fast-tracking of young offenders through the criminal justice system was prioritised as a key aim that contributed to better cost-effectiveness.

Muncie (2004) alleges that by the late 1980s, principles of welfare and/or justice had somewhat dissolved into a 'developing corporatist strategy which removed itself from the wider philosophical arguments of welfare and punishment . . . The aim was not necessarily to deliver "welfare" or "justice" but rather to develop the most cost-effective and efficient way of *managing* the delinquent problem.' Causational issues are largely ignored when applying this approach and traditional youth justice was 'reconceptualised as a delinquency management service' (Muncie, 2004, p272). This new model fitted well with the bifurcated strategy adopted by the Thatcher government in the 1980s (see Part 3, below), whereby serious and persistent offenders were dealt with harshly (with custody) whereas other offenders were diverted from custody by the development of a range of community sentence packages for use as alternatives to an expensive custodial disposal.

The move towards managerialism and multi-agency strategies in youth justice in the 1990s followed a pattern being adopted generally over the whole of the public sector. This posited the notion that social issues such as health, poverty, crime and delinquency were problems that needed to be properly managed using corporate techniques (Clarke and Newburn, 1997). According to Muncie, this approach negated the possibility that these 'problems' needed to be resolved rather than merely managed. Adopting the perspective of managerialism in relation to social problems such as youth crime arguably by implication suggests a pessimistic recognition that such problems simply exist in our society and are probably irresolvable. Therefore learning to manage these problems more effectively is the only way forward. This method appears to mirror developments in theoretical criminology over the latter part of the twentieth century. Following Martinson's (1974) nihilistic claim that 'nothing works', theoretical criminology seemed to reach a crisis in theory development, which arguably led to an era of philosophical stagnation. This resulted in both essentialism – a focus on empiricism (largely funded by the Home Office) – and implosion in the form of the development of postmodern criminologies which either attempted to rework old theories or simply dismantle all that had been achieved so far.

Authoritarianism/correctionalism/popular punitiveness

Linked partially to the justice rationale is a classicist notion (see Chapter 3) that crime is chosen rather than caused, that young people are capable of wickedness and that they deserve to be punished for their sins. The post-Bulger media moral panic, which led to the rise of what has been called 'popular punitiveness', reveals that it would be electoral suicide for any political party to appear to be 'soft' on serious and persistent young offenders. Hence, despite the reduction in youth crime figures over the last ten years (see the Home Office youth justice annual statistics on the Youth Justice Board website) the figures for receptions into custody in terms of both remanded and sentenced youths has risen. This 'law and order' approach that is reflected (created?) in newspapers such as the *Daily Mail* and the *Sun*, has ensured that any proposals that involve a radical element in terms of diversion or de-incarceration, are subject to a popular (and sometimes judicial/magisterial) backlash. The conclusion reached by politicians and policy-makers is that custodial sentencing options must be preserved and used robustly where considered necessary.

The justification for incarcerative disposals is further assisted by the historically developed notion that custodial establishments for young people are educative and reforming in nature. As Muncie and Hughes (2002) note, reformatories were viewed as reformative in nature, borstals as places that fostered rehabilitation through training, while detention centres are viewed as 'softer' than adult custodial organisations, secure training centres (12–14 year olds) as places of education, and the detention and training order introduced by the Crime and Disorder Act 1998 emphasises training and community support upon release. All these examples have created the impression that depriving a young person of their liberty is not as severe as depriving an adult, as the regime they will face is not as bad as in an adult prison and has their reformation and education as a central focus. This attitude has perhaps helped to justify rises in youth incarceration, despite the harsh reality of the severely detrimental impact of custody upon young people, both in terms of potential reformation and recidivism, clearly documented in research (NACRO, 2003c) in addition to the tragic cases of deaths in youth custody that have happened over the last few years. Given the recent focus on the actuarially based risk management or the 'what works' agenda (see below) it is, perhaps, astounding that clear evidence is repeatedly ignored by policy-makers with regard to custodial effectiveness. Their selectivity in this regard is pure political pragmatism. The transparency of their motives is clear, but their failure to follow evidence-based results in this area reveals an unjustifiable inconsistency of approach that panders to neo-conservative authoritarian rhetoric.

Authoritarianism is further in evidence through other measures introduced by the Crime and Disorder Act and subsequent legislation, such as tagging from the age of ten, the introduction of civil orders such as ASBOs, ABCs, curfew orders and parenting orders and the removal of state benefits for those who fail to comply with community orders.

Responsibilisation

David Garland (1996) developed the notion of the responsibilisation perspective as a description of government policies that seek to tackle the problem of crime by subtly encouraging the transfer of some responsibility for crime control away from formal agencies (e.g. the police, community support officers) to informal controls and mechanisms (e.g. private security, Neighbourhood Watch, local community groups). Under these initiatives, the message to individuals, businesses and communities is clear: the chance of becoming a victim of crime is not something that official agencies can alter, rather it is a matter of personal risk management – each person is responsible for the management of their risks of becoming a victim of crime. All citizens must practise practical avoidance methods in order to reduce the opportunity for crimes to be perpetrated against them, including target-hardening measures (burglar alarms, steering locks) and increased private surveillance (security lighting, CCTV). Muncie and Hughes (2002) describe this as a 'neo-liberal' method of government, which diverts the responsibility for crime away from the state. It is somewhat ironic that, in tandem with the growth of victim rights in this country, we have witnessed the concomitant rise of victim blaming: the latter is a logical result of the upsurge in the responsibilisation strategy.

In the area of youth justice, responsibilisation has further meant a devolution of control of crime to local authorities who have been made responsible for crime control strategies in terms of multi-agency panels of various managers within authorities (police, probation, social services, education) devising local youth justice plans. Consequently, local agencies are accountable for the 'crime problem' in their locality.

Furthermore, as Muncie and Hughes (2002) note, the responsibilisation strategy is arguably also in evidence in two other areas of youth justice reform following the Crime and Disorder Act 1998. It is noticeable first in terms of the growth of focus on restorative justice, part of the purpose of which is to make the young person face up to the reality of their action and take full responsibility for their law-breaking behaviour. Second, the abolition of the principle of *doli incapax* ('incapable of evil') – whereby it had to be shown that young people aged 10 to 13 possessed the ability to form the required level of culpability necessary for the offence for which they were accused – abandoned a 'buffer zone' of protection for the youngest people who come before our courts. Now these young people are automatically considered able to form the required level of *mens rea* ('guilty mind'). This now forsaken principle of *doli incapax* had been in evidence in our criminal justice system since the Middle Ages (Allen, 1996).

Paternalism

From the advent of the Welfare State after the Second World War onwards, it is arguable that the state has acted as guardian of its citizens. Even prior to this era, Section 44 of the Children and Young Persons Act 1933 enshrined what became known as 'the welfare principle' in relation to young offenders. This provided recognition of the young offender as a vulnerable, developing character and stated that all courts dealing with young people must primarily have regard to their welfare. This ethos of the state as the protective guardian continued to be in evidence in youth justice legislation and practice up to the 1980s, having its heyday in the 1960s and 1970s (see below). When the Thatcher government promoted principles of individualism and autonomy evidenced in Mrs Thatcher's famous statement, 'There is no such thing as society, there are individual men and women and there are families', (published in *Woman's Own* magazine, 31 October 1987) this led to a return to a classicist analysis of crime causation (see Chapter 3) and a belief that crime was simply an activity *chosen* by individuals. Alongside the resurgence in this notion came the belief that individuals were, therefore, responsible for their law-breaking behaviour – they could no longer blame deprivation, poverty or other social causes.

This attitude was part and parcel of the responsibilisation strategy, noted above. However, as Muncie and Hughes (2002) assert, aspects of youth justice legislation have still clung on to the notion of paternalism, despite a general move towards individualism and responsibility. This is witnessed not only by the British government being a signatory of international treaties in relation to the treatment of young suspects (see Chapter 1) but also in measures such as parenting and curfew orders, which are couched in the language of assisting and supplementing parental guidance (though their true purpose might be seen by some as merely an extension of state control into family and private life).

Remoralisation

Muncie and Hughes refer to a further perspective which they label the 'neo-conservative remoralisation approach' (2002, p9). As hinted in the previous section, an alternative analysis of the changes that have taken place in youth justice could argue that rather than the government moving away from being responsible for the crime problem by responsibilising its citizens and stepping back from micro-management of communities, in fact the opposite has happened. The advent of additional civil orders such as ASBOs, parenting orders, curfew orders and individual support orders, is testimony to a desire on the part of government to supplement and amend child-rearing practices as part of a control via re-education by force strategy. This re-education is, in reality, a form of remoralisation of a targeted community – the 'underclass'.

The fear of the underclass is the catalyst that has prompted this move towards remoralisation. Ken Auletta, the journalist who coined the phrase 'underclass' in 1982, referred to them as representing the 'peril and shame' of governments. The reason the remoralisation approach is dubbed 'neo-conservative' is that the movement gained academic credence through the theories of underclass, crime and anti-social behaviour developed by right-wing ('right-realist') criminologists in both the USA and the UK (Murray, 1984, 1988, 1990; Dennis, 1993). It has a moral agenda, as its proponents allege that a great deal of crime and social disorder is caused by feckless young male members of the underclass and that their behaviour is linked to a decline in moral standards, a rise in single parenthood (the youths have no positive male role models) and teenage pregnancies, a lack of application to education/employment, the use of drugs, etc. (see Chapter 3). Behind this notion of dysfunctional and anti-social families is a moralistic notion of how a 'proper/normal' family should behave. However, state control of these populations is 'clouded in a rhetoric of "child protection" or "family support"' (Muncie and Hughes, 2002, p9). Thus, the targeting of surveillance and social control strategies not only at the criminal population but at families and communities who are deemed to be disorderly or 'at risk' of offending is justified by this approach: 'By proclaiming that the principle aim of the youth justice system is to prevent offending, action against legal *and* moral/social transgressions is legitimised' (Muncie and Hughes, 2002, p9).

Restorative justice

In practical terms, principles of restorative justice underpinned the introduction of the referral order by the Youth Justice and Criminal Evidence Act 1999 (the referral order came into effect in England and Wales in April 2002). The rationale behind this order was that the young offender would have the opportunity in a Youth Offending Panel meeting to face up to the full consequences of their actions and that a practical package could be put into place whereby the young person would make amends for the wrong committed. Ideally, it was envisaged that the victim would attend panel meetings and that an individual agreement of restoration could be forged through the young person apologising or making amends in some practical or financial way. Unfortunately, the participation of victims in panel meetings has been low (Earle, 2005). The referral order is examined in more depth in Chapter 4.

Although notions of general redress appear initially to be related to the justice approach, it can be argued that at the heart of the principle of reparation is the belief that, having been forced to confront the full impact of their offending, the young person will experience self-reproach and desist from offending behaviour in the future. In essence, therefore, restorative justice prompts rehabilitation and as a consequence falls within a positivistic criminological analysis, believing in the reformation of the subject. As such its natural home is, perhaps, within a welfare-oriented perspective.

Prior to the introduction of the referral order, other sentences were available (and still are) that fell within the restorative ethos. Reparation is surely three-pronged: it relates to reparation to the victim, to the community, and of the offender. Thus any sentence aimed at restoration in any of these three senses falls within this category. Specifically though, disposals such as fines, reparation orders, community punishment orders and any reparation or community work undertaken as part of a supervision order are directly aimed at making amends. The principles of restoration are arguably linked to civil law ideals about restitution and compensation and as such represent a move away from ideas of punitiveness.

The theoretical grounding and rationale for restorative justice is perhaps most famously attributed to John Braithwaite. Braithwaite (1989) examined the concept of 're-integrative shaming' as an ideal in any justice system. This involved practices such as those used in Japan and New Zealand Maori culture whereby the focus of justice procedures was on the wrongness of the act rather than on the actor, and that once an offender had confessed to the crime, they would be welcomed back into the community after making amends for the wrong. He contrasted these practices with our criminal justice system, arguing that the focus on the offender being bad (rather than the offence) amounted to 'dis-integrative shaming', whereby court procedures led to stigmatisation and the offender being treated as what Becker referred to as 'an outsider' (Becker, 1963). Braithwaite (and other criminologists) examined restorative justice models as they operate in Aboriginal, Native American and Maori cultures – more particularly family group conferencing and other community mediation practices – and concluded that it leads to a more satisfactory form of community-based justice and a sense of justice being done (Braithwaite, 2003).

In this country, the Labour government adopted principles of restorative justice when it stated in its White Paper *No more excuses* (Home Office, 1997d) that the three principles underpinning their reform of the youth justice system were 'restoration', 're-integration' and 'responsibility' (the three Rs). The pursuit of the first and second of these aims can be seen in the introduction of the reparation order and the referral order. It is arguable that the growth of and continuing focus on restorative justice is a concomitant part of the recognition and expansion of victims' rights within our criminal justice system generally over the last 20 years, culminating in the new *Code of Practice for Victims of Crime* (Home Office, 2005a) which came into force in April 2006 (see Chapter 8).

Treatment model

Fionda (2005) refers to the treatment model of youth justice. She states that this model is very similar to the welfare approach; indeed, it developed in tandem with welfarism. The treatment ethos however, is specifically linked to the positivist school of criminology (see Chapter 3) which posited that crime is 'caused' by forces beyond the offender's control (early positivists examined biological/genetic causes, then psychological causes, and finally social and environmental causes of crime and delinquency). However, whatever the causational triggers for crime, under the treatment approach the young person is assumed to be not fully responsible for their actions, but instead is reacting to social, psychological and/or biological prompts.

The treatment approach became weakened in the 1980s with a return to the classicist notion of crime as choice and a focus on individual responsibility. The treatment model had always had more credence when applied to juveniles who have been generally regarded as less responsible for their actions than adults due to developing capacities. However, arguably this approach was largely abandoned post-Bulger – by the mid-1990s.

Developmental model

Though the popular notion in relation to the Thatcher years is that of a tough stance on criminality across the board, in fact the Conservative government of the 1980s adopted a bifurcated strategy towards youth justice: a twin-track method that separated serious and persistent offenders from low-level offenders who were largely diverted away from the full rigours of the criminal justice system. This is evidenced by the sharp rise in the use of cautions and the officially sanctioned practice of multiple cautioning for non-serious offenders (Home Office, 1985). This practice was boosted in many local areas by the existence of diversion panels, run by youth justice teams (see Rutherford, 2002 for further details of this model). Such panels would regularly issue a 'caution plus', the equivalent of the final warning, whereby a young person would receive a caution from the local youth liaison police officer and be required to attend for voluntary support sessions at the youth justice team.

However, at the opposite end of the spectrum, despite the rhetoric, numbers entering custody fell over this period due to the development of robust alternatives to custody by the Government, in the form of restricted criteria for youth custody (Criminal Justice Act 1982) alongside the introduction of funded Intermediate Treatment schemes and the Specified Activities disposal. This reduction in the use of the custodial sanction was further assisted by youth justice team practitioners being largely opposed to custody (some teams even operated 'no custody' policies) and being proactive in devising high-tariff alternatives to custody, regarded as acceptable by some local magistrates. Rutherford argues that additionally some magistrates at that time had become sceptical about the usefulness of custody as reformatories for young offenders.

Fionda argues that the developmental model grew as a result of the above factors and that this model regards the adolescent as a developing subject.

> The key feature of this model is that crime is viewed as part of the adolescent or traumatic 'storm and stress' phase in a teenager's life. Therefore most . . . young offenders are likely, . . . to grow out of their offending behaviour . . . The response to youth crime therefore needs to . . . not hinder the child's growth. (Fionda, 2005, p39).

Under this approach, where intervention is necessary it should be kept to a minimum in order to avoid stigmatisation. Furthermore, custody should be reserved for only a few of the most serious offenders.

Communitarianism

It is possible to link communitarianism to the responsibilisation approach as it involves placing the responsibility for and the solution to crime firmly within designated communities or areas. Local crime strategies and local youth justice plans are formed from within the community for that community (by local multi-agency experts) in order to directly address the particular crime issues or 'hotspots' within that community. According to Hester (2000), the acceptance of the concept of 'community safety' as a key factor of the communitarian approach can lead to tensions, in that on the one hand it implies the ability to reach a consensus within local areas but on the other it seems to have sanctioned the adoption of exclusionary tactics such as those that inevitably stem from, for example, an acceptance of 'zero tolerance' strategies or from the proactive targeting of ASBOs against certain communities/families. In this vein, the communitarianism approach can be viewed as negatively linked to the remoralisation strategy and thus can be regarded as feeding into an agenda that stigmatises and represses certain target (underclass) communities. As Hester states, 'the fact remains that in times and places where there is fractured consensus, attempts to create a spirit of community might involve the exclusion of those unable or unwilling to "belong"' (2000, p162).

Actuarialism/risk management/'what works' approach

The crime risk management model is partly related to the preventionist approach in that its aim is to reduce youth offending within a community. Prior to the Crime and Disorder Act 1998, the Morgan Report on crime prevention (Home Office, 1991) had been influential in stressing the need for a community-based multi-agency approach. Such strategies should be based on effective empirical research that will produce accurate crime-mapping of localities so that problem areas and issues can be specifically targeted. This evidence-based practice is part of the 'what works' agenda, favoured by the Audit Commission's *Misspent youth* report (1996) and reviewed by the Home Office (Goldblatt and Lewis, 1998) which posits that action needs to be targeted as a result of constantly reviewed data about effectiveness and that alternative inefficient approaches should be abandoned.

This ideology follows what has been called 'actuarial justice' principles or the 'new penology' (Feeley and Simon, 1992). It is linked to positivistic techniques of identification and management of individual offenders on the basis of levels of 'dangerousness' – an assessment requirement that has gained statutory force since the Criminal Justice Act 2003 in relation to both adult and young offenders (see Chapter 4). In addition, Youth Offending Teams (YOTs) are required to evaluate the risks to the public in relation to all the young people they deal with by means of the completion of the Asset assessment (see Chapter 6).

Muncie alleges that when compared with the old justice vs welfare approaches, the whole risk management ethos amounts to a 'less philosophically defensible aim of preventing offending by any pragmatic means possible. In place of the pessimistic "nothing works" paradigm evidence-based research and fiscal audit were turned to reveal interventions that might "work" . . . in the search for "value for money" and cost-effective, measurable *outputs*' (Muncie, 2004, pp271–2).

A meze of theoretical approaches, or a maze?

While Ashworth (2000) has referred to the growth of youth sentencing options as creating a 'cafeteria' style justice (which Fionda describes as 'à la carte' sentencing), it could be argued that in terms of youth justice theory we have a meze of approaches (though for some students it might appear to be a maze). Indeed, Fionda alleges that 'Contemporary policy attempts to try all approaches at the same time, . . . in the hope that within the melting pot we will discover that "something works"' (2005, p58).

In addition to the list of philosophical approaches listed above, Muncie and Hughes (2002) further discuss 'hybrid agendas', saying that it is difficult to state that one approach is prioritised above another or to assert that while one particular strategy is in the ascendant another is necessarily falling out of favour. Indeed they refer to

> *a diverse array of strategies that is available to achieve the governance of young people. It is an array that is capable of drawing in the criminal and the non-criminal, the deprived and the depraved, the neglected and the dangerous. This broad ambit is secured because the discourse . . . is sufficiently imprecise to be all-encompassing. (2002, p13)*

ACTIVITY *2.3*

Having examined all the models/approaches in relation to youth justice, discuss which one(s) you prefer and why.

Part 3: A brief legislative history

The development of youth justice practice over the last ten years (1997 onwards) is discussed in Chapter 4; this section briefly describes the historical development of youth justice policy prior to 1997. I refer to my previous analysis of this period (Pickford, 2000).

ACTIVITY *2.4*

As we trace the legislative history of youth justice (below) see if you can spot which of the theoretical approaches outlined above apply to each legislative enactment. Can you spot any incompatibility of approaches and if so (how) has this tension been resolved?

Prior to 1908 there existed no separate system for dealing with young offenders. The Children Act 1908 created juvenile courts and although these were presided over by the same magistrates who sat in the adult courts their establishment indicated a vague understanding that the reasons why children and young people commit crime, and the needs of children and young people who come before the courts, might be different from those of adults. However, it can be argued that some confusion arose at this inception stage between the quite different approaches required for those children in need of care, and those who had committed criminal offences, as the Act gave the juvenile court jurisdiction over both criminal and care issues. The unfortunate coupling of these dual roles of care and control had the practical effect of the same judicial body being called upon to deal with both the so-called 'depraved' and 'deprived'.

A recognition of the differences between adults and young people in terms of responsibility and blameworthiness, embodied in the 1908 Act by the creation of a distinct system of youth justice, gave birth to a latent and perhaps concomitant acknowledgement of a process of distinguishing between the different types of young people who came before the juvenile justice system – those who deserved punishment and those who needed help to overcome their difficulties. The tacit appreciation of this difference is arguably a tenuous but early manifestation of a bifurcated approach to dealing with different kinds of young people who came before the juvenile courts which was to develop over the course of the twentieth century.

The next significant piece of legislation was the Children and Young Persons Act 1933. The Act was passed as a result of the report of the Moloney Committee (Home Office, 1927) which contained a blend of classicist and positivist explanations of criminality in children and young people (the classicist and positivist approaches are outlined in Chapter 3). The Committee regarded law-breaking as a deliberate act of defiance, which had to be dealt with by formal court procedures and sanctions, while recognising that delinquent behaviour may be caused by psychological or environmental factors that were beyond the young person's control. Morris and Giller (1987) contend that the report thus presented:

> dual images of the delinquent [which] were placed not side by side but in sequence. In the first instance . . . the offence was used as a conscious act of wickedness. Once the act was proved or admitted, however, it was viewed as a product of personal or external forces. (1987, p71)

The 1933 Act was instrumental in establishing what became known by professionals as 'the welfare principle', which is still of paramount importance for the court when dealing with young offenders. Under Section 44 of the Act, a court must: 'have regard to the welfare of the child or young person and shall in a proper case take steps for removing him from undesirable surroundings or for securing that proper provision is made for his education or training'.

An early recognition of the inappropriateness of young people in social need being dealt with by the same institutions that dealt with juvenile offenders, can be seen in the report of the Care of Children Committee in 1946, which accepted that it was undesirable for approved schools to provide identical services and regimes for non-offenders and offenders. The report also precipitated the formation of the local government children's authorities, effectively a social service department established by the Children Act 1948, to deal with both deprived children and children subject to criminal court orders.

The Children and Young Persons (Amendment) Act 1952 allowed courts to remand young offenders to local authority accommodation and created an approved school licence release whereby those released from approved schools were to be supervised within the community by local child-care officers. This Act in effect created two provisions whereby the systems of control (the criminal justice system) and of care (the welfare system) became intertwined when dealing with young people made subject to such orders.

In the 1960s, as a result of the Ingleby Report (Home Office, 1960), a more liberal understanding of youth criminality than had been seen previously began to be evident, perhaps reflecting a recognition of the influence of criminological debates of the time which focused upon social and environmental rather than individualistic causes of crime. There was also an acknowledgement of the labelling perspective that flourished in criminological circles at that time. This promoted recognition of the probable negative results of stigmatising young people and the impact of this stigma on their life chances. The report recommended a reduction in the criminal jurisdiction of the juvenile court via the diversion of non-serious offenders away from the formal criminal justice system and a focus upon welfare provision for those who came before it. This warming towards welfarist models, coupled with professional doubts about the effectiveness of punishment for young offenders amongst social work personnel, continued throughout the 1960s and was reflected in the policy debates concerning youth criminality over that period.

An appreciation of deprivation and social inequality as causal factors in juvenile delinquency, together with a recognition of the stigmatising effects of early criminalisation, was also clearly visible in a radical white paper (Home Office, 1965). It proposed that young offenders should be completely removed from the court system and dealt with exclusively by social service departments. This radicalism of the mid-1960s met with vociferous opposition, mainly from lawyers within the Conservative party, and led to a justice-oriented backlash that resulted in an uneasy compromise in the form of the Children and Young Persons Act 1969 introduced by the then Labour government. Some of the more welfare-oriented provisions of that Act, such as the raising of the age of criminal responsibility to 14 and the proposal to allow local authorities to deal with most juvenile delinquents by means of supervision and care arrangements, never came into force due to the incoming Conservative government's refusal to implement them. However, in the same period in Scotland there was little opposition to a welfare model of youth justice as proposed by the Kilbrandon Report in Scotland (Home Office, 1964). A treatment approach was implemented north of the border at the same time as a justice backlash was occurring in England and Wales (see Pickford, 2000, Chapters 8 and 9).

The Act also granted the criminal court the power to pass a criminal sanction on a young person that in effect amounted to a welfare provision – the criminal care order (abolished in 1989). In that sentence, the 'deprived' and the 'depraved' became as one; the welfare measure became a criminal sanction.

The battlefield of the debates surrounding the passing and implementation of the 1969 Act resulted in a youth justice landscape that produced, in the 1970s 'a widening of the net of control as elements of the new system brought into being by the 1969 Act were absorbed into a larger system which retained its traditional commitment to imprisonment' (McLaughlin and Muncie, 1996, p267).

In effect, the 1969 Act created greater powers of discretion for social workers and did nothing to stem a rising tide of custodial disposals. Social workers were given wider professional discretion, which enabled them to expand their client group – a kind of professional entrepreneurialism – and this resulted in many non-serious delinquents being drawn into the social control net of the youth justice system under the guise of preventionism.

The Conservative victory in the 1979 general election saw the start of the Thatcher era and a move towards individualism and consumerism. The 'rule of law' and 'law and order' rhetoric, which dominated the Conservative's election campaign, began to be made flesh by the introduction of the (soon abandoned) 'short, sharp shock' militaristic custodial sentence.

The Criminal Justice Act 1982 restricted the criteria for custodial disposals and transformed borstals into youth training centres, aimed at giving young offenders an experience more akin to an adult prison. A policy of bifurcation was pursued in the succeeding years of the Conservative government, and arguably continued until the post-Bulger panic in the 1990s. This practice involved 'getting tough' on those deemed serious and persistent young offenders, while endeavouring to divert first-time and non-serious juvenile offenders away from the more stigmatising effects of the criminal justice system. Indeed, a general trend away from incarceration can be seen as early as the 1982 Act, which created the specified activities order as a high-tariff community disposal that was later to become a direct alternative to custody under the Criminal Justice Act 1988.

The Home Office circulars during the 1980s officially encouraged the use of cautions for young offenders (Home Office, 1985) and in many areas this resulted in the practice of multiple cautioning of some young people. This arguably allowed flexibility for professionals in dealing with young offenders whom they regarded as non-serious and who were likely to 'grow out' of their delinquency. This discretion has largely been lost by the creation of the more rigid final warning system in the Crime and Disorder Act 1998. Additionally, the Conservative government of the 1980s provided local authorities with funds to set up intermediate treatment centres and programmes for young offenders as custodial alternatives (unfortunately, funding for these was reduced by the end of that decade). Similarly, the Children Act 1989 placed a duty upon local authorities to establish diversionary schemes; attendance at these schemes could be ordered as part of a court sentence. The Act also required social service departments to provide alternatives to secure accommodation remands for young people awaiting trial.

The Criminal Justice Act 1991 represented an unusual fusing of various approaches. In terms of sentencing policy generally (adults and juveniles) the Act can be regarded as a move towards justice ideas of proportionality in sentencing (including fines). However, welfare-oriented provisions for young offenders are in evidence by a number of measures introduced by that Act (Gibson, 1994). These include an expansion of the upper age limit in the youth court to include 17 year olds; a reduction of the maximum custodial sentence in a young offender institution to 12 months (excluding 'grave' offences – see Chapter 4); a raising of the minimum age that a young person can be sentenced to a custodial punishment to 15; the expansion of community sentences for 16 and 17 year olds; and the creation of new remand arrangements (including remand fostering) for 15 and 16 year olds.

Ironically, perhaps, certain more general provisions of the Criminal Justice Act 1991 regarding proportionality of sentencing were not received well by the more conservative magistrates who seemed to believe in a type of 'welfarism' that was expressed in individualised disposals and who felt that their discretionary powers to sentence the offender (rather than the offence) had been severely curtailed. As a result of these criticisms, the Criminal Justice Act 1993 removed the classicist tariff-based restrictions placed by the 1991 Act on those sentencing, in both adult and youth courts, and allowed the full offending history of the defendant to be taken into account when deciding an appropriate disposal. Also, offences committed on bail were to be regarded as an aggravating factor, and the unit fine system was abolished.

The 1993 Act can be viewed as the beginning of a march towards more justice-oriented policies within the criminal justice system generally. However, this march was to become a sprint after the killing of James Bulger by two 10 year old boys in 1993 and the populist crisis in morality debate that ensued. This was largely fuelled by the media highlighting cases of persistent young offenders who, it was argued, were simply 'getting away with it' due to the youth justice system's inability to deal with them adequately. The Bulger case eventually led to the abolition of the presumption of innocence for 10–13 year olds in the Crime and Disorder Act 1998. Children were no longer to be regarded as innocent; they were potentially capable of evil deeds. Notions of childhood innocence were replaced by demonising images of young people. As a result, the Criminal Justice and Public Order Act 1994 arguably represented a politically motivated lurch towards a more punitive response in relation to children and young offenders. The use of police detention and secure remand was introduced for those as young as 12 years old; secure training centres were to be established as a custodial sentence for persistent offenders aged 12 and over; the maximum young offender institution sentence was increased to two years; and the 'grave crimes' procedure became operational from the age of 10. This statute was followed up by a Home Office circular (Home Office, 1994), which officially restricted the use of more than one caution for young offenders.

This was the last major piece of youth justice law-making under the then Conservative Government. We will examine the policy debates of the mid-1990s and the 'New Labour' transformation of youth justice practice in Chapter 4.

C H A P T E R   S U M M A R Y

In this chapter we have examined the various theoretical perspectives of youth justice that have developed over the last one hundred years. We analysed, first, the traditional philosophies of justice and welfare and noted both the contrasting nature of these approaches and their historical dominance of youth justice theory. We then went on to trace the emergence of other philosophies that have been developed (or recognised) by various academics over the more recent history of youth justice policy. There now seems to be a myriad of approaches and analyses of the juvenile justice system, each one backed by evidence from examination of policy by various academics. Though this may appear to be a theoretical maze through which students and practitioners of youth justice are left to wander, the variety of approaches has certainly enriched contemporary debates about ways of addressing youth criminality. Last, we took a short historical tour through the development of youth justice legislation. There we saw no evidence of a consistent approach to tackling juvenile criminality being adopted by successive governments. However, friction between the dominant philosophies of justice and welfare was notable in policy debates and legislative content over the course of the last century.

FURTHER READING

Muncie, J (2004) *Youth and crime*, 2nd edn. London: Sage.
This text provides a critical analysis of a wide range of issues surrounding young people, disorder and crime.

Muncie, J, Hughes, G and McLaughlin, E (2002) *Youth justice: Critical readings*. London: Sage.
This collection provides a critical introduction to the intellectual reframing of the history, theory, policy and practice of youth justice.

Smith, R (2003) *Youth Justice: Ideas, policy, practice*. Cullompton: Willan.
This book analyses changes in youth justice theory and policy, as well as examining various government initiatives relating to youth criminality.

Chapter 3

Criminological theories in relation to young people who offend

Jane Pickford

ACHIEVING A SOCIAL WORK DEGREE

This chapter will help you begin to meet the following National Occupational Standards.

Key Role 1: Prepare for and work with individuals, families, carers, groups and communities to assess their needs and circumstances

- Review case notes and other relevant literature.
- Evaluate all information to identify the best form of initial involvement.

It will also introduce you to the following academic standards as set out in the social work subject benchmark statement:

3.1.1 Social work services and service users

- The social processes (associated with, for example, poverty, unemployment, poor health, disablement, lack of education and other sources of disadvantage) that lead to marginalisation, isolation and exclusion and their impact on the demand for social work services.
- Explanations of the links between definitional processes contributing to social differences (for example, social class, gender and ethnic differences) to the problems of inequality and differential need faced by service users.
- The nature of social work services in a diverse society (with particular reference to concepts such as prejudice, interpersonal, institutional and structural discrimination, empowerment and anti-discriminatory practices).
- The nature and validity of different definitions of, and explanations for, the characteristics and circumstances of service users and the services required by them.

3.1.4 Social work theory

- Research-based concepts and critical explanations from social work theory and other disciplines that contribute to the knowledge base of social work, including their distinctive epistemological status and application to practice.
- The relevance of sociological perspectives to understanding societal and structural influences on human behaviour at individual, group and community levels.
- The relevance of psychological and physiological perspectives to understanding individual and social development and functioning.
- Social science theories explaining group and organisational behaviour, adaptation and change.
- Knowledge and critical appraisal of relevant social research and evaluation methodologies.

3.2.2.3 Analysis and synthesis

- Assess human situations, taking into account a variety of factors (including the views of participants, theoretical concepts, research evidence, legislation and organisational policies and procedures.
- Analyse information gathered, weighing competing evidence and modifying their viewpoint in light of new information, then relate this information to a particular task, situation or problem.

- Consider specific factors relevant to social work practice (such as risk, rights, cultural differences and linguistic sensitivities, responsibilities to protect vulnerable individuals and legal obligations).
- Assess the merits of contrasting theories, explanations, research, policies and procedures.
- Synthesise information and lines of reasoning and sustain detailed argument at length and over time.
- Employ understanding of human agency at the macro (societal), mezzo (organisational and community) and micro (inter- and intra-personal) levels.
- Analyse and take account of the impact of inequality and discrimination in work with people in particular contexts and problem situations.

Introduction

Having examined theories in relation to perspectives of youth justice in the previous chapter, here other theories that are useful in youth justice practice are analysed. These theories relate to understanding why young people commit crimes and take part in anti-social or delinquent behaviour. The theories have been developed by criminologists and study of them requires us to undertake a basic theoretical tour of some of the mainstream criminological theories. Due to constraints of space and considering that you are being trained to be reflective in your studies, the mainstream theories are outlined in their basic form without critiques. You can assess their usefulness yourself in terms of how they might assist your future practice as you go through them.

A note on two significant features of recorded crime

Before we examine causational explanations, it should be noted that two major criminological issues/themes regarding gender and race permeate through youth justice practice and relate to other areas of social work studies regarding anti-discriminatory practice (see Chapter 1). It is well documented and evident to all youth justice practitioners that there is an over-representation of (a) male and (b) minority ethnic young people coming before our penal system (visit www.homeoffice.gov.uk/rds/section951.html for the most recent Home Office statistics relating to women and crime and race and crime). If you take a cursory glance at the criminal statistics, the most obvious peculiarity is the shortage of women and girls: they are conspicuous by their absence. Various explanations have been given by criminologists for female under-representation (see Heidensohn, 1996; Walklate, 2004) and for male over-representation (see theories of masculinity and crime such as, especially, Campbell 1993; Jefferson, 1997; Messerschmidt, 1993) within the criminal justice system. According to official statistics, females contribute to only a modest part of the overall crime problem and when they come before the penal system, they are often treated differently from males who have committed similar offences (see references listed, above). As a practitioner, you must be aware of this differential treatment and of some explanations for it.

The reasons for the over-representation of young black males within our criminal justice system has been well documented by the Home Office and criminologists (see especially Bowling and Phillips, 2002) but little effective work seems to have been done to address this issue. The latest Section 95 Statement on Race and Crime was published in 2004 (see website reference above) and notes several areas of concern relating to the criminalisation of young black people:

- Blacks are 6.4 times more likely to be stopped and searched than whites.
- Black youths are more likely than white youths to be sentenced to a detention and training order.
- Black defendants are more likely to be remanded in custody (than white or Asian defendants).
- If given bail, blacks are more likely to get conditional bail (than white or Asian defendants).
- Black defendants are less likely to receive fines or discharges than whites.

Solomos (1993) has argued that the criminal justice system has become 'racialised' and that black defendants cannot expect to be treated fairly by agents and agencies of the justice system. The inquiries into the death of Stephen Lawrence by a racist gang in 1993 and that of Zahid Mubarek by a known racist in Feltham Young Offenders Institution in 2000 have fuelled public concern about the treatment black people receive while in contact with police and penal establishments. Questions as to why Lawrence's killers were never prosecuted and why Mubarek was sharing a cell with a violent racist psychopath on the day he was due to be released have never been satisfactorily answered.

Major theories of criminology

Let's now examine some of the main perspectives of criminality, while being aware of the concerns relating to possible anti-discriminatory practice issues, regarding the gender and race factors noted above.

Classicism

In tracing the genealogy of criminology, it is generally accepted that modern criminological thoughts can be tracked to writings of the eighteenth century. Mannheim (1960) cites Cesare Beccaria and his classical school of criminology (as outlined in *On Crimes and Punishments*, first published in 1764), as the pioneer of criminological thought. However, it could be said to be misleading to describe classical and neo-classical schools of thought as criminology, as classicism does not concern itself with aetiological (causational) questions in an empirical way (Garland, 2002). The classicist theories can be described as 'pre-criminology', in that they were concerned with philosophical questions about the nature of society and the nature of human behaviour, and were based on speculation as to both.

Relating the justice and welfare perspectives examined in Chapter 2 to theoretical criminology, it can be argued that the philosophy of the classical school of thought supports the justice approach to youth justice, as it views offending behaviour as basically a matter of choice. Splitting the classical approach into principles, Beccaria asserted that:

- All people are free but are by nature self-seeking – they will seek out pleasure and try to avoid pain – and so all people are capable of committing a crime if they think that crime would benefit them and that the benefits would outweigh the costs.

- However, there exists a consensus in society regarding the need to protect personal welfare and property.

- To prevent anti-social behaviour, all people freely enter into the 'social contract' whereby they abandon some of their freedoms in return for protection from the state.

- Education (via the Enlightenment) helps to prevent crime. Crime is essentially irrational behaviour. Beccaria advocated that laws should be made more understandable. He thought that education of young minds would be more effective in decreasing crime rather than mere coercion: 'leading them towards virtue . . . and directing them away from evil' (1963, p62).

- Punishment must be used in order to deter people from violating the rights of others and to demonstrate the irrationality of law-breaking behaviour. The state has been given the right to punish via the 'social contract' and punishment must be prompt, certain and public in order to act as a deterrent.

- Punishment must be proportionate to the interests violated (i.e. the harm done) not for reformation or retribution.

- Laws and legal procedures should be few and simple and legal procedures should adhere to a strict process so that everyone is treated equally. Discretion in sentencing should be avoided.

- All people are responsible for their actions; people are rational actors, choice-makers. There should, therefore, be no excuses or mitigations for criminal behaviour. (However, under neo-classicist revisionism lack of criminal capacity of young children was acknowledged and mitigation was allowed, but only as explanation, not as an excuse for criminal behaviour).

The positivist approach

The positivist school of thought, in contrast to the classicist paradigm, can be regarded as a critique of the legal system, viewing it as an inept means of dealing with crime as a social problem because of its focus on the morality of acts rather than the dangerousness or reformability of the offender. The focus for positivism is upon the person of the criminal. The studies undertaken by positivist researchers have represented an attempt to present empirical facts in order to confirm their ideas that crime was determined, rather than an act of individual choice that was the exercise of free will. The early positivists believed that they could scientifically prove that certain identifiable features within an individual caused a person's criminality. Using this approach, the offender is destined to become a criminal due to:

- Biological or genetic factors (biological positivism).

- Psychological factors (psychological positivism).

- Social or environmental factors (sociological positivism).

A positivist believes that crime is not chosen but caused largely by factors beyond the offender's control. In essence, the belief is that offenders simply can't help themselves. Certain genetic, psychological or environmental factors have influenced their behaviour and the existence of these factors means that offenders are almost pre-programmed to become criminals. With this in mind, one of the great contradictions of the positivist approach to crime is its focus on reformation and rehabilitation. Taylor et al. (1973) refer to this as the 'therapeutic paradox': if the criminal is totally determined, how is reform possible? While this has sometimes been seen as a confusion, the argument has been advanced that what is necessary is an alteration of the determining factors.

It could be argued that the classical and the positivist approach are oppositional. Further, the classicist theory seems to support the justice approach to youth offending (crime is chosen, the offender should take full responsibility for his or her actions and punishments should be proportionate) while the positivist paradigm seems to support the welfare approach (crime is caused by a variety of possible factors, these factors should be taken into account regarding culpability and individualised treatment packages are required to address these causational factors).

A positivistic system of justice requires a broad range of possible sentences/treatments so that professional discretion can be used to choose the disposal most likely to produce reformation. It is arguable that the Crime and Disorder Act 1998 and the Youth Justice and Criminal Evidence Act 1999 have created a vast range of possible disposals for young people who come before the penal system (see Chapter 4). This, coupled with a focus on preventionism, indicates a possible move towards a positivist approach within the youth justice system.

Matza (1964) has argued that there are three identifiable major assumptions within the positivistic framework. These are:

- *Determinism*. This is the idea that criminal behaviour is caused by factors outside the individual's control. These could be biological, psychological, or, as later positivists acknowledge, sociological causes of behaviour.

- *Differentiation*. Criminals are viewed as different from non-criminals due to their biological constitution, psychological traits or socialisation process.

- *Pathology*. Criminals are viewed as different from non-criminals because something has gone 'wrong' biologically, psychologically or sociologically.

In summary, therefore, the positivist school promised to utilise science in order to objectively discover the causes of criminality and provide a cure. While a thorough examination of biological and psychological positivism would be very interesting, it is beyond the scope of this book. Some of the other theories of criminology below (ecology, anomie and subcultures) fall within the third category of sociological positivism.

ACTIVITY **3.1**

Discuss the crime control measures that might be used in a youth justice system based purely on (a) classicist principles, and (b) positivist principles.

Ecology or crime and the environment

Ecological theory is basically concerned with the geography of criminality. The original theory has been developed extensively by various criminologists and is utilised practically within the youth justice industry in terms of crime mapping, local crime plans and identification of crime 'hotspots'. The theory tries to explain why crime and disorder often seem to be concentrated in particular locations – often inner-city areas. It examines what it might be about the nature and characteristics of that area (and the people who inhabit it) that appears to precipitate criminal and anti-social behaviour.

The zonal hypothesis

Park (1936, Park and Burgess, 1925) Thrasher (1927), Wirth (1928) and Shaw (1931, Shaw and McKay, 1942) developed a theory about the ecology of crime. They studied the geographical development of different groups in relation to their evolution in the context of the city of Chicago. They used the metaphor of the city as a living organism and examined ecology from the biological perspective of habitat. They asserted that people displayed the aggregation characteristics of animals in their habitat. The theory of ecology was a segmental view of the problem of crime and incivilities in the context of the city. Park contended that the growth of a city is natural rather than planned and that its differential development merely reflects the different tasks each area is called upon to perform. Using the metaphor of plant ecology, he contended that areas of the city experience changes much like a process of balancing in nature, where a new species may move into an area and then come to characterise that area in a process of invasion, domination and succession.

In devising the 'zonal hypothesis' the Chicago sociologists were responding to their interest in how cities tended to become 'internally differentiated'. They claimed that cities tend to evolve in a series of concentric zones of activity and life (see Figure 3.1).

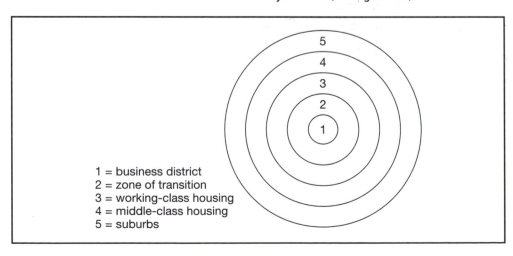

1 = business district
2 = zone of transition
3 = working-class housing
4 = middle-class housing
5 = suburbs

Figure 3.1 *Burgess's 'zonal hypothesis'*

The sociologists asserted that each of the areas had distinctive characteristics that differentiated them one from another. The areas represented unplanned groupings of similar people, and as such mirror the natural world, where there is a division of species in terms of habitat. The effect of this is to transform a geographical area into a 'neighbourhood', which Park described as a 'locality with sentiments, traditions and a history of its own' (1925, p6).

The Chicago sociologists began to fix their attention on the zone in transition. In this area the population was fluid; people would move out as soon as they bettered themselves. Further, the area seemed to have a concentration of what was called 'pathological behaviour', including mental disorder, prostitution, suicide, alcoholism, juvenile mortality, disease, poverty, juvenile delinquency and crime. In examining the characteristics of the zone in transition they discovered that it tended to be an area of cheap rents and poor housing and was home to the most recent groups of immigrants; a succession of ethnic groups tended to live there, and each of these groups seemed in turn to produce similar patterns of behaviour. The area was also characterised by its lack of settled institutions and poor provision of local resources and facilities. The zone was distinguished by what was described as its 'unruly' nature and it tended to house people who were unaccustomed to city life, to America and to one another.

Park found that many of the inhabitants of this area had left very different cultures in order to establish a new lifestyle in a strange and unfamiliar environment. This lack of cohesion was described as 'disorganisation' and 'moral dissensus'. The latter term was later described by Wirth as 'the degree to which the members of a society lose their common understanding', and argued that 'the degree to which consensus is undermined, is the measure of a society's state of disorganisation' (1964, p46). This disorganisation was characterised by the fragmented, fluid and anonymous features of urban life.

In examining the internal relationships within the zone in transition it was noted that poor social and economic conditions had led to mistrust and heterogeneity. As populations moved in and out of the area, change became normal: life became unpredictable leading to instability in terms of social cohesion. A focus of the external relationship of the zone in transition with the rest of the city and the wider American society revealed that in periods of change the instability of the zone was exaggerated, which in turn may precipitate a breakdown in social order. This may further lead to the zone in transition becoming dislocated from the larger society and taking on a characteristic of its own (e.g. the Italian community in Chicago in the 1930s). If this occurs, the community becomes isolated and independent and the master institutions of social control (such as law, the church, the courts, the police), become unable to control the area.

Park asserted that in such a community moral habits could not be effectively implanted. People formed few commitments outside of their immediate family or community and thus ideas of any neighbourhood initiative of crime control was doomed to failure. Wirth argued that the proliferation of different ethnic communities in the zone in transition led to 'amoral familiarism', which eventually could transform the zone in transition into an unsettled and unsafe region. Gangs may spring up to protect their own community and territory and impose their own brand of security. However, the 'protection' provided by the gangs only resulted in exacerbating the insecurity of the region.

People who moved to the USA were faced with the problems of both cultural discontinuities and coping with instability in the area in which they lived. Park argued that this was a particular problem for second-generation immigrants; language, custom and tradition could fall into disuse or change its significance or importance. Young second-generation males in particular, he argued, often saw themselves as marginalised from the culture they had left behind, from their family and from America. These boys often created their own social order that would correspond neither to the culture of their parents nor to the wider culture of the USA, but amounted to an order that moved unstably between both. A resort to crime by these young men was seen as a solution to the problems of their exclusion from wider society due to prejudice, lack of opportunity and economic and political impotence. In effect, rebellion was a structural response to deprivation, to growing up in an insecure city environment, deprived of economic control and resources.

ACTIVITY 3.2

Apply the 'zonal hypothesis' to a city you are familiar with. Does the 'zone in transition' correspond with known crime hotspots? Are local crime and disorder control mechanisms targeted at that area?

Anomie

In order to examine the question of what factors cause some people to become conformist and others to be non-conformist, Merton utilised Durkheim's (1893, 1897) conception of anomie as a state of normlessness and used it as a springboard for developing a general theory of crime. He borrowed Durkheim's notion of infinite aspiration and linked this to dissymmetry between social culture in the USA and social structure in developing his theory of anomie. The basis of his work can be seen in his 1938 article, 'Social structure and anomie'. However, one crucial difference between the ideas of Durkheim and Merton is that Durkheim asserted that human aspirations are not socially learned, as Merton contended, but are innate and natural. Merton was concerned with 'how some social structures exert a definite pressure upon certain persons in the society to engage in non-conformist rather than conformist conduct' (1938, p672).

Goals and means

In examining American society, Merton noticed the social pressure (which he called 'strain') people experienced in terms of their desire to achieve financial success and status. He asserted that the capitalist nature of the USA, coupled with the all-pervading notion of meritocracy, produced an image of America as the land of opportunities where anyone, no matter how lowly their background, could achieve success with hard work and enterprise. He called this the 'American Dream'. Merton used two concepts as the basis of his theorising:

- 'Cultural goals' he described as people's aspirations and desire to succeed. He asserted that such goals are socially learned.

- 'Institutional means' he defined as the availability and distribution of legitimate structural opportunities to achieve the cultural goals.

In a society where there is an emphasis on goals without sufficient provision of equal opportunities to the means of achieving those goals, people may develop a willingness to use any means to achieve the goals. Merton said that the 'most feasible procedure, whether legitimate or not, is preferred to the institutionally prescribed conduct. As this process continues, the integration of society becomes tenuous and anomie ensues' (1938, p674).

It is possible for societies to overemphasise either the cultural goals or the institutional means. Merton alleged that in the USA there is an over-emphasis on achieving the cultural goals, without sufficient attention to the institutional means. He asserted that there is an overwhelming desire for monetary success and material gain but that the institutional means of fulfilling those goals are not available or are denied to a substantial proportion of the population. Merton's so-called ideal situation, where there is an equilibrium within society between the goals and the means, implies that either an equality of opportunity is provided by the government in order to enable people to achieve their desires, or that the learned cultural goals are constricted, so that people's aspirations do not fix upon the unobtainable. The problem with the first position is that as in a capitalist society greed is endemic and addictive, there will always be winners and losers (we can't all be multi-millionaires). In relation to the second proposition, that people would have to be socialised to fix their cultural goals or aspirations upon the achievable, implies notions of Victorian principles of everyone knowing their proper place and of a structured hierarchical society.

Reaction types

According to Merton, deviant behaviour results when cultural goals are accepted (people would like to be financially successful and to have status), but access to these goals is structurally limited (e.g. a well-paid job and career structure is unavailable). It is this 'strain' that Merton described as a state of anomie. He went on to outline possible reactions or adaptations or types of people who may be socially produced due to this strain, which may occur when the goals that have been internalised cannot be legitimately attained. These possible adaptations will occur when the means of a society are not distributed fairly due to the political structure of a society.

- *The conformist* – someone who has accepted the goals of society and is able to achieve them by legitimate means.

- *The innovator* – a person who has accepted the goals but is unable to achieve them by legitimate means and so resorts to illegitimate means in order to achieve them (i.e. the criminal).

- *The ritualist* – an individual who has not accepted societal goals but adopts only legitimate ways of behaviour.

- *The retreatist* – This is the person who neither accepts the cultural goals of society nor has the means of achieving them. Using the language of his day, Merton described these people as 'drop-outs' or 'tramps' and also included within this category alcoholics and addicts.

- *The rebel* – an individual who has rejected the goals and the legitimate means of achieving these goals and seeks to replace them by a different system (the political activist).

Merton's prime concern was with the innovator, the person who uses illegitimate means to achieve their goals: (e.g. a person who, for instance, achieves financial success by theft and robbery rather than obtaining a well-paid job, investing in a savings account, etc). He asserted that inequalities in the social structure encourage criminality as people are indoctrinated to strive for financial and material success but are denied the means of achieving it. It is the lack of co-ordination of the goals and means that in Merton's view leads to a state of anomie. Merton stated that the dream of financial success encourages everyone to have 'exaggerated anxieties, hostilities, neurosis and anti-social behaviour' (1938, p680).

ACTIVITY 3.3

Discuss whether there is a 'British Dream'. If so, is it the same as the 'American Dream'? Can strain theory/anomie explain criminality among young people in Britain?

Subcultural theory

The research of the subcultural theorists essentially amounted to extensions of Merton's approach to explaining deviance – an extension that involved the investigation of youth gangs in urban areas. In order to attempt to make sense of even the most hedonistic non-utilitarian youth delinquency, sociologists began to develop the notion that far from these actions being disorganised and senseless, they did indeed make sense in that the behaviour was a result of some sort of adherence to an alternative cultural pattern.

I will briefly examine a few of the ideas of the 'founding fathers' of the subcultural explanation of delinquency.

Albert Cohen

In accepting the basic tenets of Merton's strain theory as a basis of his theorising about the development of gangs, Albert Cohen in *Delinquent Boys* (1955) attempted to examine the features of the dominant mainstream culture that may lead young men into committing delinquent acts. Cohen also accepted Merton's basic notion that delinquency may be related to impediments to success in conventional terms, which lower-class males in particular may experience.

Cohen examined delinquent subcultures in lower-class life and concluded that the patterns of behaviour he observed within these groups were very different from the larger dominant culture. He proposed that gang delinquency was a group solution to status frustrations that may be experienced by lower-class males. These boys, who were denied status in middle-class terms, would be led to seek status through alternative means, in this case via the gang. Essentially, Cohen proposed that boys who experience similar problems in relation to their lack of success in conventional terms would group together in order to resolve their somewhat masculine problems of failing to achieve status in normatively accepted ways. They would develop a subculture in which they could achieve status by creating their own alternative social order. He argued that criminal behaviour, like any other behaviour, is learned behaviour transmitted by interaction and communication with others largely within interpersonal groups.

In relation to those juveniles belonging to subcultural groups, Cohen asserted that they displayed six prevalent features. They were

- *Non-utilitarian*. The boys may undertake activities that seem nonsensical as they would lead to no particular gains, e.g. breaking a window, or stealing goods and disposing of the items.

- *Malicious*. The boys felt excitement in observing rules being broken, taboos being challenged and viewing other people being disconcerted by their activities and destructiveness.

- *Negativistic*. This was a general trend to invert the values of the wider culture, e.g. whereas studying and doing well at school would be viewed as 'good' by mainstream society, this may be viewed as 'bad' by the boys in the gang.

- *Versatile*. The boys showed an ability to become involved in a variety of delinquent activities and anti-social behaviour, including committing criminal offences.

- *Short-run hedonism*. This included the need for instant gratification without any assessment of the long-term effects of their activities.

- *Group autonomy*. The group viewed itself as being separate from the wider society and there was an acknowledgement among the boys that the gang was to be their first priority.

Cohen asserted that the gang was made up of like individuals 'with similar problems of adjustment' to society (1955, p59). Working-class boys become dependent upon their peer groups when they encounter status problems through not being able to adhere to predominant middle-class norms or values. They turn to the gang for status when they encounter middle-class values that would classify them as failures. In effect, Cohen alleged that boys who form into subcultures do so as a means of hitting back at a society that has branded them as worthless; this is what Downes and Rock call 'the D Streams Revenge' (2003, p146). According to Cohen, 'the hallmark of the delinquent subculture is the explicit and wholesale repudiation of middle class standards and the adoptions of their very antithesis' (1955, p129).

The gang is created due to 'reaction formation' against middle-class values: the gang not only violates middle-class norms, it 'expresses contempt for a way of life by making its opposite a criterion of status' (1955, p134).

Cloward and Ohlin

In *Delinquency and Opportunity* (1960) Cloward and Ohlin suggested that class was a primary element in the formation of delinquent gangs, while criticising Cohen's emphasis on the negativistic nature of delinquent gang activity. They examined subcultural formation and subcultural group types and argued that the type of gang that will develop in a particular area will be dictated by the opportunities available, the pressures suffered and the situation in which the young men find themselves. They asserted that all subcultures are not alike and that there will be different forms of adaptation to strain, which will result in different outcomes.

They focused specifically on urban gangs asserting that the particular strains caused by urbanality lead to a greater prevalence of gangs in city areas. They contended that there were three types of delinquent subcultures:

- *Criminal*. This type of gang may take part in property-related offences as a means of gaining success and prestige. They tend to form where delinquents and criminal adults are closely connected. The adult criminal will provide a role model for the juvenile and help develop their criminal skills. Stable patterns of relationship are present and often networks may develop to facilitate law-breaking behaviour. In such a gang, there appears to be an acceptance of a level of criminal behaviour, which usually focuses upon theft and other property offences.

- *Conflict*. This type of subculture displays violent behaviour as an expression of frustration due to the absence of conventional opportunities and stable relationships, either criminal or non-criminal. Violence is a symbol of discontent, which is used to gain status and to exhibit courage. The rampant frustration leads to chaotic displays of intermittent violence.

- *Retreatist*. This grouping is made up of young people who are unable to achieve success in either legitimate or illegitimate ways and who resort to alcohol or drugs instead of violence as a way of 'leaving' mainstream society in which they have not had much success. This group is reminiscent of Merton's category of the retreatist; of the 'double failure' who rejects both the goals and means of society.

Cloward and Ohlin asserted that the lower-class gang is formed as a response to the problems faced by lower-class males due to the acceptance of culturally induced goals and access to limited means in order to achieving those goals. Moreover, lower-class males do not, they alleged, accept middle-class values (as Cohen asserted); instead, they refuse to accept the legitimacy of middle-class norms. The gang is essentially a 'collective adaptation' to strain and is formed due to 'solidarity' of situation among lower-class males.

Walter Miller

In his 1958 article 'Lower class culture as a generating milieu of gang delinquency', Miller presented a different picture of subcultural formation. He challenged Cohen's assumptions that boys from the lower classes form gangs due to frustrations they feel about not being able to achieve success in middle-class terms. On the contrary, Miller alleged that these subcultures form as an attempt to conform to lower-class traditions, not as a reaction to middle-class traditions. The subculture does not amount to a response to middle-class norms, but in fact is a positive attempt to achieve status in lower-class terms. Thus the gang is normal, not oppositional: Miller argued that life among the lower-classes displayed certain key features or 'focal concerns' – issues that receive a high level of commitment among the lower-class communities. He contended that these 'focal concerns' can be used to characterise lower-class life, but that they are particularly noticeable among lower-class delinquent gangs. These can be outlined as follows:

- *Trouble*. The tendency to conflict with institutions of authority as a way of generating status also involves the use of physical confrontation, sexual activity and the use of drugs.

- *Toughness*. The display of manliness, prowess, physical ability and courage is used when young men feel the necessity to assert their masculinity.

- *Smartness*. The ability to outwit others without being tricked oneself is a of skill that can lead to more status than displays of toughness.

- *Excitement*. This is a concern with generating excitement by drinking, drug-taking, gambling, sex, etc., and is used as a means of escape from the boredom that may otherwise dominate their lives.

- *Fate, fortune and luck*. This relates to feelings that they are not able to change their lifestyle and that their lives are often subject to forces beyond their control.

- *Autonomy*. There is a resentment of the restrictions that may be put on their behaviour by institutions of authority and a desire to be liberated from any external controls.

Miller argued that, by adhering to these lower-class focal concerns and cultural patterns, legal norms may be violated. Also, law-breaking may produce more immediate results with less effort – it may be easier to steal than to get a highly paid job. Essentially, Miller asserted that illegal behaviour is the expected response to certain situations of lower-class life.

Matza and Sykes

Perhaps the most influential work of Matza and Sykes is *Techniques of neutralisation* (1957). They asserted that delinquents often rationalise their criminal behaviour in advance; they present justifications for committing infractions of the law that are seen as defences or valid excuses for the law-breaking act using their own personal assessment. Thus, Matza and Sykes proposed that delinquency is not in opposition to mainstream society but in fact amounts to an 'apologetic failure'.

These justifications, called 'techniques of neutralisation', can be outlined as follows:

- *Denial of responsibility*. The young person contends that their behaviour is beyond their control – that it is the result of a deprived background, poor parenting, etc.

- *Denial of injury*. The young person argues that no one has really been hurt – for example, in the case of a burglary, the person can claim the money back from an insurance company.

- *Denial of victim*. This is the idea that the victim somehow deserved what happened to them, or that the criminal actions were in some way justified – for example, the victim was foolish to be walking home late at night on their own with their handbag open and their purse visible, or that the victim will quickly get over the incident.

- *Condemnation of the condemners*. The young person criticises those who condemn him/her as hypocrites, as spiteful, or as corrupt.

- *Appeal to higher loyalties*. This is the notion that the young person must support the group or gang, even if this necessitates breaking the law.

Sykes and Matza also discussed the notion that delinquency is made attractive by the exaggeration of what they call 'subterranean values'. These include three factors: the seeking out of excitement; the disdain for routine work; and the interlinked values of toughness and masculinity. They argued that these 'subterranean values' are visible throughout society and are in fact leisure ideas, but that the young delinquent will exaggerate these. The combination of these three elements, they argue, encourage lower-class males in the 'limbo' of adolescence to manufacture excitement by rule-breaking.

ACTIVITY 3.4

Discuss whether we can use the subcultural perspective to explain crime perpetrated by girl gangs.

The labelling perspective

In Chapter 2 we noted that more and more young people are being drawn into the net of youth justice services. Over the last few years we have witnessed a massive increase in the numbers of workers within the youth justice industry. This professional entrepreneurialism is resulting in an extension of the labelling process to ever increasing numbers of young people. Why as a society are we producing ever more young people who are coming into contact with the broad sweep of youth justice and anti-social agencies? How will this impact upon their lives: upon their image of themselves, how others perceive them and upon their life chances? Let's examine the ideas of two of criminology's most prominent labelling theorists in an attempt to answer these questions.

Lemert's primary and secondary deviations

Lemert, in Social Pathology (1951), examined the meaning of action upon the actor and others within the subject's interpersonal and social groups. He noted that while some types of interaction may lead to the actor normalising their behaviour and therefore regarding the behaviour as insignificant in the context of their personality, some interactions may lead the actor to fully take on board the self-perception of being labelled as deviant. Such a process, which Lemert argued promotes secondary deviation, is a kind of realignment or adjustment of self-identity based upon symbolic reactions. As a result of this a secondary deviation may be sparked off; the person now labelled as deviant will realign themselves within this definition and this may provoke the development of defensive or antagonistic feelings due to the isolating effects of the social stigma.

Lemert asserted that primary deviance has many causes but secondary deviance results from being labelled until one accepts the deviant role. This is an eight-stage process:

- The commission of the act of primary deviance.

- Social penalties that follow from this act.

- Possible further primary deviations.

- This results in stronger social penalties and possibly isolation and rejection.

- Further deviation may take place, which may lead to the formation of resentment, anger and hostility focused upon those who are administering sanctions.

- A crisis may then ensue in relation to the 'tolerance quotient' of society which may be expressed in terms of taking formal action against the deviant and stigmatising them.

- The deviant behaviour may be strengthened as a reaction to the stigmatisation and the application of sanctions.

- The person may eventually accept the label of 'deviant' and their self-image may be adjusted in order to accommodate this new social status.

Lemert argued that primary deviation refers to the initial acts of (usually) a juvenile that may provoke societal reaction; he contended that such primary acts of deviation may occur at random or have been precipitated by a diversity of factors. It is important to note that Lemert stressed that the initial act of deviance will have little effect upon the person's self-concept. However, secondary deviation has a direct causational link with the societal reaction and flows directly from it. Thus Lemert proposed that secondary deviations result as a realignment or reconsideration of self-concept. His thesis involved an acceptance that secondary deviation may lead to the creation of a new self-image, which is often overtly recognisable: 'Objective evidences of this change will be found in the symbolic appurtenances of the new role, in clothes, speech, posture and mannerisms, which in some cases heightened social visibility' (1951, p76).

Becker's outsiders

In his book *Outsiders: Studies in the sociology of deviance* (1963) Becker suggested that societies create deviance by generating and applying rules that cast certain people out of mainstream or normal society. These 'outsiders' are then left to wander beyond the limits of conventionality, suffering the sanctions that are meted out by respectable society and often being forced to adopt an alternative lifestyle as a result of this rejection. Becker did not just focus upon the creation of criminality but specifically investigated the creation of concepts of deviance and concluded that all deviants become the cast-outs of society; these include not only criminals but also those who are mentally ill or have mental disabilities, the homeless, political activists and homosexuals. The labelling theory essentially tackles the processes involved in creating 'difference' as a justification for the use of social and penal sanctions. He said:

> Social rules define situations and the kinds of behaviour appropriate to them, specifying some actions as 'right' and forbidding others as 'wrong'. When a rule is enforced, the person who is supposed to have broken it may be seen as a special kind of person, one who cannot be trusted to live by the rules agreed by the group. He is regarded as an outsider. (Becker, 1963, p1).

Becker argued that there is no inherent quality to deviance, but that it is purely relative. He stressed that definitions of deviance are variable and asserted that society creates deviance by the application of rules that provide the facility to label and stigmatise those who breach the rules. Thus deviant behaviour is not related to the quality of the behaviour; there is no inherent definition of behaviours that are deviant within all societies. Deviance is a relative concept and is identified solely by the actions that follow the behaviour – the social sanction.

This process of manufacturing a deviant may depend upon perceptions of the person who has committed certain acts. Becker notes that boys from the lower classes are more likely to be perceived as delinquent than boys from middle-class backgrounds. Similarly, he alleged that the stigmatisation processes are also more likely to be applied to people of colour. Lastly, he noted that crimes committed by companies are not perceived as being as threatening as those committed by individuals, and thus white-collar 'criminals' may avoid social and criminal sanctions. As Becker suggested:

> deviance is not a simple quality, present in some kinds of behaviour and absent in others. Rather, it is the product of a process which involves responses of other people to the behaviour. The same behaviour may be an infraction of the rules at one time and

not at another; may be an infraction when committed by one person, but not when committed by another; some rules are broken with impunity, others are not. In short, whether a given act is deviant or not depends in part on the nature of the act . . . and in part on what other people do about it. (1963, p14)

Additionally, Becker maintained that we cannot know whether or not an act is deviant until we have waited to see the reaction to it:

we must recognise that we cannot know whether a given act will be categorised as deviant until the response of others has occurred. Deviance is not a quality that lies in behaviour itself, but in the interaction between the person who commits an act and those who respond to it. (1963, p14)

Becker conjectured that there is no consensus within society and an absence of homogeneity leads to differing opinions about the acceptability of behaviours. He noted that society is highly differentiated on class, occupational, cultural and ethnic grounds.

Becker, like Lemert, was also interested in examining the effect upon individuals of the application of labels, and of how this may create a deviant career. In relation to this he commented that 'one of the most crucial steps in the process of building a stable pattern of deviant behaviour is likely to be the experience of being caught and publicly labelled as deviant' (1963, p31).

In this assertion, Becker echoes Lemert's ideas about the process of 'secondary deviation', whereby the person labelled eventually readjusts their self-concept and views themselves as criminal/deviant. In effect, he/she becomes what the label implies; this process amounts to an adaptation of the popular 'give a dog a bad name' argument. So Becker asserted that the process of labelling is a process which creates a self-fulfilling prophecy and that the formal and informal vehicles of stigmatisation that spring into action following the discovery of certain behaviour is, in effect, a course of action that seeks to 'conspire to shape the person in the image people have of him' (1963, p34).

ACTIVITY 3.5

Discuss the following question: To what extent is contact with the youth justice system counter-productive for children and young people who encounter it?

Radical/Marxist perspective

Becker's insistence that criminality and deviance were essentially social constructs, and that certain groups of people, who just happened to be the least powerful in society, had been singled out for special categorisation and stigmatisation, opened the floodgates for further critical appraisals that were to challenge the very nature of social order and lead to the politicalisation of crime, deviance and difference. The developments in the late 1960s and early 1970s within the field of sociology of deviance cannot be examined without a brief reference to the political climate in both Europe and the USA at the time. Anti-establishment demonstrations were taking place across Europe and the USA. Students

were occupying their universities; Sartre and Foucault were challenging the very foundation of knowledge and power; civil rights marches demonstrated outrage at the arrogance
of the USA in relation to Vietnam; Malcom X represented black indignation and exhaus-
tion at the barbarism of racism and social apartheid; women were angrily marching out of
their kitchens; and the Stonewall riots encouraged lesbians and gay men to march out of
their closets. All this, together with flower power, Woodstock and free love, challenged
the very fabric of the status quo. Things would never be quite the same again.

It was the age of politicalisation, demonstration and rebellion. There was a re-examination
of Marxist ideology by sociologists, and they liked what they saw. Demonstrations signalled
a rebellion against traditional lifestyles and morality; they amounted to celebration of diversity. Politics were radicalised and resistance was not viewed as counterproductive, but as
meaningful and political. Deviance itself became politicalised: it was not only criminals who
were pushed under the umbrella of deviance – they were now in the company of nuts, sluts
and queers. All 'difference' began to be seen as good, as political, positive, a challenge to
the system. The labels themselves, which had once been the most powerful objects of
oppression, were claimed and seen for what they really were – the instruments those in
authority utilised to socially control those to whom they were directed. The deviant was not
a passive actor (as the labelling theorists had implied) but a political rebel.

Radical theory viewed the deviant as active, as a rebel whose actions were in essence political. Personal deviance amounted to public challenge; breaking the law was a way of
confronting the pervasive power of the state. As Sumner says, 'any sign of resistance was
to be welcomed as political and meaningful . . . Deviance was politicised . . . it was politicised completely' (1994, p253).

The social and resistance movements that were emerging resulted in the growth of a
unique perspective within the field of criminology/sociology of deviance. These contributions generally had a Marxist framework and have been called, variously, 'new
criminology', 'radical criminology' and 'conflict criminology' (Quinney 1970; Young 1971;
Taylor et al., 1973). The concerns of the theorists within this perspective were generally
what they perceived had been seen as lacking from other theories (especially labelling),
including: first, a full structural analysis; second, a focus on the unequal distribution of
wealth and power within society; and last, a radical social and political analysis. Criminal
law, it was argued, does not reflect the views of the majority but in fact serves the interest
of the ruling class. Law corresponds with the economic conditions within society and will,
therefore, inevitably support those conditions. The focus of the new movement in criminology was to provide an analysis of the nature of law. Crime, it was alleged, is a result of
contradictions and inequalities inherent within a capitalist society. Crime is inevitable in an
unequal society. The unequal distribution of wealth and power will foster rebellion and
criminality. The solution to crime, therefore, does not lie in individual treatment or punishment, but in the creation of a new type of society.

ACTIVITY 3.6

Discuss whether you agree with the left idealists that all crimes are political in nature?

Realist criminologies

In the 1980s the Home Office began to fund research programmes that would consider cost-effective methods of crime control, based on neo-classicist notions that crime control interventions should focus upon the cost-benefit analysis of criminality: the idea that crimes are committed due to the availability of opportunities, and that resources should be targeted to decrease those opportunities and increase the risks in taking part in criminal activity. This new wave of criminological research was called 'new administrative criminology' and was posited on the acceptance that rather than sitting around discussing the possible causes of criminality, effective measures were needed to tackle the impact of crime. Two new strands of criminological thought began to develop over this period: the first was based on left-wing pragmatism and the second based in a neo-conservative remoralisation paradigm.

Left realism

Left realism came to life in 1984 with the publication of Lea and Young's text *What is to be done about law and order?* This work acknowledges that the lived realities of crime are indeed problematic and recognises the need to address victimisation in a practical and constructive manner. Jock Young in 1994 described left realism as follows:-

Left realism, as a critique of existing criminological theory, emerged in the 1980s . . . Its central aim is to be faithful to the reality of crime – to the fact that all crimes must, of necessity, involve rules and breakers (criminal behaviour and reaction against it) and offenders and victims. (1994, p102)

This approach espoused a practical criminology, based on empirical research: an acceptance that crime is inevitable and a recognition that crime is experienced disproportionately by those who are the least powerful within society. The left realists conducted local crime surveys in Islington the early 1980s in and these were later replicated across other metropolitan areas. It is arguable that the left realists are to be credited with providing the momentum for the (now yearly) British Crime Survey, a comprehensive survey of victimisation that is widely regarded as criminologically more valid than any other official method of collecting and recording statistics about crime. This movement also contributed to the recognition of the value of local crime statistics, local crime plans and the targeting of crime control strategies on the basis of sound evidence. Left realism can also arguably be credited with the adoption by the Government of the benefits of a multi-agency approach to tackling local crime problems.

Young posits ten points of left realism to comprise a co-ordinated, systematic approach to tackling the reality of crime. Of these we will concentrate on three pivotal facets, namely the square of crime, the theory of relative deprivation and the multi-agency strategy.

The square of crime

Left realism puts forward the idea of the 'square of crime' (see Figure 3.2). Any analysis of a criminal event should take into account factors that might impact upon each of the four corners/points of the square, namely the interaction between (1) the police; (2) other agencies of social control; (3) the offender; and (4) the victim; ((1) and (2) cover the reaction to the crime event and (3) and (4) cover the act itself).

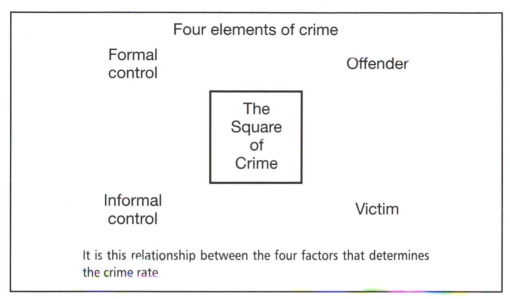

Figure 3.2 *The square of crime*

Figure 3.2 illustrates the concept of the 'square of crime'. At each point of the square we observe a factor that has contributed to the official measurement of crime in the form of the official crime statistics. In examining the creation of crime statistics we must refer to this four-fold aetiology, namely:

- Causes of offending (the domain of traditional criminology).

- Factors that make victims vulnerable (e.g. lifestyles).

- Social factors that affect public tolerance (e.g. towards smoking cannabis, violence, etc.).

- Police practice and enforcement.

The traditional focus of criminology was to concentrate only upon the factor in the top right-hand corner, namely the offender, and to consider causational aspects of their offending. Within this point on the square of crime we should, according to Young, analyse theories of crime causation which may go some way towards explaining the triggers of deviant behaviour.

Victims, at the bottom right-hand point of the square, are the second factor contributing towards the production of the crime rate. In relation to this factor, it is assumed that the victimised individual may in some way contribute towards their own victim status by their behaviour. For example, in order to avoid becoming a victim of crime a person may change their behaviour: not walking alone late at night, walking purposefully instead of slowly, wearing clothing that does not attract attention. A person's lifestyle might impact upon the chance of them becoming a victim of crime. Further other factors might affect their potential for becoming a victim by, for example, fitting car alarms, window locks, etc. Additionally, the victim's relationship with the offender may have a precipitative effect upon the outcome of their interactions.

Young asserts that most citizens of western societies are becoming more sensitive to and less tolerant of violence. This heightened sensitivity, to violent crimes in particular and all crimes in general, will lead to an increased willingness of the public to report incidences of perceived criminal behaviour to the police, thus contributing towards the increase in officially recorded crime. Indeed, Young says, realist criminology recognises that crime rates are a product not only of changes in behaviour, but also of changes in definitions of what is seriously criminal. A number of 'new crimes' have seemingly been discovered over the last 20 years, such as racial violence, child abuse, violence against women. He argues that the so-called 'civilising factor' within western societies has led to an increased sensitivity to anti-social behaviour generally.

Having examined the right-hand side of the square, we can see that these two points that contribute to the production of crime, the offender and victim interaction, provide an explanation of the criminal act but not of the societal reaction to it. Moving to the left-hand side of the square, we see that the other two points deal with the official and unofficial reactions to crime; Young calls these the social control elements that contribute towards the production of crime. With regard to the formal control agencies – the police, private security – Young asserts that these formal mechanisms contribute towards the production of crime statistics in a number of ways. The health of the relationship between the police and the public within a particular locality will contribute towards the production of crime statistics. A community that trusts its local police to investigate crime properly and fairly will be more willing to report crime than one that has lost faith in police fairness and efficiency. Further, this relationship will be affected by the level of perceived accountability of the police to the locality. Lastly a police force may decide to target particular types of crime and concentrate resources in certain areas, but this may produce a crime wave in another area.

The fourth point on the square of crime, informal public control, involves those controls the public may initiate, such as surveillance of a neighbour's property. It also includes the issues discussed earlier in relation to examining the victim's contribution towards crime statistics. There is less tolerance of criminality in general and specific types of crime in particular such as violent crime, and this increased sensitivity towards anti-social behaviour will in turn be transmitted via the democratic system into public opinion and media debate. Eventually it may lead to the creation of new crime by the legislature responding to public opinion and pressure groups.

Young asserts that it is the relationship between these four factors that determines the crime rate.

Relative deprivation

Left realists view the theory of relative deprivation as the most forceful explanation of crime, and note that other theories of criminology (e.g. anomie, subcultural theories) utilise the concept of relative deprivation. Young argues that relative deprivation is a potent notion because (a) it is not limited to the lower-class criminal and thus can be used to explain middle-class and corporate crime; (b) it is not concerned only with economic crimes but can be utilised to explain violent offences committed as a response to relative deprivation; and (c) it is not limited to absolute poverty and can explain the paradox of why some crimes of the economically deprived may focus upon obtaining the symbols of material wealth (e.g. designer clothes), rather than obtaining food and basic survival items.

The realists assert that there is no evidence to support a proposition that absolute deprivation leads to crime. They assert that this assumes that the causational flow is non-problematic. The process is not automatic. Not all people who are desperately poor commit crime; only some do. Young cites crime statistics of the 1930s during the Great Depression that indicate that crime rates decreased during this period of severe economic restraint. The realists propose that relative deprivation, coupled with the experience of unfairness with regard to the allocation of resources, leads the individual to seek a solution: this solution may involve law-breaking.

Multi-agency strategy

Young explains this as the co-ordinated response of social institutions to the issues of crime and disorder. He argues that the problem with unco-ordinated intervention based on a variety of policy of initiatives with no overarching rationale will inevitably be doomed to failure. Such interventions are often poorly resourced and may indeed overlap and possibly even conflict with each other.

The system of dealing with crime should not involve a uniform approach as different crimes require different processes. It is not merely the police, the Crown Prosecution Service and the courts who are involved in processing crime; various other agencies may handle a case at particular stages of its process. For example, the action taken to deal with an allegation of burglary will be markedly different from actions taken to deal with an allegation of child abuse. Young contends that any social control interventions in relation to crime reduction should involve all the agencies who may be involved in processing all types of crime. Table 3.1 illustrates the left realist's approach to multi-agency intervention in relation to crime control.

Table 3.1 The left realist's approach to multi-agency intervention

Stages in the devlopment of crime	Factors	Agencies
Causes of crime	Unemployment Housing Leisure time	Local authority Central government Businesses
Moral Context	Peer group values Community cohesion	Schools Public Family Mass media
Situation of commission	Physical environment Lighting Security	Local authority Public Police
Detection of crime	Public reporting Detective work	Public Police
Response to offenders	Punishment Rehabilitation	Courts Police Social services Probation
Response to victims	Insurance Public support	Local authority Victim support Local community groups Social services

Can you spot any similarities between left realism and the Labour government's approach to tackling youth crime?

Right realism

In the 1980s there was a growing cynicism about the effectiveness of the criminal justice process and pessimism regarding the perceived failure of criminology to put forward any viable proposals for the reduction of crime. Martinson's (1974) phrase 'nothing works' was adopted to describe a general dissatisfaction with crime control policies. These growing seeds of scepticism found fertile soil in the burgeoning conservatism that characterised the political landscape of both the USA and UK in the 1980s; there was a revitalisation of classicist notions of free will, choice, crime control, proportionality and deterrence. Further, there was a refocusing upon the individualistic theories of crime and a shift away from critical criminologies that had firmly placed the blame for crime on the state due to its failure to alleviate poverty, deprivation and inequalities that allegedly precipitated criminal behaviour.

The new right gurus of the underclass school in Britain were led by Charles Murray (1984, 1990), who transported his theory over the Atlantic in the mid-1980s. It was further developed in a UK context by Norman Dennis (1993) who asserted that many inner cities in the UK and other peripheral estates were becoming dominated by a growing 'underclass'. This underclass or 'yob culture' supposedly consists of feckless young men who show disdain for work and of irresponsible single mothers who live on benefits and are unable to instil any traditional moral values into their children, who consequently fall into a life of crime. According to Murray, these people who are supported by welfare, seek pleasure in drugs and try to gain further income from illegal activities. This underclass culture is cyclical: without positive role models, young men who are inadequately socialised will take part in illegal activity to create excitement and to supplement their welfare benefits.

Murray claims that the underclass can be identified by reference to certain behavioural traits that are in evidence among sections of the poorer population. These factors, he alleges, are two-fold: welfare dependency and the tendency to commit petty crime. He stresses that these two behavioural tendencies are not irrational when contextualised in the lifestyles of the underclass and the incentives that are built into the system of welfare provision. He maintains that the behaviour is rational but only in terms of short-term gain. It is destructive in the long term, but the under-educated have no ability to defer gratification.

Murray traces the origins of the resurgence of the idea that there are two categories of poor people, the deserving and the undeserving. It could be argued that this split in the lower classes in the UK was caused by the 'drawbridge effect' of the policies of Thatcherism in the 1980s. The 'yuppyisation' of parts of the UK in the 1980s, which began to slow down by the end of the decade, had created a radical re-evaluation of the traditional class structure in Britain. In relation to the working classes it had caused disjunction – a lack of solidarity between the non-working and the working lower classes.

Murray made several assumptions about the nature of criminal behaviour. He claimed that single parenthood is a predictive factor in criminal behaviour and that habitual criminals are invariably young, male members of this underclass. Single parenthood, he alleged, is encouraged by the provision of welfare and housing benefits. The welfare state produces a dependency culture and the proliferation of a 'culture of poverty'. Referring to young men and fatherhood, Murray argues that the growth of single parenthood among females has led to a loss of fatherhood responsibilities and the consequential 'civilising' effects of having to provide for children. He suggests that the welfare state encourages this situation and also promotes unstable and multiple relationships. Young boys in such an environment have no positive adult role models and the pattern of dependency is then repeated through generations. Murray describes the young male members of the 'underclass' as 'essentially barbarians, civilised by marriage' and argues that the features of the 'underclass' include crime, promiscuous self-indulgence, ungovernability, inability to defer gratification and lack of self-control. Murray concludes that crime is an easy option for these young men because of slim chances of being caught, low clear-up rates, and the tendency of magistrates and judges to give light sentences.

C H A P T E R   S U M M A R Y

In this chapter we have examined some of the major theories that have shaped the historical development of criminological theory. An insight into mainstream causational explanations of offending behaviour should help your knowledge of the nature of crime, criminality and criminalisation. It is vital that you develop skills of criminological analysis to assist your understanding of young people who come before the courts who you will deal with in your youth justice practice. Pre-sentence reports produced by youth justice practitioners must analyse the reasons why the young person has committed the crime in question and assess possible risk factors. An ability to apply criminological theory to casework is, therefore, vital in terms of enhancing your professional practice and the quality of your reports.

ACTIVITY 3.8

Bob and Sam are twins aged 18. Both live in the family home on a run-down inner-city council estate and they went to the same school. Their secondary school was average in terms of school league tables but had a high level of exclusions. Their parents are unemployed and in receipt of social benefits. Both boys associated with the same friends until the age of 15. Their mother is a recovering alcoholic and their father is a habitual criminal who has been convicted of burglary and several domestic assaults.

Bob was excluded from school at the age of 15 and has three convictions for possession of heroin, robbery and assault. Sam achieved three A grades in his A levels and is currently studying law at UCL.

Account for the criminality of Bob and the non-criminality of Sam.

FURTHER READING

Jones, S (2006) *Criminology.* Oxford: Oxford University Press.
This new edition provides a focus on explanations of criminality which are predominantly based on societal influences. The author also summarises genetic and psychological perspectives of crime causation and thus produces a full summary of major theories.

Tierney, J (2006) *Criminology: Theory and context.* London: Pearson Longman.
A second edition of an excellent textbook covering the major theoretical explanations of crime causation. It has an accessible style and provides an analysis of criminological thought within a historical context.

Walklate, S (2006) *Criminology: The basics.* London: Routledge. Chapter 4, 'The search for criminological explanation', provides an interesting summary of theory.

Chapter 4

The current legal framework of youth justice practice

Jane Pickford

This chapter will help you begin to meet the following National Occupational Standards.

Key Role 1: Prepare for and work with individuals, families, carers, groups and communities to assess their needs and circumstances

- Evaluate all information to identify the best form of initial involvement.
- Assess needs, risks and options taking into account legal and other requirements.

Key Role 4: Manage risks to individuals, families, carers, groups, communities, self and colleagues

- Identify and assess the nature of the risk.
- Balance the rights and responsibilities of individuals, carers, families, groups and communities with associated risk.
- Work within the risk assessment and management procedures of your own and other relevant organisations and professions.

Key Role 6: Demonstrate professional competence in social work practice

- Review and update your own knowledge of legal, policy and procedural frameworks.
- Identify and assess issues, dilemmas and conflicts that might affect your practice.
- Assess needs, risks and options, taking into account legal and other requirements.

It will also introduce you to the following academic standards as set out in the social work subject benchmark statement:

3.1.1 Social work services and service users

- The relationship between agency policies, legal requirements and professional boundaries in shaping the nature of services provided in interdisciplinary contexts and the issues associated with working across professional boundaries and within different disciplinary groups.

3.1.2 The service delivery context

- The complex relationships between public, social and political philosophies, policies and priorities and the organisation and practice of social work, including the contested nature of these.
- The issues and trends in modern public and social policy and their relationship to contemporary practice and service delivery in social work.
- The significance of legislative and legal frameworks and service delivery standards (including the nature of legal authority, the application of legislation in practice, statutory accountability and tensions between statute, policy and practice).
- The significance of interrelationships with other social services, especially education, housing, health, income maintenance and criminal justice.

3.1.3 Values and ethics
- The moral concepts of rights, responsibility, freedom, authority and power inherent in the practice of social workers as moral and statutory agents.
- The complex relationships between justice, care and control in social welfare and the practical and ethical implications of these, including roles as statutory agents and in upholding the law in respect of discrimination.
- The conceptual links between codes defining ethical practice, the regulation of professional conduct and the management of potential conflicts generated by the codes held by different professional groups.

3.1.4 Social work theory
- Models and methods of assessment, including factors underpinning the selection and testing of relevant information, the nature of professional judgement and the processes of risk assessment.

3.1.5 The nature of social work practice
- The factors and processes that facilitate effective inter-disciplinary, inter-professional and inter-agency collaboration and partnership.
- The processes of reflection and evaluation, including familiarity with the range of approaches for evaluating welfare outcomes, and their significance for the development of practice and the practitioner.

3.2.2.3 Analysis and synthesis
- Assess human situations, taking into account a variety of factors (including the views of participants, theoretical concepts, research evidence, legislation and organisational policies and procedures).

Introduction

In Chapter 2 we examined the philosophies and history of our youth justice system. This chapter outlines the policy discussions and legislation that shapes contemporary youth justice practice. As a social worker within the youth justice industry you will need to be familiar with the law underpinning your practice and the rationales that guide the contemporary legal framework. We examine the contemporary legal framework governing youth justice and set out the current sentencing options for young offenders. We also analyse non-criminal orders, which have the force of civil law constraints on young people who take part in anti-social and disorderly behaviour.

ACTIVITY **4.1**

As the contemporary legislation is discussed in this chapter, try to analyse the law in terms of the theoretical perspectives we examined in Chapter 2. For instance, which philosophical approach(es) are evident in current youth justice laws? Examine whether current legislation is similar to past statutes. Ideologically, does current practice represent a revolutionary break from history, or is it simply a reworking of old ideas?

The shaping of current laws

In order to understand fully the political momentum for the existing legal framework, it is necessary to revisit some of the debates about youth justice that were raging in the mid-1990s. I mentioned earlier (in Chapter 2) that various academics (Fionda, 2005; Hendrick,

2002; Jenks, 1996) have agreed that one case in 1993 changed the direction of youth justice policy and public opinion in relation to young offenders. This was the killing of the toddler James Bulger by two 10-year-old boys. The public outcry (largely media fuelled) that followed this case led to a 'moral panic' (Cohen 1973) about the law-breaking behaviour of children and young people. Indeed Jenks (1996) argued that the case led to the 'death' of childhood innocence and the subsequent 'demonisation' of youth.

From that point on, the tide of youth justice turned. Children were no longer pure and incorrupt; they were capable of the greatest evils. Hendrick (2002) argued that images of childhood became readjusted: we abandoned the 'romantic' model of childhood (that children are born innocent and so need protection from a corrupt society) and adopted the 'evangelical' model – that children are born capable of evil and so need to be firmly controlled. Media stories about young offenders allegedly being treated 'softly' by the juvenile justice system swayed public and political opinion towards an era of 'getting tough' on youth criminality.

The quasi-hysteria about the 'problem' of youth crime appears to make little sense when we analyse the statistical data for that era. According to published criminal statistics the number of young offenders aged 10 to 17 found guilty or cautioned of an indictable offence fell by 30 per cent between 1987 and 1997. According to NACRO (1999), 'since 1987, the number of male juvenile offenders has fallen by 33% and female young offenders by 17%'.

However, the number of young people receiving custodial sentences rose over that period. Whereas the numbers of young offenders detained under sentence fell by approximately 50 per cent between 1980 and 1993, this figure rose by almost 56 per cent in the four years up to and including 1997. In addition to the media frenzy, this rise also corresponded with the development of a definition of the so-called 'persistent offender' over this period and the 'getting tough' policies in relation to those so categorised.

The political debates surrounding the run-up to the 1997 general election promised a 'law and order' agenda from all the major parties. The Labour Party's promise to get 'tough on crime, tough on the causes of crime' extended to youth crime. Once in office, they established a Youth Crime Task Force and the momentum for reform of criminal justice continued, with no less than seven consultation papers being released, five of which were directly related to youth justice:

- *Tackling youth crime* (Home Office, 1997g)

- *Preventing children offending* (Home Office, 1997e)

- *Getting to grips with crime* (Home Office, 1997b)

- *Tackling delays in the youth justice system* (Home Office, 1997f)

- *No more excuses: A new approach to tackling youth crime in England and Wales* (Home Office, 1997d)

- *Community safety order* (Home Office, 1997a)

- *New national and local focus on youth crime* (Home Office, 1997c)

The government argued that the reason for change stemmed from the negative comments about the organisation of youth justice practice discovered by the Audit Commission and noted in their report *Misspent youth* (1996). The consultation papers of 1997 outlined the Labour Party's stated proposals for youth justice practice, noting that the current system was in disarray:

> *The youth justice system in England and Wales is in disarray. It simply does not work. It can scarcely be called a system at all because it lacks coherent objectives. It satisfies neither those whose principal concern is crime control nor those whose principal priority is the welfare of the young offender.* (Home Office, 1997g*)*

The Crime and Disorder Act 1998

Following these 'consultation' papers (Fionda (2005) points out that the consultation deadline allocated for *No more excuses* ended *after* the Bill had been published!) the Crime and Disorder Act was passed in 1998. The Act promised a 'root and branch' overhaul of the youth justice system to be implemented over a number of years, following the establishment of and feedback from pilot schemes and pathway sites, which tested the ground of the new reforms (one might argue that pilot schemes and viability should be tested prior to passing legislation). Section 37 of the Act emphasises the primary aim of prevention and states: 'It shall be the principal aim of the youth justice system to prevent offending by children and young persons'. It also places a duty on all personnel working within the youth justice arena to have regard to this paramount aim while carrying out their duties.

In order to deliver the principal aim, the Home Office Juvenile Offenders Unit set out a number of key objectives for the reformed youth justice system:

- Tackling delays – halving how long it takes for young offenders to be processed from arrest to sentence from an average of 142 days in 1996 to a target of 71 days (this has been achieved).
- Confronting the young offender with the consequences of their offending and encouraging responsibility for actions.
- Intervention into 'risk factors', including family, social, personal and health factors.
- Introduction of a new range of penalties in order to enable sentencers to punish in proportion to the seriousness and persistence of offending.
- Encouragement of reparation.
- Reinforcement of parental responsibilities.

The Act set out six key themes (noted below) that would assist in achieving the above objectives.

Partnership and multi-agency working

Sections 6 and 7 of the Act encourage the development of local partnerships to provide a local framework and strategy for identifying crime and disorder problems within a particular locality. Section 39 required local authorities to establish multi-agency Youth Offending Teams (YOTs) by April 2000, bringing together professionals from social services, police, health, education and probation. Teams must produce an annual youth justice plan for tackling crime within their area of responsibility. (Multi-disciplinary YOTs are discussed in Chapter 5.)

Tackling offending behaviour and providing early intervention

This key theme is actioned by the following measures:

- Child safety orders (Section 11), placed on a child under the age of 10 to prevent him/her from growing into criminal behaviour.

- Local child curfews (Section 14), aimed at preventing anti-social behaviour in local areas by children under the age of 10 (raised to 16).

- Final warnings (Section 65), replacing the cautioning system with a fixed procedure for diversionary disposals.

- Action plan order (Section 69), a three-month, intensive order that combines elements of reparation, punishment and rehabilitation to help prevent re-offending and include parental involvement.

The first two of these orders have been subsequently supplemented by the Anti-Social Behaviour Act and the introduction of acceptable behaviour contracts and individual support orders (see Chapter 2 for a discussion of these and a list of agencies that have developed to implement this expansionist agenda). This reflects the government's commitment to tackle both crime and social disorder. These civil measures (many of which have criminal consequences if breached) are part of a focus on preventionism and extend the reach of the youth justice system beyond offenders to those who are deemed anti-social or at risk of offending. (The human rights implications of these orders are discussed in Chapter 1; the dangers of net-widening and stigmatising are covered in Chapter 2.)

The action plan order, which was introduced in 2000, is aimed at young people who are low-level offenders or who find themselves in front of a courtroom for the first time. The order is a short term (three-month) package of YOT intervention aimed at 'nipping offending in the bud'. This order was widely used over the first two years of its availability but has been less in evidence since the availability (from April 2002) of the (mainly compulsory) sentence of a referral order for young people appearing in court for the first time.

Focus on reparation

Section 67 establishes the reparation order, designed to help the young person face up to the consequences of their offending behaviour. The young person may be required to make reparation to the actual victim of their crime or to the local community generally. The theme of responsibilisation is evidenced in this order, which encourages the offender to contemplate the actual impact of their law-breaking in terms of the injury and suffering caused to victims. Anecdotal accounts from practitioners indicate that this order is not widely used, as elements of reparation can be part of several more comprehensive community sentences. Reparation is also a central theme of the referral order, introduced in 2002.

Focus on parenting

Section 8 of the Act reinforces parental responsibility by introducing the parenting order. This is aimed at 'helping' parents, through support and guidance, to control the anti-social behaviour of their children. Such an order may place specific responsibilities on a parent, for example to impose a curfew on their child. In addition to the existing powers to fine and bind-over parents, the order represents a further move to hold parents responsible for the sins of their offspring and provides the Government with a way of punishing parents by means of a potentially criminalising sanction for their presumed failure to properly care for or bring up their child. It remains to be seen how much further this country will move down the pathway of parental punishment and also, how far we will continue to usurp and supplant the parental rights of those we consider to be bad parents by the use of anti-social behaviour orders, acceptable behaviour contracts, curfew orders, individual support orders, child safety orders and even remands in local authority accommodation. You may find it useful to monitor the types of parents who become subject to parenting orders and other intrusive orders in your area of practice in terms of their socio-economic backgrounds; for instance, whether it is predominantly single parents or co-parents who are targeted for such interventions.

More effective custodial sentences

Section 73 established a new detention and training order, implemented from April 2000. This purported to be a constructive and flexible custodial sentence with a clear focus on preventing re-offending behaviour. The order can be used by Youth and Crown Courts in respect of all young offenders under the age of 18 who have been convicted of an offence that if committed by an adult would be an imprisonable offence. If the child is aged 10 or 11, a further order will be required by the Home Secretary to allow such a sentence to be passed. The sentence is supposed to be 'seamless', though half the order is spent in detention and the other half under supervision in the community. The numbers of young people being sentenced to custody has continued to increase. As Bateman has noted (2003) though, the number of children and young people locked up in this country has received 'damning' criticism from the UN Committee on the Rights of the Child. Indeed the Youth Justice Board noted that: the expansion in the use of youth custody which began in the 1990s has continued unchecked since the implementation of the Crime and Disorder Act'. Recent statistics show that this rise has continued (Youth Justice Board, *Annual Statistics* 2004/05; see YJB website for the most recent figures).

A national framework

Section 41 sets up the framework for the national Youth Justice Board's operation. This is to encourage and monitor nationwide consistency in the implementation of the system of youth justice, to draw up standards for service delivery and to help disseminate good practice. (The role of the YJB is discussed in Chapter 5.)

ACTIVITY 4.2

In reference to Activity 4.1 above, can you identify which theoretical perspectives underpin the Crime and Disorder Act 1998?

The Youth Justice Criminal Evidence Act 1999

The Youth Justice and Criminal Evidence Act 1999 (as amended by the Powers of the Criminal Courts (Sentencing) Act 2000) gave effect to further reforms proposed in the 1997 White Paper *No more excuses* (Home Office, 1997d). It created a new (largely compulsory) sentence of a referral order for young people convicted for the first time. The young person is referred by the court to a Youth Offender Panel (YOP) drawn from the local community (established by YOTs) and serves the sentence for a period of between three and 12 months. A 'contract' is drawn up with the young offender and their parents, specifying the details of the order; each contract is tailor-made to suit the needs of the young person. The referral order is designed to address offending behaviour, in an attempt to prevent further offending. The order should include reparation and can also involve community work, curfews, mediation, contact with the victim and participation in specified activities or education programmes.

The new YOPs resemble the system adopted in 1971 in Scotland to deal with young offenders (see Pickford, 2000, Chapters 8 and 9). The similarities with the Children's Hearings north of the border are clear: parents are to play a crucial role in attending and being asked to help prevent anti-social behaviour; other significant adults, such as social workers or teachers, may also be required to be present, victims are able to attend panel meetings and explain to the young offender the effects of their criminal behaviour and suggest appropriate reparation; the meetings are conducted informally, without the presence of a legal representative; and the young person is encouraged to participate fully in the proceedings. Once the order is completed, the young person's offence is 'spent' for the purposes of the Rehabilitation of Offenders Act 1974.

Basically, a referral order will be made against all young people who are convicted of a first offence, except where:

- the court orders an absolute discharge;
- the sentence for the offence is fixed by law;
- the court decides to make a custodial sentence; or
- the offence is one that is non-imprisonable (2003 amendment).

It should be noted that the offender must have pleaded guilty to the offence (or to one offence, if charged with more than one offence). The type of requirements that can form part of a 'contract' include:

- Financial or other reparation.
- Attendance at mediation sessions.
- The carrying out of unpaid work in the community.
- Being at home at specified times.
- Attendance at school, training or work.

- Participation in specified activities (e.g. attending drug treatment centre).

- Presenting to named persons or institutions as and when specified.

- Avoiding specified places or persons.

Some problematic issues have arisen despite the 'flagship' status this order seems to have been given by the Government. These include:

- A low level of attendance of victims at panels – 13 per cent during the pilot period (Earle, 2005).

- The fact that legal representation is prohibited.

- These informal meetings follow no set procedures, due process requirements are not followed and each Panel tends to reflect the character and attitude of the Panel members. Thus 'justice' is meted out in an inconsistent, non-standardised manner (see Crawford and Newburn, 2003).

- A 'contract' implies equality of bargaining power, yet the young person must 'agree' to the 'contract' or be referred back to court for non-compliance (see Pickford, 2000).

- No appeal is allowed.

- As this sentence is largely compulsory, young people who have committed trivial offences may face a minimum of a three-month order. This may be considered an 'overreaction' to the original wrongdoing.

- Sentencers are not able to exercise discretion in sentencing: if the criteria for the referral order sentence are satisfied, sentencers must make a referral order – although they have discretion as to length of the order. Earle (2005) remarks that youth magistrates resented the curtailment in their powers following the implementation of the order in April 2002; this led to the government (Home Office, 2003b) extending discretion to issue other sentences where the offence is non-imprisonable. However, this concession only related to a small number of situations, e.g. motoring offences.

- In some areas panel volunteers might not reflect the social class, economic, sex, religious or racial background of the community from which they are drawn (Crawford and Newburn, 2002).

- The system relies on volunteers who are unqualified to make decisions about the sentence content of young offenders on court orders. How does this square with the overall move towards professionalisation, standardisation and evidence-based practice of youth justice?

However, as Earle remarks: 'Stationed at the gateway of the new system are over 5000 volunteers. Each year they greet approximately 27,000 young people with a novel experience of justice' (2005, p105).

ACTIVITY 4.3

In reference to Activity 4.1 above, can you identify which theoretical perspectives underpin the Youth Justice and Criminal Evidence Act 1999?

The current sentencing framework

Issues relating to bail, remand and the diversionary disposals of reprimand and final warning are covered in Chapter 5. This section examines the current disposals available to youth magistrates and crown court judges in relation to young people aged 10 to 17 years. Table 4.1 details the various disposals that can be used.

Table 4.1 The current disposals available in relation to young people aged 10 to 17 years

Sentence	Age range	Nature and content of sentence	Possible length of sentence
Discontinued or dismissed or withdrawn	10–17 years	The case is dropped because it is decided by the Prosecution Service that there is not enough evidence against the young person or that it is not in the public interest to prosecute.	Not applicable
Reprimand	10–17 years	A verbal warning given by a police officer for a minor first offence where guilt has been admitted.	One meeting
Final warning	10–17 years	A verbal warning given by a police officer for a first or second offence where guilt has been admitted. A short intervention/series of meetings takes place, usually co-ordinated by police officers attached to the local Youth Offending Team (YOT).	Up to 12 weeks
Absolute discharge	10–17 years	The young person has admitted guilt or been found guilty but no formal sentencing action is taken.	Not applicable
Conditional discharge	10–17 years	The young person must stay out of trouble for a specified period. If they do, no immediate punishment is given: if they don't they can be re-sentenced.	Between 6 months and 3 years
Referral order	10–17 years	Given to a young person who pleads guilty and is appearing in court for the first time. Compulsory unless the court issues custody, an absolute discharge or the offence is non-imprisonable or fixed by law. (Content noted above.)	Between 3 and 12 months
Fine	10–17 years	This should be proportionate to the crime and means are taken into account. If the young person is under 16 the parents/guardians will be responsible for payment.	Not applicable
Compensation order	10–17 years	As main sentence or as an ancillary order. Paid to the victim for loss/damage. Should take into account the amount of loss/damage and the means of the offender (or parents, if under 16 years).	Not applicable
Reparation order	10–17 years	Requires that the young person makes amends for the offence either directly to the victim or indirectly via community work. Supervised by YOT.	Up to 24 hours over 3 months

Sentence	Age range	Nature and content of sentence	Possible length of sentence
Action plan order	10–17 years	A short, intensive order supervised by YOT to address the offending triggers for that young person. Can include attending YOT for offence counselling and victim awareness sessions, drugs awareness, community work, education and training sessions, etc.	3 months
Curfew order	10–17 years	As main sentence or as an ancillary order (or as part of an ISSP). Must remain at a specified place for a specified period. Electronically tagged or with a 'doorstep' requirement. (Curfew can also be given as part of a bail package – see Chapter 5.)	Between 2 and 12 hours a day for up to 6 months (16 and above) or 3 months (under 16s)
Attendance centre order	10–17 years	Must attend the local attendance centre (usually run by the local police) on Saturdays and undertake posit-ive activities prescribed by the co-ordinating officer.	From 4 to 24 hours
Supervision order	10–17 years	Order run by YOT tailored to fit the needs of the offender with regard to preventing recidivism. Content can be decided by the YOT but the court can add specific conditions. Typical conditions include attending YOT offence counselling and victim awareness sessions, drugs awareness, community work, anger management, education and training sessions, etc. Can also include residence requirement and a curfew. Voluntary conditions (such as sessions with a psychotherapist) can be added. Since 2003, an intensive supervision and surveillance condition can be attached – for a period of up to 6 months.	6 months to 3 years
Intensive supervision and surveillance order	10–17 years	Includes 25 hours of specified activities per week attached to the start of a supervision order or community rehabilitation order as an intensive alternative to custody for serious/persistent offenders. The activities must be specified in the pre-sentence report and can include any of those noted under supervision orders above. The young person can also be subject to surveillance for part or all of the ISSP period (e.g. by electronic tagging). (Note: an ISSP can also be given as part of a bail package – see Chapter 5; or as part of the community element of a detention and training order – see below). Supervised by local provider (e.g. NACRO) in tandem with YOT/probation.	6 months – intensive (25 hours) for first 3 months then at a reduced level for second 3 months
Community rehabilitation order	16-17-year-olds	This is similar to a supervision order (see above) but aimed at older offenders. It can be supervised by YOT or transferred to the probation service when the young person reaches 17/18. An ISSP can be attached (see above).	6 months to 3 years
Community punishment order	16 and 17-year-olds	The young person must do unpaid community work for a specified time period.	40 to 240 hours
Community punishment and rehabilitation order	16 and 17-year-olds	A combination of the above two orders.	12 months to 3 years plus 40 to 100 hours

Sentence	Age range	Nature and content of sentence	Possible length of sentence
Detention and training order	12–17-year-olds	The young person spends the first half of the sentence in custody and the other half under supervision (usually by the YOT) within the community doing activities listed in the supervision order, above. The sentencing court can specify that for this second part of the order the young person should be placed on an ISSP (see above).	4 months to 2 years
Sentence under S90 or 91 for grave offences	10–17 years	Under the Powers of the Criminal Court (Sentencing) Act 2000 a young person who is convicted of a murder or a 'grave crime' (i.e. one for which an adult could be sentenced to 14 years in custody) can receive the same statutory maximum as an adult. They will be automatically released at the halfway point on licence (CJA 2003). YOT/probation will supervise them up to the three-quarter point. (See also the Criminal Justice Act 2003 sentencing powers regarding 'dangerousness', below.)	Indefinite

If a young person does not comply with the community penalties listed in Table 4.1 s/he will be brought before the court and the relevant supervising authority (the local YOT, the probation service or the curfew monitoring body) will initiate breach proceedings. It is the practice of many YOTs to breach orders after three failures to comply/attend. If the supervising body can prove the breach (or it is admitted) the court is able to reinstate the order or to re-sentence (usually to a harsher disposal).

It is apparent from Table 4.1 that a wide range of sentences are available to magistrates and judges. As noted in Chapter 2, academics have commented on the vast choice and referred to a 'cafeteria' style of justice for young offenders (Ashworth, 2000). In terms of criminological theory, the sentencer is able to hand pick a 'bespoke' (Fionda, 2005) sentence to fit the particular circumstances and needs of the young person. This is arguably a positivist's dream system! However, are there too many sentencing options? The government is currently (summer 2006) discussing a reduction in sentencing choice, which we will examine in Chapter 9.

Additional orders

Further to the above sentences, the following additional orders can be made. These orders were introduced either by the Crime and Disorder Act 1998 or by later statutory amendments (see next section, below). The orders listed in Table 4.2 include civil orders that can be sought as controlling measures for young people who have not been found guilty of any criminal offence. It should be noted that a child curfew order is a civil order that should be differentiated from a curfew order that can be used as a single or additional sanction for a criminal act. The restrictive nature of these measures in terms of civil liberties is commented on in Chapter 1.

Table 4.2 Additional orders

Type of order	Age range	Nature content of order	Time limits
Anti-social behaviour order (ASBO)	10 years and above	This is a civil order. ASBOs can be made by local authorities, the police, British Transport Police, Social Landlords and Housing Action Trusts or by other relevant authorities. An ASBO is made where the person has acted in an anti-social manner which has caused or is likely to cause harassment, alarm or distress. Individualised conditions can be attached requiring the person not to go to certain areas, near certain people, participate in certain activities, etc. Breach can amount to a criminal offence with a maximum punishment of a 2-year DTO. An interim ASBO can be obtained, pending a full ASBO hearing.	2 years plus (no specified upper time limit)
Acceptable behaviour contract (ABC)	Any age group – primarily aimed at 10–17 year olds	This is a civil order whereby a local authority draws up an agreement that specifies that the young person must desist from certain lower-level anti-social behaviour. Intervention by a YOT or social worker may additionally be agreed. Breach of an ABC can be used as evidence for the issuing of an ASBO.	No specified upper time limit
Individual support order (ISO)	10–17 years	A civil order introduced in May 2004. It is applied for by local authorities (usually the anti-social behaviour unit/team of a local authority) and intended to provide support for young people subject to ASBOs to prevent the behaviour that led to the ASBO being made. Managed by YOTs. Breach can be deemed a criminal offence with a fine of up to £1,000 (payable by parents if the young person is under 16).	Up to 6 months
Disperal order	No age limit	Introduced by the Anti-social Behaviour Act 2003, this order enables the police and local authority to identify problem areas where people feel threatened by groups congregating, causing intimidation and acting in an anti-social manner. Police or community support officers can direct individuals to leave an area for up to 24 hours. Until 2005 the police had been able to take under-16s home after 9pm if they were within a designated area and not under the control of an adult. However, this power was successfully	Up to 6 months

Type of order	Age range	Nature content of order	Time limits
		challenged in *R (On the Application of W) v Commissioner of Police of the Metropolis and Richmond Borough Council [2005]* EWCA Civ 1568. Now the police can only ask that the young person return home.	
Child safety order (CSO)	Under 10s	A civil order imposed on a child (i) who does an act that, had they been aged 10 or above, would have amounted to a criminal offence; (ii) has caused distress, alarm or harassment or (iii) has breached a child curfew order. Supervised by a social worker. Breach can result in the child being placed under a care order.	Up to 12 months
Local child curfew	Under 16 (including under 10s)	A civil order (obtained by a local authority or police) that bans the child/young person from a particular area during specified hours due to them causing distress to residents. If a child under 10 breaches this order, they can be given a child safety order (above).	Between 9pm and 6am for a period up to 90 days
Parenting order	Not applicable	A civil order given to parents/guardians of young people who have offended, truanted, been subjected to an ASBO, CSO or sex offender order. Parent must attend guidance sessions and could additionally be required to ensure that the child attends school, is supervised when visiting certain places and/or is home by a specified time. Failure to comply can lead to prosecution and a criminal offence.	Between 3 to 12 months
Drug treatment and testing order	10–17 years	Used in addition to any community sentence for young people who have committed drug offences or are assessed as having offended due to drug-related issues. (Any offender can now be tested for drug use at the police station when charged with an offence.) Supervised by YOT or probation service.	Between 6 months to 3 years
Costs order	10–17 years	(In existence prior to the 1998 Act). After a court hearing where the young person has pleaded or been found guilty, they (or their parents if under 16) can be ordered to pay a contribution towards prosecution costs.	Will be given a specified time to complete payment

From the discussion of all the sentencing disposals and other additional measures that can be used by the state in its endeavours to control youth disorder, it is possible to understand why some academics (noted above) have indicated that the current system may amount to overkill and that some re-evaluation of the direction in which youth justice is moving is becoming increasingly necessary.

ACTIVITY 4.4

Jim (aged 15) has been convicted of an offence of Attempted Theft (found guilty after trial). In evidence, Jim admitted that he was in the area at the time of the offence with the co-defendant (aged 18) as they had been to the West End to see a film. He stated that after the film ended both he and the co-defendant made their way to the nearest tube station (which he believed was Piccadilly Circus) in order to make their way home. Jim recounted that the tube station had been temporarily closed and that guards were not allowing anyone onto the platforms, so he and the co-defendant made their way out of the tube station in order to take a bus home. Jim stated that he was then stopped by a police officer, asked several questions, and was then processed for this offence.

This version of events did not accord with the account of events provided by the Crown Prosecution Service. Jim denied observing a man withdrawing money from a cashpoint machine, denied following him into a newsagent's shop and denied making any attempts to remove any items from the man's bag or being a secondary party to any such activities. The Magistrates accepted the Prosecution's evidence and found Jim guilty. However, although Jim has been found guilty for this matter, he maintains his innocence incontrovertibly and refuses to take any responsibility for this offence.

Jim is a refugee from Romania. According to Jim and his elder cousins with whom he fled Romania and with whom he now resides, they have been in the UK for about two years. The borough's Children and Families Team now accommodates this family unit. Jim's allocated social worker is responsible for Jim's general welfare. The borough pays for the accommodation and Jim receives a subsistence allowance of approximately £142 every four weeks. His cousins are also in receipt of subsistence money. Jim has lost contact with his mother and father. His father left Romania with Jim's elder brother aged 16, and while Jim believes that his mother is still in Romania he has not been able to contact her. Jim has not had any formal schooling for approximately three years; attempts to find special educational placements for him since he has been under the guidance of the council have not yet borne fruit. In terms of career ambitions, Jim stated that he wishes to become a mechanic. Jim recounted that he spends his time watching TV and videos (which, he stated, assist him to learn English), reading English self-learning texts and playing football in a team with some friends.

Jim received a four-month referral order a year ago (which he has completed successfully) for a matter of handling stolen goods.

- What risk factors are in evidence?

- How can these be reduced?

- What sentence might you recommend for Jim and why?

- Are any ancillary orders appropriate?

Other significant legislative changes

Alhough no statute specifically addressing youth justice practice has been passed following the 1998 and 1999 Acts, the staged implementation meant that many of the reforms are still considered to be relatively 'new' by seasoned youth justice practitioners. However, other statutes covering criminal justice generally have been passed and some of these have impacted upon youth disorder and criminal justice procedures (some of which are included in the Tables 4.1 and 4.2 above). Social workers need to be familiar with these recent changes. Furthermore, the government has released various consultation papers in relation to children and young people that have implications for future practice. In this section we explore further recent measures that are currently in force. The most important reform proposals for the future will be examined in Chapter 9.

Powers of the Criminal Courts (Sentencing) Act 2000

This Act introduced special measures for young people who have committed 'grave crimes' (see Table 4.1). Section 90 deals with young offenders convicted of murder and requires them to be detained 'during Her Majesty's pleasure'. This is an indeterminate sentence and the sanction is equivalent to the mandatory 'life' sentence for adults. The young person must serve a mandatory minimum (tariff) period fixed by the court. They will stay in custody until the end of that period. After that, they can then be released only with the permission of the parole board and will remain on 'licence' for the rest of their life.

Section 91 covers the procedure for other 'grave crimes' – primarily crimes for which an adult can be sentenced to 14 or more years in custody. Generally, the court is given the same maximum sentencing limits for young people charged with these crimes as adults. As Bateman (2005) has noted, since this Act 'a succession of legislative changes has brought an ever greater number of offences within the ambit of section 91' leading to a dramatic increase in long-term custodial sentences for young offenders (2005, p160).

Criminal Justice and Police Act 2001

Section 23 allowed electronic tagging as a condition of bail, including those on remand to local authority accommodation. Prior to this Act a court could only deprive a young person of their liberty while on remand if this was the only measure that could protect the public from serious harm. However, Section 130 allows a remand to custody (or secure accommodation) of a young offender whose offending is deemed persistent (including offending while on bail).

Justice for All

This White Paper (Home Office, 2002) proposed that trials for serious offences, now held in the Crown Court, should be heard in the Youth Court by a judge sitting with youth magistrates. This has not been implemented.

Criminal Justice Act 2003

This statute introduced new provisions for custody regarding young people (and adults) convicted of certain violent or sexual offences who are judged by the court to be 'dangerous'. New orders were introduced in December 2005 giving additional sentencing powers; these include (1) extended sentencing and (2) indeterminate sentence for public protection. The philosophical approach to these provisions is preventionism (see Chapter 2) and custodial orders are made on the basis of protection of the public rather than on the basis of proportionality. Under the new provisions the maximum sentence for such crimes committed by young people who fall within these categories can be increased.

Under category (1) if the young person has committed a sexual or violent offence for which an adult could receive two years or more and the court deems that there is a significant risk of serious harm to the public, they could receive extended detention which involves a licence extension of up to eight years for a sexual offence and five years for a violent offence. Young offenders who fall within the latter category (2) have committed a violent or sexual offence carrying a maximum penalty of ten years or above for an adult, and thus become eligible for an indeterminate sentence. Practitioners should monitor the use of these provisions, which could potentially further increase the use of long custodial disposals for young offenders.

Other provisions of the CJA that impact upon youth justice include:

- The use of a generic term for all community based disposals for young offenders – 'youth community order';

- While the community punishment and community rehabilitation orders are no longer available to adults, they are still available to 16 and 17 year olds.

- The general admissibility of 'bad character' introduced in criminal proceedings.

- YOTs are to comply with risk assessments under Multi-Agency Public Protection Arrangements (MAPPA).

- Privacy issues regarding the hitherto protective restrictions imposed on courts: courts can now release the names of those convicted of a crime and those against whom a post-conviction ASBO has been made.

Anti-Social Behaviour Order Act 2003

This Act extended the powers of public bodies in relation to civil orders associated with anti-social behaviour (as noted in Table 4.2). Significant extra measures, in addition to powers already granted (in relation to ASBOs and ABCs), included:

- Expansion of the range of authorities/bodies that can seek ASBOs.

- Introduction of a presumption in favour of making a parenting order where an ASBO is made against a young person under 16.

- Introduction of a presumption against reporting restrictions.

- Allowing hearsay evidence to be used.

- Introduction of individual support orders (ISOs) which can be ordered to run alongside ASBOs.

- Introduction of penalty notices for disorderly behaviour by young people (largely proved to be unworkable).

- Introduction of group dispersal orders.

Youth justice – *The next steps* and *Every child matters*

The Green Paper *Every child matters* (Home Office, 2003a) outlined proposals for reforming children's services generally and led to the Children Act 2004 (below). Alongside this paper the government published a companion document, *Youth justice – The next steps* (Home Office, 2003d), a separate consultation document covering proposed future reforms to the youth justice system. Though these have not been passed into legislation at the time of writing (summer 2006) it is useful to outline the major proposals, as they indicate the government's current plans for youth justice reform. These proposals are discussed in Chapter 9.

The Children Act 2004

This Act puts into effect many of the proposals relating to reforms in children's services outlined in *Every child matters*. While the Act deals with issues raised in relation to the investigation into the death of Victoria Climbié and covers mainly non-youth offending matters, some areas of reform will impact upon social work practice generally. Especially notable are:

- The establishment of the Children's Commissioner for England to raise awareness of best interests of children and young people, to examine how public bodies deal with them and consider their wishes, to examine how complaints are investigated and report annually to Parliament.

- Local authorities are to create Directors of Children's Services to cover education and social services.

- The encouragement of local authorities to create co-operation and to pool resources between agencies who deal with children and young people in order to improve their well-being in five key areas: health, safety, achievement, making a positive contribution and economic well-being.

- Placing a duty on key agencies to make sure that they safeguard and promote the welfare of children and young people and the creation of Local Safeguarding Children's Boards.

- Secondary legislation and guidance will be issued to allow the creation of databases to assist information sharing about children and young people.

- The creation of a new inspection format and regular Joint Area Reviews.

- Promoting the educational achievement of looked after children.

- Strengthening local fostering arrangements.

Youth justice 2004: A review of the reformed youth justice system (Audit Commission)

The comments of the Audit Commission in its latest review of youth justice services (2004), could have some impact upon future government proposals. These are covered in Chapter 9.

ACTIVITY 4.5

Discuss whether there are now too many options for dealing with young people who offend or take part in behaviour deemed to be disorderly or whether it is right for the government to have a variety of measures to deal with non-conforming youths. What are the implications of this expansion of youth control measures?

Future youth justice legislation

This chapter has discussed current law and practice. We review future legislation – the consultation paper *Youth justice – The next steps*, the Government's 2005 Green Paper *Youth matters*, the non-enacted Draft Youth Justice Bill 2005 and the most recent proposals for youth justice – in Chapter 9.

C H A P T E R S U M M A R Y

In this chapter the political context and debates that led to the restructuring of the youth justice system over the last ten years have been discussed. We examined the rationale expressed by the Labour Government to justify sweeping reforms of the system and noted some academic commentary relating to these changes. We have analysed the content of the two main sources of contemporary youth justice practice, namely the Crime and Disorder Act 1998 and the Youth Justice and Criminal Evidence Act 1999 and examined the current sentencing options and ancillary orders available. We have further analysed other legislative enactments relating to anti-social behaviour and children and young people passed since the major statutes and looked at their impact upon the youth justice system. We have noted the growth in the range and scope of sentencing options for young people who have committed offences and the burgeoning of other (mainly civil law) measures introduced to prevent and deter disorderly activities that do not amount to crimes.

FURTHER READING

Audit Commission (2004) *Youth justice 2004: A review of the reformed youth justice system.* London: TSO.
This report comments on the state of the current youth justice system and cites possible reforms.

Bateman, T and Pitts, J (eds) *The RHP companion to youth justice.* Lyme Regis: Russell House Publishing.
An up-to-date edited collection that provides papers discussing most areas of contemporary youth justice practice.

Fionda, J (2005) *Devils and angels: Youth policy and crime.* Oxford: Hart.
A comprehensive outline and excellent critique of youth justice policy and practice.

Chapter 5

Working within a Youth Offending Team and in the youth justice system

Paul Dugmore

A C H I E V I N G   A   S O C I A L   W O R K   D E G R E E

This chapter will help you begin to meet the following National Occupational Standards:

Key Role 2: Plan, carry out, review and evaluate social work practice, with individuals, families, carers, groups, communities and other professionals

- Prepare, produce, implement and evaluate plans with individuals, families, carers, groups, communities and professional colleagues.

Key Role 4: Manage risk to individuals, families, carers, groups, communities, self and colleagues

- Assess, minimise and manage risk to self and colleagues.

Key Role 5: Manage and be accountable, with supervision and support, for your own social work practice within your organisation

- Manage, present and share records and reports.
- Work within multi-disciplinary and multi-organisational teams, networks and systems.

Key Role 6: Demonstrate professional competence in social work practice

- Work within agreed standards of social work practice and ensure own professional development.
- Manage complex ethical issues, dilemmas and conflicts.
- Contribute to the promotion of best social work practice.

It will also introduce you to the following academic standards as set out in the social work subject benchmark statement:

3.1.1 Social work services and service users

- The relationship between agency policies, legal requirements and professional boundaries in shaping the nature of services provided in inter-disciplinary contexts and the issues associated with working across professional boundaries and within different disciplinary groups.

3.1.2 The service delivery context

- community-based, day-care, residential and other services and the organisational systems inherent within these.
- The significance of interrelationships with other social services, especially education, housing, health, income maintenance and criminal justice.

3.1.5 The nature of social work practice

- The factors and processes that facilitate effective inter-disciplinary, inter-professional and inter-agency collaboration and partnership.

3.2.4 Skills in working with others

- Act co-operatively with others, liaising and negotiating across differences such as organisational and professional boundaries and differences of identity or language.

3.2.5 Personal and professional development

- Identify and keep under review their own personal and professional boundaries.
- Handle inter-personal and intra-personal conflict constructively.

Introduction

In this chapter we consider the role of the social worker in the context of the multi-agency Youth Offending Team and the wider youth justice system. We look at how the system has changed since the Labour government came to power in 1997 and the 1998 Crime and Disorder Act was passed. Working within a YOT means working with a range of other professionals from diverse disciplines and we will also be considering their roles. The chapter provides an overview of the youth justice process so you can see the other agencies involved in dealing with young people who offend or who are at risk of committing crime and the stages a young person may go through before arriving at the door of the YOT. The chapter should provide you with a real sense of the inter-agency and inter-professional contexts involved in youth justice.

Introduction to YOTs

As identified in Pickford (2000), and in Chapter 2, prior to 1998 and the passing of the Crime and Disorder Act, the remit of working with young people involved in offending was held by juvenile or youth justice teams which were part of social services departments. These teams were staffed by a combination of social workers and unqualified workers, perhaps from a social care or youth work background. The role of the teams was to work with young people involved with the police or courts, having been cautioned or charged with a criminal offence. As is the case now with YOTs, youth justice teams prepared pre-sentence reports for courts and supervised children and young people subject to community sentences such as supervision orders and those subject to detention in a young offender institution. Juvenile justice teams developed following the intermediate treatment initiative implemented in the 1980's as an alternative to custody, where:

> Progressive policy makers and radical practitioners with young people in trouble insisted that whenever and wherever possible, we should 'leave the kids alone', maintaining that the most effective intervention was 'radical non-intervention'. (Pitts, 2003, p8)

This approach contrasts with the evidenced-based interventionist and correctionist approach that has been central to the Labour reforms of the youth justice system (Bottoms and Dignan, 2004).

Following an inspection by the Audit Commission which led to the publication of *Misspent youth* in 1996, it was perceived that the youth justice system was failing to intervene effectively with young offenders and that the same young offenders were being repeatedly processed by the courts. The report concluded:

> The current system for dealing with youth crime is inefficient and expensive, while little is done to deal effectively with juvenile nuisance. The present arrangements are failing the young people who are not being guided away from offending to constructive activities. They are also failing victims. (Audit Commission, 1996, p96)

Following this damning indictment on the youth justice system the incoming Labour government set about a radical overhaul of the entire system, proposing to replace youth justice teams with multi-agency YOTs. A number of pilots – nine – were established to test out some of the proposed reforms and these were evaluated. This was so that evidence-based practice could be seen to be at the heart of these reforms; however, criticism arose following the full roll-out of the legislation before the evaluations were complete (Holdaway et al., 2001 cited in Bottoms and Dignan, 2004).

Multi-agency working

Working in a YOT involves being a member of possibly the most diverse and wide-ranging multi-agency team within social care. Prior to 1998, there was evidence of some multi-disciplinary working in existence, for instance, community mental health teams, which were very much a joint health and social services venture, and also social workers placed in other health areas such as hospitals, health centres and in substance misuse teams. In children's settings, multi-disciplinary working was evident in relation to child protection, with Area Child Protection Committees (now Local Safeguarding Children Boards) established with representatives from all relevant agencies collaborating to ensure children are protected. However, the Crime and Disorder Act legislated for the first time that in the field of youth justice, in each local authority area the local authority social services and education departments must work with the police, probation service and health authority to establish and fund a new multi-agency Youth Offending Team. The Act went further, stipulating in section 39(5) that each YOT must have at least one of the following:

- A social worker.

- A police officer.

- A probation officer.

- A nominated person from the education department.

- A nominated person from the health authority.

The Act also stated that while this was a minimum requirement, other staff could also be included, from the statutory or voluntary sector. Section 37 of the act states: 'It shall be the principle aim of the youth justice system to prevent offending by children and young persons.'

As well as this primary aim being laid down in statute, the Act also sets out that each local authority, in consultation with its partner agencies, has a statutory duty to formulate, publish and implement an annual youth justice plan, to be submitted to the YJB, outlining how the YOT is to be composed and resourced, its functions, how it will operate and how youth justice services are to be provided and funded. Section 38(4) defines the services to be provided as:

- Appropriate adults.

- Assessment of young people for rehabilitation programmes after reprimand/final warning.

- Support for those remanded in custody or bailed.

- Placement in local authority accommodation when remanded.

- Court Reports and assessments.

- Allocation of referral orders.

- Supervision of those sentenced to community orders.

- Supervision of those sentenced to custody.

So multi-agency YOTs should co-ordinate the provision of these services with YOT staff drawn from a broad range of professions associated with the care of young people in order to tackle youth crime. Latterly, an additional requirement has been set for YOTs to provide preventative services to target those young people who may be deemed to be at risk of offending.

Youth Justice Board

The Crime and Disorder Act also introduced the Youth Justice Board, a new body to oversee the operation and monitoring of the youth justice system, specifically YOTs and the secure estate. The YJB, described by some as a quango (Smith, 2003b), has considerable influence (Pitts, 2001). Section 41 of the Act prescribed the functions of the board as being:

- To monitor the operation of the youth justice system and the provision of youth justice services.

- Advising the Secretary of State on the operation of the system especially with regard to how the statutory aim could be achieved.

- Monitoring the extent to which that aim is being achieved and any set standards met.

- Obtaining information from relevant authorities.

- Publishing information.

- Promoting good practice.

- Commissioning research into good practice.

- Awarding grants to develop good practice.

At its inception, the YJB produced the *National standards for youth justice services* in 2000, updated in 2004 (YJB, 2004b), which give guidance on the expected quality and level of service required of YOTs and the secure estate, as well as the Asset assessment framework (outlined in Chapter 6). It has also produced the *Key elements of effective practice*, guides for YOT practitioners on a range of practice areas and a quality assurance process. The YJB also has responsibility for commissioning secure beds from the secure estate.

ACTIVITY 5.1

Consider the key agencies within the youth justice system: police, YOTs, Crown Prosecution Service, courts, and prison service. Identify the key functions of each of these.

How difficult you found this activity will have depended on your prior knowledge of the youth or criminal justice system. You will see from the discussion below that each agency has quite distinct roles but that all should work alongside each other to ensure the system works effectively.

The youth justice process

The youth justice system is comprises a number of agencies each performing a particular role relating to young offenders. Figure 5.1 depicts the large number of organisations involved and how these interrelate to each other.

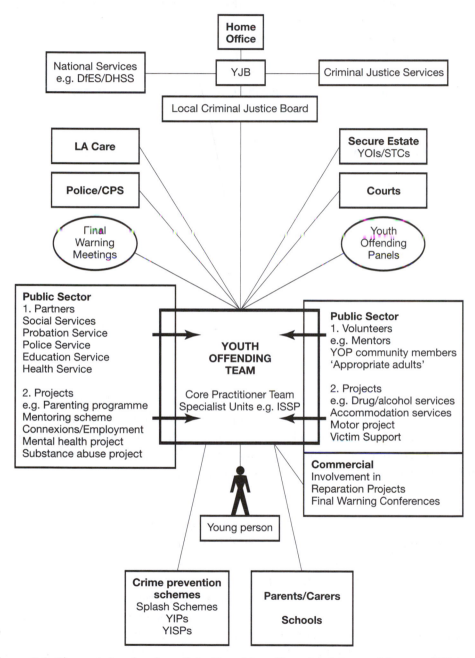

Figure 5.1 *Elements in a local youth justice system (from Appleton and Burnett, 2004, p9)*

The police

The police act as the gateway to the youth and criminal justice systems, as if they did not detect crime and arrest suspects there would be no offenders. The role of the police has changed significantly over time and is now much more complicated than it was historically (Reiner, 2000; Uglow, 2002). However, the main functions of the police are to prevent, detect and investigate crime. The work of the police in relation to the investigation of crimes and the detention of suspects is guided by the Police and Criminal Evidence Act 1984 and the Code of Practice accompanying the Act. If a young person is arrested on suspicion of committing, having committed or being about to commit an offence, they will be taken to a local police station where the police will start their investigation into the alleged offence. Once a person has been interviewed regarding an offence, hopefully in the presence of a solicitor and certainly an appropriate adult if the suspect is under 17, the police have a number of options open to them. These are:

- Take no further action.
- Bail the young person to return on another date.
- Issue the young person with a reprimand.
- Refer the young person to the YOT for a final warning assessment. (They can also issue a final warning immediately, although this is bad practice.)
- Charge the young person.

Appropriate adults

YOTs have to ensure that an appropriate adult service is provided in the local area. This is often run by specially recruited and trained volunteers, who offer 24-hour provision as young people may be arrested at any time. The role of the appropriate adult is to ensure that the young person's welfare needs are met during their detention in police custody and to facilitate communication between the young person and the police during the interview. The appropriate adult should be satisfied that the interview is being undertaken in accordance with the Police and Criminal Evidence Act 1984 and the Code of Practice. For more information on the role of the appropriate adult, there is a useful chapter in the *RHP companion to youth justice* (Bateman and Pitts, 2005).

Police Bail

Young people are usually allowed home on police bail while they wait for an appearance before the Youth Court. The police may impose conditions on bail, e.g. to sleep at their home address, to report daily to a police station. The police may however, refuse bail where they believe that the person may not appear in court or may commit further offences while on bail, or for their own protection. If an offence is very serious and the police have decided to prosecute, the person may be detained until they can be brought to the earliest available court, usually the same day or the following morning. Where it is a young person, if they have to be held overnight, the 'detention' should be transferred to local authority accommodation such as a children's home, foster placement or secure unit.

Reprimands and final warnings

The Crime and Disorder Act 1998 replaced the cautioning of young offenders (it still exists with adults) with a new system of reprimands and final warnings. Prior to the act, a young person could be cautioned indefinitely following an approach that saw young people being diverted from the criminal justice system as a way of preventing further offending based on a minimal intervention philosophy. Pitts comments on the Thatcherist approach to youth justice that consisted of 'Cost-cutting imperatives and its commitment to "small government", articulated with the desire of the youth justice lobby to limit the state's intervention in the lives of children and young people in trouble' (Pitts, 2003, p7). However, as young people were being repeatedly cautioned, concern was developing that its impact was lessened and the Audit Commission criticised its use. *Misspent youth* (1996) found that cautioning was 'reasonably effective on up to three occasions, but subsequent use was not only ineffective but brought the system into disrepute' (Marlow, 2005, p68). The final warning scheme guidance (Home Office/Youth Justice Board, 2002) states that:

> *The final warning scheme aims to divert children and young people from their offending behaviour before they enter the court system. The scheme was designed to do this by:*
>
> - *ending repeat cautioning and providing a progressive and effective response to offending behaviour;*
>
> - *providing appropriate and effective interventions to prevent re-offending; and*
>
> - *ensuring that young people who do re-offend after being warned are dealt with quickly and effectively by the courts.* (2002, p5)

Since June 2000, where there is sufficient evidence for a realistic prospect of conviction should the young person be prosecuted, a reprimand or final warning may be given, providing the person admits to the offence and consents to the reprimand or warning, and it is not in the public interest for a prosecution. The guidance on the final warning scheme states that a reprimand can only be given if a young person has not been reprimanded or finally warned before. Thus reprimands are designed for first-time offenders and the YOT must be notified when a young person is reprimanded. A final warning can only be given when a young person has re-offended having already received a reprimand. However, if the offence is serious enough to warrant it, a final warning can be given for a first offence. At this stage, the YOT must be notified so that the young person can be contacted, and assessed, using Asset (see Chapter 6) and a programme of intervention planned and offered. Compliance with this is not mandatory but if a young person fails to comply, this may be mentioned in subsequent hearings if they re-offend and are prosecuted and the police are informed of the non-compliance. If a young person offends after previously receiving a final warning, they must be charged unless the warning was given two years before the new offence was committed. A study undertaken in 2000 found that many of the young people and YOT workers saw the final warning system as 'arbitrary, unfair and disproportionate' with the way young offenders are dealt with contrasting very unfavourably with that for adults (Evans and Pugh, cited in Ball, 2004).

Sarah, aged 14, is arrested for stealing from a shop. She is stopped outside the shop by a store detective who calls the police. She is arrested and taken to the police station. She has not been arrested before and is very anxious. Outline the process that will follow, through to what action the police can take.

You will have considered the fact that as a child under the age of 17, Sarah would need to have an appropriate adult present and therefore the custody officer should have made every effort to contact her parents or carers and inform them of the arrest. If one of her parents/carers is able to attend the police station and act as the appropriate adult, this is preferable; if not, an appropriate adult will have to be provided by the YOT. You may have identified that the appropriate adult will be able to see Sarah when they arrive at the police station and check that she is all right and understands what is going on. She will probably be worried and anxious about being in a police station, especially if she has not been arrested before. The parent or carer may also be anxious. The custody officer should explain to Sarah her rights, in the presence of her appropriate adult; this will include the fact that she is entitled to free legal advice, which should always be obtained, and that she can have access to a copy of the Code of Practice. Once the solicitor arrives, she or he will speak to the police about why Sarah has been arrested and what the evidence against her is. The solicitor will also want to meet with Sarah and talk to her about her version of events. This should be a confidential interview between the two of them. Providing Sarah is feeling well enough, the police interview will take place with the appropriate adult present; Sarah will be questioned by the police under the advice of her solicitor.

If the police feel they have enough evidence to charge Sarah, the interview should stop and they should consider what action they are going to take. You may have thought about the different options open to the police; if, for instance, there is not enough evidence they may decide to take no further action. If they want to continue the investigation they could bail her to come back to the police station at another time. If Sarah admitted the offence the police could charge her and give her a date to attend court. However, as this is the first time that she has come to the attention of the police and she has admitted the theft, she could be issued with a reprimand or final warning. Either way, the YOT must be informed and they may offer some intervention to Sarah and her family.

Crown Prosecution Service (CPS)

The CPS is an integral part of the youth justice system, working alongside the police in making decisions about whether or not to charge a suspect. If the police are unsure whether to prosecute a young person, the CPS will advise on the appropriate action to take. In reaching a decision, the prosecutor (a qualified lawyer) will consider the case in relation to the Full Code Test, which looks at the evidence and the public interest. The Code for Crown Prosecutors, issued under the Prosecution of Offenders Act 1985 and available at www.cps.gov.uk/publications/docs/code2004english.pdf details the evidential and public interest tests that must be applied to each case in order to determine whether or not a prosecution should be sought. In order to continue with a prosecution brought by the police, the prosecutor must be satisfied that there is sufficient admissible evidence to secure a conviction, and that it will be in the public interest. The prosecutor has to consider issues such as the defence case, reliability of witnesses and credibility of the evidence, as well as the likely outcome of a conviction, the vulnerability of the victim and the defendant's previous offending. If a decision to prosecute is made, the young person will be given a date to appear in court or be detained by the police and taken to court the following day. The CPS is also responsible for ensuring you receive any documentation required in order for you to complete a pre-sentence report. This usually consists of evidence papers, the transcript of the police interview with the young person, witness statements, details of previous convictions, etc.

Court

Since the passing of the Children Act 1989, young people charged with criminal offences have been dealt with by the Juvenile Court, renamed the Youth Court by the Criminal Justice Act 1991. If they are charged with an adult, they will appear in the magistrates' court, or if charged with a grave offence the case has to be committed to the Crown Court.

The Youth Court has responsibility for dealing with all young people who are charged. The Youth Court setting is more informal and is presided over usually by a panel of two or three lay magistrates, volunteers who are trained in youth matters, or sometimes by a district judge who is legally qualified and sits alone. The Youth Court deals with:

- Issues of bail and remand for young people whose cases are progressing through the court system.

- Deciding a defendant's innocence or guilt following a trial when a young person pleads not guilty.

- The committal of serious cases to the Crown Court where a custodial sentence of more than two years may be appropriate (as the Youth Court does not have the power to sentence beyond this time).

- Sentencing young people pleading guilty to, or convicted of, an offence. The Youth Court also deals with breaches of sentences when young people do not comply with the requirements of a court order. (See chapter 4 for the sentencing framework for young people.)

If a court is unable to deal with the case straight away it has to consider what should happen to the person in the meantime. Arrangements should allow children and young people to remain living 'at home' wherever possible but it might be necessary for local authority accommodation or secure facilities to be used.

Remands to local authority accommodation

Section 23 of the Children and Young Persons Act (CYPA) 1969 gives courts the power to remand children and young people to local authority accommodation where they are charged with an offence and not released on bail. Subsection (7) of Section 23 allows the court to impose any conditions that can be imposed under Section 3(6) of the Bail Act 1976 on a defendant who has been granted bail. Some of the more common conditions are:

- To reside at a specific address.

- To observe a curfew between specified hours.

- A curfew may be enforced by electronic monitoring (a tag fitted to the leg).
- Not to enter a specific area.
- Not to associate with prosecution witnesses or pervert the course of justice.
- Not to contact other young people jointly accused.
- To comply with a YOT bail supervision and support programme which may involve numerous sessions a week.
- To report to a police station.

Remand to local authority accommodation confers 'looked after' status on a young person and requires the appropriate social services department to provide accommodation for the young person. Local authority accommodation is defined by the Children Act 1989, Section 22 and may include:

- residential children's homes;
- remand foster placements;
- placement with members of the defendant's family.

The local authority has considerable discretion as to the choice of accommodation, although the court may stipulate that the young person is not placed with a named individual or at a named address. Whether a young person who is subject to a remand into local authority accommodation is placed with parents or other family or not, they are also 'looked after' children and should therefore be subject to Children Act requirements.

The YOT and Youth Court panel within each authority are required to meet at least twice a year to discuss issues regarding young people at court. This can also be an opportunity for the YOT to provide training or briefings on particular aspects of practice. It is important for you to attend these where possible, as among other things magistrates will get to know you and as in all areas of work, building professional relationships across the whole youth justice system can only seek to enhance the quality and effectiveness of your practice.

Judge and jury

If a young person has committed a serious offence such as murder, rape or grievous bodily harm, the Youth Court may be of the view that the likely sentence the young person should receive will be more than the two years maximum period of imprisonment available to it. In such a situation, the case will be committed to the Crown Court for a plea and directions hearing. If the young person enters a not guilty plea, the matter will be adjourned (put back) for a trial with a judge and jury. Here, the jury, 12 randomly selected men and women, will sit through the trial, hear the evidence and have to reach a verdict, on the direction of the judge who will advise them on matters of law. If the jury finds the young person guilty of the charges, the judge could sentence there and then if it is a very serious offence such as murder. More than likely, the judge will request a pre-sentence report from the YOT which will need to be completed by the date the case is adjourned to. The judge will then sentence on the next occasion.

Appearing in court can be a very traumatic event for young people, their families and social workers, and the Crown Court is particularly intimidating with its formalities, dress code and size. Johns (2005) provides some useful advice on appearing in court and strategies to manage the anxieties it may present for you: these are, in essence, preparation, practice, prediction and professionalism. (See Further Reading at the end of the chapter.) The youth justice system in this country has been criticised for its formal court system which does not facilitate active participation from young people and their parents/carers, and magistrates are now required to undergo training in communication skills. While some may be effective at engaging young people in the court setting, there is still huge room for improvement. The government, in responding to the European Court's ruling in the case of Thompson and Venables (V v UK and T v UK (2000) 30 EHRR 121), in the White Paper *Justice for all* (Home Office, 2002) proposed changes to the way most serious trials are heard. It suggested that the current Crown Court be replaced by cases being heard by a judge and two youth magistrates in a Youth Court. However, no such changes have occurred or seem to be planned. The Thompson and Venables case did, however, bring about some changes to the way children are tried. As Bandalli (2005) states:

> *Article 6 of the European Convention on Human Rights, guarantees the right to a fair trial and childhood has been recognised as having an impact on fairness. As a result, when a child or young person is charged with a criminal offence, they should be dealt with in a manner that takes into account age, immaturity and understanding. There should be less formality and attempts should be made to ensure the child understands what is happening and to make proceedings more child-friendly.* (2005, p42)

Given the formality of the court environment, it is useful, therefore, if you can visit a range of courts during your training so that you gain some experience in how they operate. Remember that the Youth Court is closed to the public so you will be allowed in only if you are undertaking a practice learning placement within a YOT. The magistrates' and Crown Courts are not closed and it is possible to sit in the public gallery and observe proceedings.

Defence solicitors

As mentioned earlier, when a young person is arrested by the police, they are entitled to free legal advice while at the police station. If the young person is charged, this legal representation will usually be available when they appear in court. The solicitor will advise the young person in relation to the process, the evidence against them and their plea as well as issues of bail and sentence. The solicitor (or barrister if instructed by a solicitor) will also advocate on behalf of the young person in court in relation to bail and sentence. It is important for you to liaise with the solicitor of a young person with whom you are working, as you may be required to address the court on your assessment in relation to whether the young person should be remanded into secure provision or subject to bail supervision by the YOT. The solicitor will need to see a copy of your pre-sentence report prior to the hearing so that he or she is aware of what sentence you are proposing. If you are encountering difficulty in obtaining CPS documentation, the solicitor may be able to forward you a copy.

YOTs

As discussed previously, multi-agency YOTs are designed to be a joined-up approach to addressing youth crime. A team comprising a number of professional disciplines is a complex operation and there needs to be a clear understanding of and respect for each other's role in order for different practitioners to be able to work together effectively. Most of the key agencies making up a YOT have very different philosophies, cultures, training and objectives, so while able to bring a wide-ranging approach to the issue of youth crime, the potential for conflict is quite significant. Bailey and Williams (2000, cited in Burnett and Appleton, 2004) found evidence of 'turf wars' in their research into YOTs whereas Burnett and Appleton (2004) observed cordial relations from the start and a very open attitude to the prospect of learning from each other. Having a range of professional identities within one team can be threatening as duties are shared across other disciplines. It is important therefore to recognise the value of each discipline's contribution to the multi-disciplinary approach and the values and knowledge that other professionals bring. As a social worker it is vital that you develop the skills and ability to practise within a range of professional networks to develop and maintain effective working relationships for the benefit of the young people with whom you are working.

The guidance on the setting up of YOTs suggested how each of the five key professionals may be deployed and what their areas of responsibility might be.

Social worker

Social workers will be involved in carrying out most of the assessments on young people for whom pre-sentence reports have been requested. (See Chapter 6 for more information on assessment and report writing.) They will also be required to provide a service to the local Youth Court as well as attending the Crown Court when young people are appearing there for sentence. Social workers will usually have a caseload of young people who have been sentenced to a range of court orders, some of which will be served in the community, others in secure settings. YOTs may be configured so that social workers are in a team that only deals with specific types of cases, for instance custodial sentences. Working with young people on court orders involves planning and reviewing cases, intervening to prevent offending behaviour and working with families (see Chapter 7), liaising with others such as victims and referral order panel members (see Chapter 8). Thus, a typical day for a YOT social worker might involve interviewing a young person as part of an assessment, writing up the assessment and perhaps a report for the court, seeing young people who are being supervised on court orders, such as a supervision order, and attending a Youth Offender Panel with a young person. Core social work tasks such as interviewing and assessing, building relationships with people, empowering and supporting young people, advocating on behalf of young people and challenging discrimination and injustice will all feature daily in your practice.

Police officer

The issuing of final warnings, the assessment of young people subject to final warnings and the delivery of the subsequent intervention programme is often undertaken by the police officer(s) in the YOT. However, social workers may also be involved in the latter two stages. If Sarah (Activity 5.2) had received a final warning following her admission of the theft, she might have been assessed by a YOT police officer who would then have worked with her on the programme of intervention. YOT police officers are also involved in working with victims, in terms of obtaining victim impact statements about an offence so that the young person knows what effects their offending has had on the victim; supporting the victim in meeting the young person who carried out the offence and maintaining links with the local police to support crime reduction initiatives. The police officer may also link with the police and probation services relating to the Multi-Agency Public Protection Arrangements (MAPPA) in relation to high-risk offenders (see Chapter 6).

Education officer

The education officer in a YOT may be a teacher, perhaps with a background in special needs, an educational psychologist or an education welfare officer. The areas the education officer in the YOT may be involved in are assessing the educational needs of young people, as part of Asset, to inform the courts or during the course of a court-ordered programme, including DTOs. Some of the work will involve getting excluded young people or those without any education provision, such as asylum-seekers, into some educational provision and ensuring their literacy and numeracy needs are being met. YOT education officers may also be involved in helping young people sustain their placements and regular attendance there. Had there been any issues around Sarah's education, these would have been identified in the assessment of her and she might have been referred to the education officer so that these could be addressed. Education officers may also be involved in working with young people around training and employment issues, although these days YOTs often have Connexions workers or careers advisers based in the team or attached to the team to carry out this function.

Health officer

The health officer may be from a variety of backgrounds including a school nurse, a community mental health nurse, a dual diagnosis (mental health and substance misuse) specialist or a psychologist. The kind of work they may be involved in could be assessing and screening a young person's physical and mental health needs, again as part of Asset to inform a court report or as part of a fuller assessment and referral to a health organisation.

Probation officer

Given their professional training and experience, it is likely that YOT probation officers will undertake very similar duties to social workers, such as undertaking assessments, attending court and supervising young people on court orders. However, it may be that probation officers work with the older young people, aged 16 and 17, and some 18 and 19 year olds serving DTOs. If young people on adult community sentences turn 18 during the court order and there is still a significant period of time to be served on the order, the case will need to be transferred to the probation service and the YOT probation officer is well placed to manage this process as they should still be linked in with the local probation team. Probation officers may also have substantial experience of running group work programmes in the probation service and this may be another aspect of their work in a YOT. Probation officers will have been using assessment tools within the probation service and should also be experienced in managing risk and attending the MAPPA meetings, for instance (see Chapter 6).

Other professionals

In addition to these roles which are mandatory within each YOT, there may be other professionals based in the team or attached to it. These could include housing workers or substance misuse workers, for whom funding is ringfenced in order to ensure their presence in a YOT. Similarly, YOTs may also have separate prevention and early intervention teams to intervene with young people at risk of offending such as youth inclusion and support panels and youth inclusion programmes. For more information on these refer to the YJB website. All of these specialist roles/services might have been available to Sarah had they been identified as an issue in relation to her offending.

ACTIVITY 5.3

Consider the case study below and identify the role of the YOT social worker.

Jermaine, aged 15, is arrested by the police having committed a serious offence of robbery while on bail for driving-related offences. He is interviewed by the police and on the advice of his solicitor makes no comment to any of the questions the police ask. He is given bail by the police so that they can investigate the offence further, with conditions that he lives at his parents' house, does not contact any witnesses, does not enter a certain area of the town and does not go out of the house between 7 p.m and 7 a.m. He is bailed to return four weeks later when the matter will either be dropped or he will be charged. When Jermaine returns to the police station, the police decide to charge him as they have examined CCTV footage showing him committing the robbery. Jermaine is charged and detained overnight to be taken to court the next day.

The CPS lawyer outlines the case against Jermaine and informs the court that the victim has been seriously affected by the robbery, physically in terms of bruising to his head and arms, and emotionally, scared to leave the house unless in the company of his parents. The lawyer also informs the court that at the time of the alleged offence Jermaine was on bail for driving offences for which he is waiting to be tried. The magistrates hearing the case ask you, the YOT officer present in court, to assess Jermaine's circumstances and to give them more information on whether they should be granting him bail or not.

What issues would you want to address in the 15 minutes the court has adjourned the case for?

You will clearly want to interview the young person in the cells to gather some basic information such as his living arrangements and education situation. Hopefully his parents/carers will also be at court so you will be able to speak to them. If not, did you think of calling them and asking them to come to court? It will be important to ascertain and assess the level of support and supervision offered to Jermaine by his family. It may be wise to ask about other extended family members who may be able to accommodate him for the duration of the court case, particularly if the victim lives near to Jermaine. The court will be concerned in making its decision that any risk of re-offending is reduced or prevented, the victim and any other witnesses are protected as well as society generally, and that Jermaine returns to court for future hearings. You will need to consider any measures that will help to secure these outcomes and a relative some distance away may prove a very valuable alternative.

How Jermaine spends his time will be an important factor to consider; if he is in school, what is his attendance like? The absence of a school place or problematic attendance means that additional supervision of Jermaine in the community will be necessary if he is to be given bail. If he cannot be placed at home safely either because parental supervision is poor or not possible, for instance due to his parents' work commitments or younger siblings, and there is no other family member that can accommodate him, the court may consider remanding Jermaine into local authority accommodation with a condition that he is not placed at home. Your response to the court must be to propose a programme of bail supervision that the court will find an adequate alternative to custody. This may include a curfew monitored electronically, bail supervision offered by the YOT or an intensive supervision and surveillance programme (ISSP), subject to resource availability (see Chapter 4 for more information on ISSP).

The secure estate

Your contact with the secure estate will occur when you work with young people who are either remanded or sentenced to a period in custody or secure accommodation. There are three types of secure settings in youth justice: local authority secure children's homes (LASCH), privately run secure training centres (STC) and prison service young offender institutions (YOI). All three are quite different and young people can end up in any, remanded or sentenced, subject to their age and gender.

For those on remand:

- 10–12 year olds cannot be remanded to secure accommodation/custody, so go to local authority accommodation.

- 12–14 year old boys and 12–16 year old girls cannot be remanded to custody so go to local authority accommodation which can be secure if certain conditions are met.

- 15–16 year old boys can be remanded into local authority secure accommodation or custody but will usually go to custody unless deemed vulnerable.

- 17 year olds are treated as adults and if refused bail go to YOIs.

For sentenced young people, the YJB placements strategy, as cited in Bateman (2005), states that:

- Children under 12 years of age will be placed in a LASCH.

- Children aged 12–14 years of age must be placed in a LASCH or STC.

- 15–16 year old girls should be given priority for places in non-prison service establishments.

- 17 year old girls will be allocated to a LASCH if places are available.

- 15–17 year old boys will usually be placed in a YOI although vulnerable 15–16 year old males should be considered for a placement outside of the prison service where places are available.

If a young person is remanded into custody, the YOT should be present in court, although if it is by an adult court, this is not always the case. However, the YOT should at least be notified. National Standards require that remanded young people are seen within five working days and a remand plan be drawn up that must then be reviewed within timescales. Once a young person receives a custodial sentence, a post-court report needs to be completed that accompanies the young person to the secure establishment, and any concerns about their welfare need to be clearly identified on this. Again, sentenced young people must be seen in custody within five working days so that a sentence plan can be drawn up that outlines what they will be doing while serving the custodial part of the sentence. The young person and parents/carers should actively contribute to this process and the plan has to be reviewed regularly. In all cases, a key worker will be allocated to the young person in secure settings and it is important that you communicate regularly with this worker and share information accordingly. Planning for resettlement should ensure a seamless response between custody and community. Research (Goldson, 2002) identifies the vulnerability of children in custody and the lack of communication between staff in the secure estate and in the community. It is therefore crucial that you ensure your assessments and any other relevant information are always forwarded to the relevant institution and that visiting young people in custody and attending planning meetings is prioritised.

C H A P T E R S U M M A R Y

This chapter has looked at the complex system that operates to deal with the detection, prosecution, sentencing and rehabilitation of young people committing crimes. Being a social worker in a YOT means being able to work closely with a range of other professionals based in the same team as you, but having also to work with other agencies such as the courts, lawyers and the prison service. We have identified the functions of some of these agencies and you have considered these in relation to case studies. One thing that you have hopefully realised is that in order to be an effective social worker within the field of youth justice, you need to be very skilled at multi-agency and inter-professional working and the greater your understanding of the complex system, the better your practice will be.

FURTHER READING

Bateman, T and Pitts, J (2005) *The RHP companion to youth justice*. Lyme Regis: Russell House Publishing.
A very readable and comprehensive overview of youth justice with contributions from a range of academics and practitioners in the field.

Burnett, R and Appleton, C (2004) *Joined-up justice: Tackling youth crime in partnership*. Lyme Regis: Russell House Publishing.
This book identifies some of the challenges faced by YOT practitioners and the impact of the recent reforms based on research into a YOT.

Johns, R (2005) *Using the law in social work*. Exeter: Learning Matters.
This text offers some useful advice for students on appearing in court.

WEBSITES

www.cps.gov.uk

This website contains the Code for Crown Prosecutors which gives more detail about the evidential and public interest tests that have to be met if a prosecution is to be considered.

www.dca.gov.uk

This website provides information about the legal system, the courts and judiciary.

www.homeoffice.gov.uk

The Home Office website contains a number of relevant publications on all aspects of crime.

www.youth-justice-board.gov.uk

This website provides information on all aspects of YOTs, the secure estate, sentencing and contains many documents that can be downloaded.

Chapter 6
Assessing young people

Paul Dugmore

A C H I E V I N G   A   S O C I A L   W O R K   D E G R E E

This chapter will help you begin to meet the following National Occupational Standards:

Key Role 1: Prepare for, and work with individuals, families, carers, groups and communities to assess their needs and circumstances
- Assess needs and options to recommend a course of action.

Key Role 2: Plan, carry out, review and evaluate social work practice, with individuals, families, carers, groups, communities and other professionals
- Prepare, produce, implement and evaluate plans with individuals, families, carers, groups, communities and professional colleagues.

Key Role 4: Manage risk to individuals, families, carers, groups, communities, self and colleagues
- Assess and manage risks to individuals, families, carers, groups and communities.
- Assess, minimise and manage risk to self and colleagues.

Key Role 5: Manage and be accountable, with supervision and support, for your own social work practice within your organisation
- Manage, present and share records and reports.

Key Role 6: Demonstrate professional competence in social work practice
- Research, analyse, evaluate, and use current knowledge of best social work practice.
- Work within agreed standards of social work practice and ensure own professional development.

It will also introduce you to the following academic standards as set out in the social work subject benchmark statement:

3.1.4 Social work theory
Models and methods of assessment, including factors underpinning the selection and testing of relevant information, the nature of professional judgement and the processes of risk assessment.

3.1.5 The nature of social work practice
The place of theoretical perspectives and evidence from international research in assessment and decision-making processes in social work practice.

3.2.2 Problem-solving skills
- Gather information from a wide range of sources and by a variety of methods, for a range of purposes.
- Take into account differences of viewpoint in gathering information and assess the reliability and relevance of the information gathered.
- Assess human situations, taking into account a variety of factors.
- Analyse information gathered, weighing competing evidence and modifying own viewpoint in light of new information, then relate this information to a particular task, situation or problem.
- Synthesise information and lines of reasoning and sustain detailed argument at length and over time.
- Analyse and take account of the impact of inequality and discrimination in work with people in particular contexts and problem situations.

3.2.3 Communication skills
- Communicate effectively across potential barriers resulting from differences (for example, in culture, language and age).

Introduction

In all areas of social work, assessment is often considered to be the initial part of social work involvement, the gateway to service provision. This is particularly apparent in youth justice with the National Standards stating that 'All children and young people entering the youth justice system should benefit from a structured needs assessment' (YJB, 2004b, p27).

Given the clear importance of assessment within youth justice, this chapter looks at the purpose of assessment, and provides a brief overview of different types of assessments. A more detailed consideration of assessment within social work can be found in Parker and Bradley (2003). The Asset assessment tool used by YOTs is discussed as well as the relationship between Asset and pre-sentence reports (PSRs) and risk assessments. The chapter concludes by considering the relationship between Asset and the Common Assessment Framework, introduced by the 2004 Children Act.

What is assessment?

Within a social work context, assessment is often described as an activity undertaken in order to identify a person's needs or problems so that the appropriate intervention can then be planned to meet those needs or address the problems. Social workers carry out assessments for a variety of reasons depending on the area in which they practise. It is generally an information-gathering exercise undertaken to establish what the presenting and underlying factors are in a service user's life, by working in partnership with the service user, their family or carer, and other professionals who may be involved. However, it is not only about gathering information, but should be seen as 'a holistic process that involves gaining an overview of the situation' (Thompson, 2005, p64). An assessment might be carried out as a one-off event and as such may be static, or it may be a fluid process occurring more than once, depending on the situation. In youth justice, it is likely to be more than a one-off event.

According to Middleton (1997), cited in Parker and Bradley (2003), assessment is:

> *The analytical process by which decisions are made. In a social welfare context it is a basis for planning what needs to be done to maintain or improve a person's situation . . . Assessment involves gathering and interpreting information in order to understand a person and their circumstances; the desirability and feasibility of change and the services and resources which are necessary to effect it. It involves making judgements based on information.* (Parker and Bradley, 2003, p5)

Thus, assessment is not simply about the collation of information, it is, equally importantly, about making sense of that information.

ACTIVITY **6.1**

Think about undertaking an assessment of a young person coming to the attention of the YOT.

- *What are important factors in carrying out a good assessment?*
- *Identify examples of when an assessment might be undertaken in a youth justice setting.*

You may have acknowledged that in order to ensure an assessment is effective, it is important that as the social worker you are clear about the purpose of the assessment, that is, what it is you are assessing and why. In the gathering of information, the obvious starting point is an interview with the young person. However, it may be more useful if you have obtained information from other sources, where possible, prior to the interview as this may help determine the areas for discussion. Skills required here include active listening, effective communication and observation in order to pick up on non-verbal cues, as well as the ability to clarify meaning. Adopting a strengths-based approach that sees the service user as an expert in their lives in order to be able to jointly identify what their needs or problems are is also important (Thompson, 2005, Trevithick, 2005).

Assessments should also be balanced so that as well as identifying problematic behaviour or risks, positive factors and strengths are also highlighted. You may also have revisited issues looked at in Chapter 1, locating the assessment task within a value-based framework. Being aware of your own background and value base and how these may impact on the situation that you are assessing is vital so that you are able to reflect upon your work and be as objective as possible. While assessment is about making judgements about a set of circumstances or facts based on evidence gained, it is not about making value judgements. Milner and O'Byrne (2002) provide a helpful distinction between 'making a judgement' and 'being judgemental': 'Social workers are required to face the challenge and responsibility of the former in order to be helpful; they need to avoid the prejudice, close-mindedness and blaming implicit in the latter' (Milner and O'Byrne, 2002, p170).

As a social worker, in carrying out an assessment you will be in a position of power over the young person being assessed and what outcome arises from your assessment could have a huge impact upon their receipt of services, the intervention or their loss of liberty. Bevan (1998, cited in Thompson, 2005) defines a high quality assessment as bringing together:

> *Information relevant to the physical, psychological, social and spiritual dimensions of the situation. Once this is gathered, the worker needs to make sense of the information by understanding the person as part of many systems – for example, family, school, friendship and the religious and cultural dimensions of their lives. For assessment to be both accurate and adequate, it is imperative to acknowledge the influential factors of race, culture, gender and disability. Importantly, the assessment needs to recognise the structural and social dimensions and the way these disparities impact on a person's coping resources* (Thompson, 2005, p143).

Framework for assessment

While not specifically focusing on youth justice practice, Milner and O'Byrne (2002, p6) suggest a comprehensive framework for assessment that has five key stages and is applicable across all social work settings:

- *Preparation* – this refers to the purpose of the task and establishing what is relevant.

- *Data collection* – undertaken with an open mind and in line with core social work values of empowerment and respect.

- *Weighing the data* – identifying if there is a problem and if so how serious it is within a theoretical and evidence-based framework.

- *Analysing the data* – interpreting the data to identify the required intervention.

- *Utilising the analysis* – finalising judgements.

This model will be useful in the subsequent activities in this chapter as well as in your practice in youth justice.

Types of assessment

Milner and O'Byrne suggest that an 'exchange model' should always be adopted which views service users as experts in their own lives with assessment as a mutual process where the social worker follows what is said by the service user rather than attaching their own interpretation. The social worker focuses on the service user's internal resources and strengths to reach jointly agreed objectives. This model is in line with government guidance and is more likely to lead to a process of re-evaluation. Milner and O'Byrne (2002, p67) state that social workers could improve their assessments if they adopt principles from sound research:

- A clear statement of intent.

- Accountability of values.

- A systematic approach to data collection, looking at not only the personal but the social aspects.

- The development of multiple and testable hypotheses.

- Decisions that lead to measurable outcomes.

- Consumer feedback.

Such a model can be usefully applied to youth justice and if followed, will enhance your practice.

Assessment in youth justice

In recent years, particularly following concerns about social workers' abilities in relation to high-profile child protection and mental health cases (Victoria Climbié and the Laming inquiry of 2003; Christopher Clunis and the Ritchie inquiry ,1994), there has been a rise in the concept and practices of risk assessment and management. As a result, government policy and legislation has ensured assessment has been at the heart of social work activity in relation to community care, children and families and youth justice. The *Department of Health's Framework for the assessment of children in need and their families* 'provides a systematic way of analysing, understanding and recording what is happening to children and young people within their families and the wider context in which they live' (DoH, 2000. pviii). The Children Act 2004 introduced the Common Assessment Framework which is discussed later in this chapter.

This structured assessment framework has been mirrored to some extent in youth justice with the introduction of Asset in 2000. Following the implementation of the Crime and Disorder Act 1998 and multi-agency YOTs, the Youth Justice Board (YJB) was established to oversee and manage the youth justice system. One of its first tasks was to commission the development and introduction of a national assessment tool to be rolled out across England and Wales. This was significant as prior to the Crime and Disorder Act 1998, there was no standardised assessment tool or process being used by the then youth justice teams; some teams adopted their own models, while practitioners undertaking assessments used a variety of approaches, some good, others poor. The research and design of the assessment tool was carried out by the Oxford University Centre for Criminological Research and involved an extensive review of the research literature relating to risk and protective factors for offending young people together with consultation with practitioners, managers and specialists from a range of relevant services (Baker, 2004). Asset was also adapted from assessments used by the probation service with adults for appropriate use with children and young people.

The kinds of risk factors identified from research-based, longitudinal studies include a range of factors that 'cluster together in the lives of some children while important protective factors are conspicuously absent' (YJB 2005b, p8), such as 'individual features, psychosocial features and societywide influences' (Rutter et al., 1998 in YJB, 2005b, p8). Research findings demonstrate the following factors (cited in YJB, 2005b) contribute to offending by young people:

- Children whose parents are inconsistent, neglectful and harsh are at increased risk of criminality as young people (Newson and Newson, 1989).

- Family conflict – quality of parent–child relationship, parental supervision and discipline, family income, the nature of relationship breakdown between parents (Utting et al., 1993, Graham and Bowling, 1995).

- Family history of criminal activity (Farrington, 1995).

- Low income, poor housing and large family size (Utting et al., 1993, Farrington, 1992).

- School factors – low achievement in primary school.

- Aggressive behaviour and bullying (Rutter et al., 1983).

- Disadvantaged neighbourhood.

- Availability of drugs.

- Hyperactivity and impulsivity.

- Low intelligence and cognitive impairment.

- Alienation and lack of social commitment.

- Early involvement in crime and drug misuse.

- Delinquent peer groups.

Research has also identified certain protective factors that can reduce the likelihood of a young person offending, including being female (Home Office, cited in YJB, 2005b), being of resilient temperament, a sense of self-efficacy, a positive, outgoing disposition and high intelligence (YJB, 2005b, pp26–7). For further information on risk and protective factors, see the YJB *Risk and protective factors* report at www.youth-justiceboard.gov.uk/Publications/Downloads/RPF%20Report.pdf

Asset

Figure 6.1 shows how Asset has been designed, based on the availability of research evidence with practitioners required to complete all the sections identified in order to assess the likelihood/risk of the young person re-offending. Each section is then rated from 0 to 4 giving a total up to a maximum of 48, the higher the rating the higher the risk of the young person re-offending.

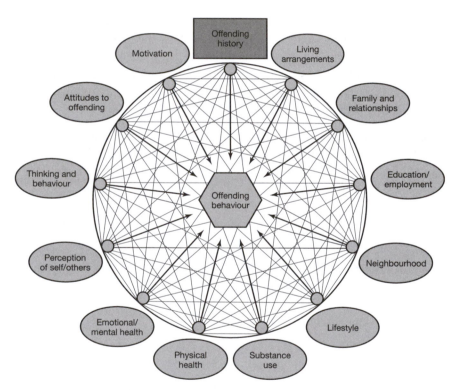

Figure 6.1 *Components of* Asset *core profile*

© *Dr C H Roberts, Probation Studies Unit, Centre for Criminology, University of Oxford*

Asset is designed to be used with every young person coming into contact with a YOT at the final warning, referral order and pre-sentence report (PSR) stages, as well as with young people appearing in court where bail is an issue. It is a tool that facilitates the systematic assessment of the circumstances and characteristics of offending young people with each factor scored according to its degree of association with the offending behaviour, providing an overall score of the risk of each young person re-offending (Burnett and Appleton, 2004).

In the YJB's *Key elements of effective practice* (KEEP) on *Assessment, planning interventions and supervision* (YJB, 2002a), good-quality assessment is seen as the basis of effective practice by helping YOT practitioners to meet the needs of young people, promoting public protection and the efficient use of resources. This document is available on line at www.youth-justice-board.gov.uk/Publications/Downloads/AssessPlanning.pdf

The YJB guidance for YOT practitioners states that:

> *Assessment should be an ongoing process that involves the young person and, where possible, the young person's parents/carers. It should provide a picture of a young person within their particular environment that will support the identification of needs, an understanding of the patterns of their offending behaviour and the planning of effective interventions. It should also take account of diverse family, ethnic and cultural backgrounds.* (YJB, 2002a, p7)

It is important to bear in mind that assessments in youth justice are generally carried out following court mandated action with young people generally presenting involuntarily. It is anticipated that Asset will be carried out by the practitioner in consultation with a range of other people. The core profile is the Asset that is used in most cases.

ACTIVITY **6.2**

List the people/sources of information that you might need to speak to or access in order to complete a thorough assessment of a young person and their offending behaviour and any barriers you may encounter in carrying out an assessment. Once you have done this, take a look at the assessment section of the KEEP guidance (YJB, 2002a) to identify if you have considered all aspects.

You will have no doubt considered that the young person will need to be interviewed in order that you can gain a picture of what is going on in their life, why they carried out the offence that has led to their contact with the YOT and how they feel about this. You may have established that this would need to be take place over a number of meetings, including a home visit, so that you can verify information obtained, seek more information and make sense of this in the context of the young person's life. As the young person is still a minor you probably also considered that contact with the young person's parent or carer is vital. If the young person is known to a social worker in a children and families team it would also be important to speak to them, and to a relevant teacher from school. Did you think about looking at the evidence from the police and Crown Prosecution Service so that you have an account of the offence other than the young person's? If the young person has offended previously, they may also be known to the YOT and case records would then need to be referred to. It is crucial that the assessment process is not carried out in isolation but in partnership with all other relevant individuals, with information shared where appropriate and necessary. It may be that other assessments have already been completed on the young person, and it is possible to obtain these. It is useful to think of the Laming (DoH/HO, 2003) criticisms in the Climbié case where agencies did not work collaboratively or share information. The setting in which the assessment is undertaken is also important and this may variously be your office, the young person's home, the court and the secure estate. How a young person responds in different settings may vary. This is not an exhaustive list and further advice is given in the Asset guidance produced by the YJB (see the Youth Justice Board website).

High-quality assessments

In order for an assessment to be of good quality, it is important that you prepare for the first interview by being aware of the purpose of the meeting so that this can be explained clearly to the young person, using language they understand that is appropriate to their age and developmental stage. Reference here to the life-course perspective mentioned in Chapter 1 is relevant. Asset is designed for use with young people aged 10 to 18. Clearly this is a wide age range with differing levels of cognitive development; in addition, some young people will have learning difficulties. These are issues you must consider in your assessment as this may influence the young person's response to some of the issues addressed. It is important that the young person and their parents/carers understand the reason why they are being assessed, the process that will follow and what the potential outcomes may be. Checking that this has been understood by asking the young person to explain what you have said to them is a useful exercise. Discussions here about the YOT's confidentiality policy and its limits should also take place; this is particularly important given the multi-agency nature of YOT's and the case management approach they adopt.

Revisiting the issues relating to values and anti-discriminatory practice introduced in Chapter 1 is important so that you are aware of the morals and beliefs that form part of your value base and how these might impact on the questions you ask, the impressions you build and judgements and decisions you make. For instance, if you are assessing a young person from a different ethnic or cultural background you need to check that you are not making any assumptions. Interpreters should be used if required by either the young person or their parents/carers, and care should be taken that eye contact and body language communication is maintained with the young person being interviewed rather than questions being directed towards the interpreter. The work of Egan (2002) is relevant here in relation to effective communication skills, such as active listening, probing and summarising, and these should be covered in your social work degree programme.

While there is an Asset self-assessment specifically designed for young people to complete which could be used at the start of the first interview, the Asset core profile should not be completed section by section in the interview, rather, each section should be addressed over the course of interviews, through for example, contact with other relevant people and available reports. By the end of the information gathering, you should be in a position to complete each of the sections, record the evidence and then give an appropriate rating for that section. As well as focusing on the criminogenic (risk) factors, it is important to look at the more positive protective factors relating to the young person and their life. You should use the young person's completed 'What do you think?' Asset to inform your final assessment, checking for any inconsistencies. Evidence must be provided in relation to each aspect of the assessment so that concrete and specific examples explain why they contribute to the likelihood of the young person re-offending or not.

Criticisms of Asset

Completing Asset for the first time can be quite difficult, particularly in deciding which rating to give to each section. While many practitioners find Asset to be a valuable tool in structuring a complex assessment process, ensuring that all areas are addressed, others (Smith, 2003b; Pitts, 2003), are critical of the routinisation it causes, seeing it as a management tool both locally and nationally. Criticism is also made of the 'tick box' nature of Asset and its over-reliance on negative risk factors to the negation of positive strengths, which is inconsistent with more recent government thinking on assessment and service-user involvement (*Framework for assessment of children in need and their families*, *National service framework for older people*, the Common Assessment Framework). Smith (2003b) summarises the concerns of practitioners in research carried out by Roberts et al. (2001) as follows:

> *The concerns of YOT members about the spurious use of an apparently objective scoring system such as this focused on a number of specific issues: uncertainty about what a specific score actually means; lack of ability to 'weight' some sections which might be more or less relevant; the negative impact of finding out more about a young person (especially significant because of the overall negative bias of the ASSET form); and possible misuse of the aggregate data by the Youth Justice Board.* (Smith, 2003b, p101)

This perspective is not uncommon in relation to standardised assessment tools, with clinical assessments perceived as enabling practitioners to exercise more skill and professional judgement. Proponents of such tools argue, however, that they are rooted in empirical data and their predictive value can be researched and evaluated. For more of a discussion on the problems with actuarial assessments see Annison (2005). Baker (2004) argues that the effective use of Asset 'requires the use of considerable professional skill and expertise' as 'practitioners are asked to make decisions about a wide range of issues, from practical assessment of the suitability of a young person's accommodation arrangements to judgements about their self-perception, levels of victim awareness and motivation to change' (Baker, 2004, p81). She suggests that the ratings are based on practitioners' own clinical judgements rather than arrived at by the number of boxes ticked in a particular area. As university students, you may wrestle with the prescriptive nature of Asset that seems to contradict the importance of critical thinking skills that you have developed during training. As your practice develops, you will need to develop the ability and confidence to use Asset as a tool to enhance your practice without being afraid of approaching every assessment critically to ensure that you are asking the right questions to acquire the right information. Asset, while comprehensive, cannot cover every eventuality so you need to probe in some areas in more depth than it may indicate, such as when trying to uncover the trauma experienced by a young person seeking asylum. While it requires you to tick boxes, Asset also contains evidence boxes and this is where you have the freedom to move away from the prescribed.

Whichever perspective you adopt, there is no escaping the fact that assessment in youth justice is a complex, detailed, time-consuming exercise, laden with professional dilemmas and ethical issues. It is important therefore, that assessment issues are reflected upon regularly and discussed with colleagues and in supervision. You need to continually acknowledge that the decisions made on the basis of an assessment can have a profound impact upon a young person's life. Ensuring you have gathered and analysed all the information you need as well as providing evidence for your decisions is crucial if your assessment is to stand any chance of being fair. Bearing in mind your assessment will probably be read by colleagues/other professionals, evidence to qualify ratings will enable those people to fully understand the issues attached to that rating. A score of 0 should also have evidence to demonstrate why this aspect of the young person's life is not problematic or related to the likelihood of them re-offending.

ACTIVITY **6.3**

Based on the information in the continuing case of Jermaine below, introduced in the previous chapter, applying your knowledge and skills of assessment, look at each section of the core Asset to assist you in completing a report from the court. The full Asset core profile can be obtained from the following link: www.youth-justiceboard.gov.uk/ PractitionersPortal/Assessment/Asset.htm

You are not expected to complete the assessment but to familiarise yourself with Asset and consider what issues you would want to address specifically in this assessment. What kind of questions would you want to ask Jermaine and who else would you want to speak to?

You are allocated the case of Jermaine to prepare a pre-sentence report for three weeks' time. He has pleaded guilty to the driving offences: taking a vehicle without consent, having no insurance and no licence and failing to stop for the police. The PSR request paperwork states that Jermaine is aged 15 years, 7 months, lives at home with his mother, stepfather and younger brother (12) and sister (9). He sees his birth father periodically. Jermaine attends the local secondary school and is a member of the football team. He has a reprimand for theft from 18 months ago. He was on bail supervision for three months in relation to a robbery charge that was committed to the Crown Court.

Your response to this activity will be determined by how much you have familiarised yourself with the Asset assessment tool and the guidance available from the YJB. In any event, you are likely to have wanted to obtain the evidence papers detailing the offence that Jermaine has pleaded guilty to so that you can interview him in order to ascertain his actions and intentions. You would want to know details of the offence – when and where it occurred, if anyone else was involved, and exactly what role Jermaine played. You may also have questioned him as to how the offence was committed, whether any planning took place, whether the victim was targeted and if Jermaine had been under the influence of any substances at the time. Your interview would want to identify whether there were any inconsistencies in Jermaine's intentions and actual behaviour. You would also want to consider any factors that make the offence more or less serious, known as aggravating or mitigating circumstances.

As well as the prosecution documents you may also be able to obtain a victim impact statement. Most YOT police officers carry out this role, which may involve contacting the victim of an offence in order to assess how they have been affected by it. (See Chapter 8 for a fuller discussion about victims.) This might be useful to have in your interview with

Jermaine in order to determine his attitude towards the offence, both at the time it was committed and now he has had the opportunity to reflect upon it: you will need to comment on what level of remorse, if any, he has demonstrated. You will also want to try and understand why Jermaine committed the offence and knowledge of his personal and social circumstances will inform your thinking as well as any motives he may have had. This may include any particular attitudes or beliefs that may have influenced the offence, such as that it is acceptable to steal cars as people have insurance and do not 'lose out'. Finally, you would want to locate this instance of offending within Jermaine's overall behaviour and therefore you would need to look at the details of any previous offences, whether there are any similarities, whether his offending is becoming more serious in nature and what response he has made to previous involvement in the youth justice system. Remember that you are supposed to be providing an analytical account that goes into detail rather than just giving a description of events. Your thinking should be firmly located in the theoretical framework outlined in Chapter 3.

You would want to raise all of these issues in your interview with Jermaine but you would also want to speak to his parents, his school and the YOT officer who worked with him on the bail supervision programme. It may be that your conversations with these people identify other areas to be pursued, for instance his football coach. It is important to remember that you are looking for evidence relating to protective factors, not just those associated with risk, so that you are giving a balanced view and that the proposed intervention resulting from your assessment focuses on his strengths as well as any problematic areas. You would also want to incorporate Jermaine's 'What do you think?' Asset as well as consider previous assessments in relation to his bail supervision.

Pre-sentence reports

The pre-sentence report that would need to be prepared in a case such as Jermaine's should follow a standard format outlined in the YJB National Standards, (2004b). This consists of:

- *Sources of information* – the people spoken to and documents referred to are stated;
- *Offence analysis* – provides the court with your analysis of the offence, its context, the impact upon the victim and an understanding of why it happened.
- *Offender assessment* – looks at the circumstances of the young person in relation to family, education, previous offending, including any mitigation.
- *Assessment of risk* – an assessment of the risk of the young person re-offending is made. The focus here should also be about the assessment of risk to the public and the risk to the young person.
- *Conclusion* – summarises the main issues and includes a realistic proposal to address the risks/issues identified in the main body of the report.

That pre-sentence reports are important is perhaps best evidenced by research findings that demonstrate that high-quality reports have a significant impact on resulting sentences. A 2000 study by the YJB cited in Bateman and Pitts (2005) found that 'PSRs in low custody areas achieved a higher score in a quality audit than areas with a higher level of incarceration' (Bateman and Pitts, 2005, p 116).

> ### RESEARCH SUMMARY
>
> *Effectiveness and evaluation of Asset*
>
> *Burnett and Appleton (2004) undertook research at Oxfordshire YOT, one of the few 'pathway' YOTs designated by the YJB to trial the new legislation and policy changes. The researchers followed the progress of the YOT for two and a half years, focusing on a wide range of issues including Asset. Feedback on the implementation and use of Asset was varied, with some practitioners finding it a useful structure to follow while other, more seasoned staff were more critical:*
>
> > *Some dissatisfaction with Asset was linked to perceptions of it as needlessly detailed, not to benefit practice but to serve as a research tool for performance monitoring and to supply statistics to the YJB. The most critical practitioners objected that their judgements were being forced into tick boxes to feed the government information machine. Managerial staff in the YOT, however, found that the tool generated invaluable aggregate information, added to the YOT's database, for monitoring work and for estimating resource requirements. (Burnett and Appleton, 2004, p33)*
>
> *The Youth Justice Board commissioned research into the validity and reliability of the Asset assessment for young offenders, which looked at findings from the first two years of the use of Asset. This evaluation took place over 18 months with 39 YOTs nationwide. The data sample consisted of 3,395 Asset completed profiles with 82 per cent male and 18 per cent female and 10 per cent from ethnic minorities. It also included 627 'What do you think' Assets. The study presents information in relation to the range of factors included in Asset, such as the young person's living arrangements, education and vulnerability. It also shows that the current Asset rating score predicted reconviction with 67 per cent accuracy which was maintained with specific groups such as females, and it was found to be predictive of frequency of reconviction and sentence at reconviction. Results in relation to reliability were seen as encouraging with a 'generally good level of reliability between teams within YOTs and between staff from different professional backgrounds' and a 'high degree of consistency in the ratings of individual assessors' (Baker et al., 2003, p7).*
>
> *Further research is planned to assess the accuracy of Asset on measuring change over time and to develop its use. Clearly this would be useful as Asset is still relatively new and its use by practitioners will hopefully improve along with training, guidance and research evidence.*

Risk assessment

In the youth justice field, the area of risk assessment is a multi-layered affair consisting of assessing the risk of re-offending of each young person, the risk to the young person in terms of their vulnerability and any risk of harm they may pose to the public. Each of these areas is addressed by Asset: the risk of re-offending and vulnerability within the core profile, and the risk of harm warranting its own additional assessment for those who trigger a positive answer to certain questions.

Vulnerability

The 'Indicators of vulnerability' section of the Asset core profile focuses on the possibility of harm being caused to the young person. It requires practitioners to assess whether there are indications that the young person is at risk of self-harm or suicide and if there are any protective factors that may reduce this vulnerability. It also considers whether the young person is likely to be vulnerable as a result of factors such as:

- The behaviour of other people (e.g. bullying, abuse, neglect, intimidation, exploitation)

- Other events or circumstances (e.g. separation, anniversary of loss, change of care arrangements)

- His/her own behaviour (e.g. risk-taking, ignorance, drugs, acting out, inappropriate response to stress)

For example, should you be working with a young person who discloses to you that they self-harm when they are feeling stressed, this would be information that would need to be recorded in the evidence box.

As with all sections of Asset, completion of this section requires that evidence is given to justify the particular rating boxes that are ticked. Given that this assessment could accompany a young person to the secure estate if they are remanded or sentenced to a period in custody, it is vital that such information is as accurate and detailed as possible as the young person may require close monitoring to ensure their own safety. Unfortunately, research shows (Goldson, 2002) that many young people in custody have a history of problems – abuse, mental health issues, educational and social exclusion to name a few – so it is highly likely that any time spent working in a YOT will include dealing with vulnerable young people, some of whom are imprisoned. In a 'civilised' society like the UK tragedies still occur, such as the death of Gareth Price, aged 16, on 20 January 2005, who was found hanging in his care and separation cell, Gareth Myatt, aged 15, who died on 19 April 2004 after losing consciousness while being restrained by staff at Rainsbrook Secure Training Centre, or 14-year-old Adam Rickwood, the youngest person to die in custody in the UK in August 2004 at the privately run Hassockfield Secure Training Centre, 100 miles from his home. It was his first time in custody and it is said he had threatened to kill himself a few days beforehand, as he was finding it difficult being so far from his family and home. While this concerns the wider issue of whether custody is suitable for many young people, it also emphasises the importance of high-quality assessments informing court reports so that courts have all the information at hand before making decisions, as well as the need for the assessment to be shared with the secure estate. There is an additional mental health assessment which provides clarity as to the level of and nature of any mental health concerns.

Risk of serious harm

The 'Indicators of serious harm' section of Asset focuses on the possibility of the young person causing serious physical or psychological harm to someone. Practitioners completing it have to state whether there is any evidence of the following:

- Behaviour by the young person which resulted in actual serious harm being caused.

- Behaviour which indicates that s/he was intending or preparing to cause serious harm.

- Other (e.g. reckless or unintentional) behaviour that was very likely to have caused serious harm.

Evidence is also required of any of the following risks indicating serious harm may be likely:

- Other features of his/her offending (e.g. unduly sophisticated methods, use of weapons, targeting).

- His/her attitudes and motives (e.g. driven by desires for revenge, control or by discriminatory beliefs).

- Current interests or activities (e.g. fascination with military paraphernalia networks/associates).

Finally, consideration is given to whether any of the following cause significant concern:

- Any other disconcerting or disturbing behaviour by the young person (e.g. cruelty to animals).

- Concerns about possible harmful behaviour expressed by the young person.

- Concerns about possible harmful behaviour expressed by other people (e.g. family, school).

- Any other intuitive or 'gut' feelings about possible harmful behaviour.

So if a young person disclosed to you that they always carry a knife when they go out with their peers because that is what they 'all do', this would be evidence that you would need to record in the appropriate evidence box along with your assessment of how likely they would be to use it based on your discussions around the use of knives. If any of the above questions warrants a 'yes' by the assessor, they must then complete the separate 'Risk of serious harm' (ROSH) Asset. Specific YJB guidance is available in relation to the completion of this form and is available at: www.youth-justice-board.gov.uk/NR/rdonlyres/5F1 AAE2B-C2D4-462D-BBBC-C0DC0D89772F/0/RiskofSH.pdf

The guidance advises that an analysis of the information recorded in the core Asset profile and other completed assessments is required, along with additional information to fill any gaps or unanswered questions to 'make a comprehensive assessment of risk of serious harm to others' (ROSH guidance, p1). The full ROSH Asset includes sections on evidence of harm-related behaviour, which is defined broadly as 'behaviour that has actually resulted in serious harm to others, and behaviour where there was a real possibility of such harm occurring'. Current risk indicators are also addressed, as is future harmful behaviour, with a concluding section in which an assessment of low, medium, high and very high risk needs to be made. On the basis of this classification, an indication is then required as to which Multi-Agency Public Protection Arrangements (MAPPA) level the young person is assessed as being at. There are three levels: at level 1 risk management should be dealt with by the YOT through normal supervision procedures; level 2 requires local interagency risk management and attendance to level 2 Strategic Management Board meetings; and level 3 requires an automatic 'referral to the Multi-Agency Public Protection Panel where a structured and detailed risk management plan is developed' (ROSH guidance, p8). YJB guidance – *Dangerous offenders – Guidance on Multi-Agency Public Protection Arrangements* – is available at: www.youth-justice-board.gov.uk/NR/rdonlyres/ C27BBD54-8FA1-4378-A841-55F92BBF28DC/0/MAPPAguidance.pdf

It is important that the assessment is reviewed and updated regularly in the light of any changes.

While assessing and managing risk is an extremely important part of the work of a Youth Offending Team social worker it is important also to bear in mind that most young people you will be working with will not be assessed as dangerous. Completion of the ROSH Asset will only be required in a minority of cases and it is imperative that young people are not identified and labelled a serious risk unless there is significant evidence to support such a claim.

Common Assessment Framework

The government's response to the Laming inquiry into the death of Victoria Climbié (DoH /HO, 2003) was published in the Green Paper *Every child matters* (Home Office, 2003a), which then led to the Children Act 2004 being passed. This proposed a Common Assessment Framework (CAF) designed to assist all practitioners working with children in universal and specialist services to 'assess children's needs earlier and more effectively' (Common Assessment Framework briefing, DfES, 2005).

The CAF aims to:

- Provide a method of assessment to support earlier intervention.

- Improve joint working and communication between practitioners by helping to embed a common language of assessment, need and a more consistent view as to the appropriate response.

- Improve the co-ordination and consistency between assessments leading to fewer and shorter specialist assessments.

- Inform decisions about whether further specialist assessment is necessary and if necessary provide information to contribute to it.

- Enable a picture of a child or young person's needs to be built up over time and, with appropriate consent, shared among professionals.

- Provide better, more evidence-based referrals to targeted and specialist services.

The CAF draws on assessment frameworks already in existence, such as the *Framework for the assessment of children in need and their families*; *Special Educational Needs Code of Practice*; Connexions APIR framework (assessment, planning, implementation and review); ASSET and others.

The government announced that it would set up a consultation exercise designed to look at how the CAF will interface with these other assessments. Draft YJB guidance (YJB, 2006a) confirms that the DfES and YJB have agreed that YOTs will continue to use Asset because of its ability to focus on offending behaviour and predict risk of reconviction, and because it is more detailed, providing a framework for thorough analysis necessary for writing reports and the research findings that demonstrate its validity and reliability. Both the YJB and DfES are currently planning how both assessments can work alongside each other so that the benefits of each are gained by young people and practitioners. This will result in full guidance, modification of Asset and training for YOT staff. It will be necessary to consider the development and implementation of the CAF as it is adopted by local authorities between April 2006 and 2008. The guidance states that sometimes a YOT needs to complete or update a CAF on a young person and the situations in which this needs to be done may vary locally. YOTs are not expected to complete CAF assessments for all the young people they deal with; however, as a minimum the YJB advises that from April 2006 a CAF should be done when a young person needs to be referred to an external organisation, and that agency requires all referrals to be made using CAF. The guidance suggests YOT practitioners should follow three key steps in using CAF to inform Asset. These are:

- collecting information;

- analysing it;

- recording it.

It is important that you are familiar with the draft guidance; it can be downloaded at: www.youth-justice-board.gov.uk/NR/rdonlyres/E8620EA1-A90D-433E-B0FB-583F61A242C9/0/CAFdraftguidanceforYOTs.pdf

One concern over the CAF identified by Piper (2004) is that: 'Without substantial extra resources, the initial common assessment could not adequately be located in universal services without reducing expenditure on specialist services' (Piper, 2004, p737). She suggests that one advantage of the CAF could be developments that break down the 'insularity' of the youth justice system. For instance, if a young person offends who is also the subject of child protection concerns, they should also be referred to a children and families team where another assessment will be undertaken under Section 47 of the Children Act 1989, using the assessment framework. Both assessments may result in different outcomes and information is not always shared although it is anticipated that this might be addressed with the introduction of the Integrated Children's System (ICS), an information-sharing project across children's services. According to the governement's *Every child matters* website ICS 'provides a conceptual framework, a method of practice and a business process to support practitioners and managers in undertaking the key tasks of assessment, planning, intervention and review'.

Piper cites a 2003 NACRO briefing that suggests YOT staff should receive training on child development and welfare if they are to effectively share the 'corporate parenting culture and associated aims and objectives' (Piper, 2004, p739). Piper suggests that the CAF may assist in bridging the gap between the separate assessment tools and systems as well as the differing professional cultures in the child protection and youth justice systems. Piper is critical of assessment questionnaires and scales which produce a numerical score to determine outcome as these 'are a visible indicator of the "actuarial justice" that is colonising penal systems and also of the preoccupation in our "risk society" with the calculation and diminution of risk' (Piper, 2004, p740). She concludes that assessment frameworks must be developed and used with caution so that they are only a tool guiding professional judgement rather than determining what the judgement should be. It is perhaps interesting that the Department of Health has commissioned a project focusing on analysis and the exercise of professional judgement with a view to helping practitioners use and critically evaluate assessment frameworks and scales. The results of this project, 'Putting analysis into assessment 2003–2005' should soon be available. Hopefully the findings will be used to tie in with the implementation of the CAF and how it will be used alongside assessment tools such as Asset.

C H A P T E R   S U M M A R Y

In this chapter we have considered what the purpose of an assessment is, when assessments are used and what makes a good assessment. We have identified that ensuring assessments are thorough information-gathering exercises with concrete evidence provided and used in making analyses, judgements and decisions is extremely important. You have been introduced to the assessment tool, Asset, used in youth justice, as well as the research that has informed its development. We have looked at the complexities and difficulties involved in carrying out an assessment and considered the issues raised in a case study which has helped you to relate the National Occupational Standards to a practice context. We have examined the concept of risk assessment and the importance of ensuring assessments are carried out properly to ensure accuracy and the obtaining of detailed information that can then be analysed so that appropriate judgements can be made. Finally, we have looked at the advent of the Common Assessment Framework and how this may impact on youth justice. In the next chapter we will begin to consider applying the assessment to the planning of, carrying out and evaluating work with young people.

FURTHER READING

Parker, J and Bradley, G (2003) *Social work practice: Assessment, planning, intervention and review*. Exeter: Learning Matters.

This text provides a useful overview of assessment within the social work process of assessment, planning, intervention and review.

Milner, J and O'Byrne, P (2002) *Assessment in social work, 2nd edn.* Basingstoke: Palgrave Macmillan.

This book summarises a range of theories relevant to the assessment process.

Chapter 7

Working with young people

Paul Dugmore

A C H I E V I N G   A   S O C I A L   W O R K   D E G R E E

This chapter will help you begin to meet the following National Occupational Standards.

Key Role 2: Plan, carry out, review and evaluate social work practice, with individuals, families, carers, groups, communities and other professionals

- Respond to crisis situations.
- Interact with individuals, families, carers, groups and communities to achieve change and development and to improve life opportunities.
- Prepare, produce, implement and evaluate plans with individuals, families, carers, groups, communities and professional colleagues.
- Support the development of networks to meet assessed needs and planned outcomes.
- Work with groups to promote individual growth, development and independence.
- Address behaviour which presents a risk to individuals, families, carers, groups and communities.

Key Role 3: Support individuals to represent their needs, views and circumstances

- Advocate with, and on behalf of, individuals, families, carers, groups and communities.
- Prepare for, and participate in decision making forums.

Key Role 4: Manage risk to individuals, families, carers, groups, communities, self and colleagues

- Assess and manage risks to individuals, families, carers, groups and communities.
- Assess, minimise and manage risk to self and colleagues.

Key Role 5: Manage and be accountable, with supervision and support, for your own social work practice within your organisation

- Manage and be accountable for your own work.
- Contribute to the management of resources and services.
- Manage, present and share records and reports.

Key Role 6: Demonstrate professional competence in social work practice

- Research, analyse, evaluate, and use current knowledge of best social work practice.
- Work within agreed standards of social work practice and ensure own professional development.

It will also introduce you to the following academic standards as set out in the social work subject benchmark statement:

3.1.4 Social work theory

- Approaches and methods of intervention in a range of community-based settings including group-care at individual, group and community levels, including factors guiding the choice and evaluation of these.

3.1.5 The nature of social work practice

- The nature and characteristics of skills associated with effective practice, both direct and indirect, with a range of service users and in a variety of settings.
- The integration of theoretical perspectives and evidence from international research into the design and implementation of effective social work intervention with a wide range of service users, carers and others.

- The processes of reflection and evaluation, including familiarity with the range of approaches for evaluating welfare outcomes, and their significance for the development of practice and the practitioner.
3.2.2 Problem solving skills:
3.2.2.4 Intervention and evaluation; and
3.2.3 Communication skills

Introduction

This chapter focuses on the different types of work that YOT social workers undertake with young people who have offended or are at risk of offending. We look at the importance of establishing an effective working relationship based on professional boundaries and the need to engage young people. We also return to the issues of diversity, equality and working with difference. One of the most important factors in the prevention of offending by young people is the intervention programme that is undertaken as part of a final warning or court order. Following on from the previous chapter and the need for assessment to be integral to the social work process, we also concentrate on planning, reviewing, ending and evaluating interventions with young people and the frameworks in place for achieving this. Finally, we consider the different approaches to working with young people in the context of one-to-one work, group work and restorative justice.

Building a relationship

Being able to form professional relationships is fundamental to good social work practice and the importance of being able to do so is enshrined in the National Occupational Standards and GSCC Code of Practice for Social Care Workers. This is particularly relevant in youth justice where as a social worker you are in a clear position of authority – an officer of the court, working with young people who are often disadvantaged, progressing through troubled adolescence, resistant to authority and who possibly have experience of abuse, emotional and/or behavioural problems and exclusion from school. As a social worker in a YOT, your first point of contact with a young person may be at court, where they may well be anxious, overwhelmed and scared about the ensuing process and possible outcomes. Being able to explain to the young person and their family in a warm and courteous way what might happen can allay some of their fears. You may meet a young person for the first time as part of the assessment process when you are assessing them in order to complete a report for the court or referral order panel or in relation to a final warning (see Chapter 6).

ACTIVITY 7.1

What do you think are the key considerations in starting a new professional relationship with a service user? Are these any different when the service user is (1) a young person? (2) a young offender? Practise introducing yourself as a social worker to a young person you are meeting for the first time.

If you are allocated a case of a young person you have previously assessed, it is generally easier to build a working relationship as you will have already started the process. If you start working with a young person who is previously unknown to you, however, it is vital that you develop a relationship based on some clear ground rules very early on.

If you find this task difficult, it may be helpful for you to think back to when you met a professional for the first time as a service user, such as going to see your doctor or bank manager. How was it? How do you expect to be treated? The things that are important to you are probably important to other people too.

Initial contact

It is essential that you always prepare before commencing work with a young person. It is crucial to be clear about the purpose of your intervention so that you can explain this clearly and easily. You will probably have previous information on the young person you are meeting that you can read to give you a useful picture of what the issues are for the young person and what has led to them being in contact with the youth justice system. It may mean that you can avoid asking questions that they have already been asked on numerous occasions, although questioning is an important part of the relationship building phase. It is also useful to bear in mind that the information you may have read prior to meeting the young person may be inaccurate, negative or the view of another person and you may form a different view. For instance, the young person may have been very uncommunicative in a previous interview with a colleague of yours perhaps due to an incident at school or at home before the interview which was not disclosed to your colleague, who may have perceived the young person in a particular way. In your first meeting with the young person they may be much more open and talkative than they were with your colleague because the events of the day are different. Therefore, be open-minded about the information you have already and be prepared to form your own opinions.

As you approach an initial social work contact, it is important to think about the first impression that you make on a service user who may have a range of feelings about social workers, from ambivalence to mistrust. Koprowska, writing about the significance of first impressions in social work practice, offers four principles (2005, p53–4):

1 *Be clear* – use simple language, free from jargon and pompous phraseology.

2 *Be concise* – prepare yourself so you know the key issues in any situation, and can communicate them succinctly.

3 *Be comprehensive* – keep in mind all the key issues, and watch out for sidelining information that makes you feel uncomfortable.

4 *Be courteous* – courtesy is much more than good manners, though these are essential, and a certain level of polite formality is important when communicating with people new to us. Courtesy is also the way in which the underpinning values of social work are communicated – our respect for individuals and their uniqueness, and our commitment to anti-discriminatory and anti-racist practices and hence our respect for diversity.

Some criminological theories such as subcultural and Marxist approaches, outlined in Chapter 3, would suppose that young people will perceive you, as a YOT social worker, as part of the state/authority and therefore as an agent of social control. This may mean you are viewed with suspicion. While being clear about your role and purpose, and the authority contained therein, you should also be able to demonstrate that you are aiming to work in the young person's best interests. Practical examples of this, such as demonstrating respect and understanding, will hopefully mean that trust begins to develop. Such theories may also attribute possible notions of collusion whereby a young person might think you are 'on their side', particularly if there are shared identities such as class or ethnic grouping. This can pose a challenge, as you have to retain professional boundaries while perhaps demonstrating some level of personal understanding or empathy.

A first meeting should start with an introduction so that you clarify your name, your role and that you are the young person's allocated social worker. Checking out what the young person likes to be called is also helpful as this may differ from their full name. Lessening the anxiety the young person may be feeling can be achieved by trying to make them feel at ease. It is important that the young person understands why they have to attend the YOT and what your role will be in working with them. This is a good time to talk about your expectations of the young person in terms of agency policy, the requirements of their order, National Standards and anything else you think is important. It is also necessary to establish if there are any expectations the young person may have of you or the service, and questions they may have about your role and what they might want from the intervention, as this can then form the basis of contract setting or planning that you will work towards over the course of the intervention. This should include:

- Giving information about the office opening hours.

- How you can be contacted.

- Establishing the best time for appointments to be made with the young person, taking into account religious observances.

- Informing the young person of the enforcement procedure and what happens when appointments are missed.

- Ensuring that the young person is aware of the complaints procedure.

- Explaining how confidentiality works, particularly in a multi-agency team.

- Introducing the young person to the notion of partnership.

- Outlining that you will also be working with parents/carers.

A welfare approach to working with young people

Core social work values such as respect, empathy, acceptance and partnership should underpin all your practice with young people and their families. The discussion that took place in Chapter 1 is relevant here, as how you view young people who have committed offences will contribute greatly to your ability to forge strong, positive and supportive working relationships with them. As well as being mindful of their age and stage of emotional, physical and intellectual development and their social circumstances, it is essential that their experiences to date are taken into account in terms of shaping who they are and why they might be displaying certain criminal or negative behaviours. Thinking back to Chapter 3 and the different criminological theories to help identify the cause(s) of criminal behaviour should help. There are many writers who emphasise the importance of the relationship in helping professions (Rogers, 1976; Egan, 2002), and there is reference to it in the *Statement of expectations* (TOPSS, 2002) accompanying the National Occupational Standards for Social Work. This importance is put into perspective if you think about the kinds of young people you will be working with. Research looking into the links between risk factors and offending behaviour, carried out by Liddle and Solanki (2002), found that the young people in their sample had an average of about six risk factors. Some of their findings are as follows (2002, p1):

- Only 14 per cent were living with both biological parents, 66 per cent lacked a good relationship with one or other parent.

- 22 per cent had suffered bereavement, 39 per cent family breakdown or divorce and 34 per cent had lost contact with significant people.

- 44 per cent had experienced neglect or physical, sexual or emotional abuse, or had witnessed violence in the family.

- 22 per cent were looked after by social services, 27 per cent had been previously.

This is only one study, but there are many more that show similar findings (Goldson, 2000; YJB, 2003b; NACRO, 2003b). Faced with such data it is important to bear in mind that building a relationship may be extremely difficult with some young people; they may not have experienced much boundary setting in their lives or have not been treated with respect or listened to. As a result, they may experience the supervisory relationship as difficult, leading them to attempt to sabotage it in a number of ways. Remaining clear about your purpose, reflecting on your practice and demonstrating understanding but firmness will all be crucial in determining a successful outcome.

However, it is perhaps easy to lose sight of the fact that you are dealing with children and young people when the system you are working within now operates according to principles of responsibility, where *doli incapax* has been removed and opportunities to adopt a 'child first' philosophy (Haines and Drakeford, 1998) have been reduced. Indeed, research undertaken in YOTs in Wales by Cross et al. (2003) found that social work students on placement in YOTs found that young people tended to be perceived as young offenders. One student commented:

> *That was something I was very conscious of coming into it. There's not as much recognition of them not being adults – and they're children not adults. The wording is all around offenders rather than young people.* (Cross et al., 2003, p159)

It is important that as both a student and a newly qualified practitioner in youth justice you strive to retain your social work identity within a multi-agency environment and keep an analytical approach to the systems and processes you work in. Youth justice, like all other areas of social work, continues to move towards more managerialist, performance-led practice. This approach, combined with the justice components of New Labour reforms, sometimes makes it difficult to remain child-focused in what can be a demoralising world.

As was identified in Chapter 2, the youth justice system is fraught with competing tensions between justice and welfare approaches and you need to be able to maximise the opportunities for practising a welfare approach. You may struggle to do this when you are working with colleagues who adopt a justice approach and a system that can be seen as the 'maze' that was discussed in Chapter 2. You may find that the different theoretical approaches presented challenge your practice. For example, you may agree with the notion of the self-fulfilling prophecy espoused by labelling theorists that can arise from young people being labelled as young offenders. You may find it difficult to do anything about this as the system perpetuates it. This is where the importance of building a trusting relationship with young people can impact positively as you are able to see them as young people not offenders, and assist them in seeing themselves as more constructive members of society with opportunities for development and success.

Working with young people in youth justice also requires you to understand the emotional context of a young person's life at the beginning and each time you see them, as this can change from one appointment to the next. Their emotions may range from anger or loss to anxiety or frustration. It is important to acknowledge how such feelings may impact upon a young person and therefore on the work you do with them at a given time. Not all emotions will be openly displayed and it is useful to be able to read body language, as well as to be aware of how your behaviour is interpreted by them. Being aware of your findings is essential if you are to work effectively with the emotions of young people, as you may sometimes feel annoyed or upset by, or irreverent to, them. Acknowledging these findings and ensuring that the young person is not aware of them, let alone affected by them, is all part of developing your own self-awareness or emotional intelligence. In his book *People Problems*, Thompson (2006) offers useful strategies for dealing with conflict and recognising the significance of loss and grief amongst others.

In order to work effectively with users of social work services you need to develop the skills to work in partnership with young people and their families. As Trevithick (2005) states:

> *Positive practice must involve service users if it is to achieve agreed objectives (empowerment and personal responsibility) and that within this process, service users must be seen not only in terms of the 'problems' they bring, but also as whole people who have an important contribution to make in terms of their knowledge and perception of the situation, personal qualities and problem-solving capabilities.* (2005, p228)

Thompson (2005, p140) suggests that social workers can take steps to ensure that partnership is enshrined in practice:

- Keep communication channels open with clients and carers.
- Consult with relevant people when undertaking assessments.
- Work *with* people when carrying out your intervention.
- Do not rely on stereotypes or assumptions about service users or colleagues.
- Remember that responsibility for resolving the situation is shared.

Working with difference

In Chapter 1 we looked at values and ethics and how these might impact on your work as a social worker within youth justice. Chapter 3 considered the over-representation of males and ethnic minorities in the youth justice system. How you practise an anti-discriminatory and anti-oppressive approach will also help determine your success in engaging young people. How you treat young people as service users and demonstrate acceptance of them as individuals in spite of their offending will also contribute to this process of engagement. Given that you will be working with young people from a range of cultural, racial, religious and social backgrounds, of different ages, sexualities and with a range of physical disabilities and learning difficulties, you will need to develop skills and competence in working with difference. It is not possible to be an 'expert' in working with difference and a complacent or arrogant attitude in this regard will soon see you coming unstuck. We are always learning, possibly nowhere more so than in the area of working with diversity, and we can never know what life is like for people from every background. Some basic principles should assist in starting to build a relationship:

- Demonstrating respect for all young people.

- Listening to what they say.

- Ensuring you are understood.

- Not making assumptions.

- Showing an interest in their culture, religion, etc. – asking them to talk about this and what it means to them in terms of how they want you to work with them.

- Identifying if they have any specific needs that you need to be aware of.

Planning your work with young people

The YJB's *Key elements of effective practice: Assessment, planning, interventions and supervision* guidance referred to in Chapter 6 (YJB, 2002a) provides the framework that YOT practitioners must follow in their work with young people. The main aim of this guidance is to impress upon practitioners the importance of ensuring that any assessment of a young person should be clearly linked to a plan of intervention that responds to the identified risks and needs in order to reduce their likelihood of re-offending. This is where knowledge of relevant criminological and social work theories will need to be applied. Plans should also take into account any positive factors in the young person's life so that these can be incorporated in the intervention programme. The KEEP guidance recommends that before meeting a young person the allocated worker:

- *Collects together all the existing information about them (e.g. Asset . . . information about their interests, activities and achievements as well as any attempts to find missing information.*

- *Should make a preliminary evaluation of the responsiveness of the young person and consider how the service can best meet their needs.*

- *Should take into account the motivation and preferred learning styles of the young person, and the resources available to them in the community (e.g. helpful school) or the opportunities to participate in specific programmes or activities within the secure estate.*

- *Should consider their own individual skills and expertise and how these could be used to support the young person.* (YJB, 2002a, p12)

Planning is an activity that underpins all social work practice and is not unique to youth justice; however, different areas of social work will use a different framework or planning process. The YJB reader *Assessment, planning and supervision* (2003a) suggests that Asset should be used to determine the key areas for intervention, focusing on the sections with the highest ratings; identifying positive factors and incorporating these into the plan to promote and sustain progress; and identifying mediating factors that may need to be managed if the young person is going to be able to complete the order successfully, such as health or literacy difficulties (YJB, 2003a, p60). Important in all planning is partnership with the service user. The purpose of a plan is to identify how the needs or risks identified will best be met, with tasks and timescales allocated to specific people who should carry out the tasks. The young person needs to agree with the plan and to participate in its formulation if it is to be effective, and a process of negotiation may be necessary. This can serve as part of the relationship-building exercise. Plans will also include other people such as specialist YOT workers, parents or carers and mentors. When a young person does not acknowledge an identified problem from the assessment, you will need to work with them, using a technique such as motivational interviewing, in order to help them recognise why you have identified this as an issue and to encourage them to address it.

YJB National Standards (2004b) state that:

Intervention plans must be drawn up within 15 working days of the making of the order (this does not apply to Curfew, Reparation, Attendance Centre and Parenting Orders). They must be based on risk factors associated with the offending identified in Asset and set out arrangements to address them. All assessments must consider the needs of the victim and plans will include restorative processes. They will take account of plans made for the young offender by other agencies (e.g. Social Services, Education, Health). The plan or contract should be discussed, agreed and signed by the young person and his/her parent(s)/carer(s) (YJB, 2004b, p47).

In order for plans to be meaningful they should be SMART (Talbot, 1996, cited in YJB, 2003c, p68):

- Specific

- Measurable

- Achievable

- Realistic

- Time-limited.

From the plan, therefore, it should be clear to the young person, you the social worker, parents/carers and any other workers involved, what the purpose of the objectives are. They should be clearly conveyed, agreed by both the young person and the worker and reviewed regularly. We will return to reviews later.

ACTIVITY 7.2

Following your assessment of Jermaine in Activity 6.3, he has been sentenced to a 12-month supervision order. Draw up a supervision plan to address the identified needs.

Would anything different need to be taken into account if the young person was a newly arrived asylum-seeker?

Types of intervention

The type of intervention that you and others undertake with a young person will depend on their assessed needs and risks, their age, sex, stage of development and learning styles, as well as the type and length of order and availability of resources to you and the service. Remember, as discussed in Chapter 6, plans should always seek to harness and strengthen protective factors. The YJB suggests that in deciding on a specific intervention, the following questions should also be addressed (2003a, p65):

- Is it proportionate to the seriousness of the offending behaviour and the assessed risk of re-offending?

- Will it help to reduce the risk that this young person will re-offend?

- Will it help to manage any risk of harm posed by the young person to other people?

- Will it contribute to reducing risks faced by the offender?

- Does the young person have a reasonable chance of being able to complete it?

- How will it address the concerns of any victims involved?

One of the greatest challenges you will come across will be working with young people who have no interest in working with you or for whom motivation levels are very low. Hopefully, if you ensure the basic factors discussed in developing a relationship are followed, you will at least have something to work with. There are various approaches, methods or models of intervention that you can use in your work. Some of these are discussed in this chapter, and some useful sources are recommended in Further Reading at the end of the chapter.

Casework/case management

You will have at your disposal a toolbox of interventions that you can use for particular aspects of work with young people. As discussed, establishing a good working relationship early on is essential as this will enable you to continually assess and update the existing assessment, in relation to the young person's strengths, motivations and difficulties. This is important particularly when you start referring them to other specialist workers in the YOT or to other organisations. One of the difficulties for YOT practitioners is that it takes time for relationships to develop, especially the trust element, and many practitioners want to get to know the young person before they start referring them elsewhere. However, as National Standards require more contact at the start of an order, referring the young person to YOT specialist workers or a group work programme is one way of utilising resources in order to manage the workload. This can result in a young person being in contact with a number of different YOT staff at the start of the order and this can be detrimental to developing that all-important relationship. Research by Burnett and Appleton (2004) found that: 'The disjointed involvement allowed by the case-management model made it harder for the individual practitioner to gain the trust of young people and prevented the relaxed communication that comes with familiarity' (2004, p33).

However, as YOT caseloads have increased, with more available sentencing options for early stage offenders, the abolition of continued cautioning and the revised National Standards, case management as a model has become the norm. Despite this, Burnett and Appleton concluded that staff 'continued to regard the development of a supervisory relationship as the necessary foundation for any other work: for achieving accurate and in-depth assessment; for engaging their interest in interventions and activities; and for motivating the young person to change their behaviour' (2004, p35).

So, one of the challenges you will face as a YOT social worker is managing to build a good relationship with young people before they start having to meet with other workers within and outside of the team, sustaining this as your contact reduces and ensuring that you liaise with all the other professionals involved so that you are able to keep a firm grasp of the case and the young person's progress.

Effective practice with young people who offend

In a Department of Health briefing, *Quality protects*, Hagell (2003) identifies a number of characteristics of successful programmes to change behaviour:

- *They should be based on a clear theoretical model of how they are meant to change behaviour.*

- *There needs to be a clear focus for all the activity involved in the programme. Everyone should know what the outcome will be, and this should be specific and measurable.*

- *They last for a reasonable length of time. Six months is usually necessary if they are to have a chance of making a difference.*

- *They need to have reasonably frequent contact with the young people. As a rule of thumb this is often suggested to be around twice a week although it depends very much on the type of work being done and the needs of the child.*

- *The programme should be focusing on rewarding positive behaviour rather than on meting out punishment.*

- *Following-through the intervention with some aftercare also seems to be* beneficial. (2003, pp5–6)

The briefing goes on to identify examples of programmes with positive outcomes. These include social skills training, cognitive behavioural programmes, parent training programmes and multi-modal interventions such as multi-systemic therapy. Such suggestions are generally based on the findings of a large number of studies, through meta-analysis (Smith, 2005), where programmes deemed as the most effective in changing behaviour are those directly addressing behaviour problems 'by using a social learning approach, teaching social and interpersonal skills and helping young people to perceive and think about their own and other people's behaviour in a different way' (Smith, 2003b, p188).

Some of the cognitive behavioural techniques used with offenders include:

- *Pro-social modelling* – modelling positive behaviour and rewarding and reinforcing pro-social behaviour in young people.

- *Motivational interviewing* – working with young people to encourage them to be motivated to making changes in their lives and a belief in their capacity to learn.

- *Problem solving* – offending is reduced by enhancing problem-solving skills, often using case scenarios and requiring young people to identify problems and solutions and develop consequential thinking skills.

- *Social skills training* – this is about improving young people's skills in social situations which may include role play and assertiveness training.

- *Moral reasoning* – giving young people a range of moral dilemmas to discuss and make decisions about.

Because the research into effective practice often focuses on new, 'flagship' programmes where resources are invested heavily and motivation is high among those delivering the programmes, Smith (2003b) suggests they are not representative of what is delivered to most young offenders. He concludes that 'these findings illustrate the danger of using the "what works" evidence as a platform for extending the scope and activity of the juvenile justice system' and that 'widening the scope of intervention to include many adolescence-limited offenders will dilute the effectiveness of efforts to help the core group of life-course persistent offenders' (Smith, 2003b, p193). Goldson (2001) also cautions against the acceptance of effective practice research:

> *The lives of young offenders are complex and reliance on a single theory of 'reasoning and rehabilitation' or a discrete form of cognitive intervention is unlikely to produce good results. We cannot expect, nor should we expect, to discover law-like universals.*
> (2001, p83)

Prior (2005) reviewed evaluations of youth justice interventions and found only minimal evidence that they are effective in reducing youth offending, suggesting that those involved in youth justice should exercise caution when approaching new initiatives. He maintains that applying a critical approach and being prepared to adapt programmes to meet the needs of the specific population being worked with are essential.

Group work with young people

As a YOT social worker you will hopefully have some discretion, in consultation with your line manager, as to how you will work with a young person in order to prevent them from re-offending. You may decide that a group work programme will be useful and appropriate. The responsibility of running a group might also be one of your roles. Payne (2005) cautions:

> *Choosing to work with a group (rather than individuals) involves a number of decisions; choosing how to work with a particular group involves yet more. Practice also involves me – the practitioner. So I need to understand how I work and behave in groups, so that I can understand how I am working with this particular group.* (2005, p122)

You may wonder how you should decide whether group work as an intervention will be an appropriate course of action. Certainly you need to consider whether the young person is ready to be in a group setting in terms of their emotional and social development. Putting someone in a group setting who already has low self-esteem may be damaging for them. You need to be aware of the learning styles of young people and any learning difficulties they may have; some may suffer from Attention Deficit Hyperactivity Disorder or Conduct Disorder in which case group work would be difficult for them. However, if managed well it can be more beneficial than one-to-one work which can be too intense for some young people. Other issues that need to be taken into account are the age and sex of other group participants and whether they have been assessed as high or low risk of offending, as it would not be sensible to mix people of significantly different ages or levels of risk together. Placing a small number of girls with a larger group of boys would also be inappropriate. Indeed many YOTs run separate groups for male and female offenders. Before referring a young person to a group programme it is important that you:

- Assess the suitability of the programme for the young person, taking into account the factors discussed above.

- Assess the young person's level of motivation and work with them to ensure that they are sufficiently motivated, particularly as non-attendance may result in you having to enforce breach proceedings.

- Explain the purpose of the programme, its requirements and expectations on the young person so that they are clear about what to expect before starting.

Once these important issues have been addressed, there are many benefits to group working with young people (Payne, 2005, pp127–8):

- The provision of a potentially fertile learning environment.

- Features of group life, such as negotiation, performing tasks, sharing thoughts and feelings, contain potential for personal development.

- Being with others with similar experiences reduces isolation and increases support.

- Supporting people to create change for themselves.

- Raising consciousness.

- Learning that there are many things that can only be achieved by co-operating with others.

However, such positive changes will only be realised provided the group is facilitated and managed well. Chapman (2005, p173) claims that effective group work requires:

- A common purpose.

- A process or set of tasks designed to achieve the purpose.

- Relationships between members which facilitate progress towards the achievement of that purpose.

- Effective facilitation.

If you are facilitating a group work programme, it is vital that you are familiar with theories and processes of group work so that you are 'in tune with the stages of development known as forming, storming, norming, performing and adjourning' (Coulshed and Orme, 2006, p254). These were originally outlined by Tuckman and Jenson (1977), cited in Coulshed and Orme (2006) where you will also find a useful summary of each stage as well as the required skills and tasks therein. Facilitating group work with young people who offend can be a very difficult and challenging experience. Chapman suggests a number of principles for workers when dealing with problematic behaviour in a group setting (2005, p178):

- Try to understand before making judgements.

- Avoid taking sides – focus on the problem in relation to group progress.

- Affirm strengths and any sign of motivation.

- Ensure the group feels safe, respected and supported.

- Move at a pace appropriate to each group member.

- Ensure that negative behaviour is not allowed to attract more attention than positive behaviour.

- Regularly review progress with the group in relation to objectives and purpose.

- Use supervision to explore their own feelings and perceptions, and to develop a skills base which contains a repertoire of responses.

Restorative justice

A central element to the Labour Government's reforms to the youth justice system is ensuring that young people take responsibility for their actions and face up to the consequences of their offending by, in part, encouraging reparation to victims. This was to be achieved by the introduction of restorative justice into the youth justice provisions, already outlined in Chapter 4 and discussed further in Chapter 8. Restorative justice has a particular philosophical base which sees offending within a wider, societal context and seeks to bring about restoration to the victim and the community affected by offending behaviour. Restorative justice has been defined as 'a process whereby the parties with a stake in a particular offence come together to resolve collectively how to deal with the aftermath of the offence and its implications for the future' (Marshall, 1996, cited in Crawford and Newburn, 2003). Elements of restorative justice are identified as being the inclusion of each stakeholder, the importance of participatory processes and the emphasis on restorative outcomes (Crawford and Newburn, 2003, p22).

Whatever part of a Youth Offending Team or Service you work in it is highly probable that you will need to be working from a restorative justice approach. As part of a police reprimand or final warning, or part of a referral, reparation, action plan or supervision order, reparation has to be addressed. This can take a number of forms: direct reparation, such as victim–offender mediation, family group conferencing, restorative conferencing or Youth Offender Panel meetings (for referral orders); or indirect reparation, which can involve community reparation or shuttle mediation where the victim and offender communicate via a third party. There are concerns about whether community reparation is restorative in nature as it may happen without the victim being consulted. However, Masters (2005) suggests that it is 'the process through which it is achieved that defines an activity as restorative' (2005, p183) and that providing the young person is able to acknowledge the harm they have caused and feels obliged to do something to remedy this, community reparation is sufficient when the victim is unwilling to engage or the offence is victimless. The types of restorative processes available will depend on the YOT you are working in.

One of the most important things to bear in mind in restorative justice work is how emotive bringing together victim and offender can be. You need to prepare the young person very well for any meeting and support them in what may be a very challenging, intimidating and anxiety-provoking event. The victim needs to be equally well briefed and supported if the meeting is to be successful. Chapter 8 will look at working with victims in more detail.

Review

Within youth justice a framework for review is provided, or even prescribed by, National Standards and the *Key elements of effective practice* (KEEP). The purpose of review is to identify if an intervention has achieved what it set out to do, to assess the progress a young person is making and to identify additional aspects of the intervention that still need to be delivered in order for it to be effective. Supervision plans are required to be reviewed every 12 weeks or any time there has been significant change in a young person's circumstances. The review process should be an opportunity for the young person to provide feedback on how the intervention programme is working for them and to identify any problems or difficulties they may be experiencing with it, and as a result of a review it may be necessary to make changes. If cases are not reviewed an intervention may be inappropriate, ineffectual or even damaging to a young person as well as cost-ineffective.

Thinking back to the SMART objectives, the review process should consider if each objective set has been achieved and if not, the reasons for this, such as a particular group work programme not running. During the review you should consider the positive successes achieved as well as the difficulties or areas where things have not gone to plan. These may be down to the young person, to you or to external factors. The review process may be carried out between you and the young person, or it may be chaired by your manager with the young person's parent/carer also present. Asset must also be looked at and possibly updated as a result of this. Depending on the length of the programme of intervention, there may be a number of reviews over the course of your involvement with a young person. The YJB (2003a) stresses the importance of the final review as 'very important'; and continues:

Cases should be closed in a positive way. It is a chance for young people to express their views on the work that has been done, and for successes, even small ones, to be celebrated and encouraged for continuation in the future. Remember that re-offending does not automatically mean that an intervention has been a failure. (2003a, p87)

Endings

As a social worker involved in youth justice you will inevitably experience the ending of your professional relationship with young people you have worked closely with. If you are involved in assessing a young person for a pre-sentence report, the result of their sentence may mean that they do not need allocating within the YOT, such as in a conditional discharge, or they may be allocated to another YOT worker. An ending can be a positive experience, with the completion of the court order they were sentenced to. This may be early – you may be able to take them back to court for the order to be discharged before it is due to end because they have worked hard and completed all aspects of the order, as outlined in the plan. It is less positive when the young person re-offends and receives another sentence, perhaps a custodial one, and this might be supervised by another member of your team. Other circumstances include a young person moving to another area who will then be supervised by a local YOT in the new area, or on turning 18 supervision is taken on by the probation service. Unexpected endings may occur which may be impossible to predict, even the death of a client. Whatever the reason for the closure, it is important that, where possible, the ending of the professional relationship is fully planned and prepared for.

Both social workers and young people may have invested a lot of energy, time, commitment and effort into a relationship, and its end may be viewed as a loss or a crisis, raising previous experiences of loss. Coulshed and Orme suggest a good model of ending as incorporating the following (2005, pp287–8):

- Clarification in the first meeting that contact will be time-limited.

- Using the experience of termination as a learning opportunity rather than a painful separating experience.

- Using a fixed time limit purposefully, using time as a therapeutic agent.

- Deciding on certain objectives to achieve in the ending phase.

- Beforehand, exploring a person's feelings about the end of a relationship.

- Introduce the new worker if there is to be one and talk about feelings of endings in the meeting.

- Help the person construct a helping network in the community.

- Explore your own feelings. Demonstrate that you will remember the person; have confidence in his or her ability to manage without you.

- In some contexts a ritual or ceremonial ending could mark the occasion.

- Write a closing record, together, if appropriate.

ACTIVITY 7.3

You have been working with Jermaine now for over a year. He has completed his 12-month supervision order and apart from a theft, for which he received a community punishment order, he has not committed any other offences. Think back to your assessment of Jermaine and the supervision plan that you completed. You are now carrying out the final review of the order. What factors would you want to address and how would you use this as part of the process of ending your relationship?

Evaluation

As mentioned earlier, reviewing your practice on a regular basis is crucially important in social work and prescribed by YJB guidance and National Standards for those practising in youth justice settings. Therefore, it could be argued that we are constantly and consistently evaluating our practice. Certainly, part of the review process is to consider how relevant, effective and cost-effective an intervention is in relation to an individual service user. Evaluation is more than this, though. It is also about being aware of how research can inform, enhance and complement your practice. Your degree course will instigate an approach that encourages you to be research-minded so that you are aware of studies that are relevant to the area you practise in as well as to develop your own research skills. You need to be competent in evaluating your own practice and able to make the necessary changes in order that you are constantly striving to progress it. You need to be confident that the work you are doing with young people is effective in relation to the stated aims and objectives.

Part of evaluation means obtaining feedback from those in receipt of the services you are providing, namely the young people and their families. The ways that this can be achieved within youth justice include the regular review process. It is your responsibility to ensure that all the young people and their parents are provided with the opportunity to give honest feedback during the intervention and after it, and that they know that their comments will be taken seriously. It may also be useful for YOTs to obtain feedback from other users of services, for instance the courts who might provide information on the quality of pre-sentence reports or bail supervision assessments. It is important to ensure that the process for providing feedback is open and transparent and that the mechanisms enable reliability.

Evaluation is a 'must do' part of the job that should not be ignored because you do not have the time or it is low on the list of priorities. As Thompson says:

> *Evaluation is a fundamental part of good practice, as it provides us with a platform from which to continue to improve. No matter how skilled, experienced or effective we are, there are, of course, always lessons to be learned, improvements to be made and benefits to be gained from evaluating our practice.* (2005, p65)

Evaluation is therefore a tool you must be competent in using as part of your commitment to reflective practice, thus ensuring your positive growth and development as a practitioner.

In order to carry out its roles of monitoring the performance of the youth justice system and the promotion of effective practice, the YJB has developed an Effective Practice Quality Assurance framework (EPQA). This includes the *Key elements of effective practice* which cover the following areas:

- Assessment, planning interventions and supervision

- Final warning interventions

- Offending behaviour programmes

- Young people who sexually abuse

- Restorative justice

- Parenting

- Education, training and employment

- Remand management

- Mentoring

- Swift administration of justice

- Mental health

- Intensive supervision and surveillance programmes

- Substance misuse

- Resettlement

- Targeted neighbourhood intervention programmes

These documents outline features of effective youth justice services informed by the latest research and legislation. The main part of the EPQA is self-assessment, with YOTs required to undertake a process of self-evaluation, to 'underpin priority-setting, business-planning and ongoing improvement'. The YJB guidance for YOTs and secure establishments published in 2006 states the EPQA framework is designed to (YJB, 2006b, p3):

- Provide a consistent system for evaluating the evidence of effective practice across all youth justice services.

- Set performance improvement targets and prioritise improvement effort within youth justice services.

- Facilitate continuing improvement in the work undertaken by youth justice services.

The framework enables YOTs to provide the YJB with qualitative feedback relating to their performance, in addition to the quantitative data provided quarterly, assisting in the identification of areas of strength and weakness. Upon completing the self-audit, which is evidenced-based against given criteria, YOTs have to develop a plan detailing how low performance will be targeted and improved.

The guidance suggests that 'feedback shows that involving staff from all levels of the service in the quality assurance process provides the most robust and accurate assessment and reaps the greatest rewards. It ensures that all services understand how effective practice relates to them and so sign up to delivering the improvement plan' (YJB, 2006b, p3).

More information on this can be found at www.youth-justice-board.gov.uk/ cgibin/ MsmGo.exe?grab_id=460&page_id=3538944&query=epqa& hiword=epqa+

Thus, as well as evaluating your own individual practice with young people, you will also be involved in the wider EPQA self-assessment process.

User perspectives

It is easy to focus on what academics and practitioners purport to be effective practice with young people or offenders or both; there is much less research engaging with the views of those receiving services within youth justice and social work settings. However, some studies have provided such findings (Hill, 1999; de Winter and Noom, 2003) where young people have been asked what they value in relationships with social workers. They suggest that being listened to, being actively involved in decision-making, confidentiality, privacy and communication that does not stress power differentials are all important (Hill, 1999). Hill adds that we should remember that we are working with children with problems rather than problem children. The key characteristics young people look for in a social worker include (1999, p141):

- A genuine willingness to understand the young person's perspective and to convey empathy.

- Reliability (keeping promises, being available, punctuality).

- Taking action.

- Respecting confidences.

Given that you will often be working with young people for whom relationships have broken down, creating a trusting environment where there is room for development is crucial (de Winter and Noom, 2003). It is also necessary to sustain support even when the young person makes mistakes. Research (Barry, 2000; Hill, 1999; de Winter, 2003) suggests that dialogue and a participatory approach, where you and the young person identify the main problems, look for causes and solutions and assess development, will yield the most positive outcomes. This ties in with the importance of establishing, harnessing and working with a young person's positive (protective) factors rather than just the problematic areas of their life.

C H A P T E R   S U M M A R Y

This chapter has looked at the importance of building a relationship with young people, focusing on issues such as the initial contact, working within a welfare approach and working with difference. We have also looked at the process of working with young people, commencing with planning – something that should be done in conjunction with the young person, using a strengths-based approach that acknowledges their positive points and protective factors. Various types of interventions have been considered within the context of effective practice, such as the traditional casework approach, and recent changes such as restorative justice. We have emphasised the essential component of reviewing practice, the significance of endings and the fundamental concept of evaluation. Finally, we have considered the young people's perspective and what they want from their involvement with social workers. Reading this chapter should have helped you to gain an understanding of some of the complexities and dilemmas in working with young people in youth justice.

FURTHER READING

Trotter, C (2006) *Working with involuntary clients: A guide to practice (2nd edn)*. London: Sage.

This book outlines a range of approaches for working with difficult and reluctant clients including problem-solving and pro-social modelling.

Thompson, N (2006) *People problems*. Basingstoke: Palgrave Macmillan.

This text provides a number of strategies or tools for dealing with a range of problems encountered in social work such as objective setting, building confidence and giving feedback.

Crawford, A and Newburn T (2003) *Youth offending and restorative justice: Implementing reforms in youth justice*. Cullompton: Willan.

Provides an exploration of the introduction of restorative justice into the youth justice system and the implementation of the referral order. It examines the difficulties of trying to marry principles of restorative justice into the UK's existing adversarial youth justice system.

Chapter 8
Working with others

Sally Angus

This chapter will help you begin to meet the following National Occupational Standards

Key Role 1: Prepare for, and work with individuals, families, carers, groups and communities to assess their needs and circumstances

- Prepare for social work contact and involvement.
- Work with individuals, families, carers, groups and communities to help them make informed decisions.
- Assess needs and options to recommend a course of action.

Key Role 2: Plan, carry out, review and evaluate social work practice, with individuals, families, carers, groups, communities and other professionals

- Interact with individuals, families, carers, groups and communities to achieve change and development and to improve life opportunities.
- Support the development of networks to meet assessed needs and planned outcomes.
- Address behaviour which presents a risk to individuals, families, carers, groups and communities.

Key Role 3: Support individuals to represent their needs, views and circumstances

- Prepare for, and participate in decision making forums.

Key Role 4: Manage risk to individuals, families, carers, groups, communities, self and colleagues

- Assess and manage risks to individuals, families, carers, groups and communities.

Key Role 5: Manage and be accountable, with supervision and support, for your own social work practice within your organisation

- Manage, present and share records and reports.
- Work within multi-disciplinary and multi-organisational teams, networks and systems.

It will also introduce you to the following academic standards as set out in the social work subject benchmark statement:

3.1.1 Social work services and service users

- The social processes (associated with, for example, poverty, unemployment, poor health, disablement, lack of education and other sources of disadvantage) that lead to marginalisation, isolation and exclusion and their impact on the demand for social work services.

3.1.2 The service delivery context

- The significance of legislative and legal frameworks and service delivery standards (including the nature of legal authority, the application of legislation in practice, statutory accountability and tensions between statute, policy and practice).

3.1.3 Values and ethics

- Aspects of philosophical ethics relevant to the understanding and resolution of value dilemmas and conflicts in both inter-personal and professional contexts.

3.1.4 Social work theory

- The relevance of sociological perspectives to understanding societal and structural influences on human behaviour at individual, group and community levels.
- The relevance of psychological and physiological perspectives to understanding individual and social development and functioning.

- Social science theories explaining group and organisational behaviour, adaptation and change.

3.2.2 Problem-solving skills

- Plan a sequence of actions to achieve specified objectives.
- Assess human situations, taking into account a variety of factors (including the view of participants, theoretical concepts, research evidence, legislation and organisational policies and procedures).
- Consider specific factors relevant to social work practice (such as risk, rights, cultural differences and linguistic sensitivities, responsibilities to protect vulnerable individuals and legal obligations).

3.2.2.4 Intervention and evaluation

- Undertake practice in a manner that promotes the well-being and protects the safety of all parties.

3.2.3 Communication skills

- Make effective contact with individuals and organisations for a range of objectives, by verbal, paper based and electronic means.
- Communicate effectively across potential barriers resulting from differences (for example, in culture, language and age).

3.2.4 Skills in working with others

- Act co-operatively with others, liaising and negotiating across differences such as organisational and professional boundaries and differences of identity or language.

Introduction

In Chapter 5 we looked at the role of the social worker working as part of a multi-agency youth offending team. The chapter focused on the specific roles of each professional making up the youth justice team. This chapter will look at how social workers in a Youth Offending Team (YOT) work with other people who are involved in the young person's life. Other people involved with a young person include those directly involved; not only parent(s), carers and guardians, but also people indirectly involved such as volunteers working with the Youth Offending Team or the crime victim.

First we consider the role of the social worker working with the parent(s), carers and guardians and the importance of working in partnership with them, but in a way that does not exclude the young person. Following this, we focus on the social work role with victims who have experienced crime perpetrated by the young person, how social workers work with victims, and consider specific skills required to undertake this role. Finally we examine the role of the volunteer community Youth Offender Panel member and how social workers can work effectively with this particular group. Working alongside volunteers in youth justice is not a new concept, but nevertheless brings with it issues of roles and responsibilities.

Working with parents and carers

Social work practice involves working not only directly with a service user, but also with their family, guardian and/or carer. This is the case for all social work practice whether working with adults or children and families as well as youth justice. Working with parents and carers remains a central tenet of New Labour's youth justice system and is one of its six key objectives. Despite considerable criticism of what was considered the criminalising of parents from some sections of the media and youth justice practice, Labour were determined to continue along the path of confronting the parenting deficit (Muncie, 1999).

'Reinforcing the responsibilities of parents' (YJB, 2006c) is based upon the premise that there is a strong correlation between inadequate parenting and youth offending. The Home Office drew upon research conducted by Graham and Bowling (1995) which revealed that almost half of young people with moderate or low levels of parental supervision had committed a criminal offence.

As a social worker working in the YOT there are three ways of working with parents:

1 *Voluntarily* – many parents want and may even ask for support. YOTs must work with parents on a voluntary basis.

2 *Voluntarily with a parenting contract* – if a more formal approach is useful or the parents are unwilling to co-operate, YOTs can suggest a parenting contract. Refusing to enter into a contract can be used as evidence to support an application for an order and may persuade a reluctant parent to engage.

3 *Parenting order* – if the parent is unwilling to co-operate, the YOT can apply for, or recommend, a Parenting Order. (Home Office/YJB/DCA, 2004).

ACTIVITY *8.1*

Consider for the moment the term 'parent'. How might you define a parent?

Defining 'parent'

You will probably find that definitions and understanding of the term 'parent' are different across professions and cultures. Certainly this issue was found to be somewhat problematic in the evaluation of the pilot YOTs where researchers found that YOT staff tended to think in rather narrow terms of 'natural' parents (Holdaway et al., 2001, p103). In addition to the subjective view of practitioners, the legislation can also appear unclear. A parenting order can be made via Sections 443 and 444 of the Education Act 1996. Here the definition of parent is virtually the same as the Children Act 1989 which is 'those with parental responsibility or care of the child' (2001, p103). Persons with 'parental responsibility' can include people other than birth parents. However if the order is made via the criminal route then the definition of 'parent' under Section 1 of the Family Law Reform Act 1987 is applied. Here the parent is defined as 'mother and father whether married to each other or not at the time of the child's birth' (2001, p103).

While the parent/guardian/carer is legally responsible in the eyes of the law, the family is equally important in the young person's life. Britain is very multicultural and while the mother and/or father might be legally responsible for the young person, it may be that the young person's day-to-day living arrangements are the responsibility of a relative or close family member. This is the case for some African and West Indian families and may well apply to other cultures as well. Alongside this, it is important to acknowledge and understand the plurality of family constructs. As Pickburn et al. point out, the 'combination of family structures are almost limitless' (2005, p198). Consideration needs to be given to diversity in terms of faith, class, race, sexuality, absent parents, culture, gender and, as advances in medicine and science continue, non-biological parents (2005, p198). For the purposes of this chapter we will use the term 'parent' but ask that you consider the term 'parent' in the wider sense to include guardian, carer or other adult in the young person's life who may have legal responsibility for them.

So let us look in more detail at how you might work directly with parents and carers.

Working voluntarily with parents

All work undertaken with young people will necessitate some contact with the young person's parent, simply because they are under the age of 18. As the parent they are the 'primary agents of care and socialisation' (Crawford and Newburn, 2003, p157) and have a significant role to play in the young person's life. It is essential to work with parents from the onset, involving them in a way that provides a framework of support, empathy and choice.

One area of work where that will require additional involvement with the parent(s) is when young people receive a referral order, a court order requiring them to attend a Youth Offender Panel. This will entail preparing the young person and parent by explaining the process of the panel and the role of the community panel members. It may seem a daunting process for all involved, but it is an opportunity for the parent to be involved in a process they can really contribute to, allowing them to take an appropriate level of responsibility in preventing further offending and help manage young people's future behaviour (Crawford and Newman, 2003, p157).

Working voluntarily with a Parenting contract

Parenting contract

The Anti-Social Behaviour Act 2003 introduced the concept of parenting contracts. They are voluntary, although formal, written agreements between parents of young offenders and YOT practitioners. The contract consists of two elements: 1) a statement by the parent to say that they agree to comply with the components of the contract for a specified period; and 2) a statement by the YOT practitioner stating they will agree to provide support to the parent 'for the purpose of complying with the contract' (Home Office/YJB/DCA, 2004).

The YOT social worker, in drawing up the contract, would include the following:

- Consultation with other agencies working with the young person to establish how the contract will fit with any existing interventions.

- Consideration as to whether another agency should be involved.

- When meeting with the parent for the first time, provision of information on the contract and what their involvement will be.

- Involvement of the young person in the process, subject to maturity, age and understanding.

- Explanation of the dedicated worker role, setting out how parents will be supported.

While parenting contracts are voluntary, refusal to co-operate could have implications. If, despite stringent efforts to engage parents, they fail to co-operate in the best interests of their child, their decision may be taken into consideration by the courts when deciding whether to issue a parenting order (Home Office/YJB/DCA, 2004).

Parenting orders

Parenting orders were introduced in the Crime and Disorder Act 1998, but extended by the Anti-Social Behaviour Act 2003 and the Criminal Justice Act 2003. This was done to allow the order to be made at an earlier stage. The idea is to involve parents earlier in order to help them to prevent their 'child's offending or anti-social behaviour to become entrenched and leading on to more serious problems' (Home Office/YJB/DCA, 2004, section 2.11). A parenting order is available in any proceedings where the child has been convicted of a criminal offence and the length of the order may range from three to 12 months. A parenting order can also be made when a child has been made subject of a child safety order, sex offender order, an anti-social behaviour order or when parents themselves have been convicted for failing to ensure their child's attendance at school or failure to attend a Youth Offender Panel (Pickburn et al., 2005).

YOTs are now able to apply to magistrates' courts under the Anti-Social Behaviour Act 2003 for 'free-standing' parenting orders without the need for the young person to appear in court (Home Office/YJB/DCA, 2004, section 2.11). The order would require a criminal standard of proof and would only be issued by the Youth Court when the court considers that it might contribute to the prevention of offending or anti-social behaviour by the young person (Pickburn et al., 2005). However, it is unlikely that you would apply for such an order unless, despite repeated attempts to work with the parent(s), they failed to engage with the YOT. The Criminal Justice Act 2003 made parenting orders available when a referral order is made or when a Youth Offender Panel refers a parent back to court for failing to attend panel meetings.

Parenting orders, while compulsory, are intended to support and give guidance to parents, focusing specifically on their parenting skills. In the Audit Commission report *Misspent youth* (1996), one of the key recommendations was the provision of support and assistance to develop parents' skills to prevent youth offending. The order will require parents to attend guidance sessions or counselling, which means they would be required to attend no more than once a week, for up to a period of three months. The order may also include additional requirements specific to the individual case. The order is likely to refer parents to a parenting programme.

Parenting programmes

Once parents have received a parenting order, then a programme of activities is devised in order to assist them in addressing their child's offending behaviour as well as developing their own parenting skills. While parenting programmes are part of the core work of a YOT, some YOTs have chosen to recruit external agencies such as Parentline Plus to deliver programmes, which should be delivered 'in a spirit of partnership' (Haines and Drakeford, 1998, p153) where YOT practitioners are working with parents in a task-centred way, rather than a prescriptive one.

This area of work is relatively new to youth justice and practitioners have struggled with the requirement to challenge parents over their competence (Burnett and Appleton, 2004). In fact Burnett and Appleton's research of a parenting programme in Oxfordshire found that practitioners would have benefited from further guidance in working with parents, particularly around the area of non-attendance. When working with parents, you need to consider the young person's offending behaviour while having an awareness of difficulties that parents might be experiencing that are quite separate from their relationship with their child. This might include issues such as domestic violence, mental health and personal welfare problems. As mentioned earlier, you need to consider the diversification of parenting styles found within multicultural Britain (Holdaway et al., 2001, p104). You will also need to have experience of, or develop skills in, working with and facilitating groups in a way that is 'welcoming and supportive, showing empathy with difficult and different situations' (2001, p103).

What do parenting programmes involve?

There are two main elements to the parenting programmes (Home Office/YJB/DCA, 2004, section 2.9(i)):

1 *The first is a parenting programme designed to meet the individual needs of parents so as to help them address their child's misbehaviour. This is not a punishment, but a positive way of bolstering parental responsibility and helping parents develop their skills so they can respond more effectively to their child's needs.*

2 *The second element specifies particular ways in which parents are required to exercise control over their child's behaviour to address particular factors associated with offending or anti-social behaviour.*

RESEARCH SUMMARY

The Youth Justice Board (YJB) funded the development of 42 parenting projects across England. These were set up by YOTs in partnership with other agencies from the voluntary and statutory sectors. The YJB also commissioned a three-year national evaluation of the effectiveness of the parenting programmes which commenced in 1999. This evaluation identified some positive changes in parenting skills, including:

- *Improved communication between parents and children;*

- *Better parental supervision and monitoring of young people's activities;*

- *Reduced parent/child conflict and better approaches to handling conflict when it arose;*

- *Better relationships, including more praise and approval of their child, and less criticism and loss of temper;*

- *Parents feeling more able to influence young people's behaviour;*

- *Parents feeling better equipped to fulfil their parenting responsibilities.*

In terms of reducing offending behaviour by young people, the research found that significant progress had been made. One year before the parents were involved in the projects, 89 per cent of their children had been convicted of a crime compared to just over 61 per cent in the year after the parents had completed the programme. In conclusion the report says: 'The study indicates that despite the controversy that surrounded the introduction of Parenting Orders, there does seem to be a role for them. They may provide a powerful way to reach vulnerable and needy parents who might otherwise never attend a parenting support service' (Youth Justice Board, 2006c).

Assessment processes in working with parents

Like any other intervention in youth justice practice the assessment process is 'critical to the success of parenting interventions' (YJB, 2002b, p7). It is crucial to work in partnership with parents because success in addressing young people's behaviour is only achievable where parents reinforce key messages at home. Where this occurs, you should begin to see the fruits of your labour and identify tangible improvements in young people's attitudes to crime and its consequences. Ghate and Ramella (2002) identify two stages in the assessment process. Stage one is the basic level of assessment which should be used to identify whether there is a need to offer parental support and be based on the premise that 'all parents may potentially benefit from parenting support' (2002, p12).

If you recall in Chapter 6 we discussed the various components of the Asset assessment tool which included the 'family and relationships' dimensions. Where this stage of assessment reveals that aspects of parenting are likely to be playing a significant role in the young person's behaviour you might usefully decide to undertake a more detailed assessment. This second stage would involve a full assessment to identify parents' needs and to ascertain how these can be met. Usually the parenting co-ordinator within the YOT would carry out this assessment and it may well be the case that this person effectively co-works with the designated person working with the young person.

According to Ghate and Ramella (2002, p11), the purpose of such an assessment is to:

- Identify risks and protective factors in parenting, in areas such as youth offending, non-school attendance and anti-social behaviour;

- Record evidence of parenting risk factors and protective factors.

- Analyse information gathered.

- Provide services to meet identified need(s) and/or make referrals to appropriate agencies.

- Provide relevant and appropriate information for magistrates in report form when required.

- Build a positive relationship with parent(s)/family.

There are a number of key factors that you should consider when undertaking an assessment involving parents/carers.

- Assessment is a continuing process, not an event.

- It should lead to and inform an action plan.

- It should be flexible in order to take account of a wide range of individual needs.

- It involves assessing parents'/carers' circumstances, identifying any possible reasons why parents/carers may find it difficult to participate in programmes (for example, issues of mental and physical health, literacy skills, personal relationships and employment).

- Assessment should lead to referral to other agencies where there is an identified need for specialist services.

- It should address the needs of all parents/carers, whether resident or non-resident, including foster carers and grandparents.

- It should inform parents subject to a parenting order of their legal rights and responsibilities in relation to the order.

- Assessment clarifies expectations, and clearly demonstrates what needs to be achieved and how this is to be measured.

- It should be linked to the young person's Asset assessment (YJB, 2002b).

ACTIVITY **8.2**

Imagine you are working with a young person on a supervision order. Upon allocation of the case, you invite the parent to your first meeting with the young person and they do not attend. The young person tells you that they cannot get the time off work. Despite your attempts to contact them, you do not manage to speak to them. What would you do next?

National Standards make it very clear that, in relation to parental participation, 'steps should be taken to explore ways of supporting them to attend' (YJB, 2004b, p 2.8). In addition National Standards require you to make initial contact with parents 'before the end of the next working day following the court hearing' (YJB, 2004b, p 8.39). In cases of difficulty, you need to inform your manager of the situation and record all attempts to contact the parent. The nature of the order means the young person has continued to offend and/or the nature of the offending behaviour is serious. Therefore it is important that you make urgent contact with the parent. You will need to establish what hours the parents work and time they return home. If this is unsuccessful then compulsion is an option. The parent(s) need to understand the importance of their involvement.

This situation is a dilemma for you as the temptation is to quiz the young person about their parent's lifestyle in order to try and understand why there is resistance. There could be a whole host of reasons for their reluctance to meet with you, ranging from embarrassment, lack of understanding of the seriousness of the situation, cultural issues or something as simple as lack of parental literacy in English.

Working with victims

In the last two decades the victim of crime has travelled from the periphery of the criminal justice system to (virtual) centre stage. Evidence of this can be found in both the Crime and Disorder Act 1998 and the Youth Justice and Criminal Evidence Act 1999. This legislation is underpinned by restorative justice principles of responsibility, reparation and reintegration and it is the first time in English law that restorative justice has been part of the criminal justice system.

While working with victims is not new to the criminal justice system (the probation service has been working in this area for some time), working with victims in the youth justice system is. Commentators have suggested that this is one of the greatest challenges to the philosophy and cultural ideology of youth justice work (Bailey and Williams, 2000; Crawford and Newburn, 2003; Holdaway et al., 2001): 'The unequivocal adoption of a victim-focused approach represents one of the most important and far reaching cultural changes required by the Crime and Disorder Act 1998' (Holdaway et al. 2001, p36).

So how are victims involved in the criminal justice system? There are a number of ways, including a key component of the youth justice system, restorative justice. If you recall, in Chapters 3 and 7 we discussed restorative justice and how the principles of restorative justice, which are responsibility, reparation and reintegration, underpin youth justice legislation.

Victims and restorative justice

YOT practitioners are expected to apply the principles of restorative justice in all work with victims. Interestingly, the YJB appears committed to the philosophy of restorative justice: 'Unlike other interventions within youth justice, the prevention of offending is not the main aim of restorative justice. The repair of harm, including harm to relationships, is what matters most' (YJB, 2003d, p7).

Restorative justice effectively provides a voice for victims in criminal justice processes. Up until the mid-nineteenth century, victims of criminal offences were responsible for taking 'their' cases to court. This changed when the state appropriated the responsibility for prosecuting offenders, a reform designed to protect victims from retribution and introduce objectivity into decision-making regarding prosecutions. While there were clear benefits for victims as a result of these changes, it has been argued that their 'conflict' had been stolen by the state – the victim had no contact with the offender, had no opportunity to say how the crime had affected them and was reduced to witness rather than victim (Christie, 1977). Restorative justice provides the victim with the opportunity to re-engage with the justice system and have a voice in the process.

Code of practice for victims

Another and very recent way of involving victims in the criminal justice system is through the code of practice for victims (Home Office, 2005a). This was introduced in April 2006. The code effectively governs the services of a number of criminal justice agencies, including YOTs, to victims and witnesses of crime, ensuring a minimum level of service to victims in England and Wales. The code does not provide 'rights' as such for victims, so there is no legal redress if the code is breached. Victims and witnesses would need to pursue any complaints they might have about the services they receive through the linked ombudsman service.

Some categories of witnesses are entitled to special treatment, including 'vulnerable' victims. Vulnerable victims are defined as such under the Youth Justice and Criminal Evidence Act 1999 and include all victims under the age of 17 years. The code states that Youth Offending Teams are 'required to take account of victims' needs' (Home Office, 2005a, p23):

> *If it decides to make contact with victims, the YOT must explain its role fully and clearly and allow victims to make informed choices about whether they want any involvement and if so, the nature of that involvement. The involvement of victims must always be voluntary; victims must not be asked to do anything which is primarily for the benefit of the offender.* (Section 11.4)

The code also requires YOTs to record the reasons for decisions not to allow victims to participate in any restorative intervention. This is an important point, because although the government is very committed to involving victims in the youth justice system, victims do not have any legal right to be involved. For example, the Youth Justice and Criminal Evidence Act 1999 states quite clearly that victims *may* attend a Youth Offender Panel. The decision is at the discretion of the YOT practitioner, based on a number of considerations such as suitability for restorative justice and health and safety reasons, more of which we will discuss later in the chapter.

Victim personal statements

Victim personal statements are yet another way victims might choose to engage in the criminal justice process. Victim personal statements were introduced in England and Wales in 2001, providing victims with the opportunity to explain the emotional, financial and other effects of a crime on them. Unlike such statements used in the United States, they can only be referred to if there is a guilty plea, or once a jury has returned a verdict (Goodey, 2005). The statement can be taken at the same time as the police officer takes the evidential statement. While this initiative provides an ideal opportunity for the victim to be heard, research suggests they are not widely used and in many areas across England and Wales both police and victims struggle to understand them (Home Office, 2004a).

Victims and Youth Offending Teams

Since their inception in 1998, Youth Offending Teams have struggled, to some degree, to embed work with victims of crime. One of the main concerns that youth justice practitioners have raised is about the possible conflict of interest if required to work with both the young person and the victim. Some practitioners feel that it is not possible to work with a young person and attempt to meet their needs if they also have to meet with the victim and hear from them about how the crime has affected them (Angus, 2001).

ACTIVITY 8.3

Take a couple of minutes to think about victims: what images come into your head? Are they adults or young people? Are they male or female?

Research has shown that there has been a significant rise in crimes against young people (Home Office, 2005c; Smith, 2003a; Victim Support, 2003). These crimes tend to be perpetrated by other young people, often people known to the victim. So, in the field of youth justice, the likelihood is that the victims you have contact with will be young people. However, there will be some exceptions to this; where a young person has committed a burglary or some kind of car crime, then the victim will almost certainly be adult. An added twist to the victim/offender relationship in youth justice is the fact that the young person may well have committed a crime against a parent. These crimes are predominantly theft and criminal damage although they may include assault. This is a complex area for practitioners who will need to consider how to balance the needs of young people (who are of primary concern) against providing some level of support to parent victims, who may well be their primary carers.

There are very few agencies offering support to victims and the largest of these is Victim Support. This is a national organisation offering practical help and emotional support to all victims of crime, irrespective of whether it is reported to the police or not. Every area will have a local scheme and the police officer in the YOT will have contact details (**www.victimsupport.org.uk**).

National Standards and work with victims

National Standards provide the framework for work with victims of crime. National Standard 5 refers to restorative justice, work with victims of crime and community payback (YJB, 2004b, p28). Broadly the National Standard requires all YOT practitioners to work with victims in a professional and sensitive manner. This is about respecting their wishes and not coercing them into engaging in restorative justice processes. But perhaps most importantly, it is about recognising that to engage victims in the youth justice system should not be primarily for the benefit of the offender, but should also be beneficial for the victim.

The idea of working with victims might be particularly difficult if you have had little experience of working with this client group. However, experience of working with young people who offend shows that many have been victims of crime. So think about your work with the young person. How have they experienced being a victim? How did they feel?

Confidentiality and work with victims

National Standards (5.4, 5.5 and 5.6) make reference to the data held by YOTs about victims and offenders. Practitioners in the YOT, working with both the victim and the young person, will need to be mindful about what information to share and with whom. No details about the young person should be disclosed to the victim and vice versa. Any information about the victim that is held by the YOT should be destroyed once the victim has disengaged from any restorative activity.

National Standards general principles in victim contact work

There are five guiding principles in relation to work with victims (YJB, 2004b, p29):

1 The wishes of victims in relation to their involvement in restorative justice processes must be respected by YOT staff at all times.

2 The need of victims to feel safe.

3 Victims should be given sufficient information to enable them to make informed choices about whether, and at what level, they wish to be involved in restorative justice processes.

4 Restorative justice services offered will include victims being able to provide information about the effects of crime, and to receive information about the results of the intervention, apologies, direct and indirect reparation and mediation.

5 Before any direct contact between victim and young person takes place, a full risk assessment must be undertaken.

ACTIVITY 8.4

Think about working with victims. We have already mentioned one possible reason why some practitioners might struggle working with this particular group of service users. What factors might you need to consider before you begin to work with victims of crime?

You might have considered training to provide essential skills to work with victims. This has been a problem for many practitioners since the introduction of Youth Offending Teams (Home Office, 2004). Williams (2000) suggests that practitioners need to consider both the impact of crime upon victims and how to work directly with them.

Impact of crime

The impact of a crime upon a victim is complex, and additional reading may help you in gaining an understanding of victimisation. However, we will endeavour to cover some key points, which should assist you in work with young people.

Even though the victim and the offender may not engage in any form of restorative justice, it is important to consider the possible impact the young person's behaviour might have had on the victim. What research does tell us is that the severity of the crime does not necessarily determine the impact upon the victim. People's responses are individual and therefore unpredictable (Williams, 1999).

The experience of a crime victim is unique in the sense that the suffering caused involves an intentional act inflicted by one person on another. The personal nature of such intrusion is likely to have a profound effect on how crime victims perceive others (Reeves and Mulley, 2000, p126). Victims can present with a number of symptoms in the aftermath of crime, which can be broadly categorised under three main headings:

Physical
Apart from obvious physical injuries sustained during a violent crime, victims may also suffer from a range of physiological effects including:

- headaches
- nausea
- insomnia and lethargy.

Emotional and psychological

Victims present with an array of responses to victimisation including:

- feelings of disempowerment

- low self-esteem

- shock

- disbelief

- fear

- anger

- guilt

- self-blame

- revenge.

These are normal responses to an abnormal situation.

Behavioural change

Behavioural change can manifest itself in a number of ways:

- Avoidance of areas and situations that remind the victim of the crime.

- Moving house.

- Withdrawing from social contact.

- Dependency or increased dependency on drugs/alcohol.

- In extreme cases attempts to alter their appearance or behaviour.

Process of recovery

The process of recovery from a crime is not dissimilar to bereavement. There is an initial response of shock and denial, giving way to a period of depression and disorganisation. The victim may blame themselves in some way. For example, a victim of a burglary may blame themselves because they failed to secure a window or door. This feeling of self-blame can often lead to low self-esteem. The victim may move on to a stage of reconstruction and acceptance, acknowledging the crime and realising they cannot turn the clock back. There is a final stage of readjustment that brings with it an acceptance and a return of self-esteem and self-worth. However, the victim's process of recovery is to some extent determined by external factors, such as the response of the criminal justice system as well as that of friends and family.

It is important to take this into account if you are working with a victim in a restorative justice intervention. Attending a Youth Offender Panel may reawaken some of the feelings the victim experienced in the aftermath of the crime. It would be useful to have a Victim Support contact number or leaflet to offer to the victim. Even if they don't necessarily appear upset at the time, it may be of use later on. Research shows that a person's ability to recover from a crime is significantly improved when others recognise the significance of the event (Victim Support, 2002).

Youth Offender Panels, victims and social workpractice

As mentioned above, a young person receiving a referral order will be required to attend a Youth Offender Panel. Section 7 of the Youth Justice and Criminal Evidence Act 1999 states that victims *may* be invited to attend the panel, but this is at the discretion of the panel, which in turn is advised by the YOT practitioner. It is important at this point to say that research shows that victim attendance at panels is very low. In the evaluation of the referral order pilots only 13 per cent of victims who were eligible to take part in referral orders did so. This is unsurprising when 50 per cent were never contacted and invited to attend (Newburn et al., 2001). However, it is likely the police officer or dedicated victim worker (if the YOT has one) would have made the initial contact with the victim and will be in a position to advise on the appropriateness of the victim attending the panel. If the victim does wish to attend, it is unlikely that a YOT practitioner will meet with the victim until the day of the panel.

ACTIVITY 8.5

Kelly is 15 and has received a four month referral order for actual bodily harm (ABH). Kelly assaulted Lucy, a girl in her class at school. You are due to meet with Kelly and her mum to discuss the Youth Offender Panel which is due to take place next week. The police officer in the YOT has informed you that Lucy wishes to attend the panel with her mum. Kelly has told you previously that Lucy had been abusive to her at school and on one occasion even hit her. However in this most recent incident Lucy was abusive again and Kelly could not take any more and lashed out, which resulted in Lucy receiving a cut to her lip and bruising on her cheek. Kelly appears to show little remorse.

- *What issues do you need to discuss with Kelly and her mum prior to the panel?*

- *What do you need to do to ensure the panel runs smoothly?*

This is both a complex and a common problem facing practitioners. Often there is a history between young victims and young offenders. This may involve simply an exchange of words – name-calling – at one end of the scale, or escalate into violence at the other.

When meeting with Kelly and her mother it is essential that you alert them to the fact that Lucy and her mother will be attending. Given the nature of the offence and the circumstances leading up to the offence, it will be important to stress to Kelly that she must make every effort to remain calm at the panel. Explain to Kelly that she will be given an opportunity to say how and why she felt angry. Kelly's mother will also have a chance to speak and give her perspective on her daughter's behaviour.

In terms of the actual panel, there are a number of issues that may need active consideration, both in relation to the specific case study but also more generally when working with young people attending a panel where the victim is also due to attend.

- The reaction of both victim and young person when they meet. Do the victim and the young person know one another?

- Expectations of the victim. Are they realistic?

- Panel members' experience and knowledge in relation to victims of crime.

In order to overcome these potential problems it is important to plan. First, it is essential that the young person is informed that the victim will be attending. You will need to explain to them the process of the panel and what contribution the victim can make. You should also meet with the victim prior to the panel commencing. At this point it is important to clarify with the victim their expectations. You will need to point out that the panel is not a rerun of the court process. You will need to explain the process of the panel to victims and their specific role in advising the panel how the crime has impacted on them. You should also discuss with the panel members, especially the member who will be chairing the meeting, any issues or concerns they may have. You may need to advise the Panel Chair of the importance of establishing ground rules at the commencement of the panel. These should include the use of respectful language, allowing everyone the chance to speak without interruption, the need to respect confidentiality and the limitations of that confidentiality (YJB, 2001).

Working with volunteers

Volunteering in youth justice work is well established and based on many years of experience. The Youth Justice Board are keen to maintain volunteer involvement in the new youth justice system and many voluntary projects in youth justice are YJB funded. In its first annual report, the YJB stated: 'Voluntary organisations have a vital role to play by providing the energy, enthusiasm and expertise to help the statutory services fulfil their role and by providing preventative services. Volunteers from all parts of society can help give young people at risk a chance' (cited in Bailey and Williams, 2000, p52).

Mentoring

Volunteers work in a number of areas within youth justice including the role of mentor, which involves a one-to-one relationship between the young person and a supportive adult mentor. The aim of mentoring is to 'make constructive changes in the life and behaviour of the young person' (YJB, 2005, p6). The YJB (2005a, p6) identifies five essential elements required by an effective mentor:

- Active listening skills.

- Ability to establish and maintain a shared agenda.

- Time to develop trusting relationships.

- Ability to sustain a high level of contact with the young person and encourage positive interactions.

- Adequate initial training and ongoing support.

YOTs often 'buy in' this service from voluntary sector mentoring agencies. It is likely that YOT involvement with the mentor may be limited to that of a supporting role. For YOT practitioners it is important to maintain regular contact with the mentor in order to support both the mentor and the young person in developing the mentoring role.

Community panel members

The largest group of volunteers working in the youth justice system are community panel members. These are men and women recruited from the local community who sit on Youth Offender Panels. Panel members are the third component of the restorative justice triangle which underpins the youth justice system. At a Youth Offender Panel we have a young offender, a victim (or victim representation) and the panel member representing the community. While the role of the panel member is to represent the wider community, panel members are unable to perform this function holistically, but provide a community perspective according to their socio-economic position. Like volunteering generally in Britain, the average youth justice volunteer is female, middle-aged and middle-class (Newburn et al., 2001).

There are approximately 7,000 panel members in England and Wales, contributing to decision-making in over 30 per cent of youth court cases (Flanagan, 2005). On average, panel members attend and sit on panels between 20 and 40 times per year (Biermann and Moulton, 2003, p5).

Working relationship with panel members

While the Home Office is pleased with the success of Youth Offender Panels and the contribution that volunteers make, not everyone perceives volunteer contributions so positively. Home Office commissioned research into panel members found that generally YOTs were pleased with the contribution that the volunteers had made and that they appeared very committed to their role (Biermann and Moulton, 2003, p8). However the research also revealed that some panel members required more support than others and identified that additional training for both panel members and staff to support them would be helpful. Others, however, have raised a number of concerns suggesting that there is a significant difference between working with voluntary agencies and working with volunteers (Bailey and Williams, 2000, p51).

Crawford and Newburn suggest that the volunteer panel member/YOT practitioner role is one of the most 'radical aspects of Youth Offender Panels in which they seek to draw lay volunteers into the decision making process' (Crawford and Newburn, 2003, p142). This research revealed some difference of opinions in how panel members were perceived by YOT staff. When they were asked about their working relationship with panel members, 62 per cent of staff questioned felt the relationship was very good (2003, p144). However, YOT managers took a slightly different view saying that some members of staff were reluctant to work with volunteer panel members. One of the main concerns for practitioners was having to 'open up their practice to outsiders' (2003, p144) with panels being led and directed by unqualified people.

We know that over a third of all disposals from the Youth Courts are referral orders and given this situation YOT practitioners will inevitably be working with victims and volunteers at the Youth Offender Panel, these being the two areas of work most new to YOTs.

RESEARCH SUMMARY

In the evaluation of the referral order pilots, researchers identified three broad approaches that YOT practitioners applied to their role at a Youth Offender Panel; the Passive Supporter, the Team Player, and the Steerer. The choice of approach was determined by the degree to which the YOT practitioner 'sought to influence the course of Panels' (Newburn et al., 2001, pvi)

Your role at the panel

When attending a Youth Offender Panel you will need to consider your role carefully. It is a role unlike any other undertaken within a YOT. The Youth Offender Panel itself is unique in as much as there are two lay members of the panel with decision-making responsibilities working within a statutory framework. In some ways the three approaches identified by Newman et al. (2001) could potentially be applied to your practice during the course of a panel. Let us consider key action points under the three headings.

Passive supporter

- *Supporting the young person* – you are not there to legally represent young people in the same way that a solicitor might represent them at court. You would have explained the panel process to both young people and their parents, who are likely to attend either voluntarily or at the request of the court.

- *Supporting the panel members* – each YOT will have a team of panel members and it is likely that you will have the opportunity to meet and work with most of them. Good practice would suggest that when meeting with panel members beforehand, you should check their understanding of the process and provide them with opportunities to discuss any queries with you.

Team player

This role has the feel of a co-ordinator and facilitator combined. There are a number of key areas you will need to consider:

- *Venue* – most panels are held away from the YOT office, often in community centres or offices belonging to social services departments or schools. You will need to arrive at the venue in sufficient time to prepare rooms, particularly if the victim is expected to attend, and you may need an additional room for them to wait in.

- *Panel report* – copies of the report should be made available to panel members, young people and parents. Give reports out in sufficient time for panel members to read and be ready to answer any queries they may have. Likewise, allow sufficient time for the young people and parents to read through reports. Ideally they should see them prior to the panel, but sometimes this is not always possible.

- *Victim attendance* – if victims are to attend consider carefully the timing of their arrival. Ideally this should be slightly later than young people and their parents. It may be that victims attend with supporters. It is very important that you provide sufficient time to explain the process of the panel and gain an understanding of their expectations. It would be helpful to have details of the victim support scheme local to the YOT area (all victim support schemes have leaflets), which you can pass to victims. If victims are due to attend, then it is important to alert panel members to this fact and answer any queries or concerns they may have.

- *Post panel* – once panels have finished it is appropriate to briefly discuss with the panel members any concerns they might have as a result of the process. It may be that panel members are fairly new, in which case a debrief of the process might be helpful, or a panel may have been particularly difficult. Again it is important that you give panel members time to discuss this.

Steerer

You may take on the role of steerer either because panel members are inexperienced or because panels lose their focus. The steering role is one that applies during the course of panels and may well include the following:

- *Panel focus* – the purpose of panels is to draw up a contract taking into account the needs of young people in the aftermath of crime. It is important that panels do not revert to the role of a court. The case has already been heard and while it is important for panels to have an understanding about how the young person was feeling and behaving during and after the crime, they are not about looking at evidence. Sometimes panel members steer towards the latter role and you will need to bring them back on track.

- *Legal status* – while it is the responsibility of Panel Chairs to explain the purpose and status of the panel, it is essential that young people and their parents are aware, when signing contracts, that these become legal documents with implications for young people if they are breached. If Panel Chairs do not make this clear, then you will need to remind them.

- *Victim attendance* – this may be a difficult issue even for very experienced panel members. As mentioned earlier, research showed that few victims choose to attend panels, so the panel members are probably unlikely to have attended a panel with a victim present. You may need to speak with panel members before panels commence, paying particular attention to the order of the proceedings and also to consider the potential risk factors and strategies to deal with situations where victims may become upset or even angry.

Clearly your role here is central to the success of panels, but needs to be carefully managed. It is about making use of your professional skill to facilitate effective communication between all parties attending panels. As Crawford and Newburn mention, the opportunity to participate in panels can 'facilitate the "opening up" of otherwise potentially introspective professional cultures, which militate against greater public participation' (Crawford and Newburn, 2003, p153).

C H A P T E R   S U M M A R Y

In this chapter we have considered the implications for working within the mixed economy that comprises the youth justice system, with particular emphasis on working with volunteers, victims and family members. Youth justice practitioners' ability to manage these pseudo-professional interactions effectively is vital to increasing the likelihood of successful youth justice outcomes. We have discussed professional roles and responsibilities in relation to these individuals and looked at some of the potential issues to consider when working with them and discussed ways of maximising effective recovery. During the activities and discussion, we have exposed and clarified the importance of developing good working relationships with young people's parents and identified strategies to deal with situations where they appear reluctant to engage. Finally we have debated and considered best practice in working with volunteers in the youth justice system.

FURTHER READING

Williams, B (ed) (2002) *Reparation and victim-focused social work*. London: Jessica Kingsley.
A useful book providing an insight into working with victims of crime, which will be helpful in both direct work with victims, and when considering the victim perspective in work with young people.

Dignan, J (2005) *Understanding victims and restorative justice*. Maidenhead: Open University Press.
A detailed overview of the role of the victim in restorative justice which will be particularly useful given the YJB focus on involving victims in the youth justice process.

WEBSITES

www.parentlineplus.org.uk
A voluntary organisation offering support to anyone parenting a child.

www.homeoffice.gov.uk/crime-victims
Specific department within the Home Office dealing with victim matters.

www.youth-justice-board.gov.uk/WorkingwithVictims
Department within the YJB relating to victim matters.

www.victimsupport.org.uk
Website for the largest victim agency in the UK.

Chapter 9
Looking forward

Paul Dugmore and Jane Pickford

Introduction

This chapter examines three key areas relating to your effective future practice as a youth justice professional: transferable skills; continuing professional development; and the possibilities for future legislation in the youth justice arena. As a youth justice practitioner you will become aware that laws and procedures are regularly subject to change. In order to face the challenges of change within your professional environment, you must keep abreast of contemporary policy debates, reports, reviews and proposals. Updating sessions and keeping your eye on professional journals and quality newspapers will assist you in keeping up to date with contemporary practice and future reforms. It is also vital that you continue to develop your skills as a practitioner and learn how some of the skills you have acquired can be transferred to other professional contexts.

This chapter will guide you in looking forward to achieving your full potential as a competent professional who is able to assimilate change and be prepared for future challenges.

Transferable skills

Hopefully, throughout this book and during the course of your professional training, you have come to recognise the vast range of skills that are required of you as a fully fledged competent social work practitioner. While we have considered these skills within the context of youth justice, most, if not all, of these skills will be applicable should you decide to move into another area of social work or an entirely different profession altogether. All your work will be within a multi-agency context so you will be used to working with a range of other professionals with different identities and philosophies from your own. In order to do this effectively you need to be able to link the knowledge you have acquired to your practice, particularly that of human behaviour and using research findings to influence your practice (Trevithick, 2005).

You should be reasonably, if not very, skilled at communicating with many different types of individuals from a range of backgrounds:

- Young people aged 10 to 19 of different gender, cultural and ethnic backgrounds, with disabilities, learning difficulties, behavioural problems, mental ill-health, and substance misuse problems. This is not an exhaustive list.

- Parents and carers from many different family compositions, foster carers, residential workers.

- Other professionals: police, social workers, health professionals, teachers and other education professionals, magistrates, judges, probation officers, prison officers, solicitors, barristers.

You will also be experienced in talking/presenting within a range of environments: young people's homes, courts, case conferences, young offender institutes, different offices. You will have experience of interviewing people and carrying out assessments, using a structured assessment tool, and writing up the assessment and subsequent reports for a range of audiences – such as the court. You will be able to make decisions based on risk and potential risk, some of which may be very difficult, and able to work to deadlines and under pressure, sometimes in crisis. You will be able to apply a number of theoretical approaches to your work with young people and their families.

All of these will be useful should you decide to move into another social work setting or out of the profession altogether. These are skills that you will continue to develop as every new situation you encounter will enable you to learn something new. It is important that you continue to approach your practice with an open mind and seek to supplement this with the acquisition of new knowledge. In such a fast-moving social care world and a youth justice system with philosophical conflicts, changes and inconsistencies, you must also hold on to the core social work values that we have discussed throughout this book such as respect for people, social justice, empowerment, anti-discriminatory and anti-oppressive practice, acceptance and partnership. Being part of a multi-agency YOT might make it easy for your professional identity to be subsumed into a generic YOT identity that takes a more justice-based, punitive approach to youth offending, rather than championing a welfare approach seeking to understand (not collude with) a young person's offending behaviour within the wider context of their life. Your role is to assess their behaviour and plan appropriate intervention within a particular theoretical framework based on research evidence. Other professionals within the YOT will not have had this education and training and therefore the knowledge you possess is specific to your profession and needs to be central to all practice with young people. As well as knowledge of a range of social work theories and models of intervention, you have also acquired knowledge of different criminological theories which help to explain offending behaviour.

Social work often receives a bad press and you are likely to be subjected to negative opinions and perceptions of you and your profession from service users and other professionals. Being part of a registered profession and working within codes of practice should help to improve the standing of social work but you also need to have confidence and pride in your practice and abilities, and in those of your peers, and to challenge some of the stereotypes that exist about social workers. Thompson (2005) offers some useful strategies for dealing with negative attitudes towards social workers.

Continuing professional development (CPD)

Once you have qualified as a social worker, your learning will not stop; some would argue that this is where it really begins. You will be required to attend training in order to increase your knowledge and skills as you join a new team and take up a post as a social worker. Remember that part of the GSCC Code of Practice requires social workers to 'Be accountable for the quality of their work and take responsibility for maintaining and improving their knowledge and skills' (GSCC, 2002). This means that it is your responsibility as a professional, as well as that of your employer, to ensure that you are able to carry out the roles and responsibilities required of you in terms of being equipped with the necessary skills and knowledge.

As a qualified social worker it is extremely important that you are registered with the GSCC; this confirms that you are qualified and registered to practise as a social worker. Part of this professional registration requires that all social workers undertake five days of CPD each year. Without this you will not have your registration renewed. This CPD is widely interpreted and the GSCC provides examples on its website of how you might undertake CPD (**www.gscc.org.uk**). For example, you may wish to:

- Arrange to shadow the work of a colleague in a related team or profession.
- Negotiate protected time to research latest policy and good practice developments in your field of practice.
- Undertake a piece of research related to your practice.

The GSCC also has responsibilty for overseeing the post-qualifying training of social workers and in 2007 a new post-qualifying framework will be introduced. If you are studying for a certificated post-qualifying award, these studies can also be used as evidence that you meet the post-registration training and learning requirements. From 2007 post-qualifying awards will be introduced allowing social workers to continue their education and training in a modular way. There will be three levels of awards, each one corresponding to a stage of professional and career development: the specialist award; the higher specialist award; and the advanced award.

There are five specialisms, none of which refer to youth justice specifically. However, one of these will cover children and young people, their families and carers. As the new framework has yet to be implemented, it is at this stage uncertain as to how it will look. However, it is anticipated that there will be consistency across some modules, such as a consolidation module that will make up part of the specialist award, which all social workers will need to complete before going on to complete more specific modules. It is envisaged that some specialist award providers will offer youth justice modules. The GSCC website will contain updated information and guidance on this as it becomes available.

The YJB has developed a National Qualifications Framework that provides a strategy for ensuring that the youth justice workforce is appropriately trained and qualified. Currently the focus has been on providing qualifications for those practitioners who do not already hold any professional qualification, and this has led to the introduction of a Foundation degree. However, the YJB has also indicated that higher level qualifications will be designed at a later stage to provide routes for continued learning. Again, how this will look remains to be seen but the YJB website will keep you updated; it is important for you to be aware of the full range of options open to you at post-qualifying level. You will not only be aware of current evidence-based, research-led, best practice but also be able to contribute to the development of such knowledge as a practitioner. You will further be equipped to reflect critically on your practice so that it retains a clear social work focus, and that young people are receiving a high-quality service that meets their need. If you are not finding your work sufficiently satisfying and rewarding, you should be able to identify an alternative challenge based on your existing knowledge and skills.

ACTIVITY **9.1**

What transferable skills do you already have and which ones would you like to develop? Which type of CPD do you think might be useful for you once in practice?

Future youth justice legislation

In this section we consider the various proposals for youth justice practice that have been discussed by the Government over the last few years. It is noteworthy that academics and practitioners have been braced for these changes for a number of years; indeed we believed that legislation would follow soon after the consultation paper *Youth justice – The next steps* (Home Office, 2003d). However, new legislation is still awaited: despite the publication of a Green Paper *Youth matters* (Home Office 2005e) and a draft Youth Justice Bill which was published but not enacted in the 2004/05 session of Parliament, no new statute has emerged. Early in 2006 it was thought that measures covering the proposed radical shake-up of youth justice practice would be contained in the criminal justice reforms contained in the Police and Justice Bill 2006, but alas they were not.

The review of proposals below will enable you to be forewarned of the probable changes to youth justice practice that are arguably forthcoming. Keep your eyes on the quality newspapers, the Home Office and the Youth Justice Board's websites!

Youth justice – *The next steps* and *Every child matters*

The Green Paper *Every child matters* (Home Office, 2003a) outlined proposals for reforming children's services generally and led to the Children Act 2004 (see Chapter 4). Alongside this paper, the Government published a companion document, *Youth justice – The next steps* (Home Office, 2003d) a separate consultation paper covering proposed future reforms to the youth justice system. Though these have not been passed into legislation at the time of writing (summer 2006) it is useful to outline the major proposals. The paper made reference to nine key areas (see NACRO, 2003a):

- *The basic approach*. Though England and Wales has the lowest age of criminal responsibility, at 10 years, compared to other European countries (apart from Scotland, where the age is 8; however here all but approximately 10 per cent of the most serious offenders are dealt with by a social work panel – a Children's Hearing – and not the courts), the government does not propose to change this. This failure to increase the age of criminal responsibility is in direct opposition to the recommendations of the UN Committee on the Rights of the Child, the Committee on Human Rights and the stated view of many children's charities.

- *Pre-court diversion*. The government wishes to increase the use of diversionary schemes, and though there are no proposals to change the current reprimand and final warning system, there are calls for views about the possible expansion of referral order type measures, which ensure the greater participation of victims and the local community.

- *Sentencing structure and rationale*. Currently the sentencing of young people is dominated by three principles: the 'welfare principle' enshrined in the Children and Young Persons Act 1933; the principle of proportionality contained in the Criminal Justice Act 1991; and the aim of preventing offending, a main focus of the Crime and Disorder Act 1998. The government proposes to scrap the first two. It is envisaged (by NACRO, 2003a) that sentencers would also take into account issues such as vulnerability, public protection, optimum punishment, parental obligation, reparation and previous interventions – but that the principal aim of preventing offending will prevail. From a criminological standpoint, this would represent a move away from classicist notions of proportionality towards the positivist ideal of preventionism and sentences tailor-made to fit the criminal as opposed to the crime. The abandonment of the long-standing welfare principle is concerning and it seems to be contrary to the focus on promotion of the well-being of the child/young person evident in *Every child matters* and enshrined in the Children Act 2004.

- *Families and communities*. The government wishes to expand the use of the parenting order and other means of ensuring 'whole family' involvement in youth crime intervention, including the active encouragement of father participation and a focus on encouraging family group conferencing.

- *Policing, public order and the courts*. This includes strengthening enforcement of anti-social behaviour measures via the youth court; providing YOT/local authority reports for courts regarding remand/bail recommendations; and promoting an increased understanding by children and young people of court processes (with the development of a 'young defendant's pack' to help young people and their families understand proceedings). In addition, specialist training is proposed for Crown Court judges. It is arguably not clear whether the latter measure will address the concerns expressed by the UN Committee on the Rights of the Child and the European Court in *Thompson and Venables* [1999] which regarded the Crown Court as essentially an adult court that was unsuitable for dealing with children and young defendants (see Chapter 1).

- *Remands*. This includes proposals for greater use of bail and non-custodial remands where possible and the expansion of ISSP bail packages to support this. An extension of the use of remand foster placements is recommended, as is the possibility of remand hostels for some upper age range youth offenders.

- *Community sentencing*. This area contains arguably the most radical proposal regarding the practice of youth justice in that it recommends the scrapping of nine current community sentences and their replacement with one generic sentence in the form of an expanded action plan order (APO). The proposed expanded APO could be ordered for a period of between 3 and 24 months and ideally would contain two or three interventions chosen from a 'comprehensive menu' of possible measures, including:

  – Fines

  – Reparation

  – Personal support from 'befrienders'

  – Drug and alcohol awareness

  – Anger management

  – Mentoring

  – Sessions on appropriate sexual behaviour

  – Reporting and supervision requirements

  – Victim–offender mediation

  – Family group conferencing

  – Attendance at junior activity/attendance centres.

These conditions might also include residence requirements – at the family home, through expanded foster placements, hostels or local authority accommodation. Mental health treatment might also be added if necessary.

It is also proposed that the referral order be expanded, including the possibility that a referral order might be allowed on a further conviction.

In order to assist implementation of these changes, there is a proposal that YOTs would be encouraged to make 'child behaviour contracts' with young people on court orders.

- *Intensive sentences and custody*. These proposals include plans to expand the use of ISSP as a high-tariff sentence and to utilise the principles of an ISSP (up to six months) as an option combined with custody in the form of a new 'intensive supervision or detention order' (ISDO) for serious and repeat offenders. This will give the court the option of *combining* ISSP with a custodial disposal. However, alongside the strengthened community ISSP and the new ISDO detention with ISSP, under the proposals it appears (though it is not clear) that the DTO will still remain largely in its current form as a further option – but that the second part of the order spent in the community could be similar to and contain some of the conditions proposed in the new expanded action plan order (above). It is proposed that restrictions relating to this sentence for 12–14 year olds be removed, with a maximum for this age group of 12 months. Practitioners might be concerned about this latter proposal. Further, it was noted that detention could include open and semi-secure facilities. There is also a promise to address safeguarding procedures for females and vulnerable males in custody.

- *Staff and organisation*. Proposals in this area relate to examining the membership of YOTs, promoting further profession-specific training and investigating multi-agency links with YOTs (with a view to joined-up service provision outlined in the Children Act 2004 – see Chapter 4).

Overall, the focus of these proposals is on diversion, reducing remand and custodial detention (the latter with a fortified ISSP), a reduction in the amount of community disposal options (with a fortified APO), a further focus on reparation and a move away from the welfare and proportionality principles of sentencing. NACRO point to the possible complexity and the risk of expansionism being created at the custodial level, but welcome some of the diversionary measures proposed. However, 'How these measures are implemented would be crucial, with the outcome in some doubt. History is littered with legislation that has failed to be implemented in practice, or that has had outcomes contrary to those intended' (NACRO, 2003a, p7).

Youth justice 2004: A review of the reformed youth justice system

It is worth noting the comments of the Audit Commission's latest review of youth justice services (2004) as it could have some impact upon future government proposals. The Audit Commission's general review was favourable, largely indicating that the new system showed considerable improvements from the old system they reviewed in 1996 (*Misspent youth*). However, they commented upon five areas of youth justice services that still needed attention following the staged implementation of the radical reforms that flowed from the Crime and Disorder Act 1998 and the Youth Justice and Criminal Evidence Act 1999.

1 *A need to focus court work towards dealing with serious and persistent offenders.* The Commission recommended an extension of the use of diversionary practice for non-serious offenders and an extended use of the referral order – specifically the possibility of a three-month order for young people who have not appeared at court before, to be issued at the discretion of the Prosecution Service. Courts would then be freed up to deal with the most complex cases and provide regular reviews.

2 *A need to improve court procedures.* The Commission commented upon the lack of understanding of court practice experienced by young defendants and their guardians. In addition, magistrates need further specialised training and the progress of specific cases should be regularly reviewed, with encouragement or changes made to interventions, as appropriate.

3 *A need to make sentencing practice more cost-effective*. The Commission noted that custody is the most expensive yet least efficient sentence. The use of ISSPs should be extended.

4 *A necessity to address the wide-ranging needs of offenders*. The Commission recommended that young people's needs should be met by a holistic approach, including (a) increasing the frequency and quality of contact with supervising officers; (b) ensuring that young people are kept in/given education and training while undertaking sentencing requirements; (c) liaising with health (including mental health) services to ensure the well-being of the young person; and (d) ensuring accessible substance misuse support and accommodation provision.

5 *The need to prevent first-time offending*. The Commission noted that young people in custody often have a history of previous local authority or other service interventions. Planned and targeted early intervention is necessary, as is greater co-ordination between various services that deal with young people.

It can be seen that some of the Audit Commission's concerns (though not all) mirror a number of the proposals outlined in *Youth justice – The next steps*, above.

Youth matters

The Green Paper *Youth matters* (Home Office, 2005e) was published (largely following the proposals set out in the consultation paper *Every child matters*) and though it did not cover youth justice specifically, it addressed four aims in relation to youths in particular: (a) positive activities and empowerment; (b) encouraging young people to become involved in their communities (including as volunteers); (c) providing better information, advice and guidance for young people; and (d) providing better and more personalised services for young people with problems or who get into trouble.

It is the latter aim that relates to youth offending. The proposals put forward in order to achieve this aim include promoting a multi-agency, integrated approach to young people who find themselves in this category and in need of help. An integrated package of support should be actioned for each young person, with one lead, named professional as co-ordinator of the package. The government proposes to merge a range of existing programmes that currently focus on specific aspects of youth services and work through children's trusts in order to address the needs of young people using a holistic approach. The issues to be tackled in this holistic manner include teenage pregnancy, young people not receiving education or training, dealing with young people with drug or alcohol problems and dealing with youth crime – the latter to help fulfil the existing duty upon local authorities under Section 17 of the Crime and Disorder Act 1998.

Draft Youth Justice Bill 2005 (not enacted)

Though a youth justice bill was mentioned in the Queen's Speech for the 2004/05 session of Parliament, no formal bill arrived (despite a Draft Youth Justice Bill appearing on government websites). The bill was not mentioned in plans for the 2005/06 timetable, though it was speculated that youth justice measures might be contained within a bill entitled

Sentencing and Youth Justice at the end of 2005 or within the Police and Justice Bill released in January 2006. However this was not the case but it is expected that the Government still wishes to produce a stand-alone statute on youth justice. It is envisaged that the forthcoming bill will reflect measures proposed in the consultation paper *Youth justice – The next steps* (Home office, 2003d, outlined above).

The Draft Youth Justice Bill, which was not enacted, mainly proposed some of the measures that were outlined in the 2003 consultation paper, namely:

- To fix the primary purpose of youth sentencing as prevention of offending.

- To establish more effective community sentences with a simplified structure and a menu of measures from which courts can compile a suitable package for the individual with the key aim of rehabilitation.

- To develop the ISSP as a robust alternative to a custodial sentence where appropriate.

- To use DTOs when there is a need to remove the offender from the community.

- To place DTO trainees in open conditions, and allow temporary release with tagging, to improve integration of the offender back into their local community after release to prevent re-offending (www.commonsleader.gov.uk).

In February 2006 the Home Office published its five-year strategy, *Protecting the public and reducing re-offending*. It restates its intention to replace nine existing community orders with a single community sentence for juveniles called a 'youth rehabilitation order'. We are currently (summer 2006) awaiting the publication of a draft bill to cover the proposals outlined for youth justice reform. As recommended earlier, you should monitor the YJB and Home Office websites for the emergence of draft legislation in this area of practice.

ACTIVITY **9.2**

Outline the most important reforms that are likely to occur in youth justice. Which changes are likely to have the most significant impact on practice? Will the proposed measures lead to a re-orientation in youth justice theory?

C H A P T E R   S U M M A R Y

In this chapter we have examined the skills you will develop as a youth justice practitioner and analysed their transferability to other professional contexts. We have also stressed the importance of continuing your professional development once *in situ* as a practitioner and outlined the various options in relation to that. Finally we have examined recent government proposals relating to potential changes to the youth justice system. Perhaps one of the things most evidenced throughout this book is what a fast-changing and evolving environment the youth justice system is, with frequent legislative and political reform: more than 50 bills to reform the criminal justice system have been introduced since Labour came to power in 1997. Even at the time of writing the criminal justice system is the subject of intense media spotlight. The *Guardian* (22 June 2006) reported that Tony Blair was warned by a leading academic expert, Professor Ian Loader, to 'think hard' before introducing any more 'headline-grabbing' law and order legislation, urging the prime minister to be the 'voice of reason and restraint' rather than the 'uncritical cipher' of public anger on the issue. The impact such change can have on practitioners should not be underestimated and some of the skills you will need to develop in order to survive will be change management and resilience skills.

In order to stay up to date in the three areas of skills, continuing development and legislation, the following sources will be useful:

Brown, K and Rutter, L (2006) *Critical thinking in social work*. Exeter: Learning Matters.
Useful guidance for social workers undertaking post-qualifying social work awards.

www.youth-justice-board.gov.uk
Youth Justice Board's website. Provides up-to-date information on policy and legislative change as well as information on development and learning.

www.nacro.org.uk
National Association for Care and Resettlement. See especially their youth crime section for briefings on changes, legislation and research.

www.homeoffice.gov.uk
Home Office website for information about current and proposed legislation.

www.communitycare.co.uk
Community Care website for news and updates for social care professionals.

www.gscc.org.uk
The General Social Care Council website has information on the Code of Practice and the revised post-qualifying framework.

www.jsboard.co.uk
The Judicial Studies Board for legal information for justice practitioners.

www.commonsleader.gov.uk
This provides information on the progress of legislation through parliament.

Conclusion

This book has sought to introduce you to social work practice within the field of youth justice by considering the different aspects of the youth justice system and the work undertaken by social workers in Youth Offending Teams. We have looked at social work practice by considering case studies of young people at differing stages of involvement in youth justice as a way of exploring some of the issues.

One of the themes running through this book is the fact that as a social worker practising in youth justice, you will encounter many practice dilemmas when working with young people involved in offending behaviour. In order to ensure that you approach these professionally, the importance of supervision and reflective practice as tools to deal with this complex area of practice have been discussed as well as the frameworks in place to ensure that practice is guided by firm ethical principles. We have tried to emphasise the importance of your practice being grounded in values that support, empower, respect, include and enable young people to make desisions, achieve and flourish, together with those values that challenge prejudice, injustice, stigma and inequality in society. All of these are enshrined in the Code of Practice for Social Care Workers and the National Occupational Standards, and are crucial if you are to become a well-rounded reflective practitioner.

The book has also introduced you to the conventional theoretical debates and highlighted the tensions between the justice and welfare philosophies of youth justice as well as an array of contemporary analyses of philosophical approaches and their applicability to contemporary practice. Your practice should now be grounded in criminological theory giving you an insight into the causational factors behind criminal behaviour. It is vital for youth justice practitioners to have some knowledge of mainstream criminological explanations of crime, because you will have to analyse causational triggers and risk factors relating to criminal behaviour with the young people you work with. Indeed, an analysis of these factors is necessary as part of the Asset assessment and is an integral part of pre-sentence reports. As well as being up-to-date with theoretical approaches to your work, it is essential that you are aware of the legislative and policy changes that impact on youth justice, and you should now be fully aware of how often such changes are implemented.

This book has focused on the mutli-agency system that you will be a part of and emphasised the importance of your understanding all aspects of the large and complex system as well as respecting the many professional disciplines involved. We have aimed to help you to consider your role as a social worker within a team of practitioners who may have undertaken different training from you and, therefore, have divergent philosophies and attitudes towards offending young people.

Finally, we hope the book has enabled you to understand how the youth justice setting should assist you in meeting the key roles, by looking specifically at the skills and knowledge required by social workers in relation to the preparation, assessment, planning, intervention and reviewing of young people involved in criminal activity, and also working with their families and victims. You will now be fully aware of the transferable skills and knowledge you should possess as a qualified social worker within the youth justice context and how these need to be continually developed, post-qualifying, in order for you to maintain and develop further competence. You will also appreciate that it is necessary to be able to respond to or positively challenge proposed reform as an effective and confident practitioner.

As this book has shown, working with young people involved in offending behaviour brings together many different aspects of social work practice. Primarily, we have encouraged you to gain an understanding of the legal and theoretical framework in which you will be practising and the areas of assessment, intervention and working with others within youth justice. We hope that this has enabled you to develop some sound skills and the knowledge required for good social work practice with young people who offend as a foundation for a long and rewarding social work career in youth justice. You will undoubtedly be qualifying and practising as a social worker in times of uncertainty and change but offering many opportunities for you as a professional and the young people you are working with. We wish you well as you begin your career as a social worker.

References

Allen, R (1996) *Children and crime: Taking responsibility*. London: Institute of Policy Research.

Angus, S (2001) *Youth Offending Teams response to victims of crime*. Unpublished dissertation. London: Middlesex University.

Annison, J (2005) Risk and protection, in Bateman, T and Pitts, J (eds) *The RHP companion to youth justice*. Lyme Regis: Russell House Publishing.

Ashworth, A (1994) Abolishing the presumption of incapacity: C v DPP. *Journal of Child Law*, 6(4): 174.

Ashworth, A (2000) *Sentencing and criminal justice*, (3rd edn). London: Butterworths.

Audit Commission (1996) *Misspent youth: Young people and crime*. London: Audit Commission.

Audit Commission (2004) *Youth justice 2004: A review of the reformed youth justice system*. London: The Stationery Office.

Bailey, R and Williams, B (2000) *Inter-agency partnerships in youth justice: Implementing the Crime and Disorder Act 1998*. Sheffield: University of Sheffield Joint Unit for Social Service Research.

Baker, K. (2004) Is Asset really an Asset? Assessment of young offenders in practice, in Burnett, R and Roberts, C (eds) *What works in probation and youth justice: Developing evidence-based practice*. Cullompton: Willan.

Baker, K, Jones, S, Roberts, R and Merrington, S (2003) *Asset – The evaluation of the validity and reliability of the Youth Justice Board's assessment for young offenders*. London: Youth Justice Board.

Ball, C (2004) Youth justice? Half a century of responses to youth offending. *Criminal Law Review*, March: 167–80.

Bandalli, S (2005) The legal framework for youth justice and its administration, in Bateman, T and Pitts, J (eds) *The RHP companion to youth justice*. Lyme Regis: Russell House Publishing.

Barry, M (2000) The mentor/monitor debate in criminal justice: 'What works' for offenders. *British Journal of Social Work*, 30: 575–95.

Bateman, T (2003) A state of affairs that shames us all. *Safer Society*, 18.

Bateman, T (2005) Court reports, in Bateman, T and Pitts, J (eds) *The RHP companion to youth justice*. Lyme Regis: Russell House Publishing.

Bateman, T and Pitts, J (eds) (2005) *The RHP companion to youth justice*. Lyme Regis: Russell House Publishing.

Beccaria, C (1963, first published 1764) *On crimes and punishments*. New York: Bobbs Merrill.

Becker, H (1963) *Outsiders: Studies in the sociology of deviance*. New York: Free Press.

Bevan, D (1998) Death, dying and inequality, *Care: The Journal of Practice and Development*, 7(1).

Biermann, F and Moulton, A (2003) *Youth offender panel volunteers in England and Wales* December 2002. London: Home Office.

Bottoms, A and Dignan, J (2004) Youth justice in Great Britain, in Tonry, M and Doob, A (eds) *Crime and justice,* vol 31: Chicago: University of Chicago Press.

Bowling, B and Phillips C (2002) *Racism, crime and justice* Harlow: Longman.

Braithwaite, J (1989) *Crime, shame and reintegration*. Cambridge: Cambridge University Press.

Braithwaite, J (2003) Restorative justice and a better future, in McLaughlin, E, Fergusson, R, Hughes, G and Westmarland, L (eds) *Restorative justice: Critical issues.* London: Sage.

Burnett, R and Appleton, C (2004) *Joined-up youth justice: Tackling crime in partnership*. Lyme Regis: Russell House Publishing.

Campbell, B (1993) *Goliath: Britain's dangerous places*. London: Methuen.

Chapman, T (2005) Group work with young people who offend, in Bateman, T and Pitts, J (eds) *The RHP companion to youth justice*. Lyme Regis, Russell House Publishing.

Christie, N (1977) Conflicts as property. *British Journal of Criminology*, 17: 1–19.

Clarke, J and Newburn, J (1997) *The managerial state*. London: Sage.

Cloward, R and Ohlin, L (1960) *Delinquency and opportunity: A theory of delinquent gangs*. Chicago: Free Press.

Cohen, A (1955) *Delinquent boys: The culture of the Gang*. Chicago: Free Press.

Cohen, S (1973) *Folk devils and moral panics: The creation of mods and rockers*. London: Paladin.

Coulshed, V and Orme, J (2006) *Social work practice*, 4th edn. Basingstoke: Palgrave Macmillan.

Crawford, A and Newburn, T (2002) Recent developments in restorative justice for young people in England and Wales: Community participation and representation. *British Journal of Criminology,* 42: 476–95.

Crawford, A and Newburn, T (2003) *Youth offending and restorative justice: Implementing reform in youth justice*. Cullompton: Willan.

Crawford, K and Walker, J (2003) *Social work and human development*. Exeter: Learning Matters.

Cross, N, Evans, J and Minkes, J (2003) Still children first? Developments in youth justice in Wales. *Youth Justice*, 2(3): 151–62.

de Winter, M, and Noom, M (2003) Someone who treats you as an ordinary human being . . . homeless youth examine the quality of professional care. *British Journal of Social Work*, 33.

Dennis, N (1993) *Rising crime and the dismembered family*. London: Institute of Economic Affairs.

Department of Health (2000) *Framework for the assessment of children in need and their families*. London: The Stationery Office.

Department of Health / Home Office (2003) *The Victoria Climbié inquiry: Report of an inquiry by Lord Laming*. London: The Stationery Office.

Downes, D and Rock, P (2003) *Understanding deviance*, 4th edn. Oxford: Oxford University Press.

Durkheim, E (1893, republished 1964) *The division of labor in society*. New York: Free Press.

Durkheim, E (1897, republished 1952) *Suicide: A study in sociology.* London: Routledge and Kegan Paul.

Earle, R (2005) The referral order, in Bateman, T and Pitts, J (eds) *The RHP companion to youth justice*. Lyme Regis: Russell House Publishing.

Egan, G (2002) *The skilled helper: A problem-management and opportunity approach to helping*, 7th edn. California: Brooks/Cole.

Farrington, D P (1992) Explaining the beginning, process and ending of antisocial behaviour from birth to adulthood, in McCord, J (ed) *Facts, frameworks and forecasts: Advances in criminological theory, Vol 3.* New Brunswick, NJ: Transaction.

Farrington, D P (1995) Teenage antisocial behaviour, in Rutter, M (ed) *Psychosocial Disturbances in Young People, Challenges for Prevention*. Cambridge: Cambridge University press.

Feeley, M and Simon, J (1992) The new penology. *Criminology*, 30 (4): 449–74.

Fionda, J (2005) *Devils and angels: Youth policy and crime*. Oxford: Hart.

Flanagan, T (2005) Working with volunteers in the youth justice system, in Bateman, T and Pitts, J (eds) *The RHP companion to youth justice*. Lyme Regis: Russell House Publishing.

Garland, D (1996) The limits of the sovereign state: Strategies of crime control in contemporary society. *British Journal of Criminology*, 36 4: 445–71.

Garland, D (2002) Of crimes and criminals: The development of criminology in Britain, in Maguire, M, Morgan, R and Reiner, R (eds) *The Oxford handbook of criminology,* (3rd edn). Oxford: Oxford University Press.

Ghate, D and Ramella, M (2002) *Positive parenting: The national evaluation of the Youth Justice Board's parenting programme*. London: Policy Research Bureau and Youth Justice Board.

Gibson, B (1994) *The Youth Court: One year on*. Winchester: Waterside.

Goldblatt, P and Lewis, C (eds) (1998) *Reducing offending*, Home Office Research Study 187. London: Home Office.

Goldson, B (2000) 'Children in need' or 'young offenders'? Hardening ideology, organisational change and new challenges for social work with children in trouble. *Child and Family Social Work*, 5: 255–65.

Goldson, B (2001) A rational youth justice? Some critical reflections on the research, policy and practice relation. *Probation Journal*, 8 (2): 76–85.

Goldson, B (2002) *Vulnerable inside: Children in secure and penal settings*. London: The Children's Society.

Goodey, J (2005) *Victims and victimology: Research, policy and practice*. Harlow: Pearson Education.

Graham, J and Bowling, B (1995) *Young people and crime*, Home Office Research Study 145. London: Home Office.

GSCC (2002) *Code of practice for social care workers.*

Hagell, A (2003) *Quality protects research briefing no 8: Understanding and challenging youth offending*. London: Department of Health.

Haines, K and Drakeford, M (1998) *Young people and youth justice*. Basingstoke, Macmillan.

Hall, S, Critchner, C, Jefferson, T, Clarke, J and Robert, B (1978) *Policing the crisis: Mugging, the state and law and order*. Basingstoke: Macmillan.

Heidensohn, F (1996) *Women and Crime*, 2nd edn. Basingstoke: Macmillan.

Hendrick, H (2002) Constructions and reconstructions of British childhood: An interpretive survey, 1800 to the present, in Muncie, J, Hughes, G and McLaughlin, E (eds) *Youth justice: Critical readings*. London: Sage.

Hester, R (2000) Community safety and the new youth justice, in Goldson, B, *The new youth justice*. Lyme Regis: Russell House Publishing.

Hill, M (1999) What's the problem? Who can help? The perspectives of children and young people on their well-being and on helping professionals. *Journal of Social Work Practice*, 13(2).

Holdaway, S, Davidson, N, Dignan, J, Hammersley, R, Hine, J and Marsh, P (2001) *New strategies to address youth offending: The national evaluation of the pilot youth offending teams*. London: Home Office.

Home Office (1927) *Report of the departmental committee on the treatment of young offenders* (Moloney Committee) Cmnd 2831. London: Home Office.

Home Office (1960) *Report of the committee on children and young persons* (Ingleby Report) Cmnd 1191. London: Home Office.

Home Office (1964) *Report of the committee on children and young persons* (Kilbrandon Report) Cmnd 3065. London: Home Office.

Home Office (1965) *The child, the family and the young offender*, Cmnd 2742. London: Home Office.

Home Office (1985) *The cautioning of offenders*, Circular 14/1985. London: Home Office.

Home Office (1991) *Safer communities: The delivery of crime prevention through the partnership approach* (Morgan Report). London: Home Office.

Home Office (1994) *The cautioning of offenders*. Home Office Circular 18/1994 London: Home Office.

Home Office (1997a) *Community safety order*. London: Home Office.

Home Office (1997b) *Getting to grips with crime*. London: Home Office.

Home Office (1997c) *New national and local focus on youth crime*. London: Home Office.

Home Office (1997d) *No more excuses: A new approach to tackling youth crime in England and Wales*. London: Home Office.

Home Office (1997e) *Preventing children offending*. London: Home Office.

Home Office (1997f) *Tackling delays in the youth justice system*. London: Home Office.

Home Office (1997g) *Tackling youth crime*. London: Home Office.

Home Office (2002) *Justice for all*. London: Home Office.

Home Office (2003a) *Every child matters*. London: Home Office.

Home Office (2003b) *Important changes to referral orders from 18 August 2003. Supplementary guidance for courts, Youth Offending Teams and Youth Offender Panels*. London: Home Office.

Home Office (2003c) *Statistics on women and the criminal justice system*. London: Home Office.

Home Office (2003d) *Youth justice – The next steps*. London: Home Office.

Home Office (2004a) *Restorative justice: The government's strategy. Responses to the consultation document*. London: Home Office.

Home Office (2004b) *Statistics on race and the criminal justice system 2004*. London: Home Office.

Home Office (2005a) *The code of practice for victims of crime*. London: Home Office.

Home Office (2005b) *Crime in England and Wales 2004/2005*. London: Home Office.

Home Office (2005c) *'Safe Week': Schoolchildren urged to 'Keep it safe – keep it hidden' to cut street crime*. London: Home Office.

Home Office (2005d) *Statistics on race and the criminal justice system – 2004*. London: Home Office.

Home Office (2005e) *Youth matters*. London: Home Office.

Home Office (2006) *Protecting the public and reducing re-offending*. London: Home Office.

Home Office/Youth Justice Board (2002) *The final warning scheme – Guidance for the police and youth offending teams*. London, HMSO.

Home Office, Youth Justice Board and Department for Constitutional Affairs (2004) *Joint Home Office/DCA/Youth Justice Board circular: Parenting orders And contracts for criminal conduct or anti-social behaviour*. London: Home Office, Youth Justice Board and Department for Constitutional Affairs.

Hudson, A (2002) 'Troublesome girls': Towards alternative definitions and policies, in Muncie, J, Hughes, G and Mclaughlin, E (eds) *Youth justice: Critical readings*. London: Sage

Jefferson, T (1997) Masculinities and crime, in Maguire, M, Morgan, R and Reiner, R (eds) *The Oxford handbook of criminology*, 2nd edn. Oxford: Oxford University Press.

Jenks, C (1996) *Childhood*. London: Routledge.

Johns, R (2005) *Using the law in social work*. Exeter: Learning Matters.

Kalunta-Crumpton, A (2005) Race crime and youth justice, in Bateman, T and Pitts, J. (eds) *The RHP companion to youth justice*. Lyme Regis: Russell House Publishing.

Koprowska, J (2005) *Communication and interpersonal skills in social work*. Exeter: Learning Matters.

Labour Party (1996) *Tackling youth crime, reforming youth justice*. London: Labour Party.

Lea, J and Young, J (1984) *What is to be done about law and order?* London: Penguin (2nd edn, London: Pluto Press, 1993).

Lemert, E (1951) *Social pathology*. New York: McGraw-Hill.

Liddle, M and Solanki, A (2002) *Persistent young offenders: Research on individual backgrounds and life experiences.* London: NACRO.

Lyon J, Dennison, C and Wilson, A (2000) *Tell them so they listen: Messages from young people in custody*. Research Study 201. London: Home Office.

Mannheim, H (ed) (1960) *Pioneers in criminology*. London: Stevens.

Marlow, A (2005) The policing of young people, in Bateman, T and Pitts, J (eds) *The RHP companion to youth justice*. Lyme Regis: Russell House Publishing Ltd.

Marshall, T F (1996) The evolution of restorative justice in Britain. *European Journal on Criminal Policy and Research*, 4(4): 21–43.

Martinson, R (1974) What works? Questions and answers about prison reform. *The Public Interest,* 35: 22–54.

Masters G (2005) Restorative justice and youth justice, in Bateman, T and Pitts, J (eds) *The RHP companion to youth justice*. Lyme Regis: Russell House Publishing.

Matza, D (1964) *Delinquency and drift*. New York: Wiley.

Matza, D and Sykes, G (1957) Techniques of neutralisation: A theory of delinquency. *American Sociological Review*, 22: 664–70.

Matza, D and Sykes, G (1961) Juvenile delinquency and subterranean values. *American Sociological Review*, 26: 712–19.

McLaughlin, E and Muncie, J (1996) *Controlling crime*. London: Sage.

Merton, R (1938) Social structure and anomie. *American Journal of Sociology*, 2: 577–602.

Messerschmidt, J (1993) *Masculinities and crime*. Maryland: Roman and Littlefield.

Middleton, L (1997) *The art of assessment*. Birmingham: Venture Press.

Miller, W (1958) Lower class culture as a generating milieu of gang delinquency. *Journal of Social Issues*, 15: 5–19.

Milner, J and O'Byrne, P (2002) *Assessment in social work*, 2nd edn. Basingstoke: Palgrave Macmillan.

Monaghan, G (2005) Children's human rights and youth justice, in Bateman, T and Pitts, J (eds) *The RHP companion to youth justice*. Lyme Regis: Russell House Publishing.

Morris, A and Giller, M (1987) *Understanding juvenile justice*. London: Croome Helm.

Muncie, J (1999) *Youth and Crime*. London: Sage

Muncie, J (2004) *Youth and crime,* 2nd edn. London: Sage.

Muncie, J and Hughes, G (2002) Modes of governance: Political realities, criminalisation and resistance, in Muncie, J, Hughes, G, and McLaughlin, E (eds) *Youth justice: Critical readings*. London: Sage.

Murray, C (1984) *Losing ground*. New York: Basic Books.

Murray, C (1988) *In pursuit of happiness and good government*. New York: Simon and Schuster.

Murray, C (1990) *The emerging British underclass*. London: Institute of Economic Affairs, Health and Welfare Unit.

Murray, C (1994) *Underclass: The crisis deepens*. London: Institute of Economic Affairs.

NACRO (1999) *Facts about young offenders in 1997*. London: NACRO Youth Crime Section.

NACRO (2003a) Implications of youth justice – The next steps. Companion to the green paper every child matters. *Youth Crime Briefing*. December.

NACRO (2003b) *Youth Crime Briefing*. Some facts about young people who offend – 2003.

NACRO (2003c) Some facts about young people who offend – 2001. *Youth Crime Briefing*, March.

Newburn, T, Crawford, A, Earle, R, Goldie, S, Hale, C, Masters, G, Netten, A, Saunders, R, Sharpe, K and Uglow, S (2001) *The introduction of referral orders into the youth justice system*, RDS Occasional Paper 70. London: Home Office.

Park, R (1936) Human Ecology. *American Journal of Sociology*, 42(1) July: 15.

Park, R and Burgess, E (eds) (1925) *The City*. Chicago: University of Chicago Press.

Parker, J and Bradley G (2003) *Social work practice: Assessment, planning, intervention and review*. Exeter: Learning Matters.

Payne, M (2005) Working with groups, in Harrison, R and Wise, C (eds) *Working with young people*. London: Sage.

Pickburn, C, Lindfield, S and Coleman, J (2005) Working with parents, in Bateman, T and Pitts, J (eds) *The RHP companion to youth justice*. Lyme Regis: Russell House Publishing.

Pickford, J (2000) *Youth justice: Theory and practice*. London: Cavendish Publishing.

Piper, C (2004) Assessing assessment. *Family Law Journal*, 34: 736–40.

Pitts, J (2001) Korrectional karaoke: New Labour and the zombification of youth justice, *Youth Justice*, 1(2).

Pitts, J. (2003) *The new politics of youth crime: Discipline or solidarity?* Lyme Regis: Russell House Publishing.

Pratt, J (1989) Corporatism, the third model of youth justice. *British Journal of Criminology*, 29(3): 236–54.

Prior, D (2005) Evaluating the new youth justice: What can practitioners learn from research? *Practice*, 17(2).

Quality Assurance Agency for Higher Education (QAA) (2001) *Social policy and administration and social work subject benchmark statements*. London: QAA.

Quinney, R (1970b) *The social reality of crime*. Boston: Little Brown.

Reeves, H and Mulley, K (2000) The new status of victims in the UK: Opportunities and threats, in Crawford, A and Goodey, J (eds) *Integrating a victim perspective within criminal justice: International debates*. Dartmouth: Ashgate.

Reiner, R (2000) *The politics of the police*, 3rd edn. Oxford: Oxford University Press.

Ritchie, J (1994) *Report of the inquiry into the care and treatment of Christopher Clunis*. London: HMSO.

Roberts, C, Baker, K Merrington, S and Jones, S (2001) *Validity and reliability of Asset: Interim report to the Youth Justice Board*. Oxford: Centre for Criminological Research.

Rogers, C (1976) *Client-centred therapy*. London: Constable and Robinson.

Rutherford, A (1992) *Growing out of crime: The new era*. Winchester: Waterside.

Rutter, M, and Garmezy, N (1983) Developmental psychopathology, in Hetherington, E M (ed) *Handbook of child psychology, Vol 4, Social and Personality Development*. Chichester: Wiley.

Rutter, M, Giller, H and Hagell, A (1998) *Antisocial behaviour by young people*. Cambridge: Cambridge University Press.

Safer Society (2003) *No. 18*.

Schon, D (1983) *The reflective practitioner*. New York: Basic Books.

Shaw, C (1931) *The natural history of a delinquent career*. Chicago: University of Chicago Press.

Shaw, C and McKay, H (1942) *Juvenile delinquency and urban areas*. Chicago: University of Chicago Press.

Smith, D (2005) The effectiveness of the juvenile justice system. *Criminal Justice*, 5(2): 181–95

Smith, J (2003a) *The nature of personal crime*. London: HMSO.

Smith, R (2003) *Youth justice: Ideas, policy, practice*. Cullompton: Willan.

Solomos, J (1993) *Race and racism in contemporary Britain*. Basingstoke: Macmillan.

Sumner, C (1994) *The sociology of deviance*: An obituary. Buckingham: Open University Press.

Talbot, C (1996) *Realising objectives in the probation service – A workbook*. London: Home Office Probation Unit.

Taylor, I, Walton, P and Young, J (1973) *The new criminology*. London: Routledge and Kegan Paul.

Thompson, N (2001) *Anti-discriminatory practice*. Basingstoke: Palgrave Macmillan.

Thompson, N (2005) *Understanding social work: Preparing for practice*, (2nd edn). Basingstoke: Palgrave Macmillan.

Thompson, N (2006) *People problems*. Basingstoke: Palgrave Macmillan.

Thrasher, F (1927) *The gang: A study of 1,313 gangs in Chicago*. Chicago: University of Chicago Press.

TOPSS England (2002) *Statement of expectations from individuals, families, carers, groups and communities who use services and those who care for them*. London: TOPSS England.

Trevithick, P (2005) *Social work skills: A practice handbook*. Maidenhead: Open University Press.

Tuckman, B W and Jenson, M A C (1977) Stages of small group development revisited. *Group and Organisation Studies*, 2 (4): 419–27.

Uglow, S (2002) *Criminal justice*, 2nd edn. London: Sweet and Maxwell.

United Nations (1966) International Covenant on Civil and Political Rights (New York).

United Nations (1985) The United Nations Standard Minimum Rules for the Administration of Juvenile Justice (New York).

United Nations (1989) The United Nations Convention on the Rights of the Child (New York).

United Nations (1990a) The United Nations Guidelines for the Prevention of Juvenile Delinquency (New York).

United Nations (1990b) The United Nations Rules for the Protection of Juveniles Deprived of their Liberty (New York).

Utting, D, Bright, J and Henricson, C (1993) *Crime and the family: Improving child rearing and preventing delinquency*. London: Family Policy Studies Centre.

Victim Support (2002) *Criminal neglect: No justice beyond criminal justice*. London: Victim Support.

Victim Support (2003) *Survey of crimes against 12–16 Year Olds*. London: Victim Support.

Walklate, S (2004) *Gender, crime and criminal justice*, 2nd edn. Cullompton: Willan.

Williams, B (1999) *Working with victims of crime: Policies, politics and practice*. London: Jessica Kingsley.

Williams, B (2000) Victims of crime and the new youth justice, in Goldson, B (ed) *The new youth justice*. Lyme Regis: Russell House Publishing.

Wilson, D and Moore, S (2004) *Playing the game: The experiences of young black men in custody*. London: The Children's Society.

Wirth, L, (1928) *The ghetto*. Chicago. University of Chicago Press.

Wirth, L (1964) Human ecology, in Wirth, L and Reiss, A, *On Cities and Social Life*. Chicago: University of Chicago Press.

Yelloly, M and Henkel, M (1995) *Learning and Teaching in Social Work: Towards reflective practice*. London: Jessica Kingsley.

Young, J (1971) *The drugtakers*. London: Paladin.

Young, J (1994) Incessant chatter: Current paradigms in criminology, in Maguire, M, Morgan, R and Reiner, R (eds) *The Oxford handbook of criminology*. Oxford: Oxford University Press.

Youth Justice Board (2001) *Good practice guidelines for restorative work with victims and young offenders*. London: Youth Justice Board.

Youth Justice Board (2002a) *Key elements in effective practice: Assessment, planning, intervention and supervision*. London: Youth Justice Board.

Youth Justice Board (2002b) *Key elements of effective practice: Parenting*. London: Youth Justice Board.

Youth Justice Board (2003a) *Assessment, planning and supervision: A reader for the professional certificate in effective practice*. London: Youth Justice Board.

Youth Justice Board (2003b) *Gaining ground in the community. Youth Justice Board Annual Review 2002/2003*. London: Youth Justice Board.

Youth Justice Board (2003c) *Key elements of effective practice*. London: Youth Justice Board.

Youth Justice Board (2003d) *Professional certificate in effective practice (youth justice): Restorative Justice*. London: Youth Justice Board.

Youth Justice Board (2004a) *Differences or discrimination?* London: Youth Justice Board.

Youth Justice Board (2004b) *National standards for youth justice services*. London: Youth Justice Board.

Youth Justice Board (2005a) *Key elements of effective practice: Mentoring*. London: Youth Justice Board.

Youth Justice Board (2005b) *Risk and protective factors*. London: Youth Justice Board.

Youth Justice Board (2006a) *Common Assessment Framework: Draft guidance for Youth Offending Teams*. London: Youth Justice Board.

Youth Justice Board (2006b) *Key elements of effective practice: Quality assurance framework: Guidance for Youth Offending Teams and secure establishments*. London: Youth Justice Board.

Youth Justice Board (2006c) *Positive parenting: A summary of the national evaluation of the Youth Justice Board's parenting programme*. **www.youth-justice-board.gov.uk**

Youth Justice Board, *Guidance for Youth Offending Teams on achieving equality*. London; Youth Justice Board.

Youth Justice Board, *Asset guidance*. London: Youth Justice Board.

Youth Justice Board, *Dangerous offenders – Guidance on multi-agency public protection arrangements*. London: Youth Justice Board.

Youth Justice Board, *Annual statistics 2004/05*. London: Youth Justice Board.

Index

Added to the index 'f' denotes a figure and 't' denotes a table.

D C Green
M Tech, CEng, MIEE

Radio Systems for Technicians

Second edition

LONGMAN

Pearson Education Limited
Edinburgh Gate, Harlow
Essex, CM20 2JE, England
and Associated Companies throughout the world.

First published by Pitman Publishing Limited 1985
Reprinted by Longman Scientific & Technical 1986
Fifth impression 1992
Second edition 1995
Second impression 1999

British Library Cataloguing in Publication Data
A catalogue entry for this title is available from the British Library

ISBN 0-582-24516-8

Set by 4 in 10/12pt Compugraphic Times
Printed in Malaysia, GPS

Contents

Preface

This book provides a comprehensive coverage of the circuits and techniques used in modern radiocommunication systems.

The Business and Technical Education Council (BTEC) scheme for the education of telecommunication technicians introduces the basic principles of radio systems in a unit intended for inclusion in certificate/diploma courses. This book has been written to provide a complete coverage of this unit.

Chapters 1 and 2 cover the principles of amplitude and frequency modulation while Chapter 3 discusses the various kinds of modulator and demodulator circuits in common use. The next chapters deal with, respectively, radio-frequency transmission lines and aerials. The propagation of radio waves is the subject of Chapter 6 and then Chapter 7 discusses the tuned radio-frequency power amplifier. Chapters 8 and 9 then deal with the principles and practice of radio transmitters and receivers operating in the HF and VHF bands. Radio receiver circuits, such as r.f. amplifiers, mixers, filters and squelch circuits, are dealt with in Chapter 10; this chapter also discusses the various ways in which AGC and AFC can be applied to a radio receiver. Lastly, Chapter 11 considers land mobile systems and Chapter 12 deals with wideband radio systems.

The book provides a comprehensive text on radiocommunication systems that should be eminently suitable for all non-advanced students of radio engineering.

Many worked examples are provided in the text to illustrate the principles that have been discussed. Each chapter concludes with a number of exercises, and concisely worked solutions to the numerical exercises are to be found at the back of the book.

I wish to express my thanks to GEC Plessey Semiconductors for their permission to include details of some of their radio integrated circuits, to the Institution of British Telecommunication Engineers for permission to use some diagrams from their journal *British Telecommunication Engineering* (*BTE*), and to Phillips Communication Systems for their assistance.

D.C.G.

1 Amplitude modulation

Amplitude modulation of a sinusoidal carrier wave is employed in radio communication systems as a means of shifting, or translating, or converting, a signal from one frequency band to another. Audio signals are transmitted and received by means of aerials but, since no kind of aerial can operate at such low frequencies, it is necessary to shift each signal to some higher frequency. It is, of course, necessary to carefully choose the frequency bands to which the signals are moved in order to ensure that each service within a given geographical area operates at a different frequency. In practice, the frequency bands which are used for particular purposes are allocated in accord with the recommendations of the International Telecommunication Union (ITU).

Principles of amplitude modulation

To obtain the maximum utilization of an available frequency spectrum, it is necessary for signals to be frequency translated to occupy different parts of that frequency spectrum. Frequency translation of a signal is accomplished by the signal amplitude modulating a carrier of appropriate frequency.

The general expression for a sinusoidal carrier wave is

$$v = V_c \sin (\omega_c t + \theta) \tag{1.1}$$

where v is the instantaneous carrier voltage, V_c is the peak value, or amplitude, of the carrier voltage, ω_c is 2π times the carrier frequency, and θ is the phase of the carrier voltage at time $t=0$. Here, θ will be taken as being equal to zero.

For the carrier wave to be amplitude modulated, the amplitude of the carrier voltage must be varied in accordance with the characteristics of the modulating signal. Suppose the modulating signal is sinusoidal and is given by $v = V_m \sin \omega_m t$, where V_m is its peak value and ω_m is 2π times its frequency. The amplitude of the carrier must then vary sinusoidally about a mean value of V_c volts. The peak value of this variation should be V_m volts, and the frequency of the variation should be $\omega_m/2\pi$ hertz. The amplitude of the modulated carrier wave is therefore $V_c + V_m \sin \omega_m t$, and the expression for the instantaneous voltage of an amplitude modulated wave is

$$v = (V_c + V_m \sin \omega_m t) \sin \omega_c t \qquad (1.2)$$

Multiplying out,

$$v = V_c \sin \omega_c t + V_m \sin \omega_m t \sin \omega_c t \qquad (1.3)$$

Using the trigonometric identity

$$2 \sin A \sin B = \cos (A - B) - \cos (A + B)$$

equation (1.3) may be rewritten as

$$v = V_c \sin \omega_c t + \frac{V_m}{2} \cos (\omega_c - \omega_m) t - \frac{V_m}{2} \cos (\omega_c + \omega_m) t \qquad (1.4)$$

This equation shows that a sinusoidally modulated carrier wave contains components at three different frequencies:

- the original carrier frequency, $f_c = \omega_c / 2\pi$
- the lower sidefrequency, $f_c - f_m = (\omega_c - \omega_m)/2\pi$ whose voltage is $V_{lsf} = V_m/2$
- the upper sidefrequency, $f_c + f_m = (\omega_c + \omega_m)/2\pi$ whose voltage is $V_{usf} = V_m/2$

The modulating signal frequency f_m is *not* present.

The maximum amplitude of the modulated wave occurs when $\sin \omega_m t = 1$, and is $V_{max} = V_c + V_m$.

The minimum amplitude occurs when $\sin \omega_m t = -1$, and is $V_{min} = V_c - V_m$.

Fig. 1.1 shows the waveform of a sinusoidally modulated wave, the outline of which is known as the *modulation envelope*. In practice, the modulating signal is rarely sinusoidal; when this is the case, each component frequency of the modulating signal produces corresponding

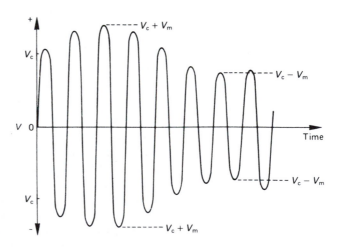

Fig. 1.1 Amplitude modulated wave

upper and lower sidefrequencies in the modulated wave, and the modulation envelope has the same waveform as the modulating signal. The band of sidefrequencies below the carrier frequency is known as the *lower sideband*, and the band of sidefrequencies above the carrier forms the *upper sideband*.

Example 1.1

A 4 MHz carrier wave is amplitude modulated by the band of audio frequencies 300–3400 Hz. Determine (a) the frequencies contained in the modulated wave; (b) the bandwidth occupied by the signal.

Solution

  (a) Using equation (1.4) the components of the modulated wave are
     (i)   the carrier frequency $f_c = 4$ MHz   (*Ans.*)
     (ii) the lower sideband frequencies 4 MHz $- (300 – 3400)$ Hz or
         3 996 600 Hz to 3 999 700 Hz   (*Ans.*)
     (iii) the upper sideband frequencies 4 MHz $+ (300 – 3400)$ Hz or
         4 000 300 Hz to 4 003 400 Hz   (*Ans.*)
  (b) The necessary bandwidth = highest frequency − lowest frequency
$$= 4\,003\,400 - 3\,996\,600$$
$$= 6800 \text{ Hz} \quad (Ans.)$$

   Note that the bandwidth occupied by the modulated wave is equal to twice the highest frequency contained in the modulating signal. This is always the case when the carrier frequency is higher than the highest modulating frequency.

Example 1.2

A carrier wave of frequency 1 MHz and amplitude 10 V is amplitude modulated by a sinusoidal modulating signal. If the lower sidefrequency is 999 kHz and its voltage is 20 dB below the carrier amplitude, calculate the amplitude and frequency of the modulating signal.

Solution

Since the carrier and lower sidefrequency voltages are developed across the same resistances, the expression

$$20 = 20 \log_{10} (V_c/V_{sf})$$

can be used. Therefore

$$10^1 = V_c/V_{sf}$$

or $V_{sf} = V_c/10 = 1$ V

From equation (1.4), the amplitude of a sidefrequency is equal to one-half of the voltage V_m of the modulating signal; therefore

$$V_m = 2 \text{ V} \quad (Ans.)$$

The lower sidefrequency is equal to the carrier frequency f_c minus the modulating frequency f_m, i.e. $f_c - f_m$, so that

$$f_m = 1000 - 999 = 1 \text{ kHz} \quad (Ans.)$$

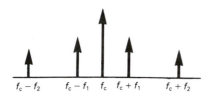

Fig. 1.2 The frequency spectrum of an amplitude-modulated wave

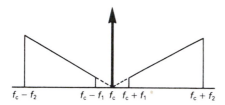

Fig. 1.3 The method of representing the sidebands of amplitude modulation

Spectrum diagrams

There are two ways in which the frequency components of an amplitude-modulated wave may be represented by a diagram. The first method is to show each component frequency by an arrow that is drawn perpendicularly to the frequency axis, as shown by Fig. 1.2; it has been assumed that the carrier wave, at frequency f_c, has been modulated by a signal containing two components at frequencies f_1 and f_2. The lengths of the arrows are drawn in proportion to the amplitudes of the components they each represent. This method of representing an AM wave is satisfactory when only a few component frequencies are involved but it rapidly becomes impractical when speech signals are involved.

The alternative method of representing sidebands is shown in Fig. 1.3. The lower and upper sidebands are each represented by a truncated triangle, in which the vertical ordinates are made proportional to the modulating frequency and no account is taken of amplitude. The upper sideband is said to be erect because its highest sidefrequency, $f_c + f_2$, corresponds to the highest frequency f_2 in the modulating signal. Conversely, the lower sideband is said to be inverted because its highest frequency component, $f_c - f_1$, is produced by the lowest modulating frequency f_1.

Modulation factor

The modulation factor m of an amplitude-modulated wave is given by

$$m = \frac{\text{Maximum amplitude} - \text{minimum amplitude}}{\text{Maximum amplitude} + \text{minimum amplitude}} \quad (1.5)$$

When expressed as a percentage, m is known as the percentage modulation, or the *depth of modulation*. For sinusoidal modulation the maximum amplitude of the modulation envelope is, from equation (1.2), $V_c + V_m$ and the minimum amplitude is $V_c - V_m$. Hence

$$m = \frac{(V_c + V_m) - (V_c - V_m)}{(V_c + V_m) + (V_c - V_m)} = V_m/V_c \quad (1.6)$$

The expression for the instantaneous voltage of an amplitude-modulated wave, equation (1.2), can be rewritten in terms of the modulation factor m:

$$v = V_c[1 + (V_m \sin \omega_m t)]/V_c \sin \omega_c t \quad (1.7)$$

$$= V_c(1 + m \sin \omega_m t) \sin \omega_c t$$

$$= V_c \sin \omega_c t + \tfrac{1}{2}mV_c[\cos (\omega_c - \omega_m)t - \cos (\omega_c + \omega_m)t] \quad (1.8)$$

Example 1.3

Draw the waveform of a carrier wave which has been sinusoidally amplitude-modulated to a depth of 25%. If the amplitude of the unmodulated carrier

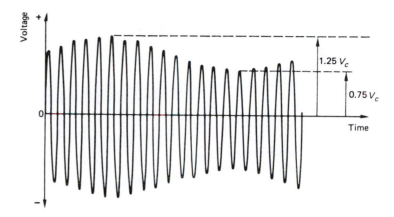

Fig. 1.4 Amplitude-modulated wave of modulation depth 25%

wave is 100 V, determine (a) the modulating signal voltage; (b) the amplitude of the lower sidefrequency component.

Solution
The maximum voltage V_{max} of the modulated wave is $V_c + V_m$ and $V_m = mV_c$. Hence

$$V_{max} = 100(1 + 0.25) = 125 \text{ V}$$

The minimum voltage of the wave is

$$V_{min} = V_c - V_m$$

or $\quad V_c(1-m) = 75 \text{ V}$

The amplitude-modulated carrier waveform is shown in Fig. 1.4.

(a) $V_m = mV_c = 0.25 \times 100 = 25 \text{ V}$ (*Ans.*)
(b) $V_{lsf} = mV_c/2 = 25/2 = 12.5 \text{ V}$ (*Ans.*)

Example 1.4

An amplitude-modulated wave is given by

$$v = 100(1 + 0.5 \sin 2000\pi t) \sin 2\pi \times 10^6 t \text{ V}$$

Determine (a) the carrier voltage; (b) the modulating voltage; (c) each sidefrequency voltage; (d) the carrier and modulating signal frequencies; (e) the peak voltage.

Solution
(a) $V_c = 100 \text{ V}$ (*Ans.*)
(b) $V_m = 0.5 \times 100 = 50 \text{ V}$ (*Ans.*)
(c) $V_{SF} = 50/2 = 25 \text{ V}$ (*Ans.*)
(d) $f_c = 1 \text{ MHz}$ and $f_m = 1 \text{ kHz}$ (*Ans.*)
(e) $V_{max} = 100 + 50 = 150 \text{ V}$ (*Ans.*)

Overmodulation

The maximum value of the modulation factor is limited to 1 since this gives a minimum value to the envelope of $V_c(1-1)$ or zero. If

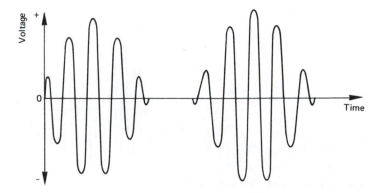

Fig. 1.5 Amplitude-modulated wave of modulation depth greater than 100%

a greater value of modulation factor is used, the envelope will no longer be sinusoidal (Fig. 1.5) and the waveform will contain a number of extra, unwanted frequency components. This means that the modulation envelope is distorted.

Power contained in an amplitude-modulated wave

The power developed by an amplitude-modulated wave is the sum of the powers developed by the carrier frequency, the upper sidefrequency and the lower sidefrequency components. The carrier power (P_c) is

$$(V_c/\sqrt{2})^2/R \quad \text{or} \quad V_c^2/2R \text{ watts}$$

and the power developed by each of the two sidefrequencies is

$$(mV_c/2\sqrt{2})^2/R \quad \text{or} \quad m^2V_c^2/8R \text{ watts}$$

so that the total power is

$$P_t = V_c^2/2R + m^2V_c^2/8R + m^2V_c^2/8R$$
$$= (V_c^2/2R)(1+m^2/2)$$
$$= P_c(1+m^2/2) \text{ watts} \qquad (1.9)$$

The theoretical maximum modulation factor which can be used without distortion is $m=1$, and for this condition P_t is one and a half times the carrier power. For maximum modulation conditions, therefore, only one-third of the total power is contained in the two sidefrequencies. Since it is the sidefrequencies that carry information, amplitude modulation is not a very efficient system when considered on a power basis.

Example 1.5

The power dissipated by an amplitude-modulated wave is 100 W when its depth of modulation is 40%. What modulation depth m is necessary to increase the power to 120 W?

Solution
From equation (1.9),

$$100 = P_c(1+0.4^2/2) \quad \text{or} \quad P_c = 100/1.08 = 92.59 \text{ watts}$$

When the depth of modulation is altered to m, the total power increases to 120 W. Therefore

$$120 = 92.59(1+m^2/2)$$

$$120/92.59 = 1.296 = 1+m^2/2$$

$$m = \sqrt{0.592} = 0.769 = 76.9\% \quad (Ans.)$$

Peak instantaneous power

The peak instantaneous power developed by an AM wave is important since it determines the required power-handling capacity of the final r.f. amplifier in the radio transmitter. If the carrier power is 1 kW and the depth of modulation is 100%, the average power in the modulated wave is 1.5 kW. The peak carrier voltage is then equal to $\sqrt{(2000R)}$ V, and the peak voltage of each sidefrequency is $0.5\sqrt{(2000R)}$ V.

When the three components are instantaneously in phase with one another the peak voltage of the modulated wave is $2\sqrt{(2000R)}$ V. Hence the instantaneous peak power is equal to $[2\sqrt{(2000R)}]^2/2R = 4$ kW.

Example 1.6

A 1 kW carrier is amplitude modulated by a sinusoidal signal to a depth of 50%. Calculate: (a) the power at the lower sidefrequency and determine what percentage it is of the total power; (b) the instantaneous peak power.

Solution
  (a) From equation (1.9)

$$P_t = 1000(1+0.5^2/2) = 1000+125 = 1125 \text{ W}$$

The carrier power is 1000 W so clearly the total sidefrequency power is 125 W. The amplitudes of the two sidefrequencies are equal and so the sidefrequencies will dissipate equal powers. Therefore

Lower sidefrequency power $= 125/2 = 62.5$ W   (*Ans.*)

The total power is 1125 W, hence the lower sidefrequency power expressed as a percentage of the total power is

$(62.5/1125) \times 100$ or 5.56%   (*Ans.*)

  (b) Peak carrier voltage $= \sqrt{(2000R)}$
       Peak sidefrequency voltage $= 0.5\sqrt{(2000R)}$
       Hence
       Peak voltage of modulated wave $= 1.5\sqrt{(20000R)}$
       Instantaneous peak power $= [1.5\sqrt{(2000R)}]^2/2R = 2250$ W   (*Ans.*)

R.m.s. value of an amplitude-modulated wave

If the r.m.s. voltage of an amplitude-modulated wave is V, then the power P_t dissipated by that wave in a resistance R is given by

$$P_t = V^2/R = P_c(1+m^2/2) \text{ W}$$

The power dissipated by the carrier component alone is

$$P_c = V_c^2/2R \text{ W}$$

Therefore

$$P_t/P_c = 2V^2/V_c^2 = P_c(1+m^2/2)/P_c$$
$$2V^2 = V_c^2(1+m^2/2)$$
$$V = (V_c/\sqrt{2})\sqrt{(1+m^2/2)} \qquad\qquad 1.10)$$

Example 1.7

The r.m.s. value of the current flowing in an aerial is 50 A when the current in unmodulated. When the current is sinusoidally modulated, the output current rises to 56 A. Determine the depth of modulation of the current waveform.

Solution
From equation (1.10),

$$56 = 50\sqrt{(1+m^2/2)}$$
$$(56/50)^2 = 1+m^2/2$$
$$m = \sqrt{2[(56/50)^2 - 1]} = 0.713 \qquad (Ans.)$$

The double-sideband full-carrier (DSB) system of amplitude modulation can be demodulated by a relatively simple circuit which responds to the variations of the envelope of the wave. Mainly for this reason, the DSB system is used for sound broadcasting in the long and medium wavebands. The disadvantage of DSB working, made apparent by Example 1.6, is that the greater part of the transmitted power is associated with the carrier component and this carries no information. Many AM radio-telephony systems use more efficient methods of working, known as single sideband and independent sideband.

Double-sideband suppressed-carrier amplitude modulation

Most of the power contained in an amplitude-modulated wave is developed by the carrier component. Since this component carries no information, it may be suppressed during the modulation process, and then all the transmitted power is associated with the upper and lower sidebands.

The waveform of a double-sideband suppressed-carrier (DSBSC) voltage is shown in Fig. 1.6. This figure has been drawn on the assumption that a 10 kHz carrier wave is amplitude-modulated by a

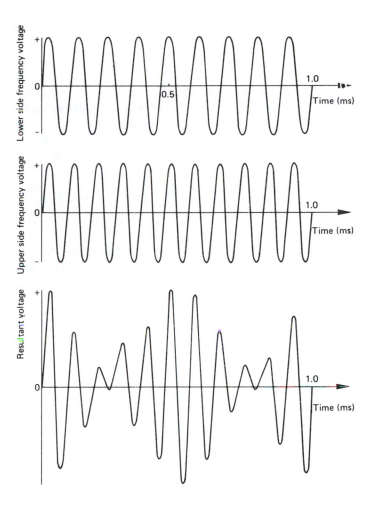

Fig. 1.6 The formation of a DSBSC wave by adding the components at the lower and upper sidefrequencies

1 kHz sinusoidal wave to produce lower and upper sidefrequencies of 9 kHz and 11 kHz respectively. With the carrier component suppressed, the DSBSC waveform is the resultant of the 9 kHz and 11 kHz waveforms (Figs 1.6(a) and (b)) and is shown in Fig. 1.6(c). The envelope of the resultant waveform is not sinusoidal and this is an indication that a DSBSC signal cannot be demodulated with the simple envelope detector which is used for full carrier demodulation.

For demodulation of a DSBSC signal, it is necessary for the carrier component to be re-inserted at the receiver with both the correct frequency and the correct phase. The first of these requirements can be satisfied if the receiver circuitry includes an oscillator of sufficiently high stability, such as a crystal oscillator. The second requirement is much more difficult to satisfy and led to the rejection of this version of amplitude modulation in the past. Nowadays, modern circuitry has considerably reduced these difficulties, and DSBSC finds an application in two particular systems. These are the transmission of the colour information in the colour television system of the UK and the transmission of the stereo information in VHF frequency-modulated sound broadcast signals.

Single-sideband suppressed-carrier amplitude modulation

The information represented by the modulating signal is contained in both the upper and the lower sidebands, since each modulating frequency f_m produces corresponding upper and lower side-frequencies $f_c \pm f_m$. It is therefore unnecessary to transmit both sidebands; either sideband can be suppressed at the transmitter without any loss of information.

When the modulating signal is of sinusoidal waveform, the transmitted sidefrequency will be a sine wave of constant amplitude. Should this signal be applied to an envelope DSB detector, a d.c. voltage output would be obtained and not the sinusoidal modulating signal. This means that demodulation using an envelope detector is not possible. For demodulation to be achieved, the carrier component must be re-inserted at the correct frequency. Now, however, the phase of the re-inserted carrier does not matter and the design of the receiver is considerably eased. This method of operation is known as single-sideband suppressed-carrier (SSBSC) amplitude modulation, frequently known simply as SSB.

The basic principle of operation of an SSB system is known in Fig. 1.7. The modulating signal is applied to a balanced modulator along with the carrier wave generated by an oscillator. The output of the balanced modulator contains the upper and lower sidebands only. The carrier component is *not* present since it has been suppressed by the action of the modulator. The DSBSC signal is then applied to the band-pass filter whose function is to remove the unwanted sideband.

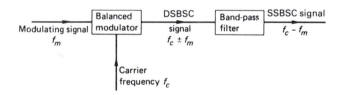

Fig. 1.7 The production of an SSBSC signal

Relative merits of single-sideband and double-sideband modulation

Single-sideband operation of a radio system has a number of advantages over double-sideband working. These advantages are as follows:

● The bandwidth required for an SSB transmission is one-half the bandwidth that must be provided for a DSB signal carrying the same information. The reduced bandwidth per channel allows a greater number of channels to be provided in a given r.f. bandwidth.

● The signal-to-noise ratio at the output of an SSB system is higher than at the output of the equivalent DSB system. The improvement in signal-to-noise ratio has a minimum value of 9 dB when the depth of modulation is 100% and becomes larger as the depth of modulation is reduced. Exactly 3 dB of this improvement comes about because the necessary bandwidth is reduced by half, and noise power is proportional to bandwidth. The rest of the improvement arises as a result of an increase in the ratio (sideband power)/(total power).

● A DSB transmitter produces a power output at all times, whereas an SSB transmitter does not. This results in an increase in the overall efficiency of an SSB transmitter.

● Selective fading of DSB radio waves may cause considerable distortion because the carrier component may fade below the sideband level. This allows the sidebands to beat together and generate a large number of unwanted frequencies. This type of distortion does not occur in an SSB system since the signal is demodulated against a locally generated carrier of constant amplitude.

The main disadvantage of SSB working is the need for the carrier to be re-inserted at the receiver before demodulation can take place. This requirement increases the complexity and, therefore, the cost of the radio receiver. It is for this reason that sound broadcast systems do not use single-sideband modulation. Nowadays, the availability of ICs means that SSBSC AM is technically feasible for domestic sound broadcasting but, politically, a change-over would be very difficult.

The frequency of the re-inserted carrier must be extremely accurate if distortion of the demodulated signal is to be avoided. For speech circuits an accuracy of perhaps ± 20 Hz may be adequate but for telegraph and data signals ± 2 Hz accuracy is needed. With modern receivers, the re-inserted carrier is generated by frequency synthesis equipment of high frequency accuracy and stability. The necessary re-insert carrier frequency accuracy is easily achieved. In older equipment a low-level *pilot carrier* is transmitted along with the wanted sideband. The pilot carrier has an amplitude of about -16 dB relative to the transmitted sideband, and is used in the receiver to operate *automatic frequency control* (AFC) circuitry. The AFC circuitry acts to maintain the frequency of the re-inserted carrier within the prescribed limits.

The output power of an SSB transmitter is usually specified in terms of the *peak envelope power* (PEP). The PEP is the power which would be developed by a carrier whose amplitude is equal to the peak amplitude of the pilot carrier and the transmitted sideband. When the pilot carrier is not transmitted, or is neglected, the term *peak sideband power* (PSP) is often used instead of PEP.

Example 1.8

The output voltage of a sinusoidally modulated SSB transmitter is applied across a 600 Ω resistance. If the amplitude of the transmitted sidefrequency is 60 V r.m.s., calculate (a) the PSP; (b) the PEP. Assume a pilot carrier is transmitted at a level of −16 dB relative to the transmitted sidefrequency.

Solution
(a) PSP $= 60^2/600 = 6$ W   (*Ans.*)
(b) 16 dB $= 20 \log_{10}(60/V_{pc})$ or $V_{pc} = 9.5$ V

Therefore peak voltage of resultant of sidefrequency and pilot carrier is $\sqrt{2}(60)+\sqrt{2}(9.5) = 98.288$ V. The r.m.s. voltage is 69.5 V and

PEP $= 69.5^2/600 = 8.05$ W   (*Ans.*)

Independent-sideband amplitude modulation

The number of SSBSC channels which can be transmitted over a given transmission medium is determined by the minimum frequency separation of the channels. This, in turn, is set by the attenuation-frequency characteristics of the band-pass filters employed, since a frequency gap between adjacent channels must be provided in which the filter attenuation can build up. Channels can be spaced closer together, and hence further economy achieved in the utilization of the available frequency spectrum, by the use of the independent sideband (ISB) system.

Fig. 1.8 The production of an ISB signal

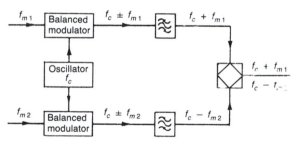

The basic principle of an ISB system is shown by Fig. 1.8. Two modulating signals at frequencies f_{m1} and f_{m2} each modulate the same carrier frequency f_c. The outputs of the two balanced modulators are DSBSC waveforms at frequencies $f_c \pm f_{m1}$ and $f_c \pm f_{m2}$ respectively. Two band-pass filters are used to select the upper sidefrequency $f_c + f_{m1}$ in one channel and the lower sidefrequency $f_c - f_{m2}$ in the other. The selected sidebands are combined in a hybrid coil to produce a DSBSC signal in which each sideband carries different information.

The differences between DSB, SSB and ISB can be illustrated by means of spectrum diagrams. Fig. 1.9 shows the spectrum diagrams for each type of modulation, assuming that a carrier of frequency f_c is modulated by a single frequency f_m or, in the case of ISB, by two sinusoidal waves at frequencies f_{m1} and f_{m2}. For a complex modulating signal, the number of arrows required is very large and an alternative kind of spectrum diagram is used in which the sidebands are represented by truncated triangles. Fig. 1.10 uses this method to

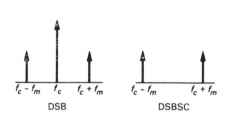

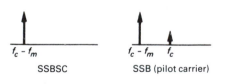

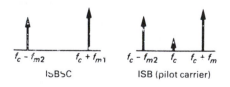

Fig. 1.9 The frequency spectrum diagrams of various amplitude-modulated signals

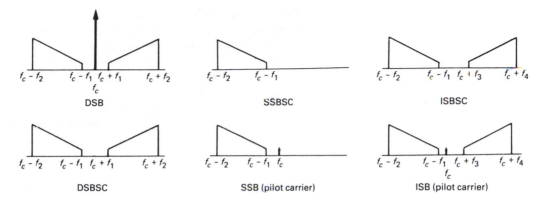

Fig. 1.10 The sidebands of various amplitude-modulated signals

illustrate the differences between the various amplitude modulation methods.

Vestigial-sideband amplitude modulation

Single- and independent-sideband operation of a radio system are possible because the lowest modulating frequency which must be transmitted is 300 Hz. A television signal, on the other hand, may include components at all frequencies down to zero hertz and this would, in consequence, present insoluble filtering difficulties if SSB operation were attempted. Conversely, the highest frequency which must be transmitted in a UHF television system is 5.5 MHz and so the use of DSB amplitude modulation would demand a minimum r.f. bandwidth of 11 MHz. As a compromise between the DSB and SSB systems of amplitude modulation, another method known as *vestigial sideband* (VSB) is employed.

A vestigial-sideband signal consists of all of the upper sideband plus a part of the lower sideband (see Fig. 1.11). The *vestige* of the lower sideband that is transmitted is not of constant maximum amplitude.

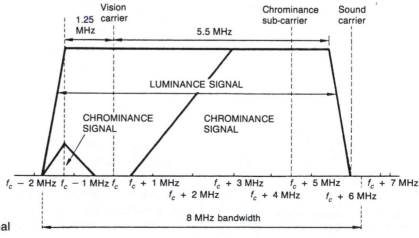

Fig. 1.11 Colour television signal

The first 1.25 MHz of the lower sideband is transmitted at full amplitude and thereafter the maximum amplitude falls linearly to zero as shown. The r.f. bandwidth occupied by the VSB signal is 8 MHz which is 72% of the bandwidth which would be required by the equivalent DSB signal. It can be seen that the carrier of the associated sound signal is positioned 6 MHz above the vision carrier frequency.

For a colour television signal, the chrominance (colour) information is superimposed upon the luminance (monochrome) signal, as shown in the figure, by making the chrominance signal amplitude modulate a 4.433 618 75 MHz *sub-carrier* frequency. Quadrature DSBSC amplitude modulation is used. *Quadrature amplitude modulation* is a system in which two signals modulate two carriers which are at the same frequency but which are 90° out of phase with each other. The two sets of sidebands produced by such a process do not become mixed up during transmission and they can be separately demodulated at the receiver if two highly stable 90°-out-of-phase oscillators are available to provide the carrier re-inserts.

Measurement of amplitude-modulated waves

With a DSB amplitude-modulated waveform, the parameter that is generally measured is the depth of modulation. This can be measured by means of a cathode oscilloscope (CRO), a modulation meter, or a true r.m.s. responding ammeter or voltmeter.

Use of a CRO

An amplitude-modulated wave can be displayed on a CRO in two different ways. The signal can be applied to the Y-input terminals and the timebase set to operate at the frequency of the modulating signal, or perhaps two or three times the modulating frequency if more than one cycle of the envelope is to be displayed. The modulation envelope is then stationary, and an amplitude-modulation envelope, such as that shown in Fig. 1.1, is displayed on the screen.

An alternative method, that makes the detection of waveform distortion easier, is to connect the modulated wave to the Y-input terminals and the modulating signal to the X-input terminals with the internal timebase switched off (see Fig. 1.12(a)). The resulting display is then trapezoidal, as shown at (b). It can be shown that the depth of modulation of the displayed waveform is given by

$$(a-b)/(a+b) \times 100 \text{ per cent} \tag{1.11}$$

The accuracy of the two methods is limited mainly by the lack of discrimination that results from the need to reduce the peak-to-peak variation of the modulated wave into the area of the CRO screen. The reduction in measurement accuracy is particularly noticeable when there is little difference between the maximum a and minimum b dimensions in centimetres, i.e. when the modulation factor is small.

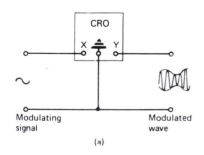

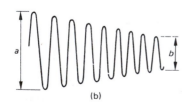

Fig. 1.12   Measurement of modulation factor using a CRO

Use of a modulation meter

A modulation meter is an instrument which has been designed for the direct measurement of modulation depth. Essentially the instrument consists of a radio receiver with a direct-coupled diode detector. If the measurement procedure specified by the manufacturer is followed carefully, accurate measurements of modulation depth can be carried out.

Use of an r.m.s. responding ammeter

The r.m.s. value of an amplitude-modulated current wave is, from equation (1.10), given by

$$I = I_c\sqrt{(1+m^2/2)}$$

where I_c is the r.m.s. value of the unmodulated current waveform. The measurement procedure is as follows. The r.m.s. value of the current, with no modulation applied, is measured first. Then the modulation is applied, and the new indication of the *true* r.m.s. responding ammeter is noted. The modulation factor can be calculated using equation (1.10) or, in practice, read off from a previously calculated graph of modulation factor plotted against the ratio I_c/I.

Example 1.9

In a measurement of modulation depth using an r.m.s. responding ammeter the unmodulated current was 50 A. Use the graph of Fig. 1.13 to determine the depth of modulation if the r.m.s. current with modulation applied is (a) 55 A; (b) 50.5 A.

Solution
    (a) $I/I_c = 55/50 = 1.1$

        Therefore, from the graph,

        Depth of modulation $m = 65\%$ *(Ans.)*

    (b) $I/I_c = 50.5/50 = 1.01$

        Therefore

        Depth of modulation $m = 14\%$ *(Ans.)*

  This method of measurement is capable of accurate results for higher values of modulation depth, but for smaller values, below about 30%, the accuracy suffers because of a lack of discrimination.
  In the case of an SSB or an ISB signal, the main feature of interest is the presence or absence of non-linearity distortion, since this will lead to the generation of intermodulation products with consequent inter-channel crosstalk. The usual method of measurement is to apply two audio-frequency sinusoidal waves, of equal amplitude but about

Fig. 1.13 The relationship between the ratio I/I_c of the r.m.s. currents of amplitude-modulated and unmodulated waves and the modulation factor

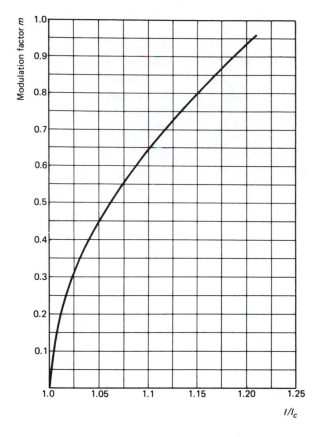

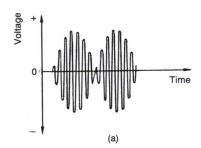

(a)

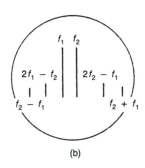

(b)

Fig. 1.14 (a) The signal waveform and (b) the spectrum diagram at the output of an ISB channel whose linearity is under test

1 kHz apart in frequency, to the input terminals of the channel. The modulated output signal is then, by some means, displayed on the screen of a CRO. If the channel operates linearly, the two frequencies should beat together to produce the waveform shown in Fig. 1.14(a). Any non-linearity present in the channel equipment will manifest itself in the form of distortion of the envelope of the beat-frequency waveform.

Alternatively, if an instrument known as a *spectrum analyzer* is available, the component frequencies of the waveform can be individually displayed on the screen of the analyzer and their amplitudes measured. Fig. 1.14(b) shows the kind of display to be expected. The required degree of linearity can then be quoted in terms of the maximum permissible amplitude of the intermodulation products.

Exercises

1.1 (a) Discuss the advantages of single-sideband operation of a radio system over double-sideband. (b) Why is the SSB system not used for sound broadcasting?

1.2 (a) Derive an expression for the output power of a double-sideband amplitude-modulated transmitter in terms of the unmodulated carrier power and the depth of modulation. (b) The output power of a radio transmitter is 1 kW when modulated to a depth of 100%. If the depth of modulation is reduced to 50% what is the power in each sidefrequency?

1.3 Explain how a CRO can be used to measure the modulation factor of a sinusoidally modulated AM signal. What are the likely sources of inaccuracy in the method?

1.4 Distinguish between the terms *sidefrequency* and *sideband*, and explain what is meant by the envelope of an amplitude-modulated waveform. Draw the waveform of a carrier wave which has been amplitude-modulated to a depth of 20% by a sinusoidal signal.

1.5 (a) A 50 V carrier wave of frequency 4 MHz is amplitude-modulated by 10 V sinusoidal voltage. Draw the spectrum diagram of the modulated wave if the system used is (i) DSB; (ii) SSBSC; (iii) ISBSC. (b) Repeat for the case when the modulating signal is the commercial speech band of frequencies 300−3400 Hz.

1.6 A 600 V carrier wave is amplitude-modulated to a depth of 60%. Calculate (a) the modulating signal voltage; (b) the voltage of the lower sidefrequency. (c) Draw the waveform.

1.7 (a) What do the initials (i) DSB, (ii) SSBSC and (iii) ISB stand for? (b) List the advantages of SSBSC over DSB. (c) What is the advantage of ISB over SSB? (d) Explain, with the aid of a block diagram, the principle of operation of the ISB system.

1.8 (a) Explain the term *depth of modulation* as applied to an amplitude-modulated wave. (b) Spectrum analysis of a signal shows that it comprises a carrier and one pair of sidefrequencies. Each sidefrequency voltage is 10 dB below the carrier. Calculate the depth of modulation and the total signal power if the power of the unmodulated carrier is 1 mW.

1.9 (a) Draw the envelope of a carrier amplitude-modulated by a sine wave, given the following:

    Maximum peak-to-peak amplitude = 80 mm
    Minimum peak-to-peak amplitude = 40 mm
    Modulating frequency = 2 kHz
    Horizontal scale 80 mm = 1 ms
(b) Calculate the modulation factor of the signal.

1.10 A 1 MHz carrier is amplitude-modulated by a 10 kHz sine wave. What frequencies are contained in the modulated waveforms if the system is (a) DSB, (b) DSBSC, and (c) SSBSC?

1.11 (a) A modulating signal occupying the frequency band 68−72 kHz amplitude modulates a 100 kHz carrier. Calculate the bandwidth occupied by the modulated wave. (b) If the power in each sidefrequency of a DSB 25 kW carrier wave is 2 kW when the carrier is sinusoidally modulated, what is the depth of modulation?

1.12 (a) Explain why the SSBSC version of amplitude modulation is not used for (i) sound broadcasting, (ii) television broadcasting, (iii) HF international radio telephony (which uses ISB). (b) When a test tone is applied to one channel in an ISB system, the pilot carrier is 18 dB down on the sidefrequency level. If the sidefrequency voltage is 25 V, determine the voltage of the pilot carrier.

1.13 A 100 V 5 MHz carrier wave is amplitude modulated to a depth of 60% by a 3 kHz sine wave and the carrier and upper sidefrequency components are suppressed. Draw the waveform of the transmitted signal.

2 Frequency modulation

Frequency modulation, in which the modulating signal varies the frequency of a carrier wave, has a number of advantages over amplitude modulation. Frequency modulation is used for sound broadcasting in the VHF band, for the sound signal of 625-line television broadcasting, for some mobile systems, and for radio relay systems operating in the UHF and SHF bands. The price which must be paid for some of the advantages of frequency modulation over DSB amplitude modulation is a wider bandwidth requirement. If the bandwidth of an FM system is no wider than the bandwidth of the comparable DSBAM system, the relative merits of the two systems are not so easy to determine.

Principles of frequency modulation

When a sinusoidal carrier wave is frequency-modulated, its instantaneous frequency is caused to vary in accordance with the characteristics of the modulating signal. The modulated carrier frequency must vary either side of its nominal unmodulated frequency a number of times per second equal to the modulating frequency. The magnitude of the variation — known as the *frequency deviation* — is proportional to the amplitude of the modulating signal voltage.

The concept of frequency modulation can perhaps best be understood by considering a modulating signal of rectangular waveform, such as the waveform shown in Fig. 2.1(a). Suppose that the unmodulated carrier frequency is 3 MHz. The periodic time of the carrier voltage is $1/3 \, \mu s$ and so three complete cycles of the unmodulated carrier wave will occur in $1 \, \mu s$. When, after $1 \, \mu s$, the voltage of the modulating signal increases to $+1$ V, the instantaneous carrier frequency increases to 4 MHz. Hence in the time interval $1 \, \mu s$ to $2 \, \mu s$ there are four complete cycles of the carrier voltage. After $2 \, \mu s$ the modulating signal voltage returns to 0 V and the instantaneous carrier frequency falls to its original 3 MHz. During the time interval $3 \, \mu s$ to $4 \, \mu s$, the modulating signal voltage is -1 V and the carrier frequency is reduced to 2 MHz; this means that two cycles of the carrier voltage occur in this period of time. When, after $4 \, \mu s$, the

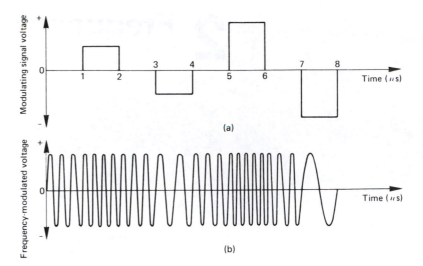

Fig. 2.1 (a) Modulating signal
(b) Frequency-modulated wave

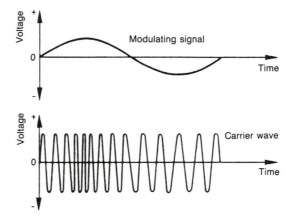

Fig. 2.2 A sinusoidally frequency-
modulated wave

modulating voltage is again 0 V, the instantaneous carrier frequency
is restored to 3 MHz. At $t = 5\,\mu s$ the modulating voltage is $+2$ V
and, since frequency deviation is proportional to signal amplitude,
the carrier frequency is deviated by 2 MHz to its new value of 5 MHz.
Similarly, when the modulating voltage is -2 V, the deviated carrier
frequency is 1 MHz. At all times the amplitude of the frequency-
modulated carrier wave is constant at 1 V, and this means that the
modulating process does not increase the power carried by the carrier
wave.

When the modulating signal is of sinusoidal waveform, the
frequency of the modulated carrier wave will vary sinusoidally; this
is shown by Fig. 2.2.

Frequency deviation

The frequency deviation of a frequency-modulated carrier wave is
proportional to the amplitude of the modulating signal voltage. There

is no inherent limit to the frequency deviation that can be obtained; this should be compared with amplitude modulation where the maximum amplitude deviation possible occurs when the modulation factor is unity.

For any given FM system, a maximum allowable frequency deviation must be specified, since the bandwidth occupied by an FM wave increases with increase in the frequency deviation. The maximum frequency deviation which is permitted to occur in a particular FM system is known as the *rated system deviation*. Since the frequency deviation is directly proportional to the modulating signal voltage, the choice of rated system deviation sets the maximum allowable modulating signal voltage that can be applied to the frequency modulator.

Example 2.1

A frequency-modulated system has a rated system deviation of 30 kHz. If the sensitivity of the frequency modulator is 4 kHz/V, what is the maximum allowable modulating signal voltage?

Solution

$$30\ \text{kHz} = 4\ \text{kHz/V} \times V_\text{m}$$

where V_m is the maximum allowable modulating signal voltage. Therefore

$$V_\text{m} = (30\ \text{kHz})/(4\ \text{kHz/V}) = 7.5\ \text{V} \quad (Ans.)$$

Most of the time the amplitude of the modulating signal voltage will be less than its maximum allowable value. Then the frequency deviation of the carrier will be smaller than the rated system deviation. This reduction can be accounted for by introducing a factor k where

$$k = \frac{\text{Modulating signal voltage}}{\text{Maximum allowable modulating signal voltage}} \quad (2.1)$$

The frequency deviation of the carrier frequency is then given by the product kf_d, where f_d is the rated system deviation. The factor k can have any value between 0, when there is no modulating signal, and 1, when the modulating signal has its maximum permitted value.

Example 2.2

An FM system has a rated system deviation of 75 kHz and this is produced by a modulating signal voltage of 10 V. Determine (a) the sensitivity of the modulator, and (b) the frequency deviation produced by a 2 V modulating signal.

Solution

   (a) Sensitivity $= 75\ \text{kHz/10 V} = 7.5\ \text{kHz/V} \quad (Ans.)$

   (b) $kf_\text{d} = (2/10) \times 75\ \text{kHz} = 15\ \text{kHz} \quad (Ans.)$

      Alternatively,

      $kf_\text{d} = 7.5\ \text{kHz/V} \times 2\ \text{V} = 15\ \text{kHz} \quad (Ans.)$

Frequency swing

The *frequency swing* of an FM wave is defined by the limits between which the carrier frequency is deviated, i.e.

$$\text{Frequency swing} = 2 \times \text{frequency deviation} \qquad (2.2)$$

Example 2.3

A 0.6 V signal is applied to the input terminals of an FM modulator whose sensitivity is 2 kHz/V. Calculate (a) the frequency swing and (b) the maximum allowable signal voltage if the rated system deviation is 2.5 kHz.

Solution

(a) Frequency deviation $= 2 \times 0.6 = 1.2$ kHz. Therefore

Frequency swing $= 2.4$ kHz   (*Ans.*)

(b) Maximum signal voltage $= 2.5/2 = 1.25$ V   (*Ans.*)

Modulation index

The modulation index m_f of a frequency-modulated wave is the ratio of the frequency deviation of the carrier to the modulating signal frequency, i.e.

$$m_f = kf_d/f_m \qquad (2.3)$$

The modulation index is equal to the peak phase deviation, in radians, of the carrier, and it determines the amplitudes and the frequencies of the components of the modulated wave.

Deviation ratio

The deviation ratio D of a frequency modulated wave is the particular case of the modulation index when *both* the frequency deviation *and* the modulating frequency are at their maximum values.

$$D = f_d/f_{m(max)} \qquad (2.4)$$

The deviation ratio is the parameter used in the design of a system and its value is fixed. Conversely, the modulation index will continually vary as the amplitude and/or the frequency of the modulating signal changes.

Example 2.4

A 100 MHz carrier wave is frequency modulated by a 10 V 10 kHz sinusoidal voltage using a linear modulator. The instantaneous carrier frequency varies between 99.95 and 100.05 MHz. Calculate (a) the sensitivity of the modulator; (b) the modulation index; (c) the peak phase deviation of the carrier.

Solution

   (a) The peak frequency deviation is 0.05 MHz. Therefore

        Modulator sensitivity $= (0.05 \times 10^6)/10 = 5$ kHz/V   (*Ans.*)

   (b) From equation (2.3),

        $m_f = (50 \times 10^3)/(10 \times 10^3) = 5$ (*Ans.*)

   (c) The peak phase deviation of the carrier is equal to the modulation index i.e. 5 radians   (*Ans.*)

Example 2.5

What will be the new values of the peak frequency and phase deviations in the system of Example 2.4 if the amplitude and frequency of the modulating signal are changed to 20 V and 5 kHz respectively?

Solution

If the amplitude of the modulating signal voltage is doubled, the frequency deviation of the carrier will also be doubled. Therefore

    $kf_d = 100$ kHz   (*Ans.*)

The peak phase deviation is given by kf_d/f_m. Therefore

    Peak phase deviation $= (5 \times 20/10)/(5/10) = 20$ radians   (*Ans.*)

Frequency spectrum of a frequency-modulated wave

When a sinusoidal carrier wave of frequency f_c is frequency-modulated by a sinusoidal signal of frequency f_m, the modulated wave will contain components at a number of different frequencies. These frequencies are the carrier frequency and a number of sidefrequencies positioned either side of the carrier. The sidefrequencies are spaced apart at frequency intervals equal to the modulating frequency. The first-order sidefrequencies are $f_c \pm f_m$, the second-order sidefrequencies are $f_c \pm 2f_m$, the third-order sidefrequencies are $f_c \pm 3f_m$, and so on.

    The amplitudes of the various components, including the carrier, depend upon the value of the modulation index or deviation ratio. This is shown by the curves given in Fig. 2.3. Only the first nine orders of sidefrequencies have been shown in order to clarify the drawing but many more orders are possible. The carrier component is zero for values of the modulation index of 2.405, 5.520 and 8.654. This is in contrast with DSB amplitude modulation where the carrier is always present in the modulated waveform.

    Fig. 2.3 can be used to determine the frequencies contained in a particular frequency-modulated wave. The amplitudes of each component frequency present in the wave are obtained by projecting from the modulation index (or deviation ratio) value on the horizontal axis, onto the appropriate curve, and thence to the vertical axis.

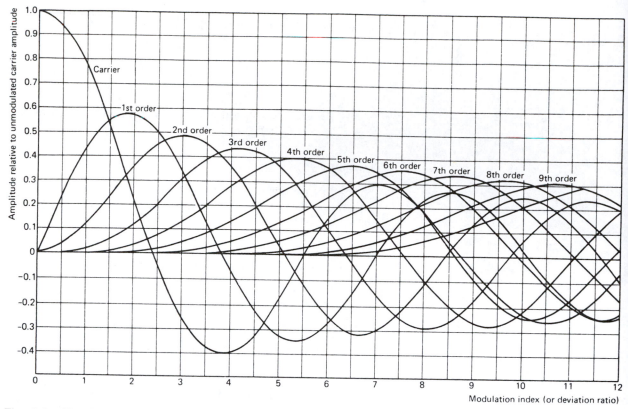

Fig. 2.3 Showing how the amplitudes of the various components of an FM wave vary with the modulation index

Negative signs are omitted, since only the magnitude of each component is wanted.

Example 2.6

Plot the frequency spectrum diagrams of frequency-modulated waves having a deviation ratio of (a) 1 and (b) 5.

Solution

The required spectrum diagrams are shown in Fig 2.4(a) and (b) respectively. These spectrum diagrams show clearly that an increase in the modulation index of an FM wave will result in an increase in the number of sidefrequencies that are generated.

The minimum bandwidth needed to transmit an FM wave is equal to $2nf_{m(max)}$, where n is the order of the highest significant sidefrequencies. When the modulation index is small, most of the information is carried by the first-order sidefrequencies and then the minimum bandwidth needed is approximately $2f_{m(max)}$. When the modulation index is fairly high, the required bandwidth is approximately equal to twice the peak frequency deviation. There are

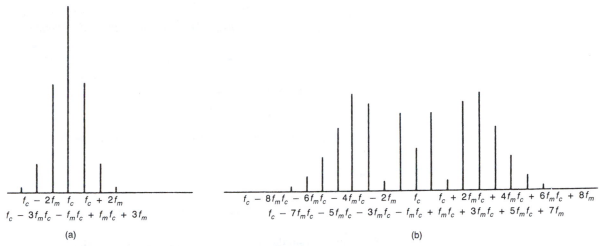

Fig. 2.4 Spectrum diagrams of FM waves with (a) $m_f = 1$, (b) $m_f = 5$

$(m_f + 1)$ pairs of sidefrequencies, each separated by f_m, in the spectrum of an FM signal. Hence the required bandwidth is

$$\text{Bandwidth} = 2(m_f + 1)f_m \tag{2.5}$$

$$= 2(kf_d + f_m) \tag{2.6}$$

where, as before, kf_d is the frequency deviation of the carrier and f_m is the modulating signal frequency. Equation (2.6) assumes that any sidefrequency whose amplitude is less than 10% of the amplitude of the *unmodulated* carrier wave need not be transmitted.

An FM system is designed to transmit the most demanding modulating signal without excessive distortion. Such a signal is the one whose maximum voltage produces the rated system deviation and whose frequency is the maximum to be transmitted by the system. The bandwidth required for the satisfactory transmission of this signal is given by equation (2.7):

$$\text{System bandwidth} = 2(f_d + f_{m(max)}) \; \cdots \tag{2.7}$$

The accuracy of equations (2.6) and (2.7) can readily be checked with the aid of Fig. 2.4. Consider, as an example, the BBC VHF frequency-modulated sound broadcast system. The parameters of this system include a rated system deviation of 75 kHz and a maximum modulating frequency of 15 kHz. The deviation ratio D is 5 and, from Fig. 2.4(b), the highest order sidefrequency that needs to be transmitted (amplitude less than ± 0.1 on the vertical scale of Fig. 2.3) is the sixth. This means that the necessary bandwidth is

$$f_c \pm 6f_m = 12f_m = 12 \times 15 \text{ kHz} = 180 \text{ kHz}$$

Using equation (2.5), the required bandwidth is

$$2(75 + 15) \text{ kHz} = 180 \text{ kHz}$$

In practice, the bandwidth is usually about 200 kHz, which allows a frequency spacing of 200 kHz between adjacent FM channels.

As a second example, consider a narrowband system in which $f_d = f_{m(max)} = 3$ kHz. For this system the deviation ratio is unity and from Fig. 2.3(a) the highest-order significant sidefrequencies are the second. The necessary bandwidth is

$$f_c \pm 2f_m = 4 \times 3 \text{ kHz} = 12 \text{ kHz}$$

From equation (2.7) the necessary bandwidth is, as before,

$$2(3+3) \text{ kHz} = 12 \text{ kHz}$$

Power contained in a frequency-modulated wave

Since the amplitude of a frequency-modulated wave does not vary, the total power contained in the wave is constant and equal to the unmodulated carrier power.

Phase modulation

When a carrier wave is phase modulated, its instantaneous phase is made to vary in accordance with the characteristics of the modulating signal. The magnitude of the phase deviation is proportional to the modulating signal voltage, while the number of times per second the phase is deviated is equal to the modulating frequency.

The maximum phase deviation permitted in a phase modulation system is known as the *rated system deviation* Φ_d and, as with frequency modulation, it sets an upper limit to the modulating signal voltage. A modulating voltage of lesser amplitude will produce a phase deviation equal to $k\Phi_d$, where k has the same meaning as before. The product $k\Phi_d$ is the modulation index of the phase-modulated wave. Modulating the phase of the carrier will at the same time vary the instantaneous carrier frequency. The frequency deviation produced is proportional to *both* the amplitude *and* the frequency of the modulating signal.

Frequency and phase modulation are sometimes grouped together and called *angle modulation* since they each deviate both the frequency and the phase of the carrier voltage. The differences between the two types of modulation are tabulated in Table 2.1.

Table 2.1

Modulation	Frequency deviation	Phase deviation
Frequency	Proportional to voltage of modulating signal	Proportional to voltage and inversely proportional to frequency of modulating signal
Phase	Proportional to both voltage and frequency of modulating signal	Proportional to voltage of modulating signal

Example 2.7

A carrier wave is angle modulated by a sinusoidal voltage and then it has a phase deviation of 3 radians and a frequency deviation of 6 kHz. If the voltage of the modulating signal is doubled and the modulating frequency is reduced by half, the frequency deviation is unaltered. Is this frequency modulation or phase modulation? What is the new phase deviation?

Solution
Referring to Table 2.1, it is clear that the carrier has been phase modulated.

(Ans.)

$$\text{New phase deviation} = 3 \times 2 = 6 \text{ rad} \quad (Ans.)$$

The frequency spectrum of a phase-modulated wave is exactly the same as that of the frequency-modulated wave having the same numerical value of modulation index.

Signal-to-noise ratio in FM systems

During its transmission, a frequency-modulated signal will be subjected to noise and interference voltages. The effect of these unwanted voltages is to vary both the amplitude and the phase of the FM signal. The amplitude variations thus produced have no effect on the performance of the system since they will have been removed by a limiter circuit in the radio receiver. The phase deviation of the signal, however, means that the carrier is effectively frequency-modulated by the noise, and a noise voltage will appear at the output of the radio receiver.

The peak phase deviation Φ_{max} of the carrier that is produced by the noise voltage is

$$\Phi_{\text{max}} = \tan^{-1}(V_n/V_c) \tag{2.8}$$

and the peak frequency deviation f_{dev} is

$$f_{\text{dev}} = f_{\text{dif}} V_n / V_c \tag{2.9}$$

where f_{dif} is the difference between the frequency of the unmodulated carrier and the frequency of the noise voltage. When the noise voltage is at the same frequency as the carrier, there is zero output noise.

Example 2.8

An NBFM signal has a signal-to-noise ratio at the detector input of 30 dB, a maximum modulating frequency of 3 kHz and a modulation index of 0.5. Calculate the signal-to-noise ratio at the output of the receiver.

Solution
30 dB is a voltage ratio of 31.62. Hence

Peak phase deviation = $\tan^{-1}(1/31.62) = 0.032$ rad
Peak frequency deviation due to the noise = $0.032 \times 3000 = 96$ Hz
Peak signal frequency deviation = $0.5 \times 3000 = 1500$ Hz

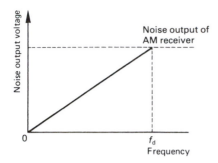

Fig. 2.5 Triangular noise spectrum of an FM system

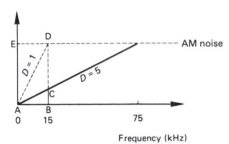

Fig. 2.6 Illustrating the effect on the noise output of an FM system of reducing the deviation ratio

Therefore

Output signal-to-noise ratio $= 20 \log_{10} (1500/96) = 23.9$ dB (*Ans.*)

Equation (2.9) shows that the magnitude of the output noise voltage is directly proportional to frequency and gives rise to the *triangular noise spectrum* shown in Fig. 2.5. The output noise voltage rises linearly from 0 V at zero frequency until, at a frequency equal to the rated system deviation f_d, it is equal to the noise output voltage from an AM system subject to the same noise voltage. Not all of this noise is able to pass through the audio amplifier of the receiver, since the frequency deviation due to the noise voltage is larger than the audio passband.

The VHF sound broadcast system of the BBC employs a rated system deviation of 75 kHz and a maximum modulating frequency of 15 kHz. Therefore the deviation ratio D is 5. Referring to Fig. 2.6, the areas enclosed by the points ABC and ABDE represent, respectively, the output noise voltages of FM and AM receivers subject to the same noise voltage. Clearly, the noise output of the FM receiver is smaller than that of the AM receiver. This means that frequency modulation can provide an increase in the output signal-to-noise ratio of a system. This is one of the advantages of frequency modulation over DSB amplitude modulation.

The size of the signal-to-noise ratio improvement depends upon the rated system deviation used and hence upon the available system bandwidth. If the frequency deviation of the BBC broadcast system were reduced to 15 kHz without changing the maximum modulating frequency, so that $D = 1$, the output noise voltage would be represented by the area ABD in Fig. 2.6. Area ABD is larger than area ABC, which is an indication that the reduction in frequency deviation has resulted in an increase in the output noise voltage.

The signal-to-noise ratio improvement of an FM system over an AM system is given by equation (2.10):

$$\text{Signal-to-noise ratio increase} = 20 \log_{10}D\sqrt{3} \text{ dB} \qquad (2.10)$$

where D is the deviation ratio.

Example 2.9

A frequency modulation system has an output signal-to-noise ratio of 30 dB when the deviation ratio is 3.5. What will be the output signal-to-noise ratio if the deviation ratio is increased to 5?

Solution

New output signal-to-noise ratio $= 30 + 20 \log_{10} (5/3.5)$

$$= 33.1 \text{ dB} \quad (\textit{Ans.})$$

The signal-to-noise ratio at the output of a frequency modulation system is a function of the rated system deviation chosen. An increase in the frequency deviation will increase the output signal-to-noise-ratio but, at the same time, will also increase the required system bandwidth. Thus, the choice of rated system deviation for a particular system must be a compromise between the conflicting requirements of maximum output signal-to-noise ratio and minimum bandwidth.

For its VHF sound broadcasts, the BBC uses a rated system deviation of 75 kHz which gives a deviation ratio of 5 and a minimum bandwidth requirement of 180 kHz. The sound signal of UHF television transmissions uses a rated system deviation of 50 kHz and this gives a deviation ratio of 3.33 and a necessary bandwidth of 130 kHz. The rated system deviation chosen for mobile systems is always less than unity. This is because the need for minimum r.f. channel bandwidth is of paramount importance, while a wide audio-frequency response is not necessary. Some typical figures for the parameters of FM mobile systems are given in Table 2.2.

Table 2.2 Mobile radio

Rated system deviation (kHz)	Maximum modulating frequency (kHz)	Deviation ratio	Minimum bandwidth (kHz)
2.5	3.5	0.71	12
5	3.4	1.47	16.8
2.8	3.4	0.82	12.4

Pre-emphasis and de-emphasis

Most waveforms transmitted by communication systems contain a large number of components at different frequencies. Usually the higher-frequency components are of smaller amplitude than the components at lower frequencies. For example, the frequencies contained in a speech waveform mainly occupy the band 100−10 000 Hz but most of the power is contained at frequencies in the region of 500 Hz for men and 800 Hz for women. Since the noise appearing at the output of a frequency-modulated system increases linearly with increase in frequency, the signal-to-noise ratio falls at high frequencies.

This is shown by Fig. 2.7 in which a signal containing components at five different frequencies has been assumed. For a multi-channel system this means that the signal-to-noise ratio will be worse in the highest-frequency channel. To improve the signal-to-noise ratio at the higher frequencies, pre-emphasis of the modulating signal is applied at the transmitter.

Refer to Fig. 2.8. The modulating signal is passed through a *pre-emphasis* network which accentuates the amplitudes of the high-frequency components of the signal relative to the low-frequency

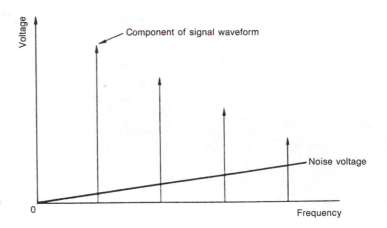

Fig. 2.7 Signal-to-noise ratio at the output of an FM system

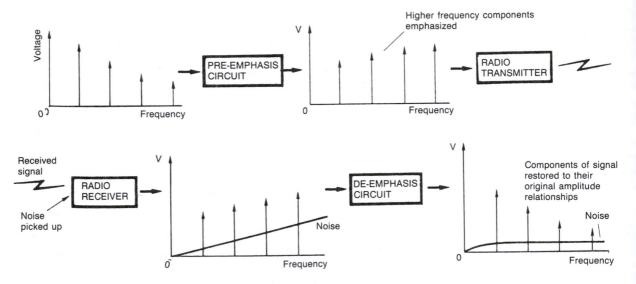

Fig. 2.8 The effect of pre-emphasis on the output signal-to-noise ratio of an FM system

components, before it is applied to the radio transmitter. During its transmission from transmitter to receiver, noise and interference will be superimposed upon the signal so that the output of the radio receiver will exhibit the triangular noise spectrum. Now, however, due to the use of pre-emphasis, the signal-to-noise ratio at the higher frequencies is greater than it would otherwise have been.

To avoid signal distortion, it is necessary to restore the frequency components of the received signal to their original relative amplitude relationships. For this the signal is passed through a *de-emphasis* circuit in the receiver. The de-emphasis circuit is a network which has an attenuation which increases with increase in frequency. The de-emphasis circuit also attenuates the high-frequency components of the noise voltage and does not, therefore, lose the signal-to-noise ratio improvement gained by the use of pre-emphasis.

To ensure that the component frequencies of the received signals

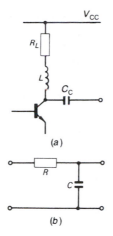

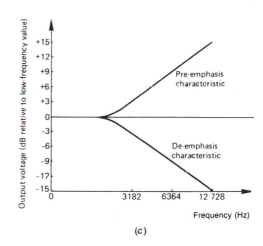

Fig. 2.9 (a) A pre-emphasis circuit, (b) a de-emphasis circuit, (c) pre- and de-emphasis characteristics for 50 μs sound broadcast systems

are restored to their orginal amplitude relationships, it is necessary for the pre- and de-emphasis networks to have equal time constants. The VHF sound broadcast system of the UK employs a time constant of 50 μs.

A variety of different networks can be used to provide pre- and de-emphasis circuits and Fig. 2.9 shows an example of each. The pre-emphasis circuit consists of an inductor L connected in series with a resistor R_L to form the collector load of a transistor. The impedance of the collector load will increase with increase in frequency and so, therefore, will the voltage gain of the circuit. The time constant of the circuit is L/R_L seconds (C_c is merely a d.c. blocking component). At the lower frequencies the impedance of the collector load is R_L ohms.

The impedance $Z = \sqrt{[R_L^2 + (\omega L)^2]}$ will be 3 dB larger than R_L ohms, i.e. $R_L\sqrt{2}$ Ω, at the frequency at which $R_L = \omega L$. The 3 dB frequency f_{3dB} is

$$f_{3dB} = R_L/2\pi L = \frac{1}{2\pi \times (\text{time constant})} \tag{2.11}$$

Therefore

$$f_{3dB} = 1/(2\pi \times 50 \times 10^{-6}) = 3182 \text{ Hz}$$

At frequencies higher than f_{3dB} the impedance of the collector load, and hence the output voltage of the circuit, will double for each twofold increase in frequency, i.e. increase at the rate of 6 dB/octave. This means that the impedance is 9 dB greater at 6364 Hz and 15 dB greater at 12 728 Hz, as shown by Fig. 2.9(c). The output voltage−frequency characteristic of the de-emphasis circuit must be the inverse of this and it is also shown in the figure.

The improvement in output signal-to-noise ratio produced by the use of pre-emphasis is not easy to assess but for sound broadcasting it is generally assumed to be about 6 dB.

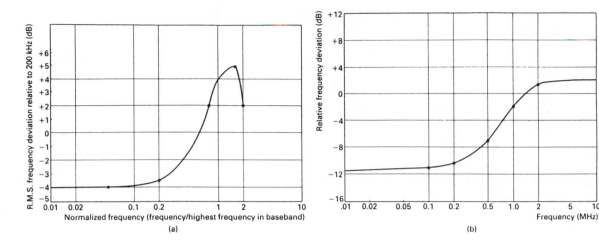

(a)

(b)

Fig. 2.10 Pre-emphasis characteristics for analogue radio-relay systems. (a) Telephony (b) Television

A mobile communication radio system will have an audio pass-band of about 300−3000 Hz and a typical pre-emphasis characteristic is 6 dB per octave over this band.

The choice of pre-emphasis characteristic to be used for a multi-channel radio relay system has been made by the ITU-R and is given in Fig. 2.10(a). Signals carried by the low-frequency channels are reduced in amplitude, while signals applied to high-frequency channels have their amplitude increased; in the case of a top channel, by 4 dB. The standard frequency deviation is produced at a baseband frequency of 60.8% of the maximum.

Many wideband SHF radio systems carry television signals as well as multi-channel telephony. The television signal is also pre-emphasized but the purpose of the operation is now to make it possible for the same modulator to be used for both telephony signals and television signals. The television signal waveform is of non-symmetrical shape, since most of its energy is contained at low frequencies and the pre-emphasis network reduces the amplitudes of the low-frequency components. The television pre-emphasis characteristic is shown in Fig. 2.10(b); standard frequency deviation is produced at 1.6 MHz.

Relative merits of amplitude, frequency and phase modulation

The advantages of frequency modulation over DSB amplitude modulation are listed below:

- The dynamic range (the range of modulating signal amplitudes from lowest to highest) is much greater.
- A frequency-modulation radio transmitter is more efficient than an AM transmitter. There are two reasons for this: firstly, Class C amplifiers can be used throughout the r.f. section of the transmitter; and secondly, since the amplitude of an FM wave is constant, each r.f. stage in the transmitter can be operated in

its optimum manner. This is not the case in a DSBAM transmitter because each of the stages must be capable of handling a *peak* power which can be considerably larger than the *average* power.

- Since an FM receiver does not respond to any amplitude variations of the input signal, selective fading is not a problem.
- The use of frequency modulation provides an increase in the output signal-to-noise ratio of the radio receiver, provided that a deviation ratio greater than unity is used. Narrowband FM systems do not share this advantage.
- An FM receiver has the ability to suppress the weaker of two signals which are simultaneously present at its aerial terminals, and are at or near the same frequency. The *capture ratio* is expressed in dB; the lower the value the better. For example, a capture ratio of 4.5 dB means that if the receiver is tuned to a particular signal, it will not respond to any other signal whose amplitude is 4.5 dB or more below the amplitude of the wanted signal.
- When a multi-channel telephony system is transmitted over a radio relay link, linearity in the output/input transfer characteristic of the equipment is of the utmost importance in order to minimize inter-channel crosstalk. The required linearity is easier to obtain using frequency modulation.

Although phase modulation is very similar to frequency modulation, it is less often used for analogue systems because frequency modulation is more efficient than phase modulation in its use of the available frequency spectrum. Also the direct demodulation of a phase-modulated wave is more difficult than FM demodulation, since it requires a very stable reference oscillator in the receiver. However, a phase-modulated signal may be received by an FM receiver that has a 6 dB de-emphasis circuit following the FM detector.

The main disadvantage of frequency modulation is, of course, the much wider bandwidth required if the possible signal-to-noise ratio improvement is to be realized. For narrowband mobile applications, the capture effect may also prove to be disadvantageous since, when a mobile receiver is near the edge of the service area, it may be captured by an unwanted signal or a noise voltage.

Measurement of a frequency-modulated wave

The parameter of a frequency-modulated wave that is usually measured is the frequency deviation. Commercial FM deviation meters are available but the measurement can be carried out by the *carrier disappearance* method. The amplitude of the carrier frequency component of an FM wave is a function of the modulation index. The carrier voltage is zero for values of modulation index of 2.405, 5.52, 8.65, etc. If, for any one of these modulation indexes, the modulation frequency is known, the frequency deviation can be calculated.

To measure the frequency deviation of an FM wave, the signal is applied to an instrument known as a *spectrum analyzer*. The spectrum analyzer is an instrument which displays voltage to a base of frequency (as opposed to a CRO, which displays voltage to a base of time). The spectrum analyzer therefore displays the spectrum diagram of the FM signal (see Fig. 2.4, for example). It is normally adjusted to display only the carrier and the first-order sidefrequencies.

With the modulating frequency kept at a constant value, the amplitude of the modulating signal is increased from zero, which varies the frequency deviation until the carrier first goes to zero. Then $m_f = 2.405$ and the frequency deviation can be calculated. Further increase in the modulating signal voltage will cause the carrier component to reappear and then again go to zero when the modulation index becomes 5.52.

Example 2.9

In a measurement of the frequency deviation of an FM signal, the frequency of a signal generator was set to 3 kHz. Calculate the frequency deviation at (a) the first and (b) the second carrier disappearance.

Solution

(a) $m_f = 2.405 = kf_d/(3 \times 10^3)$

$kf_d = 2.405 \times 3 \times 10^3 = 7.215 \text{ kHz}$ (*Ans.*)

(b) $kf_d = 5.52 \times 3 \times 10^3 = 16.56 \text{ kHz}$ (*Ans.*)

PSK, QPSK and QAM

Digital radio relay systems operating in the SHF band may employ *phase shift keying* (PSK), *quadrature phase shift keying* (QPSK), or *quadrature amplitude modulation* (QAM) as the modulation method.

Phase shift keying

Phase shift keying (PSK) is a form of digital modulation in which 2^n different phase states of the carrier are employed; $n = 1$ gives binary PSK (BPSK), $n = 2$ gives 4 PSK, $n = 3$ gives 8 PSK, and so on. Radio relay systems often employ 8 PSK.

The instantaneous voltage of a carrier modulated to give BPSK is

$$v = V_c \cos (\omega_c t \pm \phi) \tag{2.12}$$

Often the angle ϕ is 90° and then

$$v = \pm V_c \sin \omega_c t \tag{2.13}$$

and this means that BPSK is similar to amplitude modulation with a constant amplitude of V_c volts.

For 4 PSK or 8 PSK, the angle ϕ may take up any one of either four, or eight, different values to represent a bit, or a group of bits, in the digital modulating signal. In all cases the modulation may be either direct or differential. For direct PSK, the actual phases of the carrier are employed to carry information and this leads to difficulties at the receiver which must be provided with a reference phase. For differential PSK, changes in phase are used to represent groups of bits, but in both systems the PSK modulator makes the carrier phase take up any one of a set of phase values.

Quadrature phase shift keying

Quadrature phase shift keying (QPSK) is a very accurate way of applying phase shifts to a carrier. The digital modulating signal is split into in-phase (I) and quadrature (Q) bit streams and applied to a pair of balanced modulators as shown by Fig. 2.11. The modulators are also supplied with the carrier voltages that are also in phase quadrature with one another. The outputs of the two balanced modulators are added to give the QPSK waveform.

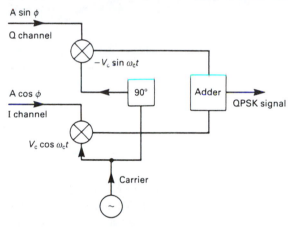

Fig. 2.11 QPSK

The output of the I modulator is $(A \cos \phi)(V_c \cos \omega_c t)$, and the output of the Q modulator is $(A \sin \phi)(-V_c \sin \omega_c t)$. The output voltage of the circuit is the sum of these voltages, i.e.

$$v_o = A \cos \phi \, V_c \cos \omega_c t - A \sin \phi \, V_c \sin \omega_c t$$

$$= AV_c \cos (\omega_c t + \phi) \tag{2.14}$$

The angle ϕ may be equal to 45°, 135°, 225° or 315° and this is shown by the constellation diagram for the system given in Fig. 2.12. Table 2.3 lists the binary states of the I and Q signals and the phase change that represents them.

Fig. 2.12 Constellation diagram for QPSK

Table 2.3

I	Q	ϕ
1	1	45°
−1	1	135°
−1	−1	225°
1	−1	315°

8 PSK

With 8 PSK the incoming bit stream is converted into groups of three bits, known as *tribits*, each of which is represented by a different carrier phase angle. One scheme uses the angles ±22.5°, ±67.5°, ±112.5° and ±157.5°.

Quadrature amplitude modulation

Quadrature amplitude modulation (QAM) is a combination of amplitude modulation and phase modulation that is used by some digital radio relay systems.

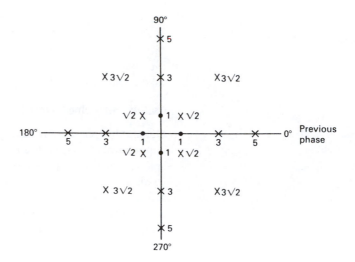

Fig. 2.13 Constellation diagram for 16 QAM

Table 2.4

Phase angle	Tribit	Phase angle	Tribit
0°	001	180°	111
45°	000	225°	110
90°	010	270°	100
135°	011	315°	101

The data is divided up into a number of bit streams, four for 16 QAM, eight for 64 QAM, and 16 for 256 QAM. The carrier is modulated in both amplitude and phase by the bit streams. Figure 2.13 shows the constellation diagram for the 16 QAM system and it can be seen that there are 16 different points that can be selected. Each phase angle is selected by a different tribit (see Table 2.4) and the amplitude is selected by the fourth bit.

Exercises

2.1 (a) Explain what is meant by the following terms in connection with frequency modulation: (i) modulation index; (ii) frequency deviation; (iii) practical bandwidth. (b) When the modulation index of a certain FM transmitter is 7 in a bandwidth of 160 kHz, what is its frequency deviation?

2.2 The r.f. bandwidth required for an FM transmitter is 100 kHz when the modulation index is 4. If the modulation signal level is increased by 6 dB, what is (a) the new modulation index and (b) the bandwidth required?

2.3 (a) Briefly explain the purpose of pre-emphasis and de-emphasis in FM systems. (b) What is the approximate improvement in output signal-to-noise ratio when pre-emphasis and de-emphasis circuits are used? (c) Draw the circuit diagram of (i) a pre-emphasis and (ii) a de-emphasis circuit.

2.4 (a) Why is the use of frequency modulation confined to the VHF band and above as a general rule? (b) Describe the meaning of the term *capture effect*.

2.5 (a) Indicate typical values of frequency deviation and highest modulating frequency used in FM broadcasting services operating in the VHF band. (b) Using these values, calculate the maximum percentage band occupancy when the minimum carrier spacing is 2.2 MHz for transmitters serving the same area.

2.6 When a sinusoidal signal is used to frequency modulate a VHF carrier, the required bandwidth is 200 kHz. It is desired to retain the same modulation index while reducing the necessary bandwidth to 100 kHz. What changes should be made to the input to the modulator to achieve the required deviation?

2.7 Discuss briefly the advantages and disadvantages of FM compared with AM in a VHF communication system.

2.8 The r.f. bandwidth of an FM transmitter is 80 kHz when a 6 kHz modulating signal is applied. What bandwidth is required if the modulating signal level is reduced by 6 dB?

2.9 Explain why FM transmission can give an improved signal-to-noise ratio compared with AM transmission of the same carrier power. What characteristics of FM transmission determine the magnitude of this improvement?

2.10 An FM radio link having a deviation ratio of 10 is to transmit speech occupying the audio band up to 3 kHz. (a) What r.f. bandwidth would normally be used for this transmission? What would be the effect on (b) the r.f. bandwidth and (c) the signal-to-noise ratio, if the deviation ratio were reduced to 5?

2.11 (a) Use the graph given in Fig. 2.3 to draw the spectrum diagram of an 80 MHz carrier wave frequency modulated with a modulation index of 4. What bandwidth is required? (b) Why will the full advantages of frequency modulation not be realised unless the signal voltage at the output of the i.f. amplifier is large?

2.12 (a) Briefly explain the differences between frequency modulation and phase modulation. (b) With which of the following modulation techniques is the triangular spectrum of noise associated: (i) AM, (ii) FM, (iii) both AM and FM? (c) At which of the following does the triangular spectrum of noise appear: (i) r.f., (ii) i.f., (iii) a.f.?

2.13 (a) What characteristic of a frequency-modulated wave determines (i) the amplitude and (ii) the frequency of the audio output of an FM receiver? (b) An FM transmitter has a frequency swing of 80 kHz. Determine its frequency deviation when the modulating signal voltage is halved.

3 Modulators and demodulators

Any radio system must operate in the frequency band that has been allocated to it by the ITU-R. This means that the modulating, or baseband, signal must be frequency-translated to a different part of the frequency spectrum. The translation process is carried out in the radio transmitter by modulating, in amplitude, frequency or phase, a carrier wave of the appropriate frequency. In the radio receiver the reverse process must be carried out, i.e. the signal must be demodulated. In this chapter the operation of the more commonly used modulators (excepting those using Class C power amplifiers) and demodulators will be considered.

Amplitude modulators

The modulator circuits used in DSB radio transmitters must permit the modulating signal to amplitude-modulate the carrier wave without the production of an excessive number of extra, unwanted frequencies. The modulator used in an SSB system must, in addition, also suppress the carrier frequency and, in some cases, the modulating signal also.

DSB modulators

The majority of DSB amplitude-modulated radio transmitters use the anode- or collector-modulated Class C r.f. tuned power amplifier circuit and this will be discussed in Chapter 7.

Other DSB modulators make use of the non-linear relationship between the applied voltage and the resulting collector or drain current of a transistor. If a carrier wave at frequency f_c and a sinusoidal modulating signal at frequency f_m are applied in series to a non-linear device, the resultant current will contain components at different frequencies. The mutual characteristic of a bipolar transistor can be represented by

$$i_c = a + bV_{be} + cV_{be}^2 + \ldots \text{ mA} \tag{3.1}$$

If the voltage applied to the base is the sum of the carrier voltage and the modulating signal voltage, i.e.

$$V_{be} = V_c \sin \omega_c t + V_m \sin \omega_m t$$

then

$$
\begin{aligned}
i_c &= a + bV_c \sin \omega_c t + bV_m \sin \omega_m t \\
&\quad + c(V_c \sin \omega_c t + V_m \sin \omega_m t)^2 \\
&= a + cV_c^2/2 + cV_m^2/2 + bV_c \sin \omega_c t + bV_m \sin \omega_m t \\
&\quad - cV_c^2/2 \cos 2\omega_c t - cV_m^2/2 \cos \omega_m t \\
&\quad + 2V_c V_m \sin \omega_c t \sin \omega_m t \text{ mA}
\end{aligned}
$$

The first three terms form a d.c. component, the fifth term is a component at the original modulating frequency, and the sixth and seventh terms give the second harmonics of the carrier and the modulating signal frequencies. If these terms are rejected and the terms $bV_c \sin \omega_c t + 2V_c V_m \sin \omega_c t \sin \omega_m t$ are selected by a tuned circuit, a DSB amplitude-modulated wave will be obtained. The non-linear device can be a diode but is more likely to be a suitably biased bipolar or field-effect transistor.

A DSBAM modulator circuit is shown in Fig. 3.1. The transistor is biased to operate over the non-linear part of its mutual characteristics. The carrier and modulating signal voltages are introduced into the base-emitter circuit of T_1 by means of transformers TR_1 and TR_2 respectively. The collector current contains the wanted carrier and sidefrequency components plus various other, unwanted components. The collector circuit is tuned to the carrier frequency and has a selectivity characteristic such that the required amplitude-modulated waveform appears across it. The various unwanted components are at frequencies well removed from resonance and so they do not develop a voltage across the collector load. The use of a non-linear modulator is restricted to low-power applications because the method has the disadvantages of low efficiency and a high percentage distortion level.

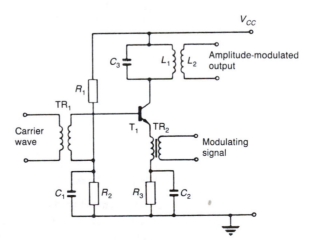

Fig. 3.1 DSBAM modulator

SSB modulators

In an SSB or an ISB system the carrier component is suppressed during the modulation process by using a *balanced modulator*. When a low-level pilot carrier is transmitted, it is added to the SSBSC signal at a later point in the transmitter.

Transistor modulator

The circuit of a transistor-balanced modulator is given in Fig. 3.2. Transistors T_1 and T_2 are biased to operate on the non-linear part of their characteristics. Since the input transformer TR_1 is centre-tapped, the modulating signal voltages applied to the bases of transistors T_1 and T_2 are in antiphase with one another. The carrier voltage is introduced into the circuit between the centre-tap on the input transformer and earth, and so appears in phase at the base terminals of the two transistors. The collector currents of each transistor contain components at a number of different frequencies, and they flow in opposite directions in the primary winding of the output transformer TR_2. The phase relationships of the various components of the collector currents are such that the current flowing in the secondary winding of TR_2 contains components at the modulating frequency and at the upper and lower sidefrequencies but *not* at the carrier frequency. In practice, the two halves of the circuit do not have identical characteristics and some carrier leak is always present at the output of the circuit.

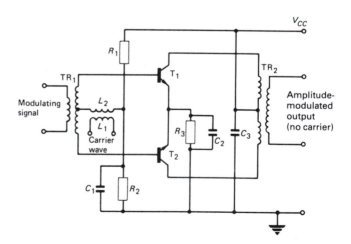

Fig. 3.2 Transistor-balanced modulator

Diode modulator

Some balanced modulators do not utilize the square-law characteristics of a transistor but instead use a diode as an electronic switch. When a diode is forward-biased its resistance is low, and when it is reverse-

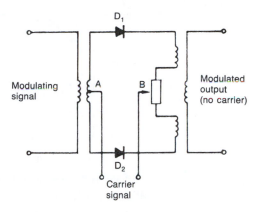

Fig. 3.3 Single-balanced modulator

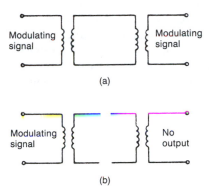

Fig. 3.4 Operation of a single-balanced modulator

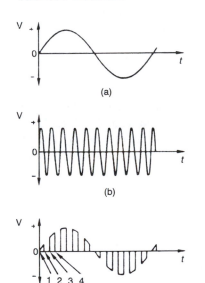

Fig. 3.5 Output waveform of a single-balanced modulator: (a) modulating signal, (b) carrier wave, (c) output waveform

biased its resistance is high. Provided that the carrier voltage is considerably greater than the modulating signal voltage, the carrier will control the switching of the diode. Ideally, the diode should have zero forward resistance and infinite reverse resistance, and this will be assumed in the next three circuits.

Figure 3.3 shows the circuit of a single-balanced diode modulator. During the half-cycles of the carrier waveform that make point A positive with respect to point B, the diodes D_1 and D_2 are forward-biased and have zero resistance. The modulator may then be redrawn as shown in Fig. 3.4(a); obviously the modulating signal will appear at the output terminals of the circuit. Similarly, when point B is taken positive relative to point A, the diodes are reverse-biased and Fig. 3.4(b) represents the modulator. The action of the modulator is to switch the modulating signal on and off at the output terminals of the circuit. The output waveform of the modulator can be deduced by considering the modulating signal and carrier waveforms at different instants. Consider Fig. 3.5: during the first positive half-cycle of the carrier wave a part of the modulating signal appears at the output (1−2 in Fig. 3.5(c)); in the following negative half-cycle the modulating signal is cut off (2−3); in the next positive half-cycle the corresponding part of the modulating signal again appears at the output terminals (3−4); and so on.

The output waveform contains the upper and lower sidefrequencies of the carrier ($f_c \pm f_m$), the modulating signal f_m and a number of higher, unwanted frequencies, but the carrier component is *not* present. In practice, of course, non-ideal diodes are employed and this has the effect of generating further unwanted frequencies and of reducing the amplitude of the wanted sidefrequency. Some carrier leak also occurs, and a potentiometer is often included to enable adjustment for minimum carrier leak.

Cowan modulator

The circuit of a Cowan modulator is shown in Fig. 3.6. The carrier voltage is applied across the points A and B and switches the four

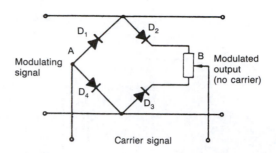

Fig. 3.6 Cowan modulator

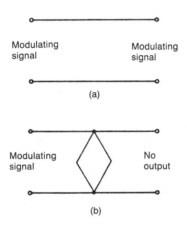

Fig. 3.7 Operation of the Cowan modulator

diodes rapidly between their conducting and non-conducting states. When point B is positive with respect to point A, all four diodes are reverse-biased and the modulator may be represented by Fig. 3.7(a); during the alternate carrier half-cycles all four diodes are turned on and Fig. 3.7(b) applies. The modulator output therefore consists of the modulating signal switched on and off at the carrier frequency. The output waveform is the same as that shown in Fig. 3.5 and it contains the same frequency components. The Cowan modulator, however, does not require centre-tapped transformers and it is therefore cheaper. The circuit also possesses a self-limiting characteristic (i.e. the sidefrequency output voltage is proportional to the input signal level only up to a certain value and thereafter remains more or less constant).

Ring modulator

Sometimes it is necessary to suppress the modulating signal as well as the carrier wave during the modulation process, and then a double-balanced modulator is used. Fig. 3.8 shows the circuit of a *ring modulator*. During half-cycles of the carrier wave when point A is positive relative to point B, diodes D_1 and D_2 are conducting and diodes D_3 and D_4 are not; D_1 and D_2 therefore have zero resistance and D_3 and D_4 have infinite resistance; Fig. 3.9(a) applies. Whenever point B is positive with respect to point A, diodes D_1 and D_2 are non-conducting, diodes D_3 and D_4 are conducting, and Fig. 3.9(b) represents the modulator. At the modulator output terminals

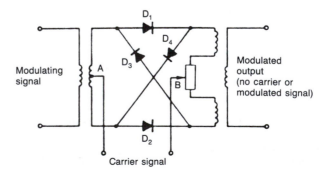

Fig. 3.8 Ring modulator

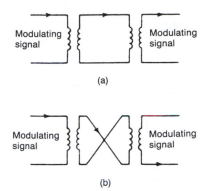

(a)

(b)

Fig. 3.9 Operation of the ring modulator

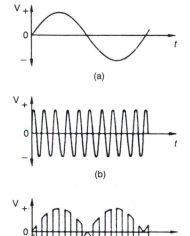

(a)

(b)

(c)

Fig. 3.10 Output waveform of the ring modulator: (a) modulating signal, (b) carrier wave, (c) output waveform

the direction of the modulating signal current is continually reversed at the carrier frequency.

The output waveform of a ring modulator is shown in Fig. 3.10(c) and can be deduced from Figs 3.10(a) and (b). Whenever the carrier voltage is positive, the modulating signal appears at the modulator output with the same polarity as (a); see points $1-2$ and $3-4$ at (c). Whenever the carrier voltage is negative, the polarity of the modulating signal is reversed (points $2-3$ and $4-5$).

Analysis of the output waveform shows the presence of components at the upper and lower sidefrequencies of the carrier wave and a number of higher, unwanted frequencies. Both the carrier and the modulating signals are suppressed.

Integrated circuit modulator

The balanced modulator is also available in integrated circuit form. Besides the usual advantages of integrated circuits over discrete circuitry, the IC modulators also offer exceptionally good carrier suppression and fully balanced input and output circuits, and they are capable of operation over a wide frequency band, typically up to about 100 MHz. Fig. 3.11 shows the basic circuit of a balanced modulator using the MC 1496. The variable resistor R_2 is provided for adjustment of the gain of the circuit. R_4, R_5, R_6 are bias components and capacitors C_1 and C_2 decouple the positive and negative power supply lines.

The SL 640 and 641 double-balanced modulators can be used at frequencies up to 75 MHz. The 640 has two output terminals, one of which has an internal 350 Ω load resistor and the other is connected

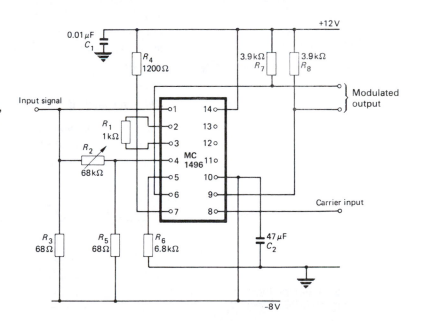

Fig. 3.11 Integrated balanced modulator

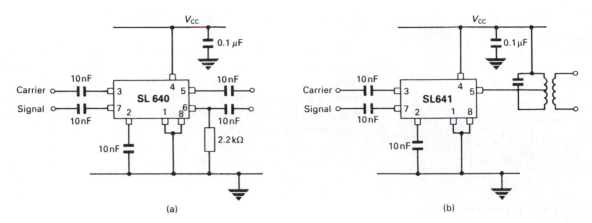

Fig. 3.12 Two SL 640 balanced modulator circuits

to a common-collector transistor. Both ICs must have input coupling capacitors and the 640 needs output coupling capacitors as well. The 641 must be provided with an external load resistor to enable the output transistor to function as an emitter follower. The 641 IC is designed to provide a current drive to a parallel-tuned circuit. Figs 3.12(a) and (b) give typical modulator circuits using the two devices. If carrier and/or signal leak is a problem, the d.c. bias voltage applied internally to the signal and carrier input terminals can be altered by an external bias network to minimize the leak.

Sideband suppression

When a complex modulating signal is applied to any of the modulator circuits described, upper and lower sidebands are produced. In an SSBSC system only one of the sidebands is to be transmitted and the other is to be suppressed. Two methods of sideband suppression are available, known respectively as the *filter method* and the *phasing method*.

The filter method

The more commonly used method of removing the unwanted sideband is to pass the output of the balanced modulator through a band-pass filter as shown in Fig. 3.13. When the modulating signal frequency

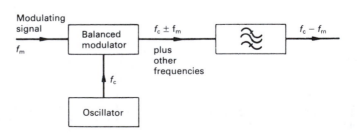

Fig. 3.13 Filter method of producing an SSBSC signal

is close to the wanted sideband, the filter may not be able to provide sufficient rejection. When this is the case, a double-balanced modulator is used so that the modulating signal will not appear at the input terminals of the filter.

The filter is required to have a flat attenuation-frequency characteristic in the passband and a rapidly increasing attentuation outside that passband.

The phasing method

The phasing method of generating an SSBSC signal avoids the use of a filter at the expense of requiring an extra balanced modulator and two phase-shifting circuits. The block schematic diagram of the phasing method is given in Fig. 3.14. Balanced modulator 1 has the modulating signal at frequency f_m applied to it, together with the output of the carrier-generating oscillator after it has been passed through a network which introduces a 90° phase lead. The other balanced modulator (2) has the carrier voltage applied directly to it but the modulating signal is first passed through a circuit which advances all frequencies by 90°. The upper sideband outputs of the two modulators are in phase, but the lower sideband outputs are in antiphase. The modulator outputs are combined in an additive circuit, with the result that the lower sidebands cancel to leave a single-sideband suppressed-carrier signal.

If the lower sideband is to be transmitted instead of the upper sideband, the phasing of the circuit must be altered so that the phase-shifted signal and carrier voltages are *both* applied to the same modulator. Then the upper sidebands are in antiphase with one another at the modulator output and cancel out in the adder.

The phasing method of SSBSC AM generation has some advantages over the filter method. Firstly, since a filter is not used, the method is able to operate at higher frequencies and, secondly, it is easy to switch from transmitting one sideband to transmitting the other sideband. The disadvantage of the phasing method is the need for a network that can introduce 90° phase shift over the whole of the audio-frequency band.

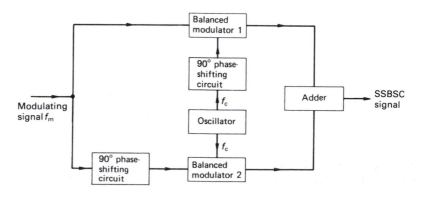

ig. 3.14 Phasing method of roducing an SSBSC signal

Frequency modulators

The function of a frequency modulator is to vary the frequency of the carrier in accordance with the characteristics of the modulating signal applied to it. There are two fundamentally different approaches to the problem. The frequency of an inductor-capacitor oscillator can be modulated by varying the capacitance or the inductance of its frequency-determining tuned circuit. Alternatively, a crystal oscillator can be phase-modulated in such a way that a frequency-modulated wave is produced.

Direct frequency modulation

Most direct frequency modulators are either some form of reactance frequency modulator or a varactor diode modulator. The basic principle of operation of a direct frequency modulator is shown by Fig. 3.15. A circuit whose reactance, generally capacitive, can be controlled by the modulating signal is connected in parallel with the frequency-determining tuned circuit L_1C_1 of the oscillator. When the modulating signal voltage is zero, the effective capacitance C_e of the variable reactance circuit is such that the oscillation frequency is equal to the nominal (unmodulated) carrier frequency, i.e.

$$f_{osc} \simeq 1/2\pi\sqrt{[L_1(C_1+C_e)]}$$
$$= 1/2\pi\sqrt{[L_1C_t]} \text{ Hz} \tag{3.2}$$

When the modulating signal is applied to the variable reactance circuit its effective capacitance is varied and this capacitance change, in turn, will frequency-modulate the oscillator.

Let C_t change by an amount δC_t; then

$$f_{osc} + \delta f_{osc} = 1/2\pi L(C_t + \delta C_t) \tag{3.3}$$

Dividing equation (3.3) by equation (3.2) gives

$$1 + (\delta f_{osc}/f_{osc}) = \sqrt{[C_t/(C_t + \delta C_t]}$$
$$= 1/\sqrt{[1 + (\delta C_t/C_t)]} \tag{3.4}$$

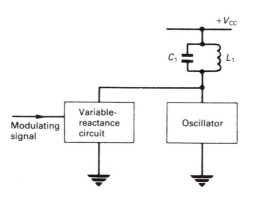

Fig. 3.15 The principle of a frequency modulator

Since $\delta C_t \ll C_t$, equation (3.4) can be written, using the Binomial Theorem, as

$$1 + (\delta f_{osc}/f_{osc}) = 1 - (\delta C_t/2C_t)$$

or

$$\delta f_{osc}/f_{osc} = -\delta C_t/2C_t \tag{3.5}$$

Thus, a fractional increase in C_t will produce a fractional decrease in f_{osc} which is approximately half as large.

Transistor reactance modulator

The circuit of a transistor reactance modulator is shown in Fig. 3.16. Resistors R_1, R_2 and R_3 and capacitor C_1 are bias and decoupling components. Capacitor C_3 is a d.c. blocking component, which is necessary to prevent L_2 shorting the d.c. collector potential of T_1 to earth, and inductor L_1 is an r.f. choke.

The current i flowing in C_2 and R_4 is

$$V_{ce}/[R_4+(1/j\omega C_2)] = (V_{ce}j\omega C_2)/(1+j\omega C_2R_4)$$

The voltage developed across R_4 is iR_4 and so the collector current of T_1 is

$$i_c = g_m i R_4$$

or

$$i_c = (g_m V_{ce}j\omega C_2 R_4)/(1+j\omega C_2 R_4)$$

The output admittance Y_{out} of the circuit is the ratio i_c/V_{ce} or

$$Y_{out} = jg_m\omega C_2R_4/(1+j\omega C_2R_4) \simeq j\omega g_m C_2 R_4$$

Thus the circuit acts as though it was a capacitor C_e whose value is

$$C_e = g_m C_2 R_4 \tag{3.6}$$

Frequency modulation of the oscillator frequency requires that the effective capacitance of the circuit is varied by the modulating signal. Since the effective capacitance is directly proportional to the mutual conductance of the transistor, it can be varied by applying the

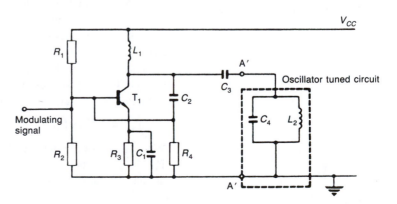

Fig. 3.16 Transistor reactance modulator

modulating signal to the base of T_1. The impedance shunted across the oscillator-tuned circuit by the modulator will have a resistive component also, and this resistance will lead to some unwanted amplitude modulation of the oscillator. Often this amplitude modulation is small and can be tolerated. If it cannot, a limiter will have to be used to remove the unwanted amplitude variations.

Example 3.1

A transistor reactance modulator has $C_2 = 22$ pF, $C_4 = 68$ pF, $R = 100\,\Omega$ and $g_m = 20$ mS. Calculate (a) its effective capacitance; (b) the frequency of the oscillator-tuned circuit if $L_2 = 3.8\,\mu$H; (c) the new frequency when an applied signal voltage decreases g_m by 10%.

Solution

(a) $C_{eff} = 20 \times 10^{-3} \times 22 \times 10^{-12} \times 100 = 44$ pF
$C_t = 44 + 68 = 112$ pF   (*Ans.*)

(b) $f_o = 1/[2\pi\,\surd(3.8 \times 10^{-6} \times 112 \times 10^{-12})] = 7.715$ MHz
(*Ans.*)

(c) New $C_{eff} = (18/20) \times 44 = 39.6$ pF
$C_t = 107.6$ pF
$f_o' = 7.715 \times \surd(112/107.6) = 7.87$ MHz   (*Ans.*)

Alternatively, variation in $C_t = 112 - 107.6 = 4.4$ pF. This is a decrease of 3.929%. Hence the increase in frequency is 1.9645%, and $100[(f_o' - 7.715)/7.715] = 1.9645$, and $f_o' = 7.87$ MHz
(*Ans.*)

Varactor diode modulator

A varactor diode modulator consists of a varactor, or voltage-variable, diode connected in parallel with the tuned circuit of an oscillator. The capacitance of a varactor diode is a function of the reverse-biased voltage applied across it and so it can be varied by an applied modulating signal. It is necessary for the oscillator frequency to be varied either side of its unmodulated value and so the varactor diode must have a mean capacitance value that is set by a bias voltage.

The basic circuit of a varactor diode modulator is shown in Fig. 3.17. The varactor diode D_1 is connected in parallel with the oscillator-tuned circuit C_1L_1. Capacitor C_2 is merely a d.c. block and L_2 is a radio-frequency choke that prevents oscillation frequency currents reaching the modulating signal circuitry. With zero modulating signal the varactor diode is reverse-biased by the bias voltage V_B. It provides the capacitance C_d necessary to tune the oscillator to the required unmodulated carrier frequency, i.e.

$$f_{osc} = 1/2\pi\surd[L(C_1 + C_d)]\ \text{Hz} \tag{3.6}$$

When the modulating signal is applied to the circuit, a voltage $V_m \sin \omega_m t$ appears across inductor L_4 and then the total voltage applied to the diode is

$$v = -V_B + V_m \sin \omega_m t\ \text{volts}$$

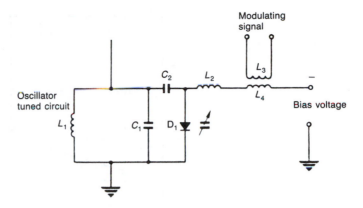

Fig. 3.17 Varactor diode modulator

This voltage varies the diode capacitance and, in so doing, frequency-modulates the oscillator.

The diode capacitance is $C_d = k/\sqrt{V_B}$ where V_B is the reverse bias voltage. When the modulating signal voltage is instantaneously zero, $v = V_B$ and so $k = C_d\sqrt{V_B}$.

When the peak modulating voltage applied to the diode is V_m, the diode capacitance will be

$$C_d + \delta C_d = (C_d\sqrt{V_B})/\sqrt{(V_B + V_m)}$$
$$= C_d/\sqrt{[1 + (V_m/V_B)]}$$
$$= C_d(1 + V_m/V_B)^{-1/2}$$
$$\simeq C_d(1 - V_m/2V_B)$$

Therefore

$$1 + \delta C_d/C_d = 1 - V_m/2V_B$$

or

$$\delta C_d/C_d = -V_m/2V_B \qquad (3.7)$$

Substituting equation (3.7) into equation (3.6) gives

$$\delta f_{osc}/f_{osc} = -(-V_m C_d)/(4V_B C_d) = V_m/4V_B \qquad (3.8)$$

Example 3.2

(a) A variable capacitance diode has the characteristic given by Table 3.1. Plot a graph of diode capacitance against diode voltage.

(b) A 90 MHz oscillator employs a parallel-tuned circuit to control the frequency of oscillation. The circuit consists of a coil of inductance $0.2\ \mu H$ in parallel with a 10 pF capacitor, across which is connected the variable capacitance diode described in (a) above. Using the given characteristic, determine the voltage which must be applied to the diode for oscillations to occur at 90 MHz.

Solution

(a) The required graph is given in Fig. 3.18.

Table 3.1

Reverse voltage (V)	Diode capacitance (pF)
−1	12.5
−2	7.5
−3	6.0
−4	5.0
−5	4.3
−6	3.8

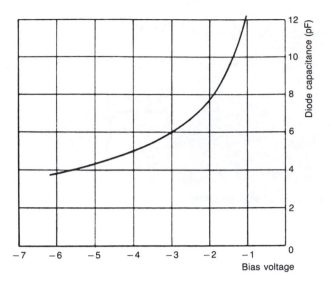

Fig. 3.18

(b) The total capacitance needed to tune the inductance to resonance at 90 MHz is

$$C_t = 1/(4\pi^2 \times 90^2 \times 10^{12} \times 0.2 \times 10^{-6}) = 15.63 \text{ pF}$$

Therefore the diode must provide a capacitance of 5.63 pF. From the graph of Fig. 3.18, this capacitance value is obtained when the applied voltage is -3.3 V.   (*Ans.*)

Indirect frequency modulation

Direct frequency modulation of an oscillator has one main disadvantage. Since an LC oscillator must be used, the inherent frequency stability of the unmodulated carrier frequency is not high enough to meet modern requirements. There are two possible solutions to this instability problem. Firstly, a direct modulation system can be used and automatic frequency control applied to the transmitter; or, secondly, a crystal oscillator can be used. With a crystal oscillator, an indirect method of modulation must be used since the frequency of a crystal oscillator cannot be modulated.

The phase deviation of a frequency-modulated signal is proportional to the amplitude of the modulating signal and inversely proportional to the modulating frequency. The phase deviation of a phase-modulated signal is proportional to the modulating signal voltage only. These relationships mean that if the modulating signal is first *integrated* before it is used to *phase modulate* a carrier wave, a *frequency-modulated* waveform is obtained. The basic arrangement of an indirect frequency modulator is shown in Fig. 3.19.

One type of phase modulator that has enjoyed considerable popularity is the Armstrong circuit shown in Fig. 3.20. The output voltage of the balanced modulator contains the upper and lower sidebands produced by amplitude modulating the 90° phase-shifted

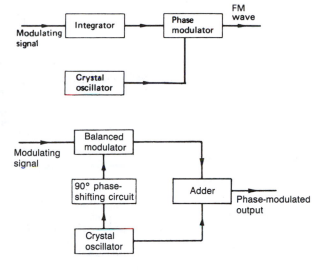

Fig. 3.19 Use of a phase modulator to generate a frequency-modulated wave

Fig. 3.20 Armstrong phase modulator

carrier with the modulating signal. The SSBSC AM signal is then added to the zero-phase-shifted carrier component. This process produces a phase-modulated wave. If the modulating signal is integrated before it arrives at the balanced modulator, a frequency-modulated ouput is produced. The frequency deviation produced is very small, being usually of the order of about 30 Hz.

The basic circuit of a phase modulator is shown by Fig. 3.21; the capacitance of the collector-tuned circuit of a transistor amplifier is partly provided by a varactor diode. The audio-frequency modulating signal is applied across the diode to alter its capacitance and thus phase-modulate the output signal.

$$i = I_o \cos \omega_o t$$

$$v = I_o Z \cos (\omega_o t - \phi)$$

where

$$Z = R/[1 + jQ\delta\omega_o/\omega_o], \quad Q = \omega_o CR \text{ and } \omega_o = 1/\sqrt{LC}$$

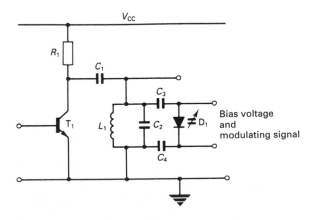

Fig. 3.21 Phase modulator

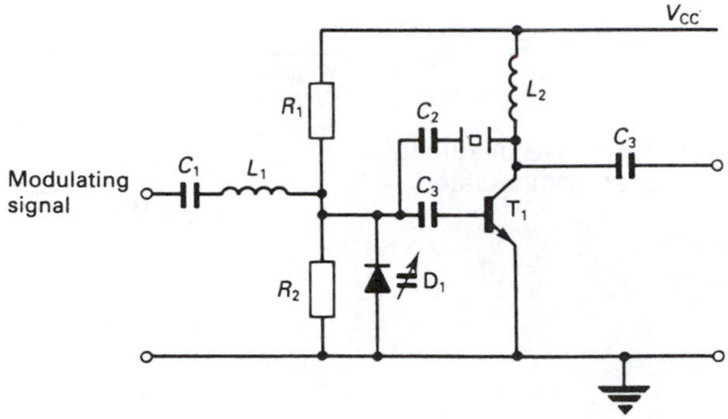

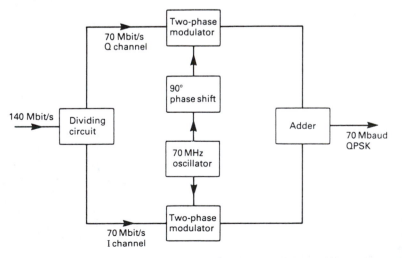

Fig. 3.22 Varactor diode phase modulator

The magnitude of the tuned circuit's impedance is

$$|Z| = R/\sqrt{[1 + Q^2(\delta\omega_o/\omega_o)^2]}$$

The phase change due to the modulating signal is

$$\phi = \tan^{-1}(Q\delta\omega_o/\omega_o)$$

Figure 3.22 shows the circuit of a varactor diode phase modulator in which the diode is used to vary the phase of a crystal oscillator. Resistors R_1 and R_2 provide the required reverse bias voltage for the diode and their values help to determine the unmodulated oscillation frequency. The applied audio-frequency signal voltage varies the reverse bias voltage to vary the capacitance of the varactor diode and so to frequency-modulate the carrier frequency. The frequency deviation produced is small.

QPSK and QAM modulators

QPSK modulator

The principle of operation of a QPSK modulator used in a digital radio relay system is shown by Fig. 3.23. The incoming 140 Mbit/s data

Fig. 3.23 QPSK modulator

is divided into two separate 70 Mbit/s bit streams. Each bit stream is applied to a phase modulator to produce a BPSK waveform. The modulators are each supplied with a 70 MHz carrier but the carrier to the Q channel is given a 90° phase shift. The two BPSK waveforms are combined at the output of the modulator to give a 70 Mbaud QPSK signal.

QAM modulator

Figure 3.24 shows the basic circuit of a 4 QAM modulator used in a radio relay system. Quadrature data streams, I and Q, are applied to digital-to-analogue converters and each DAC output is first filtered and then applied to a double-balanced mixer. Both mixers are also fed with a 70 MHz carrier but the supply to the Q channel is passed through a 90° phase-shifting circuit. The output signals of the two mixers are added together and then filtered to give a 4 QAM output signal. For the 4 QAM system the I and Q channels each carry a single data stream but for a 16 QAM system each channel carries two data streams. Usually the I and Q input bit streams have been differentially encoded so that changes in the modulation state, rather than the state itself, are signalled.

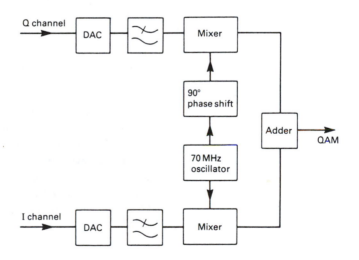

Fig. 3.24 QAM modulator

Amplitude demodulators

Demodulation or detection is the process of recovering the information carried by a modulated wave. Some DSB amplitude modulation sound broadcast receivers employ the diode detector, although often the detection stage is included within an IC and then another kind of detector circuit is used. Many communication receivers operate with either SSB or ISB signals and they often use some form of product detector.

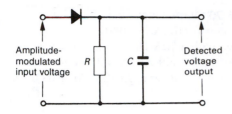

Fig. 3.25   Diode detector

Diode detector

Fig. 3.25 shows the circuit of a diode detector. It consists of a diode in series with a parallel resistor-capacitor network.

If an unmodulated carrier voltage of constant amplitude is applied to the detector, the first positive half-cycle of the wave will cause the diode to conduct. The diode current will charge the capacitor to a voltage that is slightly less than the peak value of the input signal (slightly less because of a small voltage drop in the diode itself). At the end of this first half-cycle, the diode ceases to conduct and the capacitor starts to discharge through the load resistor R at a rate determined by the time constant, CR seconds, of the discharge circuit.

The time constant is chosen to ensure that the capacitor has not discharged very much before the next positive half-cycle of the input signal arrives to recharge the capacitor (see Fig. 3.26). The time constant for the charging of the capacitor is equal to Cr seconds, where r is the forward resistance of the diode and is much smaller than R. A nearly constant d.c. voltage is developed across the load resistor R; the fluctuations that exist are small and take place at the frequency of the input carrier signal.

If now the input signal voltage is amplitude modulated, the voltage across the diode load will vary in sympathy with the modulation envelope, provided that the load time constant is small enough. The capacitor must be able to discharge rapidly enough for the voltage across it to follow those parts of the modulation cycle when the modulation envelope is decreasing in amplitude (see Fig. 3.27). The capacitor voltage falls until a positive half-cycle of the input signal makes the diode conduct and recharge the capacitor. When the modulation envelope is decreasing, one positive half-cycle is of lower peak value than the preceding positive half-cycle and the capacitor is recharged to a smaller voltage. If the time constant of the discharge path is too long, relative to the periodic time of the modulating signal, the capacitor voltage will not be able to follow the troughs of the modulation envelope. When this happens the falling capacitor voltage passes right over the top of one or more input voltage peaks, as shown by the dotted line in Fig. 3.27, and waveform distortion takes place.

The time constant must not be too short, however, or the voltage

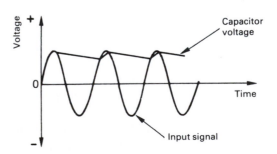

Fig. 3.26   Output voltage of a diode detector handling a signal of constant amplitude

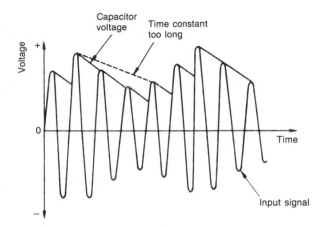

Fig. 3.27 Output voltage of a diode detector handling an amplitude-modulated signal

across the load resistor will not be as large as it could be, because insufficient charge will be stored between successive pulses of diode current. The time constant determines the rapidity with which the detected voltage can change, and must be long compared with the periodic time of the carrier wave and short compared with the periodic time of the modulating signal.

The voltage developed across the diode load resistor has three components:

(a) A component at the wanted modulating signal frequency
(b) A d.c. component that is proportional to the peak value of the unmodulated wave (this component is not wanted for detection and must be prevented from reaching the following audio-frequency amplifier stage)
(c) Components at the carrier frequency and harmonics of the carrier frequency that must also be prevented from reaching the audio-frequency amplifier.

To remove the unwanted component frequencies, the detector output is fed into a resistance-capacitance filter network before application to the audio-frequency amplifier.

Fig. 3.28 shows a possible filter circuit. Capacitor C_2 acts as a d.c. blocker to remove the d.c. component of the voltage appearing across load resistor R_1. Capacitor C_3 has a low reactance at the carrier frequency and its harmonics and, in conjunction with resistor R_2, filters out voltages at these frequencies. The voltage appearing across R_3 is therefore just the required modulating signal.

Another filter circuit is shown in Fig. 3.29. Capacitor C_2 is the d.c. blocker and C_3R_3 is the r.f. filter; R_3 also functions as the volume control.

Example 3.3

A diode detector has an input resistance of 1.5 kΩ and a load resistance of 3 kΩ. The peak value of the 70% modulated input signal voltage is 1.7 V.

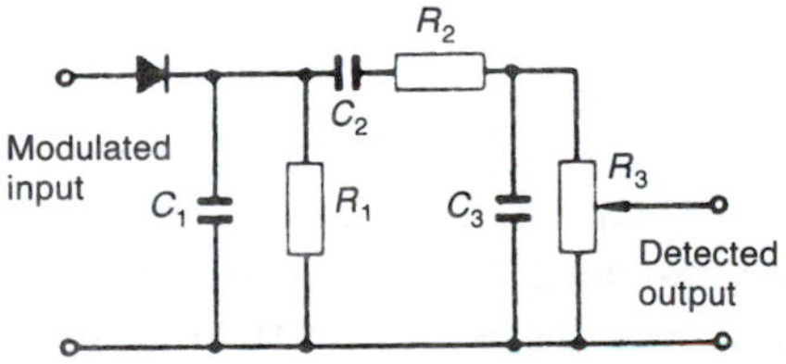

Fig. 3.28 Diode detector filter circuit

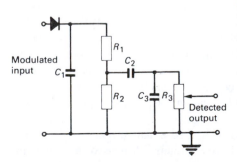

Fig. 3.29 Another diode detector filter circuit

Calculate (a) the power input to the circuit and (b) the minimum, maximum and d.c. output voltages of the circuit if the diode voltage drop is 0.2 V.

Solution

(a) $V_{max} = 1.7 = V_c(1 + 0.7)$, so $V_c = 1$ V

$P_c = (1/\sqrt{2})^2/1500 = 333\ \mu$W (*Ans.*)

(b) $V_{out(max)} = 1.7 - 0.2 = 1.5$ V (*Ans.*)

$V_{out(min)} = 0.3 - 0.2 = 0.1$ V (*Ans.*)

$V_{out(DC)} = (1.5 + 0.1)/2 = 0.8$ V (*Ans.*)

Transistor detector

The circuit of a common-emitter transistor detector is shown in Fig. 3.30. Rectification takes place in the emitter-base circuit and the rectified signal is amplified by the transistor in the usual way.

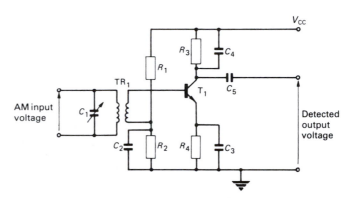

Fig. 3.30 The transistor detector

Components R_1, R_2, R_4, C_2 and C_3 provide bias and d.c. stabilization and R_3 is the collector load resistor. C_4 is a by-pass capacitor whose function is to prevent voltages at the carrier frequency appearing across R_3 and thence at the output terminals of the circuit.

The input amplitude-modulated signal is fed into the base-emitter circuit via r.f. transformer TR_1, the primary winding of which is tuned to the carrier frequency. The base-emitter junction of transistor T_1 acts as a semiconductor diode and together with R_2 and C_2 forms a diode detector. The detected voltage appears across R_2 and varies the emitter-base bias voltage of the transistor. This voltage variation causes the collector current to vary in accordance with the modulation envelope. A voltage at the modulating signal frequency appears across the collector load resistor R_3 and this is coupled to the load by capacitor C_5.

The transistor detector has a limited dynamic range and for this reason it is rarely used in discrete circuitry. It is used, however, in the detector section of some ICs.

Balanced demodulator

Demodulation of an SSB or an ISB signal can be achieved with any of the balanced modulators previously discussed. The carrier component which was suppressed at the transmitter must be re-inserted at the same frequency and the input signal is the transmitted sideband.

Suppose that the modulating signal is a sine wave of frequency f_m and that the lower sideband is transmitted. Then the input to the demodulator is at frequency $f_c - f_m$ and the demodulator output contains components at frequencies $f_c \pm (f_c - f_m)$. The lower sidefrequency is selected by a low-pass filter and is equal to $f_c - (f_c - f_m)$, or f_m, which is the required modulating signal (see Fig. 3.31).

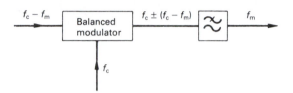

Fig. 3.31 Use of a balanced modulator as a demodulator

The frequency of the re-inserted carrier must be very close to the frequency of the carrier which was suppressed at the transmitter. Otherwise the frequency components of the demodulated output waveform will bear the wrong relationships to one another. The maximum permissible frequency error depends upon the nature of the signal. It may be as large as ± 15 Hz for voice transmissions but only ± 2 Hz for data signals. It is essential for the carrier amplitude to be considerably larger than the signal amplitude to ensure that the diodes are switched by the carrier. When digital data is being received, it is necessary also for the re-inserted carrier to be inserted with the correct phase. An example of the use of a double-balanced modulator as a mixer is in the SL 6700 i.f. amplifier and AM detector.

Product detector

Another method of demodulating an SSB signal is known as product detection, two versions of which are shown in Figs 3.32(a) and (b). In both of these circuits the a.c. current conducted by the transistor is proportional to the product of the SSBSC and carrier voltages.

Assuming sinusoidal modulation and that the lower sideband has been transmitted, the input SSBSC signal is

$$v = (mV_1/2) \cos (\omega_c - \omega_m)t \text{ volts}$$

The re-inserted carrier voltage V_2 must have the same frequency as

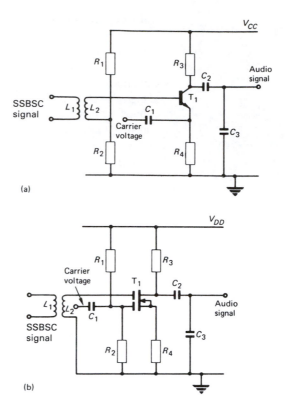

Fig. 3.32 Two product detectors

the carrier suppressed at the distant transmitter. The collector (or drain) current i_c of the transistor is therefore given by

$$i_c = (g_m m V_1 V_2/2) \cos (\omega_c - \omega_m)t \sin \omega_c t$$

or, using the trigonometric identity $2 \sin A \sin B = \cos (A - B) - \cos (A + B)$,

$$i_c = (g_m m V_1 V_2)/4[\sin \omega_m t + \sin (2\omega_c t - \omega_m)t]$$

This current flows in the load resistor R_3 and develops a voltage $R_3 i_c$ which contains a component at the original modulating frequency $f_m = \omega_m/2\pi$ hertz. The higher-frequency unwanted components are filtered out by the shunt capacitor C_3.

The product detector is often used in integrated circuits, although normally within a package that also provides other circuit functions, such as i.f. amplification. The product demodulator is also capable of detecting DSBAM signals but usually only the IC versions are used for this purpose.

Frequency detectors

The function of a frequency detector is to produce an output voltage whose magnitude is directly proportional to the frequency deviation of the input signal, and whose frequency is equal to the number of times per second the input signal frequency is varied about its mean value. Frequency demodulation can be achieved in several different ways. Most receivers using discrete circuitry employ either the ratio detector or the Foster–Seeley discriminator, but receivers which employ ICs for much of their circuitry generally use either the quadrature detector or a phase-locked loop.

Foster–Seeley discriminator

The circuit diagram of a Foster–Seeley discriminator is given in Fig. 3.33. The tuned circuit C_1L_1 acts as the collector load for the final stage of the i.f. amplifier, which is generally operated as a *limiter*. Both tuned circuits C_1L_1 and L_2C_3 are tuned to resonate at the unmodulated carrier frequency and have bandwidths wide enough to cover the rated system deviation of the FM signal. Capacitors C_2, C_4 and C_5 all have negligible reactance at radio frequencies and so L_1 is effectively connected in parallel with L_3. Thus the voltage V_1 developed across L_1 also appears across L_3.

Suppose the voltage appearing across L_1 is at the unmodulated carrier frequency. The current flowing in L_1 induces an e.m.f. into the secondary winding L_2 and this causes an in-phase current to flow in the series circuit L_2C_3. A voltage is developed across C_3 which lags this current, and hence the induced voltage, by 90°. Since inductor L_2 is accurately centre-tapped, one-half of this voltage appears across each half of L_2.

If the voltage appearing across the upper half of the winding is V_2, and V_3 is the voltage across the lower half, then the total voltages V_{D1} and V_{D2} applied across the diodes D_1 and D_2 are, respectively, the phasor sums of the voltages V_1 and V_2, and V_1 and V_3. The phase relationships are such that V_2 leads V_1 by 90° and V_3 lags V_1 by 90° as shown by the phasor diagram of Fig. 3.34(a). Since $V_{D1} = V_{D2}$, equal amplitude detected voltages appear across the diode load resistors R_1 and R_2. Because of the diode connections, these two

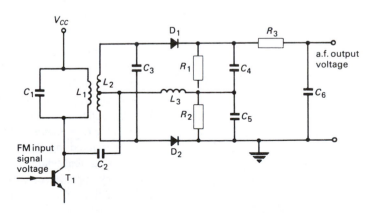

Fig. 3.33 Foster–Seeley detector

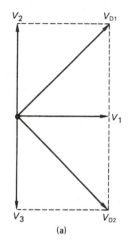

(a)

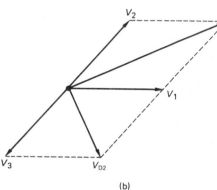

(b)

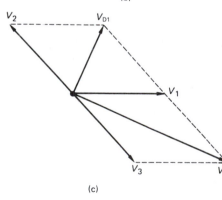

(c)

Fig. 3.34 Operation of a Foster–Seely detector

voltages act in opposite directions and cancel out, so that the voltage appearing across the output terminals of the circuit is zero.

When the frequency of the signal voltage developed across L_1 is higher than the unmodulated carrier frequency, the voltage across C_3 will lead the e.m.f. induced into L_2 by an angle greater than 90°. This results in V_2 leading V_1 by an angle less than 90° and V_3 lagging V_1 by more than 90°. See Fig. 3.34(b). Now the voltage V_{D1} applied across diode D_1 is larger than the voltage V_{D2} applied to D_2 and so the voltage developed across load resistor R_1 is greater than the voltage across R_2. A positive voltage, equal to the difference between the two load voltages, appears at the output terminals. If the frequency deviation of the carrier is increased, the larger will become the difference between the magnitudes of the diode voltages V_{D1} and V_{D2}, and so the output voltage will increase in the positive direction.

When the modulated frequency is below its unmodulated value, voltage V_2 leads V_1 by more than 90°, while V_3 lags V_1 by less than 90° as shown in Fig. 3.34(c). As a result, V_{D2} is of greater magnitude than V_{D1} and the detected voltage across R_2 is bigger than the detected voltage across R_1. The output voltage of the circuit is now negative with respect to earth. Now an increase in the frequency deviation of the carrier will increase the output voltage in the negative direction.

The way in which the output voltage of the circuit varies as the frequency of the input signal is changed is shown by the typical discriminator characteristic of Fig. 3.35.

Operation of the detector should be restricted to the linear part of the characteristic. The turn-over points are produced by the limited bandwidth of the tuned circuits C_1L_1 and C_3L_2, reducing the voltages applied to the diodes.

The output voltage of the circuit will also vary if the amplitude of the input signal should vary. This is an unwanted effect and to prevent it happening the detector should be preceded by one or more stages of amplitude limiting. De-emphasis of the output signal is provided by R_3 and C_6.

Ratio detector

A commonly used FM detector, particularly for sound broadcast receivers, is the ratio detector, one form of which is given by Fig. 3.36. The main advantage of this circuit over the Foster–Seely detector is that it incorporates its own amplitude-limiting action and hence a separate limiter is often not needed.

Inductor L_1 is inductively coupled to both L_2 and L_3 but L_2 and L_3 are not coupled together. The tuned circuits C_1L_1 and C_3L_3 are each tuned to the unmodulated carrier frequency. When a voltage at this frequency appears across L_1, voltages are induced into both L_2 and L_3. Capacitors C_2, C_4 and C_5 all have negligible reactance at radio

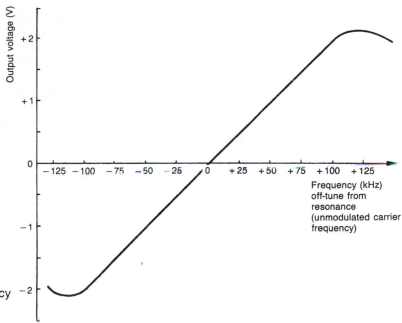

Fig. 3.35 Output voltage–frequency characteristic of a Foster–Seeley detector

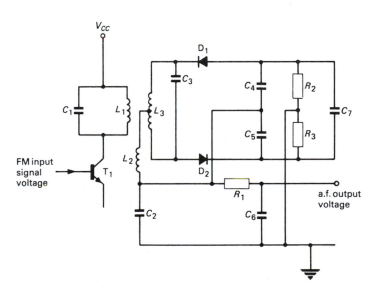

Fig. 3.36 The ratio detector

frequencies and so the voltage applied across diode D_1 is the phasor sum of the voltages across L_2 and the upper half of L_3. Similarly, the voltage applied to D_2 is the phasor sum of the voltages that appear across L_2 and the lower half of L_3. If the voltage across L_2 is labelled as V_1 and the other two voltages are labelled V_2 and V_3 respectively, the phasor diagram given in Fig. 3.34 will represent the voltages. The resultant voltages V_{D1} and V_{D2} applied to the diodes will vary with frequency to produce voltages across the load capacitors C_4 and C_5. The voltage across the d.c. load capacitor C_7

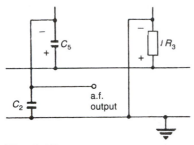

Fig. 3.37

is the sum of the voltages across C_4 and C_5 and, since $R_2 = R_3$, one-half of this voltage appears across each resistor. The time constant $C_7(R_2+R_3)$ is sufficiently long to ensure that the voltage across C_7 remains more or less constant at very nearly the peak voltage appearing across C_3.

The audio load capacitor C_2 is connected between the junctions of C_4/C_5 and R_2/R_3, and this part of the circuit is re-drawn in Fig. 3.37. The voltages across C_5 and R_3 have the polarities shown and, when the frequency of the input signal is at the unmodulated carrier frequency, are of equal magnitude. The two voltages act in opposite directions, with the result that zero current flows, and the voltage across the audio load capacitor C_2 is zero. When the input signal frequency increases, the voltage applied to diode D_1 increases and the voltage across D_2 decreases. As a result the voltage across C_4 increases while the voltage across C_5 falls; but, since the *sum* of these voltages remains constant, the voltage across R_3 does not change. A current now flows in the circuit of Fig. 3.37 and a positive voltage, equal to the difference between V_{C5} and V_{R3}, appears across C_2. If the frequency deviation is increased, the voltage across C_5 will fall still further and the voltage across C_2 will increase. Conversely, if the input frequency is reduced, the voltage across C_5 will become bigger than the voltage across R_3, and a current will flow in the opposite direction to before to produce a negative output voltage.

When the frequency of the input signal voltage is modulated, the modulating signal voltage will appear across C_2. Components R_1 and C_6 provide de-emphasis of the output voltage. The output voltage–input frequency characteristic of a ratio detector has the same shape as the Foster–Seeley curve shown in Fig. 3.35. However, the output voltage available for a given frequency deviation is only one-half that provided by the Foster–Seely circuit, and the linearity of the detection characteristic is not as good.

The advantage of the ratio detector has been previously mentioned; it provides some degree of self-limiting in the following manner. If the amplitude of the input signal is steady, the voltage across the d.c. load capacitor C_7 is constant because of the long time constant $C_7 (R_2 + R_3)$. An increase in the input signal voltage will cause both diodes to conduct extra current, and this results in an increased voltage drop across the tuned circuit which tends to keep the voltage applied to the diodes more or less constant. A similar action takes place if the input signal voltage should fall; the diodes pass a smaller current and the voltage drop across the tuned circuit is reduced, allowing the diode voltage to rise. The variable voltage drop across the tuned circuit in conjunction with the long time constant of the diode load ensures that the output voltage responds very little, if at all, to any changes in input signal amplitude.

The ratio detector shown in Fig. 3.36 is balanced since the d.c. voltage appearing across the d.c. load capacitor C_7 is balanced with respect to earth potential. Sometimes it is convenient to have an

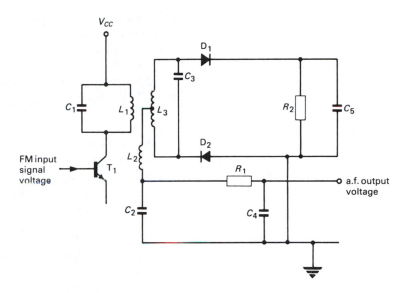

Fig. 3.38 Unbalanced ratio detector

unbalanced output voltage and then an unbalanced circuit is used. Fig. 3.38 shows the circuit of one version of the unbalanced ratio detector.

Quadrature detector

The action of a quadrature detector depends upon two voltages, which are both derived from the FM signal to be detected and which are 90° out of phase with each other at the unmodulated carrier frequency.

The basic circuit of a quadrature detector is shown in Fig. 3.39. It consists of a product detector, a parallel-tuned circuit, a capacitor and an RC low-pass filter. The function of the capacitor and the tuned circuit is to convert frequency changes into phase changes.

The tuned circuit is adjusted so that it is at resonance, and hence has a purely resistive impedance, at the unmodulated carrier frequency. The detector's input signal voltage V_1 is directly applied to one of the detector inputs and also to the capacitor and tuned circuit

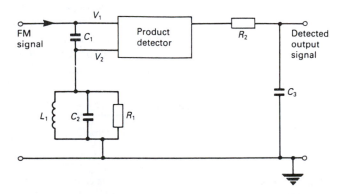

Fig. 3.39 Quadrature detector

in series. A voltage V_2 is developed across the tuned circuit and this is applied to other input of the product detector. At the unmodulated carrier frequency the phase difference between the voltages V_1 and V_2 is $90°$.

The output voltage of the product detector is

$$v_o = k[V_1 \cos \omega_c t \times V_2 \sin \omega_c t] = kV \sin (2\omega_c t)/2$$

This voltage is removed by the output low-pass filter so that the detected voltage is zero.

At any frequency deviation $\delta\omega_c$ from the unmodulated carrier frequency, the tuned circuit introduces an extra phase shift ϕ (lagging or leading depends upon whether the modulated carrier frequency has increased or decreased). This angle ϕ is equal to

$$\phi = \tan^{-1}[Q(\delta\omega_c)/\omega_c] \qquad (3.9)$$

where Q is the Q factor, ω_c is the resonant frequency of the tuned circuit, and $\delta\omega_c$ is the deviation of the signal frequency from the resonant frequency.

Now the output voltage of the product detector is

$$v_o = k[V_1 \cos \omega_c t \times V_2 \sin (\omega_c t + \phi)] \qquad (3.10)$$

The output of the product detector now contains a component at $k^1 V_1 \sin \phi$ and all other, higher-frequency, components are filtered off. This means that the detected output voltage is directly proportional to the fractional deviation from the unmodulated carrier frequency.

Quadrature detectors are generally ICs, either on their own or within a radio IC that includes several other circuit functions. With such ICs it is necessary to provide the tuned circuit external to the ICs connected to the appropriate pins. Fig. 3.40 shows how the quadrature detector components are added externally to an IC, in this case the SL 6652 IF/AF circuit.

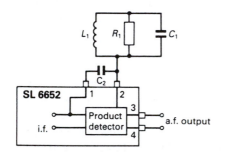

Fig. 3.40 SL 6652 uses a quadrature detector

Phase-locked loop detector

Another method of FM detection is the phase-locked loop (PLL), whose block diagram is shown in Fig. 3.41.

If a signal at a constant frequency is applied to the input terminals of the circuit, the phase detector produces an output voltage that is proportional to the instantaneous phase difference between the signal and oscillator voltages. This voltage is known as the *error voltage*.

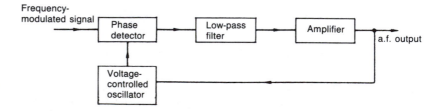

Fig. 3.41 Phase-locked loop frequency detector

The error voltage is filtered and amplified before it is applied to the input of the voltage-controlled oscillator (VCO). The error voltage varies the oscillator frequency in the direction which reduces the difference between signal frequency and the VCO frequency. This action continues until the VCO frequency is equal to the signal frequency. The VCO is then said to be *locked*; when it is in this condition a small phase difference will exist between the signal and oscillator voltages in order to generate the error voltage needed to maintain the lock. If the input signal frequency should change, the error voltage will change also, with the appropriate polarity, and will cause the VCO frequency to vary in the direction that reduces the difference between the two frequencies until the difference is again zero.

When the input signal is frequency-modulated, the error voltage will vary in the same way as the required modulating signal. The voltage that is applied to the VCO is also the output voltage of the detector and is the wanted detected signal voltage. Hence the circuit acts as an FM demodulator.

Fig. 3.42 shows the basic circuit of an IC PLL FM demodulator. Capacitors C_1 and C_2 couple the previous stage in the radio receiver to the detector and C_3 is the tuning capacitor of the voltage-controlled oscillator; C_5 is a part of the low-pass filter between the phase detector and the amplifier; and lastly, C_4 and R_1 are the de-emphasis components.

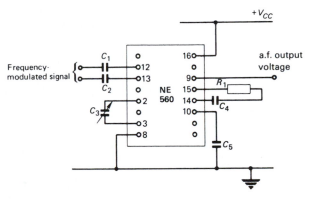

Fig. 3.42 IC PLL frequency detector

The advantages of the PLL detector are as follows:

- The detector is tuned to the unmodulated carrier frequency by a single external capacitor.
- The upper frequency limit is high.
- It introduces little noise or distortion.
- It does not require an inductance.

QPSK and QAM demodulators

QPSK demodulator

The circuit of a QPSK demodulator is shown by Fig. 3.43. The 70 Mbaud input signal is divided by four before it is applied to a phase-

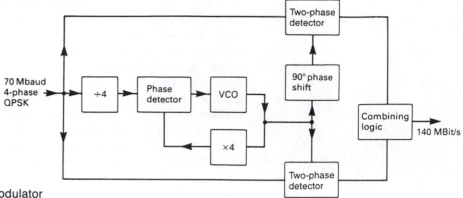

Fig. 3.43 QPSK demodulator

locked loop to recover the carrier component which is required for signal detection. The recovered carriers are applied to the two two-phase detectors, one of which has first been phase-shifted by 90°. The 70 Mbaud signals are detected by the two-phase detectors and the detected outputs are suitably combined to give the wanted 140 Mbit/s output signal.

QAM demodulator

Figure 3.44 shows the block diagram of a QAM demodulator. The input QAM signal is filtered before it is applied, along with a 70 MHz carrier, to two double-balanced mixers. The carrier supplied to one of the mixers is first phase-shifted by 90°. The demodulated signals are each then applied to an analogue-to-digital converter to obtain the I and Q channel data streams.

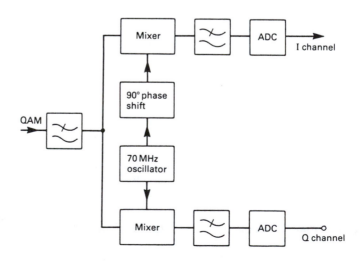

Fig. 3.44 QAM demodulator

Exercises

3.1   (a) Draw a circuit diagram of a ratio detector. Briefly explain its operation. (b) Explain how a ratio produces amplitude limiting.

3.2   Draw a block schematic diagram of a phase-locked loop frequency-modulation detector. Explain the principle of operation of the circuit. What are the advantages of this type of detector?

3.3   (a) Draw the circuit diagram of a Foster–Seeley discriminator. (b) Describe its operation as an FM demodulator.

3.4   Fig. 3.45 shows a discriminator. (a) What type is it? Draw phasor diagrams relating V_1 to each of V_2, V_3 and V_4 when the signal is (i) at the carrier frequency, (ii) above the carrier frequency. (c) Draw a typical input–output characteristic for such a discriminator, labelling the axes. (d) What happens to the output if the incoming carrier drifts from its nominal frequency?

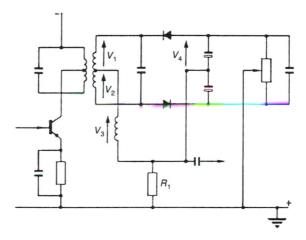

Fig. 3.45

3.5   Describe the principle of operation of a quadrature detector. Why is this type of detector commonly used inside radio ICs?

3.6   Explain, with the aid of appropriate diagrams, how an SSBSC signal can be produced (a) by the filter method and (b) by the phasing method. Compare the relative merits of the two methods.

3.7   Draw the circuit diagram of a diode detector suitable for the demodulation of DSB amplitude-modulation signals. Explain the operation of the circuit and give typical component values.

3.8   Explain, with the aid of block diagram, how a frequency-modulated wave can be produced using (a) a direct method and (b) an indirect method. Why is the indirect method employed?

3.9   (a) What is a varactor diode? (b) Draw the circuit diagram of a varactor diode modulator and explain its operation.

3.10 Describe with circuit diagrams the operation of a reactance modulator.

3.11 Fig. 3.46 shows the pin connections of an integrated-circuit double-balanced modulator. The pin functions are as listed:

   1 + signal in   8 + power supply voltage
   2 − signal in   10 + output

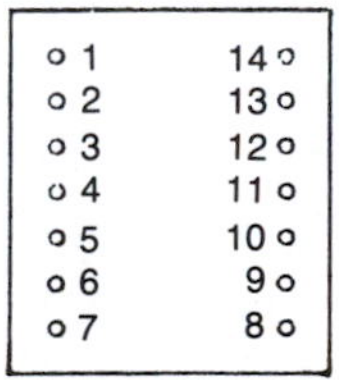

Fig. 3.46

3 + carrier in   12 − output
4 decouple   13 carrier leak adjust
7 + carrier in   14 earth

(a) Draw a suitable modulator circuit using this IC. (b) List the advantage
of ICs over the use of discrete components.

3.12 What are the requirements for the demodulation of an SSBSC signal in term
of (a) the magnitude of the re-inserted carrier, (b) the frequency of the re
inserted carrier and (c) the phase of the re-inserted carrier?

4 Transmission lines

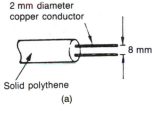

2 mm diameter
copper conductor

8 mm

Solid polythene

(a)

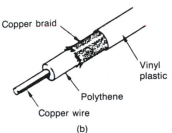

Copper braid

Vinyl
plastic

Polythene

Copper wire

(b)

Fig. 4.1 Construction of (a) a twin cable and (b) a coaxial cable

The basic purpose of a transmission line is to transmit electrical energy from one point to another. The length of a line may be some tens or hundreds of metres in the case of a feeder used to connect a radio transmitter or receiver to its aerial, or perhaps only a fraction of a metre when the line is used as a component in a UHF equipment.

Essentially, a transmission line consists of a pair of conductors separated from one another by a dielectric. The two main types of line used in radio communication systems are the two-wire or twin line and the coaxial pair shown in Fig. 4.1(a) and (b). Both types of cable are available with air as the dielectric, or with some insulating material such as polythene. Each conductor of a pair has both series resistance and inductance, and shunt capacitance and leakance exists between the conductors. The magnitudes of the four *primary coefficients* depend upon the physical dimensions of the conductors and the nature of the dielectric used. The values of the resistance and the leakance also depend upon the frequency of the signal propagating along the line.

The *electrical length* of a line is measured in wavelengths, where the wavelength is obtained from

$$\lambda = c/(f\sqrt{\epsilon_r}) \qquad (4.1)$$

where c is the velocity of light $= 3 \times 10^8$ m/s, ϵ_r is the relative permittivity of the dielectric, and f is the frequency of the signal.

Example 4.1

Calculate the electricial length of a 10 m length of line at (a) 1 MHz and (b) 200 MHz. The permittivity of the dielectric is 2.25.

Solution

(a) $\lambda = (3 \times 10^8)/(\sqrt{2.25} \times 1 \times 10^6) = 200$ m
Electrical length $= (10/200) = 0.05\,\lambda$ *(Ans.)*

(b) $\lambda = (3 \times 10^8)/(\sqrt{2.25} \times 200 \times 10^6) = 1$ m
Electrical length $= 10\,\lambda$ *(Ans.)*

When a line is electrically short, generally taken as being less than 0.1 λ, there is no need to employ transmission line theory. All calculations can be carried out with lumped values of capacitance, inductance and resistance.

Primary coefficients of a line

The four primary coefficients of a transmission line are the series resistance and inductance of the conductors, and the capacitance and leakance between the conductors. All four of the primary coefficients are uniformly distributed along the length of the line.

The *leakance* represents the flow of current through the finite insulation resistance between the conductors and the power dissipated in the dielectric as the line capacitance is alternately charged and discharged. In addition, further losses may occur at the higher radio frequencies if the conductors should radiate energy. A coaxial pair is nearly always operated with its outer conductor earthed and the outer conductor then acts as a screen. The screening effect then reduces very considerably the radiation of energy by a coaxial pair to the outside world and it also ensures that little, if any, externally produced energy can reach the inner conductor. The efficiency of the screening depends upon the construction of the outer conductor; when a solid copper tube is used, radiation is negligible, if present at all, but when a copper braid forms the outer conductor, as with flexible coaxial cables, the screening efficiency is not as good and decreases with increase in frequency.

Radiation from a balanced two-wire line will occur if the distance between the two conductors is an appreciable fraction of a wavelength; if the two conductors are electrically close together the energy radiated by one conductor will cancel out the radiation from the other. This is because at any point along the line the two wires are carrying currents of equal amplitude but of opposite phase, i.e. the current is flowing in one direction in one conductor and in the reverse direction in the other conductor.

Fig. 4.2(a) shows the current flowing in a line whose conductors are spaced λ/100 apart. The energy radiated by the bottom conductor is in antiphase with the radiation from the top conductor and, since λ/100 corresponds to an angle of 3.6°, the two fields almost entirely cancel out. At a much higher frequency the same two conductors may be λ/2 apart as in Fig. 4.2(b); now the magnetic field radiated by the lower conductor, initially 180° lagging, has a λ/2 distance to travel before reaching the upper conductor. This means that it will have a total phase lag, relative to the field due to the upper conductor, of (180° + 180°) or 360°. Hence at this frequency the fields produced by the two conductors are in phase with one another and so do not cancel.

At radio frequencies the attenuation of a line can often be neglected since its magnitude is small for the lengths of line employed. This means that both the resistance and the leakance of the line can also

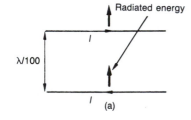

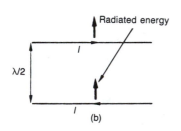

Fig. 4.2 Radiation from a two-wire line

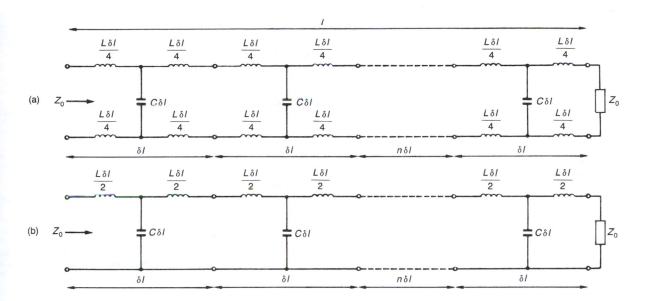

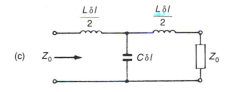

(c)

Fig. 4.3 Equivalent circuit of a loss-free line

be neglected. The line is said to be *loss-free* and then can be represented by the network given by Fig. 4.3(a). The line is considered to consist of a large number of very short lengths, δl, of line connected in cascade as shown. Each short section of line has a total shunt capacitance of $C\delta l$. The series inductance is uniformly distributed along the line and so it is shown in both conductors forming the pair. It is generally more convenient to lump all the inductance into the upper conductor as shown in Fig. 4.3(b); this does not upset the operation of the line, in theory, since the total series inductance per section is still $L\delta l$.

Secondary coefficients of a line

The behaviour of a transmission line when a signal is applied across its input terminals is determined by its *secondary coefficients*. The four secondary coefficients of a line are its characteristic impedance, its attenuation and phase change coefficients, and its phase velocity of propagation.

Characteristic impedance

The characteristic impedance Z_0 of a transmission line is the input impedance of an infinite length of that line. Fig. 4.4 shows an infinite length of line; its input impedance is the ratio of the voltage V_s applied across the sending-end terminals to the current I_s flowing into the line, i.e.

Fig. 4.4 Definition of the characteristic impedance of a line

$$Z_0 = V_s/I_s \tag{4.2}$$

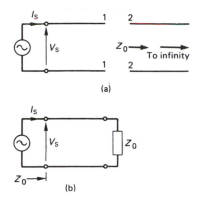

(a)

(b)

Fig. 4.5 Alternative definition of the characteristic impedance of a line

Similarly, at any point x along the line the ratio V_x/I_x is always equal to Z_0.

Suppose now the line is cut a finite distance from its sending-end terminals as shown in Fig. 4.5(a). The remainder of the line is still of infinite length and so the impedance measured at terminals 2-2 is equal to the characteristic impedance. Thus, before the line was cut, terminals 1-1 were effectively terminated in an impedance Z_0. The conditions at the input terminals will not be changed if terminals 1-1 are closed in a physical impedance equal to Z_0, as shown in Fig. 4.5(b). This leads to a more practical definition of Z_0: the characteristic impedance of a transmission line is the input impedance of a line that is terminated in the characteristic impedance.

A line is said to be *correctly terminated* when it is terminated by its characteristic impedance. Thus, when the equivalent circuit of a loss-free line, shown in Figs. 4.3(a) and (b), is terminated in the characteristic impedance Z_0, the impedance measured at the input terminals of the line is also Z_0. Similarly, the input impedance of the second network is also Z_0. This means that the first of the cascaded networks is effectively terminated by Z_0 and so the equivalent circuit of the line can be replaced by the circuit given in Fig. 4.3(c). The characteristic impedance of a radio-frequency transmission line is given by

$$Z_0 = \sqrt{L/C} \text{ ohms} \tag{4.3}$$

where L and C are the distributed inductance and capacitance per metre.

Example 4.2

A radio-frequency transmission line has an inductance of 178.57 nH/m and a capacitance of 71.43 pF/m. Calculate its characteristic impedance.

Solution
From equation (4.3)

$$Z_0 = \sqrt{[(178.57 \times 10^{-9})/(71.43 \times 10^{-12})]} = 50 \, \Omega \quad (Ans.)$$

The values of the series inductance and shunt capacitance of a line depend upon the physical dimensions of the line, according to equations (4.4) and (4.5).

For an air-spaced coaxial line,

$$Z_0 = 138 \log_{10} (R/r) \text{ ohms} \tag{4.4}$$

For a twin line,

$$Z_0 = 276 \log_{10} (D/r) \text{ ohms} \tag{4.5}$$

In equation (4.4), R is the inner radius of the outer conductor and r is the radius of the inner conductor, while in equation (4.5) D is the spacing between the centres of the two conductors and r is the radius of each conductor. If either cable employs a continuous insulating material between its conductors, the characteristic impedance is reduced from Z_0 to $Z_0/\sqrt{\epsilon_r}$, where ϵ_r is the relative permittivity of the insulating material.

Example 4.3

A twin cable has conductors of 2 mm diameter separated 8 mm from each other by continuous solid polythene insulation. If the relative permittivity of the polythene is 2.3, calculate the characteristic impedance of the cable.

Solution
From equation (4.5)

$$Z_0 = (276/\sqrt{2.3}) \log_{10} (8/1) = 164.4\,\Omega \quad (Ans.)$$

Example 4.4

A radio-frequency transmission line has a characteristic impedance of 75 Ω and is connected across the terminals of a signal generator. The signal generator has an internal impedance of 75 Ω and its voltage control is set to give an internal e.m.f. of 10 V. Determine (a) the current which flows into the line and (b) the voltage across the input terminals of the line. The line is correctly terminated.

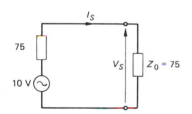

Fig. 4.6

Solution
Since the input impedance of a correctly terminated line is Z_0, the conditions at the sending end of the line can be represented by the circuit of Fig. 4.6.

(a) From Fig. 4.6,
$$I_s = 10/(75+75) = 66.67 \text{ mA} \quad (Ans.)$$
(b) $V_s = I_s Z_0 = 66.67 \times 10^{-3} \times 75 = 5 \text{ V} \quad (Ans.)$

The practical determination of the characteristic impedance of a line is best carried out by measuring its input impedance when its far-end terminals are (i) open-circuited and (ii) short-circuited. If these two input impedances are represented by Z_{oc} and Z_{sc} respectively, then

$$Z_0 = \sqrt{(Z_{oc} Z_{sc})} \tag{4.6}$$

Example 4.5

Measurement of the input impedance of a line with its far-end terminals first open-circuited and then short-circuited gave the following results: $Z_{oc} = 1200\,\Omega$ and $Z_{sc} = 300\,\Omega$. Calculate the characteristic impedance of the line.

Solution
From equation (4.6),

$$Z_0 = \sqrt{(1200 \times 300)} = 600\,\Omega \quad (Ans.)$$

Attenuation coefficient

As a current or voltage wave is propagated along a line, its amplitude is progressively reduced or *attenuated*, because of losses in the line.

These losses are of three types: firstly, there are conductor losses caused by I^2R power dissipation in the series resistance of the line; secondly, there are dielectric losses; and thirdly, there are radiation losses. Radiation losses will occur in a balanced twin line at frequencies high enough for the conductor separation to be an appreciable fraction of the signal wavelength. Radiation loss does not occur in a coaxial pair in which the outer is made of solid copper, but some losses will take place when a braided outer is used.

The radiation losses are difficult to determine but should be small if the correct type of cable is used. Neglecting the radiation losses, it is found that, if the current or voltage at the sending end of the line is I_s or V_s, then the current or voltage one metre along the line is

$$I_1 = I_s e^{-\alpha} \quad \text{or} \quad V_1 = V_s e^{-\alpha}$$

where e is the base of natural logarithms (2.7183) and α is the *attenuation coefficient* of the line in nepers per metre, where 1 neper = 8.686 dB. In the next metre length of line, the attenuation is the same and so the current I_2, two metres along the line, is

$$I_2 = I_1 e^{-\alpha} = I_s e^{-\alpha} e^{-\alpha} = I_s e^{-2\alpha}$$

Similarly $\quad V_2 = V_s e^{-2\alpha}$

If the line is l metres in length, the current and voltage received at the output terminals of the line are given, respectively, by

$$I_r = I_s e^{-\alpha l} \tag{4.7}$$

$$V_r = V_s e^{-\alpha l} \tag{4.8}$$

Alternatively, of course, the magnitude of the received current or voltage can be determined using decibels.

Equations (4.7) and (4.8) show that both the current and voltage waves decay exponentially as they propagate along the length of the line.

At radio frequencies the attenuation coefficient of a line is given by equation (4.9):

$$\alpha = R/(2Z_0) + GZ_0/2 \text{ nepers/metre} \tag{4.9}$$

$R/(2Z_0)$ represents the conductor losses and $GZ_0/2$ represents the dielectric losses, where R is the series resistance per metre loop and G is the leakance per metre.

The attenuation coefficient is not a constant quantity but increases with increase in frequency. The two contributory parts of the attenuation coefficient vary with frequency in different ways; the conductor losses are proportional to the square root of frequency but the dielectric losses are directly proportional to frequency. Normally, the conductor losses are several times larger than the dielectric losses and often, particuarly with coaxial lines, the dielectric loss is small enough to be neglected. Then the line attenuation is proportional to the square root of frequency, while the single wavelength is inversely proportional to frequency. This means that the attenuation per wavelength *decreases* with increase in frequency. Often, particularly at the VHF and higher bands, the loss of a line is small enough to be neglected; then the line is usually described as being *low-loss* or, if a very short line, as *loss-free*.

Phase change coefficient

As a current or voltage wave travels along a line, it experiences a progressive phase lag relative to its phase at the sending end of the line. The *phase change coefficient* β of a line is the number of radians or degrees phase lag per metre. If, for example, $\beta = 2°$ per metre, then a 10 metre length would introduce a phase shift of 20°.

At radio frequencies the phase change coefficient is given by equation (4.10):

$$\beta = \omega\sqrt{(LC)} \text{ radians/metre} \tag{4.10}$$

Clearly the phase change coefficient is directly proportional to frequency.

Example 4.6

A transmission line has a phase change coefficient β of 30° per metre at a particular frequency. If the physical length of the line is 1.5 m, calculate its electrical length.

Solution

$$\beta l = 30° \times 1.5 = 45°$$

In one wavelength a phase shift of 360° takes place. Therefore

$$\text{Electrical length} = 45\lambda/360 = \lambda/8 \quad (Ans.)$$

Phase velocity of propagation

The phase velocity of propagation V_p of a transmission line is the velocity with which a sinusoidal current or voltage wave is propagated along that line. Any sinusoidal wave travels with a velocity of one wavelength per cycle and, since there are f cycles per second, this corresponds to a velocity of λf metres per second. Therefore

$$V_\text{p} = \lambda f \text{ m/s} \tag{4.11}$$

where λ is the wavelength and f is the frequency of the sinusoidal wave.

In a distance of one wavelength, a phase lag of 2π radians occurs and so

$$\beta = 2\pi/\lambda \text{ radians}$$

Therefore

$$\lambda = 2\pi/\beta$$

and

$$V_p = 2\pi f/\beta = \omega/\beta \tag{4.12}$$

At radio frequencies,

$$V_p = \omega/\omega\sqrt{(LC)} = 1/\sqrt{(LC)}\,\text{m/s} \tag{4.13}$$

and V_p has the same value at all frequencies. This means that all the component frequencies of a complex signal will propagate along a line at the same velocity and will arrive at the end of the line together. The *group velocity* of a radio-frequency line is equal to the common phase velocity of the component frequencies. Thus, the signal envelope will not suffer group delay—frequency distortion.

The phase velocity of propagation on a line is always somewhat smaller than the velocity of light ($c = 3 \times 10^8$ m/s). Usually, the phase velocity is somewhere in between 0.6c and 0.9c.

Example 4.7

A radio-frequency transmission line has an inductance of 263.2 nH per metre and a capacitance of 46.8 pF per metre. Calculate (a) its characteristic impedance; (b) its phase change coefficient at 30 MHz; (c) its phase velocity of propagation.

Solution

(a) $Z_0 = \sqrt{(L/C)} = \sqrt{[(263.2 \times 10^{-9})/(46.8 \times 10^{-12})]} = 75\,\Omega$
   (Ans.)

(b) $\beta = \omega\sqrt{(LC)}$
   $= 2\pi \times 30 \times 10^6 \times \sqrt{(263.2 \times 10^{-9} \times 46.8 \times 10^{-12})}$
   $= 0.66\,\text{rad/m} = 38°/\text{m}$ *(Ans.)*

(c) $V_p = 1/\sqrt{(LC)}$
   $= 1/\sqrt{(263.2 \times 10^{-9} \times 46.8 \times 10^{-12})}$
   $\simeq 2.85 \times 10^8\,\text{m/s}$ *(Ans.)*

The phase change coefficient β can be determined using an alternative method:

$$\lambda = v/f = (2.85 \times 10^8)/(30 \times 10^6) = 9.5\,\text{m}$$
$$\beta = 2\pi/\lambda = 2\pi/9.5 = 0.66\,\text{rad/m (as before)}$$

Matched transmission lines

The input impedance of a matched line, i.e. one that is terminated in Z_0, is equal to Z_0. Suppose a generator of e.m.f. E_s and impedance Z_s is connected across the input terminals of the line. The voltage appearing across the terminals is then

$$V_s = E_s Z_0/(Z_s + Z_0)$$

and the input current I_s is equal to

$$E_s/(Z_s + Z_0)$$

The input current and voltage propagate along the line and are attenuated and phase shifted as they travel. At any point along the line the ratio of the voltage and the current at that point is equal to the characteristic impedance Z_0. At the receiving end of the line, *all* the power carried by the waves is dissipated in the load impedance.

Progression of a wave along a line

Table 4.1 Phase angles on line

Distance from sending end (m)	Phase lag (°)
0	0
10	45
20	90
30	135
40	180
50	225
60	270
70	315
80	360
90	405
100	450

Consider a loss-free radio-frequency line that is 100 metres in length and is correctly terminated at its far end. Suppose the phase change coefficient at a particular frequency is equal to 4.5° per metre and that a sinusoidal voltage of 1 volt peak value is maintained across its sending-end terminals. Since the line is loss-free, the voltage will not be attenuated as it travels along the line but it will experience a progressively increasing phase lag. At a distance of 10 metres from the input terminals the voltage will lag the sending-end voltage by 45°, at 20 metres along the line the phase lag will be 90°, and so on for the remainder of the line. The phase lag of the line voltage, relative to the sending-end voltage, at 10 metre intervals along the length of the line is listed in Table 4.1.

A polar diagram can be drawn to show the magnitude and phase, relative to the sending end, of the voltage as it travels along the line. The diagram consists of a series of phasors drawn with the correct length and at the correct angle to represent the line voltages at various points on the line. The polar diagram for the line under consideration is shown in Fig. 4.7.

At the instant when the sending end voltage is zero and is about to go positive, the voltages existing at various distances along the line can be found by projecting from the tips of the various phasors to the corresponding points on axis A; this is shown in the figure by the dotted lines. The waveform showing how the line voltage varies with distance at this particular instant in time is obtained by drawing a smooth curve to join the plotted points. A quarter of a period later the instantaneous value of the input voltage is at its positive peak value of 1 volt. This condition is obtained by rotating the polar diagram in the anticlockwise direction through an angle of 90° and then projecting from the tips of the phasors on to axis B. The phasor representing the sending end voltage is now pointing vertically upwards to indicate maximum positive value. Joining the points plotted in this way on axis B produces the waveform showing how the line voltage varies with distance at this instant in time. The waveforms of the line voltage at the instants in time when the input voltage is, firstly, zero and about to go negative and, secondly, peak negative, are shown plotted on axes C and D respectively. To obtain waveform C the polar diagram must be rotated in the anticlockwise direction by a further 90°, and then by another 90° for waveform D.

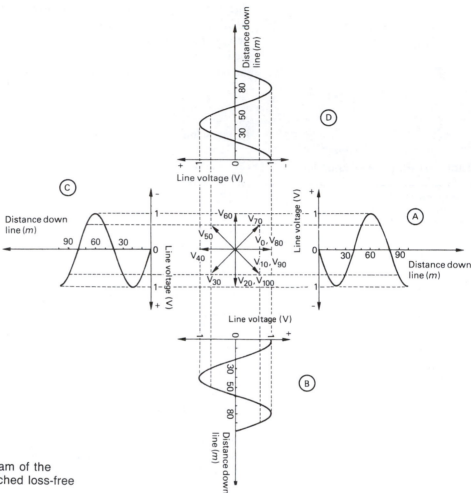

Fig. 4.7 Polar diagram of the voltages along a matched loss-free line

If the four voltage waveforms shown on axes A, B, C and D in Fig. 4.7 are redrawn beneath one another, as shown by Fig. 4.8, it is possible to see that a particular part of the voltage waveform travels along the line. Consider, for example, the negative peak value of -1 volt. In Fig. 4.8(a) this value occurs at a point 20 metres from the sending end of the line; in Fig. 4.8(b), which shows the line waveform $T/4$ later, where T is the periodic time of the input voltage waveform, the negative peak has moved another 20 metres along the line. Similarly, in each of the following two $T/4$ intervals of time the negative peak of the voltage waveform travels another 20 metres (see Fig. 4.8(c) and (d)). The wavelength of the signal is 80 metres. Since the characteristic impedance of a radio-frequency line is purely resistive, the waveform of the current is in phase with the voltage waveform.

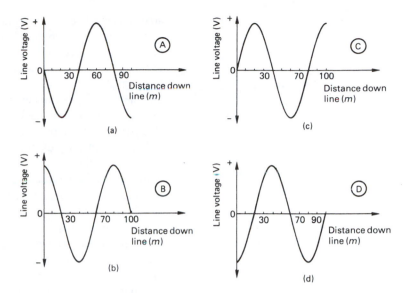

Fig. 4.8 Progression of a voltage wave along a line

Mismatched transmission lines

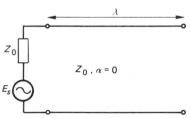

Fig. 4.9 Open-circuited loss-free line

Very often a transmission line is terminated by an impedance that is not equal to the characteristic impedance of the line. In a radio system feeder the terminating impedance is usually an aerial. This will have an impedance which depends upon the type of aerial and it is not always convenient to use a line having the same value of characteristic impedance.

When the impedance terminating a line is not equal to the characteristic impedance, the line is said to be *incorrectly terminated* or *mismatched*. Since the line is not matched, the load is not able to absorb all the power incident upon it and so some of the power is reflected back towards the sending end of the line.

Consider Fig. 4.9 which shows a loss-free line whose output terminals are open-circuited. The line has an electrical length of one wavelength and its input terminals are connected to a source of e.m.f. E_s volts and impedance Z_0 ohms.

When the generator is first connected to the line, the input impedance of the line is equal to its characteristic impedance Z_0. An *incident* current of $E_s/2Z_0$ then flows into the line and an *incident* voltage of $E_s/2$ appears across the input terminals. There are, of course, the same values of sending-end current and voltage that flow into a correctly terminated line. The incident current and voltage waves propagate along the line, being phase-shifted as they travel. Since the electrical length of the line is one wavelength, the overall phase shift experienced is 360°.

Since the output terminals of the line are open-circuited, no current can flow between them. This means that all of the incident current must be reflected at the open circuit. The total current at the open circuit is the phasor sum of the incident and reflected currents and, since this must be zero, the current must be reflected with 180° phase shift. The incident voltage is also totally reflected at the open circuit but with zero phase shift. The total voltage across the open-circuited terminals is twice the voltage that would exist if the line were correctly terminated. The reflected current and voltage waves propagate along the line towards its sending end, being phase-shifted as they go. When the reflected waves reach the sending end, they are completely absorbed by the impedance of the matched source.

At any point along the line, the total current and voltage is the phasor sum of the incident and reflected currents and voltages. Consider Fig. 4.10. At the open circuit the phasors representing the incident and reflected currents are of equal length (since *all* the incident current is reflected) and point in opposite direcitons. The current flowing in the open circuit is the sum of these two phasors and is therefore zero as expected. At a distance of $\lambda/8$ from the open circuit, the incident current phasor is 45° leading, and the reflected current phasor is 45° lagging on the open-circuit phasors. The lengths of the two phasors are equal to one another, since the line loss is zero, but they are 90° out of phase with one another. The total current at this point is $\sqrt{2}$ times the incident current. Moving a further $\lambda/8$ along the line, the incident and reflected current phasors have rotated, in opposite directions, through another 45° and are now in phase with one another. The total current $\lambda/4$ from the open circuit is equal to twice the incident current. A further $\lambda/8$ along the line finds the two phasors once again at right angles to one another so that the total line current is again $\sqrt{2}$ incident current. At a point $\lambda/2$ from the end of the line, the incident and reflected current phasors are in antiphase with one another and the total line current is zero. Over the next half-wavelength of line the phasors continue to rotate in opposite directions, by 45° in

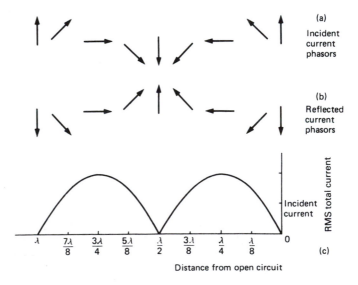

Fig. 4.10 (a) The incident current, (b) the reflected current at $\lambda/8$ intervals along a loss-free open-circuited line, (c) the r.m.s. value of the total current at each point

each λ/8 distance, and the total line current is again determined by their phasor sum.

It is usual to consider the r.m.s. values of the total line current and then phase need not be considered. The way in which the r.m.s. line current varies with distance from the open circuit is shown by Fig. 4.10(c). The points at which maxima (*antinodes*) and minima (*nodes*) of current occur are always the same and do not vary with time. Because of this, the waveform of Fig. 4.10(c) is known as a *standing wave*.

If, now, the voltages existing on the line of Fig. 4.9 are considered, the phasors shown in Fig. 4.11 are obtained. At the open-circuited output terminals, the incident and reflected voltage phasors are in phase with one another and the total voltage is twice the incident voltage. Moving from the open circuit towards the sending end of the line, the phasors rotate through an angle of 45° in each λ/8 length of line; the incident voltage phasors rotate in the anticlockwise direction and the reflected voltage phasors rotate clockwise. The total voltage at any point along the line is the phasor sum of the incident and reflected voltages, and its r.m.s. value varies in the manner shown in Fig. 4.11(c).

Two things should be noted from Fig. 4.10(c) and Fig. 4.11(c). First, the *voltage standing-wave* pattern is displaced by λ/4 from the *current standing-wave* pattern; i.e. a current antinode occurs at the same point as a voltage node and vice versa. Secondly, the current and voltage values at the open circuit are repeated at λ/2 intervals along the length of the line; this remains true for any longer length of loss-free line.

When the output terminals of a loss-free line are short-circuited, the conditions at the termination are reversed. There can be no voltage across the output terminals but the current flowing is twice the current

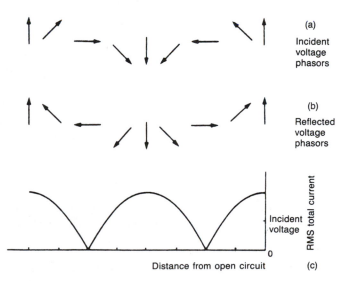

Fig. 4.11 (a) The incident voltage, (b) the reflected voltage at λ/8 intervals along a loss-free open-circuited line, (c) the r.m.s. value of the total voltage at each point

that would flow in a matched load. This means that at the short circuit the incident current is totally reflected with zero phase shift and the incident voltage is totally reflected with 180° phase shift. Thus, Fig. 4.10(c) shows how the r.m.s. voltage on a short-circuited line varies with distance from the load, and Fig. 4.11(c) shows how the r.m.s. current varies.

Clearly, neither an open-circuited nor a short-circuited line can be used for the transmission of information from one point to another. Either condition might arise because of a fault or might be intended, particularly the short circuit, when the line is to be used to simulate either a capacitance or an inductance.

Reflection coefficient

Open- and short-circuited terminations are the two extreme cases of a mismatched line and in most cases the mismatched load will have an impedance somewhere in between zero and infinity. The fraction of the incident current or voltage that is reflected by the load is determined by the *reflection coefficient* of the load.

The *voltage reflection coefficient* ρ_v is the ratio (reflected voltage)/(incident voltage). The *current reflection coefficient* ρ_i is the ratio (reflected current)/(incident current) at the load. Always

$$\rho_i = -\rho_v$$

Example 4.8

The incident current at the output terminals of a mismatched line is 5 mA. If the current reflection coefficient of the load is 0.5, what is the reflected current?

Solution

Reflected current $= 0.5 \times 5 = 2.5$ mA   (*Ans.*)

The voltage reflection coefficient is determined by the values of the characteristic impedance of the line and the load impedance. Thus

$$\rho_v = (Z_L - Z_0)/(Z_L + Z_0) \qquad (4.14)$$

The magnitude of the voltage reflection coefficient lies in the range ± 1, the limits corresponding to the cases of open- and short-circuited loads.

Example 4.9

Calculate the voltage reflection coefficient of a line of 50 Ω characteristic impedance terminated by an impedance of (a) 50 Ω, (b) 30 Ω, (c) 100 Ω.

Solution
 (a) From equation (4.14)
     $\rho_v = (50 - 50)/(50 + 50) = 0$ (*Ans.*)

This answer is to be expected since, if the line is matched, $Z_0 = Z_L$ and there is no reflection.

(b) $\rho_v = (30-50)/(30+50) = -0.25 = 0.25 \angle 180°$ (*Ans.*)

(c) $\rho_v = (100-50)/(100+50) = 0.33 = 0.33 \angle 0°$ (*Ans.*)

When the reflection coefficient is less than unity, the reflected current and voltage at any point along a loss-free line will be smaller than the incident values. Then the maximum current or voltage on the line will be less than twice the incident current and voltage, and the minimum current or voltage will not be equal to zero. Suppose, for example, that $\rho_v = 0.5 \angle 0°$, then the maximum line voltage will be 1.5 times the incident voltage and will occur at the load and at multiples of $\lambda/2$ from the load. The minimum line voltage will be 0.5 times the incident voltage and will occur $\lambda/4$ from the load and then at multiples of $\lambda/2$ from that point. Similarly, the maximum line current will be 1.5 times, and the minimum line current will be 0.5 times the incident current. Maxima of voltage will occur at the same points as minima of current and vice versa. Fig. 4.12 shows the standing waves of current and voltage on a loss-free line with a load voltage reflection coefficient of 0.5 $\angle 0°$.

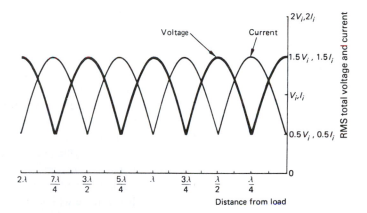

Fig. 4.12 Standing wave patterns on a mismatched line with $\rho_v = 0.5 \angle 0°$

Standing wave ratio

An important parameter of any mismatched low-loss transmission line is its *voltage standing-wave ratio* or VSWR. The VSWR is the ratio of the maximum voltage on the line to the minimum voltage, i.e.

$$S = V_{max}/V_{min} \qquad (4.15)$$

The maximum voltage on a mismatched line occurs at those points where the incident and the reflected voltages are in phase with one another. Also, the minimum line voltage exists at those points along the line at which the incident and reflected voltages are in antiphase. Therefore

$$S = [V_i + |\rho_v| V_i]/[V_i - |\rho_v| V_i] = (1 + |\rho_v|)/(1 - |\rho_v|) \qquad (4.16)$$

where V_i is the incident voltage.

Example 4.10

A low-loss line whose characteristic impedance is 70 Ω is terminated by an aerial of 75 Ω impedance. Determine the VSWR on the line.

Solution
From equation (4.14),

$$\rho_v = (75-70)/(75+70) = 0.035 \; \angle 0°$$

Therefore, from equation (4.16),

$$S = (1+0.035)/(1-0.035) = 1.07 \qquad (Ans.)$$

The presence of a standing wave on an aerial feeder is undesirable for several reasons and very often measures are taken to approach the matched condition and hence to minimize reflections. The reasons why standing waves on a feeder should be avoided if at all possible are as follows:

- Maximum power is transferred from a transmission line to its load when the load impedance is equal to the characteristic impedance. When a load mismatch exists, some of the incident power is reflected at the load and the transfer efficiency is reduced.
- The power reflected by a mismatched load will propagate, in the form of current and voltage waves, along the line towards its sending end. The waves will be attenuated as they travel and so the total line loss is increased.
- At a voltage maximum the line voltage may be anything up to twice as great as the incident voltage. For low-power feeders, such as those used in conjunction with radio receivers, the increased voltage will not matter. For a feeder connecting a high power radio transmitter to an aerial, however, the situation is quite different. Care must be taken to ensure that the maximum line voltage will not approach the breakdown voltage of the line's insulation. This means that for any given value of VSWR there is a corresponding peak value for the incident voltage and hence for the maximum power that the feeder is able to transmit. A high VSWR on a feeder can result in dangerously high voltages appearing at the voltage antinodes. Great care must then be taken by maintenance staff who are required to work on or near the feeder system.

Example 4.11

A loss-free 50 Ω line is connected to a 100 Ω load. Calculate the percentage of the incident power that is dissipated in the load.

Solution

$$\rho_v = (100-50)/(100+50) = 1/3$$

$$P_L = P_i[1-(1/3)^2] = (8P_i)/9$$

Therefore, percentage load power $= 88.9\%$ *(Ans.)*

Measurement of VSWR

The VSWR on a mismatched transmission line can be determined by measuring the maximum and minimum voltages that are present on the line. In practice, the measurement is generally carried out using an instrument known as a *standing-wave indicator*. Measurement of VSWR not only shows up the presence of reflections on a line but also offers a most convenient method of determining the nature of the load impedance.

The measurement procedure is as follows. The VSWR is measured, using a detector, a galvanometer or a VSWR meter, and the distance in wavelengths from the load to the voltage minimum nearest to it is determined. The values obtained allow the magnitude and angle of the voltage reflection coefficient to be calculated. Then, using equation (4.14), the unknown load impedance can be worked out. Unfortunately the arithmetic involved in the later calculation is fairly lengthy and tedious, and it is customary to use a graphical aid known as the Smith chart which simplifies the work.

If the load impedance is *purely* resistive, a much easier method of measurement is available. Suppose, for example, $Z_L = R_L = 3R_0$ (remember that Z_0 is always purely resistive at radio frequencies). Then

$$\rho_v = (Z_L-Z_0)/(Z_L+Z_0) = (3R_0-R_0)/(3R_0+R_0) = 0.5 \angle 0°$$

Therefore

$$S = (1+|\rho_v|)/(1-|\rho_v|) = (1+0.5)/(1-0.5) = 3$$

Now suppose that, instead, $Z_L = R_L = R_0/3$. Then

$$\rho_v = [(R_0/3)-R_0]/[(R_0/3)+R_0)] = 0.5 \angle 180°$$

and, as before,

$$S = (1 + 0.5)/(1 - 0.5) = 3$$

Note that the VSWR is equal to the ratio R_L/Z_0 or Z_0/R_L. This simple relationship is always true provided that the line losses are negligibly small and the load impedance is purely resistive.

Example 4.12

The VSWR on a loss-free line of $50\,\Omega$ characteristic impedance is 4.2. Determine the value of the purely resistive load impedance which is known to be larger than $50\,\Omega$.

Solution

$$R_L/Z_0 = S = 4.2$$

Therefore

$$R_L = SZ_0 = 4.2 \times 50 = 210\,\Omega \quad (Ans.)$$

Methods of matching

λ/4 transformer

A quarter-wavelength (λ/4) length of low-loss line possesses an important impedance-transforming property which is used for a wide variety of purposes at the higher frequencies. The input impedance of a λ/4 length of low-loss line is given by

$$Z_{in} = Z_0^2/Z_L \qquad (4.17)$$

This means that a load impedance Z_L can be transformed into any desired value of input impedance Z_{in} by the suitable choice of the characteristic impedance Z_0 of the λ/4 length of low-loss line. The required value of the characteristic impedance is obtained by transposing equation (4.17) to give

$$Z_0 = \sqrt{(Z_L Z_{in})} \qquad (4.18)$$

One common application of the *quarter-wave* (λ/4) *transformer* is the matching of a transmission line to a load impedance which is not equal to Z_0. Fig. 4.13(a) shows a 600 Ω transmission line which is to be connected to a 300 Ω load impedance. If the line is directly connected to the load, reflections will occur and a voltage standing-wave pattern will appear on the line. To avoid this happening, the load impedance must be transformed into 600 Ω so that a matched system is obtained. A λ/4 matching section should be connected between the end of the 600 Ω line and the 300 Ω load, as shown by Fig. 4.13(b). For the input impedance of the λ/4 section to be equal to 600 Ω, its characteristic impedance must be

$$Z_0 = \sqrt{(600 \times 300)} = 424.3\,\Omega$$

If the load impedance has a reactive component, the design of the matching section is more complicated. It may be possible to tune out the reactive component, or the λ/4 section can be inserted into the system at a certain distance from the load where the line's impedance has become purely resistive.

The λ/4 matching section is widely used at all frequencies high enough to keep the physical dimensions practically small, but it will only operate correctly at one frequency. Any change in the frequency will mean that the electrical length of the section is no longer equal to λ/4. Techniques are available that give a wideband matching section but these are beyond the scope of this book.

Another method of using a λ/4 length of low-loss line as a matching device is shown by Fig. 4.14. The λ/4 section has one pair of terminals short-circuited and its other pair connected across the load impedance. The impedance of the λ/4 line will vary along its length from Z_L to zero and at some point it will be equal to the characteristic impedance

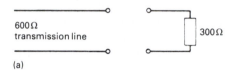

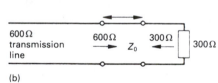

Fig. 4.13 (a) 600 Ω line and mismatched 300 Ω load (b) Use of a λ/4 section of low-loss line to obtain a matched system

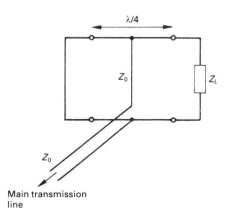

Fig. 4.14 Use of a λ/4 matching stub

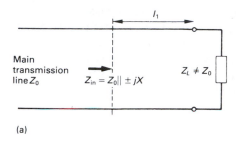

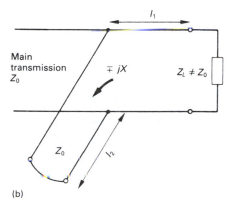

Fig. 4.15 Stub matching: (a) Line impedance at distance l_1 from the load is Z_0 in parallel with a pure reactance $\pm X$; (b) use of a stub of length l_2 to cancel out the reactance $\pm X$ of the line

of the main line. If the main line is connected to the $\lambda/4$ section at this point, it will be effectively correctly terminated and there will be no reflections.

Stub matching

A *stub line* is a length of low-loss line which is short-circuited at one end and whose length is chosen so that the stub has a particular value of input reactance. If the electrical length of the stub is less than $\lambda/4$, the input reactance will be inductive: if the electrical length is between $\lambda/4$ and $\lambda/2$, the input reactance will be capacitive.

The impedance of a mismatched line varies with distance from the load; sometimes the impedance will be larger than the characteristic impedance and sometimes it will be smaller. At some particular distance l_1 from the load, the impedance of the line will be equal to its characteristic impedance in parallel with some value of reactance, as shown in Fig. 4.15(a). The stub is then connected across the line at this point, as in Fig. 4.15(b). The length l_2 of the stub is chosen so that its input reactance is of the same magnitude but of the opposite sign to the reactance of the line at that point. The two reactances will then cancel out so that the *total* impedance of the line at this point will be equal to the characteristic impedance of the line. This means that the main line to the left of this point is effectively correctly terminated.

Example 4.14

A load of resistance $100\,\Omega$ in series with an inductive reactance of $50\,\Omega$ is connected to a $300\,\Omega$ transmission line. The line is to be matched to the load by means of a $\lambda/4$ line and a stub that are connected across the load. Calculate the necessary characteristic impedance of the $\lambda/4$ line and the reactance of the stub.

Solution

$$Y_L = 1/(100 + j50) = 8 - j4\,\text{mS}$$
Susceptance of stub $= +j4\,\text{mS}$
Stub reactance $= 1/(4 \times 10^{-3}) = 250\,\Omega$ (*Ans.*)

With the stub connected across the load,

$$Y_L' = G_L' = 8\,\text{mS}$$
or
$$Z_L' = 125\,\Omega \quad (\textit{Ans.})$$

Hence, for the $\lambda/4$ line,

$$Z_0 = \sqrt{(300 \times 125)} = 194\,\Omega \quad (\textit{Ans.})$$

Baluns

At high frequencies the direct connection of a balanced line to an unbalanced line will result in the radiation of energy and/or the pick-up of noise and interference. A *balun* is a circuit used to connect a balanced line to an unbalanced line without any adverse effects. For radio-frequency powers up to about 5 kW and up to about 30 MHz, it is generally possible to use a conventional wire-wound transformer as a balun. For higher powers and/or higher frequencies, a transmission line balun must be used.

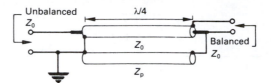

Fig. 4.16   1:1 impedance ratio balun

Figure 4.16 shows the arrangement of a transmission line balun which provides an impedance transformation ratio of 1:1. At the unbalanced end of the balun, the outer conductor of the coaxial pair is connected to a cylindrical conductor. These two conductors form a two-wire line of characteristic impedance Z_p. The line is $\lambda/4$ in length and so the impedance seen looking into the right-hand end of the balun is equal to $Z_p^2/0$, i.e. an open circuit. Hence, one of the balanced line's conductors can be connected to the outer of the coaxial pair. The other balanced conductor can be connected to the linked inner conductor and the cylindrical conductor *without* being connected to earth potential.

Usually, unbalanced lines have a characteristic impedance of the order of 50–75 Ω, while two-wire line characteristic impedances are several hundreds of ohms. There is thus usually a need for the magnitude of the line impedance to be transformed also. Fig. 4.17 shows the arrangement of a line transformer with an impedance ratio of 4:1. Two coaxial pairs are used and are connected in parallel with one another at their left-hand end and connected in series at their right-hand end. If the characteristic impedances of the coaxial pairs are equal to one another *and* to Z_0 ohms, an impedance of $2Z_0$ connected across the right-hand terminals will appear as an impedance of $Z_0/2$ at the left-hand terminals. For example, a 300 Ω impedance can be converted into 75 Ω.

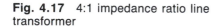
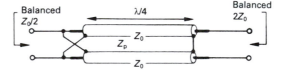

Fig. 4.17   4:1 impedance ratio line transformer

The cascade connection of the arrangements shown in Figs 4.16 and 4.17 would give a 4:1 impedance ratio balun. More complex baluns can be built up using suitable combinations of the circuits described and $\lambda/4$ sections, and many different circuits have been produced.

Radio station feeders

A feeder is employed to connect an aerial to the radio transmitter or receiver with which it is associated. Usually, feeders are either two-wire or twin conductors, about 0.3 m apart mounted on top of wooden poles, or they are coaxial pairs. The twin feeders are normally operated *balanced* with respect to earth, but the coaxial feeders have their outer conductor earthed and are therefore *unbalanced*. The two types of feeder have various advantages and disadvantages relative to one another and these are listed below.

- Twin feeders are cheaper to provide than coaxial pairs.
- It is easier to carry out VSWR measurements and locate faults on a twin feeder.
- Matching devices are commonly used in feeder systems to convert a mismatched aerial load into a more or less matched load. These matching devices are easier and therefore cheaper to make when manufactured for use in a twin feeder system.
- A coaxial feeder is less demanding in its use of space than a twin feeder.
- Both the conductors comprising a twin feeder are exposed to the atmosphere and this leads to the two-wire feeder's transmission characteristics being much more variable than those of a coaxial feeder.
- At higher frequencies the two conductors of a twin feeder are electrically spaced well apart and tend to radiate energy. Because of this the two-wire feeder has greater losses.
- In many radio stations it is often necessary to switch feeders between aerials and between station equipment as propagation conditions vary. The necessary switching arrangements are much easier to augment in conjunction with a coaxial feeder than with a twin feeder.

Most high-frequency transmitting stations use a combination of the two types of feeder in an attempt to make use of the advantages of each type. Within the radio station building coaxial feeders are used, but to connect the building to the aerials the twin feeder is employed.

Exercises

4.1 (a) A 1000 Ω feeder is to be matched to a 600 Ω aerial by a $\lambda/4$ matching section. Calculate the necessary characteristic impedance of the section. (b) Explain, with the aid of suitable sketches, the action of a stub matching system.

4.2 Explain what is meant by the term *balun*, and state where one of these devices would be employed. Draw a balun and describe its operation.

4.3 (a) A radio-frequency line has an inductance of 1.2 μH/m and a capacitance of 13.32 pF/m. Calculate the characteristic impedance of the line. (b) A loss-free line has a characteristic impedance of 500 Ω and is correctly terminated. At the sending end a current of 1 mA flows into the line. Calculate the power dissipated in the load.

4.4 What is meant by a *reflected wave* on a line and when does it occur? Explain how a standing wave is set up on a mismatched line.

4.5 A loss-free transmission line has a characteristic impedance of 600 Ω and a phase change coefficient of 30° per 10 m at a particular frequency. A sinusoidal voltage at this frequency and of 3 V peak value is applied to the input terminals of the line. Use a polar diagram to draw the waveform of the current in the first 120 metres of the line at the instant when the input voltage is zero and about to go positive.

4.6 A loss-free line is λ/4 long and its output terminals are short-circuited. Draw phasors to represent the currents and voltages on the line and hence draw curves to show how the r.m.s. current and voltage on the line vary with distance from the short circuit. Consider points which are λ/16 apart.

4.7 (a) The attenuation of a transmission line increases with increase in frequency, yet the attenuation of a radio-frequency line is often neglected. Discuss why this is so. (b) A transmission line has a characteristic impedance of 50 Ω. A 100 metre length of this line has its far end terminals closed by a 50 Ω resistor. What is the input impedance of the line? What would be the input impedance if the 50 Ω resistor were removed and the terminals were instead connected to the input terminals of a 25 metre length of another line? The second line also has a characteristic impedance of 50 Ω and is correctly terminated.

4.8 (a) Why is it necessary to match an aerial to its feeder? The voltage reflection coefficient at the end of a loss-free line is $0.6 \angle 180°$. Calculate the VSWR on the line. (b) A transmission line is 20 metres long. Is it an electrically short or long line? Give reasons for your answer.

4.9 (a) Explain how a line discontinuity or mismatch will produce standing waves of current and voltage. (b) Explain why a VSWR is undesirable on a radio feeder. The voltage reflection coefficient of a line is $0.25 \angle 180°$. Calculate the current reflection coefficient and the VSWR.

4.10 A line has a VSWR of 3. Calculate the magnitudes of (a) the voltage and (b) the current reflection coefficients.

Table 4.2

	Balanced feeders	Unbalanced feeders
	best	worst
Parameter stability		
Cost		
High-power handling		
Use at VHF		
Use with HF log-periodic aerial		
Use with Yagi aerial		
Fault location		
Ease of matching		

4.11 Complete Table 4.2 for the relative merits of balanced and unbalanced feeders in radio systems.

4.12 Given a choice between typical balanced and unbalanced feeder systems, which would you choose (a) on a cost basis, (b) for a high-power handling application, (c) for a VHF application, (d) to connect a transmitter to an HF log-periodic aerial, (e) to connect a receiver to a Yagi aerial?

4.13   (a) A radio-frequency transmission line has a characteristic impedance of 75 Ω and a phase velocity of propagation of 2.4×10^8 m/s. Determine its inductance and capacitance per metre. (b) The line is terminated by an aerial. Calculate the standing wave ratio along the line when the aerial impedance is 500 Ω.

4.14   (a) What is meant by the following terms when applied to a radio-frequency transmission line: (i) voltage reflection coefficient, (ii) voltage standing wave ratio, (iii) wavelength? (b) The VSWR on a line is 1.05. Calculate its voltage reflection coefficient.

4.15   Using the expression for the voltage reflection coefficient of a mismatched transmission line explain why there are no reflections on a correctly terminated line. List the reasons why the presence of a standing wave on an aerial feeder is undesirable.

4.16   A correctly terminated line is 2000 m in length and has a characteristic impedance of 600 Ω. (a) What is the impedance (i) at the load, (ii) 1000 m from the load, (iii) 1500 m from the load? (b) Explain why the current 100 m from the sending end of the line will lag the sending-end current. (c) The line has an attentuation coefficient of 2 dB/km at a particular frequency. What is its overall loss at twice this frequency?

5 Aerials

In a radio system, whether for point-to-point communication or for sound and/or television broadcasting, the information, or baseband signal is used to modulate a radio-frequency carrier wave and the modulated wave is radiated into the atmosphere, in the form of an electromagnetic wave, by a transmitting aerial. For the radiated signal to be received the electromagnetic wave must be intercepted by a receiving aerial. The main differences between practical transmitting and receiving aerials are the (often) tremendously different powers which have to be handled. For example, a transmitting aerial may radiate many kilowatts of power while a receiving aerial may have only a few milliwatts dissipated in it. Other than this, the main requirement of a transmitting aerial is that it should match its feeder in order to ensure maximum power input to the aerial. For a receiving aerial, the priority is for maximum gain and directivity and for minimum sidelobes to minimize the pick-up of unwanted signals.

In the low-frequency and medium-frequency bands, vertical monopole aerials mounted on the earth are employed. Point-to-point communications in the HF band generally use some form of log-periodic aerial although HF sound broadcasting employs curtains of $\lambda/2$ dipoles. In the VHF and UHF bands, arrays of $\lambda/2$ dipoles are often used for transmitting and Yagi aerials for receiving. Log-periodic aerials also find application. Mobile radio normally uses vertical whip aerials but helical aerials are also employed.

Radiation from an aerial

Whenever a current flows in a conductor, the conductor is surrounded by a magnetic field, the direction of which is determined by the direction of current flow. If the current changes, the magnetic field will change also. Now, a varying magnetic field *always* produces an electric field that exists *only* while the magnetic field continues to change. When the magnetic field is constant the electric field disappears. The direction of the electric field depends on whether the magnetic field is growing or collapsing and it can be determined by the application of Lenz's law. Similarly, a changing electric field

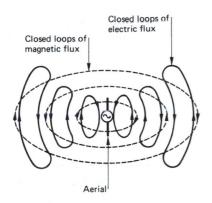

Closed loops of electric flux

Closed loops of magnetic flux

Aerial

Fig. 5.1 Radiation from an aerial

always produces a magnetic field; this means that a conductor carrying an alternating current is surrounded by continually changing magnetic and electric fields that are completely dependent on one another. Although a stationary electric field can exist without the presence of a magnetic field and vice versa, it is impossible for either field to exist separately when changing.

If a sinusoidal current is flowing in a conductor, the electric and magnetic fields around the conductor will also attempt to vary sinusoidally. When the current reverses direction, the magnetic field must first collapse into the conductor and *then* build up in the opposite direction. A finite time is required for a magnetic field and its associated electric field to collapse, however, and at frequencies above about 15 kHz not all the energy contained in the field has returned to the conductor before the current has started to increase in the opposite direction to create new electric and magnetic fields. The energy left outside the conductor cannot then return to it and, instead, is propagated away from the conductor at the velocity of light (approximately 3×10^8 m/s). This is shown by Fig. 5.1. The amount of energy radiated from the conductor increases with increase in frequency, since more energy is then unable to return to the conductor.

The energy radiated from the conductor or aerial, known as the *radiated field*, is in the form of an *electromagnetic wave* in which there is a continual interchange of energy between the electric and magnetic fields. In an electromagnetic wave the electric and magnetic fields are at right angles to each other and they are mutually at right angles to the direction of propagation, as shown in Fig. 5.2 for a particular instant in time. The plane containing the electric field and the direction of propagation of the electromagnetic wave is known as the *plane of polarization* of the wave. For example, if the electric field is in the vertical plane, the magnetic field will be in the horizontal plane, and the wave is said to be vertically polarized. A vertically polarized wave will induce an e.m.f. into any vertical conductor that it passes, because its magnetic field will cut the conductor, but it will have no effect on any horizontal conductor.

In the immediate vicinity of an aerial, the electric and magnetic fields, compared to those in the radiated field, are of greater magnitude and have a different relative phase. This is because there is, in addition to the radiated field, an *induction field* near the aerial. The induction field represents energy that is not radiated away from the aerial, i.e.

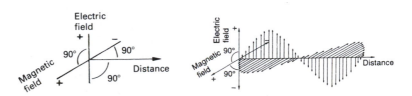

Fig. 5.2 The electromagnetic wave

the energy that does succeed in returning to the conductor, and its magnitude diminishes inversely as the square of the distance from the aerial. The magnitude of the *radiated field* is proportional to the frequency of the wave and inversely proportional to the distance from the aerial. Near the aerial, the induction field is larger than the radiation field, but the radiation field becomes the larger at distances greater than $\lambda/2\pi$, where λ is the wavelength of the signal radiated from the aerial.

Impedance of free space

The amplitudes of the electric field E, and the magnetic field H, in an electromagnetic wave bear a constant relationship to each other. This relationship is known as the *impedance of free space* and is the ratio of the electric field strength to the magnetic field strength, i.e.

$$\text{Impedance of free space} = \frac{E \text{ (volts/metre)}}{H \text{ (ampere-turns/metre)}}$$

$$= 120\pi \text{ ohms} = 377\,\Omega \qquad (5.1)$$

It is customary to refer to the amplitude of a radio wave in terms of its electric field strength.

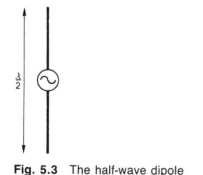

Fig. 5.3 The half-wave dipole

Example 5.1

The magnetic field strength 10 km from a transmitting aerial is 0.053 At/km. Calculate the electric field strength 50 km from the aerial in the same direction.

Solution

$$E/H = 377\,\Omega$$

or

$$E = 377H = 377 \times 0.053 \simeq 20\,\text{mV/m}$$

At 50 km from the aerial the electric field strength is therefore

$$E = 20/5 = 4\,\text{mV/m} \qquad (Ans.)$$

Current and voltage distribution in aerials

A resonant aerial is one which is an integral number of half-wavelengths long, the most common example being the half-wavelength ($\lambda/2$) dipole shown in Fig. 5.3.

The r.m.s. current and voltage distributions on an open-circuited loss-free line that is one wavelength long are shown by Figs 4.10(c) and 4.11(c) respectively. Using these graphs, the standing waves of current and voltage on a $\lambda/4$ length are easily obtained and are shown by Fig. 5.4.

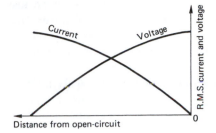

Fig. 5.4 Standing waves of current and voltage on a λ/4 open-circuited loss-free line

Similar standing-wave patterns will result if the two conductors forming the transmission line are each opened out through 90° to form a dipole aerial. As the conductors are opened out they will begin to radiate energy, since their separation will be an appreciable fraction of a wavelength and the resultant losses will slightly modify the standing-wave pattern. Since each conductor is a quarter-wavelength long, a λ/2 dipole will be formed. Reference to Fig. 5.4 shows that for a λ/4 length of open-circuited line the current increases from zero at the open circuit to a maximum, while the voltage falls from its maximum value at the open circuit to zero at the input terminals. Hence the r.m.s. current and voltage distributions on a λ/2 dipole are as shown in Fig. 5.5(a). If peak values are considered, Fig. 5.5(b) will give the current and voltage distributions.

Electrically short aerials are employed at low and medium frequencies where it is impracticable to construct an aerial whose length is comparable with the signal wavelength. For example, one half-wavelength at 300 kHz is 500 m, and at 30 kHz it is 5 km.

In the low and medium wavebands, therefore, transmitting aerials are mounted immediately above the earth, and are fed between the base of the aerial and earth. In such an aerial, whose length is very short compared to the wavelength of the signal (say, λ/16 or less), the current distribution is linear, as shown in Fig. 5.6.

Impedance of an aerial

Impedance is the ratio of voltage to current. It is evident from the current and voltage distributions shown in Figs 5.5 and 5.6 that the impedance will vary along the length of an aerial. It is necesary, therefore, to specify the point in the aerial at which the impedance is measured, and usually the input terminals of the aerial are chosen. It would appear from Fig. 5.5 that the input impedance of a centre-fed λ/2 dipole is zero, since in the middle of the aerial the voltage is zero and the current is a maximum. It should be remembered, however, that Fig. 5.5 is based on the assumption of zero losses; this, of course, is not so, since the aerial radiates power and hence the actual current and voltage distributions are slightly different from those shown. As a result, the input impedance of a dipole is not zero but is approximately 73 Ω. If the physical length of the aerial is exactly one half-wavelength, the input impedance has a small inductive component. To obtain a purely resistive input impedance, a length slightly less than half a wavelength should be used. Sometimes it is more convenient to end-feed a dipole; the input impedance is then high, at about 3600 Ω.

If the signal frequency is changed to make the dipole slightly longer than the resonant length, the input impedance is inductive; conversely, if the dipole is less than the resonant length, the input impedance is capacitive. The feed current of the aerial is at its maximum value when

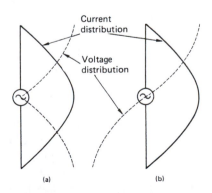

Fig. 5.5 Current and voltage distributions on a half-wave dipole showing (a) r.m.s. values and (b) peak values

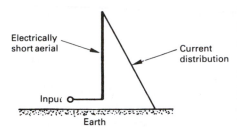

Fig. 5.6 Current distribution on an electrically short aerial

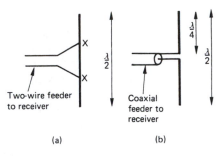

Fig. 5.7 Half-wave dipole fed by (a) two-wire feeder and (b) coaxial feeder

Radiation patterns and directivity

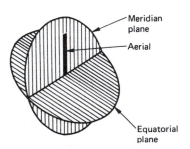

Fig. 5.8 The meridian and equatorial planes of an aerial

the input impedance is purely resistive, and, since the energy radiated from the aerial is proportional to the square of the aerial current, the aerial is at its most effective as a radiator when it is resonant.

The reactive component of the input impedance of an aerial is a function of the diameter of the conductor; an increase in diameter reduces the reactance. If an aerial is to handle signals of wide bandwidth, its input impedance should have as low a reactive component as possible, and hence a thick conductor should be employed.

Energy must be fed into, or taken away from, an aerial by means of a transmission line known as a *feeder*. If a two-wire feeder is employed, it cannot be connected directly to the input terminals of a $\lambda/2$ dipole because considerable resistance mismatch would occur. A two-wire line has a characteristic impedance of a few hundred ohms, and for correct matching the feeder must be connected to a point of higher impedance. Connection between the feeder and the aerial can be made by the method shown in Fig. 5.7(a), the tapping points selected being those where the voltage/current ratio is reasonably close to the feeder impedance. If a coaxial feeder is employed it can be connected to the mid-point of the aerial (Fig. 5.7(b)) because the 75 Ω characteristic impedance of a coaxial feeder is very nearly equal to the 73 Ω aerial input impedance.

The radiation pattern of the $\lambda/2$ dipole will be slightly modified because an unbalanced coaxial feeder is connected to a balanced dipole. If this small degradation in performance is of importance, the feeder can be connected to the dipole via a balun.

All aerials have the property of being able to radiate power better in some directions than in others. The directional characteristics, or *directivity*, of a transmitting aerial is very useful because it allows most of the transmitted power to be radiated in the wanted direction and very little radiated in unwanted directions. This reduces the transmitter power required to produce a given field strength at a distant point in the wanted direction. The directivity of a transmitting aerial is expressed by its *radiation pattern* (or polar diagram).

Radiation patterns

The radiation pattern of an aerial is a graphical representation of the way in which the electric field strength produced by the aerial varies at equal distances from the aerial. Since an aerial radiates energy in all directions, other than along its axis, two radiation patterns are needed to give a reasonable idea of the aerial's performance. The two planes normally chosen are shown in Fig. 5.8: the *meridian* plane contains the axis of the aerial, while the *equatorial* plane is at right angles to the aerial. For example, for a vertical aerial, the meridian plane is vertical and the equatorial plane is horizontal.

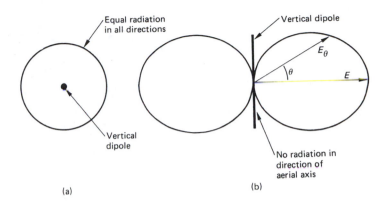

Fig. 5.9 Radiation patterns of a vertical λ/2 dipole: (a) horizontal plane pattern and (b) vertical plane pattern

A radiation pattern refers to the performance of the aerial itself, i.e. when it is mounted well away from any objects, such as buildings or the earth, which by reflecting signals might affect the shape of the pattern. Since aerials are generally mounted near to some object or other, a radiation pattern does not give a true indication of the performance to be expected from a particular aerial installation. However, a radiation pattern does give a method of comparing different types of aerial.

An aerial may be used for receiving signals as well as for transmitting them, and the radiation pattern also gives an indication of the receiving capabilities of the aerial. Directivity in a receiving aerial is useful because it enables the aerial to distinguish, to some extent, between wanted and unwanted signals.

A vertical dipole aerial will radiate, or receive, equally well in all directions in the horizontal plane; hence its horizontal plane radiation pattern is a circle, as shown in Fig. 5.9(a). In the vertical plane such an aerial does not radiate or receive at all in the line of the aerial axis, its vertical plane radiation pattern having a figure-of-eight shape. The horizontal and vertical plane radiation patterns of a vertical λ/2 dipole are shown in Figs 5.9(a) and (b).

Front-to-back ratio

Many radiation patterns exhibit much greater directivity in one direction than in any other. The *front-to-back ratio* of an aerial is the ratio of the electric field strengths produced at the same distance from the aerial but in opposite directions. Thus in Fig. 5.10 the front-to-back ratio is E_f/E_b.

Example 5.2

The field strength produced x kilometres in the wanted direction from an aerial is 10 mV/m and at the same distance in the opposite direction it is 1 mV/m. Calculate the front-to-back ratio of the aerial.

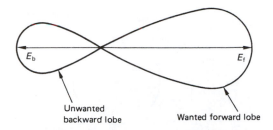

Fig. 5.10 Front-to-back ratio of an aerial

Solution

Front-to-back ratio $= E_f/E_b = (10 \times 10^{-3})/(1 \times 10^{-3}) = 10$ (*Ans.*)

or, in decibels, $= 20 \log_{10} 10 = 20\,\text{dB}$ (*Ans.*)

Beamwidth

The *beamwidth* of an aerial is a convenient measure of the directivity of the aerial. It is the angle subtended by the points at which the radiation power has fallen to half its maximum value or the field strength has fallen to $1/\sqrt{2}$ of its maximum voltage, i.e. the angle subtended by the 3 dB points on the radiation pattern of the aerial. Thus, in Fig. 5.11, the angle θ is the beamwidth. Sometimes the 6 dB beamwidth is quoted instead.

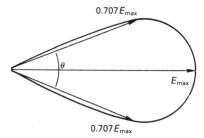

Fig. 5.11 Beamwidth of an aerial

Bandwidth

The *bandwidth* of an aerial is the band of frequencies over which its operation can be considered to be satisfactory. The performance of an aerial can be specified in two ways: (a) referring to the main lobe of the radiation pattern, (b) referring to the input impedance.

(a) For many aerials, maximum radiation in the wanted direction takes place when the lengths and/or spacings of the elements making up the aerial are particular sub-multiples of the signal wavelength. If the frequency is varied, the critical dimensions are no longer correct and the radiation in the wanted direction is reduced. Then, the bandwidth of an aerial is the band of frequencies over which the power radiated by the aerial in the wanted direction is not more than 3 dB down on the maximum radiation.

(b) The bandwidth is the range of frequencies over which the input impedance of the aerial has not changed from its resonant value by more than a specified amount.

Gain of an aerial

The gain of an aerial is not, as with amplifiers, the (power output)/(power input) ratio. Instead, the gain of an aerial is a measure of its directional properties and indicates the extent to which radiation is concentrated in a particular direction, or the extent to which the aerial receives signals better from one direction than from all others. Aerial gain is defined with respect to a reference aerial and it has the same value whether the aerial is used for transmission or reception, but may be defined in terms of either.

The gain of a transmitting aerial is the square of the ratio of the field strength produced at a point in the direction of maximum radiation from the aerial to the field strength produced at the same point by the reference aerial, both aerials transmitting the same power. Alternatively, it may be expressed as the ratio of the powers required to be transmitted by the two aerials to produce the same field strength at a particular point in the direction of maximum radiation.

The gain of a receiving aerial is the ratio of the power delivered by the aerial to a matched load connected to its terminals to the power delivered by the reference aerial to a matched load, the field strengths at the locations of the aerials being the same.

The reference aerial may be a short monopole ($< 0.1\lambda$), a $\lambda/2$ dipole or an *isotropic radiator*. An isotropic radiator is one which will radiate equally well in all directions. Such an aerial is not a practical possibility but it is a useful concept in aerial work.

In the LF and MF bands the short monopole is used as the reference aerial and gain is quoted in dBM. The isotropic radiator is used as the reference in the HF band and then gain is quoted in dBi. Lastly, in the VHF and UHF bands the reference is the $\lambda/2$ dipole and gains are calculated in dBD. Note that dBi = dBD + 2.15 = dBM + 4.8 and dBD = dBM + 2.65.

Example 5.3

An aerial must be fed with 10 kW of power to produce the same field strength at a given point as a $\lambda/2$ dipole fed with 20 kW of power. Calculate the gain of the aerial (a) relative to a $\lambda/2$ dipole; (b) relative to an isotropic radiator; (c) relative to a short monopole. (d) If a modification to the aerial results in the 10 kW input power producing double the field strength at the same point, calculate the new aerial gain relative to a $\lambda/2$ dipole.

Solution
    (a) Gain of aerial relative to $\lambda/2$ dipole $= 10\log_{10}(20 \times 10^3)/(10 \times 10^3)$
$$= 3\,\text{dBD} \quad (Ans.)$$
    (b) Gain of $\lambda/2$ dipole relative to an isotropic radiator $= 2.15\,\text{dBi}$
        Therefore
        Gain of aerial relative to isotropic radiator $= 2.15 + 3 = 5.15\,\text{dBi}$
$$(Ans.)$$

(c) Gain of aerial = 3 + 2.65 = 5.65 dBM   (*Ans.*)

(d) The aerial modification doubles the field strength at the point in question, so that

Gain due to modification = 20 $\log_{10}2$ = 6 dB
and
New gain relative to a λ/2 dipole = 3+6 = 9 dBD   (*Ans.*)

Example 5.4

In a test to determine the gain of an aerial, a standard aerial of known gain is used. Both aerials are situated in a particular field strength and the powers delivered to matched loads are measured. It is found that the power delivered to its load by the aerial under test is 2 μW and the power delivered by the standard aerial is 8 μW. If the gain of the standard aerial is 30 dBi, calculate the gain of the aerial under test.

Solution

Gain of standard aerial relative to aerial under test

= 10 $\log_{10}$ $(8 \times 10^{-6})/(2 \times 10^{-6})$ = 6 dB

Gain of aerial under test = 30−6 = 24 dBi   (*Ans.*)

Effective radiated power

An isotropic radiator is an aerial that is (theoretically) able to radiate energy equally well in all directions, and which therefore produces a constant field strength at a given distance from the aerial in all directions. In practice, however, no aerial possesses such a radiation characteristic; instead it will concentrate its radiated energy in one or more particular directions. This means that a practical aerial will need to radiate a smaller total power than an isotropic radiator to produce the same field strength at a particular point in the direction of maximum radiation. The *effective radiated power* (ERP) of an aerial is the power that an isotropic radiator would have to radiate to produce the same field strength at a particular point in the direction of maximum radiation. Numerically, the effective radiated power of an aerial is equal to the product of the total transmitted power P_t and the numerical gain G of the aerial, i.e.

$$ERP = P_t G \tag{5.2}$$

Example 5.5

An aerial with a gain of 10 dBi radiates a power of 1000 watts. Determine the effective radiated power of the aerial.

Solution

10 dB is a power ratio of 10:1. Therefore

$$ERP = 10 \times 1000 = 10 \text{ kW} \quad (\textit{Ans.})$$

Radiation resistance and radiation efficiency

It is often convenient in aerial work to regard the power radiated from an aerial as being dissipated in a fictitious resistance, known as the *radiation resistance*. The power radiated from an aerial is then given by

$$\text{Power radiated} = I^2 R_r \qquad (5.3)$$

where I is the current fed into the aerial and R_r is the radiation resistance.

The radiation resistance of an aerial is usually equal to the resistive part of its input impedance. For a $\lambda/2$ dipole it is equal to its impedance, i.e. 73 Ω, while the radiation resistance of an electrically short aerial (say, $\lambda/50$) is only about 0.1 Ω.

The power radiated from an aerial is always less than the power fed into it because some power is lost in or near the aerial. Sources of power loss are $I^2 R$ losses in the aerial conductor and in the ground adjacent to the aerial, corona losses and dielectric losses in insulators. The aerial losses can be lumped together and represented by a *loss resistance* R_L, in which all the lost power is assumed to be dissipated.

The radiation efficiency η of an aerial is the ratio of the power radiated to the power fed to the aerial, usually expressed as a percentage:

$$\eta = I^2 R_r / (I^2 R_L + I^2 R_r) = [R_r / (R_L + R_r)] \times 100\% \qquad (5.4)$$

Example 5.6

A low-frequency transmitting aerial has a radiation resistance of 0.3 Ω and a loss resistance of 1.5 Ω. If the current fed into the aerial is 50 A, calculate the radiated power, the input power and the radiation efficiency.

Solution

$$
\begin{aligned}
\text{Power radiated} \quad &= I^2 R_r = 50^2 \times 0.3 = 750\ \text{W} \quad (Ans.) \\
\text{Input power} \quad &= I^2 R_r + I^2 R_L \\
&= (50^2 \times 0.3) + (50^2 \times 1.5) = 4500\ \text{W} \quad (Ans.) \\
\text{Radiation efficiency} &= 100 R_r / (R_L + R_r) = (100 \times 0.3)/(0.3 + 1.5) \\
&= 16.67\% \quad (Ans.)
\end{aligned}
$$

At very low frequencies, radiation efficiencies may be only a few per cent, but at VHF and UHF, efficiencies greater than 90% can be obtained.

Effective aperture of an aerial

The *effective aperture* A_e of an aerial is the imaginary cross-sectional area that would absorb the same power from an incident radio wave as does the aerial when it is matched to its load. The effective aperture of an isotropic radiator is

$$A_e = \lambda^2 / 4\pi\ \text{m}^2 \qquad (5.5)$$

Any practical aerial having a gain G_r with respect to the isotropic radiator has an effective aperture of

$$A_e = G_r \lambda^2 / 4\pi \, \text{m}^2 \qquad (5.6)$$

Example 5.7

Calculate the effective aperture of a $\lambda/2$ dipole at 60 MHz.

Solution

$$\lambda = (3 \times 10^8)/(60 \times 10^6) = 5 \, \text{m}$$

$$A_e' = (5^2 \times 1.64)/4 = 3.26 \, \text{m}^2 \qquad (Ans.)$$

Monopole aerials

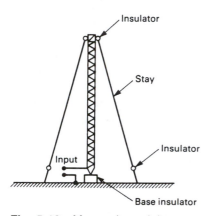

Fig. 5.12 Monopole aerial

Fig. 5.13 Self-supporting tower monopole aerial

Fig. 5.14 Monopole aerial

Transmitting aerials operating at frequencies in the VLF, LF and MF bands must employ structures of considerable height and be mounted vertically upon the earth, because at these frequencies the wavelength of the signal is long. A monopole aerial is driven between the base of the aerial and earth, as in Fig. 5.12. The aerial mast is held erect by a number of stays which are insulated from the aerial itself and from earth by a number of insulators. Sometimes a self-supporting aerial tower is employed, as shown by Fig. 5.13.

Fig. 5.14 shows a $\lambda/4$ monopole aerial that is mounted on the earth's surface and is supplied with r.f. current at the bottom of the aerial.

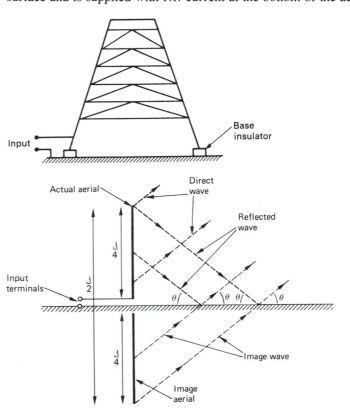

The aerial will radiate energy equally well in all directions in the horizontal plane. In the vertical plane some energy is radiated towards the sky and some is directed downwards towards the earth, as shown by the dotted lines. The downward-directed waves strike the earth and are reflected, provided the earth is flat, with equal angles of incidence and reflection.

At a point distant from the aerial, energy is received by means of both the direct wave and the wave that has been reflected from the earth. The field strength produced at this point is the resultant of the individual field strengths produced by the two waves. From the point of view of an observer located at the distant point, it appears as though the reflected wave has originated from an extension of the aerial beneath the earth. In the diagram this apparent extra length of aerial has been labelled as the *image aerial*. This means that, electrically, the aerial is operating as though its height was twice as great as it actually is. The effective increase in the height of the aerial is advantageous because the field strength produced by an aerial at a given point is proportional to the height of that aerial. The total height of the aerial and its image is $\lambda/2$ and so the current and voltage distributions on the aerial are the same as those on the $\lambda/2$ dipole illustrated by Fig. 5.5. The input impedance of the aerial is purely resistive and is equal to 37 ohms.

The current standing-wave pattern results in the existence of a current maximum at the lower end of the aerial. As a result, large currents will flow in the earth in the vicinity of the aerial and these will dissipate power. To minimize such power losses, and so keep the aerial efficiency at as high a figure as possible, the earth should be of high conductivity. To ensure this, it is usually necessary to install a network of radial conductors, known as a *ground mat*, which is buried beneath the surface of the earth to a depth of about one-third of a metre. The ground mat should extend around the aerial for a distance about equal to the height of the aerial. If the earth is too rocky or too sandy near the aerial, a *counterpoise* earth may well be employed. A counterpoise earth consists of a network of radial copper conductors that is supported on low-permittivity, insulated poles at a height of about two metres above the surface of the earth.

At low frequencies the aerial height needed to make an aerial $\lambda/4$ long is too large to be economically viable. The use of an electrically short aerial results in the input impedance of the aerial possessing a capacitive component, in a reduction in the radiation resistance of the aerial, and in a reduction in the aerial current (the current in a series-tuned circuit is a maximum at resonance). The aerial can be tuned to be resonant by the addition of a suitable inductance in series with its input terminals. Unfortunately, the maximum value of the aerial current is now found to exist in the series inductance and not in the aerial itself. Because of this, the transmitted power is not as great as might be anticipated.

Effective height

The current flowing in an aerial is not of uniform amplitude at all points along the aerial but varies; for example, as shown for two particular aerials in Figs 5.5 and 5.6.

The *effective height* or *effective length* of a transmitting aerial is that length which, if it carried a uniform current having the same magnitude as the input current I of the aerial, would produce the same field strength at a given point. This means that the product of the actual height of the aerial and the mean value of the current flowing must be equal to the product of the effective length and the uniform current. That is

$$l_{phys}I_{mean} = l_{eff}I$$

or $l_{eff} = l_{phys}I_{mean}/I$ (5.7)

In the case of an electrically short aerial in which the aerial current varies linearly from a maximum value of I amperes at the base to zero at the top, the mean aerial current is $I/2$. Hence, from equation (5.7),

$$l_{eff} = l_{phys}/2$$

Since the apparent height of an earthed monopole is twice its physical height, because of earth reflections, its effective height is equal to its physical height.

Example 5.8

An electrically short aerial that is mounted normal to perfectly conducting earth is 100 m high and carries a current that varies linearly from a maximum of 10 A at the base to 0 A at the top. Determine the effective height of the aerial.

Solution
From equation (5.7), the effective height of the aerial is $(100 \times 5)/10$ or 50 m, but since the aerial is mounted on perfectly conducting earth, the effective height is doubled. Therefore

Effective height = 100 metres   (*Ans.*)

The effective height of a receiving aerial is also an important parameter since the e.m.f. induced into the aerial by an incident electromagnetic wave is given by

$$e = El_{eff}$$ (5.8)

where E is the electric field strength of the wave in V/m. Hence the voltage induced into a receiving aerial is directly proportional to the electric field strength.

Example 5.9

An aerial of effective length 1 m is situated in a field strength of 10 mV/m. Calculate the voltage induced into the aerial.

Solution

$$e = 1 \times 10 \times 10^{-3} = 10\,\text{mV} \qquad (Ans.)$$

Top loading

If the mean value of the aerial current could be increased without a corresponding increase in the current at the input terminals, the effective height of the aerial would be increased by the same ratio. This, in turn, would mean that the radiation resistance of the aerial would be higher and more power would be transmitted. The ratio I_{mean}/I of the mean to input aerial currents could be improved if the current could be prevented from falling to zero at the top of the aerial. This is the function of top loading. A horizontal conductor, or system of conductors, is fitted to the top of the aerial and has a relatively large capacitance to earth. Current will now flow in the top loading as well as in the aerial and so the aerial current does not fall to zero at the top of the aerial (see Fig. 5.15). The top loading can also be provided by means of a horizontal conductor which is suspended between the top of the aerial and one, or two, posts. Two examples of this type of top loading are known as the inverted-L and the T aerials.

Inverted-L aerial

The *inverted-L aerial* is designed to transmit and/or receive low- and medium-frequency vertically-polarized signals, and the construction of a receive aerial is shown in Fig. 5.16. The aerial proper in which

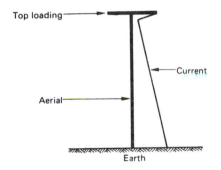

Fig. 5.15 The use of top loading

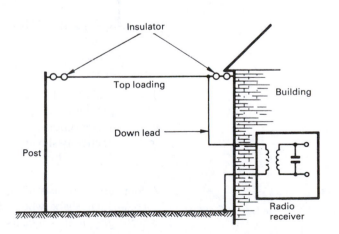

Fig. 5.16 The inverted-L aerial

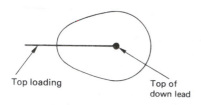

Fig. 5.17 The equatorial plane pattern of an inverted-L aerial

e.m.f.s are induced is the downlead, and this is much less than $\lambda/2$ in length. The downlead must be cut by the horizontal magnetic field of the incident electromagnetic wave, and so it should be as nearly vertical as possible. No e.m.f. is induced in the long horizontal section of the aerial, which is provided to increase the effective length of the aerial and thereby increase the mean aerial current.

The equatorial radiation pattern of an inverted-L aerial is shown in Fig. 5.17, and it can be seen that the aerial exhibits slight directivity, receiving or transmitting somewhat better in the direction from top loading to downlead.

For the best results the aerial should be mounted as high as possible and be well clear of buildings that might reduce the field strength of the signals to be received. This type of aerial can be used for domestic radio installations and is ideal when reception of distant stations is required.

T aerial

For some installations it may be more convenient to have the downlead connected to the centre of the capacitance top, as shown in Fig. 5.18. Such an arrangement, known as a *T aerial* because of its appearance, is employed, for example, on board a ship. The T aerial transmits or receives equally well in all directions in the horizontal plane and so its equatorial radiation pattern is a circle.

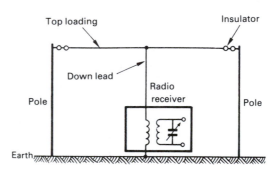

Fig. 5.18 The T aerial

Use of stays

Top loading may also be obtained by locating the highest insulators of a stayed aerial mast some way down each stay and making an electrical connection between the aerial and the stays. An example of this practice is shown by Fig. 5.19.

Loop aerial

A loop aerial consists of one or more turns of wire wound to form a rectangular shape whose dimensions are much smaller than the wavelength of the signal(s) to be received. Fig. 5.20 shows a rectangular loop aerial which has four turns of wire and which is tuned

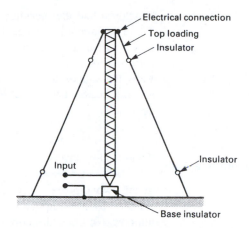

Electrical connection
Top loading
Insulator
Insulator
Input
Base insulator

Fig. 5.19   Stays provide top loading

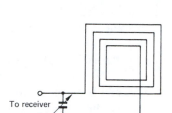

To receiver

Fig. 5.20   The loop aerial

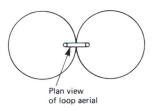

Plan view
of loop aerial

Fig. 5.21   The equatorial plane
radiation pattern of a loop aerial

Ferrite rod aerial

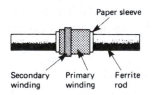

Paper sleeve

Secondary   Primary   Ferrite
winding   winding   rod

Fig. 5.22   The ferrite rod aerial

High-frequency aerials

to the signal frequency by a variable capacitor. The voltage delivered to the receiver by an aerial of this type depends upon the area of the loop and the number of turns of wire; the maximum possible area is limited by the need to fit the aerial into a confined space. A loop aerial has a figure-of-eight radiation pattern, as shown by Fig. 5.21. Clearly, no radiation is received from the directions normal to the plane of the loop and this property makes the loop aerial eminently suited for direction finding.

If the turns of wire are wound around a former made of a magnetic material such as ferrite, the magnetic field of any incident electromagnetic wave will be concentrated within the area of the loop. This will increase the flux density of any field that cuts the loop and will thereby increase the e.m.f. induced into the loop. Effectively, this considerably increases the dimensions of the loop.

Transistor radio receivers usually have ferrite rod aerials. Such an aerial consists of one or more turns mounted on a ferrite rod of about 0.25–0.5 inch diameter. This kind of aerial has the advantage of a small physical size, enabling it to be mounted on the printed circuit of the receiver. Fig. 5.22 shows the construction of a typical ferrite rod aerial. Two coils, giving coverage of one waveband, are wound on the rod; if coverage of two wavebands (e.g. long and medium) is required, another pair of coils must be wound as well. The meridian plane radiation pattern of a ferrite rod aerial is shown by Fig. 5.23; clearly for maximum response to a signal the aerial should be orientated to lie 90° to the direction of the incident radio wave.

In the HF band (3–30 MHz), the signal wavelength is short enough to allow the $\lambda/2$ dipole to be used as the basic element for many types of resonant aerial *array*. The radiation patterns of a $\lambda/2$ dipole in the

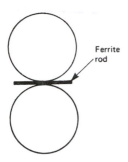

Fig. 5.23 Radiation pattern of a ferrite rod aerial

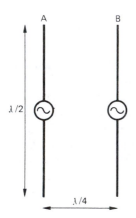

Fig. 5.24 Two λ/2 dipoles spaced λ/4 apart

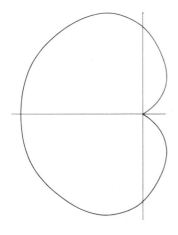

Fig. 5.25 Horizontal plane radiation pattern of two vertical λ/2 dipoles spaced λ/4 apart, fed with equal-amplitude currents

equatorial and the meridian planes have been given earlier in Fig. 5.8. The directivity and gain provided by a single λ/2 dipole is often inadequate and, in order to obtain a considerable improvement, an array of dipoles is very often employed. The radiation pattern depends upon the radiation patterns of each of the individual dipoles, the spacing between the dipoles, and the relative phases of the dipole currents.

Two-dipole arrays

When two dipoles are placed close enough together, the energy radiated by each dipole will be in phase in some directions and in antiphase in other directions. Because of this, the radiation pattern of the two-dipole array is not the same as the pattern of an individual dipole.

Fig. 5.24 shows two vertical λ/2 dipoles A and B which are λ/4 apart at a particular frequency. They form a two-dipole array. The two dipoles are fed with currents of equal amplitude but the current fed into dipole A leads the input current of dipole B by 90°. In the horizontal plane, each dipole will radiate energy equally well in all directions. In the direction A to B, the energy radiated by dipole A has to travel a distance of λ/4 before it reaches dipole B and will experience a phase lag of 90°. The field strengths produced by dipoles A and B are therefore in phase with one another and add. In the reverse direction B to A, the energy radiated by dipole B has a distance of λ/4 to travel before it reaches dipole A. It will, therefore, have a total phase of −180° relative to the energy radiated by dipole A. In the direction B to A, the field strengths produced by dipoles A and B cancel out and so there is no radiation in this direction. In all other directions the field strengths produced by the two dipoles have a phase angle, other than 0° or 180°, between them, and the resultant field strength is given by their phasor sum.

The radiation pattern of the two-dipole array is shown in Fig. 5.25. Greater directivity and gain can be achieved by the addition of a third dipole C, λ/4 apart from dipole B. Dipole C is fed with a current of equal amplitude to, but lagging by 90°, the current into dipole B. Similarly, a fourth, a fifth, and more dipoles can be added to further increase the directivity of the aerial. Unfortunately, the operation of an *end-fire array* depends critically on the spacings of its component dipoles, and this means that the aerial is only suitable for operation at a single frequency.

Different radiation patterns are obtained if the dipole spacing and/or the dipole current phases are altered. Fig. 5.26 shows how the horizontal plane radiation pattern of two vertical λ/2 dipoles varies when the dipole currents are, respectively, 180°, 120°, 60° and 0° out of phase with one another and when the dipole spacing is (a) λ/4 and (b) λ/2. If the radiation patterns for equal dipole currents are

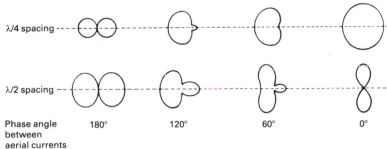

Phase angle between aerial currents: 180° 120° 60° 0°

Fig. 5.26 Effect of varying the phase of the currents in two spaced aerial elements in an array

compared, it can be seen what a large effect a change in the aerial spacing can produce.

Clearly, the greatest directivity, and hence gain, is obtained for the case of λ/2 spacing together with in-phase dipole currents. Unfortunately, this two-dipole array radiates equally well in two opposite directions, whereas the usual requirement is for the radiated energy to be concentrated in one direction only. This requirement can be satisfied by mounting a *reflector* (a conductor which is *not* connected to the aerial feeder) behind the array at a distance of exactly λ/4. The energy radiated in the unwanted direction will travel for a distance of only λ/4 before it is totally reflected to travel in the wanted direction. Because of the dipole-reflector spacing, the reflected energy will be in phase with the directly-radiated energy and so an increase of 6 dB in the gain of the aerial will be obtained. The addition of the reflector to the aerial system reduces the input impedance of the array.

Further increase in the directivity and gain of a resonant aerial can be achieved by increasing the number of λ/2 dipoles employed in the array.

Aerials mounted above earth

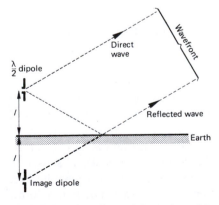

Fig. 5.27 Image aerial produced by ground reflections

When a λ/2 dipole is mounted above the earth at a distance of up to one wavelength, its vertical-plane radiation pattern will be modified because of the effect of earth reflections. Waves will be radiated by the dipole in various directions, as predicted by its radiation pattern, and some of these waves will strike the earth as shown by Fig. 5.27. Such waves are reflected by the earth and then propagate in the same direction as the direct wave. From the viewpoint of a distant observer, it would seem that the reflected wave has originated from an *image dipole* as indicated by the dotted line. The image dipole is as far beneath the earth as the real dipole is above it and so the spacing of the 'two-dipole array' is $2l$, where l is the height of the real dipole above the earth. The vertical-plane radiation patterns for a vertical λ/2 dipole and a horizontal λ/2 dipole at different heights above the ground are shown by Figs 5.28(a) and (b) respectively.

Clearly, the vertical dipole heights up to λ produce a main lobe horizontal to the surface of the earth. For a horizontal dipole, the

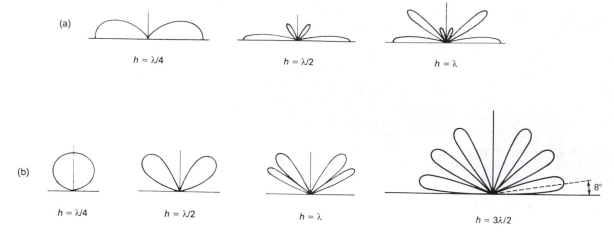

Fig. 5.28 Radiation patterns of (a) a vertical λ/2 dipole, (b) a horizontal λ/2 dipole, mounted at a height *h* above earth

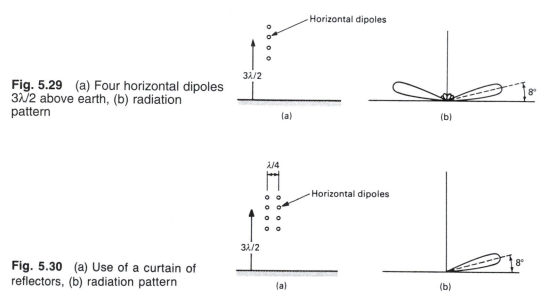

Fig. 5.29 (a) Four horizontal dipoles 3λ/2 above earth, (b) radiation pattern

Fig. 5.30 (a) Use of a curtain of reflectors, (b) radiation pattern

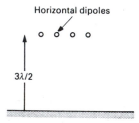

Fig. 5.31 End-fire array of horizontal dipoles

lowest lobe of the 3λ/2 height is at an angle of 8° to the horizontal. If four horizontal diodes are stacked one above the other with an average height of 3λ/2, as in Fig. 5.29, the four higher lobes will be considerably reduced in amplitude; see Fig. 5.29(b). Only one of the remaining large lobes is wanted and the unwanted one can be eliminated by the use of a curtain of reflectors mounted at a distance of λ/4 on the unwanted side of the dipoles. This is shown by Fig. 5.30(a) and the resulting radiation pattern is shown by Fig. 5.30(b). The same result can be obtained by the use of four horizontal dipoles connected as an end-fire array, as in Fig. 5.31.

An array or curtain of horizontal dipoles driven by equal-amplitude in-phase currents is often used as an HF sound broadcasting aerial.

Slot aerial

If a narrow rectangular slot is cut in a sheet of metal, the slot will be able to act as a transmitting aerial if r.f. energy is fed to both sides of the slot (see Fig. 5.32). The slot will not radiate in the plane of the metal sheet. In the *equatorial plane*, the electric field has very nearly the same radiation pattern as the $\lambda/2$ dipole, which would just fit into the slot, would have in the *meridian plane*. The input impedance of the $\lambda/2$ slot aerial is higher than the input impedance of the $\lambda/2$ dipole; that is, 471 ohms as opposed to 73 ohms.

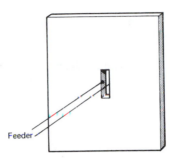

Feeder

Fig. 5.32 Slot aerial

Yagi aerial

The Yagi aerial is made up of a $\lambda/2$ dipole and a number of parasitic elements. The radiation pattern in the horizontal plane of a vertical $\lambda/2$ dipole is a circle as shown in Fig. 5.9(a). This means that the dipole will radiate or receive energy equally well in all directions in the horizontal plane. In the vertical plane, the vertical $\lambda/2$ dipole does *not* radiate or receive energy equally well in all directions. Indeed, in some directions it does not radiate at all, as shown by the radiation pattern of Fig. 5.9(b). For many radiocommunication systems (for example, television broadcasting services), the reception ability should be concentrated in one or more particular directions, and so some degree of directivity is needed.

An increase in the directivity of a $\lambda/2$ dipole can be obtained by the addition of a parasitic element known as a *reflector*. A reflector is a conducting rod, approximately 5% longer than $\lambda/2$, mounted on the side of the aerial remote from the direction in which maximum radiation should be directed. This is shown by Fig. 5.33(a). The reflector is said to be a parasitic element because it is not electrically connected to either the dipole or the feeder. The reflector will affect the radiation pattern of the $\lambda/2$ dipole because e.m.f.s are induced into it and cause it to radiate energy. The exact effect produced depends upon the length of the reflector and its distance from the dipole. Figs 5.34(a) and (b) illustrate one possibility for particular dimensions; clearly, the directivity of the array is better than that of the dipole on its own.

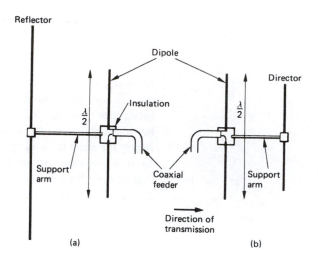

Fig. 5.33 λ/2 dipole with (a) a reflector and (b) a director

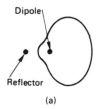

(a)

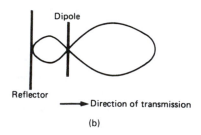

(b)

Fig. 5.34 Radiation patters for λ/2 dipole and reflector in (a) equatorial plane, (b) meridian plane

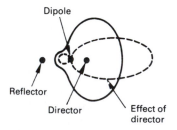

Fig. 5.35 Radiation pattern for λ/2 dipole, reflector and director in equatorial plane

When a voltage, at the resonant frequency of the dipole, is applied to the aerial, an in-phase current flows and the dipole radiates an electromagnetic wave that is in phase with the current. This energy is radiated equally well in all directions perpendicular to the dipole. Some of this energy will arrive at the reflector and induce an e.m.f. in it that will *lag* the voltage applied to the dipole by an angle determined by the element spacing. If, for example, the spacing is 0.15λ, the induced e.m.f. lags the dipole voltage by 180°. The induced e.m.f. will cause a *lagging* current to flow in the reflector. The reflector will now also radiate energy in all directions normal to it. If both the length of the reflector and the dipole/reflector spacing have been chosen correctly, the energy radiated by the reflector will add to the energy radiated by the dipole in the wanted direction. Conversely, in the opposite direction (i.e. dipole to reflector), the dipole and reflector radiations will subtract from one another.

Further increase in the directivity and gain of a dipole aerial can be achieved by the addition of another parasitic element on the other side of the dipole. This element, known as a *director*, is made about 5% shorter than the λ/2 dipole. When the dipole radiates energy, an e.m.f. is induced into the director (as well as the reflector) and a *leading* current flows in it. The director then radiates energy in all directions normal to it. The length of the director and its distance from the dipole are both carefully chosen to ensure that the field produced by the dipole is aided in the wanted direction and is opposed in the opposite, unwanted direction. The effect of the director on the radiation pattern of the dipole/reflector array can be seen in Fig. 5.35.

A further increase in the gain and directivity of the aerial cannot be obtained by using a second reflector because the magnetic field behind the reflector has been reduced to small value. The addition of further directors will give extra gain, although the increase per director falls as the number of directors is increased. This is shown by the graph given in Fig. 5.36.

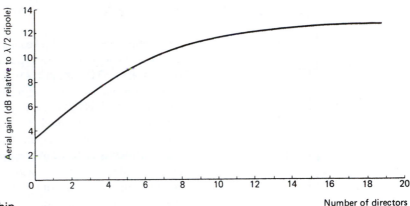

Fig. 5.36 Showing the relationship between the gain of a Yagi aerial and the number of directors employed

In practice, the choice of element spacing must be a compromise dictated by the gain and front-to-back ratio requirements of the array. Usually, the dipole/reflector spacing is between 0.15λ to 0.25λ while the common dipole/director spacing is selected as a value somewhere in the range 0.1λ to 0.15λ.

Example 5.10

An aerial array consists of a vertical $\lambda/2$ dipole with a reflector and one director. Calculate approximate dimensions and spacings for the elements if operation is to be at 100 MHz.

Solution
At 100 MHz,

$$\lambda = (3 \times 10^8)/(100 \times 10^6) = 3 \text{ m}$$

Therefore

$$\lambda/2 = 1.5 \text{ m}$$

In practice, the dipole would be made slightly shorter because the electric field fringes out at each end of the dipole, making its electrical length effectively longer. Therefore

Dipole length $= 1.48$ m   (*Ans.*)

The reflector should be about 5% longer than $\lambda/2$ and should be, say, 0.15λ behind the dipole. Therefore,

Reflector length $= 1.57$ m   (*Ans.*)
and
Reflector/dipole spacing $= 0.6$ m   (*Ans.*)

The director should be about 5% shorter than $\lambda/2$. Therefore

Director length $= 1.43$ m   (*Ans.*)
and
Director/dipole spacing $= 0.4$ m   (*Ans.*)

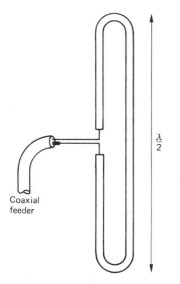

Fig. 5.37 The folded λ/2 dipole

Folded dipole

The input impedance of a resonant λ/2 dipole is 73 Ω resistive. The addition of one or more parasitic elements reduces the input impedance to, perhaps, 50 Ω with just a reflector and single-director assembly, or perhaps only 20 Ω if several directors are fitted. Normally a 50 Ω or 75 Ω coaxial feeder is used with a Yagi array, and so an impedance mismatch may exist at the aerial terminals which will produce a standing-wave pattern on the feeder.

The difficulty could be overcome if the input impedance of the dipole could be increased in some way to a higher value. Then the reduction in input impedance caused by the addition of parasitic elements would result in an impedance somewhere in the region of the 50 Ω or 75 Ω characteristic impedance of the cable. The higher dipole impedance needed is easily obtained by using the *folded dipole* shown in Fig. 5.37. The input impedance of the folded dipole is four times larger than that of the straight dipole, i.e. it is equal to $4 \times 73 = 292\,\Omega$. Impedance multiplying factors other than four are possible by making the two halves of the folded dipole from different-diameter rods. The bandwidth of the Yagi array is also increased by the use of a folded dipole. A typical Yagi array is shown in Fig. 5.38.

Since the correct operation of a Yagi aerial depends critically upon the lengths and spacings of the elements in terms of the signal wavelength, the aerial is only employed at VHF and UHF. The phsyical dimensions necessary to operate in the HF band would make the mechanical structure inconveniently large and correspondingly expensive, and the situation would be even worse if operating in the medium waveband. The bandwidth of the aerial is the range of frequencies over which the main lobe of its radiation pattern is within specified limits, generally −3 dB, and is in the order of ±3%.

Yagi aerials are commonly used for the reception of television

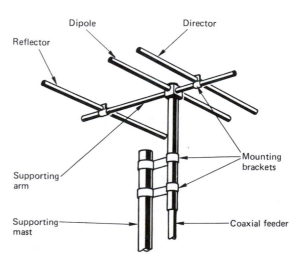

Fig. 5.38 A practical Yagi aerial

Table 5.1

Aerial	Input impedance Ω	Frequency MHz	Bandwidth MHz	Gain dBD
A	50	90	2	10
B	50	87–100	1–2	10
C	50	47–54	1	8.5

broadcast signals in the home and are visible on many rooftops. The aerial also finds considerable application in VHF point-to-point radio-telephony systems for both transmission and reception.

Typical performance figures for Yagi aerials are given in Table 5.1.

Rhombic aerial

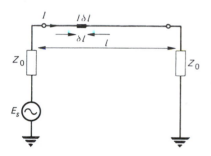

Fig. 5.39 A long-wire radiator

Point-to-point radio links operating in the HF band (3–30 MHz) are allocated three to five different frequencies to ensure a satsifactory service, as sky-wave propagation conditions vary. The HF radio transmitters must be capable of rapidly changing frequency as and when required, and it is desirable, for economic reasons, to use the same aerial as much as possible. This requirement rules out the use of a resonant aerial such as the Yagi. A wideband aerial which was used for many HF links was the rhombic aerial; the rhombic is a travelling wave type of aerial, since its operation depends upon r.f. currents propagating along the full length of the aerial, and the formation of standing waves is avoided.

Fig. 5.39 shows a conductor that is several wavelengths long and which, together with the earth, forms a transmission line of characteristic impedance Z_0 and negligible loss. At the sending end of the line, a generator of e.m.f. E_s and impedance Z_0 ohms is connected, and at the far end a terminating impedance of Z_0 ohms is used. The input impedance of the line is Z_0 and an input current $I = E_s/2Z_0$ flows and propagates along the line towards the far end. Since the line is correctly terminated, there are no reflections at the load and therefore no standing waves on the line. The line length l metres can be considered to consist of the tandem connection of a very large number of extremely small lengths δl of line. Since the line losses are negligible, the current flowing in the line has the same amplitude at all points. This means that each elemental δl of line carries the same current I and is said to form a current element $I\delta l$.

Each current element will radiate energy. The radiation from each element has its maximum value in the direction making an angle of 90° to the conductor and is zero along the axis of the conductor. The total field strength produced by the line at any point around it is the phasor sum of the field strengths produced by all of the current elements. The phase of the line current varies along the length of the line and in half-wavelength distances a 180° phase shift occurs. Because of this, the field strengths produced by the current elements

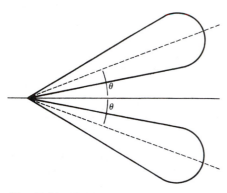

Fig. 5.40 Radiation pattern of a long-wire radiator

cancel out in the direction normal to the conductor to produce a null in the radiation pattern. Also, since no element radiates along the axis of the conductor, another null exists in this direction. Thus, the radiation pattern of an electrically long wire is as shown in Fig. 5.40 (a number of small lobes are also present but are not shown). The angle the two main lobes make with the conductor axis is dependent upon the electrical length of the conductor, decreasing as the conductor length is increased. When the length is between 4λ and 8λ, the relationship between lobe angle and frequency is a linear one between limits of 24° and 17°.

The rhombic aerial consists of four such long wires connected together to form, in the horizontal plane, the geometric shape of a rhombus (Fig. 5.41). All the four wires will radiate energy in the directions indicated by its radiation pattern. The aerial is designed

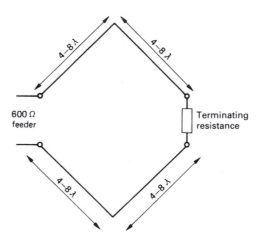

Fig. 5.41 The rhombic aerial

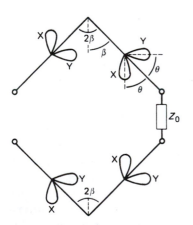

Fig. 5.42 Illustrating the correct choice of tilt angle for a rhombic aerial

so that the main lobes of the radiation pattern of the wires are additive in the wanted direction and self-cancelling in the unwanted directions. This feature of the rhombic aerial is achieved by suitably choosing the angle 2β subtended by two conductors. The tilt angle β (Fig. 5.42) is chosen so that the lobe angle θ is equal to $(90 - \beta)°$. Then the lobes marked X will point in opposite directions and the radiations they represent will cancel, and the lobes marked Y will point in the same (wanted) direction and their radiations will be additive. Since the lobe angle θ varies with frequency, it is not possible to choose the tilt angle to be correct at all the possible operating frequencies, and it is usual to design for optimum operation at the geometric mean of the required frequency band.

Example 5.11

A rhombic aerial is to operate over the frequency band 7–14 MHz. Determine a suitable value for the tilt angle.

Solution

The physical lengths of the four wires will be such that at 7 MHz they are 4λ and at 14 MHz they are 8λ long. Then at 7 MHz the lobe angle is 24° and at 14 MHz it is 17°. Since there is a linear relationship between the lobe angle and the frequency of operation, at the geometric mean of 7 MHz and 14 MHz, i.e. at 9.9 MHz, the lobe angle is approximately 20°. Therefore

$$\text{Tilt angle} = 90° - \theta° = 90° - 20° = 70° \quad (Ans.)$$

At the design frequency the horizontal plane radiation pattern of a rhombic aerial is shown in Fig. 5.43 with the radiated electromagnetic wave being horizontally polarized. The parts of the unwanted lobes that do not cancel are responsible for the sidelobes shown. At frequencies within the bandwidth of the aerial but not at the design frequency, the wanted lobes do not point in exactly the same direction, and the effect on the radiation pattern is to increase its beamwidth and lower its gain in the wanted direction. Typically, a rhombic aerial will operate over a 2:1 frequency ratio, e.g.

Fig. 5.43 Radiation pattern of a rhombic aerial

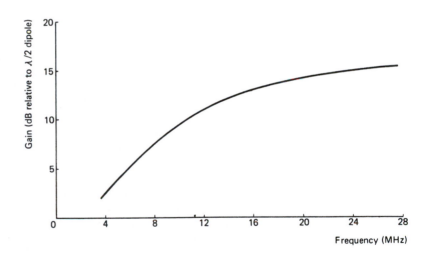

Fig. 5.44 Gain-frequency characteristic of a rhombic aerial

7–14 MHz with a gain relative to a $\lambda/2$ dipole, that varies with frequency in the maner indicated by Fig. 5.44.

When the rhombic aerial is used with sky-wave propagation systems, the energy radiated by the aerial must be directed towards the ionosphere at the correct angle of elevation. The angle of elevation of the main lobe is determined by the height at which the four conductors are mounted above the earth. For the main lobe to be at the required angle of elevation, the energy radiated downwards towards the ground must be reflected at such an angle that it is then in phase with the directly-radiated energy (Fig. 5.45). The field strength produced in the wanted direction is then doubled, which corresponds to an increase in gain of 6 dB.

The input impedance of a rhombic aerial is determined by both the signal frequency and the diameter of the wires and is in the range

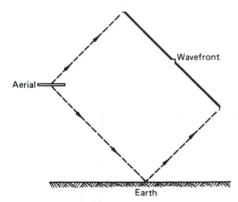

Fig. 5.45 Optimum height above ground for a rhombic aerial

600 Ω to 800 Ω. The input impedance is frequency-dependent and can be made more nearly constant by using more than one wire to form each arm of the rhombus. The input impedance is then also a function of the number of wires used and their distance apart.

The terminating impedance must match the characteristic impedance of the lines forming the aerial in order to prevent reflections taking place and this means that one-half of the power fed into the aerial will be dissipated in the terminating impedance; the aerial, therefore, has a maximum efficiency of 50%. When the powers involved are small, as with a receiving rhombic aerial, a carbon resistor will often suffice as the terminating impedance. For high-power installations, such a simple solution is not available and commonly the impedance consists of a two-wire line using iron conductors.

A typical rhombic aerial is illustrated by Fig. 5.46.

The rhombic aerial possesses two disadvantages which are tending to lead to its replacement by the log-periodic aerial. Firstly, its radiation pattern exhibits relatively large sidelobes. Sidelobes in a radiation pattern are undesirable since, in a transmitting aerial, they mean that power is radiated in unwanted directions. The energy may interfere with other systems but, in any case, represents a waste of power. In the case of a receiving aerial, the unwanted sidelobes indicate a response to interference and noise arriving from unwanted directions. The second disadvantage, made clear by the typical dimensions given in Fig. 5.46, is the large site area which must be provided to accommodate a rhombic aerial. Rhombic aerials are still commonly employed at VHF where their physical dimensions are much smaller.

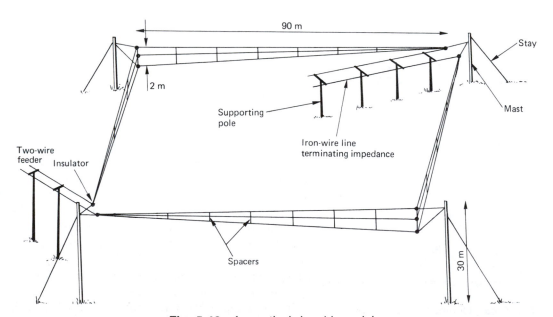

Fig. 5.46 A practical rhombic aerial

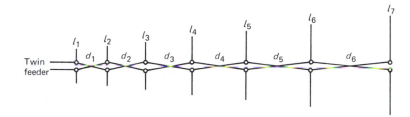

Fig. 5.47 The log-period dipole aerial: general principle

Log-periodic aerial

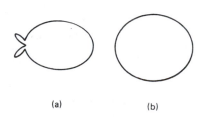

(a)   (b)

Fig. 5.48 Radiation pattern of a log-periodic dipole aerial

The log-periodic aerial (LPA) provides an alternative to the rhombic aerial in the HF band and is particularly suitable when the available site area is limited and/or an elevation angle in excess of about 40° is required. The aerial can operate over a wide frequency band and has very small sidelobes and backlobes.

The LPA provides an end-fire radiation pattern over a wide frequency band. The aerial is manufactured in various forms and Fig. 5.47 shows the principle of the log-periodic dipole array which is used at VHF. The lengths l_1, l_2, l_3, etc. of the dipoles increase from left to right with the relationship $l_2/l_1 = l_3/l_2 = l_4/l_3$ etc., the common ratio being known as the *scale factor τ* of the aerial. The spacings d_1, d_2, d_3, etc. between adjacent dipoles also increase from left to right. Successive spacings are also related by the same scale factor $τ$.

The input signal is applied to the LPA via a twin feeder and is applied to adjacent dipoles with 180° phase change because the connections to successive dipoles are reversed. At any given frequency within the bandwidth of the aerial, only two, or perhaps three, dipoles are at, or anywhere near, resonance, i.e. approximately $λ/2$ long. These dipoles take a relatively large input current and radiate considerable energy; because of the phasing of the dipole currents, an end-fire effect is obtained, with the main lobe being in the direction of from longer elements to shorter elements. All the other dipoles are now either much longer or much shorter than $λ/2$ and radiate little or no energy. The radiation pattern of an LPA is shown in Fig. 5.48. The equatorial plane pattern is given in (a) and the meridian plane pattern in (b).

As the frequency of the input signal is varied, the active region of the aerial will move in one direction or the other. If the frequency is reduced, the active region will move towards the end of the aerial where the dipoles are longer. If the frequency is increased, shorter dipoles become resonant or nearly resonant and the active region moves towards the short element end of the aerial.

The range of frequencies that can be radiated or received by an LPA is very large. It is limited by the maximum dimensions of the longest dipoles in the array. The dipole array can be mounted on top of a pole or mast and orientated to operate with either vertical or horizontal elements. Fig. 5.49 shows a typical example of a log-periodic VHF aerial.

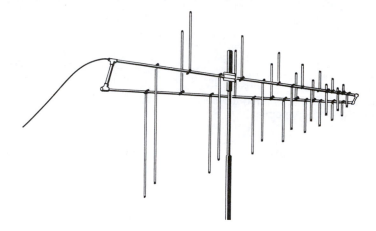

Fig. 5.49 VHF log-periodic aerial

HF log-periodic aerial

A high-frequency version of the log-periodic aerial is shown in Fig. 5.50. Since the aerial is mounted close to the earth, its vertical plane radiation pattern is modified by earth reflections. If it is desired to have the same elevation angle for the radiation pattern at all frequencies, each element must be at the same *electrical height* above the ground. This, of course, means that the physical height of the aerial above earth must vary along the length of the aerial, as shown in the figure.

Log-periodic aerials are used for HF communication links and sound broadcasting, where the wide bandwidth, 4–30 MHz, is often an advantage. The input impedance of the aerial lies in the range of 50–300 Ω and the gain is about 10 dBi, which can be increased to about 14 dBi by earth reflections.

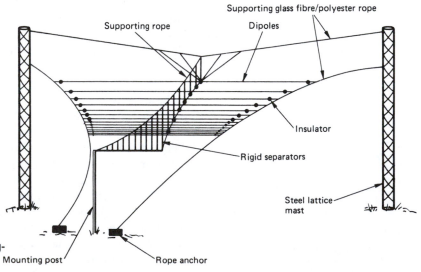

Fig. 5.50 A high-frequency log-periodic aerial

The gain is less than that of the rhombic aerial, which is an indication of a radiation pattern that is not very directive. On the other hand, its sidelobe and backlobe levels are small. Compared to the Yagi aerial, the VHF log-periodic aerial has a smaller gain (for the same number of elements), and smaller sidelobes and backlobes. Two or more LPAs can be connected in a broadside array to give increased gain and directivity.

Whip aerial

Since the direction of a mobile radio receiver, or transceiver, is continually changing, its aerial must have an omni-directional radiation pattern in the horizontal plane. The *whip aerial* consists of a number of sections of metal rod, each of which is of reducing diameter so that the sections are retractable within the thickest section. The thickest section of rod is mounted on an insulator on the body of a vehicle, or on the case of a portable receiver. The aerial used in conjunction with a car radio is expected to receive signals in all broadcast wavebands and in the MF band its electrical length is small. The gain of the aerial depends upon its physical length (it may not always be fully extended) and the frequency of the signal being received. A whip aerial is driven at its lower end and has a circular radiation pattern in the horizontal plane; in the vertical plane its radiation pattern is, typically, as shown in Fig. 5.51.

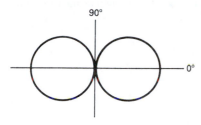

Fig. 5.51 Radiation pattern of a whip aerial

Helical aerial

The length of a whip aerial may often be inconveniently large and sometimes a *helical aerial* may be employed instead. A helical aerial consists of a helix of copper wire that is driven between one end and the body of the vehicle, as shown by Fig. 5.52(a). For a portable radio receiver, the helix is connected to a coaxial socket mounted on the body of the receiver, as in Fig. 5.52(b). A helical aerial can be operated in either one or two different modes, known as the *axial mode* and the *normal mode*. With the axial mode of operation, both the diameter of the helix and the spacing of the helix turns are comparable with the signal wavelength and then the aerial has a circularly polarized pattern with maximum radiation along the axis of the helix; see Fig. 5.52(c).

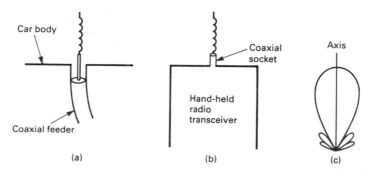

Fig. 5.52 Helical aerial (a) mounted on car body, (b) on hand-held radio, (c) radiation pattern

If both the diameter of the helix and the pitch of the helix turns are much smaller than λ/2, maximum radiation occurs in the directions at right angles, or normal, to the helix axis. In the normal mode of operation, there is negligible radiation along the axis of the helix. Normal radiation is essentially elliptically polarized, but if the helix dimensions are less than about 0.1λ it becomes almost linearly polarized. Then the radiation pattern is very similar to that of a λ/2 dipole, but for the same performance the physical dimensions are much smaller.

Parabolic dish aerial

At frequencies at the upper end of the UHF band and in the SHF band, the signal wavelength becomes sufficiently small to allow a completely different kind of aerial to be used. The aerial is known as the *parabolic dish* aerial and it is capable of producing a very directive, high-gain radiation pattern.

The aerial consists of a large metal dish which is used to reflect into the atmosphere the radio energy directed onto it by a smaller radiator (often a dipole/reflector array) mounted at the focal point. The idea of the aerial is illustrated by Fig. 5.53. A property of a parabolic dish is that the distance from the focal point of the dish to an arbitrary plane the other side of the focal point is a constant, regardless of which point on the dish is considered, i.e.

$$\text{RAX} = \text{RBX} = \text{RCX} = \text{RDX} = \text{REX} = \text{RFX}$$

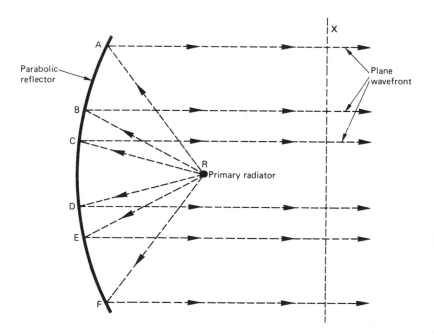

Fig. 5.53 Reflection from a parabolic reflector

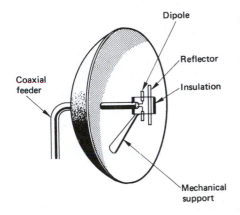

Dipole

Reflector

Coaxial feeder

Insulation

Mechanical support

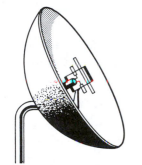

Fig. 5.54 Two views of a parabolic dish aerial

Because of this property, the spherical wavefront signal originating from the radiator and reflected by the dish arrives at the plane X with a plane wavefront. The reflected waves are all parallel to one another and form a concentrated, highly directive radio wave.

When used as a receiving aerial, the action of the dish is reversed; the incoming plane wavefront radio wave is reflected by the dish and brought to a focus at the focal point where a small receiving aerial, such as a $\lambda/2$ dipole, is mounted and is connected to the feeder.

Fig. 5.54 shows the apperance of a dish aerial.

The gain of a parabolic dish aerial depends upon its diameter in terms of the signal wavelength. If the diameter is made several times larger than the signal wavelength, very high gains can be obtained.

The gain (G) of the aerial, relative to an isotropic radiator, is

$$G = \pi(D/2)^2/(\lambda^2/4\pi) = \pi^2 D^2/\lambda^2 \tag{5.9}$$

The gain relative to a $\lambda/2$ dipole is

$$G = 6(D/\lambda)^2 \tag{5.10}$$

The sidelobes in the radiation pattern are mainly caused by the position of the primary radiator and its supports which block a part of the radiated signal path. The effective gain of the aerial is reduced by the illumination efficiency being less than 100%; typically it is 50–55%.

The effective gain, relative to an isotropic radiator, is

$$\begin{aligned} G &\simeq 0.5\pi^2 D^2/\lambda^2 \\ &\simeq 0.5\pi^2 D^2 \, (f \times 10^9)^2/(3 \times 10^8)^2 \\ &\simeq 55f^2 D^2, \text{ where } f \text{ is in GHz} \end{aligned} \tag{5.11}$$

Example 5.12

A parabolic dish aerial has a diameter of 1 m. Determine its gain at (a) 1 GHz, (b) 6 GHz.

Solution
(a) $G = 55 \times 1 \times 1 = 55 = 17.4$ dBi   (*Ans.*)
(b) $G = 55 \times 1 \times 36 = 1980 = 33$ dBi   (*Ans.*)

The radiation pattern of a parabolic reflector has one main, very-narrow-beamwidth lobe and a number of much smaller sidelobes. The main lobe is so narrow that the radiation pattern cannot conveniently be plotted in the usual manner. Usually, the radiation pattern is only drawn for a small angular distance either side of the direction of maximum radiation, and Fig. 5.55 shows a typical pattern.

The beamwidth of the aerial is also a function of the dish diameter:

$$\text{Beamwidth} = 70\,\lambda/D \tag{5.12}$$

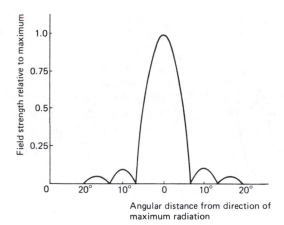

Fig. 5.55 Radiation pattern of a parabolic dish aerial

Angular distance from direction of maximum radiation

Exercises

5.1 (a) Draw radiation patterns in the horizontal plane for the following: (i) a vertical half-wave dipole aerial; (ii) a horizontal half-wave dipole aerial; (iii) a vertical half-wave dipole aerial with reflector; (iv) a horizontal half-wave dipole aerial with reflector. (b) Calculate suitable dimensions for an array comprising a half-wave dipole and reflector for use at 559.25 MHz.

5.2 (a) Explain carefully what is meant by the radiation pattern of an aerial array. (b) Sketch the radiation patterns, in the horizontal plane, of the following types of aerial: (i) a horizontal $\lambda/2$ dipole; (ii) a $\lambda/2$ vertical dipole with reflector; (iii) an inverted-L; (iv) a ferrite rod as used in a portable broadcast receiver; (v) a parabolic dish aerial; (vi) a log-periodic aerial.

5.3 (a) Explain the terms (i) radiation resistance, (ii) isotropic radiator, (iii) aerial efficiency. (b) Sketch an earthed monopole aerial which has a height of $\lambda/8$ at the operating frequency and say why its apparent height is greater than this value. What is meant by a *counterpoise earth* and when is it employed?

5.4 (a) Sketch the radiation patterns of a half-wave vertical dipole in free space, in the vertical and horizontal planes. Illustrate the influence of (i) a reflector and (ii) a director on the radiation patterns in the horizontal plane only. (b) An aerial array for use at 805 MHz consists of a vertical half-wave dipole with a reflector and one director. Calculate approximate dimensions and spacings. Sketch the radiation pattern of the array in the horizontal plane. (c) A dipole aerial requires to be fed with 20 kW of power to produce a given signal strength at a particular distant point. If the addition of a reflector makes the same field strength available with an input of only 11 kW, what is the gain in decibels obtained by the use of the reflector?

5.5 (a) With the aid of a diagram, describe the principle of operation of a monopole aerial and sketch its radiation pattern. (b) Explain any similarity between the monopole aerial and the dipole aerial. (c) State one application of the monopole aerial. (d) An aerial radiates 8 kW power when the power supplied by the feeder is 10 kW. What is the efficiency of the aerial? (e) If the aerial has a gain of 8 dB what is the effective radiated power?

5.6 (a) Explain, with the aid of diagrams, each of the following terms used in relation to aerials: (i) radiation pattern; (ii) aerial gain; (iii) half-power bandwidth; (iv) beamwidth. (b) Explain why aerials designed for use at VHF are generally more efficient than low-frequency aerials. Write down an expression for the efficiency of an aerial and state the meaning of each symbol used. (c) An aerial has a loss resistance of 2.5 Ω and a radiation resistance of 1.8 Ω. If the current fed into the aerial has an r.m.s. value of 10 A, calculate the power radiated by the aerial and the aerial efficiency.

5.7   (a) A dipole aerial must be fed with 20 kW power in order to produce an electric field strength of 5 mV/m at a particular point. The addition of a reflector and a director to the aerial enables the same field strength to be produced by a power of 8 kW. What is the gain, in dB, of the array relative to the dipole alone? (b) When an aerial radiates a power of 5 kW, a field strength of 5 mV/m is set up at a distant point. Another aerial located at the same site needs to radiate 10 kW to produce the same field strength at the same point. If the first aerial has a gain of 10 dB relative to an isotropic radiator, determine the gain of the second aerial.

5.8   (a) What is meant by the effective height of an aerial? What effect does the earth have on the effective height of a monopole aerial? (b) A monopole aerial is 75 metres in height and is mounted vertically on perfectly conducting earth. The aerial current varies linearly from 20 A at the base of the aerial to 0 A at the top. Calculate the effective height of the aerial.

5.9   (a) Describe the construction and operation of a parabolic dish aerial and sketch a typical radiation pattern. How are the gain and beamwidth of such an aerial related to its diameter and the frequency of transmission? (b) Calculate the gain in dBi of such an aerial at 2 GHz if the diameter of the dish is 2 m.

5.10 Sketch and describe a log-periodic aerial suitable for HF transmission. What are the main design features that determine its performance? State typical values for (a) the gain, (b) the frequency bandwidth and (c) the angle of elevation of the main lobe.

5.11 (a) Draw a dimensioned sketch of a rhombic aerial. (b) Why are three wires often employed on each leg of a rhombic aerial? (c) Upon what factors does the impedance of a rhombic aerial depend? (d) Why is it desirable to be able to alter the height of a rhombic aerial? (e) What is the most noticeable difference between a rhombic aerial used for receiving and one used for transmitting? (f) Complete Table 5.2.

Table 5.2

	Parabolic dish	Log-periodic	Yagi
Operating frequency range			
Bandwidth			
Gain			
Input impedance			
Dimensions			
For what service is it commonly used?			
Is it a travelling-wave aerial?			

5.12 Sketch the construction of a log-periodic aerial suitable for use in the HF band. Label the sketch with dimensions suitable for use at a frequency of (a) 45 MHz, (b) 490 MHz. Give typical values of gain and input impedance and state whether your aerial produces a horizontally polarized or a vertically polarized wave.

5.13 Sketch the radiation pattern of a half-wave dipole in both the equatorial and meridian planes. Show the current and voltage distributions in the aerial. Draw the arrangement of a simple Yagi aerial with one director and show how the radiation pattern differs from that of the dipole alone.

5.14 (a) Describe the way in which energy is radiated from a conductor carrying a high-frequency current. Hence explain why aerials for use at VHF are more efficient than those used at medium frequencies. Quote typical figures for aerial efficiency. (b) When an aerial radiates a power of 1 kW, a field strength of 10 mV/m is set up at a certain distant point. Another aerial located alongside the first needs only to radiate 250 W to produce the same field strength at the same point. If the first aerial has a gain of 20 dB relative to an isotropic radiator, determine the gain of the second aerial.

5.15 Explain the meaning of the following terms used in aerial work: (a) polarization; (b) gain; (c) radiation patterns; (d) beamwidth; (e) isotropic radiation; (f) front-to-back ratio; (g) parasitic element.

5.16 (a) Fig. 5.56 shows the path of a wave from a source, S, located at the focus of a parabolic dish aerial. Calculate the focal length of the reflector. (b) Explain how a parabolic reflector is able to convert a spherical wave into a plane wave. (c) The transmitting aerial of a microwave link has a gain of 600 with respect to an isotropic radiator. Calculate the power that must be supplied to this aerial to ensure that a receiving aerial of effective aperture 4 m^2 will receive 1 μW power at a distance of 12 km.

5.17 (a) Which parameters of a parabolic dish aerial determine (i) beamwidth, (ii) size of sidelobes, (iii) bandwidth? (b) The parabolic dish aerials used at both ends of a UHF link are replaced by others having diameters 1.5 times that of the original. Calculate in dB the overall gain improvement which would be expected from this modification.

5.18 An aerial has a beamwidth of 2.7° in a particular plane and a gain of 30 dBD. For propagation in this plane and radiated power of 1.8 W, calculate the power density at a range of 10 km (a) in the direction of maximum radiation; (b) at an angle of 1.35° to the direction of maximum radiation.

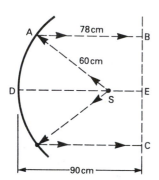

Fig. 5.56

6 Propagation of radio waves

When a radio-frequency current flows into a transmitting aerial, a radio wave at the same frequency is radiated in a number of directions as predicted by the radiation pattern of the aerial. The radiated energy will reach the receiving aerial by one or more of five different modes of propagation. Four of these modes, the *ground wave*, the *sky wave*, the *space wave* and the use of a *communication satellite*, are illustrated by Fig. 6.1.

- The ground wave is supported at its lower edge by the surface of the earth and is able to follow the curvature of the earth as it travels.
- The sky wave is directed upwards from the earth into the upper atmosphere where, if certain conditions are satisfied, it will be returned to earth at the required location.
- The space wave generally has two components, one of which travels in a very nearly straight line between the transmitting and receiving aerials, and the other which travels by means of a single reflection from the earth.
- The fourth method uses a communication satellite orbiting the

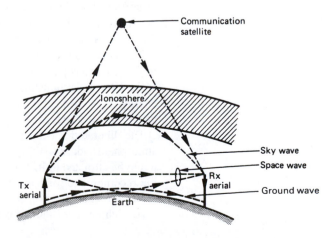

Fig. 6.1 Modes of propagation

127

Table 6.1 Radio frequency bands

Frequency band	Classification	Abbreviation
10–30 kHz	Very low	VLF
30–300 kHz	Low	LF
300–3000 kHz	Medium	MF
3–30 MHz	High	HF
30–300 MHz	Very high	VHF
300–3000 MHz	Ultra high	UHF
3–30 GHz	Super high	SHF

earth to receive a signal, amplify it, and then transmit it at a different frequency towards the earth.

- The fifth method of propagation, which is not shown in Fig. 6.1, is know as scatter and it is used only when, for one reason or another, one of the other methods is not available.

The radio frequency spectrum has been subdivided into a number of frequency bands which are listed in Table 6.1.

The ground wave is used for world-wide communication in the VLF and LF bands and for broadcasting in the MF bands.

The sky wave is used for HF communication systems, including long-distance radio-telephony and sound broadcasting.

The space wave is used for sound and television broadcasting, for radio relay systems, and for various mobile systems operating in the VHF, UHF and SHF bands.

Communication satellite systems are used to carry international telephony systems and television signals.

Lastly, scatter systems operate in the UHF band to provide multi-channel telephony links.

The ionosphere

Ultra-violet radiation from the sun entering the atmosphere of the earth supplies energy to the gas molecules in the atmosphere. This energy is sufficient to ionize some of the molecules, i.e. remove some electrons from their parent atoms. Each atom losing an electron in this way has a resultant positive charge and is said to be *ionized*.

The ionization thus produced is measured in terms of the number of free electrons per cubic metre and is dependent upon the intensity of the ultra-violet radiation. As the radiation travels towards the earth, energy is continually extracted from it and so its intensity is progressively reduced.

The liberated electrons are free to wander at random in the atmosphere and, in so doing, may well come close enough to a positive ion to be attracted to it. When this happens, the free electron and the ion recombine to form a neutral atom. Thus a continuous process of ionization and recombination takes place.

At high altitudes the atmosphere is rare and little ionization takes place. Nearer the earth the number of gas molecules per cubic metre is much greater and large numbers of atoms are ionized; but the air is still sufficiently rare to keep the probability of recombination at a low figure. Nearer still to the earth, the number of free electrons produced per cubic metre falls, because the intensity of the ultra-violet radiation has been greatly reduced during its passage through the upper atmosphere. Also, since the atmosphere is relatively dense, the probability of recombination is fairly high. The density of free electrons is therefore small immediately above the surface of the earth, rises at higher altitudes, and then falls again at still greater heights. The earth is thus surrounded by a wide belt of ionized gases, known as the *ionosphere*.

The region of the earth's atmosphere between the surface of the earth and up to a height of about 10 km is known as the *troposphere*.

In the ionosphere, layers exist within which the free electron density is greater than at heights immediately above or below the layer. Four layers exist in the daytime (the D, E, F_1 and F_2 layers) at the heights shown in Fig. 6.2.

The heights of the ionospheric layers are not constant but vary both daily and seasonally as the intensity of the sun's radiation fluctuates. The electron density in the D layer is small when compared with the densities of the other layers. At night-time, when the ultra-violet radiation ceases, no more free electrons are produced and the D layer disappears because of the high rate of recombination at the lower altitudes. The E layer is at a height of about 100 km and so the rate of recombination is smaller. Because of this, the E layer, although becoming weaker, does not normally disappear at night-time. In the day-time, the F_1 layer is at a more or less constant height of 200–220 km above ground but the height of the F_2 layer varies considerably. Typical figures for the height of the F_2 layer are 250–350 km in the winter and 300–500 km in the summer.

The behaviour of the ionosphere when a radio wave is propagated through it depends very much upon the frequency of the wave. At low frequencies the ionosphere acts as though it were a medium of

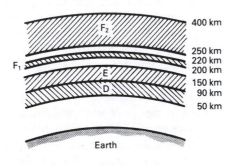

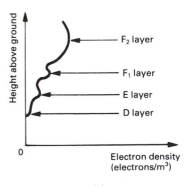

Fig. 6.2 Layers in the ionosphere   (a)   (b)

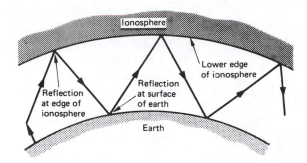

Fig. 6.3 Multi-hop transmission of a low-frequency wave

high electrical conductivity and it reflects, with little loss, any signals incident on its lower edge. It is possible for a VLF or LF signal to propagate for considerable distances by means of reflections from both the lower edge of the ionosphere and the earth. This is shown by Fig. 6.3. The wave suffers little attenuation on each reflection and so the received field strength is inversely proportional to the distance travelled.

In the MF band the D layer acts as a very lossy medium whose attenuation reaches its maximum value at a frequency of 1.4 MHz, often known as the *gyro-frequency*. Generally, MF signals suffer so much loss in the D layer that little energy reaches the E or F layers. At night-time, however, the D layer has disappeared and an MF signal will be *refracted* by the E layer and perhaps also by the F layer(s) and returned to earth. With further increase in frequency up to the HF band, the ionospheric attenuation falls and the E and F layers provide refraction of the sky wave. At these frequencies the D layer has little, if any, refractive effect but it does introduce some loss.

The amount of refraction of a radio wave that an ionospheric layer is able to provide is a function of the frequency of the wave, and usually, at VHF and above, no useful reflection is obtained. This means that a VHF or SHF signal will normally pass straight through the ionosphere.

Ground wave

At VLF and LF the transmitting aerial is electrically short but physically very large and must therefore be mounted vertically on the ground. The aerial will radiate energy in several directions. The field strength is proportional to distance but the field strength near the ground falls off more rapidly than this because of losses in the ground and the curvative of the earth. For this reason, it is useful to consider the radiated field as being the sum of two components, known as the *space wave* and the *surface wave*.

The combined surface and space wave is known as the *ground wave*. At VLF and LF, the signal wavelength is long and the aerial height is only a small fraction of a wavelength. The reflected component of the space wave experiences a 180° phase shift upon reflection and, since the difference, in wavelengths, between the lengths of the direct and reflected space waves is very small, the two waves cancel out.

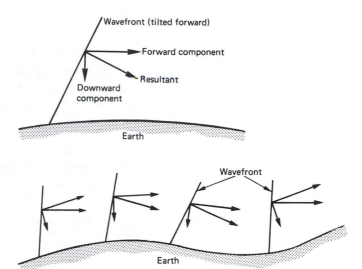

Fig. 6.4   Wavefront of the ground wave

Fig. 6.5   Propagation of ground wave over undulating terrain

Because of this, VLF and LF propagation is predominantly by means of the surface wave. Very often the term *ground wave* is used to represent the surface wave.

The ground wave is one which leaves the transmitting aerial very nearly parallel to the ground. Vertically polarized waves must be used because horizontal polarization would result in the low resistance of the earth short-circuiting the electric component of the wave. The surface wave follows the curvature of the earth as it travels from the transmitter because it is *diffracted*.† Further bending of the wave occurs because the magnetic component of the wave cuts the earth's surface as it travels and induces e.m.f.s in it. The induced e.m.f.s cause a.c. currents to flow and dissipate power in the resistance of the earth. This power can only be supplied by the surface wave, and so a continuous flow of energy from the wave into the earth takes place. The signal wavefront, therefore, has two components of velocity, one in the forward direction and one downwards towards the earth. The resultant direction is the phasor sum of the forward and downward components, and this results in the wave being tilted forward, as shown in Fig. 6.4. The downward component is always normal to the earth and the forward component 90° advanced; hence the tilted wavefront follows the undulations of the ground (Fig. 6.5).

Field strength of the ground wave

With ground wave propagation, the electric field produced by a short monopole aerial mounted on earth is taken as the reference. Such an

† Diffraction is a phenomenon which occurs with all wave motion. It causes a wave to bend round any obstacle it passes. For a surface wave, the earth itself is the obstacle.

aerial has a gain of 3 with respect to an isotropic radiator. Hence,

$$E = \sqrt{(90P_{\mathrm{t}})}/d \ \mathrm{V/m} \tag{6.1}$$

where P_{t} is the transmitted power and d is the distance in kilometres from the transmitter. Further, the reference transmitted power is taken to be 1 kW, so that equation (6.1) becomes

$$E = 300/d \ \mathrm{V/m} \tag{6.2}$$

In practice, the field strength actually received will always be less than that predicted by equation (6.2) because of losses produced as a result of the close proximity of the wave to the earth. These ground losses are accounted for by the introduction of an attenuation factor K:

$$E = 300K/d \ \mathrm{V/m} \tag{6.3}$$

For any other transmitted power, the received field strength given by equation (6.3) must be multiplied by the square root of the power quoted in kW.

$$E = (300K\sqrt{P_{\mathrm{t}}})/d \ \mathrm{V/m} \tag{6.4}$$

If, for example, the transmitted power were 4 kW, then the received field strength would be $600 \ K/d$ V/m. Usually the field strength 1 km from the transmitter is taken as the reference field, since at this distance the induction field is negligibly small. Then

$$E_{\mathrm{d}} = E_1 K/d \ \mathrm{V/m} \tag{6.5}$$

Table 6.2

Frequency	Range (km)
100 kHz	200
1 MHz	60
10 MHz	6
100 MHz	1.5

The attentuation factor K depends upon the frequency of the wave, and the conductivity and permittivity of the earth. The attenuation at a given frequency is least for propagation over expanses of water and greatest for propagation over dry ground, such as desert. For propagation over ground of average dampness, with a radiated power of 1 kW, the distance giving a field strength of 1 mV/m varies approximately with frequency, as shown in Table 6.2.

At MF, particularly at the higher end of the band, the height of the aerial is a much larger fraction of the signal wavelength. Now complete cancellation of the direct and reflected components of the space wave no longer occurs and the space wave partially contributes to the field strength over shorter distances. Field strengths are usually quoted in decibels relative to $1 \ \mu$ V/m (dBμV).

Example 6.1

Calculate the field strength at a point (a) 20 km and (b) 40 km from a radio transmitter if the transmitted power is 10 kW. Assume K $\simeq$ 1

Solution

   (a) $E = (300\sqrt{10})/(20 \times 10^3) = 47.434 \ \mathrm{mV/m}$
          $= 20 \ \log_{10}[(47.434 \times 10^{-3})/(1 \times 10^{-6})] = 93.5 \ \mathrm{dB\mu V}$ (*Ans.*)
   (b) $E = 47.434/2 = 23.717 \ \mathrm{mV/m} = 87.5 \ \mathrm{dB\mu V}$ (*Ans.*)

Example 6.2

Calculate the field strength produced at a distance of 40 km from a transmitting aerial with a gain of 1.76 dBi if the transmitted power is 10 kW, the frequency is 1 MHz, and the attenuation factor K is 0.02.

Solution

$$1.76 \text{ dBi} = 1.5 \text{ power ratio}$$
$$E = (300 \times 0.02)/(40 \times 10^3) \times \sqrt{(10 \times 1.5)} = 581 \ \mu V/m \qquad (Ans.)$$

Refraction of an electromagnetic wave

When an electromagnetic wave travelling in one medium passes into a different medium, its direction of travel will probably be altered. The wave is said to be *refracted*. The ratio

$$\frac{\text{sine of angle of incidence, } \phi_i}{\text{sine of angle of refraction, } \phi_r}$$

is a constant for a given pair of media and is known as the *refractive index* for the media. If one of the two media is air, the *aboslute refractive index* of the other medium is obtained.

If a wave passes from one medium to another medium that has a lower absolute refractive index, the wave is bent away from the normal, as shown by Fig. 6.6(a). Conversely, if the wave travels into a region of higher absolute refractive index, the wave is bent towards the normal, as in Fig. 6.6(b).

Suppose a wave is transmitted through a number of thin parallel strips, as in Fig. 6.7, each strip having an absolute refractive index lower than that of the strip immediately below it. The wave will pass from higher to lower absolute refractive index each time it crosses

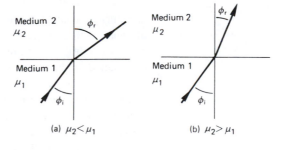

Fig. 6.6 Refraction of electromagnetic waves: wave passing into a medium of (a) lower absolute refractive index, (b) higher absolute refractive index

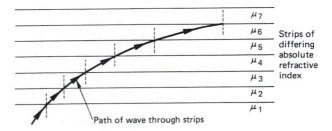

Fig. 6.7 Refraction of an electromagnetic wave passing through media of progressively lower absolute refractive index

the boundary between two strips, and it is therefore progressively bent away from the normal. If the widths of the strips are made extremely small, the absolute refractive index will decrease steadily and the wave will be continuously refracted.

Within an ionospheric layer, the electron density increases with increase in height above the earth. Above the top of the layer, the density falls with further increase in height until the lower edge of the next higher layer is reached. At heights greater than the top of the F_2 layer, the electron density falls until it becomes negligibly small.

The refractive index n of a layer is related to both the frequency of the wave and the electron density according to equation (6.6):

$$n = \sin \phi_i / \sin \phi_r = \sqrt{(1 - 81N/f^2)} \qquad (6.6)$$

Here f is the frequency of the radio wave in hertz, N is the number of free electrons per cubic metre and, as before, ϕ_i and ϕ_r are respectively the angles of incidence and refraction.

Equation (6.6) shows that the refractive index of a layer decreases as the electron density is increased. This means that *within a layer* the refractive index *falls* with increase in height above ground. Also note that an increase in frequency results in an increase in the refractive index of a layer.

Sky wave

A radio wave at a particular frequency entering a layer with angle of incidence ϕ_i will always be passing from lower to higher refractive index as it travels upwards through the layer. Therefore, the wave is continuously refracted away from the normal. If, before it reaches the top of the layer, the wave has been refracted to the extent that the angle of refraction ϕ_r becomes equal to 90°, the wave will be returned to earth. Should the angle of refraction be less than 90°, the wave will emerge from the top of the layer and travel on to a greater height. If, then, the wave enters another higher layer, it will experience further refraction and may now be returned to earth. If the frequency of the wave is increased, n will fall and the wave will be refracted to a lesser extent and it will have to travel further through a layer before it is returned to earth.

Figure 6.8 shows sky waves at frequencies 5, 10, 20 and 30 MHz that are incident on the lower edge of the E layer with an angle of incidence ϕ_1. The 5 MHz wave is refracted to the greatest extent and is returned to earth after penetrating only a little way into the E layer. The 10 MHz wave must penetrate much farther into the E layer before it is returned to earth, while the 20 MHz wave is hardly refracted at all by the E layer and passes on to the F_1 layer. The 20 MHz wave meets the F_1 layer with a much larger angle of incidence ($\phi_3 > \phi_1$). A smaller change in direction is now required to return the wave to earth, and sufficient refraction is produced by the F_1 layer. The

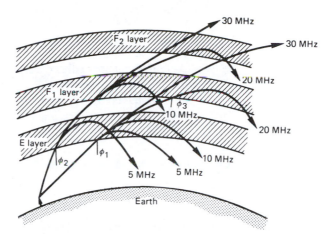

Fig. 6.8 Effect on ionospheric refraction of angle of incidence and frequency of wave

30 MHz wave is not refracted to the extent required to return it to earth and escapes from the top of the F_2 layer.

If the angle at which the waves are incident on the E layer is reduced to ϕ_2, greater refraction is necessary to return the waves to earth. Consequently, only the 5 MHz wave is now returned by the E layer, the 10 MHz and 20 MHz waves pass right through and arrive at the F_1 layer. The refractive index of the F_1 layer is lower at 10 MHz than at 20 MHz; hence the 10 MHz wave is refracted sufficiently to be returned, but the 20 MHz wave is not. The 20 MHz wave passes on to the F_2 layer and is then returned. Once again, the 30 MHz wave is not returned and it escapes from the upper edge of the ionosphere.

Further decrease in the angle of incidence of the waves on the E layer may well result in the 20 MHz wave escaping the F_2 layer also and not returning to earth at all, and the 5 MHz and 10 MHz waves being returned by a higher layer.

Example 6.3

An ionospheric layer has a maximum electron density of 6×10^{11} electrons/m^3. Calculate the maximum frequency that will be returned to earth if the angle of incidence is (a) 60°, (b) 30°.

Solution

    (a) From equation (6.6),

$$\sin 60° = 0.866 = \sqrt{[1 - (81 \times 6 \times 10^{11})/f^2]}$$
$$0.75 = 1 - (81 \times 6 \times 10^{11})/f^2$$
$$f^2 = (81 \times 6 \times 10^{11})/0.25$$
$$f = 13.943 \text{ MHz} \quad (Ans.)$$

    (b) $\sin 30° = 0.5 = \sqrt{[1 - (81 \times 6 \times 10^{11})/f^2]}$

$$0.25 = 1 - (81 \times 6 \times 10^{11})/f^2$$
$$f^2 = (81 \times 6 \times 10^{11})/0.75$$
$$f = 8.05 \text{ MHz} \quad (Ans.)$$

Critical frequency

The *critical frequency* of an ionospheric layer is the highest frequency that can be radiated vertically upwards by a radio transmitter and returned to earth. The condition corresponds to a wave that travels to the top of the layer, where the electron density is at its maximum value, before its angle of refraction becomes 90°. The angle of incidence is 0°. Using equation (6.6),

$$\sin 0° = 0 = \sqrt{[1 - (81 N_{max}/f^2_{crit})]}$$

Therefore

$$f^2_{crit} = 81 N_{max}$$
$$f_{crit} = 9\sqrt{N_{max}} \tag{6.7}$$

The critical frequency of a layer is of interest for two reasons: firstly it is a parameter which can be measured from the ground and, secondly, it bears a simple relationship to the maximum usable frequency of a sky-wave link.

Virtual height

From the ground it seems as though the radio wave at the critical frequency has travelled in a straight line to a point of total reflection and then straight down to the earth. The *virtual height* of an ionospheric layer is the height at which the apparent reflection has taken place. The concept of virtual height is illustrated by Fig. 6.9.

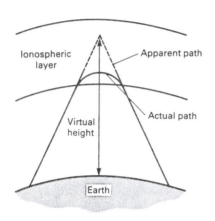

Fig. 6.9 Virtual height of an ionospheric layer

Maximum usable frequency

The maximum usable frequency (MUF) is the highest frequency that can be used to establish communication, using the sky wave, between two points. If a higher frequency is used, the wave will escape from the top of the layer and the signal will not be received at the far end of the link. The MUF is determined by both the angle of incidence of the radio wave and the critical frequency of the layer; thus

$$MUF = f_{crit}/\cos \phi_i \tag{6.8}$$

The MUF is an important parameter in sky wave propagation. Since the attentuation suffered by a wave is inversely proportional to the frequency of the wave, it is desirable to use as high a frequency as possible.

Example 6.4

Calculate the maximum usable frequency of a sky-wave link if the angle of incidence is 45° and the maximum electron density of the layer used is 4×10^{11} electrons/m³.

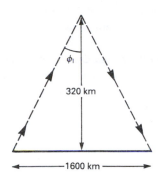

Fig. 6.10

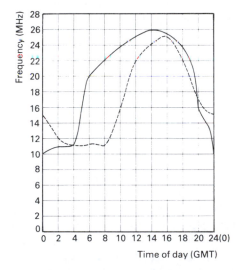

Fig. 6.11 Variations of MUF with time of day

Solution
From equation (6.7)

$$f_{crit} = 9\sqrt{(4 \times 10^{11})} = 5.692 \text{ MHz}$$

Therefore, from equation (6.8)

$$\text{MUF} = 5.692/(\cos 45°) = 8.05 \text{ MHz} \quad (Ans.)$$

Example 6.5

The ground range of a sky wave link is 1600 km and the virtual height of the ionospheric layer used is 320 km. If the critical frequency is 5 MHz, calculate the MUF of the link. Assume the earth to be flat.

Solution
Figure 6.10 shows the link. The angle of incidence ϕ_i is

$$\phi_i = \tan^{-1}(800/320) = 68.2°$$

Therefore

$$\text{MUF} = 5/(\cos 68.2°) = 13.5 \text{ MHz} \quad (Ans.)$$

Optimum working frequency

The electron density of an ionospheric layer is not a constant quantity but is subject to many fluctuations, some regular and predictable and some not. As a consequence, the MUF of any given route is also subject to considerable variation over a period of time. The MUF of a link will vary throughout each day as the intensity of the sun's radiation changes. Maximum radiation from the sun occurs at noon, while after dark there is no radiation. There is always a time lag of some hours between a change in the ultra-violet radiation passing through the ionosphere and the resulting change in electron density, and so the MUF may be expected to vary in the manner shown by the typical graphs of Fig. 6.11.

In addition to the predictable MUF variations, further fluctuations often take place and, because of this, operation of a link at the MUF prevailing at a given time would not produce a reliable system. Usually a frequency of about 85% of the MUF is used to operate a sky-wave link. This frequency is known as the *optimum working (traffic) frequency* (OWF), or the *frequency of optimum transmission* (FOT). Since the MUF will vary over the working day, the OWF will do so also, and it is therefore necessary to change the transmitted frequency as propagation conditions vary. The number of available frequencies is limited and international frequency-sharing is necessary. Usually, an individual radio transmitter is allocated several carrier frequencies, any one of which can be employed if necessary. When propagation conditions are poor, it may prove necessary to transmit on more than one frequency and even, when conditions are particularly bad, to re-transmit when conditions improve.

The attenuation of a sky-wave link increases with decrease in the frequency of the transmission and, if the transmitted power is maintained at a constant level, the received field strength is inversely proportional to frequency. The *lowest useful frequency* (LUF) is the lowest frequency at which a link with a given signal-to-noise ratio at the receive aerial can be established. The LUF varies with time of day and year in a similar manner to the MUF.

Skip distance

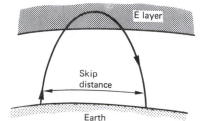

Fig. 6.12 Skip distance

There is a minimum distance over which communication at a given frequency can be established by means of the sky wave. Usually, the frequency considered is the MUF of the link. If an attempt is made to reduce this minimum distance by using a smaller angle of incidence, the wave will not be returned to earth by the E layer but will pass through it. This minimum distance is known as the *skip distance* and it is shown in Fig. 6.12. For a given frequency each of the ionospheric layers has its particular skip distance. The higher the frequency of the wave, the greater is the skip distance.

Multiple-hop transmissions

When communication is desired between two points which are more than about 3000 km apart, it is necessary to employ two or more hops, as shown in Fig. 6.13. The sky wave is refracted in the ionosphere and returned to earth, and the downward wave is reflected at the surface of the earth to be returned skywards. The overall MUF of a multi-hop link is the lowest of the MUFs of the individual links.

The number of hops that are possible depends upon both the transmitted power and the losses incurred at each ground reflection and ionospheric refraction. The main disadvantage of a multi-hop route is the likelihood of pronounced selective fading and more than two hops tend to give unreliable service.

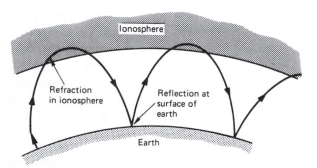

Fig. 6.13 Multi-hop transmission of sky wave

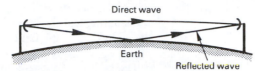

Fig. 6.14 Space wave

Space wave

At frequencies in the VHF, UHF and SHF bands, the range of the surface wave is severely limited and the ionosphere is unable to refract radio waves. Because the signal wavelength is short, the transmitting and receiving aerials can both be installed at a height of several wavelengths above earth. Then the space wave can be used for communication since its direct and reflected waves will not (always) cancel.

The principle of a space-wave radio link is illustrated by Fig. 6.14. The direct wave travels in a very nearly straight line path, slight refraction being caused by the temperature and water vapour gradients in the troposphere. The reflected wave is incident upon the earth and here it is reflected towards the receive aerial.

Direct wave

An isotropic radiator is a theoretical aerial that is supposed to be able to radiate energy equally well in all directions. It therefore produces a spherical wavefront, and so the radiated power P_t is uniformly spread over the surface area of a sphere. The power density P_d of the wavefront is

$$P_d = P_t/4\pi d^2 \ \text{W/m}^2$$

where d is the distance from the radiator.

The power density is also equal to $E^2/$(impedance of free space) and hence

$$P_t/4\pi d^2 = E^2/120\pi$$

or

$$E = \sqrt{(30P_t)}/d \ \text{V/m} \tag{6.9}$$

For a practical aerial with a gain G_t with respect to an isotropic radiator, the field strength at distance d from the aerial is

$$E = \sqrt{(30P_tG_t)}/d \ \text{V/m} \tag{6.10}$$

Direct plus reflected waves

The total field strength at the receiving aerial is the phasor sum of the field strengths produced by the direct and the reflected waves. The total field strength is given by equation (6.11):

$$E_T = 2E_d[\sin(2\pi h_t h_r)/\lambda d] \tag{6.11}$$

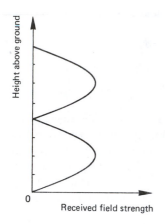

Fig. 6.15 Variation of field strength with height above ground at the receive end of a space-wave radio link

where h_t and h_r are the respective heights above ground of the transmitting and the receiving aerials, and d is the distance between the aerials. E_d is the field strength produced at the same point by the direct wave on its own; (see equation 6.10).

The total field strength at the receive aerial will vary with height above ground, (see Fig. 6.15), and it has a maximum value of $2E_d$ whenever $(2\pi h_t h_r)/\lambda d = \pi/2$. Obviously, careful choice of the height at which the receive aerial is to be mounted is essential.

Example 6.6

A $\lambda/2$ dipole radiates 10 W power at 150 MHz. The signal is received by another $\lambda/2$ dipole 25 km distant. Calculate (a) the field strength, and (b) the voltage picked up by the receiving aerial.

Solution

Wavelength $\lambda = (3 \times 10^8)/(150 \times 10^6) = 2$ m
$G_t = 1.64$
$l_{eff} = \lambda/\pi = 2/\pi$

(a) Field strength $= [\sqrt{(30 \times 10 \times 1.64)}]/(25 \times 10^3) = 887 \, \mu\text{V/m}$
                                                                          (Ans.)
(b) Received voltage $= 887 \times 10^{-6} \times (2/\pi) = 565 \, \mu\text{V}$ *(Ans.)*

Received power

An aerial having a gain G_r with respect to an isotropic radiator has an effective aperture of

$$A_e = G_r \lambda^2/4\pi \text{ m}^2 \tag{6.12}$$

If the power density of an incident radio wave is P_a W/m^2 then the power absorbed by the aerial will be

$$P_r = P_a A_e \tag{6.13}$$

or

$$\begin{aligned}
P_r &= (E^2/120\pi) \times (G_r \lambda^2/4\pi) \\
&= (30 P_t G_t)/(120\pi d) \times (G_r \lambda^2/4\pi) \\
&= (\lambda/4\pi d)^2 \, P_t G_t G_r \text{ W}
\end{aligned} \tag{6.14}$$

The factor $(\lambda/4\pi d)^2$ is known as the *free-space attenuation*, or the *space loss*, of the radio wave. It is the minimum power loss caused by the divergence of the wave during propagation, and practical losses are somewhat greater.

Example 6.7

A transmitting aerial has a gain of 40 dBi and radiates 10 W power at a frequency of 6 GHz. Calculate the power received by a similar aerial 30 km distant.

Solution

$$\lambda = (3 \times 10^8)/(6 \times 10^9) = 0.05 \text{ m}$$
$$P_r = [0.05/(4\pi \times 30 \times 10^3)]^2 \times 10 \times 10^4 \times 10^4 = 17.6 \,\mu\text{W}$$

(*Ans.*)

Example 6.8

A communication satellite system radiates a power of 140 W at 6 GHz. The gains of the transmitting and receiving aerials are $G_t = 60$ dBi and $G_r = 22$ dBi. If the space loss is 200 dB, calculate (a) the length of the radio path; (b) the received power.

Solution

(a) $200 \text{ dB} = $ power ratio of $1 \times 10^{20} = [(4\pi d)/\lambda]^2$
$$\lambda = 0.05 \text{ m}$$
$$d = [\sqrt{(1 \times 10^{20})} \times 0.05]/(4\pi) = 39\,790 \text{ km}$$ (*Ans.*)

(b) $P_t = 10 \log_{10} 140 = 21.5 \text{ dBW}$
$$P_r = 21.5 + 60 - 200 + 22 = -96.5 \text{ dBW} = 224 \text{ pW}$$ (*Ans.*)

The maximum distance of a space-wave link is determined by the curvature of the earth. Figure 6.16 shows how the *radio horizon* depends upon the height of the transmitting aerial. Beyond the radio horizon the received field strength decreases rapidly, particularly at UHF. In practice, link lengths are shorter than this in order to improve the reliability of the system. Most links are some 25–40 km in length.

The direct wave must be well clear of any obstacles, such as trees and buildings which might block the path, and this factor will determine the necessary aerial heights.

The majority of point-to-point space-wave radio systems are of considerably longer route length than 40 km and must of necessity require a number of relay stations.

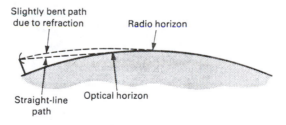

Fig. 6.16 Radio horizon

Polarization

The electric field strength produced by a horizontally polarized space wave varies with height above the ground (equation 6.11), and becomes zero at ground level. This is not so for a vertically polarized space wave; its field strength varies with height in the same way as does a horizontally polarized wave down to a height of about 10 m above the ground. At heights less than 10 m right down to ground level, the field strength remains more or less constant at the 10 m value.

Most household portable and car radio receivers are operated at heights less than 10 m, and hence vertical polarization is normally preferred, since it gives a larger field strength and it can be received by a vertical whip aerial.

Television aerials are often mounted on rooftops or in lofts and so either horizontal or vertical polarization will give good results. Co-channel interference is considerably reduced by using different polarizations for adjacent co-channel stations.

Propagation via communication satellite

The basic principle of a communication satellite system is shown in Fig. 6.17. Since different frequencies in the SHF band are used in both directions of propagation, the ionosphere has negligible effect on the path of the radio waves, and so these waves travel in straight lines. This method of propagation can transmit wideband telephony systems and television signals over distances of thousands of kilometres with the utmost reliability. Propagation is by means of the direct space wave only, since there is no reflected wave.

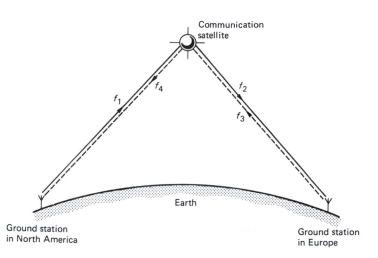

Fig. 6.17 An earth satellite commmunication system

Example 6.9

A communication satellite is 35 800 km from an earth station. The earth station aerial has a gain of 48 dBi and transmits 1 kW power at 6 GHz to the satellite. If the gain of the satellite's aerial is 35 dBi, calculate the power input to the satellite's transponder.

Solution

$\lambda = (3 \times 10^8)/(6 \times 10^9) = 0.05$ m; 1 kW is 30 dBW. From equation (6.14)

$$\text{Path loss} = 20 \log_{10}[(4\pi \times 35\,800 \times 10^3)/0.05] = 199 \text{ dB}$$

Hence

$$P_r = 30 + 48 + 35 - 199 = -86 \text{ dBW} = 2.5 \text{ nW} \qquad (Ans.)$$

Tropospheric scatter propagation

Another method of providing a number of radio-telephony channels over a long distance is known as *tropospheric scatter* and is illustrated by Fig. 6.18. A high-power radio wave is transmitted upwards from the earth and a very small fraction of the transmitted energy is *forward-scattered* by the troposphere and directed downwards towards the earth. This occurs at frequencies above about 600 MHz, but particularly at 900 MHz, 2 GHz and 5 GHz. The forward-scattered energy is received by a high-gain aerial, often of the parabolic reflector type, to provide a reliable long-distance wideband UHF radio link. The distance between the transmitting and receiving stations is usually in the range of 300 to 500 km and nearly always covers geographically hostile terrain, such as mountains, jungle or ocean. Since only a small fraction of the transmitted power arrives at the aerial, the system is very inefficient and demands the use of high-power transmitters and high-gain, low-noise radio receivers. For this reason, a tropospheric scatter system is only provided when no other alternative is available.

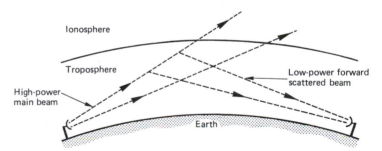

Fig. 6.18   Scatter propagation

Fading

Fading, or variation in the amplitude of a received signal, is of two main types: *general fading*, in which the whole signal fades to the same extent; and *selective fading*, in which some of the frequency components of a signal fade while at the same time others increase in amplitude.

In an analogue system, fading results in a degradation of speech quality. In a digital system, error-correcting circuitry will be able to correct any errors, provided that the bit error rate is not too high.

General fading

As it travels through the ionosphere, a radio wave is attenuated but, since the ionosphere is in a continual state of flux, the attenuation

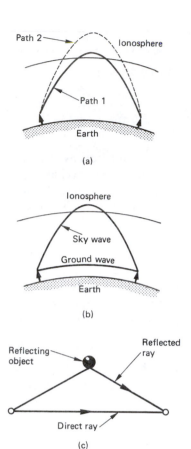

Fig. 6.19 Multi-path propagation

is not constant, and the amplitude of the received signal varies. Under certain conditions, a complete fade-out of signals may occur for up to two hours, usually caused by solar flares. With the exception of complete fade-outs, general fading can be combated by *automatic gain control* (AGC) in the radio receiver.

Selective fading

The radio waves arriving at the receiving end of a sky-wave radio link may have travelled over two or more different paths through the ionosphere. Three kinds of multi-path propagation are shown in Fig. 6.19. In each case, the total field strength at the receive aerial is the *phasor* sum of the field strengths produced by each wave. Since the ionosphere is subject to continual fluctuations in its ionization density, the difference between the lengths of paths 1 and 2 in Fig. 6.19(a) will fluctuate and this will alter the total field strength at the receiver. Suppose, for example, that path 2 is initially one wavelength longer than path 1; the field strengths produced by the two waves are then in phase and the total field strength is equal to the algebraic sum of the individual field strengths. When a fluctuation occurs in the ionosphere that causes the difference between the lengths of paths 1 and 2 to be reduced to a half-wavelength, the individual field strengths are now in antiphase and the total field strength is given by their algebraic difference.

The phase difference between the field strengths set up by the two waves is a function of frequency and hence the phasor sum of the two field strengths is different for each component frequency in the signal. This means that some frequencies may fade at the same instant as others are augmented; the effect is particularly serious in double-sideband amplitude-modulated systems because, if the carrier component fades to a level well below that of the two sidebands, the sidebands will beat together and considerable signal distortion will be produced.

Selective fading cannot by overcome by the use of AGC in the receiver since this is operated by the carrier level only. Several methods of reducing selective fading do exist; for example, the use of frequencies as near to the MUF as possible, the use of a transmitting aerial that radiates only one possible mode of propagation, the use of single-sideband or frequency-modulated systems, or the use of a specialized equipment such as *Lincompex*. Selective fading of the sky wave is most likely when the route length necessitates the use of two or more hops. Suppose, for example, that a two-hop link has been engineered. Then, because of the directional characteristics of the transmitting aerial, there may well also be a three-hop path over which the transmitted energy is able to reach the receiving aerial.

Selective fading can also arise with systems using the ground and space waves. In the daytime the D layer of the ionosphere completely absorbs any energy radiated skywards by a medium-wave broadcast aerial. At night the D layer disappears and any skywards radiation is returned to earth and will interfere with the ground wave, as shown in Fig. 6.19(b). In the regions where the ground and sky waves are present at night, rapid fading, caused by fluctuations in the length of the sky path, occurs. This is why reception of medium-waveband broadcasts is much worse at night than in the daytime; this effect can be minimized by the use of transmitting aerials having maximum gain along the surface of the earth and radiating minimum energy skywards.

Fig. 6.19(c) illustrates how multi-path reception of a VHF signal can occur. Energy arrives at the receiver by a direct path and by reflection from a large object such as a hill or gas-holder. If the reflecting object is not stationary, the phase difference between the two signals will change rapidly and rapid fading will occur.

Rayleigh fading

Rayleigh fading occurs when the signal received by an aerial is the resultant of reflected signals from a number of nearby objects and there is no direct signal path between the transmitter and the receiver. Such a situation often occurs with land mobile systems. The multiple reflections create a service area in which the amplitude and phase of the resultant received signal both vary significantly as the receiver is moved around. This causes the signal picked up by a mobile receiver to vary in an almost random manner.

Rician fading

Rician fading is similar to Rayleigh fading, but now there is also a direct radio path between the transmitter and the receiver. This generally occurs when the transmitting aerial is mounted high above the ground and/or the receiver is situated fairly close to the transmitter.

Multi-path fading

Both Rayleigh and Rician fading occur when the reflected signals are delayed in time by a period that is comparable with the carrier frequency's periodic time but is short compared to the periodic time of the modulation signal. Multi-path fading is said to have occurred when the time delay of the reflected signals is long compared to the modulation periodic time.

Use of the frequency bands

At frequencies in the VLF and LF bands, aerials are very inefficient and high-power transmitters must be used. The radiated energy is vertically polarized and will propagate reliably (no fading) for thousands of kilometres using the ground wave or by means of multiple reflections between ionosphere and earth. Services provided in this band are ship-to-shore telegraphy, navigation systems and sound broadcasting (LF band). In the MF band the range of the ground wave is limited to some hundreds of kilometres and the main use of the band is for sound broadcasting (657–1546 kHz). Also provided are ship telephonic and telegraphic links in, respectively, the bands 405–525 kHz and 1.6–3.8 MHz.

At high frequencies the main mode of propagation is the sky wave, the surface wave giving, if required, service for distances of up to the skip distance. The HF band is used for international point-to-point radio-telephony links on a number of sub-bands, for sound broadcasting, and for marine and aero mobile systems.

In the VHF and higher bands, the ground wave has a very limited range and the ionosphere (normally) does not return waves to earth. The modes of propagation used are therefore the space wave and, at certain frequencies in the SHF band, the communication satellite. Scatter is also sometimes used. Services provided are sound broadcasting in the VHF band (88.1–96.8 MHz), land, marine and aero mobile systems in the VHF and UHF bands, television broadcasting in the UHF band, and point-to-point multi-channel telephony systems in the UHF and SHF bands.

Exercises

6.1 (a) Describe two methods of obtaining long-distance radio communication at frequencies above 300 MHz. (b) Explain why it may be easier to establish a low-frequency link using reflection from the lower edge of the D layer in a north–south direction than in a west–east direction.

6.2 (a) Explain how selective fading of radio waves occurs. (b) Explain why selective fading cannot be overcome by AGC in a radio receiver.

6.3 (a) Draw a sketch of the ionosphere (i) in the daytime and (ii) at night. (b) Briefly explain the following terms in connection with radio wave propagation: (i) skip distance (ii) sky wave; (iii) fading.

6.4 With the aid of simple sketches, explain the following terms in connection with radio-wave propagation: (a) ground waves; (b) sky waves; (c) critical frequency of an ionospheric layer; (d) skip distance; (e) maximum usable frequency.

6.5 (a) Explain how a radio wave incident on an ionized region is returned to earth by refraction. (b) How does the refraction vary with (i) frequency, (ii) electron density in the ionized region, (iii) angle of incidence?

6.6 (a) Explain the mode of propagation whereby low radio frequencies can be used for world-wide communication. (b) How does field strength vary with the distance from the transmitter and with radiated frequency? (c) What are the advantages and disadvantages of low-frequency propagation?

6.7 Why is the range of a broadcast transmitter using the ground wave limited even when the ground is lossless? Does loss in the ground wave increase or decrease with increase in (a) conductivity, (b) frequency, (c) permittivity?

6.8 Fig. 6.20 is a simplified diagram of an ionospheric region in the atmosphere. (a) Explain how the radio wave incident on the ionized region represented

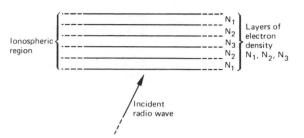

Fig. 6.20

in Fig. 6.20 is returned to earth when it is below the MUF. (b) Why does a wave at a frequency above the MUF penetrate the region? (c) Where is the maximum electron density in the ionospheric region shown in Fig. 6.20?

6.9 Explain why VHF and UHF radio signals can be received beyond the line of sight distance from the transmitter. Explain why the height above ground of the aerial at the receiving end of the link is important.

6.10 (a) Explain how a long-distance wideband radio link can be established using tropospheric scatter in the UHF band. (b) A parabolic reflector aerial used in a 2 GHz tropospheric scatter system has a diameter of 6 m and radiates a power of 1 kW. Calculate the effective radiated power.

6.11 (a) Distinguish between the terms *ground wave* and *surface wave* used in radio wave propagation. (b) For which frequency bands is the surface wave the main mode of propagation? (c) Give typical ranges for each band. (d) Why does the surface wave suffer less attenuation over sea than over land?

6.12 (a) Explain the meanings of the terms *critical frequency, maximum usable frequency* and *lowest useful frequency* when used in radio propagation work. (b) Give two reasons why a frequency as near the MUF as possible is used for a sky-wave radio link.

6.13 (a) Explain, with the aid of a diagram, why multi-hop sky-wave paths are prone to selective fading. (b) What is meant by the term *skip distance*? (c) Does the skip distance increase or decrease if (i) the frequency is raised, (ii) the transmitted power is increased, (iii) the electron density of the refracting layer is increased?

6.14 (a) What is meant by (i) the refraction of an electromagnetic wave, (ii) the diffraction of an electromagnetic wave? (b) Explain why, in practice, UHF transmissions may reach distances approximately 15 per cent greater than the uninterrupted line-of-sight distance.

6.15 (a) If a power, P watts, is radiated by an isotropic radiator, show that the power density at a range d metres is equal to $P/4\pi d^2$ W/m^2. (b) Calculate the power reaching a parabolic dish aerial with an aperture of 3 m^2, at an unobstructed range of 20 km, if the transmitter radiates 1 W from an aerial having a gain of 2000.

7 Radio-frequency power amplifiers

Radio-frequency power amplifiers are used in radio transmitters to amplify the carrier frequency to the wanted power output level. The amplifiers are often expected to provide frequency multiplication at the same time as power amplification. For many radio transmitters the output power is of the order of tens, or perhaps hundreds, of kilowatts.

All solid-state radio transmitters are available with output powers of 100 kW or more. High-power transmitters employ a number of r.f. power transistors connected in parallel, since the maximum power that a single transistor is able to provide is limited. The use of paralleled transistors increases the complexity of the transmitter circuitry. Many high-power transmitters therefore employ thermionic valves in their output stage. The earlier stages will use transistors. On the other hand, a low-power transmitter will be completely transistorized. Hence an r.f. power amplifier may use either a transistor or a valve to provide amplification.

The choice between the triode valve and the tetrode valve for the output stage must be made with due regard to a number of factors. The tetrode has a larger gain than the triode, which means that a smaller input voltage is needed to develop a given output power. The anode—grid capacitance is considerably reduced by the screen grid, and usually the tetrode can be operated without *neutralization* circuitry. Unless the triode is operated in the earthed-grid configuration, it will need to be neutralized to avoid positive feedback via its anode—grid capacitance. It is usually necessary to drive the triode valve into its grid current region in order to obtain a sufficiently large output power, and this practice results in distortion of the output waveform. The tetrode has the disadvantage that power is dissipated at its screen grid and so its overall efficiency is reduced; also some means of removing this heat may be necessary.

Normally, tetrode valves are employed but, to simplify the circuit diagrams, triode valves are shown in the following figures.

With Class B operation, shown in Fig. 7.1(a), the operating point is set at cut-off. The output current flows only during alternate half-

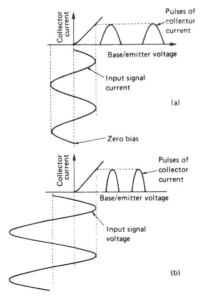

Fig. 7.1 (a) Class B bias; (b) Class C bias

cycles of the signal waveform. The output current waveform is highly distorted; Class B bias can therefore only be employed with circuits that are able to restore the missing half-cycles of the signal waveform. Class B operation has a maximum theoretical efficiency of 78.5%.

Even greater efficiency can be obtained with Class C bias. With Class C bias, shown in Fig. 7.1(b), the operating point is set well beyond cut-off. The output current flows in the form of a series of narrow pulses having a duration which is less than half the periodic time of the input signal waveform. Class C bias is used with r.f. power amplifiers because the anode efficiency can be very high, perhaps as much as 80%. Such a high efficiency is extremely important when high-power applications are concerned. For example, to obtain an output power of 60 kW, an input power of 75 kW is required if the efficiency is 80%, but the input power must be 85.7 kW when the efficiency is reduced to 70%.

Class C radio-frequency power amplifier

The basic circuit of a Class C radio-frequency power amplifier is given in Figs 7.2(a) and (b). A triode valve has been shown but a tetrode valve could be used instead. The difference between the two circuits shown lies in the way in which the anode-tuned circuit has been connected. In the series-feed circuit of Fig. 7.2(a) the tuned circuit is connected in series with the power supply, while in the parallel-feed circuit of Fig. 7.2(b) the tuned circuit is connected in parallel with the valve and is isolated from the power supply by the d.c. blocking capacitor C_2. The parallel-feed circuit uses another extra component, namely L_4, which stops r.f. currents entering the power supply instead of the tuned circuit $C_3 L_5$. In both circuits the valve

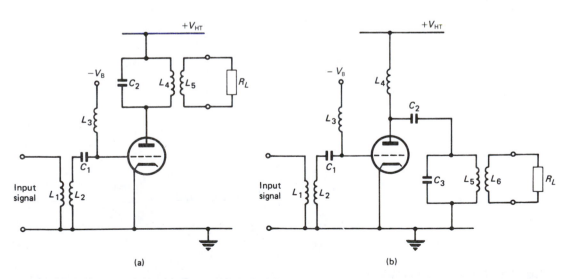

Fig. 7.2   Class C tuned power amplifiers: (a) series-fed, (b) parallel-fed

is biased to operate under Class C conditions by the negative bias voltage V_B. Usually V_B is more than twice the cut-off voltage of the valve. The bias voltage is applied via inductor L_3 to stop signal frequency currents being shunted, via the bias supply, to earth. Capacitor C_1 prevents the bias voltage being shorted to earth by L_2. The parallel-feed arrangement ensures that the tuned circuit components are at zero d.c. potential, which makes insulation and safety less of a problem.

When a sinusoidal voltage is applied to the input terminals of the amplifier, the valve will only conduct at the positive peaks of the signal voltage (Fig. 7.3). This means that the anode current flows as a series of pulses, each of which lasts for a time period smaller than one-half the periodic time of the input signal waveform. Clearly, the anode current is not sinusoidal but consists of a d.c. component and a fundamental frequency component, plus components at a number of harmonically related frequencies. The amplitude of the fundamental is greater than that of any of the harmonics. The anode circuit is tuned to be resonant at the signal frequency. A parallel-tuned circuit has its maximum impedance at its resonant frequency and this impedance, known as the *dynamic resistance R_d*, is a pure resistance. At all other

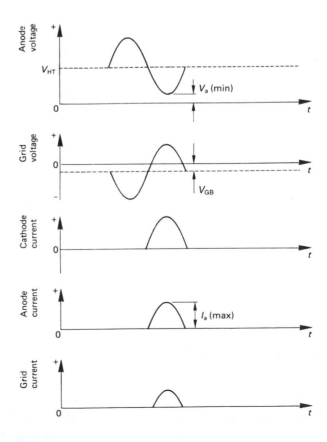

Fig. 7.3 Current and voltage waveforms in a Class C amplifier

frequencies the impedance of a parallel-tuned circuit is much smaller and is not purely resistive. The voltage developed across the anode circuit is therefore produced only by the fundamental (signal) frequency component of the anode current and is of sinusoidal waveform.

Very often with triodes (but not with tetrodes) the grid potential is taken positive with respect to the cathode at its peak positive half-cycles. This practice does result in the flow of grid current but it also produces anode current pulses of larger peak value than would otherwise be possible. Since the amplitude of the fundamental-frequency component of the anode current is proportional to the peak anode current, a larger output voltage is thus obtained.

The anode voltage of the valve is equal to the h.t. supply voltage minus the voltage developed across the anode-tuned circuit and is in antiphase with the grid voltage. The current and voltage waveforms at various points in a Class C tuned amplifier are shown in Fig. 7.3. The following points should be noted:

- The anode current flows whenever the positive half-cycles of the input signal voltage make the grid potential less negative than the cut-off voltage of the valve.
- Grid current flows whenever the grid potential is positive.
- The minimum value of the anode voltage occurs at the same times as the positive peaks of the input signal voltage. It is necessary to ensure that at no time does the grid potential become more positive than the minimum anode voltage. If this should happen, a large grid current will flow and damage the valve.
- The circuit has a high anode efficiency because anode current flows only at those times when the instantaneous anode voltage is at or near its minimum value. This reduces the power dissipated at the anode of the valve.

If the voltage of the h.t. suppply is increased, the peak value of the anode current pulses will increase in the same ratio and this, in turn, will increase the signal output voltage. This means that for a Class C tuned amplifier, the output voltage is *directly proportional* to the power supply voltage.

Angle of flow

The anode current of a Class C tuned power amplifier flows in a series of less-than-half sinewave pulses. The conduction time is expressed in terms of a parameter known as the *angle of flow*. The anode current flows whenever the total grid voltage is less negative than the cut-off voltage of the valve. Thus, referring to Fig. 7.4, θ is the angle of anode current flow. In this figure V_{CO} is the cut-off voltage of the valve and V_B is the bias voltage applied. Also shown is the angle ϕ of grid current flow, always $\phi < \theta$.

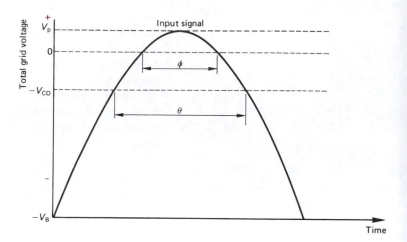

Fig. 7.4 Angle of flow

When $\omega_s t = \pi/2 \pm \theta/2$, $v = V_s \cos \theta/2$. Then

$$\cos \theta/2 = (V_B - V_{CO})/V_s = (V_B - V_{CO})/(V_B + V_p) \qquad (7.1)$$

Example 7.1

Calculate the angle of flow if the cut-off voltage is 40 V, the grid bias voltage is 100 V and the peak signal voltage at the grid is 110 V.

Solution

$$\cos \theta/2 = (100 - 40)/110, \ \theta = 114° \qquad (Ans.)$$

The angle of flow is always less than 180° ($\theta = 180°$ gives Class B conditions), the actual value chosen being a compromise between the conflicting requirements of anode efficiency and power output. A reduction in the angle of flow reduces the power output of the amplifier but increases its efficiency. Generally, the angle of anode current flow is chosen to be somewhere in the region of 120°.

When θ is approximately 120°, the anode current flows for only one-third of each cycle and the current waveform can be considered, without the introduction of undue error, to be of triangular shape. This is a convenient assumption to be able to make, since it allows the mean value of the anode current to be easily calculated using equation (7.2):

$$I_{a(mean)} = (I_{a(peak)}/2)(\theta/360) \qquad (7.2)$$

The mean value of the anode current is the direct current which is taken from the h.t. power supply.

Power relationships

The d.c. power supplied by the h.t. power supply to the amplifier is equal to the product of the power supply voltage V_{HT} and the mean value of the anode current:

$$P_{DC} = V_{HT} I_{a(mean)} \qquad (7.3)$$

Some of this power is dissipated at the anode of the valve and is known as the *anode dissipation*. The remainder of the input power is converted into a.c. power and is delivered to the anode tuned circuit. A small amount of this power is dissipated in the resistance of the tuned circuit inductance but the rest is passed on to the load to provide the power output of the amplifier. Usually, the power lost in the tuned circuit is small and it will be neglected in this book. The a.c. power P_{ac} delivered to the anode tuned circuit, i.e. the a.c. output power, is equal to the square of the r.m.s. value of the fundamental frequency component $I_{a(f)}$ of the anode current times the dynamic resistance R_d of the tuned circuit:

$$P_{ac} = I_{a(f)}^2 R_d \tag{7.4}$$

Anode efficiency

The *anode efficiency* η of a Class C amplifier is the ratio P_{ac}/P_{DC} expressed as a percentage:

$$\eta = (P_{ac}/P_{DC}) \times 100\% \tag{7.5}$$

Alternatively, the power output of the circuit can be expressed in terms of the anode and h.t. supply voltages. The fundamental frequency component of the anode current develops a voltage $V_L \sin \omega t$ across the tuned circuit, where $V_L = I_{a(f)}R_d$. Therefore the output power is

$$P_{ac} = (V_L/\sqrt{2})^2/R_d \tag{7.6}$$

The anode voltage V_a of the valve is

$$V_a = V_{HT} - V_L \sin \omega t$$

When $\sin \omega t = 1$, the anode voltage is at its minimum value $V_{a(min)}$, and

$$V_L = V_{HT} - V_{a(min)}$$

and hence

$$P_{ac} = (V_{HT} - V_{a(min)})^2/2R_d \tag{7.7}$$

Example 7.2

The anode current pulses in a Class C tuned amplifier are of approximately triangular waveform with a peak value of 3 A and an angle of flow of 100°. (a) Calculate the mean value of the anode current. (b) If $V_{HT} = 2000$ V and the power output is 600 W, calculate the anode efficiency.

Solution

(a) From equation (7.2),

$$I_{a(meam)} = (3/2) \times (100/360) = 0.417 \text{ A} \quad (Ans.)$$

(b) $P_{DC} = 0.417 \times 2000 = 834$ W
  $\eta = (600/834) \times 100 = 72\% \quad (Ans.)$

Example 7.3

In a Class C tuned power amplifier the anode current is of approximately triangular waveform of peak value 4.6 A and angle of flow 120°. If the anode efficiency of the circuit is 75% and the h.t. supply voltage is 1 kV, calculate the output power.

Solution

$$P_{DC} = (4.6/2) \times (120/360) \times 1000 = 766.7 \, W$$

Therefore

$$P_{ac} = \eta P_{DC} = 0.75 \times 766.7 = 575 \, W \qquad (Ans.)$$

Earthed-grid Class C amplifier

When a triode valve is used in the common-cathode connection, feedback of radio-frequency energy from the anode (output) circuit to the grid (input) circuit via the anode–grid capacitance of the valve will take place. This positive feedback will produce instability and possibly unwanted oscillations. To overcome the instability problem it will be necessary to use extra circuitry, known as *neutralization*, to cancel or neutralize the unwanted feedback. In modern transmitters the need for neutralization is overcome by connecting the triode in the earthed-grid configuration (Fig. 7.5). The earthed grid now acts

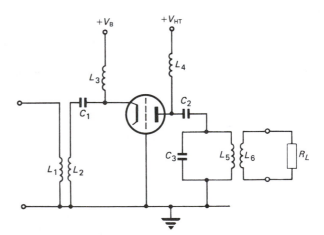

Fig. 7.5 Earthed-grid Class C tuned power amplifier

as a screen between the cathode and anode electrodes which reduces the cathode–anode capacitance to a very small value. Now unwanted feedback from the output (anode) to the input (cathode) circuit is at very low level and generally neutralization circuitry is not needed.

Grid bias

The valve must be biased to operate under Class C conditions and the required bias voltage can be obtained from a separate power

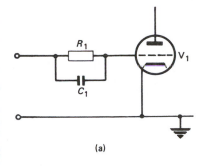

(a)

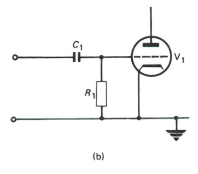

(b)

Fig. 7.6 Leaky-grid bias

Class B tuned power amplifier

supply, as shown in the circuits of Fig. 7.2(a) and (b). An alternative arrangement which can be used instead of, or as well as, a grid power supply is the leaky-grid bias circuit. The action of a leaky-grid bias circuit, two versions of which are shown in Fig. 7.6, is, very briefly, that the required bias voltage is developed across capacitor C_1 by the flow of grid current. The use of leaky-grid bias has the disadvantage that if, for some reason, the input signal voltage is removed, the bias voltage will disappear. The valve may then pass a very large anode current and quite possibly suffer damage. To prevent such an occurrence, a small cathode resistor can be fitted or some fixed bias can be provided.

Effect of loading

The anode-tuned circuit must be tuned to the required frequency of operation and it then possesses sufficient selectivity to be able to discriminate against the harmonic content of the anode current. These requirements are satisfied by using an inductor of high Q-factor and a low-loss capacitor. In addition, the tuned circuit must provide a suitable load impedance for the valve and must also transfer the power from the anode circuit to the load. The effective resistance of the tuned circuit is equal to its dynamic resistance in parallel with a coupled resistance. The magnitude of this coupled resistance depends upon both the coupling between the anode circuit and the load and the load impedance itself. By suitable adjustment of this coupling, the optimum load for the valve can be obtained.

The efficiency with which energy is transferred from the anode circuit to the load depends upon the ratio (loaded Q)/(unloaded Q). This means that the unloaded Q-factor should be high but should fall to a low value once the load is connected. The Q-factor cannot be permitted to fall to too low a figure, however, or insufficient discrimination against harmonics will be provided. Typically, the loaded Q-factor is about 12.

The Class C tuned power amplifier has the advantage of a very high anode efficiency but it can only be used when the input signal voltage is of constant amplitude. If an amplitude-modulated signal were applied to the amplifier, considerable distortion would be introduced. The reason for this is illustrated by Fig. 7.7 which shows a 75% modulated wave applied to a Class C biased valve characteristic. The peaks of the modulation envelope produce anode current pulses of varying peak value, but during the troughs of the envelope the grid voltage is unable to drive the valve into conduction. This form of distortion can only be prevented by ensuring that all positive half-cycles of the input signal voltage, no matter how small, cause anode current to flow. This effectively means that the bias voltage should be reduced until it is equal to the valve's cut-off voltage, i.e. the valve must be operated under Class B conditions.

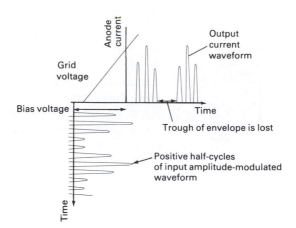

Fig. 7.7 Class C amplifier handling an amplitude-modulated waveform

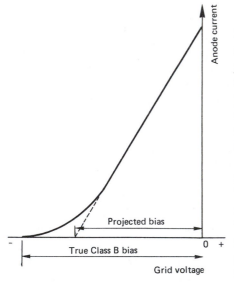

Fig. 7.8 Projected Class B bias

In practice, the mutual characteristics of a valve tend to be non-linear for the lower values of the anode current and it is usual, in order to minimize distortion caused by this non-linearity, to use *projected grid bias*, as shown in Fig. 7.8. The valve is not now operated under true Class B conditions, since a small anode current will flow for zero input signal voltage, but little error is introduced into calculations by assuming that true Class B bias is used. The circuit of a *linear* Class B tuned amplifier is the same as given earlier for Class C circuits but leaky-grid bias cannot be used.

When a sinusoidal voltage is applied to a Class B tuned amplifier, the anode current will flow as a series of half-sinewave pulses (Fig. 7.8) of peak value $I_{a(max)}$. The fundamental frequency component of this current will develop a voltage V_L across the anode tuned circuit. The mean value of this current is $I_{a(max)}/\pi$ and the peak value of its fundamental frequency component is $I_{a(max)}/2$. A number of components at other freuencies are also present in the current waveform but they will have little contribution to make to the output voltage.

Anode efficiency

The d.c. power taken from the power supply is

$$P_{DC} = (I_{a(max)}/\pi)V_{HT}$$

The a.c. power output is

$$(I_{a(max)}/2\sqrt{2})(V_L/\sqrt{2})$$

Therefore

$$P_{ac} = (I_{a(max)}/2\sqrt{2})(V_{HT} - V_{a(min)})/\sqrt{2}$$
$$= (I_{a(max)}/4)(V_{HT} - V_{a(min)}) \tag{7.8}$$

The anode efficiency η of a Class B tuned amplifier is the ratio $(P_{ac}/P_{DC}) \times 100\%$. Therefore

Fig. 7.9 Anode current waveform in a Class B amplifier

$$\eta = (I_{a(max)}/4)(V_{HT} - V_{a(min)}) \times (\pi/I_{a(max)}V_{HT})$$
$$= (\pi/4)(1 - V_{a(min)}/V_{HT}) \times 100\% \tag{7.9}$$

Maximum anode efficiency is obtained when the voltage developed across the anode-tuned circuit has its maximum possible value. This occurs when the valve is driven so that its anode voltage varies between zero and twice the h.t. supply voltage so that $V_L = V_{HT}$. Then $V_{a(min)} = 0$ and

$$\eta_{max} = (\pi/4) \times 100\% = 78.5\% \tag{7.10}$$

Practical efficiencies must fall short of this figure because varying the anode voltage over such a wide range of values would lead to considerable signal distortion. Generally, Class B tuned amplifiers have an anode efficiency in the region of 35−45% when amplifying a sinusoidal signal. The anode efficiency will rise by about 10% when an amplitude-modulated wave is amplified.

Example 7.4

A Class B tuned power amplifier operates with a power supply voltage of 1000 V and a peak anode current of 6 A. If the effective dynamic resistance of the anode tuned circuit is 200 Ω, calculate (a) the output power and (b) the anode efficiency of the amplifier.

Solution

(a) The fundamental frequency component of the anode current has a peak value of $6/2 = 3$ A. Therefore

$$P_{ac} = (3/\sqrt{2})^2 \times 200 = 900 \text{ W} \quad (Ans.)$$

(b) The mean anode current $= 6/\pi$ A and the power taken from the power supply is $6000/\pi$ W. Therefore

$$\eta = 900/(6000/\pi) \times 100\% = 47.1\% \quad (Ans.)$$

The Class B tuned power amplifier is often operated in the earthed-grid configuration, both to avoid neutralization and because of its improved linearity.

Example 7.5

In the amplifier of Example 7.4 the input signal is amplitude-modulated to a depth of 60%. Calculate the anode efficiency of the amplifier.

Solution
From equation (1.9),

$$\text{Total output power} = 900(1 + 0.6^2/2) = 1062 \text{ W}$$

The d.c. power taken from the supply is unchanged and so

$$\eta = 1062/(6000/\pi) \times 100\% = 55.6\% \quad (Ans.)$$

Transistor-tuned power amplifier

The transistor versions of the Class B and Class C tuned power amplifiers are used in low-power radio transmitters, in particular for

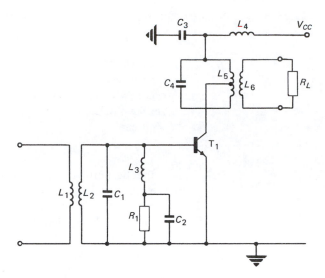

Fig. 7.10 Class C transistor tuned amplifier

those in mobile systems. The circuit of a Class C transistor tuned power amplifier is shown in Fig. 7.10. Leaky-base bias is provided by R_1 and C_2 with L_3 acting to prevent signal-frequency currents passing to earth via C_2. Alternatively, a separate bias supply could be used. The collector tuned circuit C_4L_5 is series fed and coupled by mutual inductance to the load R_L. The anode circuit is tapped to obtain the optimum load impedance for T_1. Inductor L_4 prevents r.f. currents passing into the power supply and C_3 is a decoupling component.

The circuit of a Class B transistor tuned power amplifier is very similar to the circuit of Fig. 7.10 but a separate base bias supply voltage must be provided to give slight forward bias; otherwise the base–emitter junction of the transistor will develop a self-bias that would give Class C operation.

VHF/UHF techniques

At frequencies in the VHF and UHF bands, the design and construction of a tuned power amplifier is more difficult than at lower frequencies. Most VHF and UHF communication transmitters are low-powered and use transistor power amplifiers.

VHF and UHF circuits are normally designed to work between 50 Ω resistances, and so input and output coupling networks are needed to convert 50 Ω into the values between which the transistor itself must work. Because of internal feedback, a transistor may be capable of self-oscillation when connected between particular source and load impedances. A transistor will be stable and not prone to oscillate if it is connected between source and load impedances somewhat lower than the matched impedances required for maximum power gain. Because of the impedance values concerned, the input and output coupling circuits are usually either T or π networks.

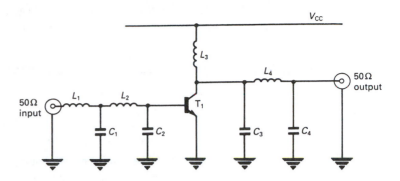

Fig. 7.11 VHF amplifier

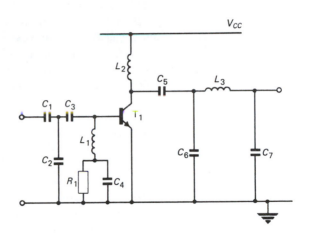

Fig. 7.12 Class C transistor tuned amplifer with π coupling to load

Figure 7.11 shows a VHF amplifier suitable for use in a radio receiver. The input network formed by C_1, C_2, L_1 and L_2 converts the 50 Ω resistance of the source into the optimum source resistance for transistor T_1. Inductor L_3 is an r.f. choke and the output network C_3, C_4, and L_4 transform the 50 Ω load resistance into the optimum collector load for T_1. The networks also act as low-pass filters to remove any unwanted high-frequency components that may be present.

A VHF Class C power amplifier circuit is shown in Fig. 7.12. Capacitors C_1, C_2 and C_3 form the input T matching network and convert, at the design frequency, the 50 Ω source impedance into the source impedance required by the transistor. C_4 and R_1 provide leaky-base Class C bias and inductors L_1 and L_2 are r.f. chokes which prevent the passage of r.f. currents. C_5 is a d.c. blocking component and C_6, C_7 and L_3 provide a π matching network which converts the 50 Ω load impedance into the load impedance required by T_1.

Example 7.6

A Class C transistor tuned power amplifier operates from a 30 V collector supply. If the collector dissipation of the transistor is 1.2 W and the mean collector current is 0.1 A, determine (a) the a.c. output power and (b) the collector efficiency of the amplifier.

Solution

(a) $P_{DC} = 30 \times 0.1 = 3 \text{ W}$

Therefore

$P_{ac} = P_{DC} - \text{collector dissipation} = 3 - 1.2 = 1.8 \text{ W}$ (*Ans.*)

(b) $\eta = (1.8/3) \times 100\% = 60\%$ (*Ans.*)

The transistor used should be a VHF type designed to have minimum internal feedback, adequate current gain, and minimum noise at the operating frequency. The inductance of the lead joining the emitter electrode to the emitter pin can have an appreciable reactance at the higher end of the VHF band and particularly in the UHF band. This reactance will cause negative feedback to be applied to the circuit and also a non-power-dissipating resistance to appear across its base−emitter terminals; both effects reduce its gain. Some transistors are manufactured with a multiple-wire emitter lead to minimize this emitter inductance.

At VHF the reactances of the various stray capacitances in an amplifier circuit are low and can adversely affect the circuit operation. To minimize the magnitudes of the stray capacitances, the layout of the circuit components must be carefully considered and carried out. The components of a circuit must be mounted as close to one another as possible so that all connections are of minimum length. Leads should cross one another at right angles. Some semiconductor manufacturers have modules available in which all components are miniature types and are very closely packed together. Usually, fault-finding on a module is not really practicable and, when faulty, the module should be discarded and replaced by another in working order. Often a printed circuit board is used for much of the circuitry and this reduces the stray capacitance problem. When a lead passes from one side to the other of the chassis, or a metal screening can, a feedthrough capacitor should be used.

The components used in a VHF amplifier must all be chosen with some care. All resistors possess both self-inductance and self-capacitance, all inductors possess resistance and capacitance, and all capacitors have both inductive and resistive components. If a component is used at a frequency higher than it was designed for, it may not provide the electrical characteristics expected. For example, Fig. 7.13 shows the electrical equivalent circuit of an inductor, and C_S represents its self-capacitance. At some particular frequency the inductor will be self-resonant and will act like a high-value resistor; at higher frequencies the component will have an effective capacitance. Clearly, an inductor must be operated at frequencies well below its self-resonant frequency.

The various stages in a circuit should be positioned in as near a straight line as possible and should be individually screened. To avoid

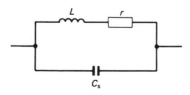

Fig. 7.13 Equivalent circuit of an inductor

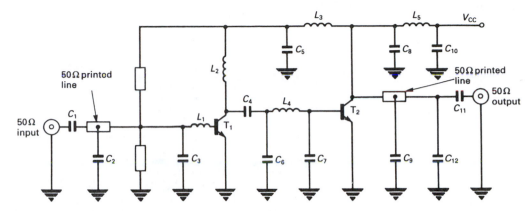

Fig. 7.14 UHF power amplifier

unwanted couplings between different parts of a circuit arising from currents flowing in the chassis and/or the earth line, all earth connections in one stage should be made to a common point. A separate common point should be used for each stage.

The circuit of a UHF power amplifier having a power output in the region of 30 W is shown by Fig. 7.14. A printed line consists of a conductor printed onto a circuit board and separated from a continuous earth plane by a dielectric material. The printed line has a high characteristic impedance and is operated so that it behaves like an inductor. The printed lines are used to match the input impedance of T_1 and the output impedance of T_2 to 50 Ω. Matching between the two stages is provided by the L_4, C_6 and C_7 network. The first stage is operated as a Class B amplifier with a small forward bias to allow small-amplitude signals to be amplified without distortion, and the second stage is operated under Class C conditions.

Frequency multiplier

The anode or collector current of a Class C tuned amplifier flows as a series of less-than-half sinewave pulses and contains components at the input signal frequency and at harmonics of that frequency. If the anode or collector tuned circuit is tuned to be resonant at a particular harmonic of the input signal frequency, the voltage developed across the load will be at that harmonic frequency. The angle of flow should be chosen to be 180°/n, where n is the order of the harmonic required. Thus, if a frequency tripler is to be designed, the angle of flow should be 60°. The higher the order of harmonic selected by the anode (collector) tuned circuit, the smaller will be the angle of flow and thus the smaller will be the output power. In practice, the frequency multiplication obtained is rarely in excess of 5. When a larger multiplying factor is wanted, two or more frequency multipliers are connected in cascade.

Anode-modulated Class C tuned amplifier

The output voltage of a Class C tuned power amplifier is directly proportional to the h.t. supply voltage. If the power supply voltage

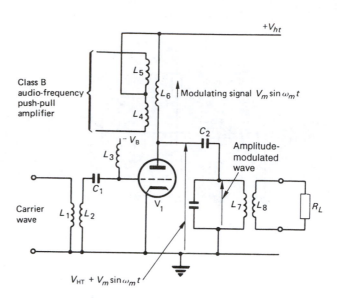

Fig. 7.15 Anode modulation of a Class C amplifier

is increased by, say, 50% the amplitude of the voltage developed across the anode tuned circuit also increases by 50%. This means that if the supply voltage is caused to vary in sympathy with a modulating signal voltage, the a.c. voltage developed across the anode tuned circuit will be amplitude-modulated.

The power supply voltage applied to the anode of a Class C tuned power amplifier can best be varied by introducing the modulating signal into the anode circuit by means of a transformer, as shown in Fig. 7.15. The total voltage applied to the anode of V_1 is the sum of the supply voltage V_{HT} and the modulating signal voltage $V_m \sin \omega_m t$ which appears across inductor L_6. The maximum voltage applied to the anode of V_1 is $V_{HT} + V_m$ and the minimum voltage is $V_{HT} - V_m$. The depth of modulation of the output voltage waveform depends upon the relative voltages of the h.t. supply and the modulating signal. If, for example, $V_m = V_{HT}/2$ the depth of modulation will be 50%.

The modulating signal voltage is produced by an audio-frequency power amplifier. Sometimes this circuit may be operated under Class A conditions but, for high-power applications, it is always a Class B push-pull amplifier. The basic circuit of a Class B modulator and its associated anode-modulated Class C amplifier is shown in Fig. 7.16.

Triodes V_1 and V_2 are connected in push-pull and operated very nearly under Class B conditions; a small forward bias voltage V_{B1} is provided via L_4. L_4, L_{10} and L_{11} are r.f. chokes. The modulating signal is first applied to inductor L_1 and, since L_2 and L_3 are the two halves of a centre-tapped secondary winding, it is then applied in antiphase to the grids of V_1 and V_2. The action of the push-pull circuit produces an amplified version of the modulating signal voltage across L_7. Thus, the effective h.t. voltage applied to the Class C

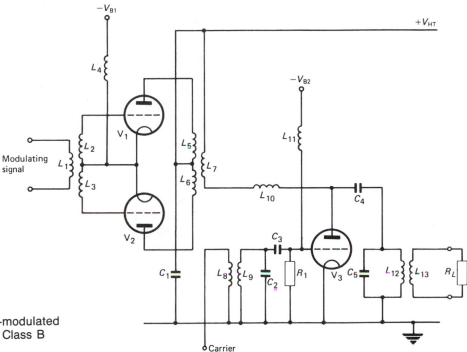

Fig. 7.16 The anode-modulated Class C amplifier with Class B modulator

amplifier is $V_{HT}+V_m \sin \omega_m t$. Leaky-grid bias, augmented by the bias supply V_{B2}, is provided by C_3 and R_1 while C_4 functions merely as a d.c. blocking component.

When there is no modulating signal applied to the circuit, the voltage applied to the anode of V_3 is the supply voltage V_{HT} and the output voltage developed across the load is of constant amplitude. The power output of the amplifier is the unmodulated carrier power. This means that the carrier power is equal to the d.c. power supplied to the Class C amplifier times its anode efficiency.

When a modulating signal is applied, the anode voltage of V_3 is varied in accordance with its characteristics and an amplitude-modulated waveform is produced across the load. The power developed across the load resistance has then been increased by an amount equal to the power contained in the upper and lower sidebands. This extra power must have been supplied by the modulator stage. Hence in an anode-modulated Class C amplifier:

- The carrier power output is equal to the d.c. power supplied to the Class C amplifier times the efficiency of the amplifier.
- The sideband power output is equal to the power provided by the Class B modulator times the efficiency of the Class C stage. The output power of the Class B modulator is equal to the d.c. power supplied to the modulator times the efficiency of the modulator. This means that the sideband power is equal to the

d.c. power input to the Class B stage times the product of the anode efficiencies of the Class B and Class C stages.

Example 7.7

A Class C anode-modulated amplifier uses a Class C stage with an anode efficiency of 75% and a Class B stage whose anode efficiency is 50%. The sinusoidally modulated output waveform has a depth of modulation of 50% and a total power of 1520 watts. Calculate the d.c. power supplied to (a) the Class C stage; (b) the Class B stage.

Solution
From equation (1.9),

$$\text{Total power } P_t = 1520 = P_c \, (1+0.5^2/2)$$
$$P_c = 1520/1.125 = 1351 \text{ W}$$
$$\text{Total sidefrequency power} = 1520 - 1351 = 169 \text{ W}$$

(a) The d.c. power supplied to the Class C stage is

$$P_{\text{DC(C)}} = 1351/0.75 = 1801.3 \text{ W} \qquad (Ans.)$$

(b) Sidefrequency power supplied to the Class C stage is

$$P_{\text{SF}} = 169/0.75 = 225.3 \text{ W}$$

Therefore, d.c. power supplied to the Class B stage is

$$P_{\text{DC(B)}} = 225.3/0.5 = 450.6 \text{ W} \qquad (Ans.)$$

The depth of modulation of the output amplitude-modulated waveform depends upon the amplitude of the modulating signal voltage introduced in series with the h.t. supply voltage of the Class C stage. For 100% modulation, the modulating signal voltage must be equal to the power supply voltage so that the effective supply voltage for the Class C stage varies between 0 and $2V_{\text{HT}}$.

The grid bias voltage must be provided wholly, or at least mainly, by means of a leaky-grid bias circuit. If, using fixed bias, the circuit is adjusted to function correctly as a Class C amplifier when the effective supply voltage is twice the d.c. supply voltage, then during the troughs of the modulation cycle the instantaneous anode voltage will be so small that an excessive grid current flows. If leaky-grid bias is used, the bias voltage will vary throughout the modulation cycle and maintain the correct bias for the instantaneous h.t. voltage.

Collector-modulated Class C tuned amplifier

A DSB amplitude-modulated wave can be generated by collector-modulating a transistor Class C tuned amplifier. The modulating signal is introduced in series with the collector supply voltage to modulate the voltage applied to the amplifier. The basic circuit of a collector-modulated Class C amplifier is given by Fig. 7.17. Transistors T_1 and T_2 form a push-pull amplifier which operates very nearly under Class B conditions, a small forward bias being given by the potential divider $R_1 + R_2$. The modulating signal voltage is developed across L_6 and so appears in series with the collector supply voltage V_{CC}.

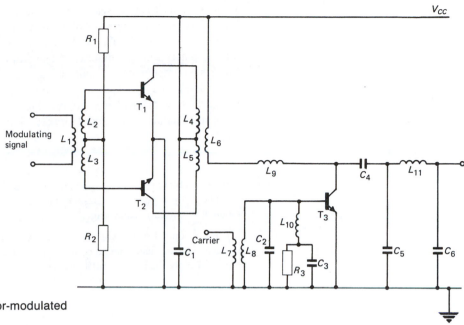

Fig. 7.17 The collector-modulated Class C amplifier

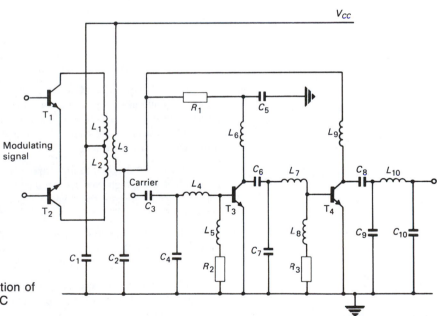

Fig. 7.18 Collector modulation of final and penultimate Class C transistor stages

Transistor T_3 operates in Class C with leaky-base bias provided by $R_3 - C_3$ and uses a π-type network to couple the output voltage to the load.

If a high depth of modulation is required, one stage of modulation is likely to prove insufficient. Then the penultimate Class C amplifier must also be modulated and Fig. 7.18 shows a possible circuit. The collector supply voltage to both the penultimate T_3 and the final T_4

Class C amplifiers passes through the inductor L_3. Both Class C amplifiers are therefore collector-modulated by the push-pull modulator T_1/T_2. The Class C stages are shown with T and π input and output coupling networks. Capacitors C_3, C_6 and C_8 are d.c. blocking components, C_1 and C_5 are decoupling capacitors, and inductors L_6 and L_9 act as the collector load impedances. Finally, the necessary base bias voltages are provided by resistors R_2 and R_3, the associated inductors L_5 and L_8 preventing r.f. currents passing to earth.

Exercises

7.1 A point-to-point high-power communication receiver has its r.f. output stage modulated by a push-pull Class B modulator. Sketch the circuit of the modulator and r.f. output stage.

7.2 The power output of an AM anode-modulated transmitter is 1245 W. The efficiency of the final stage is 60%. If the modulation depth is 0.7 and the efficiency of the modulator is 50%, calculate (a) the modulation power supplied to the anode of the final stage; (b) the anode dissipation of the modulator stage. Ignore losses in the modulation transformer.

7.3 A push-pull Class B modulator is used to modulate sinusoidally a push-pull Class C r.f. amplifier. The maximum anode dissipation of the r.f. amplifier is 250 W and its anode efficiency is 75%. The Class B modulator has an anode efficiency of 60% and a maximum anode dissipation of 200 W. (a) Calculate the maximum carrier power output from the Class C amplifier. (b) What is the maximum modulation power that the modulator can supply to the r.f. amplifier? (c) What is the maximum depth of modulation?

7.4 Explain briefly how a Class C amplifier may be used as a frequency multiplier. Illustrate your answer by waveforms of collector voltage, collector current, base voltage and base current. Indicate how the harmonic number of a multiplier influences the choice of (a) angle of collector current flow and (b) collector load impedance.

7.5 Draw the circuit diagram of the output stage of a high-frequency telephony transmitter using high-power modulation, and explain the operation of the circuit. Briefly discuss the relative merits of high-power and low-power modulation.

7.6 Draw the circuit diagram of a Class C tuned power amplifier which uses a p-n-p transistor as the active device and is designed to operate between source and load impedances of 50 Ω. Explain the operation of the circuit.

7.7 (a) Make a list of the components of the collector-modulated Class C amplifiers of Fig. 7.17 and for each one state its function. (b) Describe the operation of the circuits.

7.8 Fig. 7.19 shows the block diagram of an anode-modulated Class C tuned amplifier. The efficiencies of the Class B and Class C stages are, respectively, 48% and 66%, and the output waveform has a depth of modulation of 60%. If the total output power is 11 kW, calculate the d.c. power inputs to the two stages.

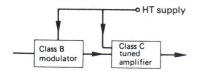

Fig. 7.19

8 Radio transmitters

The purpose of any radio communication system is to transmit intelligence from one point to another; the communication may be unidirectional, as in the case of sound and television broadcasting, or it may be bi-directional, as with most radio-telephony systems. At the transmitting end of the system the signal must modulate a suitable carrier frequency to translate the signal to the allocated part of the frequency spectrum, and then be amplified to the necessary transmitted power level.

In the VHF and UHF bands both amplitude- and frequency-modulation transmitters are used, but in the lower frequency bands only amplitude modulation finds application. Sound broadcast transmitters use DSB amplitude modulation but radio-telephony systems use either single- or independent-sideband operation. To maintain a reliable service, HF communication transmitters must be able to alter frequency rapidly as ionospheric propagation conditions change. Modern HF transmitters are designed to be self-tuning to facilitate the frequency-changing process.

Frequency synthesis

The frequency at which a radio transmitter operates must be maintained constant to within internationally agreed limits to avoid interference with adjacent (in frequency) channels. In the case of SSB and ISB systems, the suppressed carrier must be re-inserted at the receiver with the correct frequency. This requirement will clearly be made harder if the carrier frequency at the transmitter is not constant. The oscillator from which the transmitter carrier frequency is derived must be of stable frequency, both short- and long-term. If the operating frequency of a transmitter is frequently changed, a variable-frequency oscillator of some kind must be fitted, but it will then be difficult to achieve the desired frequency stability.

A frequency synthesizer is an equipment which derives a large number of discrete frequencies, singly or simultaneously, from an accurate high-stability crystal oscillator source. Each of the derived frequencies has the accuracy and stability of the source. A synthesizer

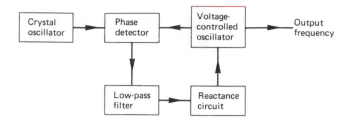

Fig. 8.1 Indirect frequency synthesis

may cover a wide frequency band; for example, any frequency at 100 Hz increments between 4 MHz and 10 MHz.

The principle of an indirect frequency synthesizer is illustrated by Fig. 8.1. The required output frequency is derived from a voltage-controlled oscillator (VCO) whose accuracy is maintained by phase-locking the oscillator to a high-stability crystal oscillator. The phase detector is a circuit which, when voltages at the same frequency are applied to its two input terminals, produces a d.c. output voltage whose magnitude and polarity are proportional to the phase difference between the two input voltages. The d.c. output voltage is applied to the VCO to vary its frequency. The change in the frequency of the VCO is in the direction necessary to reduce the error voltage at the phase detector's output.

Any tendency for the VCO to change frequency is opposed by the phase-locked loop. As the VCO frequency starts to vary, an error voltage is generated by the phase detector which changes the VCO frequency in the direction necessary to correct the frequency drift. The error voltage must be free from alternating components produced by noise or distortion, otherwise the output frequency will not be stable. This is the reason for the inclusion of the low-pass filter in the phase-locked loop.

There are various methods by which the output of the VCO can be used to derive all the wanted frequencies. One method is shown by Fig. 8.2. The output of a crystal oscillator is fed into a frequency-multiplication circuit which can produce an output frequency at any integral number of megahertz between 4 and 10. The selected

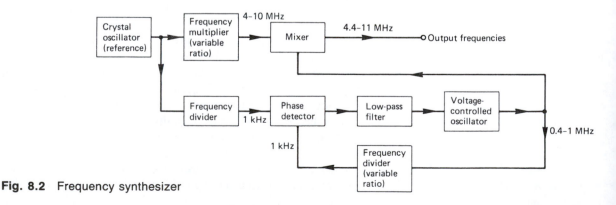

Fig. 8.2 Frequency synthesizer

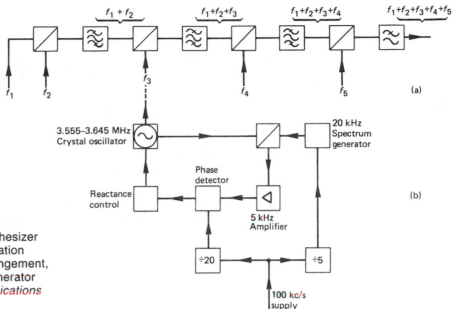

Fig. 8.3 Frequency synthesizer used in an HF communication transmitter: (a) basic arrangement, (b) 10 kHz component generator (from *British Telecommunications Engineering, BTE*)

frequency is mixed with the output of the VCO and the sum frequency is selected. The outputs of the crystal oscillator and the voltage-controlled oscillator are both divided down to 1000 Hz and applied to the phase detector. The voltage-controlled frequency can be set to any frequency in the range 0.4−1 MHz and is maintained accurately at this frequency by the phase-locked loop. 1 kHz increments of frequency are available at the output of the synthesizer.

Another version of a frequency synthesizer is shown in Fig. 8.3. Any frequency in the band 4−8 MHz is made available by generating five different frequencies f_1, f_2, etc. and combining them by repeated mixing and filtering. Each of the five frequencies is produced by the phase-lock circuit of Fig. 8.3(b) which shows the frequencies used for the f_3 decade (10−100 kHz). The crystal oscillator can operate at any one of ten frequencies in the band 3.555−3.645 MHz by switching different crystals into circuit.

Amplitude modulation transmitters

In an amplitude-modulated radio transmitter, the carrier wave generated by a high-stability crystal oscillator or a frequency synthesizer is amplified, and then, perhaps, frequency-multiplied, before it is applied to the aerial feeder. At some stage in the process the carrier is amplitude-modulated by the information signal. The modulation can be carried out when the carrier is at a low level or after the carrier has been amplified to a high power level, and transmitters are broadly divided into two classes, namely low-level and high-level, for that reason.

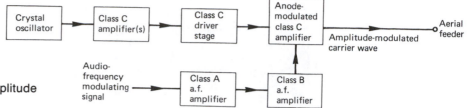

Fig. 8.4 High-level amplitude modulation transmitter

High-level modulation

The block diagram of a high-level transmitter is given by Fig. 8.4. The carrier frequency is generated by the crystal oscillator and is amplified by a number of Class C tuned r.f. amplifiers to the level necessary to fully drive the output stage. One or more of these amplifiers may be operated as frequency multipliers. The modulating signal is amplified by the Class A a.f. amplifier and then applied to the Class B modulator. The output of the modulator is connected in the anode circuit of the final Class C stage. Here it varies the anode voltage and, in so doing, amplitude-modulates the amplified carrier wave. The frequency stability of the transmitter is dependent upon the stability of the crystal oscillator. Since this is generally improved if overtone operation of the crystal can be avoided, it is often the practice to operate the crystal at its fundamental frequency and to use frequency multiplication to obtain the required carrier frequency. Another practice which is sometimes employed is to use a crystal oscillator at a higher frequency than the required carrier and then to use frequency division. An improved frequency stability can then be achieved.

The advantage of the high-level method of operating a radio transmitter is that high-efficiency Class C tuned amplifiers can be used throughout the r.f. section. The disadvantage is that the a.f. modulating signal must be amplified to a high power level if it is to adequately modulate the carrier. This demands the use of a high-power Class B a.f. amplifier and this, mainly because of the need for two large iron-cored output transformers, is expensive. When high-level modulation is used in a low-power transistorized mobile transmitter, this disadvantage is of smaller importance. High-level modulation is used for DSB amplitude-modulated sound broadcast, and VHF/UHF mobile transmitters.

Low-level modulation

The low-level method of operating an amplitude-modulation transmitter is shown in Fig. 8.5. The carrier voltage receives little, if any, amplification before it is modulated by the audio signal. The

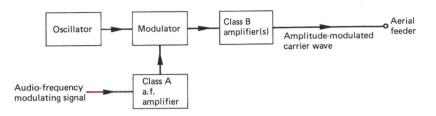

Fig. 8.5 Low-level amplitude modulation transmitter

amplitude-modulated wave is then amplified by one or more linear Class B r.f. power amplifiers to the wanted output power level.

In general, Class C tuned amplifiers cannot amplify amplitude-modulated waveforms without generating excessive distortion. Some modern low-level transmitters use Class C amplifiers with envelope negative feedback to reduce the distortion.

The low-level transmitter does not require a large a.f. modulating power, which simplifies the design of the a.f. amplifier. On the other hand, compared with high-level operation its overall efficiency is much lower because Class B amplifiers are used in place of Class C circuits.

The majority of DSB amplitude-modulation transmitters use the high-level method of modulation mainly because of the greater efficiency offered. Low-level operation is most suited to fixed-frequency applications and high-level operation is most suited to applications where frequent changes in frequency are necessary.

Doherty system

Increased efficiency (about 55%) and linear amplification can be obtained by use of the Doherty arrangement shown in Fig. 8.6. Two valves are employed, one to carry r.f. signals whose amplitude is anything up to the amplitude of the unmodulated carrier, and the other to carry the peaks of the modulation cycle. The grids of both the carrier valve and the peaking valve are fed with the modulated signal. The

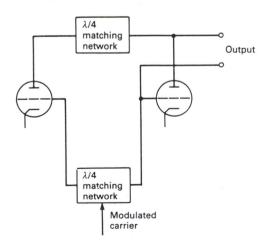

Fig. 8.6 Doherty system

peaking valve only conducts during the positive half-cycle of the modulation envelope and is cut off when the modulation voltage is at the unmodulated carrier value or less. The use of an expensive modulation transformer is avoided.

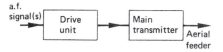

Fig. 8.7 Low-level SSB/ISB transmitter

Independent-sideband transmitters

The low-level method of operation is widely used for SSB and ISB transmitters, the modulation process being carried out in a separate *drive unit* (Fig. 8.7). The audio-frequency signal is applied to the drive unit and is there converted into an SSB or ISB waveform which is then passed on to the main transmitter. In the main transmitter the SSB/ISB signal is amplified to the required power level and translated to the appropriate part of the frequency spectrum. The HF communication ISB transmitters used in the UK for international radio links employ a standard drive unit, and all variations in the transmitted frequency and/or power are provided by the main transmitter.

The block diagram of the standard drive unit is given in Fig. 8.8. The audio input signal to a channel is applied to a balanced modulator together with a 100 kHz carrier signal. The wanted sideband, upper for channel A and lower for channel B, is selected by the channel filter. The outputs of the two filters are combined in the hybrid coil and then passed through a 100 kHz stop filter. This filter is provided to remove any carrier leak that may be present at the outputs. If required at the receiver, a low-level *pilot carrier* is then re-inserted into the composite signal, the function of this pilot carrier being to operate the automatic gain control and automatic frequency control circuitry in the receiver. The 94–106 kHz ISB signal is then translated to the band 3.094 – 3.106 MHz by modulation of the 3 MHz carrier. The output of the drive unit is passed to the main radio transmitter to be amplified to the required power level before it is fed to an aerial for radiation at the required frequency. Each 6 kHz sideband can carry two speech channels.

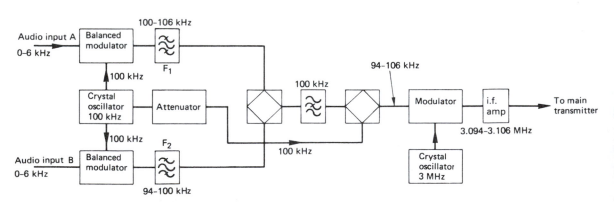

Fig. 8.8 Drive unit of an ISB transmitter

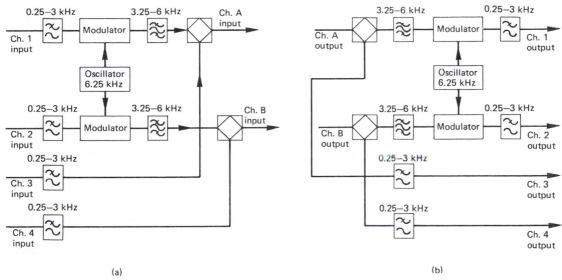

(a)

(b)

Fig. 8.9 Method of deriving four a.f. channels for transmission over an ISB system

One method generally employed for obtaining four 3 kHz telephony channels for application to the channel A and B input terminals of the ISB drive unit is shown in Fig. 8.9. Fig. 8.9(a) shows the transmitting-end equipment, while Fig. 8.9(b) shows the equipment required at the receiving end. The equipment is not usually located at the site of the radio transmitter but is installed at the radio telephony terminal, and each pair of channels, in the band 250−6000 Hz, is sent to the transmitter over a four-wire line circuit.

Single-sideband transmitters

The block diagram of an SSB transmitter is given in Fig. 8.10. The signal produced by the microphone is applied to a balanced modulator and either the upper or the lower sideband is selected by the appropriate band-pass filter. The filtered signal is amplified before it is applied to a balanced mixer, together with the local oscillator voltage, to shift the frequency of the signal to the allocated frequency band. The up-converted signal is amplified and then passed on to the

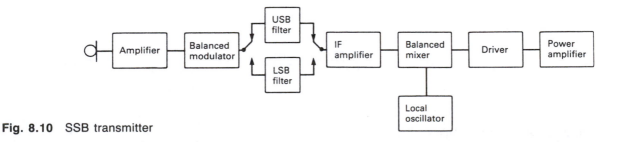

Fig. 8.10 SSB transmitter

final high-power amplifier to obtain the wanted transmitted power of 150 W. The transmitter operates in the 2−16 MHz frequency band with an audio bandwidth of 300−2700 Hz.

Self-tuning HF transmitters

Communication transmitters operating in the HF band must be capable of rapid and frequent changes in operating frequency, as ionospheric propagation conditions vary. Tuning to a new frequency is carried out automatically in a self-tuning transmitter. The operator has merely to reset some dials at a control position when the tuning/loading process is carried out automatically in about 20−30 seconds. The simplified block schematic diagram of a self-tuning transmitter is shown in Fig. 8.11.

The ISB output of the ISB drive unit is first amplified and then frequency translated to its allocated carrier frequency in the band 4−27.5 MHz. The translation process is carried out by mixing the ISB signal with the appropriate frequency in the band 7.1−30.6 MHz. The mixing frequencies are derived from a frequency synthesizer. The difference frequency component of the mixer output waveform is selected, and amplified, by several cascaded tuned amplifiers, to the voltage required to drive the earthed-grid Class B output stage to give the rated output power. The tuned amplifiers and the Class B output stage are tuned automatically to the required frequency.

Another version of the self-tuning transmitter, shown in Fig. 8.12, employs a wideband amplifier. It does not require tuning in order to amplify the signal provided by the drive unit to the level necessary to operate the tuned power output amplifier. The wideband amplifier operates over the entire frequency band covered by the transmitter.

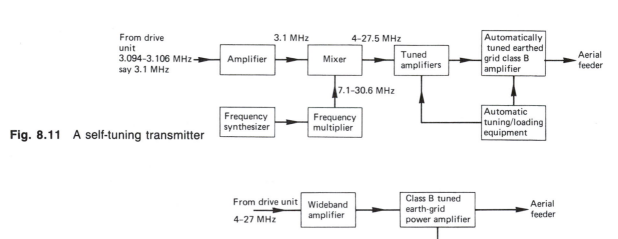

Fig. 8.11 A self-tuning transmitter

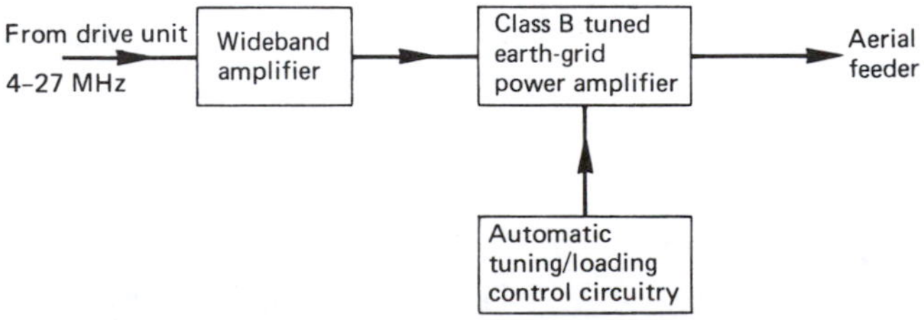

Fig. 8.12 Another self-tuning transmitter

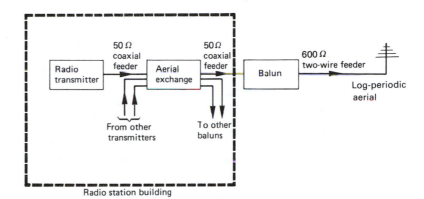

Fig. 8.13 Use of an aerial exchange

The drive unit for this transmitter must be able to produce the ISB or SSB signal at the desired frequency of operation and hence differs from the unit shown in Fig. 8.8 in that its output frequency is not constant. The output frequency of the drive unit, and thus of the transmitter, is determined by a frequency synthesizer. When the transmitted frequency is to be altered, the synthesizer is set to generate the appropriate frequency which, after mixing with the ISB/SSB signal, produces a signal at the new wanted frequency. The tuning and loading of the tuned Class B output stage is automatically adjusted to the correct value in about 20 seconds.

The power output of a self-tuning HF transmitter is several kilowatts, typically 20 kW. A self-tuning transmitter may be called upon to work at any frequency in the band 4−27.5 MHz. Since this is a wider bandwidth than a rhombic or a log-periodic aerial can efficiently work over, some kind of aerial switching is often used and Fig. 8.13 shows a possible arrangement. A number of transmitters are connected to the *aerial exchange*; this is a switching array that makes it possible for any of the transmitters to be switched to any particular aerial.

Medium-frequency sound broadcast transmitters

The block diagram of a 10 kW sound broadcast radio transmitter is shown in Fig. 8.14. The drive voltage obtained from the oscillator has a stability of typically ± 10 Hz and it is amplified to the level necessary to drive the output stage of the transmitter. Solid state circuitry is employed in this part of the transmitter. The output stage uses two tetrodes connected in a Doherty circuit. The modulation is usually carried out in two stages in the manner shown in Fig. 7.18.

Continuous wave transmitters

A sinusoidal carrier wave can be used to transmit telegraphy signals if it is switched on and off in accordance with the chosen telegraph

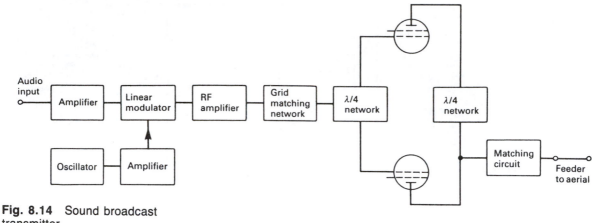

Fig. 8.14 Sound broadcast transmitter

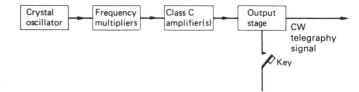

Fig. 8.15 CW telegraphy transmitter

code. Usually the Morse code is chosen. The carrier wave is said to be continuous because, when it is switched on, none of its parameters (i.e. its amplitude, frequency or phase) are varied. The carrier frequency can be switched on and off at a number of different points in a radio transmitter but it is most usual to key the output stage. This practice means that the keying is carried out at a point remote from the oscillator and ensures that the keying process does not alter the carrier frequency.

The block schematic diagram of a CW telegraphy transmitter is shown in Fig. 8.15. A crystal oscillator is used to ensure that the carrier frequency radiated by the transmitter is extremely stable. The oscillator frequency is multiplied to the desired transmission frequency and is then amplified, by one or more Class C tuned amplifiers, to the level required to fully drive the output stage. The output stage increases the carrier power to the desired transmitted power and is keyed on and off. The process of suddenly interrupting a sinusoidal carrier wave generates a large number of harmonics and these are liable to cause interference with neighbouring carrier frequencies. To reduce the bandwidth occupied by a CW signal, it is customary to fit a suitable filter circuit to the keying arrangement.

Output stages

The output stage of an HF transmitter must be designed to satisfy a number of requirements which are listed below:

● It must transfer the wanted output power to the aerial feeder with the utmost efficiency.

- It must have sufficient selectivity to discriminate against the unwanted harmonic components of the anode current, but not against the sidefrequencies of the signal.
- It should operate in a stable and linear manner.
- Tuning the stage to the required operating frequency and optimizing its coupling to the aerial feeder should be as easy and rapid a process as possible. This process is carried out automatically.

For a transmitter output stage to deliver the maximum possible power to the feeder connecting it to the aerial, two requirements must be satisfied. Firstly, the anode, or collector, circuit must be resonant at the frequency of operation and, secondly, the input impedance of the feeder must be transformed by the coupling network into the optimum load for the output stage. The anode, or collector, circuit is tuned by the correct adjustment of its inductance and/or capacitance, and the optimum load is obtained by varying the inductive coupling between the anode circuit and the feeder. The optimum load for the output stage is that value which provides the maximum output power possible without exceeding the voltage, current or power ratings of the output device(s). To achieve the maximum output power, it is also necessary for the voltage driving the output stage to be large enough and this may require careful adjustment of the coupling between the driver stage and the output stage.

Sound broadcast transmitters usually employ a Class C biased output stage but communication transmitters, handling ISB/SSB signals, use an output stage that is operated under Class B conditions; Fig. 8.16 shows a typical circuit. The circuit is tuned to the wanted frequency in the band 4–27.5 MHz by the π-type network consisting of C_1, C_2 and L_1. Unwanted second harmonics of the selected frequency are suppressed by the series-tuned circuit C_3L_3 which provides a low-resistance path to earth at its resonant frequency. Optimum coupling to the 50 Ω coaxial feeder is obtained by suitable adjustment of the value of inductor L_2. All the variable components are motor-driven and automatically adjusted when the operating frequency of the transmitter is to be altered.

Two other methods of coupling an output stage to a feeder are shown in Figs 8.17 and 8.18. Fig. 8.17 shows how a Class B push-pull output

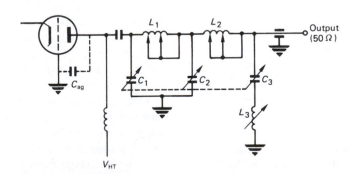

Fig. 8.16 Earthed-grid Class B output stage (from *BTE*)

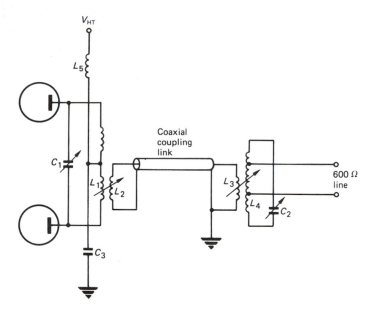

Fig. 8.17 Method of coupling a push-pull output stage to a balanced feeder (from *BTE*)

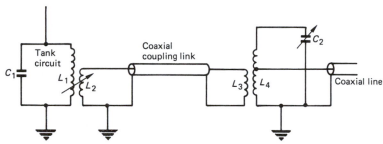

Fig. 8.18 Method of coupling a tank circuit to an unbalanced feeder (from *BTE*)

stage would be coupled to a 600 Ω twin feeder. The 600 Ω impedance of the feeder is changed to the required load impedance by the settings of the tapping points on inductor L_4. The coupling between the output stage and the feeder is optimized by adjustment of the mutual inductance coupling between L_1 and L_2 and between L_3 and L_4. The coupling arrangement is tuned to the required frequency by means of capacitors C_1 and C_2. L_5 and C_3 are power supply decoupling components.

Fig. 8.18 shows how an anode tuned circuit could be connected to an unbalanced coaxial feeder. The components of the coupling network have similar functions to those shown in Fig. 8.17. Coupling an output tuned circuit to a balanced twin feeder can be achieved in a simpler manner, as shown by Fig. 8.19. The secondary winding of the output transformer is centre-tapped to ensure that both conductors are at the same potential relative to earth.

Often a voltage standing-wave ratio meter or monitor is fitted between the output stage and the feeder. This circuit continuously monitors the VSWR presented to the transmitter, and if the VSWR exceeds some critical value, it disconnects the feeder and removes the supply voltage from the output stage.

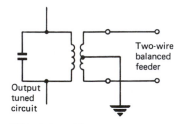

Fig. 8.19 Method of coupling a tank circuit to a balanced feeder

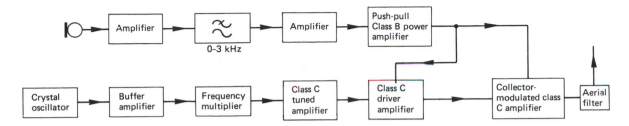

Fig. 8.20 Amplitude-modulation VHF transmitter

Mobile VHF AM transmitters

The output power of most VHF AM transmitters is only a few tens of watts and so completely solid state equipments can be designed. The block schematic diagram of a VHF amplitude-modulated transmitter is shown in Fig. 8.20. The voltage generated by the microphone is amplified and then band-limited by the 3 kHz cut-off low-pass filter. The band-limited signal is amplified to the power level necessary for it to collector-modulate the driver and output stages of the transmitter. A transmitter of this type often has the facility for switching different crystal oscillators into circuit to permit operation at different frequencies. The carrier frequency can be generated directly at frequencies up to about 150 MHz or so using the crystal in an overtone mode.

However, overtone crystal operation tends to be more expensive and of poorer frequency stability than operation by a lower-frequency crystal oscillator followed by one or more frequency multipliers. Mobile VHF channels are positioned very close to one another in the frequency spectrum and it is important that a transmitter radiates little, if any, power at other frequencies. To ensure the adequate suppression of spurious frequencies, an aerial filter is connected between the output stage of the transmitter and the aerial.

Frequency modulation transmitters

Frequency modulation is used for sound broadcasting in the VHF band, for VHF and UHF mobile systems, and for wideband UHF and SHF radio-relay systems. Radio-relay transmitters are discussed in Chapter 12.

Mobile transmitters

Many mobile transmitters use the indirect method of frequency-modulating a carrier because of the improved frequency stability then provided. The block diagram of a typical narrowband FM communication transmitter is given by Fig. 8.21. The microphone output voltage is amplified, integrated (a.f. correction), amplitude-limited and finally band-limited before being used to frequency-modulate the carrier voltage generated by the crystal oscillator. The frequency

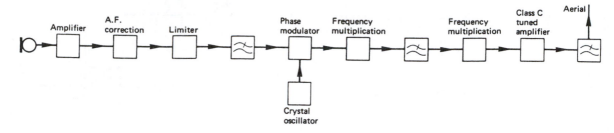

Fig. 8.21 Frequency-modulation VHF transmitter

deviation of the modulated wave is very small, often less than 100 Hz, and must be increased by several stages of frequency multiplication before the final Class C output power amplifier stage.

If a carrier at frequency f_c is frequency modulated with a frequency deviation of kf_d and is then passed into a frequency doubler, the output voltage of the doubler will be at a frequency of $2(f_c \pm f_d)$ or $2f_c + 2kf_d$. This means that the deviation ratio of the wave has been doubled. Thus the use of frequency multiplication will increase both the carrier frequency and the deviation ratio by the same ratio.

Use of mixing

The process of mixing produces the sum and the difference of the frequencies of two signals. Suppose a frequency-modulated wave is mixed with a frequency f_0; the output of the mixer then contains components at frequencies of $f_0 \pm (f_c \pm kf_d)$ and either the sum or the difference frequency can be selected. It can be seen that the selected output frequency is either

$$(f_0 + f_c) \pm kf_d \quad \text{or} \quad (f_0 - f_c) \pm kf_d$$

but the frequency deviation kf_d and hence the deviation ratio are unchanged. To obtain a particular value of carrier frequency together with a particular deviation ratio, it may well be necessary to use a suitable combination of both frequency changing and frequency mixing as shown by Fig. 8.22.

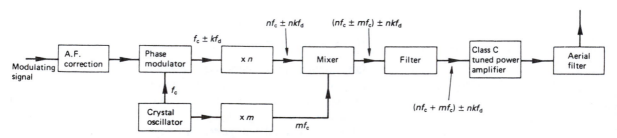

Fig. 8.22 Method of obtaining particular values of carrier frequency and deviation ratio

Some VHF and UHF transmitters are capable of operating using either amplitude modulation (DSB and SSB) or frequency modulation (including FSK).

VHF/UHF mobile transceivers

Mobile transceivers mounted under the dashboards of cars and other vehicles operate at different frequencies in both the VHF and UHF frequency bands. A modern transceiver uses a microcomputer to control the frequency synthesizer and to perform audio signalling. The signalling may be either tone-sequential signalling or CTCSS (p. 253). Frequency modulation is generally employed with an output power in the range 1–25 W. The block diagram of a VHF/UHF mobile FM transmitter is shown by Fig. 8.23. The signal generated by a microphone is filtered and amplified before it is first pre-emphasized and then amplitude-limited. The processed audio signal is then applied to a summing amplifier where signalling information is added. The composite signal is filtered and amplified, and is then applied to a voltage-controlled oscillator (VCO) to vary its frequency. The output of the VCO is the wanted FM signal, and this is amplified to the wanted output power level before it is fed to the aerial for transmission.

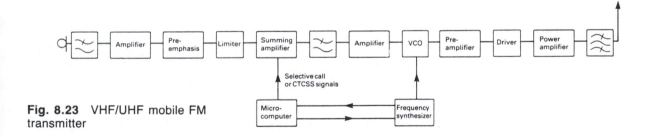

Fig. 8.23 VHF/UHF mobile FM transmitter

Sound broadcast transmitters

The block schematic diagram of an FM sound broadcast transmitter is shown in Fig. 8.24.

The centre frequency of the FM modulator output signal is 5.1 MHz and this is frequency-multiplied in three steps to 91.8 MHz. At each step of frequency, multiplication increases the frequency and phase deviations of the carrier as well as the centre frequency, but the frequency of the modulating signal is not altered. This means that the modulation index m_f is also multiplied. When an FM wave is mixed with an oscillator voltage, it can be either up-converted or down-converted without any change in the frequency or phase deviations, so that m_f is not altered. The requirement of the FM sound broadcast system is for a maximum frequency deviation of

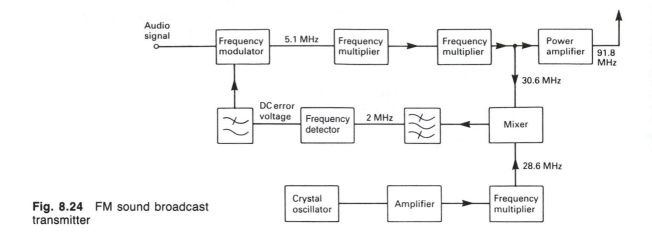

Fig. 8.24 FM sound broadcast transmitter

75 kHz. Hence the frequency deviation at the modulator's output should be 75 kHz/18 = 4166.7 Hz which gives m_f = 4166.7/15 000 = 0.2778. Therefore the modulation index at the aerial is 18 × 0.2778 = 5.

Frequency stability is obtained by the application of *automatic frequency control* (AFC) to the transmitter (page 208).

The sound signal is applied to the drive unit which generates a stereo baseband signal.

Example 8.1

The output of a frequency modulator is at a centre frequency of 5 MHz with a frequency deviation of 3948 Hz. The radiated signal is to be at 95 MHz with 75 kHz rated system deviation. Calculate (a) the necessary frequency multiplication; (b) the output deviation ratio ($f_{m(\text{max})}$ = 15 kHz).

Solution
    (a) Frequency multiplication = 95/5 = 19   (*Ans.*)
    (b) D = 75/15 = 5   (*Ans.*)
        or
        D at modulator output = 3.948/15 = 0.2632
        D = 19 × 0.2632 = 5   (*Ans.*)

High-voltage components and precautions

The thermionic valves and other components used in a high-power stage of a radio transmitter must be able to withstand voltages of several thousands of volts and so special high-voltage types must be used. The maximum permissible voltage which can be safely applied across a resistor is limited because of the danger of a dielectric breakdown. Any such breakdown appears in the form of sparking. Another factor which must be considered is the power rating of a resistor. If this is exceeded, excessive heat will be dissipated within the component and its resistance will change, possibly by a significant amount. Ceramic carbon resistors are probably the best type to use, since they have voltage ratings of 20 kV or more. Similarly, the voltage rating of a capacitor is determined by the need to ensure that the dielectric between the plates does not break down.

The design of a high-voltage inductor is constrained by the need to avoid the insulation (very likely air) between adjacent turns breaking down because of the electric field across it. This means that the turns must be spaced well apart from one another and should probably be self-supporting. Also, the inductor in a series-feed circuit will have a current of several amperes flowing in it and so it must be manufactured using a conductor of large cross-sectional area. Often the power dissipated within a high-voltage inductor is so large that the component must be cooled by blowing cool air around it. In all cases high-voltage components must not be allowed to become too hot and the equipment design must ensure adequate ventilation.

The valve in the output stage, and perhaps the penultimate stage also, of a high-power transmitter may be called upon to dissipate several kilowatts of power at its anode and, in the case of a tetrode, at its screen grid also. The anode will become extremely hot because of the power dissipated at it and this heat must be removed to keep the temperature of the anode within acceptable limits. When the anode dissipation is not very large (say, less than 1.5 kW), sufficient heat can be removed by fabricating the copper anode as an integral part of the valve's envelope and relying on direct radiation. When the anode dissipation is larger than 1.5 kW, the rate of removal of heat must be speeded up by passing cooling air, or water, around the anode. In modern transmitters, cooling of the anode is achieved using a vaporization technique. The basic idea of a water vapour cooling system is that cooling water is converted into steam by the heat of the anode; this steam is removed and condensed back into water, and then the water is re-circulated past the anode.

Because of the very high voltages present at various points in a high-power transmitter, various precautions must be taken to ensure the safety of the persons required to carry out tests or repairs on the equipment. All high-voltage points in a transmitter are mounted inside interlocking cabinets or cages. Entry within a cage can only be made by following a procedure which ensures that the panel giving access to the interior of the equipment can be opened only *after* the high voltage has been removed. This is generally arranged by feeding in the power supplies via an isolating unit that is interlocked with an earthing switch. The keys necessary to unlock the panel can be obtained only after the isolating unit has been operated to disconnect the power supply and earth the equipment. Usually, different parts of the transmitter are housed inside different cabinets; for example, one cabinet might contain the power supply circuitry and another the r.f. power output stage. When work on the equipment is completed, it is necessary to follow the reverse procedure, i.e. all entry panels must be replaced and locked and the keys restored *before* the power supplies can be switched on again.

Exercises

8.1 Describe, with the aid of a block diagram, the drive and r.f. stages of a high-power independent-sideband HF transmitter. How is crosstalk between sidebands minimized?

8.2 (a) Briefly discuss the considerations which enter into the design of the output stage of an HF transmitter. (b) Give two reasons why each aerial at an HF transmitting station is not permanently associated with a transmitter.

8.3 Fig. 8.25 is the block diagram of an FM transmitter. (a) State the purpose of the limiter in the microphone amplifier. (b) What is the purpose of the audio-frequency corrector? (c) How is the stability of the frequency generator maintained for different channels? (d) Explain briefly the function of the modulator. (e) If the frequency generator has a 8.7 MHz output what is the frequency band required for speech signals?

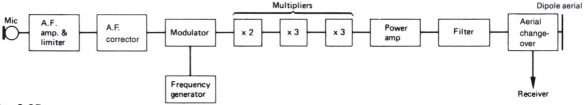

Fig. 8.25

8.4 (a) Draw the block diagram of a medium-frequency broadcast transmitter. (b) What is the class of operation of each stage? (c) How is frequency control obtained? (d) For such a transmitter, what is the typical (i) frequency range, (ii) frequency stability, (iii) power delivered to the aerial?

8.5 (a) What do you understand by the terms (i) high-level modulation, (ii) low-level modulation? Illustrate your answers with block diagrams of amplitude-modulation transmitters. (b) What class of operation is usual for the final stage amplifiers for each of these types of transmitter?

8.6 Describe briefly how rapid frequency changing in an HF transmitter is obtained. Why is regular frequency changing necessary, and about how long does it take in a modern transmitter? Using a sketch, explain how, in a modern system, a transmitter of this type is switched from one aerial to another.

8.7 List the advantages and disadvantages of the following as the drive unit for a transmitter: (a) variable-frequency oscillator; (b) crystal-controlled oscillator; (c) frequency synthesizer.

8.8 A 5 MHz carrier is frequency-modulated by a 2 kHz audio signal. The carrier frequency is converted to 90 MHz by (a) frequency multiplication, (b) mixing with output of an 85 MHz oscillator. Assuming the deviation produced by the varactor diode to be 3 kHz, deduce the final deviation in each case.

8.9 (a) What is meant by the term *frequency synthesis*? Use a block diagram to illustrate how frequency synthesis is used in a modern radio telephony transmitter. (b) In a frequency synthesizer a $2(n-2)$ divider chain output is equal to a 500 kHz reference frequency. If the input to the dividers is the difference between ten times the reference frequency and the synthesized frequency, what value of n should be selected to derive a 158 kHz output?

8.10   (a) Why is frequency stability necessary in a radio transmitter? How is it obtained in (i) an HF communications transmitter, (ii) a VHF FM communications transmitter? (b) Refer to the block diagram of a VHF AM transmitter given in Fig. 8.20 and answer the following questions. (i) Why is the modulating signal band-limited? (ii) Why are two stages of r.f. power gain collector-modulated? (iii) How is the transmitted frequency changed? (iv) Why is an aerial filter fitted?

9 Radio receivers

The functions of a radio receiver are: to select the wanted signal from all the signals picked up by the aerial, whilst rejecting all others; to extract the information contained in the modulated signal; and to produce an audio-frequency output of sufficient power to operate the loudspeaker or other receiving device.

Figure 9.1 shows the block diagram of a simple radio receiver, known as a *tuned radio frequency* (TRF) receiver. The wanted signal frequency is selected by the tuned circuits in the r.f. amplifier, amplified and applied to the detector stage. If sufficient r.f. gain is provided, a diode detector can be employed; if not, some form of non-linear detection will be required. The detected output is amplified by the a.f. amplifier to the level necessary to operate the loudspeaker.

It is also necessary for the receiver to be able to reject various other unwanted signals that may appear at the aerial. It is not possible for a TRF receiver to achieve the high selectivity required by a modern receiver and therefore radio receivers are almost always of the *superheterodyne* type.

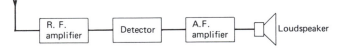

Fig. 9.1 The TRF radio receiver

The superheterodyne radio receiver

In a superheterodyne radio receiver the wanted signal frequency is converted into a constant frequency — known as the *intermediate frequency* — at which most of the gain and the selectivity of the receiver is provided.

The basic block diagram of a superheterodyne radio receiver is shown in Fig. 9.2. The wanted signal, at frequency f_s, is passed, together with many other unwanted frequencies, by the radio-frequency stage to the mixer. The main function of the r.f. stage is not to select the wanted signal but to prevent certain particularly

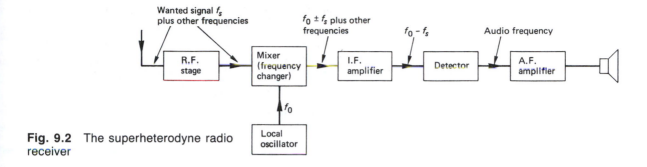

Fig. 9.2 The superheterodyne radio receiver

troublesome frequencies reaching the mixer stage. In the mixer stage the input frequencies are combined with the output of the local oscillator, at a frequency f_o, to generate components at a large number of new frequencies. Among the newly generated frequencies are components at the sum and the difference of the wanted signal frequency and the local oscillator frequency, i.e. at $f_\mathrm{o} \pm f_\mathrm{s}$.

The difference frequency $f_\mathrm{o} - f_\mathrm{s}$ is known as the *intermediate frequency* and it is selected by the intermediate frequency (i.f.) amplifier. The intermediate frequency is a fixed frequency and this means that, when a receiver is tuned to receive a signal at a particular frequency, the local oscillator frequency is adjusted so that the correct difference frequency is obtained. The amplified output of the i.f. amplifier is applied to the detector stage and it is here that the information contained in the modulated signal is recovered. The detected signal is amplified to the required power level by the audio-frequency amplifier before it is applied to the loudspeaker, telephone or other output device.

A number of differences exist between receivers designed for the reception of amplitude- and frequency-modulated transmissions and ISB/SSB radio-telephony signals. The main differences are as follows:

- The r.f. stage in an AM broadcast receiver may not include amplification whereas the other types of receiver always provide r.f. gain.
- The bandwidths of the r.f. and the i.f. stages are considerably different; often HF communication receivers have a variable bandwidth facility since they may be designed to cater for a number of different kinds of signal.
- Mainly because of the different bandwidths required, different intermediate frequencies are used.
- Different types of detector circuit are used.

Choice of local oscillator frequency

The intermediate frequency of a superheterodyne radio receiver is equal to the difference between the wanted signal frequency and the local oscillator frequency. Two possibilities exist: the local oscillator frequency may be higher than the signal frequency, or it may be lower.

A sound broadcast receiver with an intermediate frequency of 470 kHz is tunable over the band from 525 kHz to 1605 kHz. If the frequency of the local oscillator is higher than the wanted signal frequency the oscillator must be tunable from

$$(525 + 470) = 995 \text{ kHz}$$

to

$$(1605 + 470) = 2075 \text{ kHz},$$

a frequency ratio of 2075/995, or 2.085:1. Such a frequency ratio would require the use of a variable capacitor having a ratio (maximum capacitance)/(minimum capacitance) of $(2.085)^2$, or 4.35:1. Such a capacitance ratio is easily obtained.

The alternative is to make the signal frequency higher than the local oscillator frequency. The oscillator frequency must then be variable from

$$(525 - 470) = 55 \text{ kHz}$$

to

$$(1605 - 470) = 1135 \text{ kHz}$$

This is a frequency ratio of 1135/55, or 20.64:1 and requires a capacitance ratio of $(20.64)^2$, or 425.9:1. Such a large capacitance ratio could not be obtained with a single variable capacitor and so tuning would not be as easy or cheap to achieve.

It is therefore usual to make the local oscillator frequency higher than the wanted signal frequency, i.e.

$$f_o = f_s + f_i \tag{9.1}$$

The frequency of the local oscillator may be chosen so that the intermediate frequency is higher or lower than the signal frequency. Making the intermediate frequency lower than the signal frequency is known as *down-conversion* and it is always used in sound broadcast receivers. Communication receivers, both HF and VHF/UHF, are often *double superheterodyne* circuits and these often employ *up-conversion* for the first intermediate frequency. With up-conversion, the difference frequency component of the mixer's output is again selected but the frequency of the oscillator is made high enough to ensure that the intermediate frequency is above the tuning range of the receiver.

Image channel signal

No matter what frequency a superheterodyne receiver is tuned to, there is always another frequency that will also produce the intermediate frequency. This other frequency is known as the image frequency. The image channel signal has a frequency f_{im} such that the difference between it and the local oscillator frequency is equal to the intermediate frequency, f_{if}, i.e.

$$f_{if} = f_{im} - f_o$$

Substituting for f_o from equation (9.1)

$$f_{if} = f_{im} - (f_s + f_i)$$

or $f_{im} = f_s + 2f_{if}$ (9.2)

The higher the intermediate frequency, the further away from the wanted signal is the image channel.

Example 9.1

A sound broadcast radio receiver has an intermediate frequency of 470 kHz and is tuned to 1065 kHz. Calculate (a) the frequency of the local oscillator; (b) the frequency of the image signal.

Solution

  (a) $f_o = 1065 + 470 = 1535$ kHz   (*Ans.*)
  (b) $f_{im} = 1065 + 940 = 2005$ kHz   (*Ans.*)

Example 9.2

An FM radio receiver has an intermediate frequency of 10.7 MHz and is tuned to 97.3 MHz. Calculate (a) the frequency of the local oscillator; (b) the image channel frequency.

Solution

  (a) $f_o = 97.3 + 10.7 = 108.0$ MHz   (*Ans.*)
  (b) $f_{im} = 97.3 + 21.4 = 118.7$ MHz   (*Ans.*)

Example 9.3

An HF receiver has a first intermediate frequency of 40 MHz and it tunes to the frequency band 3–30 MHz. Calculate the frequency range of (a) the local oscillator; (b) the image channel signal.

Solution

  (a) When $f_s = 3$ MHz, $f_o = 40 + 3 = 43$ MHz.
        When $f_s = 30$ MHz, $f_o = 40 + 30 = 70$ MHz.

        Frequency range = 43 to 70 MHz   (*Ans.*)

  (b) When $f_s = 3$ MHz, $f_{im} = 3 + 80 = 83$ MHz
        When $f_s = 30$ MHz, $f_{im} = 30 + 80 = 110$ MHz

        Frequency range = 83 to 100 MHz   (*Ans.*)

Image channel rejection

The image signal must be prevented from reaching the mixer or it will produce an interference signal which, since it is at the intermediate frequency, cannot be eliminated by the selectivity of the i.f. amplifier.

In a sound broadcast receiver, r.f. tuned circuits are used to provide the selectivity necessary to reject the image channel signal. Tuning is necessary because the wanted signal frequency, and hence the image signal frequency, will vary. It is not difficult to obtain a resonant circuit with good enough selectivity to accept the wanted signal and reject the image signal when their separation is an appreciable fraction of the wanted signal frequency. As the signal frequency is increased, the fractional frequency separation becomes smaller and the image rejection less efficient.

In an HF communication receiver, image channel rejection is usually obtained either from a bank of band-pass filters or from a single low-pass filter. The appropriate band-pass filter is automatically switched into circuit in a receiver that uses frequency synthesis to produce the local oscillator frequency. A low-pass filter is able to provide adequate image rejection when up-conversion is used, since then all the possible image channel signals are above the tuning range of the receiver.

The *image response ratio* is the ratio, in decibels, of the voltages at the wanted signal and image signal frequencies necessary at the receiver input terminals to produce the same audio output. Typically, it is 70–90 dB.

Selectivity

The *selectivity* of a radio receiver is its ability to discriminate between the wanted signal and all the other signals picked up by the aerial, particularly the adjacent-channel signals. In other words, it is the ability of a receiver to tune to a wanted signal while rejecting all other signals.

The selectivity of a receiver is usually specified by its 6 dB and 60 dB bandwidths which are known, respectively, as the nose and the skirt bandwidths. The *nose bandwidth* is the range of frequencies over which a signal can be received with little practical loss of strength. The *skirt bandwidth* is the band of frequencies over which it is possible to receive a strong signal. The ratio of the skirt bandwidth to the nose bandwidth is known as the *shape factor*. An HF SSB receiver may have a nose bandwidth of 3 kHz, a skirt bandwidth of 12 kHz, and a shape factor of 12 kHz/3 kHz or 4.

Example 9.4

An HF communication receiver has a nose bandwidth of 2.7 kHz and a skirt bandwidth of 4.4 kHz. Calculate its shape factor.

Solution

Shape factor = 4.4/2.7 = 1.63   (*Ans.*)

Fig. 9.3 shows typical selectivity curves for AM sound broadcast,

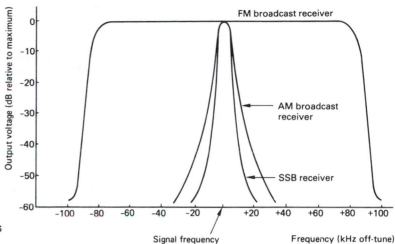

Fig. 9.3 Selectivity characteristics of radio receivers

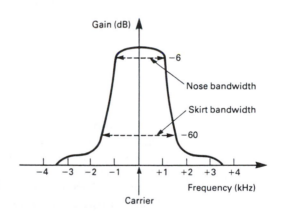

Fig. 9.4 Selectivity of a VHF NBFM receiver

FM sound broadcast, and HF SSB communication receivers. Clearly, there are large differences between the 3 dB bandwidths of the three receivers: the AM sound broadcast receiver has a 3 dB bandwidth of about 9 kHz, the SSB receiver approximately 3 kHz, but the FM broadcast receiver's bandwidth is about 200 kHz.

The adjacent channel selectivity of a radio receiver is mainly determined by the gain-frequency characteristic of the i.f. amplifier.

A typical selectivity curve for a VHF mobile receiver is shown in Fig. 9.4.

The selectivity curves shown in Figs 9.3 and 9.4 relate to a single input frequency and do not entirely predict the performance of a receiver when signals at several different frequencies are simultaneously received. The effective selectivity of a receiver when interfering signals are present is determined by:

(a) the selectivity provided by the r.f. stage;
(b) the ability of the r.f. stage to handle strong signals;
(c) the adjacent-channel selectivity provided by the i.f. stage.

Factors (a) and (b) arise because of the possibility of spurious frequencies at or near the intermediate frequency being produced by intermodulation.

The *adjacent channel ratio* is the ratio, in dB, of the input voltages of the wanted and the adjacent channel frequencies necessary for the adjacent channel to produce an output power 30 dB smaller than the signal power.

Example 9.5

A radio receiver is tuned to a certain frequency at which an input signal of 15 μV produces an output of 50 mW. If the input voltage at the adjacent-channel frequency needed to produce -30 dB output power is 1.5 mV, calculate the adjacent channel ratio.

Solution

$$\text{Adjacent channel ratio} = 20 \log_{10} (1.5 \times 10^{-3})/(15 \times 10^{-6}) = 40 \text{ dB}$$
$$(Ans.)$$

Sensitivity

The *sensitivity* of a radio receiver is the smallest input signal voltage that is required to produce a specified output power with a specified signal-to-noise ratio. For AM receivers, the specified output power is usually 50 mW with a signal-to-noise ratio of 20 dB and with the input signal modulated 30% at 1000 Hz (or 400 Hz). For an FM receiver a signal-to-noise ratio of 12 dB is required with the input signal modulated by a 1000 Hz signal to give a quoted r.m.s. frequency deviation, e.g. 12 dB signal-to-noise ratio with 2.1 kHz (r.m.s.) deviation.

It is necessary to include signal-to-noise ratio in the definition of sensitivity, otherwise the output power could consist mainly of noise and be of little use.

The sensitivity of a radio receiver is determined by

(a) the overall voltage gain of its individual stages;
(b) the gain-frequency characteristic of the r.f. stage;
(c) the noise generated by thermal agitation in its input stages.

This means that the sensitivity is directly related to the *noise figure* of the receiver.

Typical figures for sensitivity are:

- 50 μV for an AM broadcast receiver
- 2 μV for an FM broadcast receiver
- 0.1−0.2μV for an HF communication receiver
- 0.1−10 μV for a VHF mobile receiver

Noise figure

The output of a radio receiver must always contain some noise and the receiver must be designed so that the output signal-to-noise ratio is always at least as good as the minimum figure required for the system. The noise appearing at the receiver's output terminals originates from two sources: noise picked up by the aerial and noise generated within the receiver. Because of the internally generated noise, the signal-to-noise ratio at the output terminals is always less than the input signal-to-noise ratio. The *noise figure* or *noise factor* of a radio receiver is a measure of the degree to which the receiver degrades the input signal-to-noise ratio. The noise figure F is related to the input and output signal-to-noise ratios by equation (9.3):

$$F = \frac{\text{Input signal-to-noise ratio}}{\text{Output signal-to-noise ratio}} \qquad (9.3)$$

An ideal receiver would have no internal noise sources and would not degrade the input signal-to-noise ratio: hence its noise figure would be unity or zero dB. Typical figures for the noise figure are 7 dB for an HF receiver and 5 dB for a VHF/UHF receiver.

Example 9.6

The signal-to-noise ratio at the input to a communication receiver is 40 dB. If the receiver has a noise figure of 12 dB, calculate the output signal-to-noise ratio.

Solution
From equation (9.3),

$$\text{Output signal-to-noise ratio} = \frac{\text{Input signal-to-noise ratio}}{\text{Noise figure}}$$

or in dB

$$\text{Output signal-to-noise ratio} = 40 - 12 = 28 \text{ dB} \qquad (Ans.)$$

Bandwidth improvement

If the bandwidth of a receiver is reduced, the noise power will be reduced in exactly the same proportion. *Bandwidth improvement* is the reduction in noise obtained by reducing the bandwidth of a receiver. The i.f. bandwidth of a receiver is usually narrower than the r.f. bandwidth and the noise improvement then obtained is given by

$$\text{Bandwidth improvement} = \frac{\text{(r.f. bandwidth)}}{\text{(i.f bandwidth)}} \qquad (9.4)$$

Example 9.7

A communication receiver has an r.f. bandwidth of 200 kHz and an i.f.

bandwidth of 20 kHz. Calculate the improvement in the noise figure of the receiver.

Solution

$$\text{Improvement} = 10 \log_{10} (200/20) = 10 \text{ dB} \qquad (Ans.)$$

The noise figure of a radio receiver is related to its sensitivity.

$$\text{Sensitivity (dB)} = F(\text{dB}) + V_n(\text{dB}) + \text{signal-to-noise ratio (dB)} \qquad (9.5)$$

where V_n is the thermal noise voltage generated in the bandwidth of the receiver.

Example 9.8

A receiver has a noise figure of 10 dB and an output signal-to-noise ratio of 10 dB in a 3 kHz bandwidth. Calculate the sensitivity of the receiver if its input resistance is 50 Ω.

Solution

$$\begin{aligned}
\text{Thermal noise voltage } V_n &= \sqrt{(4 \times 1.38 \times 10^{-23} \times 290 \times 3000 \times 50)} \\
&= 49 \text{ nV} \\
&= 20 \log_{10} (49 \times 10^{-9})/(1 \times 10^{-6}) \\
&= -26 \text{ dB}\mu\text{V}
\end{aligned}$$

Therefore

$$\text{Sensitivity} = 10 + (-26) + 10 = -6 \text{ dB}\mu\text{V} = 0.5 \ \mu\text{V} \qquad (Ans.)$$

Spurious responses

I.f. breakthrough

If a signal at the intermediate frequency is picked up by an aerial and allowed to reach the mixer, it will reach the i.f. amplifier and interfere with the wanted signal. Such a signal must therefore be suppressed in the r.f. stage by an *i.f. trap*. The i.f. trap consists of either a parallel-resonant circuit, tuned to the intermediate frequency, connected in series with the aerial lead, or a series-resonant circuit, also tuned to the intermediate fequency, connected between the aerial lead and earth. In the first circuit the i.f. trap has a high impedance and blocks the passage of the unwanted i.f. signal; in the second circuit the i.f. trap has a low impedance and shunts the unwanted signal to earth.

Example 9.9

A superheterodyne radio receiver has an intermediate frequency of 465 kHz and is tuned to receive an unmodulated carrier at 1200 kHz. Calculate the frequency of the audio output signal if present at the mixer input there are also (a) a 1208 kHz and (b) a 462 kHz sinusoidal signal.

Solution

(a) The local oscillator frequency is $465 + 1200 = 1665$ kHz, and hence the 1208 kHz signal produces a difference frequency output from the mixer of $1665 - 1208 = 457$ kHz. If the i.f. bandwidth is only 9 kHz centred on 465 kHz, the 457 kHz signal will be rejected.

(b) The 462 kHz signal will appear at the mixer output and will be passed by the i.f. amplifier and will beat with the 465 kHz signal to produce a 3 kHz tone at the receiver output.

Co-channel interference

Co-channel interference is due to another signal at the same frequency and cannot be eliminated by the receiver itself. When it occurs, it is the result of unusual propagation conditions making it possible for transmissions from a geographically distant station to be picked up by the aerial. Harmonics of the local oscillator frequency may combine with unwanted stations or with harmonics produced by the mixer to produce various difference frequency components, some of which may fall within the passband of the i.f. amplifier. It is also possible for two r.f. signals arriving at the input to the mixer to beat together and produce a component at the intermediate frequency.

Intermodulation

The transfer and mutual characteristics of a bipolar transistor or a FET exhibit some non-linearity and as a result the output waveform of an amplifier will contain components at frequencies which were not present at the input. If, for example, the input signal contains components at frequencies f_1 and f_2, the output may contain components at frequencies $f_1 \pm f_2$, $2f_1 \pm f_2$, $2f_2 \pm f_1$, etc. These new frequencies are known as *intermodulation products*. Intermodulation can take place in both the r.f. amplifier and the mixer if the input signal level is so high that the active device is operated non-linearly. If two unwanted strong signals, separated in frequency by the intermediate frequency, or near to it, are present at the r.f. amplifier or mixer stages, they will produce an interfering component that will not be rejected by the i.f. amplifier.

Half-i.f. interference

One example of intermodulation which particularly affects VHF FM receivers is known as *half-i.f. interference*. Consider two signals at frequencies f and $f + f_{if}/2$ to be present at the r.f. stage and to produce a voltage at their difference frequency. The second harmonic of this component is $2[f - (f + f_{if}/2)]$ which is equal to the intermediate frequency of the receiver.

Intermodulation interference can be reduced by operating the r.f. stage as linearly as possible and, if possible, by rejecting one of the input voltages generating the interference.

Local oscillator radiation

The local oscillator operates at a radio frequency and may well radiate either directly or by coupling to the aerial. Direct radiation is limited by screening the oscillator. Radiation from the aerial is reduced by using an r.f. amplifier to prevent the oscillator voltage reaching the aerial. Radiation of the local oscillator frequency does not have a detrimental effect on the receiver in which it originates but is a source of interference to other nearby receivers.

Cross-modulation

Cross-modulation is the transfer of the amplitude modulation of an unwanted carrier onto the wanted carrier and is always the result of non-linearity in the mutual characteristic of the r.f. amplifier or of the mixer. If the amplitude of the input signal is small, or the mutual characteristic is essentially square law, cross-modulation will not occur. The unwanted signal may lie well outside the passband of the i.f. amplifier but, once cross-modulation has occurred, it is not possible to remove the unwanted modulation from the wanted carrier.

Cross-modulation is only present as long as the unwanted carrier producing the effect exists at the aerial, and it can be minimized by linear operation of the r.f. stage and by increasing the selectivity of the r.f. stage to reduce the number of large-amplitude signals entering the receiver. It is also helpful to avoid applying AGC to the r.f. stage, and, if large amplitude signals are expected, to use a switchable aerial attenuator to reduce the signal level and avoid overload with its consequent non-linearity. Cross-modulation does not occur in an FM receiver because the unwanted amplitude variations will be removed by the limiter stage.

Blocking

Blocking is an effect in which the gain of one or more stages in a radio receiver is reduced by an interfering signal of sufficient strength to overload the stage, or to excessively operate the AGC system of the receiver. The practical result of blocking is that the wanted signal output level falls every time the interfering signal is received.

The double superheterodyne radio receiver

To obtain good adjacent channel selectivity, the intermediate frequency of a superheterodyne radio receiver should be as low as possible, but to maximize the image channel rejection, the intermediate frequency must be as high as possible. For receivers operating in the low and medium frequency bands, it is possible to choose a reasonable compromise frequency. In the HF band it may prove difficult to select a suitable frequency and for this reason many receivers use two or, more rarely, three different intermediate frequencies.

The first intermediate frequency is chosen to give a good image channel rejection ratio and the second frequency is chosen for good adjacent channel selectivity. Typically, for an HF receiver the first intermediate fequency might be 3 MHz and the second 35—90 MHz, when a low-pass filter can give adequate image signal rejection.

The disadvantages of the double superheterodyne principle are the extra cost and complexity involved and the generation of extra spurious frequencies because there are two stages of mixing. The most serious of these new frequencies is the second image channel frequency.

Stages in a superheterodyne radio receiver

The radio-frequency stage

The radio-frequency stage of a superheterodyne radio receiver must perform the following functions:

- It must couple the aerial to the receiver in an efficient manner.
- It must suppress signals at or near the image and the intermediate frequencies.
- At frequencies in excess of about 3 MHz it must provide gain.
- It must operate linearly to avoid the production of cross-modulation.
- It should have sufficient selectivity to minimize the number of frequencies appearing at the input to the mixer that could result in intermodulation products lying within the passband of the i.f. amplifier.

At frequencies up to about 3 MHz, the noise picked up by an aerial is larger than the noise generated within the receiver. An r.f. amplifier will amplify the aerial noise as well as the signal and produce little, if any, improvement in the output signal-to-noise ratio. At higher frequencies, the noise picked up by the aerial falls and the constant-level receiver noise becomes predominant; the use of r.f. gain will then improve the output signal-to-noise ratio. An r.f. amplifier also permits the use of two or more tuned circuits in cascade, with a consequent improvement in the image response ratio.

In an HF receiver the r.f. stage is often a low-pass filter, or a bank of band-pass filters, followed by an r.f. amplifier. VHF and UHF receivers always employ one or more stages of r.f. amplification.

The mixer stage

The function of the mixer stage is to convert the wanted signal frequency into the intermediate frequency of the receiver. This process is carried out by *mixing* the signal frequency with the output of the local oscillator and selecting the resultant difference frequency.

It must be possible to set the local oscillator to any frequency in the band to which the receiver is tuned plus the intermediate frequency, i.e. $f_o = f_s + f_{if}$. The ability of a receiver to remain tuned to a particular frequency without drifting depends upon the frequency stability of its local oscillator. In an AM broadcast receiver the demands made on the oscillator in terms of frequency stability are not stringent, since the receiver is tuned by ear.

HF receivers often employ frequency synthesis since their frequency stability must be good, mainly because the channel bandwidth is narrow. Receivers operating at one or more fixed frequencies can use a crystal oscillator, when frequency changes involve crystal switching. When a receiver is to be tunable over a band of frequencies either an LC oscillator with automatic frequency control or a frequency synthesizer must be used.

The frequency stability of an ISB/SSB receiver should be good enough to ensure that the tuning of the receiver will not drift from its nominal value by more than about 20 Hz over a long period of time. This is necessary because any change in the local oscillator frequency will cause a corresponding shift in the frequency of the output signal. If, for example, the oscillator frequency should be 10 Hz too high, then all the components of the output signal will also be 10 Hz too high. If data and/or v.f. telegraph signals are to be received, the maximum permissible frequency drift is only ± 1 Hz. Generally, the long-term frequency stability of an HF communications receiver is better than 1 part in 10^7.

Ganging and tracking

When a sound broadcast radio receiver is tuned to receive a particular signal frequency, the resonant circuit(s) in the r.f. stage must be tuned to that frequency and the tuned circuit of the local oscillator must be tuned to a frequency equal to the sum of the signal and the intermediate frequencies. Clearly, it is convenient if the tuning of these circuits can be carried out by a single external control. To make this possible the tuning capacitors are mounted on a common spindle so that they can be simultaneously adjusted; this practice is known as *ganging*. The maintenance of the correct frequency difference (the intermediate frequency) between the r.f. stage and local oscillator frequencies is known as *tracking*.

It is possible to achieve nearly perfect tracking over one particular waveband if the plates of the oscillator tuning capacitor are carefully shaped, but this practice requires a different capacitor for each waveband and involves design problems. Most sound broadcast radio receivers use identicial tuning capacitors for the r.f. and oscillator circuits and modify the capacitance values by means of *trimmer* and/or *padder* capacitors.

Consider an AM sound broadcast receiver designed to tune over the medium frequency band of 525−1605 kHz that has an intermediate frequency of 470 kHz. Suppose that the (identical) variable tuning capacitors used in the r.f. and oscillator circuits have a capacitance range (maximum capacitance−minimum capacitance) of 400 pF. The r.f. stage must tune over the band 525−1605 kHz; this is a frequency ratio of 1605/525 or 3.057:1 and requires the tuning capacitance to provide a capacitance ratio of 3.057^2:1 or 9.346:1. Therefore, if the minimum capacitance needed is denoted by x, then

$$9.346x = x + 400$$
$$x = 400/8.346 = 47.93\,\text{pF} \simeq 48\,\text{pF}$$

The maximum capacitance must then be 48+400 = 448 pF. If the minimum capacitance of the variable capacitor plus the inevitable stray capacitances is not equal to 48 pF, a trimmer capacitance must be connected in parallel with the tuning capacitance. For example, if the minimum tuning capacitance plus stray capacitances adds up to 40 pF, an 8 pF trimmer will be required (see Fig. 9.5). The inductance L_1 required to tune the r.f. stage to the wanted signal frequency can be calculated using the expression $f_0 = 1/2\pi\sqrt{(LC)}$, remembering that the minimum capacitance corresponds to the maximum frequency and vice versa. Thus

$$L_1 = 1/(4\pi^2 \times 1605^2 \times 10^6 \times 48 \times 10^{-12}) \simeq 205\,\mu\text{H}$$

The oscillator must be able to tune over the frequency band from

$$(525+470) = 995\,\text{kHz}$$

to

$$(1605+470) = 2075\,\text{kHz}$$

This is a frequency ratio of 2075/995 or 2.085:1 and requires a capacitance ratio of 2.085^2 or 4.349:1. This capacitance ratio must be obtained using the same tuning capacitor as before and so either the minimum capacitance must be increased or the maximum capacitance must be decreased.

Use of a trimmer capacitor

Let the minimum capacitance needed in the local oscillator be x pF. Then

$$4.349x = x + 400$$
$$x = 400/3.349 = 119.4\,\text{pF} \simeq 119\,\text{pF}$$

The minimum capacitance of the oscillator tuning circuit can be increased to this value by connecting a trimmer capacitor in parallel with the variable capacitor. Assuming the minimum capacitance of the variable capacitor, plus stray capacitances, to be the same as in the r.f. circuit, i.e. 40 pF, then a trimmer capacitor of 119−40 = 79 pF is needed (see Fig. 9.6). The tuning inductance is

$$L_2 = 1/(4\pi^2 f_{o(max)}^2 C_{min})$$

and is equal to 49.4 μH. Unfortunately, correct tracking will not be

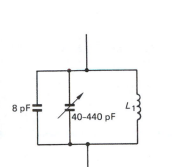

Fig. 9.5 Use of a trimmer capacitor in the r.f. stage

8 pF

40–440 pF

L_1

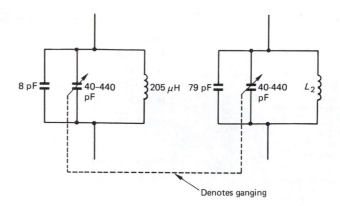

Fig. 9.6 Use of a trimmer capacitor in the oscillator

maintained between the r.f. and local oscillator circuits as the receiver is tuned over its frequency bands.

Example 9.10

A superheterodyne radio receiver employs ganged capacitors in its aerial and local oscillator circuits with an additional parallel capacitor in the local oscillator circuit. As the capacitance in the signal circuit varies from 80 pF to 320 pF, the receiver is tuned from 1200 kHz to 600 kHz. If the local oscillator capacitance variation is from 160 pF to 400 pF, and the intermediate frequency is 433 kHz, calculate (a) the frequency to which the receiver is tuned when the signal circuit capacitance is 200 pF; (b) the local oscillator frequency when the local oscillator capacitance is 280 pF; (c) the tracking error when the capacitance is at the mid-point of its range.

Solution

For both the r.f. and the local oscillator circuits, the maximum frequency corresponds to the minimum capacitance. Therefore

$$\text{(a)} \quad 1200 \times 10^3 = 1/2\pi\sqrt{(L \times 80 \times 10^{-12})} \tag{9.6}$$

$$f = 1/2\pi\sqrt{(L \times 200 \times 10^{-12})} \tag{9.7}$$

Dividing equation (9.6) by equation (9.7),

$$(1200 \times 10^3)/f = \sqrt{(200/80)}$$

$$f = (1200 \times 10^3)/1.581 = 758.95 \text{ kHz} \quad (Ans.)$$

(b) Maximum oscillator frequency $= 1200 + 433 = 1633$ kHz

$$1633 \times 10^3 = 1/2\pi\sqrt{(L \times 160 \times 10^{-12})}$$

$$f = 1/2\pi\sqrt{(L \times 280 \times 10^{-12})}$$

$$(1633 \times 10^3)/f = \sqrt{(280/160)} = 1.323$$

$$f = (1633 \times 10^3)/1.323 = 1234.43 \text{ kHz} \quad (Ans.)$$

(c) The mid-point of the capacitance range corresponds to the values used in parts (a) and (b). Therefore

$$\text{Tracking error} = 1234.43 \text{ kHz} - (758.95 + 433) \text{ kHz}$$

$$= 42.48 \text{ kHz} \quad (Ans.)$$

Use of a padder capacitor

The alternative method of reducing the capacitance ratio in the local oscillator circuit is the connection of a padder capacitor in series with the tuning capacitor. Suppose that the same tuning capacitor and frequencies as before are used. The minimum and maximum capacitances are then 40 pF and 440 pF. If the padder capacitor is denoted by C_p, then, since the required capacitance ratio is 4.349:1,

$$440C_p/(440+C_p) = (4.349 \times 40C_p)/(40+C_p)$$

$$440 \times 40 + 440C_p = 4.349 \times 40 \times 440 + 4.349 \times 40C_p$$

$$C_p(440 - 4.349 \times 40) = 40 \times 440(4.349 - 1)$$

$$C_p = (40 \times 440 \times 3.349)/[400 - (4.349 \times 40)] = 221.6 \text{ pF}$$

$$\simeq 222 \text{ pF}$$

Fig. 9.7 shows the arrangement of the r.f. and local oscillator circuits. The total capacitance of the circuit will now vary from

$$(40 \times 222)/(40+222) \text{ or } 33.89 \text{ pF}$$

to

$$(440 \times 222)/(440+222) \text{ or } 147.55 \text{ pF}$$

The inductance L_3 required to tune the circuit can be calculated using the maximum frequency of 2075 kHz and the minimum capacitance of 33.89 pF (or vice versa). Thus

$$L_3 = 1/(4\pi^2 \times 2075^2 \times 10^6 \times 33.89 \times 10^{-12}) = 173.6 \text{ } \mu\text{H}$$

$$\simeq 174 \text{ } \mu\text{H}$$

Again, correct tracking is not obtained over most of the tuning range of the receiver.

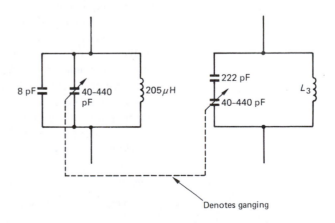

Fig. 9.7 Use of a padder capacitor

Denotes ganging

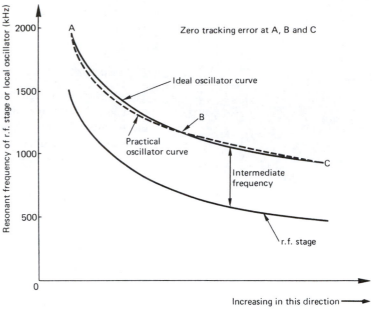

Fig. 9.8 Tracking curves

The tracking error does not have much effect on the quality of the audio output signal, since the tuning of the receiver positions the wanted signal into the middle of the passband of the i.f. amplifier. This means that the intermediate frequency is correct and the tracking error exists in the r.f. stage. The error in tuning the r.f. stage has little, if any, effect upon the adjacent channel selectivity, but both the sensitivity and the image channel rejection are worsened. Tracking is not a problem in FM sound broadcast receivers because the required frequency and capacitance ratios are small and modern HF, VHF and UHF communication receivers employ frequency synthesis to derive the oscillator frequencies.

If both a trimmer and a padder capacitor are used, *three-point tracking* can be obtained and the tracking error can be reduced to a small figure. Three-point tracking is illustrated by the curves of Fig. 9.8. The r.f. circuit and the ideal oscillator curves are always separated by a frequency difference equal to the intermediate frequency of the receiver. The practical curve, shown dotted, has zero tracking error at the three points marked A, B and C; elsewhere the error is small.

Modern HF communication receivers employ a frequency synthesizer to generate the local oscillator frequency and use up-conversion. Ganging and tracking problems can then be eliminated by obtaining the r.f. selectivity from switched band-pass filters or by having no r.f. selectivity at all.

Example 9.11

A radio receiver with an intermediate frequency of 465 kHz and a maximum

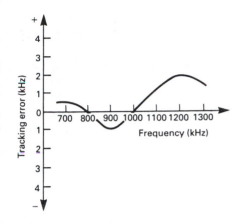

Fig. 9.9

modulation frequency of 5 kHz has the tracking error shown in Fig. 9.9. Calculate the minimum bandwidth for the i.f. amplifier.

Solution
The maximum intermediate frequency occurs for the r.f. signal that corresponds with the maximum tracking error, i.e. 1200 Hz, and the minimum for the signal frequency with the smallest tracking error, i.e. 900 Hz.

$$IF_{min} = 465 + 2 + 5 = 472 \text{ kHz}$$

$$IF_{max} = 465 - 1 - 5 = 459 \text{ kHz}$$

Therefore minimum i.f. bandwidth = 472 − 459 = 13 kHz   (*Ans.*)

The intermediate frequency amplifier

The purpose of the i.f. amplifier in a superheterodyne radio receiver is to provide most of the gain and the selectivity of the receiver. Most broadcast receivers utilize the impedance−frequency characteristics of single- or double-tuned circuits to obtain the required selectivity, but many receivers use *ceramic filters*, particularly when an integrated circuit is used as the i.f. amplifier. Narrow-band communication receivers must possess very good selectivity and very often employ one or more *crystal filters* to obtain the necessary gain−frequency response. The use of a ceramic or a crystal filter to provide the selectivity of a radio receiver offers a number of advantages over the use of LC networks:

- A very narrow bandwidth can be obtained.
- The selectivity of the receiver does not depend upon the correct alignment of the i.f. amplifier.
- The selectivity of the filter is not affected by the application of automatic gain control to the receiver.

Choice of intermediate frequency

The main factors to be considered when choosing the intermediate frequency for a superheterodyne radio receiver are

- the required i.f. bandwidth;
- interference signals;
- the required i.f. gain and stability;
- the required adjacent channel selectivity.

 The minimum bandwidth demanded of an i.f. amplifier depends upon the type of receiver (see Figs 9.3 and 9.4). Since the bandwidth of a coupled-tuned circuit is proportional to its resonant frequency ($B = \sqrt{2}f_o/Q$), the larger the bandwidth required, the higher must be the intermediate frequency. The intermediate frequency should not lie within the tuning range of the receiver, so that the r.f. stage can include an i.f. trap to prevent i.f. interference. Adequate adjacent channel selectivity is easier to obtain using a low intermediate frequency, but on the other hand, image channel rejection is easier if a high intermediate frequency is selected.

The intermediate frequency chosen for a receiver must be a compromise between these conflicting factors. Most amplitude-modulated sound broadcast receivers employ an intermediate frequency of between 450 and 470 kHz; but frequency-modulation broadcast receivers, which require an i.f. bandwidth of about 200 kHz, use an intermediate frequency of 10.7 MHz.

HF communication receivers often employ two different intermediate frequencies: the first intermediate frequency is above the highest frequency to which the receiver is able to tune, and the second intermediate frequency is usually somewhere between 5 and 12 MHz. VHF and UHF mobile receivers also often employ two stages of i.f. amplification, with the first intermediate frequency typically 10.7 MHz and the second 450 kHz. When the choice of first intermediate frequency is determined by the need to use either a crystal or a surface acoustic wave (SAW) filter to determine the i.f. amplifier's selectivity, the frequency chosen may be either 40−90 MHz or perhaps some hundreds of megahertz.

The detector stage

The function of the detector stage in a radio receiver is to recover the information modulated onto the carrier wave appearing at the output of the i.f. amplifier. Many AM broadcast receivers use the diode detector because of its simplicity and good performance, but when the detector is within a radio IC the transistor detector is often used. The transistor detector is not often used in discrete form for AM broadcast receivers because of its limited dynamic range, but it is used in some VHF communication receivers where its ability to provide an amplified AGC voltage and its gain are an advantage. Many FM sound broadcast receivers with discrete circuitry use the ratio detector, but high-quality broadcast receivers may use the Foster−Seeley circuit; when the latter circuit is used, the detector must be preceded by a limiter stage. When the detector stage is included within a radio IC, the quadrature detector or, less often, the phase-locked loop detector is commonly used. HF ISB/SSB communication receivers generally use some form of balanced or product demodulator.

The audio-frequency stage

The function of the audio-frequency stage of a radio receiver is to develop sufficient a.f. power to operate the loudspeaker or other receiving apparatus. The a.f. stage will include a volume control and sometimes treble and bass controls. The a.f. stage may also include a *squelch* or *muting* facility. A sensitive receiver will produce a considerable output noise level when there is no input signal, because there will then be no AGC voltage developed to limit the gain of the receiver. The noise unavoidably present at the input terminals of the receiver than receives maximum amplification. This noise output can cause considerable annoyance to the operator of the receiver and, to reduce or eliminate this annoyance, a squelch circuit is fitted which disconnents the a.f. amplifier, or severely reduces its gain, whenever there is no input signal present.

Automatic gain control

The field strength of the wanted signal at the receiving aerial is not a constant quantity: instead, it fluctuates widely because of changes in propagation conditions. Automatic gain control (AGC) is applied to a radio receiver to maintain the carrier level at the input to the detector at a more or less constant value even though the level at the aerial may vary considerably. AGC ensures that the audio output of the receiver varies only as a function of the modulation of the carrier and not with the carrier level itself. The use of AGC also ensures that a large receiver gain can be made available for the reception of weak signals without causing overloading of the r.f. amplifier stages (with consequent distortion) by strong signals. Further, a reasonably constant output level is obtained as the receiver is tuned from one station to another.

In an FM receiver automatic gain control is often fitted to ensure (a) that the signal arriving at the input terminals of the limiter is large enough for the limiting action to take place and (b) that overloading of the r.f. and i.f. amplifier stages does not occur. In some cases, the automatic gain control of a communication receiver may mean switching into the r.f. stage of one or more stages of an attenuator.

The basic idea of an AGC system is illustrated by Fig. 9.10. A d.c. voltage is developed, either in the detector stage or in the amplitude limiter, that is proportional to the amplitude of the carrier signal appearing at the output of the i.f. amplifier. The gain of a transistor amplifier is a function of the d.c. operating point of the transistor; hence if the AGC voltage is applied to each of the controlled stages to vary their bias voltages, the gains of these stages will be

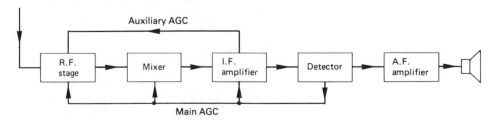

Fig. 9.10 Application of AGC to a radio receiver

under the control of the AGC system. The polarity of the AGC voltage should be chosen so that an increase in the carrier level, which will produce an increase in the AGC voltage, will reduce the gain of each stage. This will, in turn, reduce the overall gain of the receiver and tend to restore the carrier level at the detector to its original value. Conversely, of course, if the carrier level should fall, the gain of the receiver must be increased in order to keep the level at the detector very nearly constant. Another AGC loop, known as *auxiliary AGC*, is often provided to give extra control of the gain of the receiver and to limit the amplitude of strong input signals to prevent overloading of the r.f. amplifier and consequent distortion and cross-modulation. In many FM receivers, only auxiliary AGC is fitted.

Automatic gain control systems are either of the *simple* or the *delayed* type.

Simple AGC

In a simple AGC system, the AGC voltage is developed immediately a carrier voltage appears at the output of the i.f. amplifier. This means that the gain of the receiver is reduced below its maximum value when the wanted signal is weak and the full receiver gain is really wanted. This disadvantage of the simple AGC system can be overcome by arranging that the AGC voltage will not be developed until the carrier level at the detector has reached some pre-determined value — generally that at which the full audio-frequency power output can be developed. Such a system is known as a delayed AGC system.

Delayed AGC

The AGC loop can establish a minimum driving voltage to the detector stage. The loop is designed so that it does not limit the output voltage before the input to the detector reaches the minimum drive level. Quadrature detectors, in particular, require close control of their input voltage level if maximum rejection of unwanted amplitude variations is to be obtained.

Fig. 9.11 shows, graphicallly, the difference between simple and delayed AGC systems; in addition, the performance of the ideal AGC system is shown. The ideal system is one in which no AGC voltage is produced until the input voltage to the receiver exceeds some critical value and thereafter it keeps the output level of the receiver perfectly constant.

AGC calculations

Suppose that the AGC voltage developed by the AGC circuit is x volts and that the gain of each of the n controlled stages of the receiver

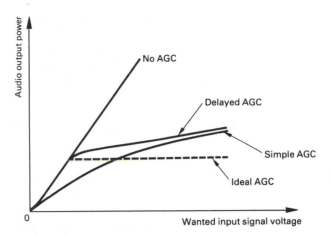

Fig. 9.11 AGC characteristics

varies by y dB per volt of AGC voltage. Then, if the maximum gain of the receiver, from r.f. stage to detector, is A_v dB, the AGC controlled gain will be $(A_v - nxy)$ dB.

When delayed AGC is used, the AGC voltage is not developed until the signal voltage at the output of the i.f. amplifier is greater than some pre-determined value, known as the delay voltage.

Example 9.12

A radio receiver has four stages which have their voltage gains controlled by a simple AGC system. Each stage has an AGC characteristic of 4 dB/V. A change in the input voltage to the r.f. stage of from 20 μV to 100 mV causes the a.f. output level to increase by 6 dB. Calculate the change in the AGC voltage that must have taken place.

Solution
The change in the input voltage expressed in decibels is

$$20 \log_{10} (100 \times 10^{-3})/(20 \times 10^{-6}) = 74 \text{ dB}$$

This means that the voltage gain of the receiver must have decreased by

$$74 - 6 = 68 \text{ dB}$$

Therefore

$$\text{AGC voltage change} = 68/4 \times 4 = 4.25 \text{ V} \quad (Ans.)$$

Example 9.13

A radio receiver has a total AGC gain control characteristic of 12 dB/V. The a.f. output is to change by only 6 dB when the r.f. input signal voltage increases from 20 μV to 100 mV. Calculate the delay voltage required to ensure that the AGC system is inoperative for r.f. input voltages of less than 20 μV.

Solution
The input signal variation expressed in dB is

$$2 \log_{10} (100 \times 10^{-3})/(20 \times 10^{-6}) = 74 \text{ dB}$$

Hence the necessary change in the AGC voltage is

74/12 = 6.2 V

The AGC voltage is proportional to the carrier level at the detector input and it is therefore proportional to the detected output level also. Thus, a 6.2 V change in the AGC voltage must correspond to a 6 dB change or a 2:1 change in the a.f. output level. Therefore

Delay voltage = 6.2 V   (*Ans.*)

Automatic frequency control

The i.f. bandwidth of a communication receiver operating in the UHF band is only a small percentage of the carrier frequency. A relatively small percentage error in the frequency of the local oscillator may lead to the wanted signal being wholly or partly rejected by the selectivity of the i.f. amplifier. Some of the necessary frequency stability can be obtained by a suitable choice of the type of oscillator to be used, but the most stable types of oscillator cannot be tuned to different frequencies.

The required frequency stability can be obtained by the use of *automatic frequency control* (AFC). To avoid distortion of the output signal caused by mistuning, many FM sound broadcast receivers also have AFC fitted.

The basic principle of an AFC system is shown by Fig. 9.12. The output of the i.f. amplifier is passed through an amplitude limiter and is then applied to the input terminals of a frequency discriminator. The input circuit of the discriminator is tuned to the nominal intermediate frequency of the receiver, and so the circuit produces zero output voltage whenever the intermediate frequency is correct. If, however, the intermediate frequency differs from its nominal value, a d.c. voltage will appear at the output of the discriminator. The polarity of this d.c. voltage will depend upon whether the intermediate frequency is higher than, or lower than, its nominal value. Thus if a negative d.c. voltage is produced by an increase in frequency, then a fall in the intermediate frequency will result in a positive d.c. voltage

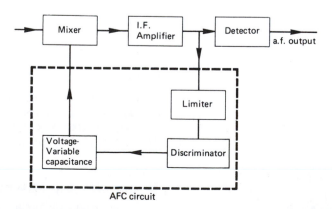

Fig. 9.12 Application of AFC to a radio receiver

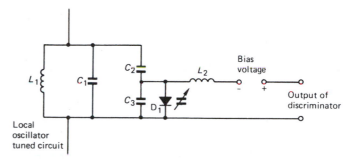

Fig. 9.13 Varactor diode control of local oscillator frequency

at the output of the discriminator. The d.c. voltage is taken to a voltage-variable capacitance, whose magnitude is a function of that voltage. The variable capacitance is a part of the frequency-determining network of the local oscillator and so a change in its value will alter the frequency of oscillation. The voltage-dependent capacitance can be provided in a number of ways but the most common is the use of a varactor diode. The basic circuit is shown by Fig. 9.13. The varactor diode D_1 is connected in parallel with the tuned circuit, and so it provides a part of the total tuning capacitance of the local oscillator.

Example 9.14

An AFC system incorporates a discriminator with an output voltage–input frequency characteristic of 1 V/3 kHz and a voltage-controlled oscillator whose output frequency–input voltage characteristic is 15 kHz/V. Calculate the tuning error with the AFC system operative if, without the AFC, the frequency error would have been 24 kHz.

Solution
Let the final frequency error be f kHz. Then the d.c. output voltage of the discriminator is $f/3$ volts and this voltage will cause the frequency of the oscillator to be shifted by $(f/3) \times 15 = 5f$ kHz. The final tuning error is equal to the original error minus the frequency correction provided by the AFC system. Therefore

$$f = 24 - 5f \quad \text{or} \quad f = 4 \text{ kHz} \quad (Ans.)$$

The *pull-in* or *capture range* of an AFC system is the maximum frequency error that can be reduced by the system. It is obviously necessary that an AFC system is designed so that the capture range is larger than the maximum expected drift in the oscillator frequency. The *hold-in range* is the band of frequencies over which the controlled oscillator frequency can suddenly change without the control exerted by the AFC system being lost.

Sound broadcast receivers

Most sound broadcast radio receivers are able to receive both amplitude-modulated, and frequency-modulated transmissions. One

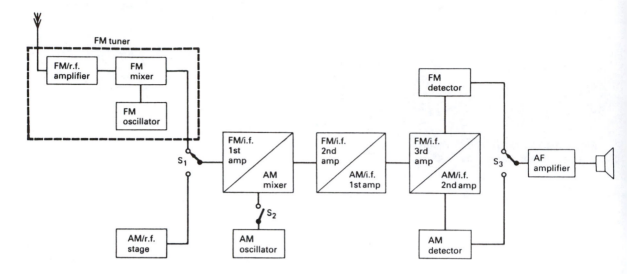

Fig. 9.14 FM/AM superheterodyne radio receiver

arrangement is shown by Fig. 9.14. The switches are shown in their FM positions. The wanted FM signal is converted to the intermediate frequency by the FM tuner and then delivered to the first common stage of the i.f. amplifier. This stage has the dual functions of first i.f. amplifier for FM signals and mixer stage for AM signals. The wanted FM signal is selected by the first i.f. amplifier, amplified, and then passed on to the next stage of i.f. amplification. The amplified FM signal is then applied to the detector where its information content is extracted and then passed to the a.f. amplifier. When amplitude modulation signals are to be received, all the switches shown are operated and the first i.f. stage then acts as the AM mixer. The amplitude modulated i.f. signal is selected by the second i.f. amplifier stage, which now acts as the first i.f. amplifier, and is then applied to the AM detector.

Integrated circuits are increasingly employed in radio receivers, and Fig. 9.15 shows the block diagram of one common arrangement. The AM and FM sections of the receiver are completely separate up to the outputs of the two detector stages. The FM signal is amplified and frequency changed by the (non-integrated) FM tuner (often in module form), and it is then passed on to an IC which performs the functions of both the i.f. amplifier and the FM detector; the selectivity of the i.f. amplifier is determined by an external inductor/capacitor network. The AM signal is received by a normal r.f. stage and is then fed to an IC which acts as the mixer, the i.f. amplifier and the AM detector. The audio-frequency outputs of the two detectors are connected, via a switch, to the common audio-frequency amplifier. The selectivity of the AM i.f. amplifier is determined by a ceramic filter.

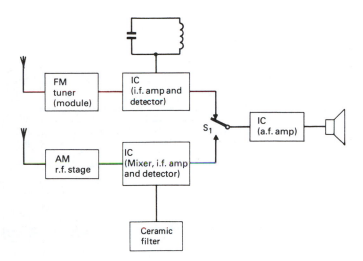

Fig. 9.15 FM/AM radio receiver using integrated circuits

Communication receivers

Most MF/HF communication receivers are able to receive several different kinds of signal, such as speech, continuous wave (CW) and data. Some receivers are also able to receive FM signals.

Most VHF/UHF communication receivers are able to receive either amplitude- or frequency-modulated signals but not both.

Some communication receivers are able to cover the HF, VHF and UHF bands, and sometimes some of the MF band as well. Such receivers are able to receive both amplitude- and frequency-modulated signals. One receiver, the Racal RA 3721, for example, covers the frequency band 20—1000 MHz (with possible extension to 10 kHz), and can detect DSB, ISB, SSB and CW amplitude-modulated signals, and NBFM and FSK frequency modulated signals with a variety of audio bandwidths.

The block diagram of an HF ISB communication receiver is shown in Fig. 9.16. The quadruple superheterodyne receiver has its first

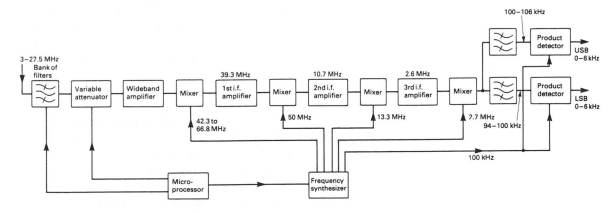

Fig. 9.16 HF ISB communication receiver

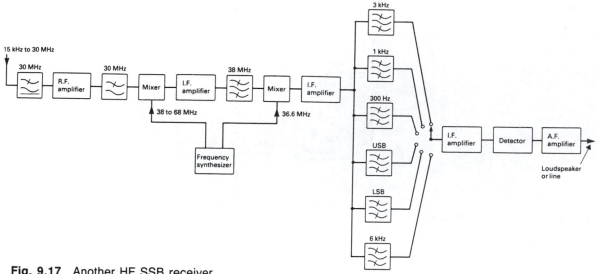

Fig. 9.17 Another HF SSB receiver

intermediate frequency above the receiver's tuning range of 3−27.5 MHz. A microprocessor-controlled frequency synthesizer provides the local oscillator frequencies to all four mixers; the microprocessor also controls the switching of the appropriate band-pass filters into the aerial circuit and the loss of the r.f. attenuator.

Fig. 9.17 shows the block diagram of an HF SSB radio receiver that covers the frequency band 15 kHz to 30 MHz with either the upper or the lower sideband transmitted. Image channel rejection is provided by the first 30 MHz low-pass filter, while the second 30 MHz low-pass filter removes unwanted signals produced by any non-linearity in the r.f. amplifier. The wanted signal is mixed with the first local oscillator signal which is derived from a 38−68 MHz frequency synthesizer to produce a first intermediate frequency of 38 MHz. The 38 MHz signal is amplified and then mixed with a 36.6 MHz second local oscillator signal, also obtained from the frequency synthesizer, to produce a 1.4 MHz second intermediate frequency. The 1.4 MHz signal is amplified and then applied to a bank of 1.4 MHz filters having various bandwidths. The appropriate filter for the type of signal being received is switched into circuit and the selected output is applied to another i.f. amplifier. The output signal of this i.f. amplifier is applied to the detector stage for detection. If a CW or SSB signal is to be received, a re-insert carrier is also applied to the detector. Finally, the detected signal is applied to an a.f. amplifier for amplification to the required level. An AGC voltage is derived from the final i.f. amplifier and it is used to control the gains of the r.f. amplifier and the first i.f. amplifier.

Typically, such a receiver might have a sensitivity of 0.8 μV for a 10 dB output signal-to-noise ratio, a nose selectivity of 2.4 kHz and

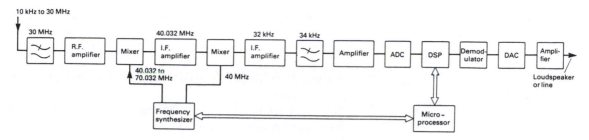

Fig. 9.18 Digital HF receiver

a skirt selectivity of 3.8 kHz. The image channel rejection is about 55 dB. The AGC system will limit a change in the output voltage to 3 dB when the r.f. input signal changes from 5 V to 100 mV.

Some modern HF receivers employ digital signal processing (DSP) now that LSI integrated circuits are available. DSP can carry out all the analogue back-end processing in a receiver, such as i.f. filtering, AGC generation, and demodulation.

The basic block diagram of a digital HF receiver that covers the frequency band 10 kHz to 30 MHz in 10 Hz steps is shown by Fig. 9.18. The r.f. signal is passed through the 30 MHz low-pass filter and a wideband amplifier. The amplified and filtered signal is applied to the first mixer, where it is mixed with the 40.032−70.032 MHz first local oscillator signal derived from a frequency synthesizer. The difference frequency of 40.032 MHz is selected by the first i.f. amplifier and further amplified. The bandwidth of the first i.f. amplifier is 12 kHz. The output signal from the first i.f. amplifier is then passed on to the second mixer, and here it is mixed with the 40 MHz second local oscillator signal, which is obtained from a crystal oscillator. The difference frequency of 32 kHz is selected and amplified by the second i.f. amplifier. The amplifier output signal is passed through a low-pass filter and another amplifier before it is routed on to the digital part of the receiver.

The 32 kHz signal is applied to a 16-bit analogue-to-digital converter (ADC) where it is converted into digital form. Another ADC measures the signal voltage and produces an AGC voltage which is applied to the first i.f. amplifier to control its gain. The digital output of the first ADC is applied to a number of DSPs where the signal is processed and demodulated. The demodulated signal is then applied to a digital-to-analogue converter (DAC) to be converted back into analogue form. Three analogue audio outputs are provided: a 600 Ω balanced output plus outputs for a loudspeaker and for headphones. Such a receiver may also provide an analogue output at 1.4 MHz and a digital output.

The microprocessor that controls the operations of the frequency synthesizer and the DSP is a device such as the Motorola 68000 with both RAM and ROM storage. The microprocessor also handles the controls and displays of the receiver.

Transceivers

Many mobile radio equipments employ a *transceiver* instead of a separate receiver and transmitter. The basic block diagram of a transceiver is shown by Fig. 9.19. The transmitter section of the transceiver is only connected to the aerial when the aerial switch is operated. Very often the aerial switch is mounted on the radio-telephone handset.

The block diagram of a VHF AM transceiver is shown in Fig. 9.20. The transmitter can operate on any one of four channels by selection of the appropriate crystal oscillator. The receiver is of the double superheterodyne type, using first and second intermediate frequencies of 10.7 MHz and 460 kHz respectively. A separate AGC detector is used, and this allows delayed AGC to be applied to the controlled stages. Finally, squelch (or muting) is applied to the a.f. section of the receiver, to prevent its operation when no signal is being received.

The block diagram of a frequency-modulated transceiver, which uses a frequency synthesizer to derive the wanted mixer frequencies, is shown in Fig. 9.21. Two stages of mixing and of i.f. amplification are provided, the selectivity of the second amplifier being provided by a crystal filter.

The block diagram of a microprocessor-controlled VHF/UHF transceiver for use in vehicles is shown in Fig. 9.22. The receiver is of the double superheterodyne type with a first intermediate frequency of 21.4 MHz and a second intermediate frequency of 455 kHz. The received signal is passed through an electronically tuned band-pass filter to the r.f. amplifier. The amplified signal is then passed on to the double-balanced mixer where it is frequency-shifted to 21.4 MHz. The selectivity of the first i.f. amplifier is provided by 21.4 MHz crystal filters. The 21.4 MHz signal is applied to the second mixer, and here it is converted to the 455 kHz second intermediate frequency. The selectivity of this amplifier is provided by a ceramic filter. The 455 kHz signal is then applied to the quadrature detector for demodulation. The second mixer, the second i.f. amplifier and the FM detector are contained within a single IC. The demodulated output signal is passed through a 300−3000 Hz band-pass filter and

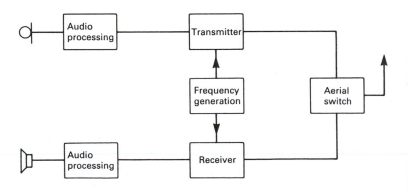

Fig. 9.19 Basic block diagram of a transceiver

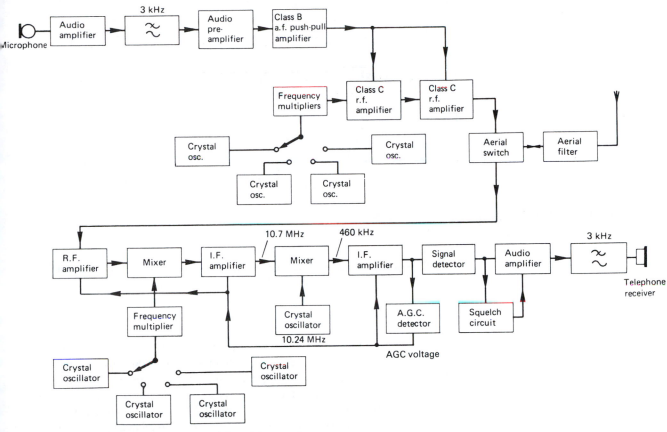

Fig. 9.20 A VHF amplitude modulated transceiver

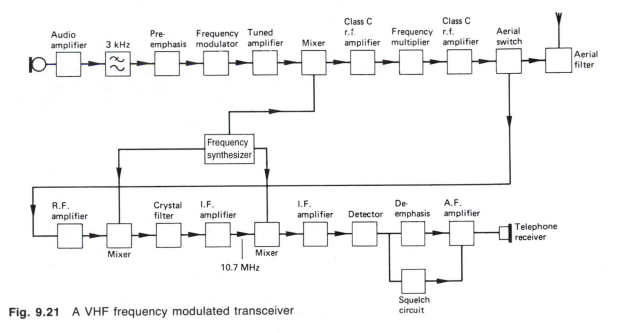

Fig. 9.21 A VHF frequency modulated transceiver

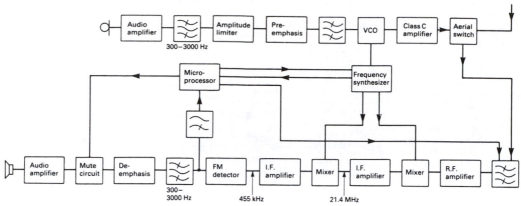

Fig. 9.22 Microprocessor-controlled transceiver

a de-emphasis circuit before it arrives at, first, a mute (or squelch) circuit and then the audio power amplifier.

The demodulated output is also passed through a high-pass filter and the filtered signal is used by the microprocessor to control the mute circuit.

In the transmitter section of the transceiver the microphone output is amplified by a pre-amplifier before it is filtered, further amplified and then applied to an amplitude limiter. The amplitude-limited signal is low-pass filtered before it is applied to the transmit voltage-controlled oscillator (VCO). The VCO, whose centre frequency is the wanted carrier frequency, is frequency modulated by the amplified audio signal, and the FM signal is applied to a wideband r.f. amplifier to produce an output power of up to 25 W.

The frequency synthesizer uses a phase-locked loop (PLL) to derive the local oscillator frequencies that are applied to the receive and transmit VCOs with the two VCOs being inside the PLL. The frequency synthesizer can be programmed to new frequencies by a digital command from the microprocessor; the microprocessor also up-dates the display on the receiver's front panel, controls the mute circuit, and monitors the front panel's buttons to detect any user instructions.

Hand-held transceivers are necessarily of small physical size, lightweight and battery-operated; Fig. 9.23 shows a simplified block diagram of a modern design. The microphone signal is pre-emphasized and amplified before it is applied to an amplitude limiter to keep its amplitude at a constant level. The amplitude-limited signal is then low-pass filtered before it is used to frequency-modulate the transmit VCO. The frequency-modulated signal is then amplified, first by a buffer amplifier and then by an r.f. power amplifier, before being passed on to the aerial via the aerial switch.

In the receiving direction, the incoming signal is filtered by a band-pass filter which covers the whole of a frequency band. The output

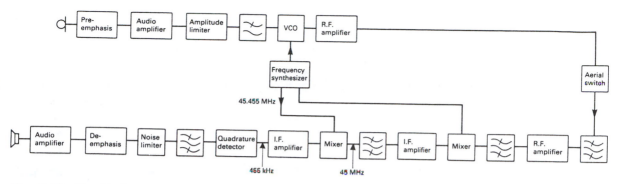

Fig. 9.23 Hand-held transceiver

of this filter is passed on to the r.f. amplifier, and the amplified signal is further filtered by an electronically controlled filter which gives the receiver an image rejection of about 80 dB. The band-limited signal is then fed to a single-balanced mixer, where it is mixed with the first local oscillator frequency to produce the first intermediate frequency of 45 MHz. The range of frequencies covered by the local oscillator depends upon which frequency band is being used. The 45 MHz signal is amplified before it is passed through a crystal filter, which provides much of the receiver's adjacent channel selectivity, before the signal is applied to the second mixer. Here the signal is mixed with the 45.455 MHz signal from the frequency synthesizer to produce a second intermediate frequency of 455 kHz. The 455 kHz signal is amplified by a limiting amplifier before it is applied to the quadrature detector for demodulation. The demodulated signal is then noise-limited and de-emphasized before it is amplified by the audio amplifier.

The transceiver operates in three VHF bands and three UHF bands with up to 250 12.5 kHz channels with ±2.5 kHz deviation and a power output of between 0.1 and 5 W. the sensitivity of the receiver is 0.35 μV and its adjacent-channel selectivity is better than 60 dB.

Radio pager

A pager operates in the frequency band 279–281 MHz with 20 kHz spacing, using a standard paging code specified by the ITU-R. The block diagram of a radio pager is shown by Fig. 9.24. The received signal is amplified by an r.f. amplifier and is then applied to two identical mixers with one signal being given 90° phase shift before it reaches the mixer. This results in two output signals, I and Q; according to the frequency deviation, one signal leads the other by 90°. The I and Q signals are filtered to remove adjacent channel signals and they are then applied to the demodulator. The phase relationships between the I and Q signals determine whether a binary 1 or a binary 0 is produced at the demodulator's output. The following low-pass filter removes all unwanted high-frequency components from the detected signal. The data stream is passed on to the decoder, where the information carried is compared with information held in memory.

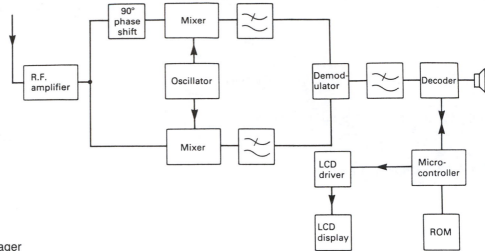

Fig. 9.24 Radio pager

If the address of the incoming message is recognized, the message is displayed on the LCD display and perhaps gives an audible indication of a received call.

Measurement of performance of radio receivers

A number of measurements can be carried out to determine the performance of a radio receiver. Some of these tests are appropriate for both amplitude- and frequency-modulated receivers, while others only apply to one type of receiver. Only the more important of the many receiver measurements will be described; these are (a) sensitivity, (b) noise factor, (c) adjacent channel ratio, and (d) image channel response ratio.

Sensitivity

The sensitivity of an amplitude modulation radio receiver is the smallest input signal voltage, modulated to a depth of 30% by a 1000 Hz (or 400 Hz) tone, needed to produce 50 mW output power with a signal-to-noise ratio of 20 dB.

The circuit used to carry out a sensitivity measurement is shown in Fig. 9.25. The signal generator is set to 30% modulation depth at the required frequency of measurement, and its output voltage is set to a value about 10 dB above the expected sensitivity. The audio-frequency gain of the receiver is then set to approximately its half-maximum position and the receiver is tuned to the measurement frequency. The signal generator frequency is then varied slightly to give the maximum reading on the output power meter. The input voltage producing the necessary audio output condition can now be determined. The input voltage is varied until the power meter indicates

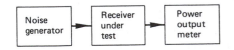

Fig. 9.25 Measurement of radio receiver sensitivity

50 mW; then the modulation of the signal generator is switched off and the power meter indication is noted: say, P mW. The output signal-to-noise ratio is then

$$10 \log_{10} (50/P) \text{ dB}$$

If this ratio is not equal to the required 20 dB, the modulation of the signal generator is switched on again and the input voltage to the receiver is increased or decreased as appropriate. The a.f. gain is adjusted to obtain 50 mW indication on the power meter before the modulation is again switched off and the new signal-to-noise ratio determined. This procedure is repeated until the required output power of 50 mW is obtained together with 20 dB signal-to-noise ratio. The input signal voltage giving the required output conditions is the sensitivity of the receiver.

For an SSB receiver, the frequency of the signal generator is made 1 kHz away from the carrier frequency so that a 1 kHz tone is produced at the receiver's output.

When an FM receiver is measured, a 1 kHz tone is used to modulate the signal generator to 60% of rated system deviation (this is usually 3 kHz). The sensitivity is then measured relative to the input signal that produces the standard audio output with 12 dB SINAD.

Noise factor

The noise factor F of a radio receiver is the ratio

$$F = \frac{\text{Noise power appearing at the output of the receiver}}{\text{That part of the above which is due to thermal agitation at the input terminals}}$$

(9.8)

This definition of noise factor is, for most conditions, equivalent to the previously quoted meaning of noise factor, i.e. equation (9.3):

$$F = \frac{\text{Input signal-to-noise ratio}}{\text{Output signal-to-noise ratio}}$$

Fig. 9.26 Measurement of radio receiver noise figure

Fig. 9.26 shows the circuit used for the measurement of the noise factor of a receiver. With the noise generator switched off, the indication of the power output meter is noted. The noise generator is then switched on and, without altering any of the receiver controls, its noise output is increased until the indication of the power meter is *exactly* double its previous value.

The noise output of the generator is directly proportional to the current indicated by an integral milliammeter and so the noise factor of the receiver is equal to

$$F = 20I_a R \tag{9.9}$$

where I_a is the indication of the milliammeter and R is the (matched) resistance of the receiver and the noise generator. If, as is often the case at VHF and at UHF, $R = 50\,\Omega$, the noise factor of the receiver is equal to the milliammeter reading.

Example 9.15

In a measurement of the noise factor of a 50 Ω input resistance radio receiver, the reading of the output power meter is doubled when the noise generator's milliammeter indicates 6 mA. Calculate the noise factor of the receiver in dB.

Solution

$$F = 6 \quad \text{or} \quad 10 \log_{10} 6 = 7.78\,\text{dB} \qquad (Ans.)$$

Adjacent channel selectivity

The selectivity of a radio receiver is its ability to select the wanted signal from all the unwanted signals present at the aerial. The selectivity curves given in Figs 9.3 and 9.4 indicate how well the receiver rejects unwanted signals when the wanted signal is *not* present. This is, of course, not of prime interest since the important factor is the adjacent channel voltage needed to adversely affect reception of the wanted signal. This feature of a receiver is expressed by its adjacent channel response ratio which can be measured using the arrangement shown in Fig. 9.27.

With signal generator 2 producing zero output voltage, signal generator 1 is set to the required test frequency and then is modulated to a depth of 30%. With the input signal voltage at 10 mV, the a.f. gain of the receiver is adjusted to give an audio output power greater than 50 mW but below the overload point. The modulation of signal generator 1 is then switched off. Signal generator 2 is then set to a frequency that is 9 kHz above the test frequency and is modulated to a depth of 30%. The output voltage of signal generator 2 is then increased until the audio output power is 30 dB less than the previous value. The adjacent channel response ratio is the ratio of these voltages. The measurement can be carried out at a number of other frequencies and the results plotted (see Fig. 9.28).

When an FM receiver is measured, two signal generators are again

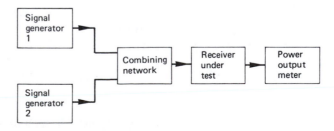

Fig. 9.27 Measurement of radio receiver adjacent channel response ratio

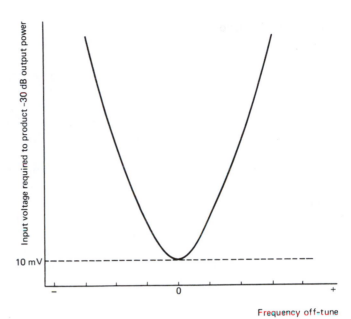

Fig. 9.28 Selectivity characteristic of a radio receiver

employed. One of the generators simulates the wanted signal modulated by a 1 kHz tone and its output voltage is adjusted to give the reference 12 dB SINAD level. The signal generator voltage is then increased by another 3 dB. The other signal generator is used to simulate the interfering signal and it is modulated with a 40 Hz tone. Its output voltage is increased until the SINAD is decreased back to its 12 dB reference level. The *desensitization* level of the receiver is then the ratio, in dB, of the off-channel signal voltage to the reference sensitivity of the receiver. The minimum acceptable figure is usually 70 dB. This measurement combines both selectivity and noise.

Image channel response ratio

The image channel response ratio (or rejection ratio) is the ratio

$$20 \log_{10}\left(\frac{\text{Input voltage at image frequency}}{\text{Input voltage at signal frequency}}\right) \quad (9.10)$$

to produce the same audio output power. The measurement can be carried out using the circuit given in Fig 9.24. The signal generator and the receiver are each tuned to the test frequency and the input voltage is adjusted to give an audio output power of 50 mW. Then, without altering any of the receiver controls, the frequency of the signal generator is altered to the image frequency. The input voltage is then increased until 50 mW audio output power is again registered by the power meter. The image response ratio is then given by the ratio of the two necessary input voltages, expressed in dB.

Frequency modulated stereo sound broadcast signals

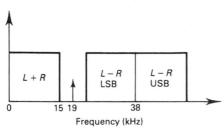

Fig. 9.29 Spectrum diagram of FM stereo radio

In a stereo radio transmitter two audio signals, known as the L and R signals, are both added and subtracted to obtain $(L + R)/2$ and $(L - R)/2$ signals. The $(L - R)/2$ signal is then used to amplitude modulate a 38 kHz sub-carrier. The carrier component is suppressed to produce a DSBSC signal. This is transmitted along with the $L + R$ signal and a 19 kHz low-level carrier; the spectrum diagram of the baseband signal is shown by Fig. 9.29. The baseband signal has a amplitude of either L or R, whichever is the larger, so that the frequency deviation of the carrier is no more than would result if it were to be frequency-modulated by the equivalent mono signal.

At the FM stereo receiver, the 19 kHz carrier is frequency-doubled to give a 38 kHz sub-carrier. The $(L - R)/2$ signal is demodulated against the 38 kHz sub-carrier and then it is added to the $(L + R)/2$ signal to give the L signal, and subtracted from the $(L + R)/2$ signal to give the R signal. A mono receiver uses only the $L + R$ term to produce an audio output signal.

Exercises

9.1 (a) Describe, with the aid of a block diagram, the functions of the various stages of a VHF communication radio receiver. (b) By means of a numerical example, illustrate the advantage of the double superheterodyne principle for the reception of a signal at a frequency of 90 MHz.

9.2 (a) Explain the terms *adjacent channel selectivity* and *image rejection*, and briefly explain which parts of the receiver principally determine its performance in each of these respects. (b) What bandwidth would be required in (i) the r.f. stages, (ii) the i.f. stages, (iii) the audio stages of a radio receiver if it is required to receive an amplitude-modulated signal in which the highest modulating frequency used is 4.5 kHz? (c) If a receiver has an intermediate frequency of 450 kHz, calculate the image frequency when it is tuned to a signal of 1400 kHz.

9.3 (a) Draw and explain a block diagram of a sound broadcast radio receiver. (b) Explain briefly the following terms: (i) image channel rejection, (ii) adjacent-channel selectivity, (iii) delayed automatic gain control. (c) List the factors which influence the choice of intermediate frequency for a radio receiver. Quote typical values of intermediate frequency for MF, HF and VHF receivers.

9.4 What is meant by (a) simple automatic gain control and (b) delayed automatic gain control? When and why are they used?

9.5 A receiver having an intermediate frequency of 465 kHz is required to tune over a range of 600 kHz to 1800 kHz with a ganged variable capacitor having a range of 320 pF per section. Calculate the values of (a) the minimum capacitance needed in the r.f. circuit; (b) the inductance required in the r.f. circuit; (c) the padding capacitance required in the local oscillator circuit, assuming that the minimum value of the capacitance is the same as that found in (a); (d) the inductance required to tune the local oscillator.

9.6 (a) Define the terms (i) *sensitivity* and (ii) *image channel response ratio* in relation to the performance of a superheterodyne radio receiver. Why is the image channel response generally lowest when the receiver is tuned to the highest frequency in its range? (b) A radio receiver with an i.f. of 465 kHz is tuned to an incoming sinusoidal signal of 1000 kHz. Assume the oscillator frequency to be above the signal frequency. What signal appears in the audio output if another unmodulated signal appears in the aerial at a frequency of (i) 1902 kHz, (ii) 1008 kHz, and (iii) 469 kHz? For each of these frequencies, state what factor in the receiver design affects the level of the output signal.

9.7 (a) With the aid of a block schematic diagram, describe the application of automatic fequency control to an FM radio receiver. Why is AFC more necessary at VHF than at lower frequencies? (b) an AFC discriminator produces 1 V of control bias for a frequency error of 50 kHz and the controlled oscillator is shifted by 250 kHz/V. Calculate the tuning error if the oscillator would have drifted 20 kHz from the correct frequency without AFC.

9.8 (a) Draw the block schematic diagram of an HF communication receiver. State the functions of each block. (b) What are the advantages of using integrated circuits in a receiver? (c) State some of the functional circuits which are currently available in IC form and draw a block diagram for a receiver using some, or all, of these ICs.

9.9 A superheterodyne receiver has $f_{if} = 470$ kHz. It is tuned over the frequency band 500−1500 kHz. (a) What range of frequencies must its local oscillator cover? What are (b) the lowest and (c) the highest image frequencies? (d) How can the image frequencies be suppressed?

9.10 (a) What is meant by *squelch* or *muting* as applied to radio receivers and why is it often applied to communication receivers? Why is it not applied to AM broadcast receivers? (b) Draw and explain the operation of a mute circuit.

10 Radio receiver circuits

The principles of operation of the superheterodyne radio receiver have been discussed in the previous chapter by considering the various sections of the receiver as blocks performing particular functions. The circuits of the various kinds of detector have been discussed in Chapter 2, while a.f. and r.f. amplifiers and oscillators are covered in *Electronics III*. Here the circuitry and principles of operation of some further radio receiver circuits will be given, namely VHF/UHF amplifiers, mixers, crystal, ceramic and SAW filters, automatic gain control, automatic frequency control and squelch or muting arrangements.

VHF/UHF amplifiers

An r.f. amplifier is always included in the r.f. stage of a radio receiver that operates at frequencies higher than about 3 MHz. In a sound broadcast receiver the r.f. amplifier is tuned to a particular frequency, but in many communication receivers a wideband amplifier is employed and image channel selectivity is obtained by the use of a filter.

A tuned amplifier is one which is required to handle a relatively narrow band of frequencies centred about a particular radio frequency. Such an amplifier has two main functions: first, to provide a specified gain over a given frequency band, and, second, to provide the selectivity necessary to ensure that frequencies outside the wanted band are not amplified. A parallel-resonant circuit is used as the collector load; this is tuned to the required operating frequency and designed to have the wanted 3 dB bandwidth. The required LC product is fairly small and is easily obtained; the capacitances inherent in the device and stray capacitances that adversely affect the performance of an untuned amplifier now contribute to the capacitance of the tuned circuit.

Very often the gain required from an amplifier is greater than can be obtained from a single stage, and then two or more stages may be coupled in cascade to produce the required gain. The overall gain A of a multi-stage amplifier is the product of the individual stage gains.

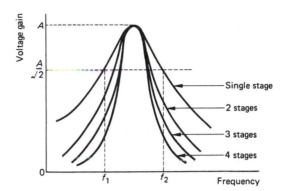

Fig. 10.1 Bandwidth shrinkage

For example, if the three stages of an amplifier have voltage gains of 10, 12, and 8 respectively, the overall gain of the circuit is 960. If four identical stages, each having a gain of 10, are cascaded, the overall gain is 10^4.

Cascading stages also has the effect of reducing the 3 dB bandwidth of the amplifier. Consider, for example, the four identical stages previously mentioned. Suppose the lower and upper 3 dB frequencies of each stage are f_1 and f_2 respectively; then the gain per stage at these frequencies is $10/\sqrt{2}$. The overall gain at frequencies f_1 and f_2 is $(10/\sqrt{2})^4$ or 1250. The overall gain at the centre frequency is 10^4 and 3 dB down on this value is $10^4/\sqrt{2} = 7071$. Clearly, the overall 3 dB bandwidth is narrower than the bandwidth f_2-f_1. The reduction in the 3 dB bandwidth caused by cascading stages is known as *bandwidth shrinkage*, which is illustrated by Fig. 10.1.

The overall bandwidth B_o of a tuned amplifier with n identical stages is

$$B_o = B\sqrt{(2^{1/n} - 1)} \qquad (10.1)$$

where B is the 3 dB bandwidth of a single stage.

Example 10.1

Calculate the overall bandwidth for a two-stage r.f. amplifier if the bandwidth of each identical stage is 12 kHz.

Solution

$$B = 12\sqrt{(2^{1/2} - 1)} = 7.723 \text{ kHz} \qquad (Ans.)$$

VHF amplifiers are often single-stage wideband transistor circuits. Fig. 10.2 shows the circuit of a VHF amplifier in which all the resistor values are low to obtain a wide bandwidth. The amplifier is connected in between two electronically tuned band-pass filters which provide all the r.f. selectivity.

A UHF wideband amplifier may have a similar circuit, except that extra power supply decoupling is necessary. Fig. 10.3 shows the circuit of a typical UHF amplifier.

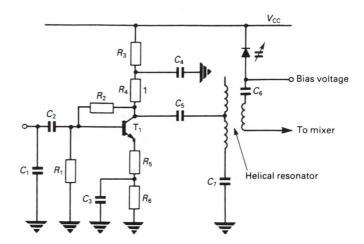

Fig. 10.2 VHF amplifier

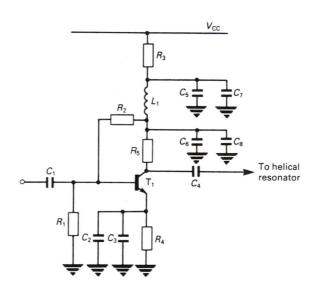

Fig. 10.3 UHF amplifier

The FET is often used in the r.f. stage of HF, VHF and UHF radio receivers because of its superior performance with regard to both cross-modulation and intermodulation. At the upper end of the UHF band, a FET connected in the common-gate configuration may be employed and Fig. 10.4 gives the circuit of a UHF FET amplifier.

Integrated circuit r.f. amplifiers

The Plessey SL 560C is a wideband r.f. amplifier whose pin connections are shown in Fig. 10.5(a). The IC can be operated with its input stage in either the common-base or the common-emitter configuration or as an amplifier connected between 50 Ω resistances. The circuit of a wideband amplifier with a common-emitter input working from a 9 V supply is shown in Fig. 10.5(b). If 6 V operation

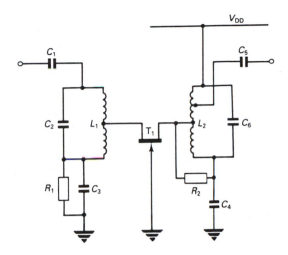

Fig. 10.4   UHF FET amplifier

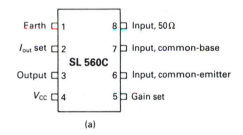

Fig. 10.5   (a) Pin connections of the SL 560C wideband r.f. amplifier, (b) typical circuit (courtesy of GEC Plessy Semiconductors)

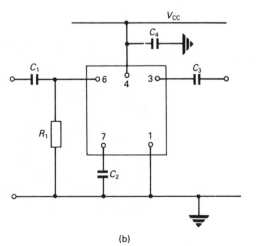

is required, the 10 kΩ resistor R_1 is removed from the circuit. The amplifier is able to provide 35 dB voltage gain with about 2 dB noise figure over a 75 MHz bandwidth. The voltage gain can be reduced and the bandwidth increased if the gain set pin 5 is connected to pin 4. Further increase in bandwidth can be obtained by connecting pin 5 to pin 1. The input transistor can be operated in common base by using pin 7 as the input terminal and decoupling pin 6 to earth via a capacitor. The maximum bandwidth is then obtained. Often the 560C

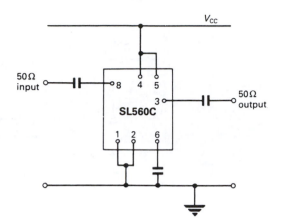

Fig. 10.6 Use of the SL 650C between 50 Ω resistances (courtesy of GEC Plessy Semiconductors)

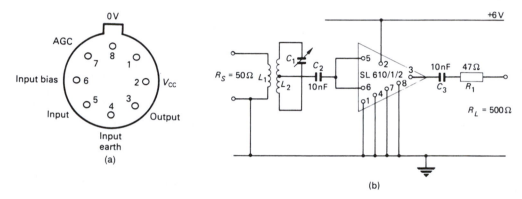

Fig. 10.7 (a) Pin connections of the SL 610/1/2 r.f. amplifier (b) r.f. amplifier using SL 610/1/2 (Courtesy GEC Plessy Semiconductors)

is used between two 50 Ω resistances, and Fig. 10.6 shows the circuit used.

Plessey also offer several other r.f. amplifier ICs, including the SL 610, 611 and 612 r.f./i.f. amplifiers. The gain of these ICs may be AGC controlled, and their maximum gains and bandwidths are 20 dB/120 MHz, 26 dB/80 MHz and 34 dB/15 MHz respectively. The pin connections of the IC are shown by Fig. 10.7(a), and Fig. 10.7(b) shows the device connected as an r.f. amplifier.

Mixers

A mixer is a circuit whose function is to translate a signal from one frequency band to another. There are two basic methods by which mixers operate: either the signal and the output of a local oscillator are *added* together and then applied in series with a square-law device, or the two signals are *multiplied* together in a dual-gate MOSFET.

An additive mixer must include a device having a non-linear input voltage–output current characteristic; this device may be a diode or a suitably biased FET or bipolar transistor.

When a sinusoidal signal at frequency f_s is applied to the input of a mixer, the output current of the circuit contains components at the following frequencies:

- the signal frequency f_s
- the sum and difference $f_o \pm f_s$ of the signal and the local oscillator frequencies
- the local oscillator frequency f_o

Additive mixing

An additive mixer is shown in Fig. 10.8. The transistor is biased with a low collector current so that it is operated on the non-linear part of its characteristics. The local oscillator signal is introduced into the base-emitter circuit via the inductances L_5 and L_6 and the signal voltage is inserted in series with the oscillator voltage via inductors L_1 and L_2. The collector current then contains the wanted difference frequency component plus various other components. The collector circuit is tuned so that the wanted component is selected and all other frequencies are rejected.

Many cheap sound broadcast receivers employ the self-oscillating mixer shown in Fig. 10.9, since it does not need a separate local oscillator. Inductors L_3, L_4 and L_6, capacitors C_1 and C_2 and the transistor form the oscillator part of the circuit. Energy is fed from the collector circuit to the L_6C_2 circuit, which is tuned to resonate at the desired frequency of oscillation. The oscillatory current set up in inductor L_6 induces a voltage, at the oscillation frequency, into the emitter circuit of the transistor in series with the signal voltage. Mixing takes place because of the non-linearity of the transistor characteristics, and the difference frequency component of the collector current is

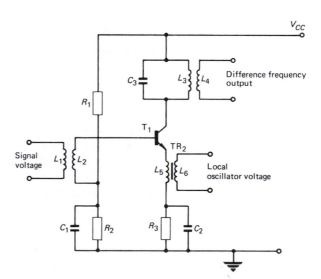

Fig. 10.8 Bipolar transistor mixer

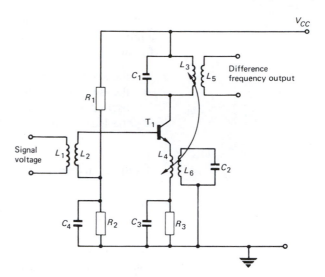

Fig. 10.9 Self-oscillating mixer

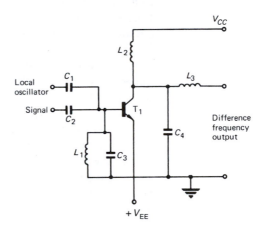

Fig. 10.10 A VHF mixer

amplified by the transistor and then selected by the collector-tuned circuit C_1L_3.

The two previous mixer circuits have both introduced the local oscillator voltage into the emitter circuit. Other methods are possible, and Fig. 10.10 shows the circuit of a VHF mixer in which both signal and local oscillator voltages are fed into the base circuit. L_1 and C_3 tune the input circuit of the mixer to the signal frequency, and C_1 and C_2 couple the local oscillator and signal frequency circuits to the mixer. L_2 is provided to prevent a.c. currents from passing into the collector supply, and C_4 and L_3 match the mixer to the output circuit and select the difference frequency component of the collector current.

Important features of a mixer are (a) its conversion conductance, given by

$$\left(\frac{\text{Difference frequency component of the output current}}{\text{r.f. input signal voltage}}\right) \quad (10.2)$$

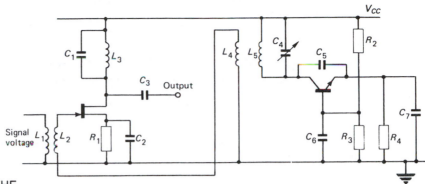

Fig. 10.11 FET mixer and VHF oscillator

and (b) its cross-modulation performance. Cross-modulation is the transfer of the modulation of an unwanted carrier onto the wanted carrier, and it can occur in a mixer if its mutual characteristic includes a cubic term. The mutual characteristic of a FET more nearly approaches the ideal square law and consequently FETs are often employed as mixers. Fig. 10.11 shows a typical FET mixer circuit together with an example of an oscillator circuit which is often used at VHF.

Multiplicative mixing

Multiplicative mixing can be achieved by applying the signal and the local oscillator voltages to the two inputs of a dual-gate MOSFET, and Fig. 10.12 shows a dual-gate MOSFET mixer circuit. The oscillator voltage is applied to gate 1 of the MOSFET and the signal

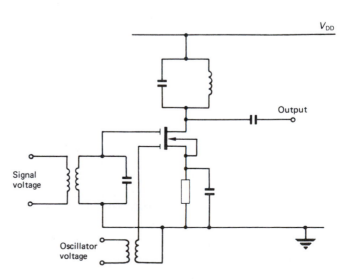

Fig. 10.12 Dual-gate MOSFET mixer

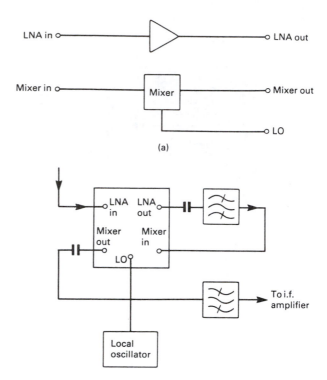

Fig. 10.13 (a) Basic block diagram of the LMX 2216B, (b) use as front end in a UHF receiver

voltage is applied to gate 2. The oscillator voltage varies the mutual conductance of the MOSFET and, since $I_d = g_m V_s$, the a.c. component of the drain current is proportional to the product of the instantaneous values of the signal and the local oscillator voltages. The drain current contains components at a number of different frequencies, among which is the wanted difference $f_o - f_s$ component. Multiplicative mixing has two advantages over additive mixing: firstly, the signal and local oscillator circuits are isolated from one another, which prevents oscillator pulling; and, secondly, its conversion conductance is higher. On the other hand, multiplicative mixing is a noisier process than additive mixing.

The balanced modulator shown in Fig. 3.11 can also be used as a mixer; then the modulating signal and carrier inputs are read, respectively, as the r.f. and local oscillator voltages. The output voltage of the circuit is then, of course, the required difference frequency component.

There are also some ICs that are a combined r.f. amplifier and mixer, and an example is shown in Fig. 10.13(a). The National Semiconductor LMX 2216B is intended for use in hand-held VHF/UHF radio receivers. The amplifier and the mixer are both wideband circuits, all the necessary selectivity being provided by external filters. This is shown by Fig. 10.13(b).

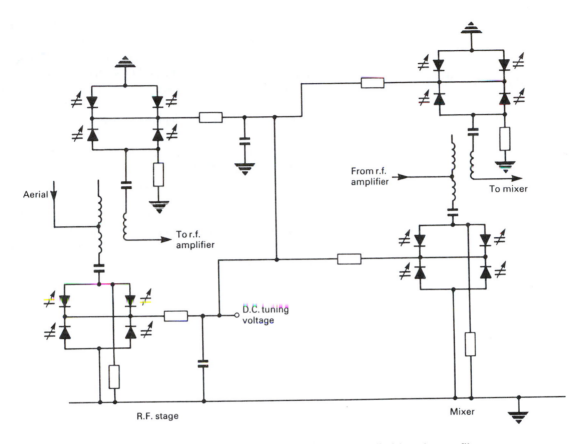

Fig. 10.14 Electronically controlled band-pass filter

Filters

Electronically controlled band-pass filters

In VHF communication receivers, r.f. selectivity is often obtained by the use of electronically tuned filters. A typical arrangement is shown in Fig. 10.14. The filter consists of two pairs of coupled helical resonators which are tuned to the required signal frequency by a number of varactor diodes. A d.c. bias voltage is applied to the diodes in both filters to vary their capacitance and hence tune the filters to the signal frequency. The tuning voltage is passed through an RC low-pass filter to remove any a.c. components that may be present.

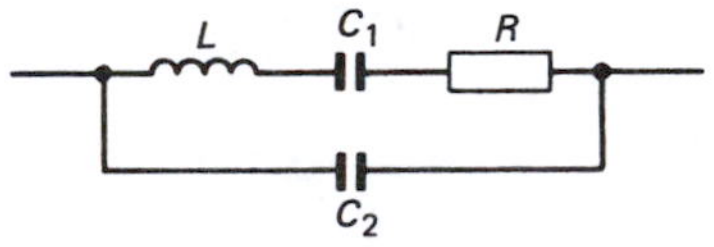

Crystal filters

The electrical equivalent circuit of a piezo-electric crystal is shown in Fig. 10.15. The inductance L represents the inertia of the crystal, capacitance C_1 represents the crystal's compliance (1/stiffness) and the resistance R provides losses which are equivalent to the frictional

Fig. 10.15 Electrical equivalent circuit of a piezo-electric crystal

losses of the crystal. Lastly, the shunt capacitor C_2 is the actual electrical capacitance of the crystal. A series-parallel circuit of this kind has two resonant frequencies: one is the resonant frequency of the series circuit LC_1R and the other is the frequency at which parallel resonance occurs between shunt capacitor C_2 and the net (inductive) reactance of the series arm. Obviously, the parallel-resonant frequency is higher than the frequency of series resonance. The crystal will pass, with little attenuation, all frequencies in between the series and parallel-resonant frequencies. Often this bandwidth is too narrow and when this is the case it can be widened by connecting an inductor of suitable value in series with the crystal. The added inductance has this effect because it will reduce the series-resonant frequency of the crystal without affecting its parallel-resonant frequency. Usually, this technique is only employed at the lower frequencies since, when the centre frequency is high, the bandwidth, as a percentage of the centre frequency, is likely to be wide enough.

A crystal filter circuit is shown in Fig. 10.16. The crystal is chosen to be one whose series-resonant frequency is equal to the required passband's lowest frequency. The parallel resonant frequency of the crystal, and hence the upper passband frequency, is adjusted to the required figure by means of the variable capacitor C_3. The selectivity of the circuit is partly determined by the load impedance of the filter and this can, to some extent, be varied by adjustment of C_4 and/or R_1.

A wider bandwidth filter can be obtained by the use of two crystals connected as shown in Fig. 10.17. The series-resonant frequencies of the crystals are chosen to differ from one another by a frequency equal to the wanted passband; this may be only a few hundred hertz if telegraphy signals are to be received, or about 3 kHz for the reception of an SSB signal. Capacitor C_4 is provided to allow for fine adjustment of the bandwidth provided.

Even better selectivity characteristics can be obtained, but at greater expense, if four crystals are connected to form a lattice network (see Fig. 10.18).

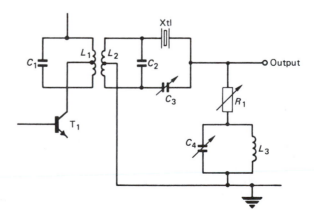

Fig. 10.16 Crystal filter

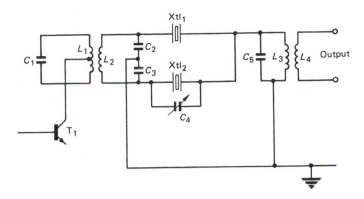

Fig. 10.17 Two-crystal filter

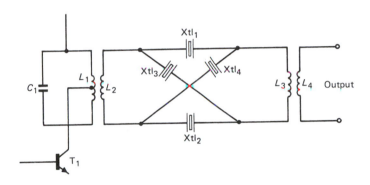

Fig. 10.18 Crystal lattice filter

The two series crystals are chosen so that their common series-resonant frequencies lie within the required passband and they offer little attentuation to a narrow band of frequencies on either side of this frequency. The two parallel crystals are selected so that their parallel-resonant frequencies are equal to the series-resonant frequencies of the series crystals. Therefore they will not shunt signals in the wanted passband. At frequencies outside the required passband, the series crystals will have a high impedance and the parallel crystals will have a low impedance, and the network will offer considerable attenuation.

Crystal filters are available in a number of standard frequencies, such as 9 MHz, 10.7 MHz, 21.4 MHz and 45 MHz, and so these values are often chosen as the intermediate frequencies of radio receivers.

Ceramic filters

The piezo-electric effect is also obtained when a ceramic disc has electrode plates mounted on each of its two faces, the resonant frequencies and selectivity characteristic being determined mainly by the shapes and dimensions of the electrodes and the disc. The make-up of a ceramic filter is shown in Fig. 10.19(a); this type of filter,

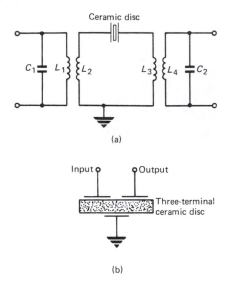

(a)

(b)

Fig. 10.19 Ceramic filter

available as a complete sealed unit, is usually manufactured for use at one of the standard AM sound broadcast receiver intermediate frequencies. The input and output tuned circuits are both arranged to be resonant at the centre frequency of the desired passband. Ceramic filters for use at the higher frequencies, such as the standard 10.7 MHz intermediate frequency of many VHF receivers, are usually of the three-electrode type shown in Fig. 10.19(b).

Ceramic resonators are available in a number of standard frequencies, such as 455, 640 and 800 kHz, and 2, 4, 5 and 6 MHz.

SAW filter

A *surface acoustic wave* (SAW) filter consists of a pair of comb-shaped transducers that have been deposited upon the surface of a piezo-electric substrate. The basic structure is shown in Fig. 10.20. When an electrical signal is applied to the input transducer, it is converted

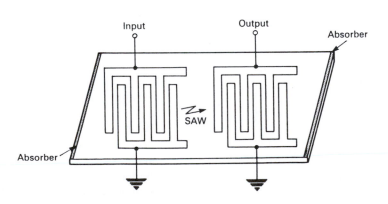

Fig. 10.20 SAW filter

into a surface acoustic wave that propagates in both directions from the transducer. The power sent in one direction is completely absorbed by the absorber and is lost. The other half of the acoustic power is transmitted along the surface of the substrate to the output transducer and here it is converted back into electrical form. The minimum loss of the SAW filter is 6 dB when the frequency of the input signal is such that the spacing of the comb teeth is equal to the signal wavelength. At all other frequencies, when the comb spacing is not equal to the signal wavelength the loss of the filter increases rapidly. This means that a SAW filter has a very selective loss-frequency characteristic.

SAW filters are available at a number of standard frequencies, such as 45,100 and 405 MHz.

Ceramic, crystal and SAW filters possess the advantages of being small in size, reliable and insensitive to external magnetic fields, requiring no alignment, and having a selectivity that is not affected by the application of AGC to an i.f. amplifier stage. Ceramic filters are cheaper than crystal or SAW filters and are used in both sound broadcast and mobile radio receivers. Crystal filters are used in both HF and VHF communication receivers.

Automatic gain control

The signals arriving at the input terminals of a radio receiver are subject to continual fading, and automatic gain control (AGC) must be employed to keep the output of the receiver more or less constant. The function of an AGC system is to vary the gain of a receiver to maintain a reasonably constant output power even though there are large variations in the input signal level. This means that the gain of the receiver must be reduced by the AGC system when a large-amplitude input signal is received, and increased for a small input signal. The variation in the receiver gain also serves to prevent the output level changing overmuch as the receiver is tuned from one station to another, and it also avoids a.f. amplifier distortion caused by overloading on larger input signals.

Simple AGC

The voltage appearing across the load resistor of a diode detector contains a d.c. component, the magnitude of which is directly proportional to the amplitude of the carrier voltage. This d.c. voltage is available for use as the AGC voltage and can be fed to the controlled stages in the manner shown in Fig. 10.21. With the diode D_1 connected as shown, the d.c. voltage developed across the load resistor R_2 is positive with respect to earth; if a negative voltage is required the diode D_1 must be reversed. The AGC voltage is fed to the controlled stages via a filter network $C_3 R_1$ to remove the various a.c. components that are superimposed upon it. The time constant of the

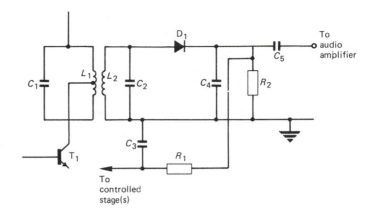

Fig. 10.21 Derivation of simple AGC voltage

filter should be chosen to ensure that the AGC voltage will not vary with the modulation envelope but will respond to the most rapid fades to be expected. The time constant is equal to $4CR$ seconds because of the sinusoidal input signal to the circuit rather than a d.c. drive. Typically, the time constant is 0.05 to 0.5 seconds.

Delayed AGC

In a simple AGC system, the AGC voltage starts to increase as soon as a signal is received and hence the sensitivity of the receiver is reduced. However, it is better if the gain of the receiver is not reduced until the signal level at the detector input has reached the level at which the rated output power of the a.f. stage can be developed. This is the function of *delayed AGC*. A delayed AGC system will not produce any AGC voltage until the carrier level at the output of the detector is greater than some predetermined value. This means that the diode that produces the AGC voltage must be biased into its non-conducting state by a delay voltage of suitable magnitude. The signal diode cannot be biased into non-conduction and so it is necessary to use a separate diode for the AGC voltage.

Fig. 10.22 shows a typical circuit. The signal diode D_1 is operated as a normal diode detector with a load resistor R_1. The AGC diode D_2 has a positive bias voltage $VR_4/(R_3+R_4)$ at its n terminal and will not conduct until the signal voltage appearing at its p terminal is greater than the bias voltage. When diode D_2 conducts, the AGC voltage is developed across R_4 and is fed to the controlled stages via the filter network C_5R_2. The AGC diode is supplied from the collector of T_1 to obtain as large a voltage as possible.

FM receiver main AGC

A main AGC loop may sometimes be applied to an FM receiver to ensure that the signal level to the input of the limiter stage is always

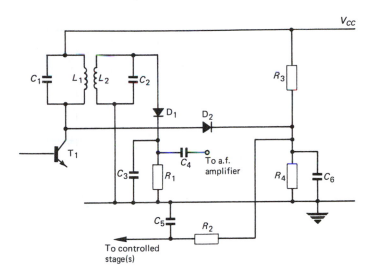

Fig. 10.22 Derivation of delayed AGC voltage

large enough for the limiting action to take place. The AGC voltage can be obtained from the d.c. load capacitor of a ratio detector or, if a ratio detector is not used, from the limiter stage itself. Alternatively, a separate AGC diode can be employed.

Applying the AGC voltage to the controlled stage

The current gain of a bipolar transistor is a function of its emitter current and Fig. 10.23 shows a typical gain-emitter current characteristic. At low values of emitter current, the current gain of a transistor increases with increase in its emitter current in a more or less linear manner. Conversely, at high values of emitter current, an increase in the emitter current produces a fall in the current gain. Two methods are therefore available for varying the gain of an AGC controlled stage in a radio receiver: increasing the gain by increasing the emitter current is known as *reverse AGC*, while increasing the gain by decreasing the emitter current is known as *forward AGC*. In either case the emitter current is most easily controlled by variation of the base-emitter forward bias voltage of the transistor, since minimum power is then taken from the AGC line.

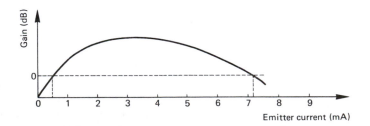

Fig. 10.23 Gain-emitter current characteristic of a bipolar transistor

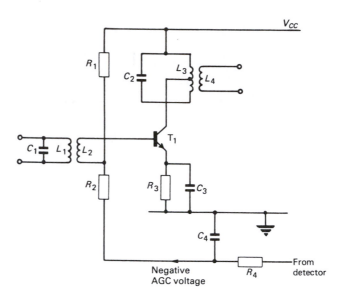

Fig. 10.24 Reverse AGC

Reverse AGC

Fig. 10.24 shows the application of *reverse AGC* to a transistor tuned amplifier. The negative polarity AGC voltage determines the forward bias voltage applied to the transistor T_1. An increase in the carrier level at the input to the detector stage will make the AGC voltage become more negative. The base potential of T_1 relative to earth will become less positive and the transistor will conduct a smaller emitter current. The voltage gain of the amplifier will therefore fall and the carrier level at the detector will be reduced, tending to compensate for the original increase.

Forward AGC

When *forward AGC* is to be applied to an amplifier, a resistor is connected in series with the collector tuned circuit to increase the gain variation produced by a given AGC voltage. A typical forward AGC circuit is given in Fig. 10.25. When the positive AGC voltage increases, because of an increase in the received carrier voltage, the forward bias of the transistor is also increased. The transistor conducts a larger current and so its current gain falls; the fall in gain is accentuated by the collector-emitter voltage also falling because of the increased voltage drop across the series resistor R_2.

Comparison of reverse and forward AGC

The relative merits of reverse and forward AGC are as follows. Reverse AGC controls the gain of a stage by varying its emitter current; to reduce the gain, the emitter current must be reduced and

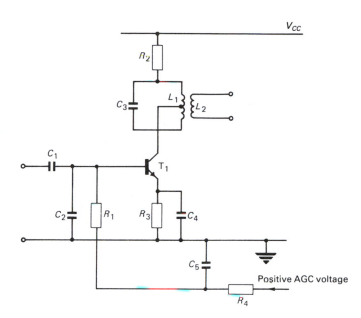

Fig. 10.25 Forward AGC

as a result the output resistance of the transistor increases. This, in turn, reduces the damping effect of the transistor on the collector tuned circuit and so reduces the bandwidth of the stage. The reduction in emitter current, and hence in the collector current, also has the effect of reducing the signal-handling capability of the stage — at the very time it is being called upon to handle a signal of larger amplitude. Conversely, with forward AGC, a decrease in the voltage gain of a stage is obtained by increasing the emitter and collector currents and is therefore associated with an increase in both the bandwidth and the signal handling capacity of the stage. Also, the d.c. collector current taken from the supply is greater with forward AGC than with reverse AGC and this is undesirable with a battery-operated equipment.

In an ISB/SSB communication receiver, the AGC system is often operated from a low-level pilot carrier which is filtered off from the wanted signal. If there is no pilot carrier, it is possible to derive an AGC voltage from the received signal itself, either at the i.f. amplifier or the a.f. amplifier stages.

AGC generator

SSB radio receivers are often provided with a circuit known as an *AGC generator* that generates an AGC voltage from the demodulated audio waveform. The block diagram of the SL 621 AGC generator is shown in Fig. 10.26(a), and Fig. 10.26(b) shows how the IC is connected in an SSB receiver.

Essentially, the circuit consists of an a.f. amplifier coupled to a d.c. amplifier by two detectors. The time constants of the detectors

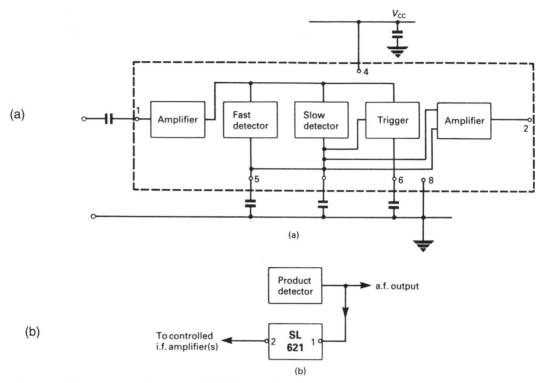

Fig. 10.26 SL 621 AGC generator (Courtesy GEC Plessy Semiconductors)

are set by externally connected capacitors, and they are given short falltimes and long risetimes. The audio input signal will quickly be rectified by the fast detector to provide an AGC voltage across C_1. The output voltage of the slow detector, which is developed across C_2, will increase and soon take control of providing the AGC voltage. C_2 is provided with a discharge path via the trigger circuit. The AGC system is able to follow signals that vary at a rate no greater than 20 dB/s. If the input signal should change at a faster rate than this, or disappear completely during pauses in the received speech, the trigger circuit will remove the discharge path for C_2. Capacitor C_2 will then hold its charge, and hence the AGC voltage, at its last value for about one second. The output of the fast detector falls to zero. At the end of the hold time, C_2 discharges so that there is no AGC voltage and then the full gain of the receiver is restored.

Automatic frequency control

The d.c. voltage needed to activate the automatic frequency control (AFC) system of a frequency-modulation radio receiver can be derived from the audio load capacitor of the ratio detector. Fig. 10.27 shows the operation of an AFC system. When the average value of the intermediate frequency of the receiver is correct, the voltage appearing across the audio load capacitor C_4 has zero d.c. component and the

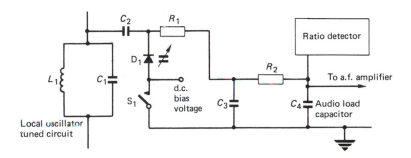

Fig. 10.27 Application of AFC voltage in a radio receiver

capacitance of the varactor diode is determined by the applied bias voltage. If the average value of the intermediate frequency should drift from its nominal value, the voltage developed across the audio load capacitor will have a d.c. component. This d.c. voltage is applied to the varactor diode to add to or subtract from (depending upon its polarity) the bias voltage and so vary the diode capacitance. This variation in the diode capacitance alters the frequency of the local oscillator in the direction necessary to reduce the error in the intermediate frequency. Capacitor C_3 and resistor R_2 act as a low-pass filter to remove all a.c. voltages from the AFC line.

Squelch or muting

A sensitive radio receiver will have a very high gain between its aerial terminals and its detector stage. When it is not receiving a carrier, and so develops zero AGC voltage, its full voltage gain will be made available to amplify the noise unavoidably present at its input stage. As a result, there will be a high noise level at the output of the audio amplifier, which may cause considerable annoyance to the user of the receiver. To reduce or eliminate this annoyance, either the a.f. amplifier can be cut off, or its voltage gain can be severely reduced, whenever there is no input carrier signal; this is the function of a squelch, or muting, circuit.

A squelch circuit is given in Fig. 10.28. When a carrier voltage

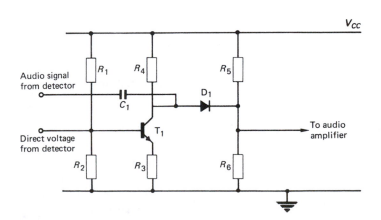

Fig. 10.28 Squelch or muting circuit

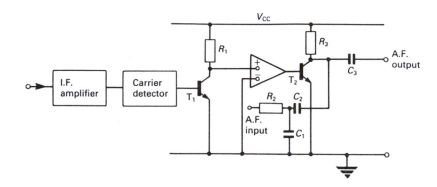

Fig. 10.29 Squelch circuit

is present at the detector input, a direct voltage, proportional to the carrier level, is applied to the base of transistor T_1. The polarity of this d.c. voltage is such that T_1 is turned off and the collector potential of the transistor rises to $+V_{CC}$ volts. The diode D_1 conducts and the audio-frequency output voltage of the signal detector is able to pass to the a.f. amplifier. With zero carrier voltage at the detector input, transistor T_1 is able to conduct and its collector potential falls to a lower positive value than is present at the junction of resistors R_5 and R_6. Diode D_1 is now biased into its non-conducting state and prevents noise voltages appearing at the detector output and passing on to the a.f. amplifier.

Figure 10.29 shows a squelch circuit used in VHF communication receivers. When the carrier level falls below the carrier detect voltage, the transistor T_1 turns OFF and the voltage applied to the + terminal of the op-amp goes high. The output of the op-amp goes into its positive saturation state and this turns T_2 ON. The collector voltage of T_2 is then very nearly zero volts and the a.f. output is muted. When the carrier detect voltage goes higher than the trip level, T_2 is turned OFF and the a.f. signal is able to pass through to the output terminal of the circuit. R_2 and C_1 form the de-emphasis circuit.

Very often it is thought desirable for operational reasons for the squelch system not to cut off the a.f. amplifier but, instead, to reduce its gain to a low value. The output noise level can generally be varied by means of an adjustable squelch circuit control.

Radio receiver integrated circuits

There are a number of ICs available that provide much of the circuitry required for a radio receiver.

SL 6601

The SL 6601 is intended for use with hand-held NBFM receivers, such as cellular telephones, and it contains an i.f. amplifier, a mixer and local oscillator, a phase-locked loop detector and an a.f. amplifier. A squelch circuit is also provided. The block diagram of the IC is shown by Fig. 10.30(a) and a typical circuit using the device is given in Fig. 10.30(b). The circuit is able to operate over the frequency band 455 kHz to 25 MHz, although usually the first intermediate frequency is 10.7 MHz and the second intermediate frequency is 100 kHz.

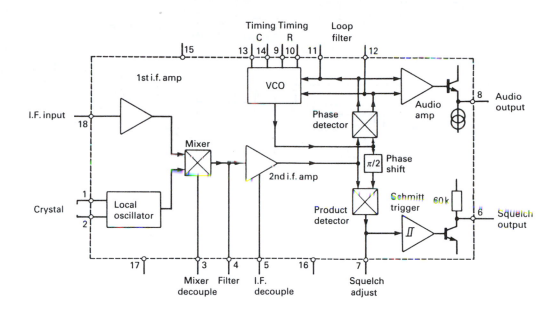

(a)

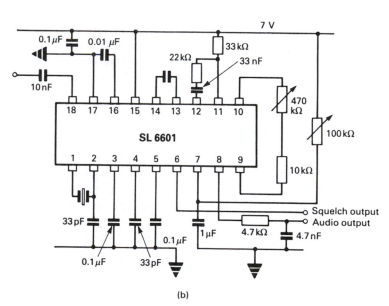

(b)

Fig. 10.30 (a) SL 6601 radio IC. (b) Typical circuit using the SL 6601 (Courtesy GEC Plessy Semiconductors)

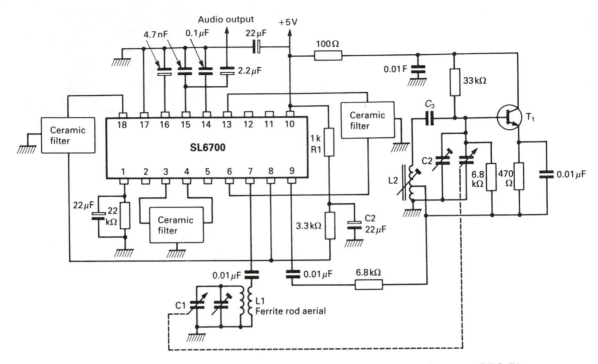

Fig. 10.31 The SL 6700 connected as AM sound broadcast radio receiver (Courtesy GEC Plessy Semiconductors)

SL 6700

The SL 6700 is intended for use in AM radio receivers and it includes first and second i.f. amplifiers, a double-balanced mixer, a detector, and AGC and noise-blanking circuits. Fig. 10.31 shows how the IC can be connected to operate as an AM sound broadcast receiver.

NE 546

The NE 546 contains an r.f. amplifier, a mixer, a local oscillator, an i.f. amplifier and an AGC detector. With any linear integrated circuits, any necessary inductors and capacitors and large-value resistors must be provided externally. Fig. 10.32 shows a simplified example of this. The gain-frequency characteristics of the r.f. and i.f. amplifiers and the mixer are determined by the tuned circuits shown. The AGC voltage line must have a particular time constant and this is provided by capacitor C_7.

Exercises

10.1 Sketch and describe the circuit of a mixer with a following i.f. amplifier stage suitable for a medium-wave radio receiver.

$C_3 = C_6 = 0.1 \mu F$
$C_8 = 22 \mu F$
$C_7 = 3 \, pF$
$C_1 = 13–190 \, pF$
$C_5 = 12–80 \, pF$

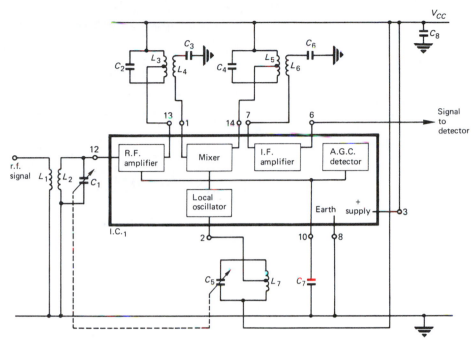

Fig. 10.32 Use of an integrated circuit in a radio receiver

10.2 (a) Give reasons for the use of AGC in a radio receiver designed for the reception of (i) AM signals, (ii) FM signals. (b) Draw and explain a circuit that shows how the AGC voltage can be applied to an i.f. amplifier.

10.3 With the aid of a circuit diagram, explain the operation of the mixer and local oscillator of an AM sound broadcast receiver. If the input signal to a mixer consists of two sinusoidal waves, at what frequencies do the significant components of the output occur?

10.4 (a) Draw the circuit diagram of a ratio detector which will produce a suitable output to control the frequency of the receiver oscillator section. (b) Explain how the AFC voltage is produced by the circuit given in (a) and describe how this voltage maintains the local oscillator at the required frequency.

10.5 Fig. 10.33 shows the block schematic diagram of an integrated circuit that has been designed for use in a radio receiver. Draw a diagram to show the external components which are necessary.

10.6 What is meant by the term *squelch* as applied to a radio receiver? Draw a squelch circuit and explain its operation.

10.7 (a) Draw the circuit of a VHF amplifier. State the precautions necessary in construction and earthing. (b) A VHF amplifier uses three identical stages, each having a gain of 5 and a bandwidth of 100 MHz. Calculate the overall gain and bandwidth of the amplifier.

10.8 (a) Draw and explain the circuit of a VHF mixer. (b) A VHF mixer has a 0.5 V signal at 90 MHz and a 2 V carrier at 100.7 MHz applied to it. If the conversion conductance is 0.5 mS, calculate the amplitude and frequency of the difference frequency component of the mixer's output current.

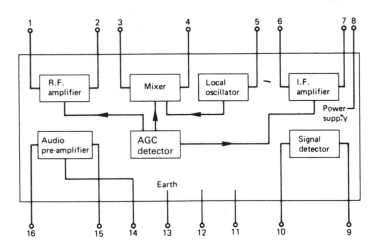

Fig. 10.33

11 Mobile radio systems

Modern telecommunication networks include a large number of different mobile radio systems which can be placed into one of several categories such as *private land mobile radio* (PMR), *cellular radio, cordless telephones*, and *paging systems*. PMR systems can be broadly divided into three groups:

(a) emergency — the ambulance, fire and police services;
(b) public utilities — the gas, electricity and water companies;
(c) private — delivery vans, taxis, mini-cabs, plumbers and various other users of mobile telephones.

The user of a PMR system does not have access to the *public switched telephone network* (PSTN) and the geographical area covered is usually no larger than about 30 miles in diameter. In a basic PMR system a dispatcher calls mobiles over a channel that is assigned for the duration of the conversation. Cellular radio provides a user with a mobile connection to the PSTN that may be used like a conventional telephone instrument (except that, since charges are high, calls ought to be as brief as possible!). Calls can also be made to other mobiles. The cellular radio system is therefore required to provide nationwide coverage.

PMR is considerably cheaper for a user to operate than cellular radio, both for connection to a network and for everyday running costs. PMR users generally require a despatch facility which allows mobiles to be simultaneously contacted via an open channel. This facility is not possible with cellular radio. In either the PMR or the cellular system a mobile transceiver may be car-mounted or it may be hand-held.

Portable computers are now widely accepted in business and may be used in conjunction with a mobile telephone to provide a data link. Such a data link may be used for such purposes as the transmission of spreadsheets and documents and the dynamic up-dating of the schedules of mobile personnel. Off-site users are able to gain access to their company's mainframe computer to obtain information.

Paging systems are also used to alert people that they are wanted on the telephone. Some paging receivers let the holder know who is calling.

Private mobile radio

A two-way PMR system may consist of just two transceivers, a base station and several mobile transceivers, or several inter-connected base stations and a large number of mobiles. Users of a PMR system are allocated a specific r.f. channel over which they can communicate. With the ever-increasing demand for mobile radio facilities, radio channels are becoming congested and users may have to share channels with other users. Also, adjacent channel interference is a potential problem. To overcome this congestion, a system known as *trunked PMR*, which allocates channels to users in a different way, is often employed.

The simplest way of operating a PMR system is shown in Fig. 11.1. The system operates in the single-frequency simplex mode and uses a single aerial that is switched between the receiver and the transmitter. A mobile is only able to communicate with the control.

A different frequency may be used for each direction of transmission to provide double-frequency simplex operation of a radio channel. The basic idea is illustrated by Fig. 11.2. Although this method of operation would appear to be more expensive in its use of the frequency spectrum than single-frequency working, it allows systems

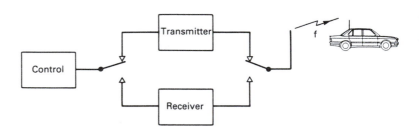

Fig. 11.1 Simplest PMR system

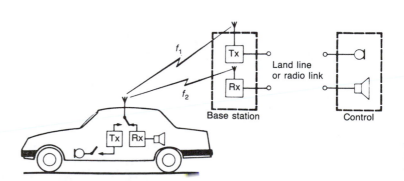

Fig. 11.2 Double-frequency simplex operation of a mobile radio link

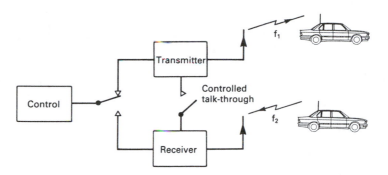

Fig. 11.3 PMR system with talkthrough

operating on the same frequency to be more closely spaced by a factor of about three. Channel carrier frequencies are allocated on an area basis and so nine times as many channels in a given area can be accommodated if double-frequency working is used instead of single-frequency. Since two frequencies are required, the net gain is about 4.5 times.

Double-frequency working also provides another advantage: all the transmitters are allocated carrier frequencies in one block and all the receivers are allocated frequencies in another block. This makes it easy to provide the necessary high receiver selectivity.

The slightly more complex arrangement shown in Fig. 11.3 provides for two-way communication between the control centre and each mobile, as well as allowing for communication between two mobiles. Talkthrough may be only possible under the control of the system operator, or it may be possible for selected mobiles to initiate talkthrough without recourse to the control. For this system it is necessary to have either separate receive and transmit aerials or a single aerial fed via a duplexer.

The allocation of the actual frequency bands to be used is determined by the telephone administration and then the blocks of frequencies are selected within a band to give the largest number of channels together with the minimum possible level of intermodulation. A considerable number of different frequency bands, of various widths, have been allocated to land, sea and air mobile services in the VHF and UHF bands. The complete list of frequencies is too long to include in this book, but Table 11.1 gives some examples.

Since frequencies in either the VHF band or the UHF band are employed, the service area provided by a base station transmitter is of limited size. This means that a number of interconnected base stations may be required to cover a large area and Fig. 11.4 shows a typical arrangement. Mobiles are not allocated a particular fixed carrier frequency; instead, a number of channels are provided and one of them is allocated to a mobile as and when required. The operation of such a system is not as simple as it perhaps might seem, largely because the signal received by a mobile may be the resultant of the signals produced by more than one base station, or,

Table 11.1

Frequency band	Used by
71.5–78.0	PMR
80.0–85.0	Emergencies
85.0–88.0	PMR
97.0–102.0	Emergencies
105.0–108.0	PMR
108.0–136.0	Aero
138.0–141.0	PMR
146.0–148.0	Emergencies
156.0–163.0	Maritime
165.0–173.0	PMR
425.0–449.5	PMR
451.0–452.0	Emergencies
453.0–462.5	PMR
465.0–466.0	Emergencies

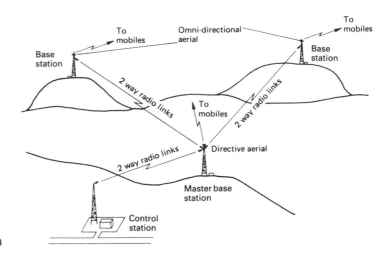

Fig. 11.4 Base-mobile radio system

alternatively, the mobile signal arriving at the control may have come via two or more base station receivers.

Selective signalling

Open channel

In many PMR systems, the driver of a vehicle must keep the radio receiver turned on at all times and must continuously listen for his/her call sign or number to be broadcast by the dispatcher. The driver can then answer the call to receive the message. This system is known as *open channel* and it has two main disadvantages:

- the need for the driver to be continually listening for his/her call sign;
- a lack of confidentiality.

Some PMR users, such as taxi and hire-car firms, are expected to continue using this system but many other users prefer a system in which an individual mobile can be contacted privately.

Five-tone signalling

The basic set-up for a five-tone signalling system is shown by Fig. 11.5. All mobile receivers automatically listen for their own identifying code to be transmitted by the base station and if this code is recognized, the receiver automatically responds and an audible signal is heard by the user. The receiver also automatically transmits back its code to the base station so that it is positively identified as the wanted mobile receiver. This system increases the overall efficiency and effectiveness of a mobile system, since it eliminates the need for unnecessary verbal messages. The identifying code is

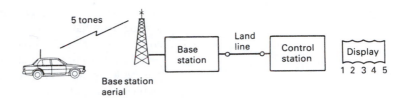

Fig. 11.5 Five-tone signalling

made up of five tones that are transmitted in sequence. When a mobile wants to initiate a call, its identifying code is sent to the base station and thence to the control centre where its number appears on a display. Further, if there is more than one control point in a system, a mobile can be given the ability to call any particular control centre.

Continuous tone controlled squelch system

The continuous tone controlled squelch system (CTCSS) is a system in which the r.f. carrier frequency is continuously modulated at the transmitter by a low audio-frequency tone. The tones used include 67, 74.4, 79.7, 85.4, 91.5 and 97.4 Hz.

When a CTCSS signal is received by a receiver that is fitted with the CTCSS facility, it can be used to provide one of the following features:

● remote selection of a facility, such as talkthrough;
● minimization of co-channel interference;
● selective calling of base stations.

CTCSS can be used to remotely switch a base station into its *talkthrough* mode, so that the base station can act as a repeater station. Figure 11.6 shows the principle of remote-controlled talkthrough. The

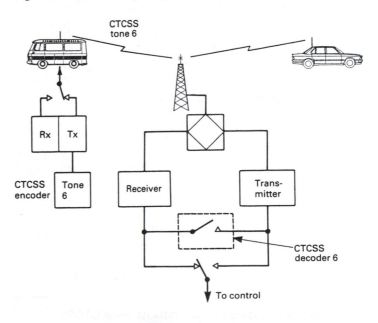

Fig. 11.6 Talkthrough controlled by CTCSS

mobile transceiver is set to operate on one of the CTCSS tones (number 6 in the figure) and the base station's CTCSS decoder is set to respond only to this tone. When the mobile transceiver transmits tone 6, the base station decoder operates the talkthrough facility to complete the path between the base station's receiver and transmitter. The calling mobile is then able to talk to another mobile transceiver.

The use of CTCSS allows a number of mobiles to use the same r.f. channel with little, if any, co-channel interference between them. The presence of a CTCSS tone in a transmitted signal means that only a receiver that has been fitted with a CTCSS decoder, set for the same tone, will be able to receive that signal. The receivers of all the other co-channel mobiles will remain muted. The way in which the system operates is illustrated by Fig. 11.7.

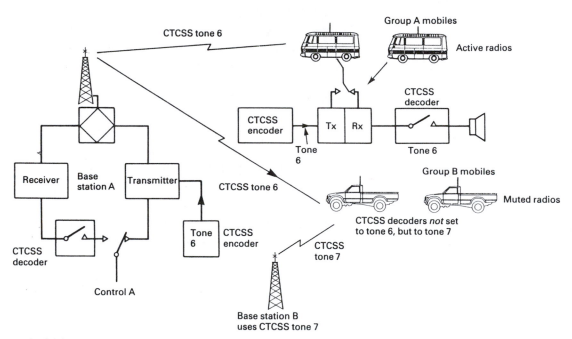

Fig. 11.7 CTCSS reduces co-channel interference

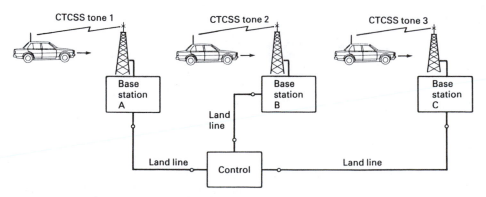

Fig. 11.8 Selective calling of base stations using CTCSS

Figure 11.8 shows how the CTCSS system can be used to provide *selective calling of base stations*. The system is employed when a number of base stations are required to provide coverage of a wide geographical area. Each mobile transceiver is fitted with a CTCSS encoder which is able to select any one of a number of CTCSS tones. Each tone corresponds to the CTCSS decoder fitted in a different base station. By transmitting the appropriate CTCSS tone, a mobile can select the base station that will provide the best signal strength for any location within the covered area.

Trunked PMR

Conventional dispatcher mobile radio systems frequently have some of their dedicated channels idle for much of the time and this means that the system has both reduced efficiency and poor cost-effectiveness. Sometimes one channel may be congested while another channel is mainly idle, but, because conventional PMR users are tied to a fixed channel, it is not possible for them to switch from one channel to another, less busy, channel. Their attempted call fails and they must then make repeated attempts to establish the wanted call. This is shown by Fig. 11.9(a). Trunking of a mobile radio system allows relatively few channels to fulfil the needs of a large number of users by considerably reducing the amount of idle time. It therefore allows for a much more efficient use of the frequency spectrum.

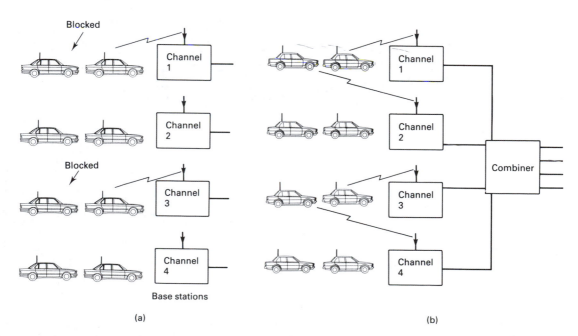

Fig. 11.9 (a) Conventional PMR may block calls. (b) Trunked PMR allows mobile access to any free channel.

A trunked mobile radio system shares a common 'pool' of r.f. channels between a large group of users, each of whom have exclusive use of a channel whenever it is needed. As a result, there is a large reduction in the number of r.f. channels that are needed to carry a certain amount of radio traffic. In a trunked system, any mobile is able to use any free channel; see Fig. 11.9(b).

Trunked mobile radio systems operate in the frequency band 174–225 MHz. The basic concept of a trunked mobile system is illustrated by Fig. 11.10. Up to 20 radio channels, each with its own base station, provide coverage of a geographical area. Each mobile within a trunked system is registered with its home node, using its address code as an identifier. If a mobile moves away from the area covered by its home node, it will automatically register with the new node into whose area it has entered. This node will inform the home node where its mobile has gone and the home node will then re-route all calls via the new node to the mobile at its new position.

Radio trunking requires the use of a control channel to which all the mobiles are connected when they are not communicating with another mobile. A computer, via the control channel, is used to allocate speech channels to mobiles as and when they are required for calls. As each call is completed, the channel is returned to the pool for allocation to another user. Each base station is given exclusive access

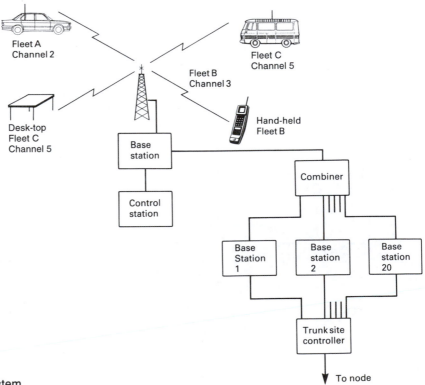

Fig. 11.10 Trunked PMR system

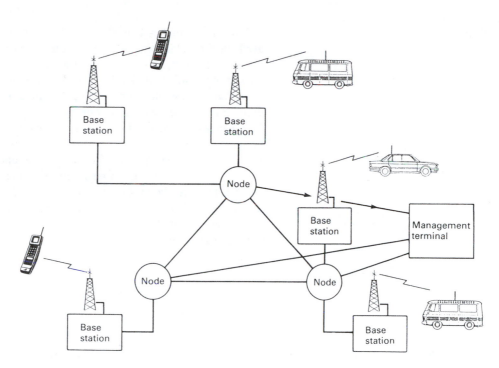

Fig. 11.11 Trunked PMR system links base station via nodes

to the control channel for a fixed period of time. This time period is divided into 20 time slots, with the base stations and the mobiles using the same slots on a 'turnabout' basis; i.e. if a mobile makes a call request in time slot 2, the base station will send an acknowledgement in time slot 3. A signalling protocol known as MPT 1327, which uses 100 baud FSK signals, is employed. The control channel may be permanently allotted as such, or the first channel to become free after a call is initiated may become the new control channel. When all the traffic channels are busy, any further calls that are initiated are placed in a queue, with emergency calls taking precedence. Callers are automatically called back when a channel has become free and the called party has answered the call. Because users are given access to a larger number of r.f. channels, the average time that they have to wait for a call to be established is reduced.

Each base station is connected to a switching centre and these centres are fully inter-connected, as shown in Fig. 11.11. The switching centres are generally referred to as *nodes*. Each node is connected to a *management terminal*, which consists of a personal computer (PC) and a printer, to both the PSTN and the dispatch operator.

To initiate a call, a mobile contacts its nearest base station and passes details of the required call over the control channel to the base station. The connection request is passed through all the relevant nodes and, if a free path is found, the called mobile is notified and both mobiles are connected to the free channel.

Cellular radio

Cellular radio makes better use of the limited frequency spectrum available for mobile radio by re-using the same frequencies many times over. Frequency re-use is achieved by dividing a large geographical area into a number of small, nominally hexagonal areas, known as *cells*, over the whole country. The transmitted power level of each base station is limited to restrict the coverage area of that base station. Frequencies are assigned in such a way that the same frequency can be used for different voice transmissions only a few cells away.

The cells are arranged in clusters and the allocated bandwidth is divided between the cells in each cluster. Three-, four- and seven-cell clusters are shown in Fig. 11.12, and 12- and 21-cell clusters are also sometimes employed. Regular patterns of clusters then give total coverage of the geographical area. Figure 11.13 shows how coverage of an area is achieved using a large number of seven-cell clusters.

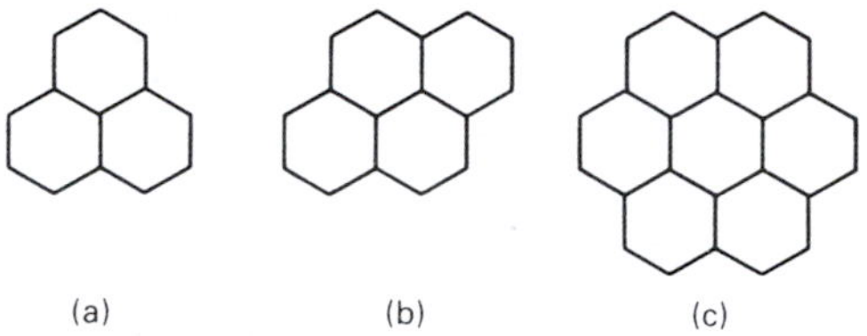

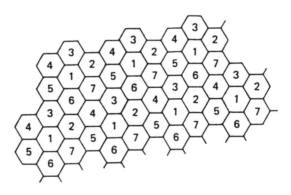

Fig. 11.12   (a) 3-cell, (b) 4-cell, and (c) 7-cell clusters

(a)   (b)   (c)

Fig. 11.13   Cell layout for cellular radio

Cellular radio uses multitudinous access points sited according to local traffic demands. The physical size of a cell is limited by radio wave propagation characteristics. At VHF and UHF, propagation is 'line-of-sight' and the coverage area is influenced by buildings and the local terrain. In a town or city it is necessary to place some base station aerials at the top of tall buildings and to position others lower down, on the top of lamp posts for example. This means that in the centre of a town, the size of a cell may be as small as 1 km in diameter and in such cases a cell is then known as a *microcell*. Within a high office block it is often necessary to use even smaller *picocells*. Figure 11.14 shows a mixed-cell cellular radio system.

Co-channel interference can be reduced by the use of a *sectored aerial* at the base station. A three-sectored aerial has a coverage angle

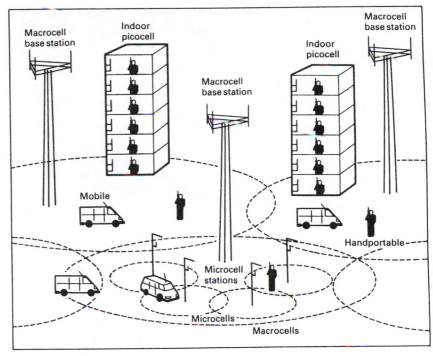

Fig. 11.14 Mixed-cell cellular radio system (from BTE)

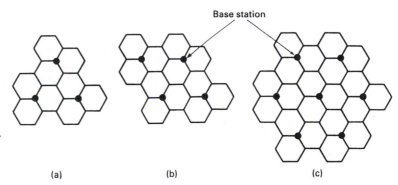

Fig. 11.15 Use of sectored aerials. (a) sectored 3-cell, (b) sectored 4-cell, and (c) sectored 7-cell clusters.

of 120° and its use effectively divides a cell into three sectors, each of which can be regarded as a new cell with its own set of channel frequencies. Each of the new cells is excited at one corner; this is shown by Fig. 11.15 which shows (a) a sectored three-cell cluster, (b) a sectored four-cell cluster and (c) a sectored seven-cell cluster. The number of cells provided are (a) 9, (b) 12 and (c) 21.

TACS

The original cellular radio system employs analogue technology, and a large number of incompatible systems have been installed in different countries. The UK system is known as the *Total Access Communication System* (TACS). It occupies the 900 MHz frequency band and has an r.f. channel spacing of 25 kHz. The main specifications are:

- Frequency range — transmit: 872.0125 to 904.9875 MHz
  receive: 917.0125 to 949.9875 MHz
- Channel spacing — 25 kHz

The base station is known as the *mobile switching centre* (MSC) or the *mobile telephone switching office* (MTSO), and it automatically controls and maintains all calls initiated by, or incoming to, a mobile in its cell. The MTSO also switches, bills and administers telephone traffic. Each MTSO is connected to the PSTN by a *local switching office* (LSO).

When a mobile is turned on, it searches for both a dedicated control channel and a paging channel in the cell in which the mobile currently is located, and then it goes into its idle state in which it continuously monitors the paging channel. If at any time the amplitude of the paging signal falls below a set value, the mobile will search for another, stronger, paging signal. At all times a mobile is automatically listening for an incoming call. As the mobile moves its position, it must register its whereabouts with the nearest base station so that its location is up-dated whenever it moves into another cell.

When a mobile wishes to initiate a call, the wanted telephone number is keyed and this information is transmitted over the control channel to the base station. If a speech channel is free, the MTSO allocates a channel to the mobile and sets up the required connection via the PSTN. Should there be no free channels at that time, the mobile will automatically try again after a random short interval of time. When the call is terminated, the mobile sends an 8 kHz tone for 1.8 seconds to the base station to signal end-of-call before it returns to its idle state.

When there is an incoming call for a mobile, the LSO pages all base stations near the last known location of the wanted mobile by sensing a paging signal on the paging channel of each base station. When the wanted mobile receives the paging signal, it automatically accesses the network. The mobile is then allocated a free speech channel by the nearest base station and the mobile automatically tunes to that channel frequency. The base station then transmits an 8 kHz tone to the mobile to indicate that there is an incoming call. When the mobile answers, this tone is turned off and the connection is set up.

If, during the progress of a call, the mobile travels from one cell to another, the received signal level will fall and this reduction in amplitude will start an *in-call hand-over*. The base station notifies the LSO and this then tells all base stations to measure the signal level from that mobile, and then the call is handed over to the base station that has the strongest signal. The mobile transceiver is automatically tuned to the new carrier frequency. The hand-over process is illustrated by Fig. 11.16. There are rarely more than one or two hand-overs in a single call. To reduce co-channel interference, adaptive power

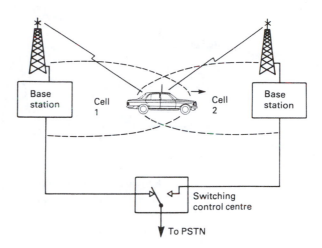

Fig. 11.16 Hand-over as mobile goes from one cell to another

control is used. This means that the power transmitted by a mobile is controlled by the base station to just above the minimum level needed to give an acceptable signal-to-noise ratio.

There are six cellular radio telephony networks in the UK. These networks are Cellnet analogue, Cellnet digital, Mercury one-2-one (digital), Orange (digital), Vodaphone analogue, and Vodaphone digital. The more modern digital networks operate to the GSM specification.

GSM

The *Global System for Mobile Communications* (GSM) method of operating a cellular radio system uses digital techniques for modulation, speech and channel coding, and also for timing and *time division multiple access* (TDMA). Besides giving a higher quality service, GSM is able to provide up to three times more traffic capacity than the earlier analogue systems. The mobile station may be a car-mounted radio telephone or a hand-held portable telephone.

The same frequency bands, 890−915 MHz for mobile transmit and 935−960 MHz for base station transmit, with 200 kHz channel spacing, have been allocated to GSM by all the countries in the European Union. A time division multiple access (TDMA) technique separates the different telephone conversations in progress between a base station and many mobile telephones in its cell by dividing each frequency channel into eight time slots. Each telephone conversation is allocated to one of the time slots, and so eight conversations can be simultaneously transmitted on each channel, eight times as many as with TACS. The basic principle of TDMA is shown by Fig. 11.17. Each channel is allocated a 0.577 ms time slot which occurs every 4.615 ms. GSM transmissions are transmitted at 270.833 kbit/s.

Speech is transmitted in digital form, using a modulation method

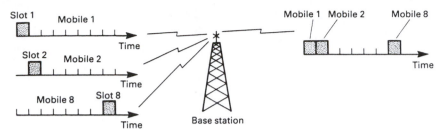

Fig. 11.17 TDMA access to GSM

known as *Gaussian minimum shift keying* (GMSK), and the data signal is encrypted both to provide security and to reduce the error rate. GMSK is a form of FSK in which the carrier frequency deviation is very accurately controlled. To generate a GMSK waveform, the signal is first passed through a Gaussian filter to shape the bits, and then it is applied to a *minimum shift keying* (MSK) modulator (see Fig. 11.18). MSK is a variant of FSK that has a frequency deviation equal to one-half of the bit rate.

Two channels are provided for each telephone call, one for each direction of transmission, to provide full duplex working. The signal-to-noise ratio of each call is continuously monitored by the mobile and it is compared with that current on adjacent channels. If another channel has the better performance, the mobile will request the base station to hand over the call to the better channel. This procedure results in a more rapid hand-over than is achieved with TACS.

The fixed part of the GSM network must keep track of the very large number of mobile telephones, located anywhere in Europe, so that any calls can be directed to each mobile.

The block diagram of a GSM mobile telephone is shown in Fig. 11.19. The operation of the telephone is controlled by a 16-bit

Fig. 11.18 Generation of a GMSK signal

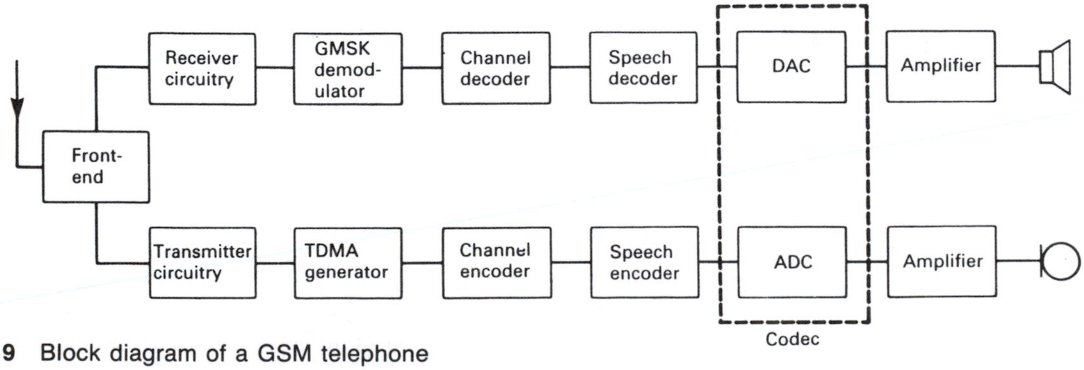

Fig. 11.19 Block diagram of a GSM telephone

microcomputer; this controls the search for a free r.f. channel, tunes the telephone to the appropriate frequency, provides forward error correction, and so on.

When a GSM mobile user initiates a call, his/her telephone will search for a free local *base station system* (BSS). Each BSS consists of a *base station controller* (BSC) and one or more *base station transceivers* (BST). Each BST serves a radio cell having one or more r.f. channels. Once a mobile has accessed, and then synchronized with, a BSS, the BSC will allocate a dedicated bi-directional signalling channel and will set up a route to a *mobile services switching centre* (MSC). An MSC routes traffic and signalling data within the network and also inter-connects with other networks. An MSC comprises a trunk telephone exchange with additional features to support mobile telephony.

When a mobile requests access to the system, the mobile must supply its *international mobile subscriber identity* (IMSI) number. The network will then check that the caller is authorized to use the network. Whenever a mobile is switched on, and at regular intervals thereafter, it will register its location with the system. The local MSC uses the IMSI to interrogate the mobile's *home location register* (HLR) and add the data thus obtained to its local *visitor's location register* (VLR). The VLR then contains the address of the mobile's HLR and the authentication request is routed back through the HLR to the subscriber's *authentication centre* (AUC).

Once a mobile has been accepted by the network, it must indicate the kind of service that it requires, such as voice or data, and the wanted telephone number. A telephone channel is then allocated to the call and the MSC will route the call to its destination.

If, during the progress of a call or while a call is being set up, the mobile should move outside the range of the BST, the call will be handed over to another BST. Hand-over takes place so fast that the user is unaware that it has happened. The choice of the new BST may be made by the BSS if the mobile is within the range of another BST under the control of the same BSS. Otherwise, hand-over is controlled by the MSC.

When a call is to be set up from the PSTN to a mobile, the mobile is first located by means of a paging signal that covers the area with which the mobile has registered. Each mobile continuously monitors the paging channel and, when it detects a call addressed to itself, accepts the incoming call. The basic arrangement of the GSM network is shown by Fig. 11.20.

Cordless telephones

A cordless telephone uses a radio link instead of a physical cord to connect the handset to the base station. Both the mobile handset and the base station are radio transceivers. The first generation of cordless telephones uses analogue techniques and it is known as CT1. CT1 has been followed by a digital system known as CT2. Both CT1 and

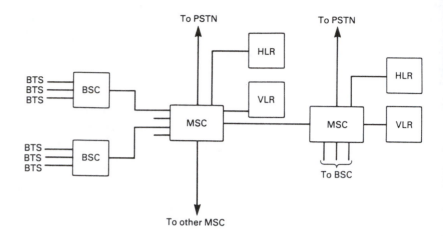

Fig. 11.20 GSM network

CT2 rely upon the base station to connect the mobile handset to the PSTN. An even more recent system is DECT; this system employs digital cellular technology to provide a mobile telephone service to large PABXs.

CT1

CT1 uses two radio frequencies and analogue technology to provide a full duplex speech path between the handset and the base station. The two frequencies are spaced well apart; in the direction base to handset the frequency is 1.7 MHz, and in the direction handset to base the frequency is 47 MHz. The CT1 system has a number of disadvantages:

- The quality of the received speech is not very good.
- Transmissions can be received by a sound broadcast radio receiver.
- Only eight r.f. channels are allocated.
- A telephone has no ability to search for a free channel and hence it can easily be blocked off by another cordless telephone that has been set to use the same channel.
- The range is limited to about 50 m.

CT2

The second generation of cordless telephones, known as CT2, uses a digital speech path in any one of forty 100 kHz wide r.f. channels in the frequency band 864–868 MHz. The channels are not allocated in pairs. Instead, full duplex operation is obtained by the use of a digital technique known as *time division duplex* (TDD). With TDD the two halves of a telephone conversation are first converted into digital form and then they are divided into a number of small packets of data. Each packet of data is then compressed to one-half its natural length before the two sets of data are interleaved on the same carrier frequency.

Each handset has up to 11 unique identity codes loaded in at manufacture. This enables each base station to be programmed to recognize up to eight separate handset identities that it is able to deal with simultaneously, and this allows base stations to provide a PABX function. Since every handset is uniquely identified, there is little risk of privacy invasion. A handset can also send recall and other tone signals to the base station which can relay them on to the PSTN. This feature allows a CT2 user at home and at the office to employ the same handset as a PABX extension.

The CT2 specification defines a *common air interface* (CAI), which means that all CT2 handsets and base stations can communicate with one another, regardless of their manufacturer. The modulation method that is employed is two-level FSK with frequency deviations of

(a) 14.4 to 25.2 kHz above the carrier frequency representing binary 1;
(b) 14.4 to 25.2 kHz deviation below the carrier frequency indicating binary 0.

This is shown by Fig. 11.21. A single r.f. channel is used for both directions of transmission using the 'ping-pong' version of TDD shown in Fig. 11.22. Speech signals in either direction of transmission

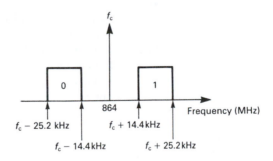

Fig. 11.21 Two-level FSK

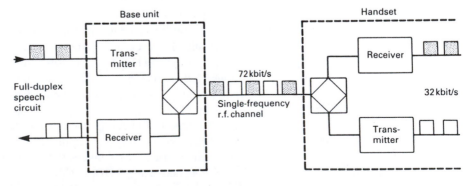

Fig. 11.22 CT2 uses a form of TDD

are sampled and coded into digital form at 32 kbit/s. The 2 ms duration samples are transmitted at 72 kbit/s in 1 ms bursts to allow the bits to be compressed into packets of data of 1 ms duration. Forty r.f. channels are available so that CT2 is a combined FDMA/TDD system.

When a call is initiated, there is initially no synchronization between the handset and the base station. For a link to be set up so that the two items are able to communicate with one another, they must first be tuned to the same r.f. channel and then they must synchronize with one another.

Incoming call to base station: When an incoming all is detected by the base station, it scans the 40 r.f. channels to find a free one that has an adequate signal-to-noise ratio. The base station then transmits a call signal over the selected channel. Periodically the handset moves out of its SLEEP state into its SCAN state, in which it scans the r.f. channels. When the call signal is detected on one of the r.f. channels, the handset remains on that frequency and achieves bit synchronization with the base station. The handset then checks that the call is for it (not for some other handset); if so, burst synchronization is obtained to establish a link to the base station. The ringer of the handset then rings until the call is answered, when speech can commence.

Handset originating a call: When a handset wishes to make a call, the CALL button is pressed and this action causes the handset to scan the 40 r.f. channels to find a free one with adequate signal-to-noise ratio. The handset then signals the base station over the selected channel. The base station is continually scanning all the 40 r.f. channels, and so it rapidly detects the call from the handset. Synchronization between handset and base station is established and then the base station seizes a line to the local telephone exchange or PABX. Dialling tone is then returned to the caller.

CT2 transmits at a power level of about 10 mW and it has a range of about 100 m.

DECT

The *Digital European Cordless Telephone* (DECT) system uses a cellular radio-like technology to support very high user densities. DECT is intended for use in conjunction with large PABXs and it is not suitable for car telephones. The block diagram of the DECT system is shown in Fig. 11.23. It uses a three-dimension cellular layout in which there may be cells above and below one another as well as side-by-side. The cell dimensions are small, typically about 100 m diameter. The DECT system uses the frequency band 1.88–1.9 GHz and this band is divided up into ten separate carrier frequencies. In turn, each carrier frequency is divided into 23 time slots, any two of which are used for a conversation. The system provides 32 kbit/s voice channels using TDD.

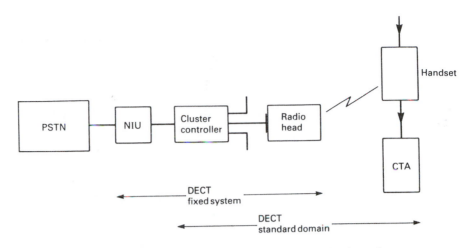

Fig. 11.23 DECT system (NIU = network interface unit, CTA = cordless terminal adaptor)

During a conversation a handset continuously compares the signal-to-noise ratio obtained in its time slot with signal-to-noise ratio in the corresponding time slot in another r.f. channel. If the other time slot is better, the handset will change over to use the better time slot. This procedure allows almost instantaneous hand-over to be achieved. A terminal is able to seize several time slots simultaneously to provide a single wideband channel which can be used for high speed data communications.

DECT uses FDMA/TDMA/TDD techniques to provide 120 duplex channels using ten separate carrier frequencies and multiplexing 12 send channels and 12 receive channels onto each carrier. The bit rate per channel is 1152 kbit/s, and the modulation is GMSK with a frequency deviation of ± 288 kHz and a carrier spacing of 1728 kHz.

Pagers

Public paging services over a wide geographical area are provided in the UK by several different companies, including BT and Mercury. In addition there are a large number of private paging services. A pager may be:

- a tone pager, providing a simple beep to alert the user when called;
- a numeric pager, incorporating a small display panel which is able to display telephone numbers or other numeric data;
- a alphanumeric pager, which is able to display both textual and numeric data and so may be used to pass a message to the user.

A paging message is broadcast by a network of long-range radio transmitters that are operated by the providers of the paging services. The message is first passed to the paging service either by calling an operator or by tone signalling. Radio paging customers must indicate to the operator which area in the country (or in Europe) they wish to be paged. When a call is made, a paging message is sent to

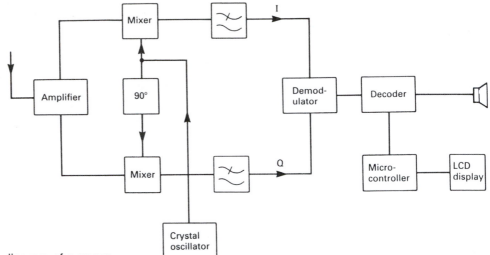

Fig. 11.24 Block diagram of a pager

all paging transmitters in the area in which the person is expected to be.

Pagers use the ITU-R paging code 1, also known as POCSAG (Post Office Code Standardization Advisory Group), which is the internationally agreed standard for radio paging. POCSAG has a system capability of 8×10^6 addresses and operates in the frequency band 138−174 MHz with a 25 kHz channel spacing. The modulation employed is NRZ FSK at 512 bit/s.

Figure 11.24 shows the block diagram of a pager. The received signal is amplified and then applied to two identical mixers that are also supplied with the local oscillator voltage. One of the oscillator voltages is given 90° phase shift before it is applied to the mixer. The output signals of the mixers are at a frequency equal to that of the carrier ± the frequency deviation, and they are in phase quadrature with one another. When the input signal is at the higher frequency $f_c + f$, the Q signal leads the I signal by 90°. When the input signal is at the lower frequency $f_c - f$, the Q signal lags the I signal by 90°. The I and Q signals are filtered, to remove the adjacent-channel signal, before they arrive at the demodulator. In the demodulator the phase relationship between the I and Q signals determines whether a binary 1 or a binary 0 output voltage is generated. The digital signal is passed on to the decoder to give the audio signal to produce a bleep and the information for the microcontroller to produce a message on the LCD display.

Exercises

11.1 (a) List the different cordless telephone systems in use in the UK. Outline the operation of each system and give the frequencies employed. (b) What is meant by the *common air interface*?

11.2 (a) Draw a block diagram of the DECT system and explain its operation.

(b) Explain how a tall office building may be divided up into a number of cells. State typical cell dimensions.

11.3   (a) What are the facilities offered by a cellular radio system? (b) How does such a system differ from a PMR system? (c) Explain how a cellular radio system makes it possible for frequencies to be 're-used' many times over. (d) What is meant by the term *hand-over* and how is it achieved?

11.4   Early cellular radio systems employed analogue technology but the newer systems employ digital techniques. Discuss the reasons for the change from analogue to digital operation.

11.5   Wide area paging services are provided in the UK by a number of companies, including BT, Mercury and Vodapage. (a) Outline the operation of a paging system. (b) State the paging code that is employed. (c) State the frequency band that is used.

11.6   With reference to a mobile radio system, what is meant by (a) single-frequency simplex, (b) double-frequency simplex, (c) duplex operation? Explain how talkthrough between two mobiles can be set up.

11.7   (a) Explain how a PMR mobile telephone network can be operated using the open-channel system. What are the disadvantages of this method of working? (b) Explain how selective signalling of mobiles is possible using (i) five-tone signalling; (ii) CTCSS.

11.8   (a) Explain how blocking can reduce a mobile's access to a base station in a conventional PMR system. (b) Use a diagram to show how a trunked system will give a more efficient use of the allocated frequency spectrum.

11.9   Discuss the differences between TACS and GSM in their methods of (a) setting up a call and (b) obtaining in-call hand-over.

12 Wideband radio systems

The public transmission network of a country is used for the communication of many kinds of information, such as commercial quality speech, data signals and sound/television signals for the broadcasting authorities. The network is made up of the access network and the core network. The core network contains trunk telephone exchanges and trunk lines. The trunk lines are routed over multi-channel pulse code modulated systems and many of these, in turn, are routed over wideband radio relay systems. Both analogue and digital radio relay systems are in use in the UK network, although all new systems are digital. Large-capacity PCM systems are built up from combinations of the basic 32-channel system and Figs 12.1(a) and (b) show how, respectively, 34 Mbit/s and 140 Mbit/s systems are transmitted over a radio relay system. The baseband PCM signal can be directly applied to a digital system but will require digital-to-analogue conversion before entering an analogue system.

Both radio relay and land PCM systems are widely used as integral parts of the UK telephone network. The two systems have a number of advantages and disadvantages relative to one another, which often means that one or the other may be best suited for providing communication over a given route. The relative merits of the two systems are listed below:

- A radio relay system is generally quicker and easier to provide.
- The problems posed by difficult terrain are easier to overcome using a radio relay system.
- It is easier to extend the channel capacity of a radio relay system.
- Difficulties may be experienced in obtaining suitable (line-of-sight distance) sites for a radio relay system.
- When relay station sites have been chosen it may be difficult to gain access to them, whereas land systems usually follow roads and so access is relatively easy.
- The transmission performance of a radio relay system is adversely affected by bad weather conditions.

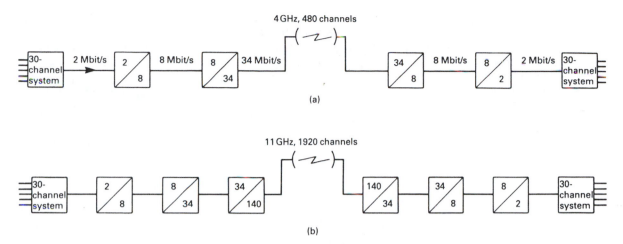

Fig. 12.1   PCM system transmitted over a radio relay system, (a) 480 channels and (b) 1920 channels

The ITU-T and the ITU-R

To ensure compatibility between the telephone networks of different countries that play a part in a particular international telephone connection, it is necessary to standardize carrier frequencies, bandwidths, noise levels and other parameters involved. The task of specifying the parameters of telecommunication systems destined for possible use in the international network has been given to the *International Telecommunication Union* (ITU). The ITU carries out its standardization work through three sectors: the *Telecommunications Standardization sector* (ITU-T), the *Radiocommunication sector* (ITU-R), and the *Telecommunication Development sector* (ITU-D).

The functions of the ITU-T are to study technical, operating and tariff questions relating to telecommunications and to produce recommendations with the aim of standardizing telecommunications

Table 12.1 ITU-T study groups

1	Service definition
2	Network operation
3	Tariff and accounting principles
4	Maintenance of networks
5	Protection against electromagnetic interference
6	Line plant
7	Data networks
8	Telematic terminals
9	Television and sound transmission
10	Telecommunication languages
11	Switching and signalling
12	End-to-end transmission performance of networks and terminals
13	General network aspects
14	Modems and data transmission techniques
15	Transmission systems and equipment

Table 12.2 ITU-R study groups

1	Management of the r.f. spectrum
2	Inter-service sharing and compatibility
3	Radio wave propagation
4	Fixed satellite services
7	Science services
8	Mobile radio services
9	Fixed radio services
10	Sound broadcasting
11	Television broadcasting

throughout the world. The ITU-T works through a number of study groups which are listed in Table 12.1.

The functions of the ITU-R are to ensure that the best use is made of the radio frequency spectrum by all kinds of radio services, and to produce recommendations on radiocommunication matters. The ITU-R works through the study groups listed in Table 12.2.

The third sector of the ITU, the ITU-D, implements telecommunication projects for the United Nations and assists with the development of telecommunications in various countries by providing technical assistance.

Radio relay systems

Radio relay systems using line-of-sight transmissions in the UHF and SHF bands can provide a large number of telephone channels and/or a television signal (see Fig. 12.2). Table 12.3 lists the frequency bands that are currently operated in the UK.

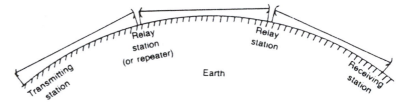

Fig. 12.2 Microwave radio relay system

Table 12.3

Frequency (GHz)	Name	Use
3.7–4.2	4 GHz band	⎰140 Mbit/s PCM
5.85–6.425	Lower 6 GHz band	⎱2 × 34 Mbit/s PCM
6.425–7.11	Upper 6 GHz band	⎧140 Mbit/s PCM
10.7–11.7	11 GHz band	⎨2 × 34 Mbit/s PCM
14.0–14.5	14 GHz band	⎩Television
17.7–19.7	19 GHz band	⎰8 Mbit/s PCM feeders
		⎱140 Mbit/s PCM

At the transmitting terminal the baseband signal (the signal produced by a multi-channel PCM system or a television system) is processed before it is used to modulate a 70 MHz carrier. The modulated wave is then up-converted to the allocated part of the frequency spectrum and is amplified before it is radiated by a parabolic dish aerial. At each relay station, the received signal is down-converted to 70 MHz before it is amplified and, for a digital system, demodulated and pulse-regenerated. The processed signal is then up-converted to the frequency band that is to be used to transmit the signal to the next relay station. At the receiving station the signal is down-converted to 70 MHz before it is demodulated, and perhaps pulse-regenerated, to recover the baseband signal.

In a digital system the received signal is down-converted to the 140 MHz intermediate frequency so that the digital bit stream can be regenerated. The regenerated signal then modulates a carrier and the modulated signal is up-converted to the required transmit frequency.

Analogue systems employ frequency modulation rather than amplitude modulation, mainly because of its better signal-to-noise ratio performance. The digital baseband input signal to a radio relay system is always at a fixed rate equal to one of the standard PCM higher-order bit rates. Such a signal will be applied to a digital-to-analogue converter (DAC) before it is used to frequency-modulate the 70 MHz carrier. Analogue systems are now only used to transmit TV signals.

Digital radio relay systems may employ QPSK, 8 PSK, 16 QAM, 64 QAM or 256 QAM. A version of QPSK in which the QPSK signal is heavily filtered, known as *reduced bandwidth QPSK* (RBQPSK), is also employed. 64 QAM is able to provide between six and eight two-way 140 Mbit/s channels. Six 140 Mbit/s channels give $6 \times 1920 = 11\,520$ telephone channels. Similarly, 256 QAM can carry 565 Mbit/s circuits which provide 7680 telephone channels. Systems with even higher capacities are being developed, such as 1.2 Gbit/s (15 360 channels) and 2.4 Gbit/s (30 720 channels).

Analogue radio relay systems

Transmitter

Figure 12.3 shows the equipment used at the transmitting end of an analogue system. The input baseband signal is either a multi-channel telephony system or a television waveform.

The baseband signal is pre-emphasized before it frequency-modulates a 70 MHz carrier wave. Different pre-emphasis networks

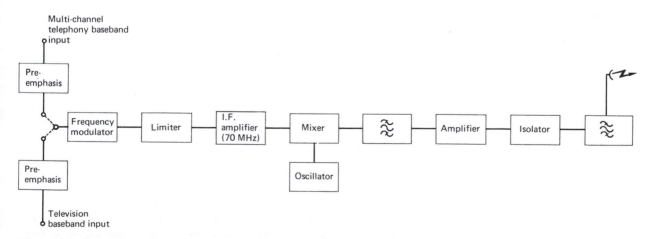

Fig. 12.3 Transmitter in an analogue radio relay system

are used for telephony and for television signals (characteristics shown in Fig. 2.10) but otherwise the same items of equipment are used. The frequency-modulated signal is amplitude-limited to remove any amplitude modulation that may be present. It is then amplified before it is up-converted to the required frequency band by the mixer. The following low-pass filter removes all unwanted frequency components from the mixer output.

The signal is then further amplified to the required transmitted power level, typically $2-10\,\text{W}$, and it is then passed on to the aerial via an *isolator* and another bandpass filter. The isolator is a ferrite device which will only allow signals to pass in one direction, and it is used to prevent any unwanted signals picked up by the aerial from passing into the transmitting equipment. Any reflected signals caused by mismatch at the aerial terminals will also be prevented from entering the transmitter. The aerial band-pass filter is provided to band-limit the transmitted signal in order to avoid interference with adjacent systems.

Receiver

The block diagram of an analogue radio relay receiver is given by Fig. 12.4. The received signal is selected by the aerial filter, which rejects any unwanted signals that are also picked up by the aerial, and it is then down-converted to the 70 MHz intermediate frequency of the receiver. The intermediate-frequency signal is amplified, group-delay equalized and amplitude limited before it is demodulated to obtain the baseband signal. The baseband signal is passed through the appropriate de-emphasis network in order to restore its frequency components to their original amplitude relationships with one another.

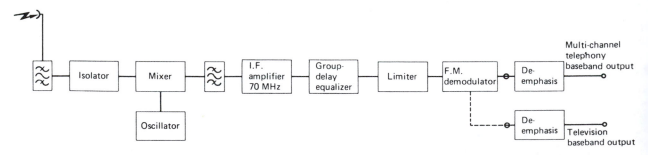

Fig. 12.4 Receiver in an analogue radio relay system

Relay station

The equipment used in an analogue relay station consists of the back-to-back connection, at the intermediate frequency, of a receiver and a transmitter equipment. The block diagram of an analogue relay

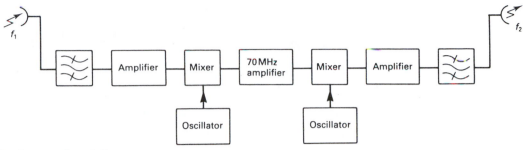

Fig. 12.5 Analogue relay station

station is shown in Fig. 12.5. The received signal at frequency f_1 is frequency shifted down to the standard intermediate frequency of 70 MHz and here it is amplified. After amplification, the signal is up-converted to the frequency f_2 that is to be used to transmit on to the next repeater station or to the receiver.

Combining r.f. channels

The parabolic dish aerials used with radio relay systems have the capability to transmit or receive more than one r.f. channel at the same time. It is therefore usual for more than one r.f. channel to be multiplexed onto a single aerial. To improve the discrimination between channels, adjacent (in frequency) channels use alternate planes of polarization. For example, if channel 1 is horizontally polarized, channel 2 will be vertically polarized, channel 3 will be horizontally polarized and so on.

The block diagram of the equipment involved is shown in Fig. 12.6. As before, only one relay station is shown but usually there will be several more. A *circulator* is a ferrite device with four input/output terminals; the operation of the device is such that a signal entering one pair of terminals will be directed only to one other pair of terminals — none of the input energy will appear at the other two pairs of terminals.

Digital radio relay systems

In a digital radio relay transmitter, the baseband signal processing must establish a clock frequency so that the data can be recovered at the receiver. The clock may be the frequency of the incoming data stream or it may be generated in the transmitter. In either case, the input baseband signal is usually in bipolar digital form and must be converted into non-return zero (NRZ) form. This conversion is carried out by the baseband processor. The data stream is divided into the appropriate number of bit streams for the modulation method that is employed, e.g. two for QPSK, four for 16 QAM, and eight for 64 QAM.

The bit streams are scrambled to remove any strong spectral lines

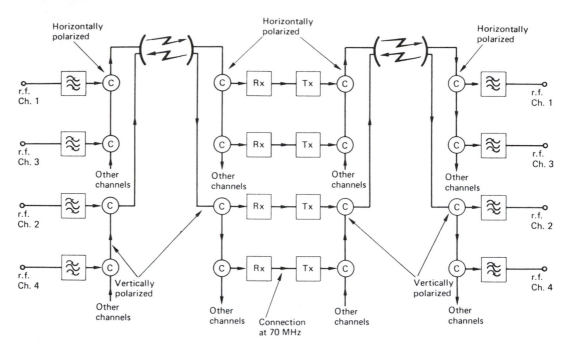

Fig. 12.6 Method of transmitting several r.f. channels over a single radio relay system (C = circulator)

and to ensure that adequate timing information is transmitted for use by the demodulator in the distant receiver. The scrambled bit streams are then retimed before the frame is established by the insertion of some extra bits. Each frame consists of a frameword, a block of data and some spare bits. Some of the spare bits are used for supervisory signals and some for error correction.

At the receiver, the baseband processing must carry out the reverse of these functions plus the regeneration of the demodulated signal.

Transmitter

The block diagram of the transmitter of a digital radio relay system is shown by Fig. 12.7. The baseband signal is processed to give an NRZ signal that is applied to the TDM multiplexer, which combines several channels together, before the combined signal is scrambled to obtain a smooth frequency spectrum and encoded to ensure that the timing signal can be recovered at the receiver.

The modulator converts the digital encoded baseband signal to the intermediate frequency of 70 MHz. The modulation method is usually QPSK, or 16 QAM or 64 QAM at 140 Mbit/s and 256 QAM at higher bit rates. The 70 MHz signal is then applied to an up-converter (mixer) to shift the signal to the allocated part of the r.f. spectrum. The local oscillator is usually a transistor crystal oscillator with a varactor diode frequency multiplier; often a phase-locked loop is employed to ensure

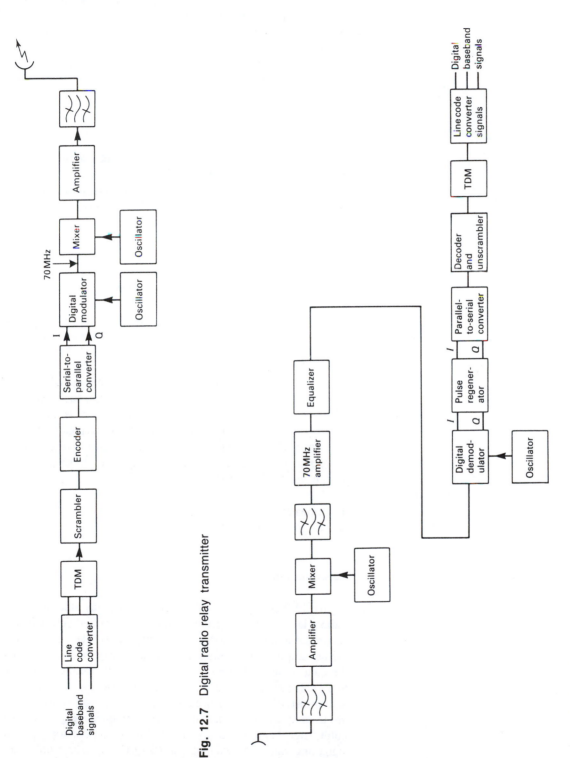

Fig. 12.7 Digital radio relay transmitter

Fig. 12.8 Digital radio relay receiver

frequency stability. The microwave signal is amplified by an r.f. power amplifier, which is generally either a gallium arsenide FET amplifier for frequencies up to about 6 GHz, or a travelling wave amplifier (TWA) at higher frequencies. Lastly, the amplified signal is passed through a filter which shapes the transmitted spectrum and limits the transmitted bandwidth.

Receiver

Figure 12.8 shows the block diagram of the receiver in a digital radio relay system. The received signal is band-limited by a band-pass filter before it is mixed with the local oscillator voltage to shift the signal to the intermediate frequency of 70 MHz. The mixer output is filtered to remove all unwanted frequency components before it is amplified to give a constant level signal at the input to the demodulator. The demodulator input signal is equalized to correct for distortion and, if it is of the adaptive type, to compensate for selective fading also. In the demodulator, a carrrier recovery circuit extracts the clock timing signal from the original data stream and this is used to synchronize the receiver to the transmitter. The demodulator also, of course, produces the encoded baseband signal. The recovered baseband signal is then decoded and de-scrambled to reconstruct the aggregate bit stream. This, in turn, is applied to the de-multiplexer, which separates the data into the appropriate channels, and the individual channel data is converted into the standard data format by the baseband decoder.

The performance of a digital radio relay system is usually quoted in terms of the allowed *bit error rate* (BER); typically this is 1×10^{-3} for a 24 dB co-channel interference signal-to-noise ratio, or for a 10dB adjacent channel interference signal-to-noise ratio. Typical parameters for such a system are

- repeater spacing: 40−50 km;
- output power: 1−10 W.

Relay stations

Figure 12.9 shows the block diagram of a relay station in a digital radio relay system. The received signal is amplified before it is down-converted to the intermediate frequency of 70 MHz. It then receives further amplification before it is applied to a demodulator to recover the data streams. The recovered data signals are then each applied to a pulse regenerator to regenerate the pulses, removing any noise and/or distortion that has been picked up. The regenerated bit streams are used to digitally modulate a carrier frequency. The regenerated output signals are directly connected to the modulator inputs at the signalling rate. For example, a 16 QAM system would have an

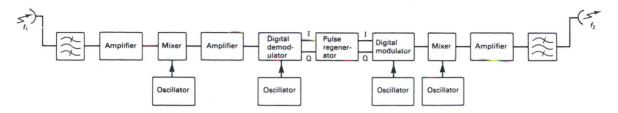

Fig. 12.9 Digital radio relay station

Table 12.4 Microwave radio relay system frequency bands

Frequency (GHz)	Name	Use
3.7–4.2	4 GHz band	2 × 34 Mb/s (8PSK), 140 Mb/s (16QAM, RBQPSK)
5.85–6.425	Lower 6 GHz band	2 × 34 Mb/s (8PSK), 140 Mb/s (RBQPSK)
6.425–7.11	Upper 6 GHz band	2 × 34 Mb/s (8PSK), 140 Mb/s (16QAM)
10.7–11.7	11 GHz band	2 × 34 Mb/s (8PSK), 140 Mb/s (QPSK, 8PSK, 16QAM, 64QAM)
14.0–14.5	14 GHz band	2 × 34 Mb/s digital (8PSK), 140 Mb/s (QPSK, 8PSK)
17.7–19.7	19 GHz band	140 Mb/s (QPSK), 555 Mb/s (QPSK)

interface with four bit streams at an approximate bit rate of 37 Mbit/s. The modualted signals are then up-converted to the required transmitted frequency and are amplified and filtered before they arrive at the transmitting aerial.

Table 12.4 gives details of the various digital radio relay systems in use in the UK.

Communication satellite systems

Most of the long-distance international telephone traffic which is not carried by submarine cable systems is routed via a broadband communication satellite system, the basic principle of which is illustrated by Fig. 12.10. The ground stations are fully integrated with their national telephone networks and, in addition, the European ground stations are fully interconnected. Four frequencies are used: the North American ground station transmits on frequency f_1 and receives a frequency f_4, while the European stations transmit frequency f_3 and receive frequency f_2. Essentially, the purpose of the communication satellite is to receive the signals transmitted to it, frequency-translate them to a different frequency band (f_1 to f_2 or f_3 to f_4), amplify them and then re-transmit them to the ground station at the other end of the link.

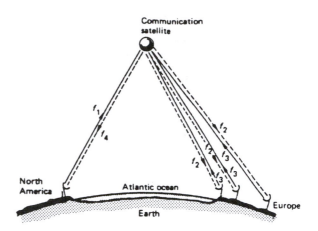

Fig. 12.10 Communication satellite system

Communication satellites which form an integral part of the public international telephone network are operated on a global basis by COMSAT (Communication Satellite Corporation) on behalf of an international body known as INTELSAT (International Telecommunication Satellite Consortium). The COMSAT system employs communication satellites travelling in the circular equatorial orbit at a height of 35 880 km. This particular orbit is known as the *geo-synchronous orbit*, because a satellite travelling in it appears to be stationary above a particular part of the Earth's surface. Seven satellites are used, positioned around the Earth so that nearly all parts of the surface of the Earth are 'visible' from at least one satellite. A large number of ground stations are in use and now number more than 100 in nearly 100 different countries.

Each ground station transmits its telephone traffic to a satellite on the particular carrier frequency allocated to it in the frequency band 5.925–6.425 GHz or 14.0–14.5 GHz. This is a bandwidth of 500 MHz and allows the simultaneous use of a satellite by more than one ground station. Different ground stations are allocated different carrier frequencies within this 500 MHz band, either permanently or for particular periods of time, depending on the traffic originated by that station. Each of the allocated carrier frequencies has a sufficiently wide bandwidth to allow a large number of telephony channels to be transmitted and, in some case, a television channel. The number of telephony channels thus provided varies from 24 in a 2.5 MHz bandwidth to 1872 in a 36 MHz bandwidth. All the signals transmitted by a satellite are transmitted towards every ground station and each station selects the particular carrier frequencies allocated to it in the band 3.7–4.2 GHz.

Other satellite systems operate in the up-band 14–14.5 GHz and in the down-band 10.95–11.2 GHz and 11.45–11.7 GHz, or 10.95 to 11.2 GHz and 11.45 to 11.7 GHz.

The block diagram of the transponder in a 6 GHz satellite is shown in Fig. 12.11. *Transponder* is the term used in satellite technology to denote a wideband channel. Signals in the 6 GHz band received

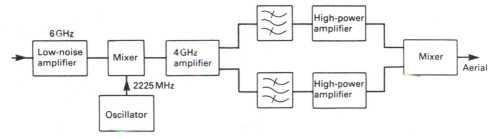

Fig. 12.11 6 GHz satellite transponder

by the satellite are amplified by a low-noise amplifier and then down-converted to the 4 GHz band. Here the signals are further amplified and filtered before they are applied to a high-power amplifier to be boosted to the transmitted power level of, typically, 4 W.

The signals transmitted by a satellite down to earth are received by all earth stations in the 'footprint' of the satellite. Each earth station selects those signals that are destined for it and rejects all others. Transmissions to earth are in the frequency bands 3.7−4.2 GHz and 11.45−11.7 GHz. Thus, some satellites work in the 4/6 GHz band and others in the 11/14 GHz band. The channel frequencies employed in both directions for a 11/14 GHz system are shown in Table 12.5 (frequencies given in MHz).

The odd-numbered transponders are horizontally polarized and the even-numbered are vertically polarized.

Access by a ground station to a satellite is based either on *frequency division multiplex access* (FDMA) or on *time division multiplex access* (TDMA). FDMA divides the transponder bandwidth between different carriers, each of which is normally allocated to a different ground station. TDMA shares the full bandwidth of a transponder between several different ground stations. Each earth station in turn transmits data for a short period of time as shown by Fig. 12.12. TDMA offers two main advantages over FDMA: firstly, it makes more effective use of the capacity of the satellite because it avoids any problems arising from intermodulation between carriers; and, secondly, it is more flexible in responding to changing traffic requirements.

Table 12.5

(a) UP							
1	3	5	7	9	11	13	15
14029	14088	14147	14206	14265	14324	14383	14442
2	4	6	8	10	12	14	16
14058.5	14117.5	14176.5	14235.5	14294.5	14353.5	14412.5	14471.5

(b) DOWN							
1	3	5	7	9	11	13	15
11729	11788	11847	11906	11965	12024	12083	12142
2	4	6	8	10	12	14	16
11758.5	11817.5	11876.5	11935.5	11994.5	12053.5	12112.5	12171.5

Other orbits

Although the use of GEO allows high-gain directive aerials to be employed and each satellite has a large footprint, the large path loss and long propagation delay are disadvantages.

A satellite system that uses the *low-earth orbit* (LEO) of between 700 and 2000 km above earth has less loss and smaller propagation delay, *but* requires the use of a larger number of satellites to cover a given area of the earth's surface. Since the satellites do not appear to be stationary the ground stations must have complex tracking equipment. LEO is employed by the GLOBALSTAR, IRIDIUM, and TELEDISIC mobile services.

The *medium-earth orbit* (MEO) is at approximately 10350 km above the earth and provides a compromise between GEO and LEO. MEO is employed by the I-CO and ODYSSEY mobile services.

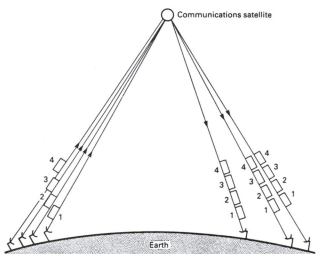

Fig. 12.12 Time-division multiple access

Noise and interference in radio systems

The output of any communication system, line or radio, will always contain some unwanted components superimposed upon the desired signal waveform. The unwanted voltages are the result of noise and interference picked up by or generated within the system. The sources of noise and interference in communication systems are many and are discussed in *Electronics III*. This section will deal with noise and interference in radio relay systems.

Thermal noise voltages developed in the input stages of a receiver, either in a relay station or at the terminal station, will have an effect on the ouput signal-to-noise ratio, which varies with the level of the incoming signal. When the incoming signal level is low, the AGC action of the receiver will increase the gain of the receiver in an attempt to maintain the output voltage at a more or less constant level; unfortunately, this means that the thermal noise generated in the input stage will be amplified to a greater extent. The other main source of noise appearing at the output of the system is known as *intermodulation noise*. Intermodulation noise is produced by non-linearity in the amplitude frequency and group-delay frequency characteristics of the various parts of the system. Intermodulation noise has components at most frequencies and so sounds very much like thermal agitation noise. However, whereas thermal noise is continually produced, intermodulation noise increases with increase in the signal level.

Adjacent-channel interference can occur on routes where all the available carrier frequencies are in use and therefore adjacent in-frequency carriers must be employed. Clearly, this form of interference can be minimized by the use of receivers of adequate selectivity.

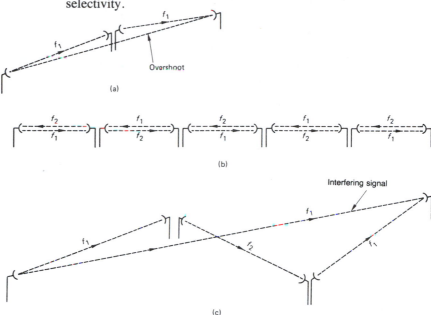

Fig. 12.13 Co-channel interference in a radio relay system

Co-channel interference can also exist if signals proper to one receive aerial are able to overshoot and be picked up by another aerial further along the route; see Fig. 12.13(a). To reduce co-channel intereference arising from this effect, two frequencies f_1 and f_2 can be allocated for use as carriers and alternate relay stations can use the same frequency; see Fig. 12.13(b). To reduce still further this form of interference, the path followed by the route can be zig-zagged in the manner shown in Fig. 12.13(c); however, the possibility of co-channel interference is not eliminated, as shown.

Choice of carrier frequency

Wideband radio relay systems must operate in the UHF and SHF bands because of the very wide bandwidths they occupy. Various frequency bands, listed in Table 12.3, have been allocated for this purpose by the ITU. The ITU-R issues recommenations regarding the division of each frequency band into a number of r.f. channels and, as an example, Fig. 12.14 gives the recommendations for the 5925−6425 MHz band. The 500 MHz bandwidth is divided into a low and a high group of frequencies. At any particular relay station, all the transmitting channels are given carrier frequencies in one group and all the receiving channels have carrier frequencies in the other group. For example, at one station r.f. channels may be transmitted on low-group frequencies and received on carrier frequencies in the

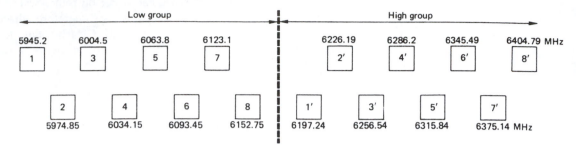

Fig. 12.14 Frequency allocation of a radio relay system

high group. Also, as shown in Fig. 12.13(b), an r.f. channel received on a low-group carrier frequency at a relay station will be transmitted on the corresponding high-group carrier frequency; e.g. a channel received at a carrier frequency of 6004.5 MHz would be re-transmitted at 6256.54 MHz.

Exercises

12.1 Give an outline description of a radio relay system for carrying television and multi-channel PCM signals. Discuss the factors that would influence the choice of radio frequencies to be used for the system.

12.2 Discuss the sources of noise and intererence in a radio relay system.

12.3 (a) Why is frequency modulation used in analogue radio relay links in preference to amplifude modulation? (b) Why is pre-emphasis used for (i) multi-channel PCM and (ii) television signals? (c) Draw the pre-emphasis characteristic used in each case.

12.4 Draw the block diagrams of (a) the transmitter and (b) the receiver of an SHF radio relay link. Explain the function of each block.

12.5 Draw and explain the block schematic diagram of the repeater in an SHF radio relay system.

12.6 Where and why in a radio relay system might (a) an isolator (b) a circulator be used?

Table 12.6

System	Cost	Time to install	Typical number of channels	Communication reliability
Land coaxial cable				
Submarine cable				
SHF radio relay				
HF radio				
Communication satellite				
Tropospheric scatter				
Land optical fibre cable				

12.7 By insertion of suitable words, complete Table 12.6 comparing different methods of wideband communication.

12.8 (a) Tabulate the various forms of digital modulation employed in radio relay systems. For each entry, give bit rates and numbers of telephony channels. (b) List the advantages of digital systems over the older analogue systems. How can the multiplex digital signal produced by a higher-order PCM system be transmitted over an analogue radio relay system?

12.9 With the aid of diagrams, explain the operation of a communication satellite system. How do many different ground stations gain access to a satellite (a) when transmitting signals to the satellite, (b) when receiving signals from it?

Answers to numerical exercises

1.2 (b) $1000 = P_c(1 + 0.5)$, $P_c = 1000/1.5 = 666.67$ W
When $m = 0.5$, $P_t = (1000/1.5)(1 + 0.25^2/2) = 750$ W
$P_{lsf} = P_{usf} = (750 - 666.67)/2 = 41.67$ W (*Ans*)

1.6 (a) $V_m = mV_c = 0.6 \times 600 = 360$ V (*Ans*)
(b) $V_{lsf} = V_m/2 = 180$ V (*Ans*)

1.8 (b) 10 dB = 3.162 voltage ratio
Therefore
$V_{sf} = mV_c/2 = V_c/3.162$
$m = 2/3.162 = 0.6325 = 63.25\%$ (*Ans*)
$P_t = 1(1 + 0.6325^2/2) = 1.2$ mW (*Ans*)

1.9 (b) $m = (80 - 40)/(80 + 40) = 0.333 = 33.3\%$ (*Ans*)

1.10 (a) 1 MHz, 990 kHz, 1.01 MHz (*Ans*)
(b) 990 kHz, 1.01 MHz (*Ans*)
(c) Either 990 kHz or 1.01 MHz (*Ans*)

1.11 (a) Bandwidth = $2 \times 72 = 144$ kHz (*Ans*)
(b) $P_t = P_c + P_{sf}$
$2 = (m^2 \times 25)/4$
$m = \sqrt{(8/25)} = 0.566 = 56.6\%$ (*Ans*)

1.12 (b) 18 dB = 7.94 voltage ratio
Pilot voltage = $25/7.94 = 3.15$ V (*Ans*)

2.1 $160 = 2(f_d + f_m)$ and $f_d = 7f_m$
$80 = 8f_m$ and $f_m = 10$ kHz
Therefore
$f_d = 7 \times 10 = 70$ kHz (*Ans*)

2.2 (a) 6 dB = 2 voltage ratio and hence new $m_f = 8$ (*Ans*)
(b) $100 = 2(f_d + f_m) = 2(5f_m)$. Therefore $f_m = 10$ kHz
Bandwidth = $2(9 \times 10) = 180$ kHz (*Ans*)

2.5 (b) $(180 \times 10^3)/(2.2 \times 10^6) \times 100 = 8.18\%$ (*Ans*)

2.6 Reduce both the voltage and the frequency of the modulating signal by 50% (*Ans*)

2.8 $80 = 2(f_d + 6)$
$f_d = 40 - 6 = 34$ kHz
A signal voltage reduction of 6 dB reduces f_d in direct proportion to 17 kHz Bandwidth = $2(17 + 6) = 46$ kHz (*Ans*)

2.10 (a) $f_d = 10 \times 3 = 30$ kHz
Bandwidth = $2(30 + 3) = 66$ kHz (*Ans*)

(b) With $D = 5$, $f_d = 15\,\text{kHz}$.
Bandwidth $= 2(15 + 3) = 36\,\text{kHz}$ (*Ans*)

(c) Signal-to-noise ratio is directly proportional to D and hence its reduction is 6 dB (*Ans*)

2.13 (b) Initial frequency deviation $= 80/2 = 40\,\text{kHz}$
Final deviation $= 40/2 = 20\,\text{kHz}$

4.1 (a) $Z_o = \sqrt{(1000 \times 600)} = 774.6\,\Omega$ (*Ans*)

4.3 (a) $Z_o = \sqrt{[(1.2 \times 10^{-6})/(13.32 \times 10^{-12})]} = 300\,\Omega$ (*Ans*)

(b) $P_L = (1 \times 10^{-3})^2 \times 500 = 500\,\mu\text{W}$ (*Ans*)

4.7 (b) $50\,\Omega$, $50\,\Omega$ (*Ans*)

4.8 (a) $S = (1 + 0.6)/(1 - 0.6) = 4$ (*Ans*)

4.9 (b) $\rho_c = 0.25\,\angle 0°$
$S = (1 + 0.25)/(1 - 0.25) = 1.67$ (*Ans*)

4.10 (a) $3 = (1 + |\rho_v|)/(1 - |\rho_v|)$
$3 - 3\rho_v = 1 + \rho_v$
$\rho_v = 0.5$ (*Ans*)

(b) $|\rho_c| = |\rho_v| = 0.5$ (*Ans*)

4.13 (a) $75 = \sqrt{(L/C)}$, $2.4 \times 10^8 = 1/\sqrt{(LC)}$
$75 \times 2.4 \times 10^8 = 1/C$, $C = 55.6\,\text{pF/m}$ (*Ans*)
$L = 75^2 \times 55.6 \times 10^{-12} = 313\,\text{nH/m}$ (*Ans*)

(b) $\rho_v = (500 - 75)/(500 + 75) = 0.739\,\angle 0°$
$S = (1 + 0.739)/(1 - 0.739) = 6.66$ (*Ans*)

4.14 (b) $1.05 = (1 + |\rho_v|)/(1 - |\rho_v|)$, $|\rho_v| = 0.024$ (*Ans*)

4.16 (a) (i) $600\,\Omega$, (ii) $600\,\Omega$, (iii) $600\,\Omega$

(c) Loss/km $= \sqrt{2} \times 2 = 2.828\,\text{dB/km}$. Overall loss $= 5.657\,\text{dB}$ (*Ans*)

5.1 (b) $\lambda = (3 \times 10^8)/(559.25 \times 10^6) = 0.536\,\text{m}$
$\lambda/2 = 0.268\,\text{m}$
Dipole length $\simeq 0.26\,\text{m}$ (*Ans*)
Reflector length $\simeq 0.268 + (5 \times 0.268)/100 \simeq 0.28\,\text{m}$ (*Ans*)

5.4 (b) $\lambda = (3 \times 10^8)/(805 \times 10^6) = 0.373\,\text{m}$
$\lambda/2 \simeq 0.186\,\text{m}$
Dipole length $\simeq 0.186\,\text{m}$ (*Ans*)
Reflector length $\simeq 0.195\,\text{m}$ (*Ans*)
Director length $\simeq 0.177\,\text{m}$ (*Ans*)

(c) Gain $= 10\log_{10}(20/11) = 2.6\,\text{dB}$ (*Ans*)

5.5 (d) $\eta = (8000/10\,000) \times 100 = 80\%$ (*Ans*)

(e) ERP $= 6.31 \times 8 = 50.48\,\text{kW}$ (*Ans*)

5.6 (c) $P_r = 10^2 \times 1.8 = 180\,\text{W}$ (*Ans*)
$\eta = [1.8/(1.8 + 2.5)] \times 100 = 41.86\%$ (*Ans*)

5.7 (a) Gain $= 10\log_{10}(20/8) = 3.98\,\text{dB}$ (*Ans*)

(b) Gain $= 10\log_{10}(10/5) + 10 = 13\,\text{dBi}$ (*Ans*)

5.8 (b) $l_{\text{eff}} = (75 \times 10)/20 = 37.5\,\text{m}$ (*Ans*)

5.9 (b) Gain $= 55D^2 f^2 = 55 \times 1 \times 4 = 220 = 46.8\,\text{dBi}$ (*Ans*)

5.14 (b) Gain $= 10\log_{10}(1000/250) + 20 = 26\,\text{dBi}$ (*Ans*)

5.16 (a) SDE $=$ SAB $= 60 + 78 = 138\,\text{cm}$
$2\text{DS} + \text{SE} = 138\,\text{cm}$, $\text{DS} + \text{SE} = 90\,\text{cm}$
Therefore
$\text{DS} = 138 - 90 = 48\,\text{cm}$ (*Ans*)

(c) $P_t = (4\pi \times 12^2 \times 10^6 \times 1 \times 10^{-6})/(4 \times 600) = 754\,\text{mW}$ (*Ans*)

5.17 (b) Gain increase per aerial $= 1.5^2 = 2.25$
Overall gain increase $= 2.25^2 = 5.06 = 7\,\text{dB}$ (*Ans*)

5.18 (a) Gain $= 30 + 2.16\,\text{dB} = 32.16\,\text{dBi} = 1644$ power ratio
$P_\text{d} = (1.8 \times 1644)/(4\pi \times 1 \times 10^8) = 2.36\,\mu\text{W/m}^2$ (*Ans*)
(b) $1.35°$ is a 3 dB point. Hence
$P_\text{d} = 1.67\,\mu\text{W/m}^2$ (*Ans*)

6.10 (b) Gain $= 55 \times 6^2 \times 2^2 = 7920$
$ERP = 7920 \times 1\,\text{kW} = 7.92\,\text{MW}$ (*Ans*)

6.15 (b) $P_\text{d} = 2000/[4\pi \times (2 \times 10^4)^2 \simeq 0.4\,\mu\text{W/m}^2$
$P_\text{r} = 3 \times 0.4 = 1.2\,\mu\text{W}$ (*Ans*)

7.2 (a) $P_\text{t} = 1245\,\text{W} = P_\text{c}(1 + 0.7^2/2) = 1.245\,P_\text{c}$
$P_\text{c} = 1245/0.7 = 1000\,\text{W}$
Total sidefrequency power $= 1245 - 1000 = 245\,\text{W}$
Modulation power $= 245/0.6 = 408.33\,\text{W}$ (*Ans*)
(b) D.c. power to Class B $= 408.33/0.5 = 816.66\,\text{W}$
Therefore anode dissipation $= 408.33\,\text{W}$ (*Ans*)

7.3 (a) $P_\text{o} = 0.75\,P_\text{DC} = P_\text{DC} - 250$, or $P_\text{DC} = 1000\,\text{W}$
Maximum output power $= 0.75 \times 1000 = 750\,\text{W}$ (*Ans*)
(b) $P_\text{o} = $ modulation input power $= 0.6\,P_\text{DC} = P_\text{DC} - 200$
$P_\text{DC} = 500\,\text{W}$ and $P_\text{o} = 0.6 \times 500 = 300\,\text{W}$ (*Ans*)
(c) Maximum modulated $P_\text{o} = 750 + 0.75 \times 300 = 975\,\text{W}$
$975 = 750(1 + \text{m}^2/2)$
Hence $m = \sqrt{0.6} = 0.775 = 77.5\%$ (*Ans*)

7.8 $11\,000 = P_\text{c}(1 + 0.6^2/2) = 1.18P_\text{c}$
$P_\text{c} = 11\,000/1.18 = 9322\,\text{W}$
Class C: $P_\text{DC} = 9322/0.66 = 14\,124\,\text{W}$ (*Ans*)
Modulation power $= 0.18 \times 9322 = 1678\,\text{W}$
Class B: $P_\text{o} = 1678/0.66 = 2542.4\,\text{W}$
$P_\text{DC} = 2542.4/0.48 = 5297\,\text{W}$ (*Ans*)

8.8 (a) Both carrier and frequency deviation are increased by the same ratio. Hence
Deviation $= (90/5) \times 3 = 54\,\text{kHz}$
Deviation ratio $= 54/2 = 27$ (*Ans*)
(b) The frequency deviation is unchanged.
$D = 3/2 = 1.5$ (*Ans*)

8.9 (b) $(5000 - 158)/2(n - 2) = 500$
$n = (5000 - 158 + 2000)/1000 = 6.842$ (*Ans*)

9.2 (c) $f_\text{im} = 1400 + 2 \times 450 = 2300\,\text{kHz} = 2.3\,\text{MHz}$ (*Ans*)

9.5 (a) Frequency ratio $= 1800/600 = 3{:}1$
Required capacitance ratio $= 9{:}1$
$9C_\text{min} = C_\text{min} + 320$
$C_\text{min} = 40\,\text{pF}$ (*Ans*)
(b) $L = 1/(4 \times \pi^2 \times 40 \times 10^{-12} \times 1800^2 \times 10^6) = 195.5\,\mu\text{H}$ (*Ans*)
(c) In the oscillator circuit, the frequency ratio is
$(1800 + 465)/(600 + 465) = 2.127{:}1$
Hence
Capacitance ratio $= 2.127^2 = 4.524$
$(360C_\text{p})/(360 + C_\text{p}) = 4.524(40C_\text{p})/(C_\text{p} + 40)$
or $C_\text{p} = 283.5\,\text{pF}$ (*Ans*)
(d) Minimum capacitance $= (40 \times 283.5)/(40 + 283.5) = 35\,\text{pF}$
$L = 1/(4 \times \pi^2 \times 2265^2 \times 10^6 \times 35 \times 10^{-12}) = 141\,\mu\text{H}$ (*Ans*)

9.6 (b) (i) 0 (ii) 0 (iii) 4 kHz (*Ans*)

9.7 (b) AFC correction = $f/50 \times 250 = 5f$ kHz

Hence $f = 20 - 5f$ or $f = 3.33$ kHz (*Ans*)

9.9 (a) 970–1970 kHz (*Ans*)

(b) $500 + 2 \times 470 = 1440$ kHz (*Ans*)

(c) $1500 + 2 \times 470 = 2440$ kHz (*Ans*)

10.7 (b) $G = 5^3 = 125$ (*Ans*)

$B = 100 \sqrt{(2^{1/3} - 1)} = 51$ MHz (*Ans*)

10.8 (b) $f = 100.7 - 90 = 10.7$ MHz (*Ans*)

$i = 0.5 \times 10^{-3} \times 0.5 = 0.25$ mA (*Ans*)

Index